Social
Change

OTHER BOOKS BY AMITAI ETZIONI

Winning without War   1964

Modern Organizations   1964

The Hard Way to Peace: A New Strategy   1962

A Comparative Analysis of Complex Organizations   1961

Complex Organizations: A Sociological Reader   1961

Diary of a Commando Soldier   1952

SOCIAL CHANGE

Sources, Patterns, and Consequences

Edited by Amitai Etzioni

and Eva Etzioni

BASIC BOOKS, INC., PUBLISHERS
New York · London

Fourth Printing

Library of Congress Catalog Card Number: 64–13894
Manufactured in the United States of America
Designed by Sophie Adler

In memory of Salomon Horowitz

Preface

Assembling this book has proved to be a frustrating experience. Again and again we were tempted to compile a multivolume series, in order to do justice to the rich variety of materials available on social change. Within the space limits we had, it was impossible to include more than a small sample of essays, excerpts from books, and new articles representing the major approaches to the study of social change.

We have tried to select writings that were brief enough in their entirety or that could be excerpted without becoming incomprehensible or distorted* and which, at the same time, would provide keys to the work that could not be included. We generally chose analytical as against descriptive material, hoping that the former would furnish the student and researcher with tools for dealing with the latter. We also tried to include concrete illustrations of analytical propositions and to give at least some examples of empirical study in various aspects of social change; but lengthy descriptions had to be excluded. The teacher may wish to enrich the students' diet by assigning the reading of one or more monographs, now often available in paperback. Or, in more advanced courses, the teacher who wishes to enlarge on one aspect of social change—such as group dynamics, industrialization, or population —may find it desirable to assign additional pertinent readings.

Though this volume draws on a variety of approaches and disciplines, it has been compiled by sociologists, concentrates on the work of sociologists, and is intended for students of sociology. The tyranny of space allowed the inclusion of only a fraction of the relevant work done by anthropologists, political scientists, economists, and psychologists.

The present collection includes rather more discussion than one might expect to find of social change on an international level. We feel that this area of change has been unduly neglected by sociologists and that it will be of much interest in the near future.

* The more important omissions are marked in the text by ellipses.

The brief introductory notes are meant to be neither novel in content nor exhaustive in scope. They are intended to stimulate the reader's interest in the material, to show some of the threads that connect the selections, and to sketch out the main lines of discussion and argument on these issues up to now. The student should also bear in mind that our interpretive comments, like the propositions made in the essays themselves, are open to refutation and should be viewed as food for thought, rather than as *obiter dicta*.

Eva and Amitai Etzioni

Contents

Part **III** Spheres of Change:

The Modern Society

Social
Change

PART I

SOURCES AND PATTERNS OF CHANGE

Classical
Theories

CHAPTER 1

Introduction

Many of the fathers of sociology were concerned with the general trend of history and its meaning. Mostly they sought to explain the past development of society and sometimes to predict its future in terms of a definite pattern.

For such nineteenth-century thinkers as Herbert Spencer and Auguste Comte, the pattern is one of linear ascent. Spencer saw the development of society as a process of evolution, which, like organic evolution, is a process of growth, increasing complexity, increasing differentiation of structure and function, and increasing interdependence among the differentiated parts. He also believed in the emergence of an industrial order which would increasingly protect the rights of the individual, decrease the emphasis on government, abolish wars, dissolve national borders, and establish a global community.

Comte, too, saw society as a process of evolution and progress and defined his task as one of establishing the uniformities governing this progress. Thus, he formulated his famous law of the three states of the development of human thought—the theological, the metaphysical, and the positive—which were also the bases of the three historical forms of social organization.

As against these optimistic conceptions, Oswald Spengler early in this century put forth an opposing, essentially pessimistic view. For Spengler, human existence is an endless series of ups and downs. Like waves in the ocean, the great cultures appear, rise to great heights, only to subside again while others rise in their turn. Like the individual organism, each culture has a life cycle of birth, childhood, maturity, old age, and death. The cycles have no cumulative meaning. At the end of each cycle, mankind is essentially where it was before. For Spengler, the West has passed its phase of maturity, which he calls "culture," and is already well advanced into the decadent period, which he refers to as "civilization."

Most other theories presented here derive from either the linear or the cyclical principle; some writers, with differing emphases, incorporate elements of both.

Arnold Toynbee, who belongs to a later period but whose enterprise has the pith and moment of those of Spencer, Comte, and Spengler, has developed a theory that is in one sense cyclical, since it is a theory of the growth and disintegration of civilizations. According to Toynbee, a civilization comes into being through a successful response to a challenge. It grows when each successful response to a challenge provokes a further challenge, which in turn meets with a successful response. These responses are worked out by the genius of "creative minorities." When a creative minority becomes stagnant and dominant, its society is no longer capable of successful responses to challenge, and a civilization disintegrates. Not all civilizations complete this cycle; some are abortive, others are arrested. Although there is a certain similarity to Spengler's approach, in contrast to Spengler's recurrent cycles, Toynbee perceives gradations among civilizations and even a long-term trend. First, some civilizations are born of primitive societies, others develop from prior civilizations, and still others constitute third generations. Civilizations that rise out of the decay of older civilizations are on a higher level than those born to primitive societies, though all pass through the same cycles. Finally, the ultimate growth potential of a civilization is defined by its ability to develop higher religions, rather than idolizing the means of production or the means of violence. Western civilization, the carrier of Christianity, has the highest growth potential. Thus Toynbee combines a rather clear cyclical theory with a less sharply defined theory of progress.

The Marxist theory, too, is basically a theory of progress, although not of linear progress. The advance toward the classless society proceeds through "dialectical" conflicts, in each of which one subordinate class overthrows its ruling class (*e.g.,* the bourgeoisie overthrows the aristocracy), only to establish a new society in which a new subordinate class rises to overthrow it. But these cycles are neither endless nor meaningless. As Marx saw it, the wheel has now reached its last turn; with the proletarian revolution, the story is about to come to an end. The proletariat's victory will give rise to a classless society, one which knows no major conflict and hence no revolutions.

The Marxist theory of history differs from that of the linear progress, not only in that it conceives history as a series of violent conflicts rather than a smooth progress to higher plateaus, but also in its view of the initial state. The typical "enlightenment" theory of progress (*e.g.,* Condorcet's) saw humanity as gradually moving from a dark, ignorant, brutal, primitive state to one of reason, virtue and happiness. For Engels, the initial state was similar to the end state; generalizing the ethnographic researches of Lewis H. Morgan, he viewed early primitive society as a classless commune, to which man is destined to return. The basic similarity of this conception to that common to many religions has often been pointed out. There was a Garden of Eden; there is a state of sin; there will be a return to the Kingdom of God.

One important aspect of Max Weber's theory is in a way quite close to the cyclical approach. According to Weber, when the legitimacy of an old historical structure is exhausted, a charismatic leader emerges outside the structure and gives it its *coup de grâce*. The leader and his followers take over and build a new structure on the ruins of the old one. The subsequent "routinization of charisma" constitutes the foundation of the new structure—which sooner or later will also be faced with the same lack of legitimacy, charismatic upheaval, new routinization, and so on.

Another aspect of Weber's theory approximates the linear-development approach, for he sees the development of culture as a process of constantly increasing rationalization, of growing inner consistency and coherence. This is most evident in the transition from magic to science; the development of religion from polytheism to monotheism is also viewed in this light; and Weber observed the same trend in the development of music.

Thus, Weber's approach to change is two-pronged; he combines a cyclical theory of social development with a linear theory of cultural development. Though Weber never fully relates these two themes, he intimates that the social structure "catches up" with cultural development under the impact of the charismatic periods; at these points, the social structure is opened up to reorganization by ever-more-"rationalized" cultural systems. The role of Calvin and other great reformers in introducing a "Protestant ethic" is a prime illustration.

The work of Toennies is second only to that of Weber in the scope and depth of its influence on contemporary sociology. Toennies, like Spencer, views society as growing more and more complex, in a linear process. Small and simple structures grow to become large and complex ones. He sees the trend from what he calls *Gemeinschaft* to *Gesellschaft* as one in which primitive, traditional, closely knit communities are torn and uprooted, to be replaced by a large, urbanized, industrial society in which human relations are impersonal and instrumental. Like the theorists of linear ascent, he sees a clear, irreversible trend; but, unlike them, he is ambivalent in evaluating this trend. Modern society has provided men with many new freedoms, with new dimensions of knowledge, and with material affluence. But it has also brought about alienation, atomization, and impersonality.

By making the pattern and direction of human history their domain, the early sociologists made certain that their theories would bear directly on the most basic questions of social life. The same holds for their concern with the forces that move history. Can men make their own history or only ride history like a wave? Most thinkers represented here are determinists up to a point; if the sheer contingency of random impulse were all that made the world go round, its course could hardly be as predictable, as "rational," as they felt it is. On the other hand, all these thinkers concede a modicum of leeway for man to interfere with his fate, though they differ greatly in the degree of freedom they grant him.

Spengler sees the course of history as more-or-less given, like the childhood, maturity, and decay of the human body. There is extremely little man can do to alter it. Spencer, too, leaves little room for individual interference. But, whereas Spengler outlines the inevitability of our culture's doom, Spencer believes in the inevitability of human progress. Man's spirit and his history point in the same direction; there is no contradiction between the two. Marx takes somewhat different positions in various writings, but basically he views human fate as predestined. The ruling class, by utilizing the state and the church, means of violence and ideology, might delay the historic process to some extent; the proletariat, if properly organized and acting in concert, might accelerate it. But ultimately the wheels of history are turning, and nobody can stop or reverse them.

Weber left history more open to human guidance. To be sure, man is caught in the institutional web he himself set up; but, at charismatic moments, he breaks in, remodeling the institutional structure to bring it closer to his wish. On the cultural level, the process of increasing rationalization indicates increased submission of the universe to man's mind; but, at the same time, there is no sign that man is free to reverse this process, should he change his mind about it.

The theories represented here view the forces of history as originating from within human society—from its economic structure or its culture. In this sense, they indeed lay the foundations of contemporary sociology, which has completely rejected several other sets of theories that regard society and its changes as determined by forces originating outside the social system. Theories that explain the course of human history predominantly by supernatural forces, environmental factors (*e.g.,* climate), or biological factors (*e.g.,* race) have all been discredited. The supernatural theories have been discarded on the ground that the factors they deal with are not amenable to scientific inquiry; the environmental and biological theories because the factors they deal with change extremely slowly and therefore could hardly explain the changes of human society, which are occasionally quite rapid. The amount of rainfall in Russia and its racial composition hardly changed from 1817 to 1917 and so cannot adequately account for the shift from a tsarist to a communist regime. Unlike the classic theories presented in this volume—many of which have exerted a strong influence on contemporary sociology—the environmental and biological theories have been so completely rejected that they are only of historical interest.

Within the range of the theories which stress that the determinants of social change arise from within society itself, the longest, deepest, and most important controversy lies between those who see the prime moving forces of human history in the "spiritual" spheres and those who see it in the "material" ones; between those who stress the role of ideas and those who stress the role of economic factors; between those who stress the role of culture and those who stress the role of technology.

Thus Comte, though he called on sociology to look, not for causes and effects in history, but rather for uniformities, nevertheless, in his own work, implicitly attributes causal primacy to the cultural sphere by describing the three successive states of human thought as giving rise to three successive states of social organization.

Marx, in contrast, believes that "the method of production in material existence conditions social, political, and mental evolution in general." Since Marxism has frequently been oversimplified, it must be stressed that it does allow for a certain range of independence of the various non-economic spheres; but, as Engels put it: ". . . the *final causes* [italics supplied] of all social changes are to be sought . . . in the modes of production and exchange."

Weber, in *The Protestant Ethic and the Spirit of Capitalism,* brought this primacy into question by demonstrating the crucial importance of the spiritual sphere in determining the economic structure itself. But he was careful to point out that this was only one side of the causal chain, that under other circumstances the economic factors might determine the cultural ones, and that *in toto* the sources of change are neither exclusively economic nor exclusively cultural.

Under the influence of Weber, sociology is outgrowing this controversy by rejecting all deterministic theories. All efforts to explain societal change as originating in one single social factor have so utterly failed, while efforts to show that a variety of factors exert some influence have proved to be so much more satisfactory, that contemporary sociology has almost unanimously adopted the multifactor approach.

Social change, it is now held, may originate in any institutional area, bringing about changes in other areas, which in turn make for further adaptations in the initial sphere of change. Technological, economic, political, religious, ideological, demographic, and stratificational factors are all viewed as potentially independent variables which influence each other as well as the course of society.

The appeal of classical theories, especially to the untutored reader, is large. Their scope is enormous, their claim to applicability limitless, their language nontechnical and arousing. Still, sociology has tended to move away from the effort to form and improve such theories, chiefly because of a drawback they had—a drawback directly related to their virtues: though they supplied valuable insights, when viewed in their entirety, they turned out to be either untestable, and hence scientifically unacceptable, or only partly true at best.

Thus, mankind obviously does not travel smoothly from a lesser to a

higher state of enlightenment, as Comte asserted. The melting of national
borders and the development of a global community which Spencer envisioned has not been brought about by industrial society so far, and, since
he did not specify *when* he expected this to happen, the theory can never be
disproved, which makes it untestable.

Similarly, Marx has been proved wrong on almost every single count on
which he made a prediction specific enough to be tested: the revolution
did not occur in highly industrialized, but rather in industrially "backward,"
countries; it did not bring about the classless society, nor did it eliminate
internal conflicts and contradictions; and the middle class did not diminish
in a process of polarization, but instead increased steadily; and so on. On
the other hand, the proposition that the "final" causes of social change lie
in the economic sphere is untestable. Since no empirical specification for
the concept "final" has been provided, any impetus originating in the economic sphere can be viewed as a final cause, whereas any impetus originating in another sphere may be viewed as nonfinal. Moreover, when he predicted the fading away of the state in a classless society, Marx, like Spencer,
did not specify the conditions or time at which he expected this to come
about. Consequently, this thesis, too, is untestable.

Weber, as we saw, put much stress on the role of charismatic upheavals
in bringing about change; his theory makes but little provision for slow, re-
formatory changes, which come about gradually and without crisis. Changes
like these took place, for instance, in modern England and the United
States, which were transformed from rural, religious, closed to urban, industrial, highly mobile societies; from what approximated a state of *laissez-
faire* to societies controlled to a considerable degree by central governments,
societies in which the welfare of the population as well as the growth of the
country are guided by the community and its political instruments—all this
without revolutionary upheaval.

Toennies, again, did not make sufficient allowance for the survival of
elements of *Gemeinschaft* in the *Gesellschaft*—like the nuclear family or
friendships—and he did not foresee the development of what could be referred to as elements of *Gemeinschaft* or quasi-*Gemeinschaft* in modern
society, expressed for instance in flourishing suburbs, clubs, and professional
communities.

Even so, the fact is that sociology has evolved from these theories.
They have laid the groundwork for modern sociology by calling attention
to various areas of inquiry (*e.g.,* Marx—to stratification) and by providing
many of the concepts used as a matter of course in present-day sociology.
But the totalistic scope of these theories soon had to be abandoned; before it
could progress, sociology had largely to give up the quest for overall patterns and for "ultimate" causes of change. Although in general this reaction was well justified, possibly it was overdone by sociologists moving to
the other extreme, avoiding not only the study of history in its broadest

sense, the inquiry into the study of change of all times, but also the changes of specific societies at particular times. Hopefully, the concepts and tools recently developed will serve as the building stones of a new theory of change that is not only grand, but also testable, and one which when tested will be found true.

CHAPTER 2

HERBERT SPENCER

The Evolution of Societies

A Society Is an Organism

Growth is common to social aggregates and organic aggregates. We do not entirely exclude community with inorganic aggregates. Some of these, as crystals, grow in a visible manner; and all of them, on the hypothesis of evolution, have arisen by integration at some time or another. Nevertheless, compared with things we call inanimate, living bodies and societies so conspicuously exhibit augmentation of mass, that we may fairly regard this as characterizing them both. Many organisms grow throughout their lives; and the rest grow throughout considerable parts of their lives. Social growth usually continues either up to times when the societies divide or up to times when they are overwhelmed.

Here, then, is the first trait by which societies ally themselves with the organic world and substantially distinguish themselves from the inorganic world.

The Evolution of Structures

It is also a character of social bodies, as of living bodies, that, while they increase in size, they increase in structure. Like a low animal, the embryo of a high one has few distinguishable parts; but, while it is acquiring greater mass, its parts multiply and differentiate. It is thus with a society. At first the unlikenesses among its groups of units are inconspicuous in number and degree; but, as population augments, divisions and subdivisions become more numerous and more decided. . . . As we progress from small groups to larger, from simple groups to compound groups, from compound groups to doubly compound ones, the unlikenesses of parts increase. The social aggregate, homogeneous when minute, habitually gains in heterogeneity along

From Herbert Spencer, *Sociology* (New York: Appleton and Co., 1892), Vol. 1, pp. 437-439, 459-463, 473-475, 584-585.

with each increment of growth, and to reach great size must acquire great complexity. Let us glance at the leading stages.

Naturally, in a state like that of the Cayaguas or Wood-Indians of South America, so little social that "one family lives at a distance from another," social organization is impossible; and even where there is some slight association of families, organization does not arise while they are few and wandering. Groups of Esquimaux, of Australians, of Bushmen, of Fuegians, are without even that primary contrast of parts implied by settled chieftainship. Their members are subject to no control but such as is temporarily acquired by the stronger, or more cunning, or more experienced; not even a permanent nucleus is present. Habitually, where larger simple groups exist, we find some kind of head. Though not a uniform rule (for . . . the genesis of a controlling agency depends on the nature of the social activities), this is a general rule. The headless clusters, wholly ungoverned, are incoherent, and separate before they acquire considerable sizes; but along with maintenance of an aggregate approaching to, or exceeding, a hundred, we ordinarily find a simple or compound ruling agency—one or more men claiming and exercising authority that is natural, or supernatural, or both. This is the first social differentiation.

Soon after it, there frequently comes another, tending to form a division between regulative and operative parts. In the lowest tribes, this is rudely represented only by the contrast in status between the sexes: the men, having unchecked control, carry on such external activities as the tribe shows us, chiefly in war; while the women are made drudges who perform the less skilled parts of the process of sustentation. But that tribal growth, and establishment of chieftainship, which gives military superiority, presently causes enlargement of the operative part by adding captives to it. This begins unobtrusively. While in battle the men are killed, and often afterwards eaten, the noncombatants are enslaved. Patagonians, for example, make slaves of women and children taken in war. Later, and especially when cannibalism ceases, comes the enslavement of male captives; whence results, in some cases, an operative part clearly marked off from the regulative part. Among the Chinooks, "slaves do all the laborious work." We read that the Beluchi, avoiding the hard labor of cultivation, impose it on the Jutts, the ancient inhabitants whom they have subjugated. Beecham says it is usual on the Gold Coast to make the slaves clear the ground for cultivation. And among the Felatahs "slaves are numerous: the males are employed in weaving, collecting wood or grass, or on any other kind of work; some of the women are engaged in spinning . . . in preparing the yarn for the loom, others in pounding and grinding corn, etc."

Along with that increase of mass caused by union of primary social aggregates into a secondary one, a further unlikeness of parts arises. The holding together of the compound cluster implies a head of the whole as well as heads of the parts; and a differentiation analogous to that which originally produced a chief now produces a chief of chiefs. Sometimes the combination is made for defense against a common foe, and sometimes it results from conquest by one tribe of the rest. In this last case, the predominant tribe, in maintaining its supremacy, develops more highly its military character, thus becoming unlike the others.

After such clusters of clusters have been so consolidated that their united powers can be wielded by one governing agency, there come alliances with, or subjugations of, other clusters of clusters, ending from time to time in coalescence. When this happens there results still greater complexity in the governing agency, with its king, local rulers, and petty chiefs; and, at the same time, there arise more marked divisions of classes—military, priestly, slave, etc. Clearly, then, complication of structure accompanies increase of mass.

This increase of heterogeneity, which in both classes of aggregates goes along with growth, presents another trait in common. Beyond unlikenesses of parts due to development of the coordinating agencies, there presently follow unlikenesses among the agencies coordinated—the organs of alimentation, etc., in the one case, and the industrial structures in the other.

When animal-aggregates of the lowest order unite to form one of a higher order and when, again, these secondary aggregates are compounded into tertiary aggregates, each component is at first similar to the other components; but in the course of evolution dissimilarities arise and become more and more decided. Among the *Coelenterata* the stages are clearly indicated. From the sides of a common hydra bud out young ones, which, when fully developed, separate from their parent. In the compound hydroids, the young polyps produced in like manner remain permanently attached and, themselves repeating the process, presently form a branched aggregate. When the members of the compound group lead similar and almost independent lives, as in various rooted genera, they remain similar—save those of them which become reproductive organs. But, in the floating and swimming clusters, formed by a kindred process, the differently conditioned members become different while assuming different functions. It is thus with the minor social groups combined into a major social group. Each tribe originally had within itself such feebly marked industrial divisions as sufficed for its low kind of life, and these were like those of each other tribe. But union facilitates exchange of commodities; and if, as mostly happens, the component tribes severally occupy localities favorable to unlike kinds of production, unlike occupations are initiated, and there result unlikenesses of industrial structure. Even between tribes not united, as those of Australia, barter of products furnished by their respective habitats goes on so long as war does not hinder. And evidently, when there is reached such a stage of integration as in Madagascar or as in the chief Negro states of Africa, the internal peace that follows subordination to one government makes commercial intercourse easy. The like parts being permanently held together, mutual dependence becomes possible; and, along with growing mutual dependence, the parts grow unlike. . . .

The Evolution of Functions

Changes of structure cannot occur without changes of function. . . . Indeed, as in societies many changes of structure are more indicated by changes of function than directly seen, it may be said that these last have been already described by implication.

There are, however, certain functional traits not manifestly implied by traits of structure. To these a few pages must be devoted.

If organization consists in such a construction of the whole that its parts can carry on mutually dependent actions, then in proportion as organization is high there must go a dependence of each part on the rest so great that separation is fatal, and conversely. This truth is equally well shown in the individual organism and in the social organism.

The lowest animal-aggregates are so constituted that each portion, similar to every other in appearance, carries on similar actions; and here spontaneous or artificial separation interferes scarcely at all with the life of either separated portion. When the faintly differentiated speck of protoplasm forming a Rhizopod is accidentally divided, each division goes on as before. So, too, is it with those aggregates of the second order in which the components remain substantially alike. The ciliated monads clothing the horny fibers of a living sponge need one another's aid so little, that, when the sponge is cut in two, each half carries on its processes without interruption. Even where some unlikeness has arisen among the units, as in the familiar polyp, the perturbation caused by division is but temporary: the two or more portions resulting need only a little time for the units to rearrange themselves into fit forms before resuming their ordinary simple actions. The like happens for the like reason with the lowest social aggregates. A headless wandering group of primitive men divides without any inconvenience. Each man, at once warrior, hunter, and maker of his own weapons, hut, etc., with a squaw who has in every case the like drudgeries to carry on, needs concert with his fellows only in war and to some extent in the chase; and, except for fighting, concert with half the tribe is as good as concert with the whole. Even where the slight differentiation implied by chieftainship exists, little inconvenience results from voluntary or enforced separation. Either before or after a part of the tribe migrates, some man becomes head, and such low social life as is possible recommences.

With highly organized aggregates of either kind, it is very different. We cannot cut a mammal in two without causing immediate death. Twisting off the head of a fowl is fatal. Not even a reptile, though it may survive the loss of its tail, can live when its body is divided. And, among annulose creatures it similarly happens that, though in some inferior genera bisection does not kill either half, it kills both in an insect, an arachnid, or a crustacean. If in high societies the effect of mutilation is less than in high animals, still it is great. Middlesex, separated from its surroundings, would in a few days have all its social processes stopped by lack of supplies. Cut off the cotton district from Liverpool and other ports, and there would come arrest of its industry followed by mortality of its people. Let a division be made between the coalmining populations and adjacent populations which smelt metals or make broadcloth by machinery, and both, forthwith dying socially by arrest of their actions, would begin to die individually. Though when a civilized society is so divided that part of it is left without a central controlling agency, it may presently evolve one; yet there is meanwhile much risk of dissolution, and before reorganization is efficient a long period of disorder and weakness must be passed through.

So that the *consensus* of functions becomes closer as evolution advances. In low aggregates, both individual and social, the actions of the parts are but little dependent on one another, whereas in developed aggregates of both kinds, that combination of actions which constitutes the life of the whole makes possible the component actions which constitute the lives of the parts.

Summary

. . . The many facts contemplated unite in proving that social evolution forms a part of evolution at large. Like evolving aggregates in general, societies show *integration*, both by simple increase of mass and by coalescence and recoalescence of masses. The change from *homogeneity* to *heterogeneity* is multitudinously exemplified; up from the simple tribe, alike in all its parts, to the civilized nation, full of structural and functional unlikenesses. With progressing integration and heterogeneity goes increasing *coherence*. We see the wandering group dispersing, dividing, held together by no bonds; the tribe with parts made more coherent by subordination to a dominant man; the cluster of tribes united in a political plexus under a chief with subchiefs; and so on up to the civilized nation, consolidated enough to hold together for a thousand years or more. Simultaneously comes increasing *definiteness*. Social organization is at first vague; advance brings settled arrangements which grow slowly more precise; customs pass into laws which, while gaining fixity, also become more specific in their applications to varieties of actions; and all institutions, at first confusedly intermingled, slowly separate, at the same time that each within itself marks off more distinctly its component structures. Thus in all respects is fulfilled the formula of evolution. There is progress toward greater size, coherence, multiformity, and definiteness.

CHAPTER 3

AUGUSTE COMTE

The Progress of Civilization through Three States

The Progress of Civilization Follows Laws

The experience of the past proves, in the most decisive manner, that the progressive march of civilization follows a natural and unavoidable course, which flows from the law of human organization and, in its turn, becomes the supreme law of all practical phenomena.

In this place it is manifestly impossible to expound the law in question with precision, or to verify it historically, even in the briefest manner. We only propose to offer some reflections on this fundamental conception.

The first reflection points to the necessity for assuming that such a law does exist in order to explain the political phenomena.

All men who possess a certain knowledge of the leading facts of history, be their historical views what they may, will agree in this, that the cultivated portion of the human race, considered as a whole, has made uninterrupted progress in civilization from the most remote periods of history to our own day. In this proposition, the term "civilization" is understood as including the social organization.

No reasonable doubt can be raised about this fundamental fact as regards the epoch which extends from the eleventh century to the present time, in other words commencing with the introduction of the sciences of observation into Europe by the Arabs and the enfranchisement of the Commons. But the truth is equally incontestable as regards the antecedent period. Savants are now well convinced that the pretensions to advanced scientific knowl-

From Auguste Comte, *System of Positive Polity* (London: Longmans, Green and Co., 1877), "General Appendix: Early Essays," Vol. IV, pp. 555-58, 572-73.

edge put forward on behalf of the ancients by *littérateurs* are devoid of all real basis. The Arabians are proved to have surpassed them. Such also has been the case, even more decidedly, as regards industry, at all events in reference to all that calls for real ability and does not result from mere accident. Even if the fine arts were deemed to constitute an exception, their exclusion is susceptible of a natural explanation which would leave the main proposition essentially untouched. Lastly, as regards the social organization, it is perfectly manifest that this, during the same period, made the greatest progress, owing to the establishment of Christianity and the formation of the feudal system, so superior to the organization of Greece and Rome.

It is therefore certain that civilization has, under every aspect, made constant progress.

On the other hand, while discarding the disparaging spirit, alike blind and unjust, introduced by the metaphysical philosophy, we cannot but perceive that, in consequence of the state of infancy which has hitherto characterized political speculations, the practical combinations that have until now guided civilization were not always those best adapted to promote its progress and frequently tended rather to impede than to assist this. There have been epochs the main political activity of which was of a purely stationary character. Such, generally speaking, were those of social systems in their decline; for example, of the Emperor Julian, of Philip II and the Jesuits, and lastly of Bonaparte. Let us also bear in mind that, as already pointed out, the social organization does not regulate the course of civilization, but, on the contrary, results from this.

Frequent cures, effected in spite of a treatment manifestly erroneous, have revealed to physicians the powerful action by which every living body spontaneously tends to rectify accidental derangements of its organization. In like manner the advance of civilization, notwithstanding unfavorable political combinations, clearly proves that civilization is governed by a natural law of progress, independent of all combinations, and dominating them. If this principle were denied, in order to explain such a fact and comprehend how it has come to pass that civilization, in place of being retarded by errors committed, has almost invariably benefited by them, we could only have recourse to direct, continuous supernatural guidance, after the fashion of theological politics.

Lastly, it is well to remark that too frequently events have been regarded as unfavorable to civilization which were only apparently so. The chief cause of this misapprehension has been the insufficient attention paid, even by the best intellects, to an essential law of organized bodies, which applies with equal force to the human race acting collectively as to a single individual. It consists in the necessity for a certain degree of resistance, in order that all forces may be fully developed. But this remark in no way affects the preceding consideration. For, though obstacles are needed to develop forces, they do not produce them.

The conclusion deduced from this fundamental consideration would be much strengthened if we took into account the remarkable identity observable in the development of the civilization of different nations, between which no political intercommunication can with probability be assumed. Such an identity could only have been produced under the influence of a natural progress of civilization, uniformly applicable to all nations as resulting from the fundamental laws of the human organization common to all. Thus, for example, the customs of the early times of Greece, as they are described by Homer, are found to be almost identical with those which subsist among the savage nations of North America. So, likewise, the feudalism of the Malays closely resembles that of Europe in the eleventh century. These points of resemblance, it is clear, can only be explained in the way above mentioned.

A second consideration will render evident the existence of a natural law regulating the progress of civilization.

If, in conformity with the view above submitted, we admit that each phase of the social order is necessarily derived from that of the corresponding civilization, we may in our observations lay out of consideration this complex element; the results arrived at for the residuary facts will equally apply to the organization of society.

Reducing thus the question to its simplest terms, it becomes easy to perceive that civilization follows a determined and invariable course.

A superficial philosophy, which would make this world a scene of miracles, has immensely exaggerated the influence of chance, that is to say of isolated causes, in human affairs. This exaggeration is peculiarly apparent in reference to the sciences and the arts. Among other remarkable examples, everyone knows the great admiration excited even in intelligent minds by the idea that the law of universal gravitation was revealed to Newton by the fall of an apple.

All sensible men in our time admit that chance plays only a very small part in scientific and industrial discoveries, that in none but insignificant discoveries does it rank as chief agent. But to this error has succeeded another which, though in itself much less unreasonable, has nevertheless almost the same disadvantages. The office of chance has been in like manner transferred to genius. This explanation hardly accounts more felicitously for the action of the human mind.

The history of human knowledge clearly proves that all our labors in the sciences and arts are so connected, whether in the same or in succeeding generations, that the discoveries of one age prepare those of the following, as the former had been themselves prepared by those of the preceding. It has been demonstrated that the isolated power of genius is greatly less than that with which it has been credited. The man most justly distinguished by great discoveries almost always owes the largest share of his success to his predecessors in the same career. In a word, the human mind follows, in the development of the sciences and arts, a definite course, one that transcends the greatest intellectual forces, which arise, so to speak, only as instruments destined to produce in due course successive discoveries.

Confining our observations to the sciences whose progress we can follow most easily from remote periods, we see, in truth, that their main historic epoch—that is to say their passage through the theological and metaphysical into the positive stage—are rigorously determined. These three states succeed one another necessarily in an order prescribed by the nature of the human mind. The transition from one to the other takes place according to a course the steps of which resemble one another in all the sciences, nor can the greatest amount of genius dispense with passing through them. Turning from this general review to the subdivisions of the scientific or definitive state, we observe the same law. Thus for example, the great discovery of universal gravitation was prepared by the labors of the astronomers and geometers of the sixteenth and seventeenth centuries, chiefly by those of Kepler and Huygens. They were indispensable to its birth and certain, sooner or later, to produce it.

It appears, therefore, from the preceding remarks that the elementary march of civilization is unquestionably subject to a natural and invariable law which overrules all special human divergencies. But since the state of the social organization of necessity follows that of civilization, the same conclusion applies to civilization, considered as a whole or in its elements.

The two considerations above announced, though insufficient to furnish a complete exposition of the progress of civilization, nevertheless prove its reality. They show the possibility of determining with precision all its attributes by a careful observation of the past and of thus creating positive polity.

Our business is next to fix exactly the practical aim of this science and its general points of contact with the wants of society, especially its connection with the real work of reorganization which is so imperiously required by the actual state of the body politic.

To effect this, it is necessary at the outset to ascertain the limits of all true political action.

The fundamental law which governs the natural progress of civilization rigorously determines the successive states through which the general development of the human race must pass. On the other hand, this law necessarily results from the instinctive tendency of the human race to perfect itself. Consequently, it is as completely independent of our control as are the individual instincts the combination of which produces this permanent tendency.

Since no known fact authorizes us to believe that the human organization is liable to any fundamental alteration, the progress of that civilization which flows from it is in essentials unalterable. To speak more precisely, none of the intermediate steps which it prescribes can be evaded, and no step in a backward direction can really be made.

Nevertheless, the progress of civilization is more or less modifiable and may vary in point of rapidity within certain limits, from various causes, physical and moral, which can be estimated. Among these causes are political combinations. In this sense only is it possible for man to influence the course of his own civilization. . . .

Law of the Three States

I believe that history may be divided into three grand epochs, or states of civilization, each possessing a distinct character, spiritual and temporal. They embrace civilization at once in its elements and its *ensemble;* which . . . evidently constitutes an indispensable condition of success.

Of these the first is the Theological and Military epoch.

In this state of society, all theoretical conceptions, whether general or special, bear a supernatural impress. The imagination completely predominates over the observing faculty, to which all right of inquiry is denied.

In like manner, all the social relations, whether special or general, are avowedly and exclusively military. Society makes conquest its one permanent aim. Industrial pursuits are carried on only so far as is necessary for the support of the human race. Slavery, pure and simple, of the producers, is the principal institution.

Such is the first great social system produced by the material progress of civilization. It existed in an elementary shape from the very commencement of regular and permanent societies. In its entirety it becomes completely established only after a long series of generations.

The second epoch is Metaphysical and Juridical. Its general character is that of possessing no well-defined characteristics. It forms a link and is mongrel and transitional.

. . . Observation is still kept subordinate to imagination, but the former is, within certain limits, allowed to modify the latter. These limits are gradually enlarged, until, in the end, observation conquers the right of examining in every direction. At first it obtains this right in reference to all special theoretical conceptions and gradually, by force of exercise, as to general theoretic ideas, which constitutes the natural termination of the transition. This period is one of criticism and argument.

Under temporal aspects, industry in this second epoch becomes more extended, without as yet acquiring the upper hand. Consequently, society is no longer frankly military and yet has not become frankly industrial, either in its elements or in its *ensemble*. The special social relations are modified. Industrial slavery is no longer direct; the producer, still a slave, begins to obtain some rights in his relations with the military. Industry makes fresh advances which finally issue in the total abolition of individual slavery. After this enfranchisement, the producers still remain subject to a collective arbitrary authority. Nevertheless, the general social relations soon undergo a modification. The two aims of activity, conquest and production, advance *pari passu*. Industry is at first favored and protected as a military resource. Later its importance augments; and finally war is regarded and systematically pursued as a means of favoring industry—which is the last term of the intermediate *régime*.

Lastly, the third epoch is that of Science and Industry. All special theoretic conceptions have become positive, and the general conceptions tend to become so. As regard the former, observation predominates over imagination; while, in reference to the latter, observation has dethroned the imagination, without having as yet taken its place.

Under temporal aspects, industry has become predominant. All the special relations have gradually established themselves on industrial bases. Society, taken collectively, tends to organize itself in the same manner, by making production its only and constant aim.

The last epoch has ended as regards the elements and is commencing as regards the *ensemble*. Its direct point of departure dates from the introduction of the positive sciences into Europe by the Arabs and the enfranchisement of the Commons, that is to say, from about the eleventh century.

In order to prevent all confusion in applying this general view, we should never lose sight of the fact that civilization necessarily progressed in reference to the spiritual and temporal *elements* of the social state before advancing in regard to their *ensemble*. Consequently, the three great and successive phases were inevitably inaugurated as to their elements before they commenced as to the *ensemble,* a circumstance which might occasion some confusion if we did not make a large allowance for this unavoidable difference.

Such, then, are the principal characteristics of the three epochs into which we can divide the entire history of civilization, from the period when the social state began to acquire real solidity until the present time. I venture to submit to savants this primary division of the past, which appears to me to fulfill the essential conditions of a good classification of the *ensemble* of political facts.

CHAPTER 4

OSWALD SPENGLER

The Life Cycle of Cultures

Cultures are organisms, and world history is their collective biography.
Morphologically, the immense history of the Chinese or of the classical culture is the exact equivalent of the petty history of the individual man, or
of the animal, or the tree, or the flower. In the destinies of the several cultures that follow upon one another, grow up with one another, touch, overshadow, and suppress one another, is compressed the whole content of human history. And, if we set free their shapes, till now hidden all too deep
under the surface of a trite "history of human progress" and let them
march past us in the spirit, it cannot but be that we shall succeed in distinguishing, amidst all that is special or unessential, the primitive cultureform, *the* Culture that underlies as ideal all the individual cultures.

I distinguish the *idea* of a culture, which is the sum total of its inner possibilities, from its sensible *phenomenon* or appearance upon the canvas of
history as a fulfilled actuality. It is the relation of the soul to the living body,
to its expression in the light-world perceptible to our eyes. This history of a
culture is the progressive actualizing of its possible, and the fulfillment is
equivalent to the end.

Culture is the *prime phenomenon* of all past and future world history.
The deep and scarcely appreciated idea of Goethe, which he discovered in
his "living nature" and always made the basis of his morphological researches, we shall here apply—in its most precise sense—to all the formations of man's history, whether fully matured, cut off in the prime, half-
opened, or stifled in the seed. It is the method of living into (*erfühlen*) the
object, as opposed to dissecting it. "The highest to which man can attain is
wonder; and, if the prime phenomenon makes him wonder, let him be
content; nothing higher can it give him, and nothing further should he seek
for behind it; here is the limit." The prime phenomenon is that in which the

idea of becoming is presented net. To the spiritual eye of Goethe, the idea of the prime plant was clearly visible in the form of every individual plant that happened to come up or even that could possibly come up. . . . It was a look into the heart of things that Leibniz would have understood, but the century of Darwin is as remote from such a vision as it is possible to be.

At present, however, we look in vain for any treatment of history that is entirely free from the methods of Darwinism—that is, of systematic natural science based on causality. A physiognomic that is precise, clear, and sure of itself and its limits has never yet arisen, and it can only arise through the discoveries of method that we have yet to make. Herein lies the great problem set for the twentieth century to solve—to explore carefully the inner structure of the organic units in and through which world history fulfills itself, to separate the morphologically necessary from the accidental, and, by seizing the *purport* of events, to ascertain the languages in which they speak.

Over the expanse of the water passes the endless uniform wave-train of the generations. Here and there, bright shafts of light broaden out, everywhere dancing flashes confuse and disturb the clear mirror, changing, sparkling, vanishing. These are what we call the clans, tribes, peoples, races which unify a series of generations within this or that limited area of the historical surface. As widely as these differ in creative power, so widely do the images that they create vary in duration and plasticity, and, when the creative power dies out, the physiognomic, linguistic, and spiritual identification marks vanish also, and the phenomenon subsides again into the ruck of the generations. Aryans, Mongols, Germans, Kelts, Parthians, Franks, Carthaginians, Berbers, Bantus are names by which we specify some very heterogeneous images of this order.

But over this surface, too, the great cultures accomplish their majestic wave cycles. They appear suddenly, swell in splendid lines, flatten again, and vanish, and the face of the waters is once more a sleeping waste.

A culture is born in the moment when a great soul awakens out of the protospirituality (*dem urseelenhaften Zustande*) of ever-childish humanity and detaches itself, a form from the formless, a bounded and mortal thing from the boundless and enduring. It blooms on the soil of an exactly definable landscape, to which plant-wise it remains bound. It dies when this soul has actualized the full sum of its possibilities in the shape of peoples, languages, dogmas, arts, states, sciences and reverts into the protosoul. But its living existence, that sequence of great epochs which define and display the stages of fulfillment, is an inner passionate struggle to maintain the Idea against the powers of chaos without and the unconscious muttering deep-down within. It is not only the artist who struggles against the resistance of the material and the stifling of the idea within him. Every culture stands in a deeply symbolical, almost in a mystical, relation to the Extended, the space in which and through which it strives to actualize itself. The aim once attained—the idea, the entire content of inner possibilities, fulfilled and made externally actual—the culture suddenly hardens, it mortifies, its blood congeals, its force breaks down, and it becomes Civilization, the thing which we feel and understand in the words Egypticism, Byzantinism, Mandarinism. As such, they may, like a worn-out giant of the primeval forest, thrust their decaying branches toward the sky for hundreds or thousands of years, as we see in China, in India, in the Islamic world. It was thus that the classical civilization rose gigantic, in the imperial age, with a false semblance of youth and strength and fullness, and robbed the young Arabian culture of the East of light and air.

This—the inward and outward fulfillment, the finality, that awaits every living culture—is the purport of all the historic "declines," among them that decline of the classical which we know so well and fully and another decline, entirely comparable to it in course and duration, which will occupy the first centuries of the coming millennium but is heralded already and sensible in and around us today—the decline of the West. Every culture passes through the age-phases of the individual man. Each has its childhood, youth, manhood, and old age. It is a young and trembling soul, heavy with misgivings, that reveals itself in the morning of Romanesque and Gothic. . . . Childhood speaks to us also—and in the same tones—out of early Homeric Doric, out of early Christian (which is really early Arabian) art and out of the works of the Old Kingdom in Egypt that began with the Fourth Dynasty. . . . The more nearly a culture approaches the noon culmination of its being, the more virile, austere, controlled, intense the form-language it has secured for itself, the more assured its sense of its own power, the clearer its lineaments. In the spring, all this had still been dim and confused, tentative, filled with childish yearning and fears witness the ornament of Romanesque-Gothic church porches of Saxony[1] and southern France, the early Christian catacombs, the Dipylon[2] vases. But there is now the full consciousness of ripened creative power that we see in the time of the early Middle Kingdom of Egypt, in the Athens of the Pisistratidae, in the age of Justinian, in that of the Counterreformation, and we find every individual trait of expression deliberate, strict, measured, marvelous in its ease and self-confidence. And we find, too, that everywhere, at moments, the coming fulfillment suggested itself; in such moments were created the head of Amenemhet III (the so-called Hyksos Sphinx of Tanis), the domes of Hagia Sophia, the paintings of Titian. Still later, tender to the point of fragility, fragrant with the sweetness of late October days, come the Cnidian Aphrodite and the Hall of the Maidens in the Erechtheum; the arabesques on Saracen

---

[1] By "Saxony," a German historian means not the present-day state of Saxony (which was a small and comparatively late accretion), but the whole region of the Weser and the lower Elbe, with Westphalia and Holstein.—TRANS

[2] Vases from the cemetery adjoining the Dipylon Gate of Athens, the most representative relics that we possess of the Doric or primitive age of the Hellenic culture (about 900 to 600 B.C.).—TRANS

horseshoe-arches; the Zwinger of Dresden, Watteau, Mozart. At last, in the gray dawn of civilization, the fire in the soul dies down. The dwindling powers rise to one more half-successful effort of creation and produce the classicism that is common to all dying cultures. The soul thinks once again and in Romanticism looks back piteously to its childhood; then finally, weary, reluctant, cold, it loses its desire to be and, as in Imperial Rome, wishes itself out of the overlong daylight and back in the darkness of protomysticism, in the womb of the mother, in the grave. . . .

The notion of life duration as applied to a man, a butterfly, an oak, a blade of grass comprises a specific time value, which is quite independent of all the accidents of the individual case. Ten years are a slice of life which is approximately equivalent for all men, and the metamorphosis of insects is associated with a number of days exactly known and predictable in individual cases. For the Romans the notions of *pueritia, adolescentia, iuventus, virilitas, senectus* possessed an almost mathematically precise meaning. . . . The duration of a generation—whatever may be its nature—is a fact of almost mystical significance.

Now, such relations are valid also, and to an extent never hitherto imagined, for all the higher cultures. *Every culture, every adolescence and maturing and decay of a culture, every one of its intrinsically necessary stages and periods, has a definite duration, always the same, always recurring with the emphasis of a symbol.* . . . What is the meaning of that striking fifty-year period, the rhythm of the political, intellectual, and artistic "becoming" of all cultures? [3] Of the 300-year period of the Baroque, of the Ionic, of the great mathematics, of Attic sculpture, of mosaic painting, of counterpoint, of Galilean mechanics? What does the *ideal* life of one millennium for each culture mean in comparison with the individual man's "three-score years and ten"? As the plant's being is brought to expression in form, dress, and carriage by leaves, blossoms, twigs, and fruit, so also is the being of a culture manifested by its religious, intellectual, political, and economic formations. Just as, say, Goethe's individuality discourses of itself in such widely different forms as the *Faust,* the *Farbenlehre,* the *Reineke Fuchs, Tasso, Werther,* the journey to Italy and the Friederike love, the *Westöstliche Diwan* and the *Römische Elegien,* so the individuality of the classical world displays itself in the Persian wars, the Attic drama, the city-state, the Dionysia and not less in the Tyrannis, the Ionic column, the geometry of Euclid, the Roman legion, and the gladiatorial contests and *panem et circenses* of the Imperial age.

In this sense, too, every individual being that has any sort of importance

---

[3] I will only mention here the distances apart of the three Punic Wars, and the series —likewise comprehensible only as rhythmic—Spanish Succession War, Silesian wars, Napoleonic Wars, Bismarck's wars, and the World War.

recapitulates, of intrinsic necessity, all the epochs of the culture to which it belongs. In each one of us, at that decisive moment when he begins to know that he is an ego, the inner life wakens just where and just how that of the culture wakened long ago. Each of us men of the West, in his child's daydreams and child's play, lives again its Gothic—the cathedrals, the castles, the hero sagas, the crusader's *Dieu le veult,* the soul's oath of young Parsifal. Every young Greek had his Homeric age and his Marathon. In Goethe's Werther, the image of a tropic youth, that every Faustian (but no classical) man knows, the springtime of Petrarch and the Minnesänger reappears. When Goethe blocked out the *Urfaust,*[4] he was Parsifal; when he finished *Faust I,* he was Hamlet, and only with *Faust II* did he become the world-man of the nineteenth century who could understand Byron. Even the senility of the classical—the faddy and unfruitful centuries of very late Hellenism, the second childhood of a weary and blasé intelligence—can be studied in more than one of its grand old men. Thus, much of Euripides' *Bacchae* anticipates the life outlook, and much of Plato's *Timaeus,* the religious syncretism of the Imperial age; and Goethe's *Faust II* and Wagner's *Parsifal* disclose to us in advance the shape that *our* spirituality will assume in our next (*in point of creative power our last*) centuries.

Biology employs the term *homology* of organs to signify morphological equivalence, in contradistinction to the term *analogy* which relates to functional equivalence. This important, and in the sequel most fruitful, notion was conceived by Goethe (who was led thereby to the discovery of the *os intermaxillare* in man) and put into strict scientific shape by Owen; this notion, also, we shall incorporate in our historical method.

It is known that for every part of the bone structure of the human head an exactly corresponding part is found in all vertebrated animals right down to the fish and that the pectoral fins of fish and the feet, wings and hands of terrestrial vertebrates are homologous organs, even though they have lost every trace of similarity. The lungs of terrestrial and the swim bladders of aquatic animals are homologous, while lungs and gills on the other hand are analogous—that is, similar in point of use. And the trained and deepened morphological insight that is required to establish such distinctions is an utterly different thing from the present method of historical research, with its shallow comparisons of Christ and Buddha, Archimedes and Galileo, Caesar and Wallenstein, parceled Germany and parceled Greece. More and more clearly as we go on, we shall realize what immense views will offer themselves to the historical eye as soon as the rigorous morphological method has been understood and cultivated. To name but a few examples, *homologous* forms are: classical sculpture and West European orchestration; the Fourth Dynasty pyramids and the Gothic cathedrals; Indian Buddhism and Roman Stoicism (Buddhism and Christianity are *not even*

---

[4] The first draft of *Faust I,* discovered only comparatively recently.—TRANS

analogous); the periods of "the Contending States" in China; the Hyksos in Egypt and the Punic Wars; the age of Pericles and the age of the Ommayads; the epochs of the Rigveda, of Plotinus, and of Dante. The Dionysiac movement is homologous with the Renaissance, analogous to the Reformation. For us, "Wagner is the *résumé* of modernity," as Nietzsche rightly saw; and the equivalent that logically *must* exist in the Classical modernity we find in Pergamene art. . . .

The application of the "homology" principle to historical phenomena brings with it an entirely new connotation for the word "contemporary." I designate as contemporary two historical facts that occur in exactly the same relative positions in their respective cultures and therefore possess exactly equivalent importance. The development of the classical and that of the Western mathematic proceeded in complete congruence, and we might venture to describe Pythagoras as the contemporary of Descartes; Archytas, of Laplace; Archimedes, of Gauss. The Ionic and the Baroque, again, ran their course *contemporaneously*. Polygnotus pairs in time with Rembrandt; Polycletus, with Bach. The Reformation, Puritanism, and, above all, the turn to civilization appear simultaneously in all cultures. In the classical, this last epoch bears the names of Philip and Alexander; in our West, those of the Revolution and Napoleon. Contemporary, too, are the building of Alexandria, of Baghdad, and of Washington; classical coinage and our double-entry bookkeeping; the first Tyrannis and the Fronde; Augustus and Shih-huang-ti; Hannibal and the World War.

. . . All great creations and forms in religion, art, politics, social life, economy, and science appear, fulfill themselves, and die down *contemporaneously* in all the cultures; the inner structure of one corresponds strictly with that of all the others; there is not a single phenomenon of deep physiognomic importance in the record of one for which we could not find a counterpart in the record of every other; and this counterpart is to be found under a characteristic form and in a perfectly definite chronological position. . . .

CHAPTER 5

ARNOLD J. TOYNBEE

The Nature of the Growth
of Civilizations

Two False Trails

We have found by observation that the most stimulating challenge is one
of mean degree between an excess of severity and a deficiency of it, since a
deficient challenge may fail to stimulate the challenged party at all, while an
excessive challenge may break his spirit. But what about the challenge with
which he is just capable of coping? On a short view, this is the most stimulating challenge imaginable; and, in the concrete instances of the Polynesians and the Eskimos and the Nomads and the Osmanlis and the Spartans,
we have observed that such challenges are apt to evoke *tours de force*. We
have also observed, however, that, in the next chapter of the story, these
tours de force exact, from those who have performed them, a fatal penalty
in the shape of an arrest in their development. Therefore, on the longer
view, we must pronounce that the evocation of the greatest immediate response is not the ultimate test of whether any given challenge is the optimum from the standpoint of evoking the greatest response on the whole and
in the end. The real optimum challenge is one which not only stimulates the
challenged party to achieve a single successful response but also stimulates
him to acquire momentum that carries him a step farther—from achievement to a fresh struggle, from the solution of one problem to the presentation of another. The single finite movement from a disturbance to a restoration of equilibrium is not enough if genesis is to be followed by growth. And,
to convert the movement into a repetitive, recurrent rhythm, there must be
an *élan vital* (to use Bergson's term) which carries the challenged party
through equilibrium into an overbalance which exposes him to a fresh

From Arnold J. Toynbee, *A Study of History,* volumes I-VI abridged by D. C. Somer-
vell (New York: Oxford University Press, 1946), pp. 187-208. Copyright 1946 by
Oxford University Press, Inc., and reprinted by permission.

challenge and thereby inspires him to make a fresh response in the form of
a further equilibrium ending in a further overbalance, and so on in a progression which is potentially infinite.

This *élan,* working through a series of overbalances, can be detected in
the course of the Hellenic civilization from its genesis up to its zenith in the
fifth century B.C.

The first challenge presented to the new-born Hellenic civilization was the
challenge of chaos and ancient night. The disintegration of the apparented
Minoan society had left a welter of social debris—marooned Minoans and
stranded Achaeans and Dorians. Would the sediment of an old civilization
be buried under the shingle which the new torrent of barbarism had brought
down in spate? Would the rare patches of lowland in the Achaean landscape
be dominated by the wilderness of highlands that ringed them round? Would
the peaceful cultivators of the plains be at the mercy of the shepherds and
brigands of the mountains?

This first challenge was victoriously met; it was decided that Hellas
should be a world of cities and not of villages, of agriculture and not of
pasturage, of order and not of anarchy. Yet the very success of their response to this first challenge exposed the victors to a second. For the victory
which ensured the peaceful pursuit of agriculture in the lowlands gave a
momentum to the growth of population, and this momentum did not come
to a standstill when the population reached the maximum density which
agriculture in the Hellenic homeland could support. Thus the very success of
the response to the first challenge exposed the infant Hellenic society to a
second, and it responded to this Malthusian challenge as successfully as to
the challenge of chaos.

The Hellenic response to the challenge of overpopulation took the form
of a series of alternative experiments. The easiest and most obvious expedient was adopted first and was applied until it began to bring in diminishing
returns. Thereupon, a more difficult and less obvious expedient was adopted
and applied, in place of the first, until this time a solution of the problem
was achieved.

The first method was to employ the techniques and institutions which
the lowlanders of Hellas had created in the process of imposing their wills
on their highland neighbors at home in order to conquer new domains
for Hellenism overseas. With the military instrument of the hoplite phalanx
and the political instrument of the city state, a swarm of Hellenic pioneers
established a Magna Graecia in the toe of Italy at the expense of barbarian Itali and Chônes, a new Peloponnese in Sicily at the expense of
barbarian Sikels, a new Hellenic pentapolis in Cyrenaica at the expense
of barbarian Libyans, and a Chalcidicê on the north coast of the Aegean at
the expense of barbarian Thracians. Yet, once again, the very success of the
response brought down a new challenge on the victors. For what they had
done was in itself a challenge to the other Mediterranean peoples; and eventu-

ally the non-Hellenic peoples were stimulated to bring the expansion of Hellas to a standstill—partly by resisting Hellenic aggression with borrowed Hellenic arts and arms and partly by coordinating their own forces on a greater scale than the Hellenes themselves were able to achieve. Thus the Hellenic expansion, which had begun in the eighth century B.C., was brought to a standstill in the course of the sixth. Yet the Hellenic society was still confronted by the challenge of overpopulation.

In this new crisis in Hellenic history the required discovery was made by Athens, who became "the education of Hellas" through learning, and teaching, how to transmute the expansion of the Hellenic society from an extensive into an intensive process—a significant transmutation of which we shall have more to say later in this chapter.

Civilizations, it would seem, grow through an *élan* which carries them from challenge through response to further challenge, and this growth has both outward and inward aspects. In the macrocosm, growth reveals itself as a progressive mastery over the external environment; in the microcosm, as a progressive self-determination or self-articulation. In either of these manifestations, we have a possible criterion of the progress of the *élan* itself. Let us examine each manifestation in turn from this standpoint.

In considering first the progressive conquest of the external environment, we shall find it convenient to subdivide the external environment into the human environment, which for any society consists of the other human societies with which it finds itself in contact and the physical environment constituted by nonhuman nature. Progressive conquest of the human environment will normally express itself in the form of a geographical extension of the society in question, whereas progressive conquest of the non-human environment will normally express itself in the form of improvements in technique. Let us begin with the former, namely, geographical expansion, and see how far this deserves to be considered an adequate criterion of the real growth of a civilization.

Our readers would be unlikely to quarrel with us if we asserted, without more ado and without troubling to marshal any of the voluminous and overwhelming evidence, that geographical expansion, or "painting the map red," is no criterion whatever of the real growth of a civilization. Sometimes we find that a period of geographical expansion coincides in date with, and is a partial manifestation of, qualitative progress—as in the case of the early Hellenic expansion just cited in another connection. More often, geographical expansion is a concomitant of real decline and coincides with a "time of troubles" or a universal state—both of them stages of decline and disintegration. The reason is not far to seek. Times of trouble produce militarism, which is a perversion of the human spirit into channels of mutual destruction, and the most successful militarist becomes, as a rule, the founder of a universal state. Geographical expansion is a byproduct of this militarism, in interludes when the mighty men of valor turn aside from their assaults on their rivals within their own society to deliver assaults on neighboring societies.

Militarism, as we shall see at a later point in this study, has been by far the commonest cause of the breakdowns of civilizations during the last four or five millennia which have witnessed the score or so of breakdowns that are on record up to the present date. Militarism breaks a civilization down by causing the local states into which the society is articulated to collide with one another in destructive fratricidal conflicts. In this suicidal process, the entire social fabric becomes fuel to feed the devouring flame in the brazen bosom of Moloch. This single art of war makes progress at the expense of the divers arts of peace; and, before this deadly ritual has completed the destruction of all its votaries, they may have become so expert in the use of their implements of slaughter that, if they happen for a moment to pause from their orgy of mutual destruction and to turn their weapons for a season against the breasts of strangers, they are apt to carry all before them.

Indeed, a study of Hellenic history might suggest a conclusion exactly the converse of that which we have rejected. We have noticed already that, at one stage in its history, the Hellenic society met the challenge of overpopulation by geographical expansion and that, after some two centuries (*circa* 750-550 B.C.), this expansion was brought to a halt by surrounding non-Hellenic powers. Thereafter, the Hellenic society was on the defensive, assaulted by the Persians from the east in its homelands and by the Carthaginians from the west in its more recently acquired domains. During this period, as Thucydides saw it, "Hellas was repressed from all sides over a long period of time," and, as Herodotus saw it, "was overwhelmed by more troubles than in the twenty preceding generations." [1] The modern reader finds it difficult to realize that, in these melancholy sentences, the two greatest Greek historians are describing the age which, in the sight of posterity, stands out in retrospect as the acme of the Hellenic civilization, the age in which the Hellenic genius performed those great acts of creation, in every field of social life, which have made Hellenism immortal. Herodotus and Thucydides felt as they did about this creative age because it was an age in which, in contrast to its predecessor, the geographical expansion of Hellas was held in check. Yet there can be no disputing that, during this century, the *élan* of the growth of the Hellenic civilization was greater than ever before or after. And, if these historians could have been endowed with superhuman longevity to enable them to watch the sequel, they would have been amazed to observe that the breakdown marked by the Atheno-Peloponnesian War was followed by a fresh outburst of geographical expansion —the expansion of Hellenism overland, inaugurated by Alexander—far surpassing in material scale the earlier maritime expansion of Hellas. During

---

[1] Thucydides i. 17; Herodotus vi. 98.

the two centuries that followed Alexander's passage of the Hellespont, Hellenism expanded in Asia and the Nile Valley at the expense of all the other civilizations that it encountered—the Syriac, the Egyptiac, the Babylonic, and the Indic. And, for some two centuries after that, it continued to expand, under the Roman aegis, in the barbarian hinterlands in Europe and North-West Africa. Yet these were the centuries during which the Hellenic civilization was palpably in process of disintegration. . . .

We will now pass on to the next division of our subject and consider whether the progressive conquest of the physical environment by improvements in technique will provide us with an adequate criterion of the true growth of a civilization. Is there evidence of a positive correlation between an improvement in technique and a progress in social growth? . . .

When we turn to the evidence we shall find cases of technique improving while civilizations remain static or go into decline as well as examples of the converse situation in which technique remains static while civilizations are in movement—either forward or backward, as the case may be.

For instance, a high technique has been developed by every one of the arrested civilizations. The Polynesians have excelled as navigators, the Eskimos as fishermen, the Spartans as soldiers, the Nomads as tamers of horses, the Osmanlis as tamers of men. These are all cases in which civilizations have remained static while technique has improved.

An example of technique improving while a civilization declines is afforded by the contrast between the Upper Palaeolithic age in Europe and the Lower Neolithic, which is its immediate successor in the technological series. The Upper Palaeolithic society remained content with implements of rough workmanship, but it developed a fine aesthetic sense and did not neglect to discover certain simple means of giving it pictorial expression. The deft and vivid charcoal sketches of animals which survive on the walls of Palaeolithic man's cave dwellings excite our admiration. The Lower Neolithic society took infinite pains to equip itself with finely ground tools and possibly turned these tools to account in a struggle for existence with Palaeolithic man in which *Homo pictor* went down and left *Homo faber* master of the field. In any case, the change, which inaugurates a striking progress in terms of technique, is distinctly a setback in terms of civilization, for the art of Upper Palaeolithic man died with him.

•

Procopius of Caesarea, the last of the great Hellenic historians, prefaces his history of the wars of the Emperor Justinian—wars which actually sounded the death knell of the Hellenic society—with a claim that his subject was superior in interest to those chosen by his predecessors because his own contemporaries' military technique was superior to that employed in any previous wars. In truth, if we were to isolate the history of the technique of war from the other strands of Hellenic history, we should find a continuous

progress from first to last, through the period of the growth of that civilization and onward through its decline as well; and we should also find that
each step in the progress of this technique had been stimulated by events
that were disastrous for civilization.

To begin with, the invention of the Spartan phalanx, the first signal Hellenic military improvement on record, was an outcome of the Second Sparto-
Messenian War, which brought the Hellenic civilization in Sparta to a premature halt. The next signal improvement was the differentiation of the
Hellenic infantryman into two extreme types: the Macedonian phalangite
and the Athenian peltast. The Macedonian phalanx, armed with long, two-
handed pikes in place of short, one-handed stabbing-spears, was more formidable in its impact than its Spartan predecessor, but it was also more un-
wieldy and more vulnerable if it once lost formation. It could not safely go
into action unless its flanks were guarded by peltasts, a new type of light infantry who were taken out of the ranks and trained as skirmishers. This second improvement was the outcome of a century of deadly war, from the outbreak of the Atheno-Peloponnesian War to the Macedonian victory over
Thebans and Athenians at Chaeronea (431-338 B.C.), which saw the first
breakdown of the Hellenic civilization. The next signal improvement was
made by the Romans, when they succeeded in combining the advantages
and avoiding the defects of both peltast and phalangite in the tactics and
equipment of the legionary. The legionary was armed with a couple of
throwing-spears and a stabbing-sword and went into action in open order
in two waves, with a third wave, armed and ordered in the old phalanx style,
in reserve. This third improvement was the outcome of a fresh bout of
deadly warfare, from the outbreak of the Hannibalic War in 220 B.C. to the
end of the Third Romano-Macedonian War in 168 B.C. The fourth and last
improvement was the perfection of the legion, a process, begun by Marius
and completed by Caesar, which was the outcome of a century of Roman
revolutions and civil wars ending in the establishment of the Roman Empire
as the Hellenic universal state. Justinian's cataphract—the armored rider on
an armored mount whom Procopius presents to his readers as the *chef
d'oeuvre* of Hellenic military technique—does not represent a further stage
in this native Hellenic line of development. The cataphract was an adaptation, by the last decadent generations of the Hellenic society, of the military
instrument of their Iranian contemporaries, neighbors and antagonists, who
had first made Rome aware of their prowess when they defeated Crassus at
Carrhae in 55 B.C.

Nor is the art of war the only kind of technique that is apt to make its progress in inverse ratio to the general progress of the body social. Let us now
take a technique which stands at the furthest remove from the art of war—
the technique of agriculture, which is generally regarded as par excellence
the sovereign art of peace. If we revert to Hellenic history, we shall find that

an improvement in the technique of this art has been the accompaniment of a decline in a civilization.

At the outset, we seem to be entering on a different story. Whereas the first improvement in the Hellenic art of war was purchased at the price of an arrest in the growth of the particular community that invented it, the first comparable improvement in Hellenic agriculture had a happier sequel. When Attica, on Solon's initiative, led the way from a regime of mixed farming to a regime of specialized agriculture for export, this technical advance was followed by an outburst of energy and growth in every sphere of Attic life. The next chapter of the story, however, takes a different and a sinister turn. The next stage of technical advance was an increase in the scale of operations through the organization of mass production based on slave labor. This step appears to have been taken in the colonial Hellenic communities in Sicily and perhaps first in Agrigentum, for the Sicilian Greeks found an expanding market for their wine and oil among the neighboring barbarians. Here the technical advance was offset by a grave social lapse, for the new plantation slavery was a far more serious social evil than the old domestic slavery. It was worse both morally and statistically. It was impersonal and inhuman, and it was on a grand scale. It eventually spread from the Greek communities in Sicily to the great area of Southern Italy which had been left derelict and devastated by the Hannibalic War. Wherever it established itself, it notably increased the productivity of the land and the profits of the capitalist, but it reduced the land to social sterility, for, wherever slave plantations spread, they displaced and pauperized the peasant yeoman as inexorably as bad money drives out good. The social consequence was the depopulation of the countryside and the creation of a parasitic urban proletariat in the cities, and more particularly in Rome itself. Not all the efforts of successive generations of Roman reformers, from the Gracchi onward, could avail to rid the Roman world of this social blight which the last advance in agricultural technique had brought on it. The plantation-slave system persisted until it collapsed spontaneously in consequence of the breakdown of the money economy on which it was dependent for its profits. This financial breakdown was part of the general social debacle of the third century after Christ; and the debacle was doubtless the outcome, in part, of the agrarian malady which had been eating away the tissues of the Roman body social during the previous four centuries. Thus this social cancer eventually extinguished itself by causing the death of the society on which it had fastened. . . .

Progress toward Self-Determination

The history of the development of technique, like the history of geographical expansion, has failed to provide us with a criterion of the growth of civilizations, but it does reveal a principle by which technical progress is governed, which may be described as a law of progressive simplification. The ponderous and bulky steam engine with its elaborate "permanent way" is replaced by the neat and handy internal combustion engine which can take to the roads with the speed of a railway train and almost all the freedom of action of a pedestrian. Telegraphy with wires is replaced by telegraphy without wires. The incredibly complicated scripts of the Sinic and Egyptiac societies are replaced by the neat and handy Latin alphabet. Language itself shows the same tendency to simplify itself by abandoning inflections in favor of auxiliary words, as may be illustrated by a comparative view of the histories of the languages of the Indo-European family. Sanskrit, the earliest surviving example of this family, displays an amazing wealth of inflections side by side with a surprising poverty of particles. Modern English, at the other end of the scale, has got rid of nearly all its inflections, but has recouped itself by the development of prepositions and auxiliary verbs. Classical Greek represents a middle term between these two extremes. In the modern Western world, dress has been simplified from the barbaric complexity of Elizabethan costume to the plain modes of today. The Copernican astronomy, which has replaced the Ptolemaic system, presents, in far simpler geometrical terms, an equally coherent explanation of a vastly wider range of movement of the heavenly bodies.

Perhaps simplification is not quite an accurate, or at least not altogether an adequate, term for describing these changes. Simplification is a negative word and connotes omission and elimination, whereas what has happened in each of these cases is not a diminution but an enhancement of practical efficiency or of aesthetic satisfaction or of intellectual grasp. The result is not a loss but a gain; and this gain is the outcome of a process of simplification because the process liberates forces that have been imprisoned in a more material medium and thereby sets them free to work in a more ethereal medium with a greater potency. It involves, not merely a simplification of apparatus, but a consequent transfer of energy, or shift of emphasis, from some lower sphere of being or of action to a higher. Perhaps we shall be describing the process in a more illuminating way if we call it, not simplification, but etherealization.

In the sphere of human control over physical nature, this development has been described with a finely imaginative touch by a modern anthropologist:

> We are leaving the ground, we are getting out of touch, our tracks grow fainter. Flint lasts forever, copper for a civilization, iron for generations, steel for a lifetime. Who will be able to map the route of the London-Peking air express when the Age of Movement is over or today to say what is the path through the aether of the messages which are radiated and received? But the frontiers of the petty vanished kingdom of the Iceni still sweep defensively

across the southern frontier of East Anglia, from drained marsh to obliterated forest.

Our illustrations suggest that the criterion of growth, for which we are in search and which we failed to discover in the conquest of the external environment, either human or physical, lies rather in a progressive change of emphasis and shifting of the scene of action out of this field into another field, in which the action of challenge and response may find an alternative arena. In this other field, challenges do not impinge from outside, but arise from within, and victorious responses do not take the form of surmounting external obstacles or of overcoming an external adversary, but manifest themselves in an inward self-articulation or self-determination. When we watch an individual human being or an individual society making successive responses to a succession of challenges, and when we ask ourselves whether this particular series is to be regarded as a manifestation of growth, we shall arrive at an answer to our question by observing whether, as the series proceeds, the action does or does not tend to shift from the first to the second of the two fields aforesaid. . . .

If we arrange the outstanding characters of the great Shakespearian gallery in an ascending order of etherealization, and if we bear in mind that the playwright's technique is to reveal characters by displaying personalities in action, we shall observe that, as Shakespeare moves upward from the lower to the higher levels in our character scale, he constantly shifts the field of action in which he makes the hero of each drama play his part, giving the microcosm an ever-larger share of the stage and pushing the macrocosm ever further into the background. We can verify this fact if we follow the series from *Henry V* through *Macbeth* to *Hamlet*. The relatively primitive character of Henry V is revealed almost entirely in his responses to challenges from the human environment around him—in his relations with his boon companions and with his father and in his communication of his own high courage to his comrades-in-arms on the morning of Agincourt and in his impetuous wooing of Princess Kate. When we pass to Macbeth, we find the scene of action shifting, for Macbeth's relations with Malcolm or Macduff or even with Lady Macbeth are equaled in importance by the hero's relations with himself. Finally, when we come to Hamlet, we see him allowing the macrocosm almost to fade away, until the hero's relations with his father's murderers, with his spent flame Ophelia, and with his outgrown mentor Horatio become absorbed into the internal conflict which is working itself out in the hero's own soul. In *Hamlet,* the field of action has been transferred from the macrocosm to the microcosm almost completely; and in this masterpiece of Shakespeare's art, as in Aeschylus' *Prometheus* or in Browning's dramatic monologues, a single actor virtually monopolizes the stage in order to leave the greater scope for action to the surging spiritual forces which this one personality holds within itself.

This transference of the field of action, which we discern in Shakespeare's presentation of his heroes when we arrange them in an ascending order of spiritual growth, can also be discerned in the histories of civilizations. Here too, when a series of responses to challenges accumulates into a growth, we shall find, as this growth proceeds, that the field of action is shifting all the time from the external environment into the interior of the society's own body social. . . .

In Hellenic history, for example, we have seen that the earlier challenges all emanated from the external environment—the challenge of highland barbarism in Hellas itself and the Malthusian challenge, which were met by expansion overseas and involved as their consequences challenges from indigenous barbarians and rival civilizations, the challenges of these latter culminating in the simultaneous counterattacks of Carthage and Persia in the first quarter of the fifth century B.C. Thereafter, however, this formidable challenge from the human environment was triumphantly surmounted in the four centuries beginning with Alexander's passage of the Hellespont and continuing with the victories of Rome. Thanks to these triumphs, the Hellenic society now enjoyed a respite of some five or six centuries during which no serious challenge from the external environment was presented to it. But this did not mean that, during those centuries, the Hellenic society was exempt from challenges altogether. On the contrary, as we have already noted, these centuries were a period of decline, that is to say, a period in which Hellenism was confronted by challenges to which it was failing to respond with success. We have seen what these challenges were, and, if we now look into them again, we shall see that they were all internal challenges resulting from the victorious response to the previous external challenge, as the challenge presented by feudalism to our Western society resulted from the previous development of feudalism as a means of response to the external pressure of the Vikings.

For example, the military pressure from the Persians and the Carthaginians stimulated the Hellenic society to forge in self-defense two potent social and military instruments, the Athenian navy and the Syracusan *tyrannis*. These produced, in the next generation, internal strains and stresses in the Hellenic body social; these resulted in the Atheno-Peloponnesian War and in the reaction against Syracuse of her barbarian subjects and of her Greek allies; and these convulsions produced the first breakdown of the Hellenic society.

In the following chapters of Hellenic history, the arms turned outward in the conquests of Alexander and the Scipios were soon turned inward in the civil wars of rival Macedonian diadochi and rival Roman dictators. Similarly, the economic rivalry between the Hellenic and Syriac societies for the mastery of the Western Mediterranean reappeared within the bosom of the

Hellenic society, after the Syriac competitor had succumbed, in the still-more-devastating struggle between the Oriental plantation slaves and their Siceliot or Roman masters. The cultural conflict between Hellenism and the Oriental civilizations—Syriac and Egyptiac and Babylonic and Indic—likewise reappeared within the bosom of the Hellenic society as an internal crisis in Hellenic, or Hellenized, souls—the crisis that declared itself in the emergence of Isis-worship and astrology and Mithraism and Christianity and a host of other syncretistic religions. . . .

Corresponding transmutations of external into internal challenges have followed the triumph of the Western civilization over its material environment. The triumphs of the so-called Industrial Revolution in the technical sphere notoriously created a host of problems in the economic and social spheres, a subject at once so complicated and so familiar that we need not enlarge on it here. Let us call to our minds the now fast-fading picture of the premechanical road. This antique road is thronged with all kinds of primitive wheeled vehicles: wheelbarrows and rickshaws and oxcarts and dogcarts, with a stagecoach as the *chef d'oeuvre* of muscular traction and a foot-propelled bicycle here and there as a portent of things to come. Since the road is already rather crowded, there are a certain number of collisions; but nobody minds, because few are hurt, and the traffic is scarcely interrupted. For the fact is, these collisions are not serious. They cannot be serious because the traffic is so slow and the force impelling it so feeble. The "traffic problem" on this road is not the problem of avoiding collisions, but the problem of getting the journey accomplished at all, roads being what they were in the old days. Accordingly, there is no sort of traffic regulation, no policeman on duty or signal lights.

And now let us turn our eyes to the road of today, on which a mechanical traffic hums and roars. On this road, the problems of speed and haulage have been solved, as is testified by the motor-lorry, with its train of trucks that comes lumbering along with more than the momentum of a charging elephant and by the sports car that goes whizzing past with the swiftness of a bee or a bullet. But, by the same token, the problem of collisions has become the traffic problem par excellence. Hence, on this latter-day road, the problem is no longer technological but psychological. The old challenge of physical distance has been transmuted into a new challenge of human relations between drivers who, having learned how to annihilate space, have thereby put themselves in constant danger of annihilating one another.

This change in the nature of the traffic problem has, of course, a symbolic as well as a literal significance. It typifies the general change that has occurred over the whole range of our modern Western social life since the emergence of the two dominant social forces of the age: industrialism and democracy. Owing to the extraordinary progress which our latter-day inventors have made in harnessing the energies of physical nature and in organizing the concerted actions of millions of human beings, everything that is now done in our society is done, for good or evil, with tremendous "drive"; and this has made the material consequences of actions and the moral responsibility of agents far heavier than ever before. It may be that, in every age of every society, some moral issue is always the challenge that is fateful for the society's future; but, however that may be, there is no doubt that it is a moral challenge rather than a physical challenge that confronts our own society today.

> In the present-day thinker's attitude toward what is called mechanical progress, we are conscious of a changed spirit. Admiration is tempered by criticism; complacency has given way to doubt; doubt is passing into alarm. There is a sense of perplexity and frustration, as in one who has gone a long way and finds he has taken the wrong turning. To go back is impossible; how shall he proceed? Where will he find himself if he follows this path or that? An old exponent of applied mechanics may be forgiven if he expresses something of the disillusion with which, now standing aside, he watches the sweeping pageant of discovery and invention in which he used to take unbounded delight. It is impossible not to ask: Whither does this tremendous procession tend? What, after all, is its goal? What is its probable influence upon the future of the human race? [1]

These moving words propound a question which has been struggling to find expression in all our hearts; and they are words spoken with authority, for they were uttered by the president of the British Association for the Advancement of Science, in his opening address at the hundred-and-first annual meeting of that historic body. Is the new social driving power of industrialism and democracy to be employed in the great constructive task of organizing a Westernized world into an ecumenical society, or are we going to turn our new power to our own destruction?

In a perhaps rather simpler form, the same dilemma once presented itself to the rulers of ancient Egypt. When the Egyptiac pioneers had victoriously responded to their first physical challenge, when the water and soil and vegetation of the Lower Nile Valley had been subjected to the wills of human beings, the question arose how the lord and master of Egypt and the Egyptians would use the marvelous human organization ready to his hand and responsive to his will. It was a moral challenge. Would he employ the material power and the manpower at his command to improve the lot of his subjects? Would he lead them upward and onward to the level of well-being that had been attained already by the king himself and a handful of his peers? Would he play the generous part of Prometheus in Aeschylus' drama or the tyrannous part of Zeus? We know the answer. He built the Pyramids; and the Pyramids have immortalized these autocrats, not as ever-

---

[1] Sir Alfred Ewing, as reported in *The Times*, September 1, 1932.

living gods but as grinders of the faces of the poor. Their evil reputations were handed down in Egyptiac folklore till they found their way into the immortal pages of Herodotus. As a nemesis for their misguided choice, death laid his icy hand on the life of this growing civilization at the moment when the challenge which was the stimulus of its growth was transferred from the external to the internal field. In the somewhat similar situation of our own world today, when the challenge of industrialism is being transferred from the sphere of technique to the sphere of morals, the outcome is still unknown, since our reaction to the new situation is still undecided.

. . . We conclude that a given series of successful responses to successive challenges is to be interpreted as a manifestation of growth if, as the series proceeds, the action tends to shift from the field of an external environment, physical or human, to the *for intérieur* of the growing personality or civilization. Insofar as this grows and continues to grow, it has to reckon less and less with challenges delivered by external forces and demanding responses on an outer battlefield and more and more with challenges that are presented by itself to itself in an inner arena. Growth means that the growing personality or civilization tends to become its own environment and its own challenger and its own field of action. In other words, the criterion of growth is progress toward self-determination; and progress toward self-determination in a prosaic formula for describing the miracle by which life enters into its kingdom.

CHAPTER 6

KARL MARX

Historical Materialism
Summarized

In the social production which men carry on, they enter into definite re-lations that are indispensable and independent of their will; these relations of production correspond to a definite stage of development of their material powers of production. The sum total of these relations of production consti-tutes the economic structure of society—the real foundation, on which rise legal and political superstructures and to which correspond definite forms of social consciousness. The mode of production in material life determines the general character of the social, political, and spiritual processes of life. It is not the consciousness (*Bewusstsein*) of men that determines their exist-ence (*sein*), but, on the contrary, their social existence that determines their consciousness. At a certain stage of their development, the material forces of production in society come in conflict with the existing relations of production or—what is but a legal expression for the same thing—with the property relations within which they had been at work before. From forms of development of the forces of production, these relations turn into their fetters. Then comes the period of social revolution. With the change of the economic foundation, the entire immense superstructure is more or less rapidly transformed. In considering such transformations, the distinction should always be made between the material transformation of the eco-nomic conditions of production, which can be determined with the precision of natural science, and the legal, political, religious, aesthetic, or philosophic —in short, ideological—forms in which men become conscious of this con-flict and fight it out. Just as our opinion of an individual is not based on what he thinks of himself, so can we not judge of such a period of transforma-tion by its own consciousness; on the contrary, this consciousness must

From the author's Introduction to Karl Marx, *A Contribution to the Critique of Po-litical Economy* (Chicago: Charles H. Kerr, 1904), pp. 11-13.

rather be explained from the contradictions of material life, from the existing conflict between the social forces of production and the relations of production. No social order ever disappears before all the productive forces, for which there is room in it, have been developed; and new, higher relations of production never appear before the material conditions of their existence have matured in the womb of the old society. Therefore, mankind always takes up only such problems as it can solve, since, looking at the matter more closely, we will always find that the problem itself arises only when the material conditions necessary for its solution already exist or are at least in the process of formation. In broad outlines we can designate the Asiatic, the ancient, the feudal, and the modern bourgeois methods of production as so many epochs in the progress of the economic formation of society. The bourgeois relations of production are the last antagonistic form of the social process of production—antagonistic not in the sense of individual antagonism, but of one arising from conditions surrounding the life of individuals in society; at the same time, the productive forces developing in the womb of bourgeois society create the material conditions for the solution of that antagonism. This social formation constitutes, therefore, the closing chapter of the prehistoric stage of human society.

CHAPTER 7

KARL MARX AND FRIEDRICH ENGELS

The Class Struggle

Bourgeoisie and Proletariat

The history of all hitherto existing society is the history of class struggles.

Freeman and slave, patrician and plebeian, lord and serf, guildmaster and journeyman, in a word, oppressor and oppressed, stood in constant opposition to one another, carried on an uninterrupted, now hidden, now open fight, a fight that each time ended either in a revolutionary reconstitution of society at large or in the common ruin of the contending classes.

In the earlier epochs of history, we find almost everywhere a complicated arrangement of society into various orders, a manifold gradation of social rank. In ancient Rome we have patricians, knights, plebeians, slaves; in the Middle Ages, feudal lords, vassals, guildmasters, journeymen, apprentices, serfs; in almost all of these classes, again, subordinate gradations.

The modern bourgeois society that has sprouted from the ruins of feudal society has not done away with class antagonisms. It has but established new classes, new conditions of oppression, new forms of struggle in place of the old ones.

Our epoch, the epoch of the bourgeoisie, possesses, however, this distinctive feature: it has simplified the class antagonisms. Society as a whole is more and more splitting up into two great hostile camps, into two great classes directly facing each other—bourgeoisie and proletariat.

The Rise of the Bourgeoisie

From the serfs of the Middle Ages sprang the chartered burghers of the earliest towns. From these burgesses, the first elements of the bourgeoisie were developed.

The discovery of America, the rounding of the Cape, opened up fresh

---

From Karl Marx and Friedrich Engels, *Manifesto of the Communist Party* (New York: International Publishers, 1932), pp. 9-21.

ground for the rising bourgeoisie. The East Indian and Chinese markets, the colonization of America, trade with the colonies, the increase in the means of exchange and in commodities generally gave to commerce, to navigation, to industry, an impulse never before known and, thereby, to the revolutionary element in the tottering feudal society, a rapid development.

The feudal system of industry, in which industrial production was monopolized by closed guilds, now no longer sufficed for the growing wants of the new markets. The manufacturing system took its place. The guildmasters were pushed aside by the manufacturing middle class; division of labor between the different corporate guilds vanished in the face of division of labor in each single workshop.

Meantime, the markets kept ever growing, the demand ever rising. Even manufacture no longer sufficed. Thereupon, steam and machinery revolutionized industrial production. The place of manufacture was taken by the giant, modern industry; the place of the industrial middle class, by industrial millionaires—the leaders of whole industrial armies, the modern bourgeois.

Modern industry has established the world market, for which the discovery of America paved the way. This market has given an immense development to commerce, to navigation, to communication by land. This development has, in its turn, reacted on the extension of industry; and, in proportion as industry, commerce, navigation, railways extended, in the same proportion the bourgeoisie developed, increased its capital, and pushed into the background every class handed down from the Middle Ages.

We see, therefore, how the modern bourgeoisie is itself the product of a long course of development, of a series of revolutions in the modes of production and of exchange.

Each step in the development of the bourgeoisie was accompanied by a corresponding political advance of that class. An oppressed class under the sway of the feudal nobility, it became an armed and self-governing association in the medieval commune; here independent urban republic (as in Italy and Germany), there taxable "third estate" of the monarchy (as in France); afterward, in the period of manufacture proper, serving either the semifeudal or the absolute monarchy as a counterpoise against the nobility and, in fact, cornerstone of the great monarchies in general—the bourgeoisie has at last, since the establishment of modern industry and of the world market, conquered for itself, in the modern representative state, exclusive political sway. The executive of the modern state is but a committee for managing the common affairs of the whole bourgeoisie. . . .

More and more, the bourgeoisie keeps doing away with the scattered state of the population, of the means of production, and of property. It has agglomerated population, centralized means of production, and has concentrated property in a few hands. The necessary consequence of this was political centralization. Independent or but loosely connected provinces with separate interests, laws, governments and systems of taxation became lumped together into one nation, with one government, one code of laws, one national class interest, one frontier, and one customs tariff.

The bourgeoisie, during its rule of scarce one hundred years, has created more massive and more colossal productive forces than have all preceding generations together. Subjection of nature's forces to man, machinery, application of chemistry to industry and agriculture, steam navigation, railways, electric telegraphs, clearing of whole continents for cultivation, canalization of rivers, whole populations conjured out of the ground—what earlier century had even a presentiment that such productive forces slumbered in the lap of social labor?

We see then that the means of production and of exchange, which served as the foundation for the growth of the bourgeoisie, were generated in feudal society. At a certain stage in the development of these means of production and of exchange, the conditions under which feudal society produced and exchanged, the feudal organization of agriculture and manufacturing industry—in a word, the feudal relations of property—became no longer compatible with the already developed productive forces; they became so many fetters. They had to be burst asunder; they were burst asunder.

Into their place stepped free competition, accompanied by a social and political constitution adapted to it and by the economic and political sway of the bourgeois class.

The Rise of the Proletariat

A similar movement is going on before our own eyes. Modern bourgeois society, with its relations of production, of exchange, and of property—a society that has conjured up such gigantic means of production and of exchange—is like the sorcerer who is no longer able to control the powers of the nether world whom he has called up by his spells. For many a decade past, the history of industry and commerce is but the history of the revolt of modern productive forces against modern conditions of production, against the property relations that are the conditions for the existence of the bourgeoisie and of its rule. It is enough to mention the commercial crises that by their periodical return put the existence of the entire bourgeois society on trial, each time more threateningly. In these crises, a great part, not only of the existing products, but also of the previously created productive forces, are periodically destroyed. In these crises, there breaks out an epidemic that, in all earlier epochs, would have seemed an absurdity—the epidemic of overproduction. Society suddenly finds itself put back into a state of momentary barbarism; it appears as if a famine, a universal war of devastation, had cut off the supply of every means of subsistence; industry and commerce seem to be destroyed. And why? Because there is too much civilization, too much means of subsistence, too much industry, too much commerce. The productive forces at the disposal of society no longer tend to further the development of the conditions of bourgeois property; on the contrary, they have become too powerful for these conditions, by which they are fettered, and no sooner do they overcome these fetters than they bring disorder into the whole of bourgeois society, endanger the existence of bourgeois property. The conditions of bourgeois society are too narrow to comprise the wealth created by them. And how does the bourgeoisie get over these crises? On the one hand, by enforced destruction of a mass of productive forces; on the other, by the conquest of new markets and by the more thorough exploitation of the old ones. That is to say, by paving the way for more extensive and more destructive crises and by diminishing the means whereby crises are prevented.

The weapons with which the bourgeoisie felled feudalism to the ground are now turned against the bourgeoisie itself.

But not only has the bourgeoisie forged the weapons that bring death to itself; it has also called into existence the men who are to wield those weapons—the modern working class, the proletarians.

In proportion as the bourgeoisie, *i.e.,* capital, is developed, in the same proportion is the proletariat, the modern working class, developed—a class of laborers who live only so long as they find work and who find work only so long as their labor increases capital. These laborers, who must sell themselves piecemeal, are a commodity, like every other article of commerce, and are consequently exposed to all the vicissitudes of competition, to all the fluctuations of the market.

Owing to the extensive use of machinery and to division of labor, the work of the proletarians has lost all individual character and, consequently, all charm for the workman. He becomes an appendage of the machine, and it is only the most simple, most monotonous, and most easily acquired knack that is required of him. Hence, the cost of production of a workman is restricted almost entirely to the means of subsistence that he requires for his maintenance and for the propagation of his race. But the price of a commodity, and therefore also of labor, is equal to its cost of production. In proportion, therefore, as the repulsiveness of the work increases, the wage decreases. Nay more, in proportion as the use of machinery and division of labor increases, in the same proportion the burden of toil also increases, whether by prolongation of the working hours, by increase of the work exacted in a given time, or by increased speed of the machinery, etc.

Modern industry has converted the little workshop of the patriarchal master into the great factory of the industrial capitalist. Masses of laborers, crowded into the factory, are organized like soldiers. As privates of the industrial army, they are placed under the command of a perfect hierarchy of officers and sergeants. Not only are they slaves of the bourgeois class and of the bourgeois state, they are daily and hourly enslaved by the machine, by the overseer, and, above all, by the individual bourgeois manufacturer himself. The more openly this despotism proclaims gain to be its end and aim, the more petty, the more hateful, and the more embittering it is.

The less the skill and exertion of strength implied in manual labor, in other words, the more modern industry develops, the more is the labor of men superseded by that of women. Differences of age and sex have no longer any distinctive social validity for the working class. All are instruments of labor, more or less expensive to use, according to their age and sex.

No sooner has the laborer received his wages in cash, for the moment escaping exploitation by the manufacturer, than he is set upon by the other portions of the bourgeoisie, the landlord, the shopkeeper, the pawnbroker, etc.

The lower strata of the middle class—the small tradespeople, shopkeepers, and retired tradesmen generally, the handicraftsmen and peasants—all these sink gradually into the proletariat, partly because their diminutive capital does not suffice for the scale on which modern industry is carried on and is swamped in the competition with the large capitalists, partly because their specialized skill is rendered worthless by new methods of production. Thus the proletariat is recruited from all classes of the population.

The proletariat goes through various stages of development. With its birth begins its struggle with the bourgeoisie. At first the contest is carried on by individual laborers; then by the workpeople of a factory; then by the operatives of one trade, in one locality, against the individual bourgeois who directly exploits them. They direct their attacks, not against the bourgeois conditions of production, but against the instruments of production themselves; they destroy imported wares that compete with their labor, they smash machinery to pieces, they set factories ablaze, they seek to restore by force the vanished status of the workman of the Middle Ages.

At this stage the laborers still form an incoherent mass scattered over the whole country and broken up by their mutual competition. If anywhere they unite to form more compact bodies, this is not yet the consequence of their own active union, but of the union of the bourgeoisie, which, in order to attain its own political ends, is compelled to set the whole proletariat in motion and is, moreover, still able to do so for a time. At this stage, therefore, the proletarians do not fight their enemies, but the enemies of their enemies, the remnants of absolute monarchy, the landowners, the nonindustrial bourgeois, the petty bourgeoisie. Thus the whole historical movement is concentrated in the hands of the bourgeoisie; every victory so obtained is a victory for the bourgeoisie.

But, with the development of industry, the proletariat not only increases in number; it becomes concentrated in greater masses, its strength grows, and it feels that strength more. The various interests and conditions of life within the ranks of the proletariat are more and more equalized, in proportion as machinery obliterates all distinctions of labor and nearly everywhere reduces wages to the same low level. The growing competition among the bourgeois and the resulting commercial crises make the wages of the workers ever more fluctuating. The unceasing improvement of machinery, ever more rapidly developing, makes their livelihood more and more precarious; the collisions between individual workmen and individual bourgeois take more and more the character of collisions between two classes. Thereupon the workers begin to form combinations (trade unions) against the bourgeoisie; they club together in order to keep up the rate of wages; they found permanent associations in order to make provision beforehand for these occasional revolts. Here and there the contest breaks out into riots.

Now and then the workers are victorious, but only for a time. The real fruit of their battles lies, not in the immediate result, but in the ever-expanding union of the workers. This union is furthered by the improved means of communication which are created by modern industry and which place the workers of different localities in contact with one another. It was just this contact that was needed to centralize the numerous local struggles, all of the same character, into one national struggle between classes. But every class struggle is a political struggle. And that union, to attain which the burghers of the Middle Ages, with their miserable highways, required centuries, the modern proletarians, thanks to railways, achieve in a few years.

This organization of the proletarians into a class and consequently into a political party is continually being upset again by the competition between the workers themselves. But it ever rises up again, stronger, firmer, mightier. It compels legislative recognition of particular interests of the workers by taking advantage of the divisions among the bourgeoisie itself. Thus the ten-hour bill in England was carried.

Altogether, collisions between the classes of the old society further the course of development of the proletariat in many ways. The bourgeoisie finds itself involved in a constant battle. At first, with the aristocracy; later on, with those portions of the bourgeoisie itself whose interests have become antagonistic to the progress of industry; at all times, with the bourgeoisie of foreign countries. In all these battles, it sees itself compelled to appeal to the proletariat, to ask for its help, and, thus, to drag it into the political arena. The bourgeoisie itself, therefore, supplies the proletariat with its own elements of political and general education; in other words, it furnishes the proletariat with weapons for fighting the bourgeoisie.

Further, as we have already seen, entire sections of the ruling classes are, by the advance of industry, precipitated into the proletariat or are at least threatened in their conditions of existence. These also supply the proletariat with fresh elements of enlightenment and progress.

Finally, in times when the class struggle nears the decisive hour, the process of dissolution going on within the ruling class, in fact within the whole range of old society, assumes such a violent, glaring character, that a small section of the ruling class cuts itself adrift and joins the revolutionary class, the class that holds the future in its hands. Just as, therefore, at an earlier period, a section of the nobility went over to the bourgeoisie, so now a portion of the bourgeoisie goes over to the proletariat and, in particular, a portion of the bourgeois ideologists who have raised themselves to the level of comprehending theoretically the historical movement as a whole.

Of all the classes that stand face to face with the bourgeoisie today, the proletariat alone is a really revolutionary class. The other classes decay and finally disappear in the face of modern industry; the proletariat is its special and essential product.

The lower middle class, the small manufacturer, the shopkeeper, the artisan, the peasant—all these fight against the bourgeoisie, to save from extinction their existence as fractions of the middle class. They are, therefore, not revolutionary, but conservative. Nay more, they are reactionary, for they try to roll back the wheel of history. If by chance they are revolutionary, they are so only in view of their impending transfer into the proletariat; they thus defend, not their present, but their future interests; they desert their own standpoint to adopt that of the proletariat.

The "dangerous class," the social scum (*Lumpenproletariat*), that passively rotting mass thrown off by the lowest layers of old society, may, here and there, be swept into the movement by a proletarian revolution; its conditions of life, however, prepare it far more for the part of a bribed tool of reactionary intrigue.

The social conditions of the old society no longer exist for the proletariat. The proletarian is without property; his relation to his wife and children has no longer anything in common with bourgeois family relations; modern industrial labor, modern subjection to capital, the same in England as in France, in America as in Germany, has stripped him of every trace of national character. Law, morality, religion are to him so many bourgeois prejudices, behind which lurk in ambush just as many bourgeois interests.

All the preceding classes that got the upper hand sought to fortify their already acquired status by subjecting society at large to their conditions of appropriation. The proletarians cannot become masters of the productive forces of society except by abolishing their own previous mode of appropriation and thereby also every other previous mode of appropriation. They have nothing of their own to secure and to fortify; their mission is to destroy all previous securities for, and insurances of, individual property.

All previous historical movements were movements of minorities or in the interest of minorities. The proletarian movement is the self-conscious, independent movement of the immense majority, in the interest of the immense majority. The proletariat, the lowest stratum of our present society, cannot stir, cannot raise itself up, without all the superincumbent strata of official society being sprung into the air.

Though not in substance, yet in form, the struggle of the proletariat with the bourgeoisie is at first a national struggle. The proletariat of each country must, of course, first of all settle matters with its own bourgeoisie.

In depicting the most general phases of the development of the proletariat, we traced the more or less veiled civil war raging within existing society up to the point where that war breaks out into open revolution and where the violent overthrow of the bourgeoisie lays the foundation for the sway of the proletariat.

Hitherto, every form of society has been based, as we have already seen, on the antagonism of oppressing and oppressed classes. But, in order to oppress a class, certain conditions must be assured to it under which it can, at least, continue its slavish existence. The serf, in the period of serfdom, raised himself to membership in the commune, just as the petty bourgeois, under the yoke of feudal absolutism, managed to develop into a bourgeois. The modern laborer, on the contrary, instead of rising with the progress of industry, sinks deeper and deeper below the conditions of existence of his own class. He becomes a pauper, and pauperism develops more rapidly than population and wealth. And here it becomes evident that the bourgeoisie is unfit any longer to be the ruling class in society and to impose its conditions of existence upon society as an overriding law. It is unfit to rule because it is incompetent to assure an existence to its slave within his slavery, because it cannot help letting him sink into such a state that it has to feed him, instead of being fed by him. Society can no longer live under this bourgeoisie; in other words, its existence is no longer compatible with society.

The essential condition for the existence and sway of the bourgeois class is the formation and augmentation of capital; the condition for capital is wage labor. Wage labor rests exclusively on competition between the laborers. The advance of industry, whose involuntary promoter is the bourgeoisie, replaces the isolation of the laborers, due to competition, by their revolutionary combination, due to association. The development of modern industry, therefore, cuts from under its feet the very foundation on which the bourgeoisie produces and appropriates products. What the bourgeoisie therefore produces, above all, are its own gravediggers. Its fall and the victory of the proletariat are equally inevitable.

CHAPTER 8

MAX WEBER

The Role of Ideas in History

In a universal history of culture, the central problem for us is not, in the last analysis, even from a purely economic viewpoint, the development of capitalistic activity as such, differing in different cultures only in form: the adventurer type or capitalism in trade, war, politics, or administration as sources of gain. It is rather the origin of this sober bourgeois capitalism with its rational organization of free labor. Or, in terms of cultural history, the problem is that of the origin of the Western bourgeois class and of its peculiarities, a problem which is certainly closely connected with that of the origin of the capitalistic organization of labor, but is not quite the same thing. For the bourgeois as a class existed prior to the development of the peculiar modern form of capitalism, though, it is true, only in the Western hemisphere.

Now, the peculiar modern Western form of capitalism has been, at first sight, strongly influenced by the development of technical possibilities. Its rationality is today essentially dependent on the calculability of the most important technical factors. But this means fundamentally that it is dependent on the peculiarities of modern science, especially the natural sciences based on mathematics and exact and rational experiment. On the other hand, the development of these sciences and of the technique resting on them now receives important stimulation from these capitalistic interests in its practical economic application. It is true that the origin of Western science cannot be attributed to such interests. Calculation, even with decimals, and algebra have been carried on in India, where the decimal system was invented. But it was only made use of by developing capitalism in the West, while in India it led to no modern arithmetic or bookkeeping. Neither was the origin of mathematics and mechanics determined by capitalistic interests. But the *technical* utilization of scientific knowledge, so important

From the author's Introduction to Max Weber, *The Protestant Ethic and the Spirit of Capitalism,* trans., Talcott Parsons (New York: Charles Scribner's Sons, 1958), pp. 23-27. Used by permission of Charles Scribner's Sons.

for the living conditions of the mass of people, was certainly encouraged by economic considerations, which were extremely favorable to it in the Occident. But this encouragement was derived from the peculiarities of the social structure of the Occident. We must hence ask, from *what* parts of that structure was it derived, since not all of them have been of equal importance?

Among those of undoubted importance are the rational structures of law and of administration. For modern rational capitalism has need, not only of the technical means of production, but of a calculable legal system and of administration in terms of formal rules. Without it, adventurous and speculative trading capitalism and all sorts of politically determined capitalisms are possible, but no rational enterprise under individual initiative, with fixed capital and certainty of calculations. Such a legal system and such administration have been available for economic activity in a comparative state of legal and formalistic perfection only in the Occident. We must hence inquire where that law came from. Among other circumstances, capitalistic interests have in turn undoubtedly also helped, but by no means alone nor even principally, to prepare the way for the predominance in law and administration of a class of jurists specially trained in rational law. But these interests did not themselves create that law. Quite different forces were at work in this development. And why did not the capitalistic interests do the same in China or India? Why did not the scientific, the artistic, the political, or the economic development there enter on that path of rationalization which is peculiar to the Occident?

For in all the cases above it is a question of the specific and peculiar rationalism of Western culture. Now, by this term very different things may be understood, as the following discussion will repeatedly show. There is, for example, rationalization of mystical contemplation, that is, of an attitude which, viewed from other departments of life, is specifically irrational, just as much as there are rationalizations of economic life, of technique, of scientific research, of military training, of law and administration. Furthermore, each one of these fields may be rationalized in terms of very different ultimate values and ends, and what is rational from one point of view may well be irrational from another. Hence, rationalizations of the most varied character have existed in various departments of life and in all areas of culture. To characterize their differences from the viewpoint of cultural history, it is necessary to know what departments are rationalized, and in what direction. It is, hence, our first concern to work out and to explain genetically the special peculiarity of Occidental rationalism and, within this field, that of the modern Occidental form. Every such attempt at explanation must, recognizing the fundamental importance of the economic factor, above all take account of the economic conditions. But at the same time the opposite correlation must not be left out of consideration. For, though the development of economic rationalism is partly dependent on rational technique and law, **it** is at the same time determined by the ability and disposition of men to adopt certain types of practical rational conduct. When these types have been obstructed by spiritual obstacles, the development of rational economic conduct has also met serious inner resistance. The magical and religious forces and the ethical ideas of duty based on them have in the past always been among the most important formative influences on conduct. In the studies collected here we shall be concerned with these forces.[1]

Two older essays have been placed at the beginning which attempt, at one important point, to approach the side of the problem which is generally most difficult to grasp: the influence of certain religious ideas on the development of an economic spirit, or the *ethos* of an economic system. In this case we are dealing with the connection of the spirit of modern economic life with the rational ethics of ascetic Protestantism. Thus we treat here only one side of the causal chain. Later studies on the economic ethics of the world religions attempt, in the form of a survey of the relations of the most important religions to economic life and to the social stratification of their environment, to follow out both causal relationships, so far as it is necessary in order to find points of comparison with the Occidental development. For only in this way is it possible to attempt a causal evaluation of those elements of the economic ethics of the Western religions which differentiate them from others, with a hope of attaining even a tolerable degree of approximation. . . .

---

[1] That is, in the whole series of *Aufsätze zur Religionssoziologie.*—TRANS

CHAPTER 9

MAX WEBER

The Routinization
of Charisma

The Nature of Charismatic Authority

The term "charisma" will be applied to a certain quality of an individual personality, by virtue of which he is set apart from ordinary men and treated as endowed with supernatural, superhuman, or at least specifically exceptional powers or qualities. These are such as are not accessible to the ordinary person, but are regarded as of divine origin or as exemplary, and on the basis of them the individual concerned is treated as a leader. In primitive circumstances this peculiar kind of deference is paid to prophets, to people with a reputation for therapeutic or legal wisdom, to leaders in the hunt, and heroes in war. It is very often thought of as resting on magical powers. How the quality in question would be ultimately judged from any ethical, aesthetic, or other such point of view is naturally entirely indifferent for purposes of definition. What is alone important is how the individual is actually regarded by those subject to charismatic authority, by his "followers" or "disciples."

For present purposes it will be necessary to treat a variety of different types as being endowed with charisma in this sense. It includes the state of a "berserker" whose spells of maniac passion have, apparently wrongly, sometimes been attributed to the use of drugs. In medieval Byzantium a group of people endowed with this type of charismatic warlike passion were maintained as a kind of weapon. It includes the "shaman," the kind of magician who in the pure type is subject to epileptoid seizures as a means of falling into trances. Another type is that of Joseph Smith, the founder of Mormonism, who, however, cannot be classified in this way with absolute

From Max Weber, *The Theory of Social and Economic Organization* (New York: Oxford University Press, 1947), pp. 358-373. Reprinted by permission of the translator, Talcott Parsons.

certainty since there is a possibility that he was a very sophisticated type of deliberate swindler. Finally it includes the type of intellectual, such as Kurt Eisner,[1] who is carried away with his own demagogic success. Sociological analysis, which must abstain from value judgments, will treat all these on the same level as the men who, according to conventional judgments, are the "greatest" heroes, prophets, and saviors. . . .

Charismatic authority is specifically outside the realm of everyday routine and the profane sphere. In this respect, it is sharply opposed both to rational, and particularly bureaucratic, authority and to traditional authority, whether in its patriarchal, patrimonial, or any other form. Both rational and traditional authority are specifically forms of everyday routine control of action; while the charismatic type is the direct antithesis of this. Bureaucratic authority is specifically rational in the sense of being bound to intellectually analyzable rules, while charismatic authority is specifically irrational in the sense of being foreign to all rules. Traditional authority is bound to the precedents handed down from the past and to this extent is also oriented to rules. Within the sphere of its claims, charismatic authority repudiates the past and is in this sense a specifically revolutionary force. It recognizes no appropriation of positions of power by virtue of the possession of property, either on the part of a chief or of socially privileged groups. The only basis of legitimacy for it is personal charisma, so long as it is proved, that is, as long as it receives recognition and is able to satisfy the followers or disciples. But this lasts only so long as the belief in its charismatic inspiration remains.

The above is scarcely in need of further discussion. What has been said applies to the position of authority of such elected monarchs as Napoleon, with his use of the plebiscite. It applies to the "rule of genius," which has elevated people of humble origin to thrones and high military commands, just as much as it applies to religious prophets or war heroes. . . .

In traditionally stereotyped periods, charisma is the greatest revolutionary force. The equally revolutionary force of "reason" works from without by altering the situations of action and hence its problems, finally in this way changing men's attitudes toward them; or it intellectualizes the individual. Charisma, on the other hand, may involve a subjective or internal reorientation born out of suffering, conflicts or enthusiasm. It may then result in a radical alteration of the central system of attitudes and directions of action, with a completely new orientation of all attitudes toward the different problems and structures of the "world."[2] In prerationalistic periods,

---

[1] The leader of the communistic experiment in Bavaria in 1919.—ED (T.P.)

[2] Weber here uses *Welt* in quotation marks, indicating that it refers to its meaning in what is primarily a religious context. It is the sphere of "worldly" things and interests as distinguished from transcendental religious interests.—ED (T.P.)

tradition and charisma between them have almost exhausted the whole of the orientation of action.

The Necessity of Routinization

In its pure form charismatic authority has a character specifically foreign to everyday routine structures. The social relationships directly involved are strictly personal, based on the validity and practice of charismatic personal qualities. If this is not to remain a purely transitory phenomenon, but to take on the character of a permanent relationship forming a stable community of disciples, or a band of followers, or a party organization, or any sort of political or hierocratic organization, it is necessary for the character of charismatic authority to become radically changed. Indeed, in its pure form charismatic authority may be said to exist only in the process of originating. It cannot remain stable, but becomes either traditionalized or rationalized, or a combination of both.

The following are the principal motives underlying this transformation: (1) the ideal and also the material interests of the followers in the continuation and the continual reactivation of the community; (2) the still stronger ideal and also stronger material interests of the members of the administrative staff, the disciples or other followers of the charismatic leader in continuing their relationship. Not only this, but they have an interest in continuing it in such a way that both from an ideal and a material point of view, their own status is put on a stable everyday basis. This means, above all, making it possible to participate in normal family relationships or at least to enjoy a secure social position, in place of the kind of discipleship which is cut off from ordinary worldly connections, notably in the family and in economic relationships.

The Problem of Succession

These interests generally become conspicuously evident with the disappearance of the personal charismatic leader, and with the problem of succession which inevitably arises. The way in which this problem is met—if it is met at all and the charismatic group continues to exist—is of crucial importance for the character of the subsequent social relationships. The following are the principal possible types of solution:

(1) The search for a new charismatic leader on the basis of criteria of the qualities which will fit him for the position of authority. This is to be found in a relatively pure type in the process of choice of a new Dalai Lama. It consists in the search for a child with characteristics which are interpreted to mean that he is a reincarnation of the Buddha. This is very similar to the choice of the new Bull of Apis.

In this case the legitimacy of the new charismatic leader is bound to certain distinguishing characteristics—thus, to rules with respect to which a tradition arises. The result is a process of traditionalization in favor of which the purely personal character of leadership is eliminated.

(2) By revelation manifested in oracles, lots, divine judgments, or other techniques of selection. In this case, the legitimacy of the new leader is dependent on the legitimacy of the technique of his selection. This involves a form of legalization. It is said that at times the *Schofetim* of Israel had this character. Saul is said to have been chosen by the old war oracle.

(3) By the designation on the part of the original charismatic leader of his own successor and his recognition on the part of the followers. This is a very common form. Originally, the Roman magistracies were filled entirely in this way. The system survived most clearly into later times in the appointment of "dictators" and in the institution of the "interrex." In this case, legitimacy is acquired through the act of designation.

(4) Designation of a successor by the charismatically qualified administrative staff and his recognition by the community. In its typical form, this process should quite definitely not be interpreted as "election," or "nomination," or anything of the sort. It is not a matter of free selection, but of one which is strictly bound to objective duty. It is not to be determined merely by majority vote, but is a question of arriving at the correct designation, the designation of the right person who is truly endowed with charisma. It is quite possible that the minority and not the majority should be right in such a case. Unanimity is often required. It is obligatory to acknowledge a mistake, and persistence in error is a serious offense. Making a wrong choice is a genuine wrong requiring expiation. Originally it was a magical offense.

Nevertheless, in such a case it is easy for legitimacy to take on the character of an acquired right which is justified by standards of the correctness of the process by which the position was acquired, for the most part, by its having been acquired in accordance with certain formalities, such as coronation. This was the original meaning of the coronation of bishops and kings in the Western world by the clergy or the nobility with the "consent" of the community. There are numerous analogous phenomena all over the world. The fact that this is the origin of the modern conception of "election" raises problems which will have to be gone into later.

(5) By the conception that charisma is a quality transmitted by heredity; thus that it is participated in by the kinsmen of its bearer, particularly by his closest relatives. This is the case of hereditary charisma. The order of hereditary succession in such a case need not be the same as that which is in force for appropriated rights, but may differ from it. It is also sometimes necessary to select the proper heir within the kinship group by some of the methods just spoken of; thus in certain Negro states brothers have had to fight for the succession. In China, succession had to take place in such a

way that the relation of the living group to the ancestral spirits was not disturbed. The rule either of seniority or of designation by the followers has been very common in the Orient. Hence, in the house of Osman, it has been obligatory to eliminate all other possible candidates.

Only in medieval Europe and in Japan universally, elsewhere only sporadically, has the principle of primogeniture, as governing the inheritance of authority, become clearly established. This has greatly facilitated the consolidation of political groups in that it has eliminated struggle between a plurality of candidates from the same charismatic family.

In the case of hereditary charisma, recognition is no longer paid to the charismatic qualities of the individual, but to the legitimacy of the position he has acquired by hereditary succession. This may lead in the direction either of traditionalization or of legalization. The concept of "divine right" is fundamentally altered and now comes to mean authority by virtue of a personal right which is not dependent on the recognition of those subject to authority. Personal charisma may be totally absent. Hereditary monarchy is a conspicuous illustration. In Asia there have been very numerous hereditary priesthoods; also, frequently, the hereditary charisma of kinship groups has been treated as a criterion of social rank and of eligibility for fiefs and benefices.

(6) The concept that charisma may be transmitted by ritual means from one bearer to another or may be created in a new person. The concept was originally magical. It involves a dissociation of charisma from a particular individual, making it an objective, transferable entity. In particular, it may become the charisma of office. In this case the belief in legitimacy is no longer directed to the individual, but to the acquired qualities and to the effectiveness of the ritual acts. The most important example is the transmission of priestly charisma by annointing, consecration, or the laying on of hands and of royal authority, by annointing and by coronation. The *caracter indelibilis* thus acquired means that the charismatic qualities and powers of the office are emancipated from the personal qualities of the priest. For precisely this reason, this has, from the Donatist and the Montanist heresies down to the Puritan revolution, been the subject of continual conflicts. The "hireling" of the Quakers is the preacher endowed with the charisma of office.

Routinization and the Administrative Staff

Concomitant with the routinization of charisma with a view to insuring adequate succession, go the interests in its routinization on the part of the administrative staff. It is only in the initial stages and so long as the charismatic leader acts in a way which is completely outside everyday social organization, that it is possible for his followers to live communistically in a community of faith and enthusiasm, on gifts, "booty" or sporadic acquisition.

Only the members of the small group of enthusiastic disciples and followers are prepared to devote their lives purely idealistically to their call. The great majority of disciples and followers will in the long run "make their living" out of their "calling" in a material sense as well. Indeed, this must be the case if the movement is not to disintegrate.

Hence, the routinization of charisma also takes the form of the appropriation of powers of control and of economic advantages by the followers or disciples, and of regulation of the recruitment of these groups. This process of traditionalization or of legalization, according to whether rational legislation is involved or not, may take any one of a number of typical forms:

1. The original basis of recruitment is personal charisma. With routinization, the followers or disciples may set up norms for recruitment, in particular involving training or tests of eligibility. Charisma can only be "awakened" and "tested"; it cannot be "learned" or "taught." All types of magical asceticism, as practiced by magicians and heroes, and all novitiates, belong in this category. These are means of closing the group which constitutes the administrative staff.

Only the proved novice is allowed to exercise authority. A genuine charismatic leader is in a position to oppose this type of prerequisite for membership. His successor is not, at least if he is chosen by the administrative staff. This type is illustrated by the magical and warrior asceticism of the "men's house" with initiation ceremonies and age groups. An individual who has not successfully gone through the initiation, remains a "woman"—that is, is excluded from the charismatic group.

2. It is easy for charismatic norms to be transformed into those defining a traditional social status on a hereditary charismatic basis. If the leader is chosen on a hereditary basis, it is very easy for hereditary charisma to govern the selection of the administrative staff and even, perhaps, those followers without any position of authority. The term "familistic state" will be applied when a political body is organized strictly and completely in terms of this principle of hereditary charisma. In such a case, all appropriation of governing powers, of fiefs, benefices, and all sorts of economic advantages follow the same pattern. The result is that all powers and advantages of all sorts become traditionalized. The heads of families, who are traditional gerontocrats or patriarchs without personal charismatic legitimacy, regulate the exercise of these powers, which cannot be taken away from their family. It is not the type of position he occupies which determines the rank of a man or of his family, but rather the hereditary charismatic rank of his family determines the position he will occupy. Japan, before the development of bureaucracy, was organized in this way. The same was undoubtedly true of China as well, where, before the rationalization which took place in the territorial states, authority was in the hands of the "old families." Other types of examples are furnished by the caste system

in India and by Russia before the *Mjestnitschestvo* was introduced. Indeed, all hereditary social classes with established privileges belong in the same category.

3. The administrative staff may seek and achieve the creation and appropriation of individual positions and the corresponding economic advantages for its members. In that case, according to whether the tendency is to traditionalization or legalization, there will develop (a) benefices, (b) offices, or (c) fiefs. In the first case a praebendal organization will result; in the second, patrimonialism or bureaucracy; in the third, feudalism. These become appropriated in the place of the type of provision from gifts or booty without settled relation to the everyday economic structure.

Case (a), benefices, may consist in rights to the proceeds of begging, to payments in kind, or to the proceeds of money taxes, or finally, to the proceeds of fees. Any one of these may result from the regulation of provision by free gifts or by "booty" in terms of a rational organization of finance. Regularized begging is found in Buddhism; benefices in kind, in the Chinese and Japanese "rice rents"; support by money taxation has been the rule in all the rationalized conquering states. The last case is common everywhere, especially on the part of priests and judges and, in India, even the military authorities.

Case (b), the transformation of the charismatic mission into an office, may have more of a patrimonial or more of a bureaucratic character. The former is much the more common; the latter is found principally in Mediterranean Antiquity and in the modern Western World. Elsewhere it is exceptional.

In case (c), only land may be appropriated as a fief, whereas the position as such retains its originally charismatic character. On the other hand, powers and authority may be fully appropriated as fiefs. It is difficult to distinguish the two cases. It is, however, rare that orientation to the charismatic character of the position disappears entirely; it did not do so in the Middle Ages.

Routinization and Economic Organization

For charisma to be transformed into a permanent routine structure, it is necessary that its anti-economic character should be altered. It must be adapted to some form of fiscal organization to provide for the needs of the group, and hence to the economic conditions necessary for raising taxes and contributions. When a charismatic movement develops in the direction of praebendal provision, the "laity" become differentiated from the "clergy"; that is, the participating members of the charismatic administrative staff which has now become routinized. These are the priests of the developing "church." Correspondingly, in a developing political body, the vassals, the holders of benefices, or officials are differentiated from the "taxpayers." The former, instead of being the "followers" of the leader, become state officials or appointed party officials. This process is very conspicuous in Buddhism and in the Hindu sects. The same is true in all the states resulting from conquest which have become rationalized to form permanent structures, also of parties and other movements which have originally had a purely charismatic character. With the process of routinization, the charismatic group tends to develop into one of the forms of everyday authority, particularly the patrimonial form in its decentralized variant or the bureaucratic. Its original peculiarities are apt to be retained in the charismatic standards of honor attendant on the social status acquired by heredity or the holding of office. This applies to all who participate in the process of appropriation, the chief himself and the members of his staff. It is thus a matter of the type of prestige enjoyed by ruling groups. A hereditary monarch by "divine right" is not a simple patrimonial chief, patriarch, or sheik; a vassal is not a mere household retainer or official. Further details must be deferred to the analysis of social stratification.

As a rule, the process of routinization is not free of conflict. In the early stages personal claims on the charisma of the chief are not easily forgotten, and the conflict between the charisma of office or of hereditary status with personal charisma is a typical process in many historical situations.

1. The power of absolution—that is, the power to absolve from mortal sins—was held originally only by personal charismatic martyrs or ascetics, but became transformed into a power of the office of bishop or priest. This process was much slower in the Orient than in the Occident because in the latter case it was influenced by the Roman conception of office. Revolutions under a charismatic leader, directed against hereditary charismatic powers or the powers of office, are to be found in all types of corporate groups, from states to trade unions. The more highly developed the interdependence of different economic units in a monetary economy, the greater the pressure of the everyday needs of the followers of the charismatic movement becomes. The effect of this is to strengthen the tendency to routinization, which is everywhere operative, and as a rule has rapidly won out. Charisma is a phenomenon typical of prophetic religious movements or of expansive political movements in their early stages. But as soon as the position of authority is well established, and above all as soon as control over large masses of people exists, it gives way to the forces of everyday routine.

2. One of the decisive motives underlying all cases of the routinization of charisma is naturally the striving for security. This means legitimization, on the one hand, of positions of authority and social prestige; on the other hand, of the economic advantages enjoyed by the followers and sympathizers of the leader. Another important motive, however, lies in the objective necessity of adaptation of the patterns of order and of the organization of the administrative staff to the normal, everyday needs and conditions of carrying on administration. In this connection, in particular, there are al-

ways points at which traditions of administrative practice and of judicial decision can take hold, since these are needed both by the normal administrative staff and by those subject to its authority. It is further necessary that there should be some definite order introduced into the organization of the administrative staff itself. Finally, as will be discussed in detail below, it is necessary for the administrative staff and all its administrative practices to be adapted to everyday economic conditions. It is not possible for the costs of permanent, routine administration to be met by "booty," contributions, gifts and hospitality, as is typical of the pure type of military and prophetic charisma.

3. The process of routinization is thus not by any means confined to the problem of succession and does not stop when this has been solved. On the contrary, the most fundamental problem is that of making a transition from a charismatic administrative staff, and the corresponding principles of administration, to one which is adapted to everyday conditions. The problem of succession, however, is crucial, because through it occurs the routinization of the charismatic focus of the structure. In it, the character of the leader himself and of his claim to legitimacy is altered. This process involves peculiar and characteristic conceptions which are understandable only in this context, and do not apply to the problem of transition to traditional or legal patterns of order and types of administrative organization. The most important of the modes of meeting the problem of succession are the charismatic designation of a successor and hereditary charisma.

4. As has already been noted, the most important historical example of designation by the charismatic leader of his own successor is Rome. For the *rex,* this arrangement is attested by tradition; while for the appointment of the "dictator" and of the co-emperor and successor in the principate, it has existed in historical times. The way in which all the higher magistrates were invested with the *imperium* shows clearly that they also were designated as successors by the military commander, subject to recognition by the citizen army. The fact that candidates were examined by the magistrate in office, and that originally they could be excluded on what were obviously arbitrary grounds, shows clearly what was the nature of the development.

5. The most important examples of designation of a successor by the charismatic followers of the leader are to be found in the election of bishops, and particularly of the Pope, by the original system of designation by the clergy and recognition by the lay community. The investigations of U. Stutz have made it probable that, though it was later altered, the election of the German emperor was modeled on that of the bishops. He was designated by a group of qualified princes and recognized by the "people," that is, those bearing arms. Similar arrangements are very common.

6. The classical case of the development of hereditary charisma is that of caste in India. All occupational qualifications, and in particular all the qualifications for positions of authority and power, have there come to be

regarded as strictly bound to the inheritance of charisma. Eligibility for fiefs, involving governing powers, was limited to members of the royal kinship group, the fiefs being granted by the eldest of the group. All types of religious office, including the extraordinarily important and influential position of *guru,* the *directeur de l'âme,* were treated as bound to hereditary charismatic qualities. The same is true of all sorts of relations to traditional customers and of all positions in the village organization, such as priest, barber, laundryman, watchman, etc. The foundation of a sect always meant the development of a hereditary hierarchy, as was true also of Taoism in China. Also in the Japanese "feudal" state, before the introduction of a patrimonial officialdom on the Chinese model, which then led to praebends and a new feudalization, social organization was based purely on hereditary charisma.

This kind of hereditary charismatic right to positions of authority has been developed in similar ways all over the world. Qualification by virtue of individual achievement has been replaced by qualification by birth. This is everywhere the basis of the development of hereditary aristocracies, in the Roman nobility, in the concept of the *stirps regia,* which Tacitus describes among the Germans, in the rules of eligibility to tournaments and monasteries in the late Middle Ages, and even in the genealogical research carried on on behalf of the parvenu aristocracy of the United States. Indeed, this is to be found everywhere where a differentiation of hereditary social classes has become established.

The following is the principal relation to economic conditions: The process of routinization of charisma is in very important respects identical with adaptation to the conditions of economic life, since this is one of the principal continually operating forces in everyday life. Economic conditions in this connection play a leading role and do not constitute merely a dependent variable. To a very large extent, the transition to hereditary charisma or the charisma of office serves in this connection as a means of legitimizing existing or recently acquired powers of control over economic goods. Along with the ideology of loyalty, which is certainly by no means unimportant, allegiance to hereditary monarchy in particular is very strongly influenced by the consideration that all inherited property and all that which is legitimately acquired would be endangered if subjective recognition of the sanctity of succession to the throne were eliminated. It is hence by no means fortuitous that hereditary monarchy is more acceptable to the propertied classes than, for instance, to the proletariat.

Beyond this, it is not possible to say anything in general terms, which would at the same time be substantial and valuable, on the relations of the various possible modes of adaptation to the economic order. This must be reserved to a special investigation. The development of a praebendal structure, of feudalism and the appropriation of all sorts of advantages on a hereditary charismatic basis, may in all cases have the same stereotyping effect on the economic order if they develop from charismatic starting points as if they developed from patrimonial or bureaucratic origins. The immediate effect of charisma in economic as in other connections is usually strongly revolutionary; indeed, often destructive, because it means new modes of orientation. But in case the process of routinization leads in the direction of traditionalism, its ultimate effect may be exactly the reverse.

CHAPTER 10

FERDINAND TOENNIES

From Community to Society

Order—Law—Mores

There is a contrast between a social order which—being based upon consensus of wills—rests on harmony and is developed and ennobled by folkways, mores, and religion and an order which—being based upon a union of rational wills—rests on convention and agreement, is safeguarded by political legislation, and finds its ideological justification in public opinion.

There is, further, in the first instance, a common and binding system of positive law, of enforceable norms regulating the interrelation of wills. It has its roots in family life and is based on land ownership. Its forms are in the main determined by the code of the folkways and mores. Religion consecrates and glorifies these forms of the divine will, *i.e.,* as interpreted by the will of wise and ruling men. This system of norms is in direct contrast to a similar positive law which upholds the separate identity of the individual rational wills in all their interrelations and entanglements. The latter derives from the conventional order of trade and similar relations, but attains validity and binding force only through the sovereign will and power of the state. Thus, it becomes one of the most important instruments of policy; it sustains, impedes, or furthers social trends; it is defended or contested publicly by doctrines and opinions and thus is changed, becoming more strict or more lenient.

There is, further, the dual concept of morality as a purely ideal or mental system of norms for community life. In the first case, it is mainly an expression and organ of religious beliefs and forces, by necessity intertwined with the conditions and realities of family spirit and the folkways and mores. In the second case, it is entirely a product and instrument of public opinion, which encompasses all relations arising out of contractual sociableness, contacts, and political intentions.

From Ferdinand Toennies, *Community and Society—Gemeinschaft und Gesellschaft,* trans. and ed., Charles P. Loomis (East Lansing, Mich.: The Michigan State University Press, 1957), pp. 223-233. Reprinted by permission of the editor and the publisher.

Dissolution

The substance of the body social and the social will consists of concord, folkways, mores, and religion, the manifold forms of which develop under favorable conditions during its lifetime. Thus, each individual receives his share from this common center, which is manifest in his own sphere, *i.e.,* in his sentiment, in his mind and heart, and in his conscience as well as in his environment, his possessions, and his activities. This is also true of each group. It is in this center that the individual's strength is rooted, and his rights derive, in the last instance, from the one original law which, in its divine and natural character, encompasses and sustains him, just as it made him and will carry him away. But under certain conditions and in some relationships, man appears as a free agent (person) in his self-determined activities, and has to be conceived of as an independent person. The substance of the common spirit has become so weak or the link connecting him with the others worn so thin that it has to be excluded from consideration. In contrast to the family and cooperative relationship, this is true of all relations among separate individuals where there is no common understanding and no time-honored custom or belief creates a common bond. This means war and the unrestricted freedom of all to destroy and subjugate one another, or, being aware of possible greater advantage, to conclude agreements and foster new ties. To the extent that such a relationship exists between closed groups or communities or between their individuals or between members and nonmembers of a community, it does not come within the scope of this study. In this connection we see a community organization and social conditions in which the individuals remain in isolation and veiled hostility toward each other so that only fear of clever retaliation restrains them from attacking one another, and, therefore, even peaceful and neighborly relations are in reality based upon a warlike situation. This is, according to our concepts, the condition of *Gesellschaft*-like civilization, in which peace and commerce are maintained through conventions and the underlying mutual fear. The state protects this civilization through legislation and politics. To a certain extent science and public opinion, attempting to conceive it as necessary and eternal, glorify it as progress toward perfection.

But it is in the organization and order of the *Gemeinschaft* that folk life and folk culture persist. The state, which represents and embodies *Gesellschaft,* is opposed to these in veiled hatred and contempt, the more so the further the state has moved away from and become estranged from these forms of community life. Thus, also in the social and historical life of mankind there is partly close interrelation, partly juxtaposition and opposition of natural and rational will.

The People and the State

In the same way as the individual natural will evolves into pure thinking and rational will, which tends to dissolve and subjugate its predecessors, the original collective forms of *Gemeinschaft* have developed into *Gesellschaft* and the rational will of the *Gesellschaft*. In the course of history, folk culture has given rise to the civilization of the state.

The main features of this process can be described in the following way. The anonymous mass of the people is the original and dominating power which creates the houses, the villages, and the towns of the country. From it, too, spring the powerful and self-determined individuals of many different kinds: princes, feudal lords, knights, as well as priests, artists, scholars. As long as their economic condition is determined by the people as a whole, all their social control is conditioned by the will and power of the people. Their union on a national scale, which alone could make them dominant as a group, is dependent on economic conditions. And their real and essential control is economic control, which before them and with them and partly against them the merchants attain by harnessing the labor force of the nation. Such economic control is achieved in many forms, the highest of which is planned capitalist production or largescale industry. It is through the merchants that the technical conditions for the national union of independent individuals and for capitalistic production are created. This merchant class is by nature, and mostly also by origin, international as well as national and urban, *i.e.*, it belongs to *Gesellschaft*, not *Gemeinschaft*. Later all social groups and dignitaries and, at least in tendency, the whole people acquire the characteristics of the *Gesellschaft*.

Men change their temperaments with the place and conditions of their daily life, which becomes hasty and changeable through restless striving. Simultaneously, along with this revolution in the social order, there takes place a gradual change of the law, in meaning as well as in form. The contract as such becomes the basis of the entire system, and rational will of *Gesellschaft*, formed by its interests, combines with authoritative will of the state to create, maintain, and change the legal system. According to this conception, the law can and may completely change the *Gesellschaft* in line with its own discrimination and purpose; changes which, however, will be in the interest of the *Gesellschaft*, making for usefulness and efficiency. The state frees itself more and more from the traditions and customs of the past and the belief in their importance. Thus, the forms of law change from a product of the folkways and mores and the law of custom into a purely legalistic law, a product of policy. The state and its departments and the individuals are the only remaining agents, instead of numerous and manifold fellowships, communities, and commonwealths which have grown up organically. The characters of the people, which were influenced and determined by these previously existing institutions, undergo new changes in adaptation to new and arbitrary legal constructions. These earlier institutions lose the firm hold which folkways, mores, and the conviction of their infallibility gave to them.

Finally, as a consequence of these changes and in turn reacting upon them, a complete reversal of intellectual life takes place. While originally rooted entirely in the imagination, it now becomes dependent upon thinking. Previously, all was centered around the belief in invisible beings, spirits and gods; now it is focalized on the insight into visible nature. Religion, which is rooted in folk life or at least closely related to it, must cede supremacy to science, which derives from and corresponds to consciousness. Such consciousness is a product of learning and culture and, therefore, remote from the people. Religion has an immediate contact and is moral in its nature because it is most deeply related to the physical-spiritual link which connects the generations of men. Science receives its moral meaning only from an observation of the laws of social life, which leads it to derive rules for an arbitrary and reasonable order of social organization. The intellectual attitude of the individual becomes gradually less and less influenced by religion and more and more influenced by science. Utilizing the research findings accumulated by the preceding industrious generation, we shall investigate the tremendous contrasts which the opposite poles of this dichotomy and these fluctuations entail. For this presentation, however, the following few remarks may suffice to outline the underlying principles.

Types of Real Community Life

The exterior forms of community life as represented by natural will and *Gemeinschaft* were distinguished as house, village, and town. These are the lasting types of real and historical life. In a developed *Gesellschaft,* as in the earlier and middle stages, people live together in these different ways. The town is the highest, *viz.,* the most complex, form of social life. Its local character, in common with that of the village, contrasts with the family character of the house. Both village and town retain many characteristics of the family; the village retains more, the town less. Only when the town develops into the city are these characteristics almost entirely lost. Individuals or families are separate identities, and their common locale is only an accidental or deliberately chosen place in which to live. But as the town lives on within the city, elements of life in the *Gemeinschaft,* as the only real form of life, persist within the *Gesellschaft,* although lingering and decaying. On the other hand, the more general the condition of *Gesellschaft* becomes in the nation or a group of nations, the more this entire "country" or the entire "world" begins to resemble one large city. However, in the city and therefore where general conditions characteristic of the *Gesellschaft* prevail, only the upper strata, the rich and the cultured, are really active and alive. They set up the standards to which the lower strata have to conform. These lower classes conform partly to supersede the others, partly in imitation of them in order to attain for themselves social power and independence. The city consists, for both groups (just as in the case of the "nation" and the "world"), of free persons who stand in contact with each other, exchange with each other and cooperate without any *Gemeinschaft* or will thereto developing among them except as such might develop sporadically or as a leftover from former conditions. On the contrary, these numerous external contacts, contracts, and contractual relations only cover up as many inner hostilities and antagonistic interests. This is especially true of the antagonism between the rich or the socalled cultured class and the poor or the servant class, which try to obstruct and destroy each other. It is this contrast which, according to Plato, gives the "city" its dual character and makes it divide in itself. This itself, according to our concept, constitutes the city, but the same contrast is also manifest in every largescale relationship between capital and labor. The common town life remains within the *Gemeinschaft* of family and rural life; it is devoted to some agricultural pursuits but concerns itself especially with art and handicraft which evolve from these natural needs and habits. City life, however, is sharply distinguished from that; these basic activities are used only as means and tools for the special purposes of the city.

The city is typical of *Gesellschaft* in general. It is essentially a commercial town and, insofar as commerce dominates its productive labor, a factory town. Its wealth is capital wealth, which, in the form of trade, usury, or industrial capital, is used and multiplies. Capital is the means for the appropriation of products of labor or for the exploitation of workers. The city is also the center of science and culture, which always go hand in hand with commerce and industry. Here the arts must make a living; they are exploited in a capitalistic way. Thoughts spread and change with astonishing rapidity. Speeches and books through mass distribution become stimuli of farreaching importance.

•

ounterpart of Gemeinschaft

Family life is the general basis of life in the *Gemeinschaft*. It subsists in village and town life. The village community and the town themselves can be considered as large families, the various clans and houses representing the elementary organisms of its body; guilds, corporations, and offices, the tissues and organs of the town. Here original kinship and inherited status remain an essential, or at least the most important, condition of participating fully in common property and other rights. Strangers are accepted and protected as serving-members or guests, either temporarily or permanently. Thus, they can belong to the *Gemeinschaft* as objects, but not easily as agents and representatives of the *Gemeinschaft.* . . . All these relationships can, under special circumstances, be transformed into merely interested and dissolvable interchange between independent contracting parties. In the city such change, at least with regard to all relations of servitude, is only natural and becomes more and more widespread with its development. The difference between natives and strangers becomes irrelevant. Everyone is what he is, through his personal freedom, through his wealth and his contracts. He is a servant only insofar as he has granted certain services to someone else, master insofar as he receives such services. Wealth is, indeed, the only effective and original differentiating characteristic; whereas in *Gemeinschaften* property it is considered as participation in the common ownership, and as a specific legal concept is entirely the consequence and result of freedom or ingenuity, either original or acquired. Therefore, wealth, to the extent that this is possible, corresponds to the degree of freedom possessed.

In the city . . . family life is decaying. The more and the longer their influence prevails, the more the residuals of family life acquire a purely accidental character. For there are only few who will confine their energies within such a narrow circle; all are attracted outside by business, interests, and pleasures, and thus separated from one another. The great and mighty, feeling free and independent, have always felt a strong inclination to break through the barriers of the folkways and mores. They know that they can do as they please. They have the power to bring about changes in their favor, and this is positive proof of individual arbitrary power. The mechanism of money, under usual conditions and if working under high pressure, is means to overcome all resistance, to obtain everything wanted and desired, to eliminate all dangers and to cure all evil. This does not hold always. Even if all controls of the *Gemeinschaft* are eliminated, there are nevertheless controls in the *Gesellschaft* to which the free and independent individuals are subject. For *Gesellschaft* (in the narrower sense), convention takes to a large degree the place of the folkways, mores, and religion. It forbids much as detrimental to the common interest which the folkways, mores, and religion had condemned as evil in and of itself.

The will of the state plays the same role through law courts and police, although within narrower limits. The laws of the state apply equally to everyone; only children and lunatics are not held responsible to them. Convention maintains at least the appearance of morality; it is still related to the folkways, mores, and religious and aesthetic feeling, although this feeling tends to become arbitrary and formal. The state is hardly directly concerned with morality. It has only to suppress and punish hostile actions which are detrimental to the common weal or seemingly dangerous for itself and society. For as the state has to administer the common weal, it must be able to define this as it pleases. In the end it will probably realize that no increase in knowledge and culture alone will make people kinder, less egotistic and more content, and that dead folkways, mores and religions cannot be revived by coercion and teaching. The state will then arrive at the conclusion that in order to create moral forces and moral beings it must prepare the ground and fulfill the necessary conditions, or at least it must eliminate counteracting forces. The state, as the reason of *Gesellschaft,* should decide to destroy *Gesellschaft* or at least reform or renew it. The success of such attempts is highly improbable.

The Real State

Public opinion, which brings the morality of *Gesellschaft* into rules and formulas and can rise above the state, has nevertheless decided tendencies to urge the state to use its irresistible power to force everyone to do what is useful and to leave undone what is damaging. Extension of the penal code and the police power seems the right means to curb the evil impulses of the masses. Public opinion passes easily from the demand for freedom (for the upper classes) to that of despotism (against the lower classes). The makeshift, convention, has but little influence over the masses. In their striving for pleasure and entertainment they are limited only by the scarcity of the means which the capitalists furnish them as price for their labor, which condition is as general as it is natural in a world where the interests of the capitalists and merchants anticipate all possible needs and in mutual competition incite to the most varied expenditures of money. Only through fear of discovery and punishment, that is, through fear of the state, is a special and large group, which encompasses far more people than the professional criminals, restrained in its desire to obtain the key to all necessary and unnecessary pleasures. The state is their enemy. The state, to them, is an alien and unfriendly power; although seemingly authorized by them and embodying their own will, it is nevertheless opposed to all their needs and desires, protecting property which they do not possess, forcing them into military service for a country which offers them hearth and altar only in the form of a heated room on the upper floor or gives them, for native soil, city streets where they may stare at the glitter and luxury in lighted windows forever beyond their reach! Their own life is nothing but a constant alternative between work and leisure, which are both distorted into factory routine and the low pleasure of the saloons. City life and *Gesellschaft* drive the common people to decay and death; in vain they struggle to attain power through their own multitude, and it seems to them that they can use their power only for a revolution if they want to free themselves from their fate. The masses become conscious of this social position through the education in schools and through newspapers. They proceed from class consciousness to class struggle. This class struggle may destroy society and the state which it is its purpose to reform. The entire culture has been transformed into a civilization of state and *Gesellschaft,* and this transformation means the doom of culture itself if none of its scattered seeds remain alive and again bring forth the essence and idea of *Gemeinschaft,* thus secretly fostering a new culture amidst the decaying one.

The Periods

To conclude our theory, two periods stand thus contrasted with each other in the history of the great systems of culture: a period of *Gesellschaft* follows a period of *Gemeinschaft.* The *Gemeinschaft* is characterized by the social will as concord, folkways, mores, and religion; the *Gesellschaft* by the social will as convention, legislation, and public opinion. The concepts correspond to types of external social organization, which may be classed as follows:

A. Gemeinschaft

1. Family life: concord. Man participates in this with all his sentiments. Its real controlling agent is the people (*Volk*).
2. Rural village life: folkways and mores. Into this, man enters with all his mind and heart. Its real controlling agent is the commonwealth.
3. Town life: religion. In this, the human being takes part with his entire conscience. Its real controlling agent is the church.

B. Gesellschaft

1. City life: convention. This is determined by man's intentions. Its real controlling agent is *Gesellschaft* per se.
2. National life: legislation. This is determined by man's calculations. Its real controlling agent is the state.
3. Cosmopolitan life: public opinion. This is evolved by man's consciousness. Its real controlling agent is the republic of scholars.

With each of these categories a predominant occupation and a dominating tendency in intellectual life are related in the following manner:

(A) 1. Home (or household) economy, based upon liking or preference, *viz.,* the joy and delight of creating and conserving. Understanding develops the norms for such an economy.
    2. Agriculture, based upon habits, *i.e.,* regularly repeated tasks. Cooperation is guided by custom.
    3. Art, based upon memories, *i.e.,* of instruction, of rules followed, and of ideas conceived in one's own mind. Belief in the work and the task unites the artistic wills.

(B) 1. Trade based upon deliberation; namely, attention, comparison, calculation are the basis of all business. Commerce is deliberate action per se. Contracts are the custom and creed of business.

2. Industry based upon decisions; namely, of intelligent productive use of capital and sale of labor. Regulations rule the factory.
3. Science, based upon concepts, as is self-evident. Its truths and opinions then pass into literature and the press and thus become part of public opinion.

Epochs of the Periods

In the earlier period, family life and home (or household) economy strike the keynote; in the later period, commerce and city life. If, however, we investigate the period of *Gemeinschaft* more closely, several epochs can be distinguished. Its whole development tends toward an approach to *Gesellschaft* in which, on the other hand, the force of *Gemeinschaft* persists, although with diminishing strength, even in the period of *Gesellschaft,* and remains the reality of social life.

The first period is formed by the influence of the new basis of social organization which results from the cultivation of the soil: neighborhood relation is added to the old and persisting kinship relations, village to the clan. The other epoch comes into existence when villages develop into towns. The village and town have in common the principle of social organization in space, instead of the principle of time which predominates through the generations of the family, the tribe, and the people. Because it descends from common ancestors, the family has invisible metaphysical roots, as if they were hidden in the earth. The living individuals in the family are connected with each other by the sequence of past and future generations. But in village and town it is the physical, real soil, the permanent location, the visible land, which create the strongest ties and relations. During the period of *Gemeinschaft* this younger principle of space remains bound to the older principle of time. In the period of *Gesellschaft* they become disconnected, and from this disconnection results the city. It is the exaggeration of the principle of space in its urban form. In this exaggeration, the urban form becomes sharply contrasted with the rural form of the same principle, for the village remains essentially and almost necessarily bound to both principles. In this sense, the whole continual development may be considered as a process of increasing urbanization. "It may be said that the whole economic history of *Gesellschaft, i.e.,* of the modern nations, is in essence summarized in the change in the relationship between town and country" (Karl Marx, *Das Kapital,* I, p. 364). That is, from a certain point on, the towns by their influence and importance achieve, in the nation, predominance over the rural organization. In consequence, country and village must use more of their own productive forces for the support and furtherance of the urban areas than they can spare for purposes of reproduction. Therefore, the rural organization is doomed to dissolution. . . .

PART II

SOURCES AND PATTERNS OF CHANGE

Modern Theories

CHAPTER 11

Introduction

The grand theories gave inadequate guidance for sociological research, but no modern theory of social change has replaced them. There is no adequate theory of social change, just as there is no fully developed general theory of society. Actually, both Talcott Parsons and Wilbert E. Moore have suggested that a theory of society and one of social change are inseparable. Parsons closes his discussion of change in *The Social System* with the statement:

> Perhaps, even, it is not too much to hope that this chapter as a whole will convince the reader that there is a certain falsity in the dilemma between "static" and "dynamic" emphases. If theory is *good theory,* whichever type of problem it tackles most directly, there is no reason whatever to believe that it will not be *equally* applicable to the problems of change and to those of process within a stabilized system.[1]

Moore states: "An 'integrated' theory of social change will be as singular or plural as sociological theory as a whole, and will include about the same subdivisions and topics." [2]

There is little doubt that, once a complete theory of society is developed, it will serve to study both "static" structures and "dynamic" processes, but the search for such a theory must progress on several fronts. Furthermore, even in a fully integrated theory, whereas statements on high levels of abstraction will probably be applicable to both structure and process, concrete statements may deal with one rather than with the other. At any rate, at present one can certainly point to such statements that are exclusively concerned with "static" relationships as: "the more ranks an organization has, the lower the morale of the lower participants." This statement discusses no

---

[1] Talcott Parsons, *The Social System* (Glencoe, Ill.: The Free Press, 1951), p. 535.
[2] Wilbert E. Moore, "A Reconsideration of Theories of Social Change," *American Sociological Review,* XXV (1960), 818.

processes, but compares the morale of lower ranks among organizations that have differing numbers of ranks. On the other hand, we have such statements as: "In order for the process of differentiation of the child's personality to continue, one (or more) of the socialization agents must sanction behavior that is conforming to the next state of equilibrium, whereas another agent (or agents) has to be supportive in a nondirective way." The statement specifies two conditions under which the personality system of a child can be kept changing, but says nothing about the power differential between the two socialization agents, which is a comparatively "static" condition as concerns this process.

The growth of sociological analysis tends to follow two lines: (1) analysis of existing structures based on case studies of social units at one point in time or comparisons of several units at the same time (or at different times, but disregarding this on the assumption that the difference in time is irrelevant); (2) follow-up studies that examine the same variable or a set of variables at different times. While some studies combine both approaches, so far these are the exception, not the rule.

Parsons' most recent work, that of Neil Smelser presented later in this volume, as well as those of several other sociologists, all suggest some elements of a general theory of change. The most important point, represented in the opening paragraphs of Parsons' article, is the progress made since the early 1950's in regarding change not just as a sort of disequilibrium, or as something that maintains equilibrium, but also as a process that can decisively change the state of equilibrium itself. Earlier writings in modern sociological theory dealt mainly with two kinds of change:

(1) A process that removed a social unit from its institutionalized pattern and thus elicited forces of social control that strove to counter it, to return the unit to its initial state. The image was one of a ball that is rolled from the bottom of a bowl against one of its walls. The force of gravity strives to return the ball to its initial position. A simple social parallel would be an increase in unemployment that elicits an increase in federal spending on public works, which reduces the unemployment to its initial state.

(2) The second kind of change or process dealt with in earlier writings, is a necessary condition for equilibrium—for instance, the changing positions of the feet of a bicycle rider, or the turning of the wheels, which are required in order for the bicycle to keep upright and on the move. A simple social illustration would be the need to keep mobility at a given level to maintain an achievement-oriented society.

Both conceptions of change assume that the basic variables (or "framework") remain unchanged. The walls of the bowl, the force of gravity, the bicycle structure, public works, the social value of mobility, are taken as constants. To the degree that their change is studied, they are viewed in a still larger framework, which in turn is assumed to be constant.

The more recent development of sociological theory permits the study of changes within a system itself, *i.e.,* changes in the "basic" variables. The study of change is no longer limited to changing subsystems of stable systems; it now allows for the study of change of an entire unit, of society itself.

The model Parsons offers below for the study of changes of a system is based on the idea of differentiation. Any given social unit has a "simple," "undifferentiated" structure in which the various functions fulfilled by the unit are "fused" together, *i.e.,* are all carried out by the same set of actors, in the same set of relationships. In the process of differentiation the various functions acquire structural units of their own. For instance, production and socialization, once carried out within the family, become vested in distinct social structures, such as the factory (or the occupational realm in general), and the school (and to a degree youth movements, clubs and the like). The process of differentiation requires at the same time that the new units, each specializing in a particular function, be related to each other; differentiation requires reintegration. This is achieved through a normative system which prescribes the relationships between, let us say, the family and the factory; through "bridging" institutions, *e.g.,* the vocational school; or through mechanisms for adjustment of conflicts, such as courts.

In sum, the study of differentiation, and that of the new modes of integration it requires, is a study of the re-formation of social structure. At the beginning of the process we see a system in a state of equilibrium being disturbed, not just in part but in its entirety; at the end of the process we see that a new equilibrium has been established. The model allows us to analyze, and within limits to forecast, the direction of certain structural changes. There can hardly be a question that the model of differentiation does provide the elements of a theory of social change.

Obviously, this model does not presume to cover all possible forms of change. The development of several social units may follow different patterns. The "differentiation model" applies to the pattern in which a developing unit builds up new subunits but serves no new functions. On the other hand, the "epigenesis model" presented below deals with the pattern in which a newly created unit first fulfills only one function autonomously, then expands to serve more and more functional needs. The expansion of international systems from rather limited, intergovernmental treaties to encompassing supranational communities is one striking example. A formal organization developing an informal structure is another.

The possibility of formulating a theory of social change, as an integral part of the structural–functional approach in sociology, is not accepted by all sociologists. Both Ralf Dahrendorf and Francesca Cancian address themselves to this question. Dahrendorf concludes that the answer will have to be found outside the structural–functional tradition. Cancian sees the answer within it.

Dahrendorf views the structural–functional effort to form a *general* theory of society as a failure. He regards it as covering one part, one set of elements, and not another. Structural–functional theory, he feels, explores the factors that hold social units together, the forces of integration, but is not adequate to handle the forces of disruption and change. Dahrendorf does not formulate a general theory that would encompass both "statics" and "dynamics," but instead advocates the formation of another partial theory that would cover the elements which he sees as neglected by the structural–functional approach, a theory of conflict and change. Together the two partial theories would cover the full range of sociological phenomena. Dahrendorf proceeds to provide an illustration of what such a partial theory of conflict and change would be like.

Cancian explicitly meets the criticism of Dahrendorf, and suggests that the structural–functional theory is indeed able to study change and actually does so. Moreover, the study of change need not be introduced in an *ad hoc,* unsystematic fashion; it can be made an integral part of the structural–functional approach. Thus, for example, *disintegration* of a particular system can be predicted: functionalism specifies the prerequisites of a system; remove these, and the system falls apart. In other words, if we make a statement about the prerequisites of a system and give this statement a negative sign—meaning that the prerequisites are not now being fulfilled—we formulate a statement about the conditions of disintegration, which is one form of change.

In addition, according to Cancian, the structural–functional theory can make statements about *changes which are prerequisites for the maintenance of stability* of the system and about *corrective changes,* in which deviations from the system's state of equilibrium are followed by attempts to restore it.

While these modes of change do not exhaust the possibilities of the structural–functional approach, they surely suffice to show that the search for one sociological theory that covers both permanence and change need not be given up yet. But it is worth pointing out that it is precisely due to the pressure of criticism by Dahrendorf, Lewis Coser, and others that more and more attention is being paid by functionalists to the study of change.

While much theoretical work conducted in sociology today is done in the framework of structural–functional analysis, the earlier approaches are far from obsolete, and some new ones are being developed as well.

As we have pointed out, Toennies' conception of the transition from *Gemeinschaft* to *Gesellschaft*—from community to society—proved to be one of the most fruitful insights of sociology. Much sociological thought and analysis has been built around these two concepts or similar ones—such as "traditional" versus "modern," or "folk" versus "urban" society, all implying a general movement from the first to the second type. Horace Miner reviews and evaluates the major criticisms which have been voiced against the idea of the folk–urban continuum and assesses what this model may still contribute to a modern theory of change. The most basic question raised is whether all societies really do move from a folk to an urban society. As Miner indicates, the model allows for a certain degree of variability, and some movement in the opposite direction need not be excluded. But, Miner points out, no one could seriously disclaim the existence of a general trend toward urbanization. The two concepts must be viewed as the poles of a continuum; we should see that any society includes both folk *and* urban elements and that the sort of transition which actually takes place increases the importance of urbanity but never eliminates the folk elements entirely. Moreover, some folk elements (*e.g.,* the nuclear family) are, as far as one can tell, a permanent feature of urbanized society, and even some new "folk" elements (*e.g.,* suburbs, clubs) have emerged. Nevertheless, globally the urban elements continue to grow.

The *Gemeinschaft–Gesellschaft* or folk–urban continuum may be viewed as an independent approach. However, an attempt was made to enhance its value by incorporating it into a general sociological theory. For this purpose the basic insights embodied in this conception were elevated to a higher level of abstraction, thus gaining wider applicability, and the two ideal types, and with them the entire continuum, were broken up into a set of variables. Parsons showed that the folk society might be described as a highly particularistic, diffuse, collective, affective, and ascriptive society while the urban society might be characterized as governed by universalism, specificity, achievement, and affective neutrality.[3] Thus Parsons tied the folk–urban continuum to the major stream of sociology by showing that the variables used in the study of this general transition are actually the same as those used to study any other social unit and its change.

The work of C. Wright Mills continues the grand-theory line, even though Mills did not make all history and all societies his domain. Actually, compared to earlier "classical" works, Mills's analysis is limited in scope—technical and empirical. But compared to most contemporary sociology, he is urgently concerned with social issues, rather than rigorously scientific. His use of terms is far from precise (his "elite," for instance, stands sometimes for holders of institutional positions, sometimes for a social class)[4] and his combination of sociological analysis and social criticism is in the best Marxist tradition.

Mills's perspective differs from that common among contemporary sociologists also in his incomplete adherence to the multifactor approach. It would be a gross error to view Mills as a pure Marxist, since his work is deeply influenced by Max Weber. He assigns a considerable role to political (*i.e.,* normative and coercive) factors, viewing the government and the

---

[3] Talcott Parsons, *The Structure of Social Action* (Glencoe, Ill.: The Free Press, 1937), pp. 686-694.

[4] This point was made by Daniel Bell, *The End of Ideology* (Glencoe, Ill.: The Free Press, 1960), pp. 46-47.

military, the church and the courts, not as mere instruments of the propertied classes, but as forces in their own right. Still, Mills puts a strong emphasis on class factors, and his view of a coalition of elites maintaining exclusive access to power certainly comes closer to a neo-Marxist approach
than most other contemporary sociological writings on social change.

Anthropologists have maintained or revived approaches which most sociologists have rejected but which are nevertheless of interest, and which,
in the future, may yet be reincorporated into sociological theories of change.
The old evolutionary theories, mostly implying linear progress, have been
rejected on the grounds that human history obviously fails to display a
general, encompassing trend toward higher and higher enlightenment; that
various sectors of any society are apt to proceed at a different pace and
possibly in different directions (science may progress cumulatively while
the enforcement of moral standards may show no or only little improvement); and that different societies follow different patterns of development and possibly are oriented to different states of "maturity." Not only
did the Russian industrialization follow a different path from that of England,
but, in addition, industrialized Russia is quite different from industrialized
England.

Julian H. Steward explores a new approach to the study of evolution
that avoids these pitfalls. First, following the general trend of the social sciences, his concepts are less value-laden and he does not assume that moral
progress is immanent in social development. Second, again in line with the
general trend, he does not seek a single path of change, but presents a theory of multilinear evolution. What then is left of the earlier evolutionary
framework? Although the multilinear evolutionist assumes that there is
more than one path of development, he makes it his working assumption
that the number of possible patterns is limited. There are several patterns
the course of civilization might follow, but not an endless number, and
empirical study may show under what conditions a society will go one way
rather than another. Moreover, while societies travel on different paths at a
different pace, to different destinations, there seem to be some basic similarities between these journeys. Thus, in spite of interruptions, cyclical
rhythms of ascent and decline, and so on; societies seem to proceed from the
small and simple to the large and complex.

A. L. Kroeber analyzes another anthropological approach markedly different from both the evolutionary and the structural–functional views. Basically, "diffusionism" tends to explain change in one society by finding its origin in another. When pushed to an extreme, it claims that every new pattern
of behavior or item of culture has spread from one original source. Most
sociologists find it difficult to accept this approach. True, many ideas
spread from one society to another, especially in modern times—with the
increase and improvement in communication—but at the same time there is
undoubtedly much parallel innovation in which two or more cultures dis-

cover or work out a similar solution to the same problem. Even more important is the fact that from the multitude of items communicated to any society, only a few are adapted; which ones are utilized and which are not depends not only on the communication (*e.g.,* its vigor, amount, and repetitiveness), but on the needs, interests, and absorptive capacities of the receiving system. Furthermore, identical items communicated will be differently adapted by various societies. Thus, as Kroeber indicates, diffusion is an important variable in the analysis of change, but diffusionism has been pushed too far in an attempt to build a framework for the study of change around this one variable.

What is needed is a *combined* study of systems of intersocial communication and patterns of intrasocial absorption, related to the study of the conditions under which innovations, whether externally or internally initiated, are integrated into society. We will return to this point below, where innovation and diffusion are examined more closely.

The cybernetic approach to the study of change is in some ways similar to that of functional analysis. Like the latter, it studies equilibrium and the conditions under which stability is maintained as against those under which it is undermined. The concept of "ultrastability," basic to cybernetics, refers to systems that have mechanisms of feedback that allow them not only to respond to the environment but also to change their pattern of response; not only to introduce corrective changes to counter deviation, but when deviation is too frequent (and so strains the correctional mechanisms) to change the point at which the system is balanced, or to introduce new corrective mechanisms. Systems that exist in environments which change rapidly and/or drastically need to be ultrastable in order to survive. Up to this point, the cybernetic approach can be completely integrated with the structural–functional approach. The main point of difference comes when we realize that the cybernetic models and their terminology, derived from the study of machines and electric circuits, are often limited to some sets of social phenomena and exclude others. Cybernetics tends to view actors as rational; for instance, little attention is paid to subconscious distortion of information or to irrational resistance to innovation. Moreover, the social structure is viewed as a communication network, not taking into account differences in power positions which are not necessarily related to communicative positions; a person or group at the end of a communication network—let us say, at the top of a corporation—might receive comparatively less communication, but have much more power, than a middle-ranking executive who is at a major intersection of the communication network. Finally, information is not the only communication that has to be taken into account; actually, expressive communication—in which symbols that carry normative and emotional meaning are transmitted—often might prove more vital. This is not to suggest that the analysis of information flow or of communication in general is marginal, but rather, that like most approaches that focus on one set of variables, it gains its fullest value when systematically related to the study of other sets of factors, such as the distribution of power and the flows of expressive communication. It may well be that one could construct a computer model that would take into account all these factors, including emotional and irrational behavior. But the fact remains that most computer models and cybernetic writings do not include them at present.

The psychological approach gained much new attention in recent years, due to David McClelland and Everett E. Hagen's contribution to the study of change, in particular development.[5] According to this approach, the main force that propels societies rests not in environmental factors, ideas, or social conflict but in individuals with high achievement motivation. This achievement drive is largely attained in the formative years and is effected by the social structure of the family and the culture.

---

[5] David C. McClelland, *The Achieving Society* (Princeton, N.J.: D. Van Nostrand, 1961); Everett E. Hagen, *On the Theory of Social Change* (Homewood, Ill.: The Dorsey Press, 1961).

CHAPTER 12

TALCOTT PARSONS

A Functional Theory
of Change

Structure and Process

The subject in general is far too vast for discussion in a brief paper, unless one confined himself to the highest level of generality. I should like, therefore, to concentrate my attention on one major type of change in social systems, that which is most closely analogous to the process of growth in the organism. This usually involves an element of quantitative increase in the "magnitude" of the system, in the social case, *e.g.,* through increase in population, but it also involves what in an important sense is qualitative or "structural" change. The type of the latter on which I should like to concentrate is the process of structural differentiation and the concomitant development of patterns and mechanisms which integrate the differentiated parts.

•

One of the most fundamental canons of scientific method is that it is impossible to study everything at once. Since the basis of generalization in science is always the demonstration of relatedness in process of variation (in one sense change), there must always somewhere be a distinction between the features of the phenomena under observation which do and which do not change under the relevant limitations of time and scope and in the respects which are defined as important for the purposes in hand. The specificities of significant change could not even be identified if there were no *relative* background of nonchange to relate them to.

To me the concept of structure is simply a shorthand statement of this basic point. The structure of a system is that set of properties of its component parts

From Talcott Parsons, "Some Considerations on the Theory of Social Change," *Rural Sociology,* XXVI (1961), No. 3, pp. 219-239. Reprinted by permission of the author and the publisher.

and their relations or combinations which, for a particular set of analytical purposes, can both logically and empirically be treated as constant within definable limits. If, however, there is built up strong empirical evidence that treating such elements as constant for particular types of systems is helpful in understanding the patterning of variation of other elements, then this structure is not simply an arbitrary methodological assumption, but propositions about it and its limits of empirical stability become empirical generalizations which are just as important as are "dynamic" generalizations.

•

Any ordinary system, therefore, is capable of description as on the one hand a structure, a set of units or components with, for the purposes in hand, stable properties, which of course may be relational, and on the other hand of events, of processes, in the course of which "something happens" to change some properties and some relations among them.

The concept of stability has obviously been used here as a defining characteristic of structure. The sense of the former term which must be distinguished from structure is that in which it is used to characterize a system as a whole, or some subsystem of such a system. In this present sense it is equivalent to the more specific concept of stable equilibrium—which in another reference may be either "static" or "moving." A system then is stable or (relatively) in equilibrium when the relation between its structure and the processes which go on within it and between it and its environment are such as to maintain those properties and relations, which for the purposes in hand have been called its structure, relatively unchanged. Very generally, always in "dynamic" systems, this maintenance is dependent on continuously varying processes, which "neutralize" either endogenous or exogenous sources of variability which, if they went far enough, would change the structure. A classic example of equilibrium in this sense is the maintenance of nearly constant body temperature by mammals and birds—in the face of continuing variation in environmental temperature and through mechanisms which operate either to produce heat, including slowing up its loss, or to slow down the rate of heat production or accelerate its dissipation.

Contrasted then with stability or equilibrating processes are those processes which operate to bring about structural change. That such processes exist and that they are of fundamental scientific importance is nowhere in question. Thus even in physics, whereas the mass of the atom of a particular element has been the prototype of the stable structural reference point, the discoveries of modern nuclear physics have now evolved a theory of change by which, through nuclear fission and/or fusion, the structures of "atomic identity" are transformed into others. The reason for insistence on the importance of keeping the concepts of structure and process and of stability and change analytically distinct is not a predilection in favor of one or the other item in each pair, but in favor of orderly procedure in scientific analysis.

As I see it now, the distinction between the two pairs of concepts is one of level of system reference. The structure of a system and of its environment must be distinguished from process *within* the system and in *interchange* between the system and its environment. But processes which maintain the stability of a system, internally through both structure and process, and in interchange with its environment, *i.e.,* states of its equilibrium, must be distinguished from processes by which this balance between structure and more "elementary" process is altered in such a way as to lead to a new and different "state" of the system, a state which must be described in terms of an alteration of its previous structure. To be sure the distinction is relative, but it is an essential and an ordered relativity. What I have been saying is that *at least two* systematically related perspectives on the problem of constancy of variation are essential to any sophisticated level of theoretical analysis.

These considerations constitute the major framework in which I should like to approach the analysis of change in social systems. I should like to attempt to discuss one type of change in the sense in which it has just been contrasted with stability and therefore will presuppose that there is a system or set of systems to which the concept of equilibrium is relevant, but which are conceived as undergoing processes of change which as such are processes of upsetting the initial equilibrium state and later "settling down" into a new equilibrium state. . . .

Let us start with the question of the structure of social systems and introduce both a formal and a substantive consideration. The formal one is that the structure of any empirical system may be treated as consisting in (1) *units,* such as the particle or the cell, and (2) *patterned relations* among units, such as relative distances, "organization" into tissues and organs. For social systems the minimum unit is the *role* of the participating individual actor (or status-role, if you will), and the minimum relation is that of patterned reciprocal interactions in terms of which each participant functions as an actor in relation to (orienting to) the others and, conversely, each is object for all the others. Higher-order units of social systems are collectivities, *i.e.,* organized action systems of the role performance of pluralities of human individuals. Perhaps it is well to speak of units on either level as units of *orientation* when they are treated as actors, as units of *modality* when they are treated as objects.[1]

In social structure the element of "patterned relation" is clearly in part

---

[1] This is the terminology used in "Pattern Variables Revisited," *American Sociological Review,* XXV (1960), 467-483.

"normative." This is to say that from the point of view of the unit it includes a set of "expectations" as to his or its behavior on the axis of what
is or is not proper, appropriate, or right. From the point of view of other
units with which the unit of reference is in interaction, this is a set of standards according to which positive or negative sanctions can be legitimated.
Corresponding to the distinction between role and collectivity for the case of
units is that between norm and value for that of relational pattern. A value
is a normative pattern which defines desirable behavior for a system in relation to its environment, without differentiation in terms of the functions of
units or of their particular situations. A norm, on the other hand, is a pattern defining desirable behavior for a unit or class of units in respects specific to it, and differentiated from the obligations of other classes.

The proposition that the relational patterns of social systems are normative, which is to say that they consist in institutionalized normative culture,
can, in fact, be extended to the structure of units as well. One way of making
this clear is to point out that what at one level of reference is a unit at another is a system. What we are calling the structural properties of the unit,
therefore, are at the next level the relational patterns which order the relations between what in turn are the subunits making *it* up. Therefore, it is
justified to assert, in the wider perspective, that the structure of social systems in general *consists* in institutionalized patterns of normative culture.
It is of course further essential that these must be understood as applying
at the two distinct levels of organization, which we call that of units and
relational pattern among units.

To return now to the paradigm of the stable system discussed above, process in a system must be conceived as a process of interchanging inputs and
outputs between units (subsystems) of the system on the one hand, and between the system, through the agency of its units, and its environment on
the other. There is thus a "flow" of such inputs and outputs as between all
pairs of classes of units, whether the relation be internal or external. What I
am calling the normative pattern governing the relationship is then to be
conceived as regulating this flow. For stable interchange to go on there must
on the one hand be flexibility for inputs and outputs to move, but there
must also be ways of "channeling" this process to keep its variability within
limits.

A prototypical case is the flow of transactions involving the exchange of
things of "value," namely goods and services and money, which constitute a
market process. The normative patterns on the other hand are the institutional patterns defining money itself, the norms of contract and of the aspects of property other than money, conceived as Durkheim did in the
famous phrase about the noncontractual elements of contract. The equilibrium of a market system is dependent on the maintenance of limits, relative
to a set of definable conditions, to the fluctuation in the rates of these flows.
The stability of the *structure* of the market system in the present sense is

on the other hand a matter of the stability of the normative pattern system, the institutions.

What, then, do we mean by the stability of an institutional complex? First, of course, is meant the stability of the normative pattern itself. The single term "norm," especially if it is equated with "rule," is probably too narrow because it seems to imply a level of simplicity which permits description in a single proposition; this would patently not be true of the institutions of property or contract. Secondly, stability implies a minimum level of commitment of acting units, *i.e.,* of dispositions to perform in accordance with the relevant expectations—rather than to evade or violate them—and to apply the relevant sanctions, positive or negative, to other units in response to performance, evasion or violation. Third, institutionalization implies acceptance of an empirical and mutually understood "definition of the situation" in a sense of understanding of what the system of reference *is;*[2] this can for example be ideologically distorted so as to make functioning impossible.[3]

Finally, institutionalization means some order of integration of the normative complex in question in the more general one governing the system as a whole, at the normative level itself. Thus the doctrine of "separate but equal" proved to be dubiously integrated with the rest of the American system of constitutional rights formulated on the basis of the constitutional right to "equal protection of the laws." It can thus be said that the 1954 decision of the Supreme Court was a step in institutional integration, or at least that this was the primary problem before the court.

Endogenous and Exogenous Sources of Change

The concept of stable equilibrium implies that through integrative mechanisms endogenous variations are kept within limits compatible with the maintenance of the main structural patterns, and through adaptive mechanisms fluctuations in the relations between system and environment are similarly kept within limits. If we look at what is meant by stable equilibrium from the perspective of the principle of inertia,[4] then it becomes a

---

[2] This definition is normative to acting units but existential to observers. Here the actor is placed in the role of an observer of his own situation of action, *i.e.,* is treated as potentially "rational."

[3] Thus it seems plausible to suggest that perhaps the most serious source of conflict in the UN at present lies in the ideological difference between the Western and the Communist powers as to what the UN itself, and the system of international order of which it is a guardian, in fact consist in. The slogans of imperialism and colonialism formulate the Communist view of everything not under their more-or-less direct control. If this is the "diagnosis" it is quite clear that the present organization is not "doing its job."

[4] The concept of inertia is here used in the sense of classical mechanics, namely to designate stability in rate and direction of process, not a state in which "nothing hap-

problem to account for alterations in this stable state through disturbances of sufficient magnitude to overcome the stabilizing or equilibrating forces or mechanisms. Once a disturbance fulfilling these criteria is present, then the problem is that of tracing its effects through the system, and defining the conditions under which new stable states can be predicted (or, retrospectively, accounted for).

Such changes may in principle be either endogenous or exogenous or both, but in approaching the problem it is essential to bear in mind that I am here dealing with the concept "social system" in a strict analytical sense. Therefore, changes originating in the personalities of the members of the social system, the behavioral organisms "underlying" these, or the cultural system as such are to be classed as exogenous, whereas common sense would have it that only the physical environment (including other organisms and societies), and perhaps the "supernatural," is truly exogenous.

The formal paradigm for the analysis of the general system of action which I with various associates have been using would suggest, first, that the immediately most important channels of exogenous influence on the social system are the culture and the personality systems and also that the modes of their influence are different. The direct influence of the cultural system in turn should involve in the first instance empirical knowledge, hence should lead into the field of the sociology of knowledge in that area. Important as this is, because of limitations of space I shall not deal directly with it here, but will confine myself to the boundary vis-à-vis the personality.

There is, however, a double reason why the boundary of the social system vis-à-vis the personality is particularly significant. In its most direct sense it is concerned with the "motivation" of the individual, in an analytical psychological sense, hence with his level of "gratification" and its negative, frustration. But indirectly the most critical point is that what is structurally the most critical component of social systems, what we call its institutionalized values, is institutionalized by way of its internalization in the personality of the individual. There is a sense in which the social system is "boxed in" between the cultural status of values and their significance to the integration of the individual personality.

The problem of analyzing the independent variability which may exist as between cultural values and personalities is beyond the scope of this paper; it may be presumed that problems such as those of charismatic innovation fall at least partly in this rubric. Given relative stability of this connection, however, we may suggest that there will be in the personality of the typical individual what may be called an integrate of value and motivational com-

---

pens." The *problem* then becomes that of accounting for change in rate or direction, including "slowing down." This of course runs counter to much of common sense in the field of human action.

mitments which can for heuristic purposes be assumed to be stable and that this in turn can be assumed to define the *orientation* component of the requisite role—expectations of the appropriate classes of individual actors. Furthermore, this should be true whether a society as a whole or a sub-system of it is under analysis. This assumption clearly implies that, for purposes of analyzing the particular process of change in question, the institutionalized values will be assumed to remain constant.

I am also assuming that the structure of normative patterns which defines the relations of the class of acting units under consideration to the objects in their situation is also given, initially, but that this is our primary independent variable; namely the problem is to account for processes of change in this normative structure, in institutions. This leaves the modalities of objects as the focus of initiation of change. I shall therefore postulate a change in the relation of a social system to its environment which in the first instance impinges on the definition of the situation for one or more classes of acting units within the system, and then has further repercussions which can put pressure for change on the normative institutional patterns. The type of pressure I have specifically in mind is in the direction of differentiation.

•

A Model of Differentiation

With these preliminaries in mind, let us now attempt to outline in general terms the main steps in a cycle of differentiation, and then apply the analysis to the case of differentiation between household and producing collectivity.

We may start with the postulation of a deficit of input at the goal-attainment boundary of the social system which is postulated as undergoing a process of differentiation, *e.g.,* the family household which also performs "occupational" functions. Looking at it from a functional point of view, it may be said that the "frustration" of its capacity to attain its goals, or fulfill its expectations, may focus at either of the functional levels which is important to it, namely its productive effectiveness or its effectiveness in performing what later come to be the "residual" family functions of socialization and regulation of the personalities of members, or of course some combination of the two. Secondly, it will of course concern the boundary between this and other subsystems of the society. In this case the important boundary conceptions are the markets for commodities and labor and the ideological "justifications" of the unit's position in the society, which may or may not take a prominently religious direction. But underlying this is the problem of input from the personality of the individual into the social system at the more general level; in the present case this is likely to be particularly important because familial and occupational roles are, for the personality of the adult, the most important foci of commitment to the performance of societal function. Third, there will be some balance between the two components of frustration just mentioned, namely with respect to the conditional components of facilities and rewards, and with respect to the normative components of expectation systems. The latter component is the indispensable condition of the process leading to differentiation.

The complexity involved in these three distinctions may seem formidable, but it may be argued that the difficulty is not so serious as it sounds. It is the last one which is the most crucial because of the importance of a normative component somewhere. The difference between the other two concerns that between exogenous and endogenous sources of change for the system in question; personalities in roles in the particular social system of reference operate "directly" on that system, not through its boundary interchanges with other social systems.

The most important point to be made here is that, *whatever its source,* if a disturbance impinges on the goal-attaining subsystem of a social system, its effects will, in the first instance, be propagated in two directions. One of these concerns the functional problem of access to facilities for the performance of primary functions, namely the kind of facilities available and the terms on which they are available. The other direction concerns the kind of integrative support which the unit receives within the system, the senses in which it can be said to have a "mandate" to "do a job." Back of that, in turn, and on a still higher level of control is the basic "legitimation" of its functioning. Support here may be defined as particularized to the specific unit or class of units. Legitimation on the other hand concerns more the functions than the particular unit and the normative more than the operative patterns.

These three problems fit into a hierarchy of control. The first is an adaptive problem and must be solved first if the groundwork of solution of the others is to be laid, and so on for the others. What is meant by "solution" in this case is provision of *opportunity* in a facilities sense for the higher level of functioning in question to be attained. Opportunity thus conceived is always double-barreled, in that it has a concrete resource aspect on the one hand, a normatively controlled "mechanism" or standard aspect on the other.

Another familiar sociological concept should be brought in here, namely "ascription." Ascription is essentially the *fusion* of intrinsically independent functions in the same structural unit. Looked at in this way differentiation is a process of "emancipation" from ascriptive ties. As such it is a process of gaining "freedom from" certain restraints. But it is also the process of fitting into a normative order which can subject the now independent units to a type of normative control compatible with the functional imperative of the larger system of which they are a part. In differentiating, however, the unit gains certain degrees of freedom of choice and action which were not open to it before the process of differentiation had taken place. Moreover, this should be the case whichever side of the division is taken as a point of reference.

•

The obverse of this emancipation from ascription to a relatively particularized source of income is the freedom to offer a much wider variety of services in exchange for income. The labor force, that is to say, may become much more highly differentiated, and a wider variety of specialized talents may find employment. A new set of conditions are of course introduced, because the more important specialized talents often involve prerequisites of training and experience which cannot be universally taken for granted.

These two are the relatively "conditional" factors from the point of view of the household. We may say that it cannot afford to let the process of differentiation take place unless certain minima in these respects are, if not guaranteed, made highly probable. These probabilities are, in turn, dependent on two further sets of considerations which involve the more ramified relationship systems in which the process takes place. These are considerations in the first place of the nature of the labor market in which the income earner has to offer his services; above all the extent to which he is protected against pressures to accept particularly disadvantageous terms. There are three main mechanisms involved in modern labor markets at the operative level, though others may operate in other ways. These are of course competition between potential employers, the self-protective measures of employee groups, *e.g.*, through collective bargaining, and establishment and enforcement of a normative order by "higher" authority, *e.g.*, public agencies. The effect of regulation of terms by any combination of these factors is to emancipate the unit from exposure to particular pressures exerted by any one source of supply, *e.g.*, of income. Through such means as the monetary mechanisms and credit instruments, there is also time-extension, in that the employee is emancipated from the pressures of immediacy to a degree to which this may not be the case for the proprietor.

•

Let us now turn to the second context, that of support for the performance of function. This is the kind of context in which farming is regarded as a "way of life" rather than a "business." Typically occupational employment is justified by the higher level of efficiency of such organization in producing a higher standard of living, but this may be problematical when it involves ceasing to be "independent" and "working for one's own" rather than for an employer. On the other side there is the problem of "loss of function" of the family, with the implication that the differentiated family is not "doing a worthwhile job," but is coming to be a consumption unit alone —a question particularly coming to a head in the alleged concentration of the feminine role on "leisure" activities. We may follow through this context in terms of the problem of degrees of freedom, being careful to distinguish the two levels which above have been called support and legitimation.

The problem in which I am calling the context of support is the position of the family in locally significant "public opinion." The support of this unit is ascribed to the conception that acceptable status in the community is bound to proprietorship of an enterprise, with all its connotations about the place of property—that the employed person is in some sense a second class citizen. It seems to follow that, just as in the context of facilities available to differentiating units the relevant frame of reference or "reference group" was the market, both for labor and for consumers' goods, in that of "support" it is the local community, since both residential unit and employing unit for the typical adult must be comprised within this. In the undifferentiated case, the core structure of the local community in America consists in proprietary kinship units—in the first instance farm families, but the same structural patterns extend to small businesses and professional practices in market towns. In the differentiated case it is residential kinship units on the one hand, employing organizations on the other.

Since the basic "goals" of residential kinship units as such are in the nature of the case ascribed, namely as socialization of children and management of the personalities of members, the community gains in this respect an exceedingly important new range of freedom in the new levels and diversities of, in the above broad sense, "productive" achievement, which higher level organizations are capable of carrying out and which are beyond the capacities of kinship units. The typical family unit need no longer look to units of its own type of structure for these benefits, thus staying within the limits imposed by this structure, and members of the community can support the functions of the community *both* in the familial realm and in the productive without making their ascription to each other a condition.

This, however, is possible only if there are standards which regulate the terms on which the two categories of functions are related to each other. This, in part, concerns market relations; but a number of other things are also involved, such as obligations for contributing to the support of common community interests, both through taxation and through voluntary channels. There must be a new set of "rules of the game" according to which both sets of operating units can live in the same community without undue friction. One major focus of these balancing institutions lies in the field of stratification, above all perhaps because the larger scale of organization of producing units in the differentiated sense makes it impossible to preserve the basis of equality of kinship units of a family–farm community.

This leads over into the problem of legitimation which concerns the justifications or questioning of the basic pattern of organization of socially important functions in terms of the institutionalized values of the system. Here the problem is that of emancipating the formulas of legitimation from the organizational particularities of the less differentiated situation. These considerations clearly get over into the ideological realm. For differentiation to be legitimated it must no longer be believed that only proprietors are really "responsible" people, or that organizations which are not controlled by locally prestigeful kinship units are necessarily concerned only with "self-interest" and are not really "contributing." On the other side, the family which has "lost functions" can really be a "good family."

Perhaps the most important focus of this new legitimation is the new conception of the adequate, socially desirable *man,* particularly as organized about the balancing of the two differentiated spheres of performance and responsibility, in his occupational role on the one hand, in his family on the other. If this is the case, then clearly there are extremely important concomitant problems of change in the feminine role. The first stage of these probably concerns the ideological legitimation of a more differentiated femininity than before, namely that even in a family which has lost function it is justified for the woman to devote herself primarily to husband and children. A later phase involves various forms of community participation and occupational involvement.

These three seem to be the main contexts in which the direct impact of the impetus to structural change must work out if it is to result in the differentiation of a previously fused structure. For the sake of completeness, it should be mentioned that there will be certain other more indirect problem areas. One of these is that of the sheer content of consumption tastes which is involved in a change in the standard of living, and its relation to the occupational contribution of the income earner. A second is the problem of the relation of values, at various levels of specification, not only to the more immediate problems of the legitimation of the various classes of structural units in the system, but to that of the more generalized norms and standards which regulate their relations. Finally, the most indirect of all seems to lie in the field of what Durkheim called organic solidarity. I interpret this to mean the normative regulation of the adaptive processes and mechanisms. As I see it, this is the primary link between what I have called support on the one hand and the realistic play of "interests" of the various units on the other.

The above discussion has dealt, in far too great a hurry, with several different "functional" contexts in which some kind of reordering has to take place if a process of differentiation, as this has been defined, is to be completed and the new structure stabilized. It is of the essence of the present view that in each of these there is involved a complex balance of input–output relationships, such that too great a tipping in either direction with respect to any one such balance could make the difference between successful differentiation and its failure. The dismal complexity of the resulting picture is, however, somewhat mitigated by considerations of the hierarchy of control and hence of the fact that firm establishment of the "proper" patterns at the higher levels may make it possible to exercise control over rather wide ranges of variation at the lower.

•

The Consequences of Differentiation

. . . In conclusion, I should like to attempt to summarize certain of the primary conditions of successful differentiation which also constitute in a sense characterizations of the outcome in the relevant respects. First there is what I have called the *opportunity* factor. This is the aspect of the structure of the situation which is most directly relevant to the process of differentiation as such. The operation of the process of course presupposes a need or demand factor, the source of disturbance to which reference was made above. The implementation of the process of differentiation in turn implies a leadership factor in that some individual or group should take responsibility, not only for routine "management" but for reorganization. The entrepreneur of standard economic discussion is a prototypical example.

But for there to be genuine differentiation there must be a process by which facilities, previously ascribed to less differentiated units, are freed from this ascription and are made available through suitable adaptive mechanisms for the utilization of the higher-order new class of units which are emerging. The prototype of such facilities for the process considered above is that of labor services, freed from ascription to the household unit, but with their availability to the employing organization institutionally regulated in terms of the market system and the institutionalization of the contract of employment. The obverse is of course the accessibility, for the residual household units, of necessary facilities through the expenditure of money income on the markets for consumers' goods. Looked at then in structural terms, the opportunity factor is essentially the possibility of institutionalizing the mutual access to facilities, in this case through the market mechanisms. In another type of case, for instance, it may be the mechanisms of communication.

The second main context of structural reorganization concerns the way in which the two new and differentiated classes of units are related to each other in the wider system, in the first instance from the point of view of the structure of collectivities. I have suggested, for the case of the producing household, that what is primarily involved here is a restructuring of the local community. The latter can no longer be an aggregate of proprietary kinship units, only supplemented by a few structures articulating it with the wider society, but it comes to be organized about the relationships between "residential" units and "employing" units. It is evident that this entails articulating the most important *differentiated* roles of the same individual, in the first instance of course the typical adult male.

This may be called the restructuring of the ways in which the particular unit, collectivity and role, is included in higher-order collectivity structures in the society. Since in the nature of the case any initial collectivity unit (or role unit) is part of a society, it is not a question whether it should or should not be included; for example, the case of absorption of immigrant kin groups into a host society is a different problem from that now under consideration. The point is rather that there must be a restructuring of collectivities on the level immediately above that of the initial unit, with either the incorporation of both the old (or "residual") unit and the new in an already available higher-order unit, or the creation of a new category of such units, or both. The essential point is that there must be established a new collectivity structure within which both types of units perform essential functions and in the name of which both can draw the kind of "support" discussed above. The problem is of course particularly acute for the newly emerging unit or class of units.

The third context in which normative components of structure have to be reorganized as part of a process of differentiation is that of the more general complexes of institutionalized norms which apply not to one collectivity structure but to many. The prototype here for largescale and highly differentiated social systems is the system of legal norms, but it is not confined to that. Standards of performance or achievement, of technical adequacy, and the like are also involved.

In the case we have used for illustration, the standards in terms of which employing collectivities are legitimized are particularly important. Here it is important to recognize two different stages beyond that of the proprietary unit which was our original point of reference, namely that in which all productive roles are performed by household members. The next step has usually been the "family firm" in which the managerial and entrepreneurial roles were ascribed to kinship, but the "labor" roles were not. This of course is still very prominent in the "small business" sector of the American economy and also in some other fields. But beyond this is the case where the organization is cut entirely loose from kinship. The most important legal aspect of this development has been the generalization of the idea of the corporation and its legitimation in many different fields, quantitatively of course most conspicuously the economic.

At the role level, an important case is that of the standards of competence which become institutionalized as defining conditions of employment in certain classes of roles, behind which in turn lie levels of education. These, like legal norms, are independent of any particular employing collectivity or kinship group—in this sense both are universalistic. The rules of corporate organization define the kinds of things certain organized groups can do and the responsibilities they assume in organizing to do them; standards of education define the kinds of legitimate requirements of eligibility for certain types of employment which may be laid down, hence both the kinds of opportunities open to individuals of various classes and the ways in which access to such opportunity is limited.

It has been suggested above that a process of differentiation, with the meaning we have given that term, involves the establishment of a unit having primary functions of a higher order, seen in terms of the system in which it operates, than was the function of the unit from which it differentiates. If this is the case, then the norms governing the performance of that function, including the relations of its performers to other units in the social structure, must be of a higher order of generality than before. This is what we mean by saying that they are more universalistic; they define standards which cannot, in their relevance, be confined to the lower-order function and the units performing it. This criterion is directly involved with the emancipation of resources from ascription. Competence as a qualification for a role, in a sense which denies the relevance of kinship membership, is prototypical. Thus we may speak of an *upgrading* of the standards of normative control of the more differentiated system as compared with the less differentiated one.

This whole discussion has been based on the assumption that the underlying value-pattern of the system does not change as a part of the process of differentiation. It does not, however, follow that nothing changes at the level of values. It is an essential proposition of the conceptual scheme used here that every social system has a system of values as the highest-order component of its structure. Its values comprise the definition, from the point of view of its members—if it is institutionalized—of the desirable type of system at a level independent of internal structural differentiation or of particularities of situation. This "system" involves both a pattern type and an element of content, namely a definition of what kind of system the pattern applies to. In our case there are the values of households and of employing-productive units. In what I am calling "pattern" terms they may be the same, *e.g.,* both of them incorporating the general American pattern of "instrumental activism." But if these values are to be implemented in either type of system there must be specifications of the more general system to the type of function (not its particularities) and to the type of situation in which the unit operates.

Where differentiation has occurred, this means that the values of the new system, which includes both the new and the residual unit, must be different in the content component from that of the original unit, though not, under present assumptions, in the pattern component. The new values must be more extensive, in the special sense that they can legitimize the functions of both differentiated units under a single formula which permits each to do what it does and, equally essential, not to do what the other does. The difficulty of institutionalizing the more extensive values is evidenced by the widespread currency of what may be called romantic ideologies in this sense, the allegation that the "loss of function," which is an inevitable feature of what I call the residual unit after the differentiation has taken place, is a measure of failure to implement the value-pattern of the system. For example, the new dependence of households on occupational earnings from employing organizations is often interpreted as loss of a sense of responsibility for independent support. This to be sure is ideology, but as such is an index of incomplete institutionalization of restructured values.

The relation between the values of a higher-order social system and those of a differentiated subsystem may be said to be one of *specification* of the implications of the more generalized pattern of the more extensive system to the "level" of the subsystem, by taking account of the limitations imposed upon the latter by function and situation. In this sense a business firm may value "economic rationality" in a sense which comprises both productivity and solvency, with considerably less qualification for more extensive values than an undifferentiated family household can, and in a complementary sense the household can devote itself in economic contexts to "consumption."

The above is sufficient to indicate only a few highlights of a very complex problem area. In this paper I have dealt with only one aspect of the field of the theory of social change. I have had to do so very abstractly and with only a tiny bit of empirical illustration. It does, however, seem to me justified to draw the conclusion that the problems of this area are in principle soluble in empirical-theoretical terms. Above all, we have at our disposal a conceptual scheme which is sufficiently developed so that at least at the level of categorization and of problem statement it is approaching the type of closure—logical of course—which makes *systematic* analysis of interdependencies possible. We can define the main ranges of variability which are essential for empirical analysis, and the main mechanisms through which variations are propagated through the system. We can quantify to the point of designating deficits and surpluses of inputs and outputs, and here and there we can come close to specifying threshold values beyond which equilibrium will break down. . . .

CHAPTER 13

RALF DAHRENDORF

Toward a Theory of
Social Conflict[1]

I

After an interval of almost fifty years, a theme has reappeared in sociology which has determined the origin of that discipline more than any other subject area. From Marx and Comte to Simmel and Sorel, social conflict, especially revolution, was one of the central themes in social research. The same is true of many early Anglo-Saxon sociologists (although in their work the problem of revolution has been characteristically somewhat neglected), for example, the Webbs in England and Sumner in the United States. However, when Talcott Parsons in 1937 established a certain convergence in the sociological theories of Alfred Marshall, Émile Durkheim, Vilfredo Pareto, and Max Weber,[2] he no longer had in mind an analysis of social conflict; his was an attempt to solve the problem of integration of socalled social systems by an organon of interrelated categories. The new question was now "What holds societies together?"—no longer, "What drives them on?" The influence of the Parsonian posing of the question on more recent sociology (and by no means only on American sociology) can hardly be overrated. Thus, it is possible that the revival of the study of social conflict in the last decades appears to many not so much a continuation of traditional research paths as a new thematic discovery—an instance of dialectic irony in the development of science.

At this time, approaches to a systematic study of social conflict are still

From Ralf Dahrendorf, "Toward a Theory of Social Conflict," *The Journal of Conflict Resolution*, XI (1958), No. 2, pp. 170-183. Reprinted by permission of the author and the publisher.

[1] This paper was translated by Anatol Rapoport, Mental Health Research Unit, University of Michigan.

[2] Cf. Talcott Parsons, *The Structure of Social Action* (New York, 1937; 2nd ed., Glencoe, Ill.: The Free Press, 1949).

relatively isolated, compared to the innumerable works on social stratification or on the structure and function of specific institutions, organizations, and societies. Still, the thesis of a revival of the study of social conflict can be justified with regard to the works of Aron, Philip, Brinton, Kerr, Coser, Brinkmann, Geiger, Gluckman and others,[3] as well as an attempt to determine a systematic locus and a specific framework for a theory of conflict in sociological analysis.

Types and Varieties of Social Conflict

To begin with a commonplace observation, the problem of conflict is no less complex than that of integration of societies. We now know that the attempt to reduce all actually occurring conflicts among social groups to a common principle, say that of classes, is sterile. It leads either to empty generalizations (such as "Every society experiences social conflicts") or to empirically unjustifiable oversimplifications (such as "The history of all societies so far has been a history of class struggles"). It seems advisable, first, to sort out and to classify the problems which are conceived under the general heading of "social conflict." Even a superficial reflection leads to the distinction of a series of types.

There are wars, and there are conflicts among political parties—evidently two different kinds of struggle. With regard to a given society, A, one could say there are *exogenous* conflicts brought upon or into A from the outside, and there are *endogenous* conflicts generated within A. Of these two categories—which, at least analytically, can be relatively precisely distinguished—there are again several types. Let us confine our attention for the moment —for reasons which will presently be given—to endogenous conflicts. Then further subdivisions are directly perceived: slaves versus freemen in Rome, Negroes versus whites in the United States, Protestants versus Catholics in the Netherlands, Flemings versus Walloons in Belgium, Conservatives versus Labourites in England, unions versus employers in many countries. All these are opposing groups in wellknown conflicts. Perhaps each of these examples does not fall into a separate category; but certainly they cannot all be subsumed under a single type of social conflict. Whatever criterion one

---

[3] Raymond Aron, "Social Structure and the Ruling Class," in *Class, Status, and Power,* ed., Reinhard Bendix and Seymour Martin Lipset (Glencoe, Ill.: The Free Press, 1954); André Philip, *Le Socialisme trahi* (Paris, 1957); Crane Brinton, *The Anatomy of Revolution* (2nd ed.; New York: Alfred A. Knopf, 1952); Clark Kerr, "Industrial Conflict and Its Mediation," *American Journal of Sociology,* XL (1954); Lewis Coser, *The Functions of Social Conflict* (Glencoe, Ill.: The Free Press, 1956); idem, "Social Conflict and Social Change," *British Journal of Sociology,* VIII (1957); Carl Brinkmann, *Soziologische Theorie der Revolution* (Tübingen, 1948); Theodor Geiger, *Klassengesellschaft in Schmelztiegel* (Köln-Hagen, 1949); Max Gluckman, *Custom and Conflict in Africa* (Glencoe, Ill.: The Free Press, 1957).

chooses for classification—for example, the objects of contention, or the structural origin of the conflicting groups, or the forms of conflict—several distinct types result.

The Limits and Goals of a Theory of Social Conflict

An ideal sociology cannot, in principle, exclude any of these categories and types of conflict from analysis. Nevertheless, the types mentioned do not all have the same importance for sociological analysis. A brief recollection of the intent of a sociological theory of conflict reveals that the contribution of sociology to the understanding of conflict (as well as the contribution of conflict to the social process) is in specific instances greater in some cases than in others.

The intent of a sociological theory of conflict is to overcome the predominantly arbitrary nature of unexplained historical events by deriving these events from elements of their social structures, in other words, to explain certain processes by prognostic connections. Certainly, it is important to describe the conflict between workers and employers purely as such; but it is more important to produce a proof that such a conflict is based on certain social structural arrangements, and hence is bound to arise wherever such structural arrangements are given. Thus it is the task of sociology to derive conflicts from specific social structures, and not to relegate these conflicts to psychological variables ("aggressiveness") or to descriptive-historical ones (the influx of Negroes into the United States) or to chance.

In the sense of strict sociological analysis, conflicts can be considered explained if they can be shown to arise from the structure of social positions, independently of the orientation of populations and of historical *dei ex machina*. This is necessarily a very abstract formulation; instead of elaborating it, it may be advisable to illustrate its meaning by the following treatment of a form of social conflict. First, however, let us draw a consequence of this formulation which will help to make our problem more precise.

Since the recognition of the inadequacy of the Marxist-Leninist theory of imperialism, the explanation of exogenous conflicts on the basis of the structure of a given society is once again an open problem, the treatment of which has scarcely begun. It seems, moreover, that the explanation of exogenous conflicts[4] by the tools of sociological structure analysis is possible only in a metaphorical sense—namely, only where entire societies (or less comprehensive "social systems") are taken to be the units of a new structure, that is, where C is analyzed in terms of the structure of its elements A and B without consideration of the inner structure of A and B. On these

---

[4] We recall here that a conflict which, from the point of view of Society A, appears as exogenous is represented from another point of view as a conflict between two societies or systems, A and B.

grounds it seems sensible to exclude exogenous conflict for the time being from a theory of social conflicts.

On the other hand, the abovementioned examples of endogenous conflict, if considered from the point of view of their structural significance, fall into two groups. On the one hand, they point to conflicts which arise only in specific societies on the basis of special historical conditions (Negroes or whites in the United States, Protestants versus Catholics in the Netherlands; Flemings versus Walloons in Belgium); on the other hand, however, there are conflicts which can be understood as expressions of general structural features of societies, or of societies in the same stage of development (Conservatives versus Labourites in England; unions versus employers' associations). Certainly in both cases an analysis leading to generalization is possible: a theory of minority or religious conflict is as meaningful as that of class conflict. Nevertheless, their respective weights within a general theory of society are evidently distinguishable. It is not surprising that the "classical" theory of conflict—I mean here primarily the class theory of conflict—has, above all, called attention to such social frictions which can be derived from the structure of societies independently of structurally incidental historical data.

The following approaches toward a theory of conflict also relate themselves to conflicts based on structure. So far, we are by no means considering a general theory of social conflict, although I would undertake to defend the assertion that we are dealing here with one of the most important, if not the most important, type of social conflict. However important as problems of social conflict St. Bartholomew's Night, Crystal Night and Little Rock may be, the French Revolution, the British General Strike of 1926 and the events in East Berlin on June 17, 1953, seem to me more germane for structural analysis. To put it less dramatically, the sociological theory of conflict would do well to confine itself for the time being to an explanation of the frictions between the rulers and the ruled in given organizations.

II

The explanation of motion requires two separate attacks. We must know the point of departure and the direction of motion or, better yet, the moving force. No theory of social change or of conflict can forego the description of the structural entity which undergoes change or within which conflicts occur. Such a description is offered by the integration theory of society. However, it is erroneous to assume that a description of how the elements of a structure are put together into a stable whole offers, as such, a point of departure for a structural analysis of conflict and change. So far, the claim of the socalled "structural–functional" theory of modern sociology to the status of a general theory of society is demonstrably unjustified.

Toward a Critique of a Structural–Functional Theory

This critique has been led in recent times repeatedly, most effectively by David Lockwood.[5] It is based on a relatively simple argument. As long as we orient our analysis toward the question as to how the elements of a society are combined into a coordinated functioning whole, then the representation of society as a social system is the last point of reference. We are therefore faced with the task of determining certain associations, institutions, or processes within this balanced whole, that is—in Merton's definition—of determining the intentional or unintentional consequences of these associations for the functioning and the preservation of the system. In this way, we come to contentions such as "the educational system functions as a mechanism of assigning social positions," or "religion functions as an agent of integrating dominant values." The majority of sociological investigations in the last years moves in this area of analysis.

However, such an approach leads to difficulties, if we put a question of a different sort. What was the function of the English trade unions in the General Strike of 1926? What was the function of the construction worker in Stalin Allee on June 17, 1953? Without doubt, it can be argued in many cases that militant trade unions or opposition political groups and parties also contribute to the functioning of the existing system.[6] But even where this was the case—and in the two cases cited it would be difficult to establish this—such a conclusion would say little about the role of the group in question. Moreover, it is clear that the intentional as well as the unintentional effects of such oppositional groups contribute toward an abolition or destruction of the existing system. The structural–functional position has a comfortable label for such cases; they are "dysfunctional" organizations, institutions or processes. But this designation again tells us less than nothing. It not only fails to explain the place of these things in the process but actually hinders such explanation by a terminology which seems to be congruent with the system but which, upon closer examination, reveals itself as a residual category. Whatever does not fit is conjured out of the world by word magic.

In every science, residual categories are a fruitful point of departure for new developments. It seems to me that a careful analysis of problems which the term "dysfunction" hides in the structural–functional theory automatically puts us on the trace of a meaningful sociological theory of con-

---

[5] David Lockwood, "Some Notes on 'The Social System,'" *British Journal of Sociology*, VII (1956), No. 2. Although Lockwood's argument leads to the same conclusion, it proceeds somewhat differently (cf. my *Social Classes and the Class Conflict*, pp. 159 ff.).

[6] This aspect of social conflict is, in fact central in the analysis of Lewis Coser (continuing that of Simmel) in his work on the functions of social conflict (cf. n. 3).

flict. At the same time, it offers a remarkable vantage point associated with an attempt of a scientific analysis of society.

Two Models of Society

If we extrapolate the analytical approaches of the structural–functional theory somewhat beyond their boundaries, and investigate their implicit postulates, we can construct a model of society which lies at the base of this theory and determines its perspectives. The essential elements of this societal model are these:

1. Every society is a relatively persisting configuration of elements.[7]
2. Every society is a well-integrated configuration of elements.
3. Every element in a society contributes to its functioning.
4. Every society rests on the consensus of its members.

It should be clear that a theory based on this model does not lend itself to the explanation, not even the description, of the phenomena of social conflict and change. For this purpose, one needs a model which takes the diametrically opposite position on all the four points above:

1. Every society is subjected at every moment to change; social change is ubiquitous.
2. Every society experiences at every moment social conflict; social conflict is ubiquitous.
3. Every element in a society contributes to its change.
4. Every society rests on constraint of some of its members by others.

The remarkable nature of our vantage point becomes evident when we examine the two groups of postulates with respect to their truth content, that is, if we ask ourselves which of the two models promises greater utility for cognition of reality. It appears that the juxtaposed pairs of postulates are in no way mutually exclusive with respect to social reality. It is impossible to decide by empirical investigation which of the two models is more nearly correct; the postulates are not hypotheses. Moreover, it seems meaningful to say that both models are in a certain sense valid and analytically fruitful. Stability and change, integration and conflict, function and "dysfunction," consensus and constraint are, it would seem, two equally valid

---

[7] There is much controversy over this implication of the structural–functional approach. Most functionalists deny that they make such an assumption. Indeed, assertions to the contrary are found in the works of Parsons, Merton, and others. Nevertheless, it can be shown that these assertions are, from the point of view of structural–functional theory, mere declarations. The notion of equilibrium and the concept of a system would have little sense if they did not make the assumption of stability of societies. However, two limitations are to be observed: (1) we have to do here (also in the implications which follow) not with a metaphysical postulate but rather with an assumption made for the purpose of analysis; and (2) stability does not mean statics in the sense of complete absence of processes within the "system."

aspects of every imaginable society. They are dialectically separated and are exhaustive only in combination as a description of the social problems. Possibly a more general theory of society may be thought of which lifts the equivalidity of both models, the coexistence of the uncombinable, onto a higher level of generality. As long as we do not have such a theory, we must content ourselves with the finding that society presents a double aspect to the sociological understanding, each side no better, no more valid, than the other. It follows that the criticism of the structural–functional theory for the analysis of conflict is directed only against a claim of generality of this theory, but leaves untouched its competence with respect to the problem of integration. It follows, on the other hand, also that the theory of conflict and change is not a general theory. Comparisons between natural and social sciences always carry the danger of misunderstanding. However, it may be maintained, without attributing to this analogy more than a logical meaning, that the situation of the sociologists is not unlike that of the physicists with respect to the theory of light. Just as the physicists can solve certain problems only by assuming the wave character of light and others, on the contrary, only by assuming a corpuscular or quantum theory, so there are problems of sociology which can be adequately attacked only with an integration theory and others which require a conflict theory for a meaningful analysis. Both theories can work extensively with the same categories, but they emphasize different aspects. While the integration theory likens a society to an ellipse, a rounded entity which encloses all of its elements, conflict theory sees society rather as a hyperbola, which, it is true, has the same foci, but is open in many directions and appears as a tension field of the determining forces.

The Tasks of a Theory of Social Conflict

The double aspect of society and the dialectics of the two types of sociological theory are in themselves a most fruitful object of reflection. Nevertheless, another problem seems to be more urgent. The theory of social integration has recently developed to a flourishing state as the structural–functional approach in ethnology and sociology. Our theory of conflict, however, is still in a very rudimentary state. It is an approach based on postulating ubiquitous social change and social conflict, the "dysfunctionality" of all the elements of social structure, and the constraining character of social unity. Our considerations put us in a position to formulate some requirements of such a theory:

1. It should be a scientific theory (as is the theory of social integration), that is, it should be formulated with reference to a plausible and demonstrable explanation of empirical phenomena.

2. The elements of the theory should not contradict the conflict model of society.

3. The categories employed should, whenever possible, agree with those of the integration theory or at least correspond to them.

4. A conflict theory should enable us to derive social conflicts from structural arrangements and thus show these conflicts systematically generated.

5. It should account both for the multiplicity of forms of conflict and for their degrees of intensity.

The last goal of a social theory is the explanation of social change. The integration theory gives us a tool for determining the point of departure of the process. To find the locus of the forces which drive the process and social change is the task of a theory of conflict. It must develop a model which makes understandable the structural origin of social conflict. This seems possible only if we understand conflicts as struggles among social groups, that is, if we make our task precise to the extent that it reduces to the structural analysis of conflicting groups. Under this supposition three questions come especially to the forefront, which conflict theory must answer:

1. How do conflicting groups arise from the structure of society?
2. What forms can the struggles among such groups assume?
3. How does the conflict among such groups effect a change in the social structures?

III

Wherever men live together and lay foundations of forms of social organization, there are positions whose occupants have powers of command in certain contexts and over certain positions, and there are other positions whose occupants are subjected to such commands. The distinction between "up" and "down"—or, as the English say, "Them" and "Us"—is one of the fundamental experiences of most men in society, and, moreover, it appears that this distinction is intimately connected with unequal distribution of power. The main thesis of the following attempt to construct a model for the structural analysis of conflict is that we should seek the structural origin of social conflict in the dominance relations which prevail within certain units of social organization. For these units I will use Max Weber's concept of "imperatively coordinated group." The thesis is not new; it is found (however often with important modifications) in the formulation of many social scientists before and after Marx. But we shall make no attempt to trace the history of this thesis.

Authority and Authority Structures

The concepts of power and authority are very complex ones. Whoever uses them is likely to be accused of lack of precision and of clarity to the extent that he tries to define them "exhaustively." Is the influence of a father on his children, the influence of an industrial combine on the government, or the influence of a demagogue on his followers an instance of an authority relation? Here, as in most other cases, it is basically not a question of a definition, but rather a question of an "operational definition," as it is often called today—a method of determination which allows us to identify as such the state of affairs when we are actually confronted with it. However, for the purpose of analysis and identification, Weber's determination of authority is sufficient: "The likelihood that a command of a certain content will be obeyed by given persons." [8] This determination contains the following elements:

1. Authority denotes a relation of supra- and subordination.

2. The supraordinated side prescribes to the subordinated one certain behavior in the form of a command or a prohibition.

3. The supraordinated side has the right to make such prescriptions; authority is a legitimate relation of supra- and subordination; authority is not based on personal or situational chance effects, but rather on an expectation associated with social position.

4. The right of authority is limited to certain contents and to specific persons.

5. Failure to obey the prescriptions is sanctioned; a legal system (or a system of quasilegal customs) guards the effectiveness of authority.

This determination of authority makes possible the identification of a cabinet minister, an employer, and a party secretary as occupants of authority positions—in contrast to an industrial syndicate or a demagogue, neither of which satisfies condition three above.

It is not the intention of our "definition" of authority to solve all analytical and empirical problems of this category. In fact, the very first step of our model leads us deep into these problems; in each imperatively coordinated group, two aggregates can be distinguished—those which have only general ("civil") basic rights, and those which have authority rights over the former. In contrast to prestige and income, a continuum of gradual transition cannot be constructed for the distribution of authority. Rather, there is a clear dichotomy. Every position in an imperatively coordinated group can be recognized as belonging to one who dominates or one who is dominated. Sometimes, in view of the bureaucratic largescale organization of modern societies—under the influence of the state—this assumption may at first sight seem problematic. However, a sharper analysis leaves no doubt that here also the split into the dominating and dominated is valid, even though in reality a considerable measure of differentiation is discernible among those in the dominating group.

---

[8] Max Weber, "Wirtschaft und Gesellschaft," in *Grundriss der Sozialökonomik,* III (3rd ed.; Tübingen, 1947), 28.

The Conflict-Theory Model

The dichotomy of social roles within imperatively coordinated groups,[9] the division into positive and negative dominance roles, is a fact of social structure. If and insofar as social conflicts can be referred to this factual situation, they are structurally explained. The model of analysis of social conflict which is developed against a background of an assumption of such a dichotomy involves the following steps:

1. In every imperatively coordinated group, the carriers of positive and negative dominance roles determine two quasigroups with opposite latent interests. We call them "quasigroups" because we have to do here with mere aggregates, not organized units; we speak of "latent interests," because the opposition of outlook need not be conscious on this level; it may exist only in the form of expectations associated with certain positions. The opposition of interests has here a quite formal meaning, namely, the expectation that an interest in the preservation of the status quo is associated with the positive dominance roles and an interest in the change of the status quo is associated with the negative dominance roles.

2. The bearers of positive and negative dominance roles, that is, the members of the opposing quasigroups, organize themselves into groups with manifest interests, unless certain empirically variable conditions (the condition of organization) intervene. Interest groups, in contrast to quasigroups, are organized entities, such as parties and trade unions; the manifest interests are formulated programs and ideologies.

3. Interest groups which originate in this manner are in constant conflict over the preservation or change of the status quo. The form and the intensity of the conflict are determined by empirically variable conditions (the conditions of conflict).

4. The conflict among interest groups in the sense of this model leads to changes in the structure of their social relations, through changes in the dominance relations. The kind, the speed, and the depth of this development depend on empirically variable conditions (the conditions of structural change).

The intent of such a model is to delimit a problem area, to identify the factors pertinent to it, to put them into order—that is, to propose fruitful questions—and at the same time to fix precisely their analytical focus. We have delimited our problem area by viewing social conflict as a conflict among groups which emerge from the authority structure of social organizations. We have identified pertinent factors in the conditions of organization,

---

[9] In what follows, I shall designate the roles to which the expectation of the exercise of authority is attached as "positive dominance roles" and, conversely, the roles without authority privileges as "negative dominance roles."

of conflict, and of change. Their order, however, can be expressed on the basis of the model in three functions: interest groups (for example, parties) are a function of conditions of organization if an imperatively coordinated group is given; specific forms of conflict (*e.g.,* parliamentary debates) are a function of the conditions of conflict if the interest groups are given; specific forms of change (*e.g.,* revolutions) are a function of the conditions of change if the conflict among interest groups is given. Thus the task of the theory of conflict turns out to be to identify the three sets of conditions and to determine as sharply as possible their respective weight—ideally, by quantitative measure.[10] The following remarks are hardly more than a tentative indication of the sorts of variables in question.

Empirical Conditions of Social Conflict

As far as the conditions of organization are concerned, three groups of factors come to mind. First, we have certain effective social conditions: for example, the possibility of communication among the members of the quasigroup and a certain method of recruitment into the quasigroups. Next, there are certain political conditions which must be fulfilled if interest groups are to emerge. Here, above all, a guarantee of freedom of coalition is important. Finally, certain technical conditions must be fulfilled: an organization must have material means, a founder, a leader, and an ideology.

Under conditions of conflict, two kinds are immediately conspicuous: the degree of social mobility of individuals (or of families) and the presence of effective mechanisms for regulating social conflicts. If we imagine a continuum of intensity of social conflict among interest groups, ranging from democratic debate to civil war, we may conjecture that the presence or absence of social mobility and of regulating mechanisms has considerable influence on the position of specific given conflicts on this continuum. Here, as with the other conditions, the determination of the exact weights of the factors is a task of empirical investigation.

Finally, a third group of conditions or variables determines the form and the extent of social structural changes which arise from the conflict of interest groups. Probably a relatively intimate connection exists between the intensity of the conflict and the change, that is, also between the conditions of conflict and of the structural changes. However, additional factors come into play, such as the capacity of the rulers to stay in power and the pressure potential of the dominated interest group. The sociology of revolutions and especially the unwritten sociology of uncompleted revolutions should contribute considerably to making these factors precise.

---

[10] By this remark is meant (1) a mathematical formulation of the functions, (2) a development of measurement scales for each of the conditions, and (3) the adjustment of the combined scales to groups of conditions.

It need hardly be re-emphasized that these unsystematic observations can, as such, hardly lay a foundation of a theory of conflict. Nevertheless, we put ourselves in a position to ask meaningful questions both on the theoretical level and with respect to empirical problems. Each of the conditions mentioned offers a fruitful object of theoretically oriented investigations. And in the empirical sphere, the systematic association of factors in such an investigation redirects our questions from a haphazard search for *ad hoc* relations in the world of coincidences to a meaningful study of specific interdependencies, whose locus and meaning are fixed by a general perspective. By the nature of the subject, our exposition up to this point had to remain somewhat abstract in form.

In spite of the tentative nature of the above-mentioned frame of reference, it is nevertheless possible to test its resolving power on an empirical problem.

•

IV

The Problem of the Totalitarian State

Since June 17, 1953, and with greater certainty since the events in Hungary and Poland in the autumn of 1956, we know that social conflict (and social change!) has by no means disappeared in the totalitarian states. Conflict theory raises this knowledge to the status of law. The state, that is, society in its political aspect, is an imperatively coordinated group. There are in it mere citizens (voters) and occupants of positions equipped with command opportunities. Therefore, political conflict is a structural fact of society under every imaginable condition. This conflict can assume mild or severe forms; it can even disappear for limited periods from the field of vision of a superficial observer; but it cannot be abolished. Now one of the aspects of a totalitarian state is an attempt to suppress the opposition, that is, to suppress social conflict. The question then arises, against the background of conflict theory: How do social frictions become manifest under such circumstances? We can analyze totalitarian states from the point of view of conditions of organization of interest groups—that of conflict and of structural change—and hope to arrive in this way at meaningful explanations of historical events and to testable predictions. Again it is possible here to make only a few indications.

Let us begin—for reasons which will soon become evident—with the conditions of conflict. The intensity of social conflicts depends on the measure of social mobility and on the presence of mechanisms for regulating the conflicts. Both mobility and regulation can be present in totalitarian states. One could argue that the regular "purges" in Communist states—that is, a replacement of the bearers of authority—function as a guarantee of stability (in the sense of alleviating social conflicts). In the same way, the systematic requirement of discussion with the aim of deciding the political "platforms" within and outside the state party may be an effective mechanism of regulation. Still, there seems to be an inherent tendency in most totalitarian states to isolate socially the leadership layer and to prevent discussions, that is, to disregard the mechanisms for regulating conflicts. Where this is the case, social conflicts threaten to increase in potential intensity and to take on a revolutionary character.

From the point of view of conditions of structural change, this means that political conflicts in totalitarian states aim more and more at sudden replacement of the ruling class. The important variable which determines the probability of realizing a radical change is the resistance of the rulers to the pressures making for change. Perhaps it is meaningful to make the empirical generalization that this resistance does increase to a certain degree with increasing pressure, but then gives way to a relatively speedy dissolution and so promotes change.

Central for the analysis of conflicts in totalitarian states, however, is our third set of conditions (first, as listed in the theory): the condition of organization. It follows in a way from the "definition" of a totalitarian state that there are no conditions in it for the organization of opposing interest groups. More specifically, although the social and technical conditions are often present, the political conditions are lacking;[11] there is no freedom of coalition. At this point, the resistance of the German eastern zone government to free elections becomes clear, as does the general threat of violent, possibly revolutionary conflict in totalitarian states. When—as expressly in Hungary or virtually on June 17, 1953 in Berlin—an opportunity for organization occurs to latent conflict groups, the total edifice of the totalitarian state collapses. Moreover, it seems very probable that this possibility can become realized at any moment in every totalitarian state.[12] In modern totalitarian societies founded on ideological state parties, there is a constant danger from the point of view of the rulers that a permitted organization, even the state party itself, may become the root of an opposition movement and of revolutionary conflict.

Our analysis will be broken off at the point where it promises testable results. It was not the intent of this discussion to treat exhaustively some empirical problem. Rather, we wanted to show that conflict theory puts us in a position to formulate more sharply urgent problems of empirical investiga-

---

[11] For certain technical conditions of organization, this is valid only within limits. Thus the liquidation of potential leaders of the opposition is a central component of totalitarian authority. In a way, both the East German and the Hungarian events can be taken as corroborations of the effectiveness of this policy.

[12] Relevant here is the wellknown slight decrease of pressure which seems to precede every revolution. Insofar, for example, as a certain relaxation of police control makes possible only an *ad hoc* organization, the emergence of open conflict becomes acute.

tion, to bring within our grasp unexplained events, to see what is known from additional points of view, and to transform tentative questions into a systematic search—that is, to do precisely what a scientific theory should accomplish. . . . In spite of all progress, the theory of social conflict is still more a challenge to the sociologist than a result of his researches.

CHAPTER 14

FRANCESCA CANCIAN

Functional Analysis
of Change

Functional analysis is frequently criticized as being of little use in describing and predicting change.[1] At the same time, many social scientists interested in investigating change hesitate to give up the functional approach. It has been fruitful in many empirical studies and crucial in many of the attempts to construct general theories of behavior.

Fortunately, a philosopher has come to aid of social scientists on this confused issue. Ernest Nagel[2] presents a formal definition of functional systems based on Merton's essay, "Manifest and Latent Functions."[3] Nagel does not explicitly consider the problem of functional analysis of change. His formal definition of a functional system, however, provides a basis for outlining several specific ways in which functional analysis can be used to study change and for concluding that most of the arguments about the static nature of such analysis are based on semantic confusion and unimaginative and incorrect methods.

The following discussion (1) summarizes Nagel's extensive formal definition of a functional system; (2) considers some of its methodological implications; (3) outlines the ways in which functional analysis, so defined,

From Francesca Cancian, "Functional Analysis of Change," *American Sociological Review*, XXV (1960), No. 6, pp. 818-826. Reprinted by permission of the author and the publisher.

[1] See, *e.g.*, Ralf Dahrendorf, "Out of Utopia," *American Journal of Sociology*, LXIV (1958), 115-127; Clifford Geertz, "Ritual and Social Change," *American Anthropologist*, LIX (1957), 32-54; Wayne Hield, "The Study of Change in Social Science," *British Journal of Sociology*, V (1954), 1-10; David Lockwood, "Some Remarks on 'The Social System,'" *British Journal of Sociology*, VII (1956), 134-146.

[2] Ernest Nagel, "A Formalization of Functionalism," in his *Logic without Metaphysics* (Glencoe, Ill.: The Free Press, 1956), pp. 247-283.

[3] Robert K. Merton, *Social Theory and Social Structure* (Glencoe, Ill.: The Free Press, 1957), pp. 19-84.

can deal with change; (4) answers some of the critics who charge that functional analysis cannot adequately treat change; and (5) presents an example of investigation of change by means of functional analysis.

A Definition of "Functional System"

To Nagel, functional analysis is distinguished by the use of a particular model, the model of a directively organized or functional system. A "model," here used in a very broad sense, is a set of general relationships. A model is useful if the relationships posited in it "fit" the data in the sense of parsimoniously yielding accurate and relevant predictions. The model of a functional system consists of a fairly complex set of properties or relationships. Two simpler models are described below for purposes of clarification and contrast.

The simplest and most general system model posits interdependence of elements within a certain boundary, that is, the interdependence has a specific referent. The model for such a *simple* system may be expressed as $x = f(y)$: one property is the function of another. This is the type of system implied by using "function" in the mathematical sense. Empirical examples are: the volume of gas at a constant temperature varies inversely with its pressure; the rate of suicide varies inversely with the strength of the collective conscience; presence of male initiation rites is associated with household composition.

These types of statements, using the model of a simple system, do not necessarily lead to predictions of either change or stability. Unless the state of part of the system at some future time is known, the future state of the system cannot be predicted. For example, to predict the suicide rate two years hence, one would have to know the strength of the collective conscience at that time.

Certain properties can be added to the definition of a simple system so that, by definition, predictions of change or stability can be made on the basis of present knowledge. In a *deterministic* system, as defined by Nagel,[4] the properties of the system at one time are a function of its properties at a certain previous time. Since it may be inconvenient to observe the whole set, one attempts to find the smallest number of properties or variables "such that the specific forms of *all* the properties . . . at any time are uniquely determined by these *n* properties at that time." [5] Nagel cites the mechanics of bodies, the several dimensions of which can be neglected, as an example of a deterministic system:

> Thus, in the case of a freely falling body, it suffices to know (in addition, of course, to the laws of motion) the position and momentum of the body at some

4 *Op. cit.,* pp. 253-256.
5 *Ibid.,* p. 255.

initial instant, in order to be able to calculate its position and momentum (and accordingly other properties of the body, such as its kinetic energy, which are definable in terms of these coordinates) at any other instant.[6]

If one knows the present values of certain key variables and the stability or rates of change of these variables, then one can predict the values of these variables, and many others, at any future time.

If one treats a social system as a deterministic system, certain types of statements may be made. For example, since a society is integrated at the community level and is beginning to develop irrigation, it can be predicted on the basis of laws of sociocultural development that it will develop cities and a national level of sociocultural integration within the next two centuries; since the present questionnaire responses of a small, task-oriented group show little agreement on role differentiation, it can be predicted on the basis of laws of progressive consensus on role differentiation that the responses will show more agreement after five meetings.

A deterministic system is a simple system—with the added restriction that the properties of the system at one time are a function of its properties at a previous time. A *functional* system is a deterministic system—with the added restriction that certain properties of the system are maintained despite potentially disruptive changes in the system or the environment or both.

A functional system, according to Nagel's definition, is made up of two types of variables: G's and "state coordinates." G is the property of the system that is maintained or is stable. State coordinates determine the presence or absence of G. The values of the state coordinates may vary to such an extent that the maintenance of G is threatened, but when one exceeds the "safe" limits for G, the other(s) compensates and G is maintained. Some of the state coordinates may lie outside the system boundary, that is, in the environment. Such a system of G and state coordinates may be called functional with respect to G and the state coordinates may be described as having the function of maintaining G.

For example, a small, task-oriented group could be treated as a functional system. Let G be the solution of the group's task or problem. Let the state coordinates be task-oriented activity and emotionally supportive activity. If these three variables can be usefully treated as a functional system, then: (1) problem solution is dependent on task-oriented activity and emotionally supportive activity; (2) at certain times, there will be such a preponderance of task-oriented activity that problem solution will be threatened because of decreased motivation or resentment over following others' suggestions—at these times emotionally supportive activity will increase and problem solution will no longer be threatened; (3) at certain

---

[6] *Ibid.*, p. 256.

times, there will be such a preponderance of emotionally supportive activity that problem solution will be threatened—at these times task-oriented activity will increase to maintain problem solution or G.

It should be noted that, by definition, more than one state of the system leads to maintenance of G. Thus, in the preceding example, eventual problem solution might result from both: initially high task-oriented activity and low supportive activity, followed by increased supportive activity; and initially low task-oriented activity and high supportive activity followed by increased task activity. In a functional system there is more than one combination of the values of certain parts of the system which will result in the same trait or will have the same consequences (maintenance of G). This is one way of stating the familiar notion of functional equivalents.

It should also be noted that stability of G is not *assumed* in a functional analysis. On the contrary, it is assumed that the environment or parts of the system or both are changing so much that it is impossible for G to persist unless there are specific mechanisms within the system to compensate for these changes. It is therefore inappropriate to use this system model if the environment and the system are treated as constant, or if there is no state of the system which threatens the maintenance of G.

The definition of "functional" as "fulfilling a basic need" does assume that there is no state of the system which threatens the maintenance of G. This definition is therefore inappropriate according to Nagel's concept of a functional system. Functional analysis, as here defined, does not assume that G (some need) is stable and then explain the existence of state coordinates in terms of their efficiency in fulfilling this need. Rather, functional analysis shows that G is or is not maintained because certain state coordinates do or do not compensate for each other's variation. An example of a *non*functional proposition is that religion and related institutions are maintained because of a need for the meaningfulness of life to be maintained, while a *functional* analysis would propose that the meaningfulness of life is maintained because of the interaction of religion and other institutions.

Thus far, no specific attention has been given to the limits on possible variation of the values of state coordinates. Three limits on the values of the variables determining G should be considered. First, there are limits dictated by physical reality. To return to our former example, the amount of task-oriented activity possible in a given time period is limited by the number of people in the group and the number of messages that can be communicated within that time. Second, within the limits of physical reality, there are limits determined by the definition of the system under consideration. If a property is used to define a system, one cannot analyze conditions under which this property disappears, unless a different definition is used. For example, if one wishes to study the relations among interaction, role differentiation, and cohesion *within social systems,* and a social system is defined by a certain amount of interaction, there cannot be less than this amount of interaction.

Within these two types of limits, there is a third which is the most relevant to this discussion. This is the limit beyond which compensation is impossible and G ceases to exist. In our previous example, it seems reasonable to assume that if either supportive activity or task-oriented activity increases or decreases beyond a certain point, no possible adjustment can result in maintenance of G or problem solution. Thus, if task-oriented activity exceeds certain limits, some of the group members may become so hostile or uninterested that no future supportive activity can regain their cooperation. Solution of the group's problem becomes impossible and the group can no longer be considered a functional system with respect to the G of problem solution.

This discussion of limits leads to a way of conceptualizing the potential stability of a given G in a given functional system. The persistence of G depends upon the amount of discrepancy between two ranges: the range of possible variation for each state coordinate and the range of variation that can be compensated for by variation in other state coordinates. G becomes less stable as the discrepancy between these two ranges increases.

In sum, a functional system is one that satisfies the following conditions: (1) the system can be analyzed into a set of interdependent variables or parts; (2) the values of some of these variables—state coordinates—determine whether or not a certain property G will occur in the system; (3) there are certain limits on the variation of the values of state coordinates, such that variation within the limits will be followed by a compensating variation of other state coordinates, resulting in the maintenance of G; (4) variation beyond these limits will not be followed by a compensating variation of other state coordinates and G will disappear.

This definition of functional systems is neither complete nor without problems of its own. However, it should suffice to show that there is no logical reason why a functional analysis cannot be useful in investigating change. There are several ways in which functional analysis can be so used. For example, the presence or absence of G can be predicted if one knows whether or not the state coordinates are exceeding the limits within which compensation is possible. Or, G itself can be a cycle or a rate of change. And there is no empirical reason why functional analysis cannot be used to investigate change if some phenomena fit the model of a functional system and if one can assume that they will continue to fit it in the future.

Before proceeding, it should be noted that Nagel's definition of functional analysis does not include all of the many meanings ascribed to the term function. Therefore, caution should be maintained in generalizing the finding that functional analysis, as conceived by Nagel, can be used to investigate change. Functional analysis has been so broadly defined that one sociologist concludes that the term is "synonymous with sociological analysis." [7] Nagel's definition elaborates and clarifies the type of "functional analysis" used, for example, by the sociologist Parsons,[8] the anthropologist Leach,[9] and the linguist Martinet.[10] This definition, of course, excludes all modes of analysis that do not meet the four criteria specified above. Semantic difficulty could be largely eliminated by clear definitions of the different types of "functional analysis" and consensus on terminology. In the meantime, the special definition presented here may help to avoid semantic confusion.

A Basic Methodological Rule

Nagel's formalization of functionalism provides a basis from which many useful methodological rules and terminological distinctions can be drawn, including some of those pointed out by Firth,[11] Levy,[12] Merton[13] and others. One rule, which has frequently been stated, is the importance of specifying the system and the G(s) in relation to which the state coordinates are functional. This rule is crucial to successful functional analysis of change (or stability) and deserves special attention. As Nagel points out in his comment on Merton's discussion of the ideological implications of functional analysis:

> Functional analyses in all domains, and not only in sociology, run a similar risk of dogmatic provincialism which characterizes some analyses in sociology, when the relational character of functional statements is ignored, and when it is forgotten that a system may exhibit a variety of G's or that a given item may be a member of a variety of systems.[14]

Specification of the system(s) and the G(s) under consideration is especially important when a plurality of systems and G's are involved. A subsystem may be functionally organized with respect to a G while the larger system is not. Or one may be interested in several G's and the conditions for maintaining some of the G's may preclude maintenance of others, that is,

[7] Kingsley Davis, "The Myth of Functional Analysis as a Special Method in Sociology and Anthropology," *American Sociological Review,* XXIV (1959), p. 757.

[8] Talcott Parsons and Neil J. Smelser, *Economy and Society* (Glencoe, Ill.: The Free Press, 1956).

[9] E. R. Leach, *Political Systems of Highland Burma* (Cambridge: Harvard University Press, 1951).

[10] André Martinet, "Function, Structure and Sound Change," *Word,* VIII (1952), 1-32.

[11] Raymond Firth, "Function," in W. L. Thomas, ed., *Current Anthropology* (Chicago: University of Chicago Press, 1956).

[12] Marion J. Levy, Jr., *The Structure of Society* (Princeton: Princeton University Press, 1952).

[13] *Loc. cit.*

[14] *Op. cit.,* p. 283.

the range of values of a state coordinate that maintains G_1 may cause G_2 to disappear.

The importance of these distinctions becomes more apparent if one considers the definition of such terms as "equilibrium" and "functional unity." Equilibrium means the maintenance of G. G can be a stable state, for example, corruption of city government, or allocation of reward according to evaluation of performance; or it can be a stable rate of change, for example, accelerating rate of technological innovation, or decreasing interpersonal communication in prepsychotics; or it can be a cycle or series of states, for example, change from a conservative power elite to an opportunistic elite and then again to a conservative elite, or change from feudalism to capitalism to communism. If only one G is being considered, equilibrium can be clearly defined. If a plurality of G's or subsystems or both is being considered and they are ranked on a scale, then the degree of stability of each G in each subsystem can be weighted and some general notion of the equilibrium of the total system can be defined. It is possible, however, that the G's and the subsystems cannot be ranked. In such a case, it would be meaningless to specify a general state of equilibrium if some G's in some subsystems are maintained while others are not. It would also be meaningless to discuss conditions of equilibrium for the system as a whole if the conditions for maintaining some G's preclude the maintenance of other G's.

A similar argument applies to the definition of the function of a phenomenon as "the contribution it makes to the total social life as the functioning of the total social system." [15]

> Such a view implies that a social system . . . has a certain kind of unity. . . . We may define it as a condition in which all parts of the social system work together with a sufficient degree of harmony or internal consistency, *i.e.*, without producing persistent conflicts which can neither be resolved nor regulated.[16]

To translate this statement by Radcliffe-Brown into our terminology, the postulate of functional unity means that the conditions for maintaining a specified set of G's in the system under consideration are not mutually exclusive or are mutually supportive. If no particular G's are specified, then "functional unity" would mean that no persistent properties conflict with each other. It seems very doubtful that functional unity, in this latter sense, characterizes many social systems. In addition, treating a social system as a functional unity without specifying the G's so unified results in a vague analysis and one that allows for no internal source of change. It is this use of functional unity that best merits Geertz's criticism of the adequacy of the functional approach in dealing with social change: "The emphasis on sys-

---

[15] A. R. Radcliffe-Brown, *Structure and Function in Primitive Society* (Glencoe, Ill.: The Free Press, 1952), p. 181.

[16] *Loc. cit.*

tems in balance, on social homeostasis, and on timeless structural pictures, leads to a bias in favor of 'well-integrated' societies in a stable equilibrium and to a tendency to emphasize the functional aspects of a people's usages and customs rather than their dysfunctional implications." [17]

Methods of Using Functional Analysis to Investigate Change

On the basis of the foregoing discussion, a more precise delineation of the resources and limitations of functional analysis in investigating change can be made. The definition of different types of system change itself raises complex problems which cannot be discussed here. However, one set of definitions is important to the problem of the functional analysis of change, namely, the distinction between change *of* and *within* the system.[18]

Change *within* the system refers to change that does not alter the system's basic structure. In a functional system, this means changes in state coordinates for which compensation is possible. G and the relationship between state coordinates remain the same. Change *of* the system is any change that alters the system's basic structure. In a functional system, this includes disappearance of G, the appearance of new state coordinates or the disappearance of old ones, and change in the range of variation of state coordinates for which compensation is possible.

The ways in which change is incorporated in functional analysis now may be specified. Their justification lies in the definition of functional systems and in the consequent possibility of ordering systems hierarchically and of treating (sub)systems as state coordinates maintaining G's in a more inclusive system.

(1) *Disappearance of G can be predicted as the result of failure to meet conditions of equilibrium.* Disappearance of G means change *of* the system. State coordinates exceed the limits within which compensation is possible and the functional system breaks down.

(2) *If G is defined as a stable rate of change or a moving equilibrium, a stable rate of change can be predicted as the result of fulfillment of the conditions of equilibrium.* In this case, state coordinates do not exceed the limits within which compensation is possible and G—a steady rate of change—is maintained.

(3) *Compensating changes in the values of state coordinates can be predicted as the result of an "initial" variation in other state coordinates that threaten the maintenance of G.* This is change *within* the structure of the system and it must, by definition, be possible in a functional system.

(4) *Systems can be treated as subsystems, that is, as state coordinates maintaining a G in a more inclusive system. Compensating changes in sub-*

---

[17] Geertz, *op. cit.,* p. 32.
[18] This distinction is discussed by Parsons and Smelser, *op. cit.,* pp. 247-248.

systems can be predicted as the result of an "initial" variation in other sub-systems that threaten the maintenance of G. In this case, change *of* a sub-system is change *within* a more inclusive system. In other words, what is a G from the point of reference of the subsystem is a state coordinate from the point of reference of the more inclusive system. Thus, the disappearance of G, as depicted in (1) above, could be treated as the variation of a state coordinate in a more inclusive system.

These four methods can be used under the following conditions: first, if it can be assumed that a set of phenomena form a functional system; second, if information about an "initial" change in a state coordinate can be obtained; and, third, if there is information about whether this change is within or outside of the limits governing the possibility of compensation. If one is interested in predicting when an "initial" change will occur and whether or not it will be confined to such limits, he might use the model of a deterministic system (if x occurs at one time, then y will occur at some future time) or of a simple system (if x then y). These two models may also be used to predict the ramifications of the disappearance of G.

Criticisms and Examples

If functional analysis can be used to investigate change in these various ways, why has it seldom been so used, and why have certain critics adamantly asserted its inherent static bias? There are several cases, in fact, in which these methods of analyzing change have been employed, as the examples presented below indicate. Both the critics and proponents of functional analysis, however, often fail to see the potential of this model, and the critics frequently misconstrue the aims of the analyses which they attack.

Functionalists themselves have often invited severe criticism. The concepts of moving equilibrium and of hierarchically ordered systems are rarely used, eliminating in most instances two of the four ways of studying change functionally. Many investigators do not attempt to formulate their analyses in terms of state coordinates—variables that are essential to the maintenance of some G and that can vary only within certain limits if G is to be maintained. In this case, none of the four methods of analyzing change can be used. There is no predictive power for change *or stability* in the statement, "the function of x is to maintain G," unless it implies that G will cease to exist if x and its functional equivalents are terminated or if certain limits are exceeded.

Failure to state functional studies in precise form, along with lack of specification of G, the state coordinates, and the system under consideration, results in inadequate analysis of both change and stability. If a functional analysis has been refined to the point where it provides an adequate explanation of stability, then it will always imply certain predictions about change; if the conditions of equilibrium are specified, the prediction can be made that change will occur when these conditions are not met.

However, lack of precision characterizes functionalists and nonfunctionalists alike, and is often unavoidable in exploratory studies. In any case, most of the critics who claim that a static bias inheres in functionalism stress neither the necessity of precise analysis nor the use of moving equilibriums and hierarchically ordered systems. Instead, they focus their attack on the defining attribute of functional systems, that is, the maintenance of a certain state of the system (G) or equilibrium.

Among anthropologists, one of the strongest criticisms has been made by E. R. Leach in the theoretical sections of his book, *Political Systems of Highland Burma*.[19] Like many other anthropologists, he assumes that functional analysis is inherently static and, *also,* that adequate descriptions of societies must be made in functional terms. Thus Leach states: "In practical field work situations the anthropologist must always treat the material of observation *as if* it were part of an overall equilibrium, otherwise description becomes almost impossible." [20] But elsewhere he writes: "While conceptual models of society are necessarily models of equilibrium systems, real societies can never be in equilibrium." [21] Firth seems to agree with this view when he comments that "the necessary equilibrium of the model as a construct means that essentially it is debarred from providing in itself a dynamic analysis." [22] Given these two assumptions, Leach appears to infer— validly—that functional analyses have been extremely inadequate in investigating change, and that major alterations in methodology will have to be made before the situation improves.

But both assumptions are invalid. The first, the assumption that social and cultural systems *must* be treated as if they were in equilibrium, ignores a possibility noted above. Functional system models may be preferable, but a simple or deterministic system model may also be used. The applicability of a functional model cannot be assumed a priori. The model should be applied in cases where it seems useful to treat specific states or parts of the system as G's and state coordinates. If the G's and state coordinates cannot be specified, the analysis will result in a great deal of confusion (and possibly some very productive hints for further research).

Secondly, an equilibrated or functional system need not be static unless "change *within* the system" is subsumed under the term "static." Moving equilibria may be used. Or systems and subsystems may be differentiated with subsystems treated as state coordinates and therefore, by definition, as changing. In addition, *using* the model of a functional system does not

---

[19] *Loc. cit.*
[20] *Ibid.,* p. 285 (emphasis in original).
[21] *Ibid.,* p. 4.
[22] Raymond Firth, Foreword in Leach, *ibid.,* p. vi.

imply that the system *is* in equilibrium, that G is being maintained. Specification of the conditions necessary to maintain G may explain why G is not being maintained. Thus Leach's criticism, at least in part, seems to be based on false premises.

If the criticisms in the theoretical sections of Leach's study are misleading, elsewhere in the volume Leach himself refutes the proposition that functional analyses are necessarily static. In the following brief (and incomplete) outline of his examination of cyclical political change in Kachin society an attempt is made to translate Leach's presentation into our terminology (G's, state coordinates).

Leach isolates certain political systems, among them the democratic (*gumlao*) and aristocratic (*gumsa*), and treats them as subsystems of Kachin society. Certain basic norms of this society are interpreted as the G of the larger system, and the different political subsystems as state coordinates. Leach also treats each political subsystem as itself a functional system. He specifies the conditions of equilibrium in each of the subsystems, and demonstrates that these conditions cannot be met for long periods of time if the basic norms of Kachin society are to be maintained. The result is a cyclical set of changes of the political systems *within* the larger Kachin social system. Political subsystems (state coordinates) change, but the basic norms (G) are maintained.

> A *gumsa* political state tends to develop features which lead to rebellion, resulting, for a time, in a *gumlao* order. But a *gumlao* community, unless it happens to be centered around a fixed territorial centre . . . , usually lacks the means to hold its component lineages together in a status of equality. It will then either disintegrate altogether through fission, or else status difference between lineage groups will bring the system back into the *gumsa* pattern.[23]

Leach shows how an aristocratic political system prospers and is maintained until it begins to undermine the Kachin norms concerning obligations towards one's wife's family. At this point, either the aristocratic system or Kachin society must disintegrate since one type of marriage system is essential to the aristocratic political system while a conflicting marriage system is "the crucial distinguishing principle of modern Kachin social structure." [24] Leach's evidence indicates that Kachin society is a functional system with respect to this marriage system. When the marriage system is threatened by the aristocratic system, the latter distintegrates, becomes democratic, and the marriage system is maintained. A similar reversal of the political order occurs when a democratic political system reaches the point of conflicting with the basic Kachin norm of higher status for the wife's family than for the husband's family. Thus, despite his criticism of structural–functional

[23] *Ibid.*, p. 204.
[24] *Ibid.*, p. 249.

analysis, Leach's presentation of cyclical change in Kachin society can be seen as a demonstration of the dynamic potential of such analysis.

The criticisms made by some sociologists are much more sweeping than those voiced by Leach, and seem to call for the abandonment of functional analysis rather than its refinement. Critics such as Dahrendorf and Hield appear to start with two assumptions: first, that functional systems must be static; second, that the G's used in functional analysis must be the values and norms that characterize the majority of the members of the group, often including those of the social scientists themselves. For example, Dahrendorf attacks "the sense of complacency with—if not justification of —the status quo, which by intention or default pervades the structure-functional school of social thought." [25] He also asserts that analyses of this "school" cannot deal with change, and since he rejects "the entirely spurious distinction between 'change within' and 'change of societies,' " [26] he charges in effect that no type of change can be incorporated into a functional analysis. The discussion above should suffice to disprove this charge.

Hield makes similar criticisms: "The 'structural functional' orientation is a set of methodological tools for the study of social control, deviance, and 're-equilibration.' " [27] Again: "Where deviance presents itself, the theoretical concern is with the processes involved in restoring or re-equilibrating a condition of equilibrium or social control." [28] And: "The study of change has thus been obscured by the formulation of theoretic constructs stressing order and stability." [29]

These criticisms have a certain validity *if* functional analysis is limited to the definition of G's in terms of a static system of shared values. The several examples presented above show the different possible definitions of G and thus of equilibrium. G may be a moving equilibrium, a state of conflict, a set of values characterizing a deviant group, or it may have nothing to do with values as, for example, in the case of an annual increase of gross national product.

These critics, then, incorrectly define equilibrium or G because they identify the inherent properties of functional analysis with the particular way such analysis has been used by many social scientists. More specifically, they attack the approach exemplified by Talcott Parsons and assume that this approach exhausts the analytic potentialities of functionalism.

Parsons has devoted a considerable part of his work to answering the Hobbesian problem of order. He defines the social system in terms of shared values: "Analytically considered, the structure of social systems as treated within the frame of reference of action, *consists* in institutionalized

---

[25] Dahrendorf, *op. cit.*, p. 122.
[26] *Ibid.*, p. 126.
[27] Hield, *op. cit.*, p. 2.
[28] *Ibid.*, p. 3.
[29] *Ibid.*, p. 10.

patterns of normative culture." [30] Parsons assumes the stability of values to "provide a reference point for the orderly analysis of a whole range of problems of variation which can be treated as arising from sources *other* than processes of structural change in the system." [31] If shared values define the system, it is difficult to treat major conflict and deviance in the area of values as part of the system. And if one assumes stability of values, major structural change *of* the system is excluded, by definition.

Thus Parsons' explicit strategy is to hold constant values and the basic structure of the system. It is extremely difficult validly to criticize a theorist's strategy, since its usefulness can be tested only by comparing prolonged research using one strategy with similar research using another and by assessing the results. Some kind of strategy is necessary and something must be held constant. Parsons, like Leach, treats certain aspects of the larger system as G's and then analyzes changes in subsystems or state coordinates. "Structural change in subsystems [state coordinates] is an inescapable part of equilibrating process in larger systems. . . ." [32]

---

[30] Talcott Parsons, "An Outline of the Social System" (Cambridge, Mass.: 1958), p. 19, mimeographed (emphasis in original).

[31] *Ibid.*, p. 25 (emphasis in original).

[32] *Ibid.*, p. 199.

CHAPTER 15

C. WRIGHT MILLS

The Sources of
Societal Power

Personal Milieu and Social Structure

I need to make clear a simple and very much overlooked distinction which, to my mind, is the single most important distinction available in the sociological sciences. It is the distinction between personal milieu and social structure. And we may think of it in this way:

> When a handful of men do not have work and do not seek jobs, we may look for the causes in their immediate situations and character. But when twelve million men are unemployed, then we cannot believe that all of them suddenly "got lazy" and turned out to be "no good." Economists call this "structural unemployment"—meaning, for one thing, that the men involved cannot personally control their job chances. Now, what individual men are usually aware of, and what they usually try to do, are limited by the horizon of their specific milieu. Most men do not transcend the boundaries of their jobs and families and local communities. In other milieux which they encounter they are and they remain visitors. That is why "great changes" are out of their control, for great changes, by definition, are those whose causes lie outside the ordinary milieu of ordinary men but which nevertheless affect their conduct and their outlook. And that is why in periods full of such changes many ordinary men feel that they are "powerless," which in all sober fact they are. Mass unemployment, for example, does not originate in one factory or in one town, nor is it due to anything that one factory or one town does or fails to do. Moreover, there is little or nothing that one man, one factory, or one town can do about it when it sweeps over their personal mileu.

From C. Wright Mills, "The Power Elite: Military, Economic and Political," in Arthur Kornhauser, ed., *Problems of Power in American Democracy* (Detroit: Wayne State University Press, 1957), pp. 154-167. Reprinted by permission of the publisher.

But the great historical changes—do not their causes lie somewhere? And cannot we trace them? Yes they do, and yes we can. Simply to tag them, we call them structural changes, and we define them by realizing in our definition that they are changes which transcend the milieux of most men. They transcend these personal milieux not only because they effect a great range of milieux, but because, by their nature, the structural principles of change have to do with the unintended, hence the unexpected consequences of what men, seated in and limited by various milieux, may be trying to do or trying to ward off.

But not all men are ordinary in the sense of being limited by narrow milieux. Some have access to many more milieux than do others, and some in addition are so placed in the social structure that they can look down, so to speak, upon the milieux of many ordinary men.

This is the most important general meaning that I wish to give the term "elite." This is *the* position of the elite.

The elite are those who command the leading institutions, and whose commanding positions so place them in their social structure that they transcend, to a greater or to a lesser extent, the ordinary milieux of ordinary men and women.

The Development of the Means of Power

From even the most superficial examination of the history of Western society, we learn that the power of any decision-maker is first of all limited by the level of technique, by the *means* of power and violence and organization that prevail in a given society. In this connection, we also learn that there is a rather straight line running upward through the history of the West, that the means of oppression and exploitation, of violence and destruction, as well as the means of production and reconstruction, have been progressively enlarged and increasingly centralized.

As the institutional means of power and the means of communication that tie them together have become steadily more efficient, those in command of these enlarged and centralized structures have come into command of instruments of rule quite unsurpassed in the history of mankind. And we are not yet at the climax of their development. We can no longer lean upon or take soft comfort from the historical ups and downs of ruling groups of previous epochs. In that sense, Hegel is correct: we learn from history that we cannot learn from it.

For every epoch and for every social structure, we must work out an answer to the question of the power of the elite. And the major questions about the American elite today—about its composition and its unity, and its power—must now be faced with due attention to the awesome means of power that are now available to them. Caesar could do less with Rome than Napoleon with France; Napoleon less with France than Lenin with

Russia; and Lenin less with Russia than Hitler with Germany. But what was Caesar's power at its peak compared with the power of the changing inner circle of Soviet Russia or of Eisenhower's temporary administration? The men of either circle can cause great cities to be wiped out in a single night and in a few weeks turn continents into thermonuclear wastelands. That the facilities of power are enormously enlarged and decisively centralized means that the decisions of small groups are now more consequential.

Within the American society, major national power now resides in the economic, the political, and the military domains. . . . Within each of these big three, the typical institutional unit has become enlarged, has become administrative, and, in the power of its decisions, has become centralized. Behind these developments, within each of them, there is a giant and fabulous technology; for as institutions, they have incorporated this technology and guide it, even as it shapes and paces their developments.

The economy—once a great scatter of small productive units in autonomous balance—has become dominated by two or three hundred giant corporations, administratively and politically interrelated, which together hold the keys to economic decisions.

The political order, once a decentralized set of several dozen states with a weak spinal cord, has become a centralized, executive establishment, which has taken up into itself many powers previously scattered, and now enters into each and every cranny of the social structure.

The military order, once a slim establishment in a context of distrust fed by state militia, has become the largest and most expensive feature of government, and, although well versed in smiling public relations, now has all the grim and clumsy efficiency of a sprawling bureaucratic domain.

In each of these institutional areas, the means of power at the disposal of centralized decision-making units have increased enormously and their central executive powers enhanced, while below each of their centers, modern administrative routines are elaborated and tightened up.

As each of these domains becomes enlarged and centralized, the consequences of its activities become greater, and its traffic with the others increases. The decisions of a handful of corporations bear upon military and political as well as upon economic developments around the world. The decisions of the military establishment rest upon and grievously affect political life as well as the very level of economic activity. The decisions made within the political domain determine economic activities and military programs. There is no longer, on the one hand, an economy, and, on the other, a political order containing a military establishment unimportant to politics and to money-making. There is a political economy, linked in a thousand ways with military institutions and decisions. On each side of the world-split running through central Europe and around the Asiatic rimlands, there is ever increasing the interlocking of economic, military, and political

structures. And if there is government intervention in the corporate economy, so is there corporate intervention in the governmental process. In the
structural sense, this triangle of power is the source of the interlocking directorate that is most important for the historical structure of the present.

The fact of the interlocking is clearly revealed at each of the points of
crisis of modern capitalist society—slump, war and boom. In each, men of
decision are led to an awareness of the interdependence of the major institutional orders. In the nineteenth century, when the scale of all institutions
was smaller, their liberal integration was achieved in the automatic economy, by an autonomous balance of market forces, and in the automatic
political domain, by bargaining and voting. It was then assumed that out
of the oscillations and frictions that followed the circumscribed decisions
then possible, a new equilibrium would in due course emerge. That can
no longer be assumed, and it is not assumed by the men at the top of each
of the three dominant hierarchies.

For given the scope of their consequences, decisions in any one of these
ramify into the others, and hence top decisions become coordinated decisions. They become decisions with the total context of the nation, and indeed of the world, in mind. In their calculated risks, men of decision must
anticipate longrange consequences, lest they be fatally overwhelmed by new
and unforeseen problems.

At the pinnacle of each of the three enlarged and centralized domains,
there have arisen the men of the higher circles, who make up the economic,
the political and the military elites. At the top of the economy, among the
corporate rich, there are the corporation executives; at the top of the political order, above the middle levels of the Congress, there are the members
of the political directorate; and at the top of the military establishment, the
elite of soldier-statesmen cluster in and around the Joint Chiefs of Staff and
the upper echelon. And as each of these domains has coincided with the
others, and as decisions tend to become total in their consequence, the leading men in each of the three domains of power—the warlords, the corporation chieftains, the political directorate—tend to come together, to form the
power elite of America.

The Formation of the Power Elite

If the power to decide such national issues as are decided were shared
in an absolutely equal way, there would be no power elite; in fact, there
would be no gradation of power, but only a radical homogeneity. At the opposite extreme as well, if the power to decide issues were absolutely monopolized by one small group, there would be no gradation of power; there
would simply be this small group in command, and below it, the undifferentiated, dominated mass. American society today represents neither the
one nor the other of these extremes, but a conception of them is nonetheless

useful. It makes us realize more clearly the question of the structure of power in the United States and the position of the power elite within it.

To say that there are obviously gradations of power and of opportunities to decide within modern society, is not to say that the powerful are united, that they fully know what they do, or that they are consciously joined in conspiracy. Such issues are best faced if we become, in the first instance, more concerned with the structural position of the high and mighty and with the consequences of their decisions, than with the extent of their awareness or the purity of their motives.

The formation of the power elite, as we may now know it, occurred during World War II and its aftermath. In the course of the organization of the nation for that war, and the consequent stabilization of the warlike posture, certain types of man have been selected and formed, and, in the course of these institutional and psychological developments, new opportunities and intentions have arisen among them.

Like the tempo of American life in general, the longterm trends of the power structure have been speeded up since World War II, and certain newer trends within and between the dominant institutions have also set in to shape the power elite:

(1) Insofar as the structural clue to the power elite today lies in the political order, that clue is the decline of politics as a genuine and public debate of alternative decisions—with nationally responsible and policy-coherent parties and with autonomous organizations connecting the lower and middle levels of power with the top levels of decision. America is now in considerable part more a formal political democracy than a democratic social structure, and even the formal political mechanics are weak.

The longtime trend of business and government to become more intricately and deeply involved with each other has, in this epoch, reached a point of explicitness not before evident. Now, in a hundred ways, they are difficult to see as two distinct worlds. And it is in terms of the executive agencies of the state that the rapprochement has proceeded most decisively. The growth of the executive branch of the government, with its agencies that patrol the complex economy, does not mean merely the "enlargement of government" as some sort of autonomous bureaucracy: it has meant the ascendancy of the corporation's man as a political outsider.

If during the New Deal the corporate chieftains joined the political directorate, since World War II they have come to dominate it. Long interlocked with government, now they moved into quite full direction of the economy of the war effort and of the postwar era. And this shift of the corporation executives into the political directorate has accelerated the longterm relegation of the professional politicians in the Congress to the middle levels of power.

(2) Insofar as the structural clue to the power elite today lies in the enlarged and military state, that clue is that, with the military ascendancy,

the warlords have, for the first time, become of decisive political relevance and have gained decisive political power. The military structure of America is now in considerable part a political structure. For the seemingly permanent military threat places a premium on the military and upon their control of men, material, money, and power. Virtually all political and economic actions are now judged in terms of military definitions of reality: the higher warlords have ascended to a firm position within the power elite. . . .

In some part at least this fact has come about by virtue of one simple historical fact, pivotal for the years since 1939: the focus of elite attention has been shifted from domestic problems, centered in the thirties around slump, to international problems, centered in the forties and fifties around war.

Since the governing apparatus of the United States has by long historic usage been adapted to and shaped by domestic clash and balance, it has not, from any angle, had suitable agencies and traditions for the handling of international problems. And such formal democratic mechanics as had arisen in the century and a half of national development prior to 1941 had not been extended to the US handling of international affairs. It is, in considerable part, in this vacuum that the power elite has grown.

(3) Insofar as the structural clue to the power elite today lies in the economic order, that clue is the fact that the economy is at once a permanent war economy and a private corporation economy. American capitalism is now in considerable part a military capitalism, and the most important relation of the big corporation to the state rests on the coincidence of interests between military and corporate needs, as defined by warlords and corporate rich. Within the elite as a whole, this coincidence of interest between the high military and the corporate chieftains strengthens both of them and further subordinates the role of the merely political men. Not politicians, but corporate executives, sit with the military and plan the organization of war effort.

The Uneasy Coincidence of the Three Powers

The shape and meaning of the power elite today can be understood only when these three sets of structural trends are seen at the point of their coincidence: the military capitalism of private corporations exists in a weakened and formal democratic system containing an already quite politicized military order. Accordingly, at the top of this structure, the power elite has taken its shape from the coincidence of interest between those who control the major means of production and those who control the newly enlarged means of violence; from the decline of the professional politician and the rise to explicit political command of the corporate chieftains and the professional warlords; from the absence of any genuine civil service of skill and integrity, independent of vested interests.

The power elite is composed of political, economic, and military men, but these instituted elites are frequently in some tension; they only come together on certain coinciding points and only on certain occasions of "crisis." In the long peace of the nineteenth century, the military were not in the high councils of state, not of the political directorate—and neither were the economic men; they made raids upon the state but they did not join its directorate. During the thirties, the political man was ascendant, and now the military and the corporate men are in top positions.

Of the three types of circles that compose the power elite today, it is the military that have benefited the most in their enhanced power, although the corporate have also become more explicitly and, in fact, more decisively entrenched in the more public decision-making circles. It is the professional politician that has lost the most, so much that, in examining the events and decisions, one is tempted to speak of a political vacuum in which the corporate rich and the high warlord, in their coinciding interests, rule.

But we must always be historically specific and we must always be open to complexities: (1) the simple Marxian view makes the big economic man the real holder of power; (2) the simple liberal view makes the big political man the chief of the power system; and (3) there are some who would view the warlords as virtual dictators. These are each an oversimplified view. And it is to avoid them that we use the term "power elite" rather than, for example, "ruling class."

"Ruling class," we feel, is a badly loaded phrase. "Class" is an economic term; "rule," a political one. The phrase, "ruling class" thus contains the theory that an economic class rules politically. That shortcut theory may or may not at times be true, but we do not want to carry that one rather simple theory about in the terms that we use to define our problems; we wish to state the theories explicitly, using terms of more precise and unilateral meaning. More specifically, the phrase "ruling class," in its common political connotations, does not allow enough autonomy to the political order and its agents, and it says nothing about the military as such. It should be clear by now that we do not accept as adequate the simple view that high economic men unilaterally make all decisions of national consequence. We hold that such a simple view of "economic determinism" must be elaborated by "political determinism" and by "military determinism"; that the higher agents of each of these three domains now often have a noticeable degree of autonomy; and that only in the often intricate ways of coalition do they make up and carry through the most important decisions. Those are the major reasons we prefer "power elite" to "ruling class" as a characterizing phrase for the higher circles, when we consider them in terms of power.

Insofar as the power elite has come to wide public attention, it has done so in terms of the "military clique," and, in fact, the power elite does take its current shape from the entrance into it in a decisive way of the military. Their presence and their ideology are its major legitimations, whenever the power elite feels the need to provide any. But what is called the "Washington military clique" is not composed merely of military men, and it does not prevail merely in Washington. Its members exist all over the country, and it is a coalition of generals in the roles of corporation executives, of politicians masquerading as admirals, of corporation executives acting like politicians, of civil servants who become majors, of vice-admirals who are also the assistants to a Cabinet officer, who is himself, by the way, really a member of an important managerial clique.

Neither the idea of a "ruling class" nor of a simple monolithic rise of "bureaucratic politicians," nor of a "military clique" is the correct view. The power elite today involves the often uneasy coincidence of economic, military and political power. . . .

CHAPTER 16

JULIAN H. STEWARD

A Neo-Evolutionist
Approach

In biology the theory of evolution today is more powerfully established than ever. In cosmology it has become the primary generator of man's thinking about the universe. But the idea of evolution in the cultural history of mankind itself has had a frustrating career of ups and downs. It was warmly embraced in Darwin's time, left for dead at the turn of the century, and is just now coming back to life and vigor. Today, a completely new approach to the question has once more given us hope of achieving an understanding of the development of human cultures in evolutionary terms.

The Nineteenth-Century Evolutionists

Before considering these new attempts to explain the evolutionary processes operating in human affairs, we need to review the attempts that failed. By the latter part of the nineteenth century, Darwin's theory of biological evolution had profoundly changed scientists' views of human history. Once it was conceded that all forms of life, including man, had evolved from lower forms, it necessarily followed that at some point in evolution man's ancestors had been completely without culture. Human culture must therefore have started from simple beginnings and grown more complex. The nineteenth-century school of cultural evolutionists—mainly British— reasoned that man had progressed from a condition of simple, amoral savagery to a civilized state, whose ultimate achievement was the Victorian Englishman, living in an industrial society and political democracy, believing in the Empire, and belonging to the Church of England. The evolutionists assumed that the universe was designed to produce man and civilization,

From Julian H. Steward, "Cultural Evolution," *Scientific American,* CXCIV (1956), No. 5, pp. 70-80. Copyright © 1956 by Scientific American, Inc., and reprinted by permission. All rights reserved.

that cultural evolution everywhere must be governed by the same principles and follow the same line, and that all mankind would progress toward a civilization like that of Europe.

Among the leading proponents of this theory were Edward B. Tylor, the Englishman who has been called the father of anthropology; Lewis H. Morgan, an American banker and lawyer who devoted many years to studying the Iroquois Indians; Edward Westermarck, a Finnish philosopher famed for his studies of the family; John Ferguson McLennan, a Scottish lawyer who concerned himself with the development of social organization; and James Frazer, the Scottish anthropologist, historian of religion and author of *The Golden Bough*. Their general point of view was developed by Morgan in his book *Ancient Society,* in which he declared: "It can now be asserted upon convincing evidence that savagery preceded barbarism in all the tribes of mankind, as barbarism is known to have preceded civilization." Morgan divided man's cultural development into stages of "savagery," "barbarism," and "civilization"—each of which was ushered in by a single invention.

These nineteenth-century scholars were highly competent men, and some of their insights were extraordinarily acute. But their scheme was erected on such flimsy theoretical foundations and such faulty observation that the entire structure collapsed as soon as it was seriously tested. Their principal undoing was, of course, the notion that progress (*i.e.,* toward the goal of European civilization) was the guiding principle in human development. In this they were following the thought of the biological evolutionists, who traced a progression from the simplest forms of life to *Homo sapiens*. Few students of evolution today, however, would argue that the universe has any design making progress inevitable, in either the biological or the cultural realm. Certainly there is nothing in the evolutionary process which preordained the particular developments that have occurred on our planet.

•

The Facts

When, at the turn of the century, anthropologists began to study primitive cultures in detail, they found that the cultural evolutionists' information had been as wrong as their theoretical assumptions. Morgan had lumped together in the stage of middle barbarism the Pueblo Indians, who were simple farmers, and the peoples of Mexico, who had cities, empires, monumental architecture, metallurgy, astronomy, mathematics, phonetic writing, and other accomplishments unknown to the Pueblo. Field research rapidly disclosed that one tribe after another had quite the wrong cultural characteristics to fit the evolutionary niche assigned it by Morgan. Eventually the general scheme of evolution postulated by the nineteenth-century theorists fell apart completely. . . . Another blow to the evolutionists' theory was the discovery that customs had spread or diffused from one group to another over the world: that is to say, each society owed much of its culture to borrowing from its neighbors, so it could not be said that societies had evolved independently along a single inevitable line. . . .

When the evolutionary hypothesis was demolished, however, no alternative hypothesis appeared. The twentieth-century anthropologists threw out the evolutionists' insights along with their schemes. Studies of culture lost a unifying theory and lapsed into a methodology of shreds and patches. Anthropology became fervently devoted to collecting facts. But it had to give some order to its data, and it fell back on classification—a phase in science which has been called the "natural history stage."

The "culture elements" used as the classification criteria included such items as the bow and arrow, the domesticated dog, techniques and forms of basketry, the spear and spear thrower, head-hunting, polyandrous marriage, feather headgear, the penis sheath, initiation ceremonies for boys, tie-dyeing techniques for coloring textiles, the blowgun, use of a stick to scratch the head during periods of religious taboo, irrigation agriculture, shamanistic use of a sweat bath, transportation of the head of state on a litter, proving one's fortitude by submitting to ant bites, speaking to one's mother-in-law through a third party, making an arrowhead with side notches, marrying one's mother's brother's daughter. Students of the development of culture sought to learn the origin of such customs, their distribution, and how they were combined in the "culture content" of each society.

Eventually this approach led to an attempt to find an overall pattern in each society's way of life—a view which is well expressed in Ruth Benedict's *Patterns of Culture*. She contrasted, for example, the placid, smoothly functioning, nonaggressive behavior of the Pueblo Indians with the somewhat frenzied, warlike behavior of certain Plains Indians, aptly drawing on Greek mythology to designate the first as an Apollonian pattern and the second as Dionysian. The implication is that the pattern is formed by the ethos, value system or world view. During the past decade and a half it has become popular to translate pattern into more psychological terms. But description of a culture in terms either of elements, ethos or personality-type does not explain how it originated. Those who seek to understand how cultures evolved must look for longer-range causes and explanations.

Multilinear Evolution

One must keep in mind Herbert Spencer's distinction between man as a biological organism and his functioning on the superorganic or cultural level, which has distinctive qualities. We must distinguish man's needs and capacity for culture—his superior brain and ability to speak and use tools —from the particular cultures he has evolved. A specific invention is not explained by saying that man is creative. Cultural activities meet various biological needs, but the existence of the latter does not explain the character of the former. . . . Thanks to his jaw and tongue structure and to the speech and auditory centers of his brain, man is capable of speech, but these facts do not explain the origin of a single one of the thousands of languages that have developed in the world. . . .

The failure to distinguish the biological basis of all cultural development from the explanation of particular forms of culture accounts for a good deal of the controversy and confusion about "free will" and "determinism" in human behavior. The biological evolutionist George Gaylord Simpson considers that, because man has purposes and makes plans, he may exercise conscious control over cultural evolution. On the other hand, the cultural evolutionist Leslie A. White takes the deterministic position that culture develops according to its own laws. Simpson is correct in making a biological statement, that is, in describing man's capacity. White is correct in making a cultural statement, that is, in describing the origin of any particular culture.

All men, it is true, have the biological basis for making rational solutions, and specific features of culture may develop from the application of reason. But since circumstances differ (*e.g.,* in the conditions for hunting), solutions take many forms.

•

The facts now accumulated indicate that human culture evolved along a number of different lines; we must think of cultural evolution not as unilinear but as multilinear. This is the new basis upon which evolutionists today are seeking to build an understanding of the development of human cultures. It is an empirical approach—an attempt to learn how the factors in each given type of situation shaped the development of a particular type of society.

Multilinear evolution is not merely a way of explaining the past. It is applicable to changes occurring today as well—for example, among peasants, small farmers, wage workers on plantations and in mines and factories, primitive tribes. These several types of societies evolved, and their customs are being changed by economic or political factors introduced from the modern industrial world. Studies of such societies should obviously have practical value in guiding programs of technical aid for these peoples.

Hunters

To illustrate the empirical approach, let us consider very briefly several different types of societies, using the ways in which they made their living as the frame of reference. The first example is the form of society consisting of a patrilineal band of hunters. This type of organization was found among many primitive tribes all over the world, including the Bushmen of the deserts in South Africa, the Negritos of the tropical rain forest in the

Congo, the aborigines of the steppes and deserts in Australia, the now extinct aboriginal islanders in Tasmania, the Indians of the cold pampas on the islands of Tierra del Fuego, and Shoshoni Indians of the mountains in Southern California. Although their climates and environments differed greatly, all of these tribes had one important thing in common: they hunted cooperatively for sparsely scattered, nonmigratory game. In each case the cooperating band usually consisted of about fifty or sixty persons who occupied an area of some 400 square miles and claimed exclusive hunting rights to it. Since men could hunt more efficiently in familiar terrain, they remained throughout life in the territory of their birth. The band consequently consisted of persons related through the male line of descent, and it was required that wives be taken from other bands. In sum, the cultural effects of this line of evolution were band localization, descent in the male line, marriage outside the group, residence of the wife with the husband's band and control by the band of the food resources within its territory.

•

Early Civilizations

Farming was one of the major factors leading to dense populations which were the basis for another line of evolution that covered a considerable span of the early prehistory and history of China, Mesopotamia, Egypt, the north coast of Peru, probably the Indus Valley, and possibly the Valley of Mexico. This line had three stages. In the first period, primitive groups apparently began to cultivate food plants along the moist banks of the rivers or in the higher terrain where rainfall was sufficient for crops. They occupied small but permanent villages. The second stage in some of these areas started when the people learned to divert the river waters by means of canals to irrigate large tracts of land. Intensive farming made possible a larger population and freed the farmers from the need to spend all their time on basic food production. Part of the new-found time was put into enlarging the system of canals and ditches and part into developing crafts. This period brought the invention of loom weaving, metallurgy, the wheel, mathematics, the calendar, writing, monumental and religious architecture, and extremely fine art products. It was also marked by the beginnings of urban centers.

When the irrigation works expanded so that the canals served many communities, a coordinating and managerial control became necessary. This need was met by a ruling class or a bureaucracy, whose authority had mainly religious sanctions, for men looked to the gods for the rainfall on which their agriculture depended. Centralization of authority over a large territory marked the emergence of a state.

That a state developed in these irrigation centers by no means signifies that all states originated in this way. Many different lines of cultural evolution could have led from kinship groups up to multicommunity states. For example, feudal Europe and Japan developed small states very different from the theocratic irrigation states.

The irrigation state reached its florescence in Mesopotamia between 3000 and 4000 B.C., in Egypt a little later, in China about 1500 or 2000 B.C., in northern Peru between 500 B.C. and 500 A.D., in the Valley of Mexico a little later than in Peru. Then, in each case, a third stage of expansion followed. When the theocratic states had reached the limits of available water and production had leveled off, they began to raid and conquer their neighbors to exact tribute. The states grew into empires. The empire was not only larger than the state, but differed qualitatively in the ways it regimented and controlled its large and diversified population. Laws were codified; a bureaucracy was developed; a powerful military establishment, rather than the priesthood, was made the basis of authority. The militaristic empires began with the Sumerian Dynasty in Mesopotamia, the pyramid-building Early Dynasty in Egypt, the Chou periods in China, the Toltec and Aztec periods in Mexico, and the Tiahuanacan period in the Andes.

Since the wealth of these empires was based on forced tribute rather than on increased production, they contained the seeds of their own undoing. Excessive taxation, regimentation of civil life and imposition of the imperial religious cult over the local ones led the subject peoples eventually to rebel. The great empires were destroyed; the irrigation works were neglected; production declined; the population decreased. A "dark age" ensued. But in each center the process of empire building later began anew, and the cycle was repeated. Cyclical conquests succeeded one another in Mesopotamia, Egypt and China for nearly 2,000 years. Peru had gone through at least two cycles and was at the peak of the Inca Empire when the Spaniards came. Mexico also probably had experienced two cycles prior to the Spanish Conquest.

Our final example of a specific line of evolution is taken from more recent times. When the colonists in America pre-empted the Indians' lands, some of the Indian clans formed a new type of organization. The Ute, Western Shoshoni and Northern Paiute Indians, who had lived by hunting and gathering in small groups of wandering families, united in aggressive bands. With horses stolen from the white settlers, they raided the colonists' livestock and occasionally their settlements.

Similar predatory bands developed among some of the mounted Apaches, who had formerly lived in semipermanent encampments consisting of extended kinship groups. Many of these bands were the scourge of the Southwest for years. Some of the Apaches, on the other hand, yielded to the blandishments of the U. S. Government and settled peacefully on reservations; as a result, there were Apache peace factions who rallied around chiefs such as Cochise, and predatory factions that followed belligerent leaders such as Geronimo.

The predatory bands of North America were broken up by the U. S. Army within a few years. But this type of evolution, although transitory, was not unique. In the pampas of South America similar raiding bands arose after the Indians obtained horses. On an infinitely larger scale and making a far greater impression on history were the Mongol hordes of Asia. The armies of Genghis Khan and his successors were essentially huge mounted bands that raided entire continents.

Biology and Culture

Human evolution, then, is not merely a matter of biology, but of the interaction of man's physical and cultural characteristics, each influencing the other. Man is capable of devising rational solutions to life, especially in the realm of technical problems, and also of transmitting learned solutions to his offspring and other members of his society. His capacity for speech gives him the ability to package vastly complicated ideas into sound symbols and to pass on most of what he has learned. This human potential has resulted in the accumulation and social transmission of an incalculable number of learned modes of behavior. . . .

The biological requirements for cultural evolution were an erect posture, specialized hands, a mouth structure permitting speech, stereoscopic vision and areas in the brain for the functions of speech and association. Since culture speeded the development of these requirements, it would be difficult to say which came first.

The first step toward human culture may have come when manlike animals began to substitute tools for body parts. It has been suggested, for example, that there may have been an intimate relation between the development of a flint weapon held in the hand and the receding of the ape-like jaw and protruding canine teeth. An ape, somewhat like a dog, deals with objects by means of its mouth. When the hands, assisted by tools, took over this task, the prognathous jaw began to recede. There were other consequences of this development. The brain centers that register the experiences of the hands grew larger, and this in turn gave the hands greater sensitivity and skill. The reduction of the jaw, especially the elimination of the "simian shelf," gave the tongue freer movement and thus helped create the potentiality for speech.

Darwin called attention to the fact that man is in effect a domesticated animal; as such he depends upon culture and cannot well survive in a state of nature. Man's self-domestication furthered his biological evolution in those characteristics that make culture possible. Until perhaps 25,000 years ago he steadily developed a progressively larger brain, a more erect posture, a more vertical face and better developed speech, auditory and associational centers in the brain. His physical evolution is unquestionably still going on, but there is no clear evidence that recent changes have increased his inherent potential for cultural activities. However, the rate of his cultural development became independent of his biological evolution. In addition to devising tools as substitutes for body parts in the struggle for survival, he evolved wholly new kinds of tools which served other purposes: stone scrapers for preparing skin clothing, baskets for gathering wild foods, axes for building houses and canoes. As cultural experience accumulated, the innovations multiplied, and old inventions were used in new ways. During the last 25,000 years the rate of culture change has accelerated.

The many kinds of human culture today are understandable only as particular lines of evolution. Even if men of the future develop an I.Q. that is incredibly high by modern standards, their specific behavior will nonetheless be determined not by their reason or psychological characteristics, but by their special line of cultural evolution, that is, by the fundamental processes that shape cultures in particular ways.

1964 POSTSCRIPT

This paper follows "Cultural Evolution" in the *Scientific American* fairly closely, except that research since 1956 has modified its factual basis while the many symposiums on evolution in celebration of the 100th anniversary of the publication of Darwin's *Origin of the Species* in 1859 have suggested refinements of its conceptual approach. Attention is called to modifications indicated in "Some Mechanisms of Sociocultural Evolution" by Julian H. Steward and Demitri B. Shimkin in *Evolution and Man's Progress,* Hudson Hoagland and Ralph W. Burhoe, eds. (New York: Columbia University Press, 1962), pp. 67-87, which has a fairly complete bibliography of recent publications on cultural evolution.

The most important factual modification of the original article results from evidence on the role of irrigation in the development of the early civilizations of Mesoamerica, Peru, the Near East, and China. These civilizations reached their culminations in arid areas and had large irrigation systems, but the hypothesis that the managerial controls required for expanding irrigation works during their developmental periods led to their final integration as irrigation or hydraulic states must be modified. In all cases, increased agricultural productivity, population expansion, and growth of urban centers or "containers of civilization" where the rulers and various nonfarming specialists lived were factors in the development of states and empires; but it is still unclear how, in the absence or weakness of militarism, the great rural and urban populations were brought under centralized theocratic control.

A conceptual refinement of neo-evolution is that, since cultures cannot be classified in a taxonomy analogous to that of biology, it is futile and misleading to attempt to discuss evolutionary transformations of whole cultures. Although all components of a culture—economics, technology, society, humanistic features, language, and others—may be described in their interrelatedness as they characterize a society at a given point in time, these components change, or evolve, in different ways. Man's understanding of and technological control over his physical universe tends to be largely cumulative. Languages, from a genetic point of view, divide and subdivide so that the larger and more remotely related linguistic stocks cross-cut many kinds of societies and technological systems. Such stylistic features as art and architecture develop according to their own rationale, except that very unlike styles may serve similar functions in sociopolitical and religious structures. Finally, sociopolitical and economic systems evolve through a series of transformations which are only partly related to the other components of culture.

Recent work on cultural evolution has paid special attention to sociocultural transformations and has sought, by means of an empirical method, technological, ecological, or other causes of the many lines of evolution. Such evolution does not negate the possibility that historical factors, such as diffusion or migration, have introduced single key features of culture or whole cultures in particular cases.

CHAPTER 17

A. L. KROEBER

Diffusionism

Diffusionism is the name currently given several theories of the development of culture which specially emphasize the factor of diffusion.

Diffusion is the process, usually but not necessarily gradual, by which elements or systems of culture are spread; by which an invention or a new institution adopted in one place is adopted in neighboring areas, and in some cases continues to be adopted in adjacent ones, until it may spread over the whole earth.

Diffusion is obviously allied to tradition in that both pass cultural material on from one group to another. As usually understood, however, tradition refers to the transmission of cultural content from one generation to another of the same population; diffusion, from one population to another. Tradition therefore operates essentially in terms of time, diffusion in terms of space, although the spread through space may be rapid or slow and therefore involves a time factor also.

Both tradition and diffusion are conservative factors in culture history as contrasted with the creative one of invention, which in its broadest sense is denotive of the origination of new culture material or new cultural organization. Tradition conserves material or organization through time lapses within a greater or smaller population. Diffusion conserves it from the point of view of human culture as a whole. This aspect of diffusion has been largely underemphasized because attention has been given to the mechanism of the spread of culture per se, or because diffusions have been studied less from an interest in them than as a means by which historical events may be reconstructed or origins determined. Such interests are legitimate, but do not exhaust the significance of diffusion. It is obvious that new cultural material which does not diffuse beyond the people among whom it originates stands little chance of permanent preservation. It is likely to

From A. L. Kroeber, "Diffusionism," in Edwin R. A. Seligman and Alvin Johnson, eds., *The Encyclopedia of the Social Sciences,* III (1937), 139-142. Copyright 1937 by the Macmillan Company, and reprinted by permission of the publisher.

perish with the particular culture to which it remains attached, or even to be squeezed out of existence by new growths within this culture. Diffusion is then a process concerned with growth as well as preservation, whereas tradition as such affects only preservation. But neither in itself produces new culture content.

•

The mechanisms of diffusion are several: migration and colonization, that is, ethnic movements; conquest; missionization; commerce; revolution; and gradual infiltration, ranging from the conscious to the unconscious, or infiltration which comes into social consciousness only after it is an accomplished fact. The older anthropologists and the less subtle among historians have relied chiefly upon the first and grosser of these mechanisms. Ethnologists, archaeologists, and culture historians, on the other hand, recognizing more and more that these simple mechanisms are inadequate to explain the phenomena they are confronting, have increasingly discerned the importance of infiltration, and have tended to emphasize it as in the long run the most important phase of diffusion. They seem to have shown that the main streams of culture permeation often run surprisingly independently of migrations and political and military events. In extreme instances this has led to an underemphasis upon these more obvious factors, or even to impatience at their recognition. They can indeed be disturbing elements in the task of unraveling the full story of cultural events, which is normally both intricate and largely below the level of historic consciousness.

Both the culture area and the age-and-area concepts presuppose and rest upon diffusion, mainly of the infiltrating kind and as a normal process. But however normal the tendency of culture material to diffuse, it is clear that the actual spread of such material has not gone on irresistibly nor in any mechanically calculable manner, else all but extremely remote populations would long since have assimilated to nearly the same culture. Among the checks or limitations to diffusion—other than the self-evident ones of lack or scantiness of communications—are the factors of resistance and displacement. Resistance is due to the presence in the recipient cultures of material and systems which are, or are felt to be, irreconcilable with the invading traits or system and therefore tend to block them, checking their further diffusion. Frequently it is the presence of cultural habits functionally analogous to the new elements which results in a block. Coffee is unlikely to invade rapidly or successfully a nation addicted to tea drinking. Christianity and Islam, which are both monotheistic, Messianic, and scriptural, have diffused into the territory of each other very much less, except by violence, than they have diffused into countries of a different type of religion. Sometimes the factors that defeat or facilitate diffusion are far more subtle or intricate than in these examples, and yet are at least approximately determinable.

Displacement affects not the process of diffusion but its results. If representative government gains at the expense of monarchy, the distribution of the latter shrinks and the products of an earlier diffusion of the idea of kingship begin to be obliterated, until perhaps the institution remains only in scattered survivals. From such territorially discrete survivals the history of the growth and decay, or diffusion and shrinkage, of monarchy could perhaps be inferred even in the absence of documentary data, as among primitive or nonliterate peoples. On the other hand, such sporadic occurrences might . . . also be due to wholly independent origins, to parallel inventions of kingship. Convergent processes may also be the cause. Monarchy may arise in one place as a product of military defense, in another theocratically, and yet the two institutions may assimilate quite closely, although independently, with the lapse of time. It is even possible that each might then undergo diffusion until they met, and their coalesced areas would then look as if they were the result of a single origin and diffusion. Considerations of this sort make the unraveling of historically undocumented culture data a difficult and delicate task, calling for intensive knowledge, reliable analysis, and a critically conservative judgment. Most of the controversies of anthropology have revolved about problems of precisely this order. The diffusionist schools, in the opinion of the others, have tried to hack their way through this intricate Gordian knot.

On the other hand, the diffusionists have developed more clearly than before the important concept of degeneration, not only of whole cultures but of culture elements, and have provided some extremely suggestive examples. Their tendency has been to operate almost exclusively with rare and unique inventions and very widespread diffusions, tempered at need with degenerations. But this oversimplification of mechanisms should not lead to overdistrust of the concept of cultural degeneration.

There are two schools of diffusionism, the German-Austrian and the British. The former posits some seven or eight original *Kulturkreise*. These are not, as the name might seem to imply, geographical spheres or areas of culture, but are culture types or blocks of cultural material, each of which at one time in the past is assumed to have existed as a discrete, internally uniform culture, presumably of independent origin, in one part of the world and then to have diffused essentially as a unit. These several culture blocks originated successively in time as well as progressively in degree of advancement or complexity; and, through each spreading more or less over the whole planet, have become represented in all cultures in an interpenetration or overlay of varying proportions. The task of culture history is the segregation of any given culture into the elements derived from the several *Kulturkreise*.

The *Kulturkreislehre* was first conceived by Foy and Graebner, promulgated chiefly by the latter, supported for Africa by Ankermann, and attacked by Father Schmidt. The latter, however, soon became a convert and has since, with his associate Koppers and others, modified and amplified the hypothesis, depriving it of its original rigor and lack of specific placing in time and space by tying the scheme in wherever possible with linguistics, archaeology, and history. The term *Kulturkreis* is being abandoned and the phrase *kulturgeschichtliche Methode* substituted, which is unfortunate in its implication that the study of culture history, at any rate among non-literate cultures, must be carried on through acceptance of the special assumptions of this school. Probably not far from half of the ethnologists of Austria and Germany either profess adherence to or have been influenced by the views of this school.

The British school originated a few years later with G. Elliot Smith, Perry, and Rivers, whose respective roles might be roughly characterized as inspirer, protagonist, and moderator. This school also has undergone some modifications and is best represented in its recent form by Smith's *Human History*. In contrast with the German school, it is monogenetic. Primitive culture is conceived as essentially stagnant, inclined to retrogression as much as to progress. It is contended that at one time and place in human history, namely, in Egypt around 3000 B.C., an unusual constellation of events produced a cultural spurt leading to the rapid development of agriculture, metallurgy, political organization and kingship, priesthood, concern with the after life and mummification, writing, and other cultural institutions. From this center of origination, this great cultural complex was carried in whole or in part, with secondary embellishments and degenerations, to Mesopotamia and the Mediterranean world, to India, Oceania, Mexico, and Peru and in fragmentary form even to remote peoples who remained otherwise primitive. The remainder of culture history is essentially the story of the minor modifications of this one great culture, until the Greeks began to dissolve and replace it by civilization.

The British school has won about the same degree of adherence at home as the German; and likewise has tended to label as evolutionists and antidiffusionists all students who showed themselves unsympathetic to its full tenets. It is perhaps significant that both schools have made practically no converts from each other nor outside their countries of origin. Scandinavia, France, and the United States have held almost unanimously aloof.

The methodological weaknesses of both diffusionist schools may be summarized as follows. Granted a certain modest empirical beginning, they very early took a long a priori leap, and since then have been forced to depend largely on selected evidence or construals of evidence to maintain the position thus taken, genuinely inductive inquiry being relegated to the background. The basic schemes are too simple to seem adequate to most culture historians and anthropologists. The mechanisms used, with their primary insistence on diffusion, are also too simple.

The virtues of the schools are in part associated with this overemphasis on diffusion, whose strength they have at any rate shown, thus helping to clear the ground of the older school of evolutionism or naïvely psychological theories of stages of progress. They have also made probable the specific connection between a number of geographically separate culture elements or complexes, and they have drawn fresh attention to culture history as a study of universal human interrelations. The future will probably characterize their theories as overshootings of a newly discerned and legitimate mark.

CHAPTER 18

HORACE MINER

The Folk–Urban Continuum

It is our purpose to examine the basic propositions of the folk–urban continuum in the light of experience and criticism, in an effort to determine its inherent advantages and limitations for research and theory-building.

Briefly stated, Redfield's scheme defines an ideal type, the *folk society,* which is the polar opposite of urban society. The ideal type is a mental construct and "No known society precisely corresponds to it. . . ." [1] It is "created only because through it we may hope to understand reality. Its function is to suggest aspects of real societies which deserve study, and especially to suggest hypotheses as to what, under certain defined conditions, may be generally true about society." [2]

The folk type of society is characterized as follows:

> Such a society is small, isolated, nonliterate, and homogeneous, with a strong sense of group solidarity. The ways of living are conventionalized into that coherent system which we call "a culture." Behavior is traditional, spontaneous, uncritical, and personal; there is no legislation or habit of experiment and reflection for intellectual ends. Kinship, its relationships and institutions, are the type categories of experience and the familial group is the unit of action. The sacred prevails over the secular; the economy is one of status rather than of the market.[3]

Redfield concerns himself largely with the folk pole of the continuum. It is the characteristics of the folk society which receive his descriptive attention. These are derived by discovering the common traits of those societies which are least like our own.[4] The definitive qualities of the urban type are

From Horace Miner, "The Folk–Urban Continuum," *The American Sociological Review,* XVII (1952), 529-537. Reprinted by permission of the author and the publisher.

[1] Robert Redfield, "The Folk Society," *The American Journal of Sociology,* LII (1947), 294.

[2] *Ibid.,* p. 295.

[3] *Ibid.,* p. 293.

[4] *Loc. cit.*

then left as the logically opposite ones to those which characterize the folk. Urban society is never actually discussed here as an ideal type and is not explicitly named. Redfield usually refers to it as "modern urbanized society" or some variant of the phrase. Implicit in the use of this pole as an ideal type, however, is the idea that it stands for urbanized society in general and that modern Western society represents the specific case most closely approximating the polar category. The term "urban society" would appear to represent the content of the ideal type more adequately.

The folk–urban continuum developed, of course, from earlier conceptual schemes. Maine, Toennies, and Durkheim contributed important dichotomies of societal characteristics. Redfield's formulation took elements of these characteristics and others which he saw to be related and put them together as the definitive traits of the polar types. A factor influencing the research work of Redfield was that of concern with empirical method. To this interest must be attributed the fact that he executed, in Yucatan, one of the rare field projects in which a series of communities was selected and studied to test a specific hypothesis. Consistent with the express purpose of the formulation of the ideal type, its characteristics suggested the hypothesis. Concerning the Yucatan study, Redfield writes:

> The problem is seen as one of the relation among variables. No one of these is the sole cause of the others, but it is assumed, subject to proof, that, as certain of these vary, so do others. *For the purposes of this investigation** the isolation and homogeneity of the community are taken together as an independent variable. Organization or disorganization of culture, secularization, and individualization are regarded as dependent variables. The choice of isolation and homogeneity as independent variables implies the hypothesis that loss of isolation and increasing heterogeneity are causes of disorganization, secularization, and individualization. Even if this should be established, it would not follow that these are the only causes of these effects or that these are the only covariant or causal relationships to be discovered in the same data.[5]

Consideration of the data from Yucatan leads Redfield to the conclusion that ". . . increase of contracts, bringing about heterogeneity and disorganization of culture, constitutes one sufficient cause of secularization and individualization." [6] No formal generalization is attempted with regard to the nature of the processes through which the variables affect one another, although the analysis of the data is full of demonstration of their specific interdependence in Yucatan . . . ; ". . . there is no single necessary cause for secularization and individualization." [7]

---

* Italics mine.

[5] Robert Redfield, *The Folk Culture of Yucatan* (Chicago: University of Chicago Press, 1941), p. 344.

[6] *Ibid.*, p. 369.

[7] *Loc. cit.*

•

In a . . . study of Timbuctoo, French West Africa, the writer did try to determine whether or not this densely populated, heterogeneous, nonisolated community showed social disorganization and was characterized by secular behavior and impersonal relationships, even in the absence of influences from Western civilization. . . .

The previous lack of interest, among anthropologists, in the urban pole of the continuum has already been alluded to. This polar type is logically also an ideal type, yet its characteristics have frankly been derived from a consideration of our own society. Further, in the series of Yucatan communities, decreasing isolation was in fact due to increased contact with Western urban civilization. This was explicitly recognized by Redfield.[8] But inherent in the continuum, as a hypothesis-provoking construct, is the idea that increased contact with any dissimilar society, not just with Western urban society, results in change in other variables of the ideal type. The Timbuctoo study was an attempt to avoid the limitations of the Yucatan research and of relevant rural–urban studies which have also been made in situations of rural contact with cities of Western civilization.

Briefly, the theoretical implications of the Timbuctoo data are that lack of isolation, marked population density and heterogeneity seem to be accompanied by disorganization, secularization and impersonalization, even in the absence of Western influences. The market economy appears as the system which makes possible the basic ecological conditions, holds the diverse cultural elements together, and mediates most relationships among them. Having said this, certain qualifications are immediately required. Evidence of disorganization and of secular and impersonal behavior, is most evident in relationships between members of different ethnic elements of the community. Familial relationships within each group seem to be strong, sacred and personal. Other intra-ethnic relationships are only somewhat less folklike in character. Any attempt to characterize the whole society, and to compare it with others, highlights the fact that the folk–urban continuum deals with problems of the relative degree of presence or absence of polar characteristics, which vary not only between cultures but within them, and that no adequate methodological techniques exist for operationalizing and quantifying the characteristics themselves. To this point we shall want to return.

Certainly the most adverse comment on the utility of the folk–urban continuum is Oscar Lewis' critique which concludes his restudy of Tepoztlán. Both because this is a restudy of a community analyzed earlier by Redfield and because of the limited amount of research conducted with the continuum explicitly in mind, Lewis' comments deserve careful consideration.

---

[8] *Op. cit., The Folk Culture of Yucatan,* p. 360.

Lewis points out that the folk concept is an ideal type and hence a matter of definition. It is upon its heuristic value that the type and its related continuum must be judged. He makes the following six criticisms of the conceptual framework, with regard to its utility for the study of culture change and for cultural analysis:[9]

(1) The folk–urban conceptualization of social change focuses attention primarily on the city as a source of change, to the exclusion or neglect of other factors of an internal or external nature. . . .

We would agree that Redfield's writing and research does neglect other sources of change than urban contact. We cannot agree that the folk–urban continuum excludes other conceptualization. Most social scientists believe that the evolution of cities and civilizations has resulted from increased cultural interaction and interdependence. The operation of this process is evident in Tax's Guatemalan data and in the Timbuctoo material. However, it would be erroneous to say that even loss of isolation need always be considered the independent variable in change. Any other variable might do, so far as the continuum is concerned. The very consideration of what other characteristics might be so employed leads immediately to the fruitful observation that some of the type traits seem to presuppose others. For example, great heterogeneity in the division of labor requires a large population, while a large population may exist with a relatively unelaborate division of labor.

(2) . . . culture change may not be a matter of folk–urban progression, but rather an increasing or decreasing heterogeneity of culture elements. For example . . . the incorporation of Spanish rural elements, such as the plow . . . did not make Tepoztlán more urban, but rather gave it a more varied rural culture. . . .

The fact that Lewis says "may not be a matter of folk–urban progression" can be taken to mean that homogeneity and the other variables of the ideal type arc interrelated only in certain circumstances. His phraseology also suggests an identification of the concepts "folk" and "rural."

While it is possible that homogeneity may vary independently from the other variables, the following excerpts from Lewis' monograph demonstrate that this was not the case with regard to the increase of heterogeneity resulting from the addition of plow cultivation to hoe agriculture in Tepoztlán.

The differences between hoe culture (*tlacolol*) and plow culture are not limited merely to the use of different tools; each system has far-reaching social and economic implications.[10]

---

[9] Quotations extracted from Oscar Lewis, *Life in a Mexican Village: Tepoztlán Restudied* (Urbana: University of Illinois Press, 1930), pp. 432-440.

[10] *Ibid.*, p. 129.

Tlacolol is practiced on communally owned land and necessitates a great deal of time and labor but very little capital. Plow culture is practiced on privately owned land and requires relatively little time and labor but considerable capital. In the former, there is dependence almost exclusively upon family labor; in the latter, there is a great dependence upon hired labor.[11]

Tlacolol is essentially geared to production for subsistence, while plow culture is better geared to production for the market. It is significant that most families who work *tlacolol* are landless and that *tlacolol* has traditionally been viewed as the last resort of the poor.[12]

[An informant says of Tepoztlán during the Diaz regime,] ". . . The presidents of the municipio, in agreement with the *caciques,* forbade the sowing of *tlacolol* and so the poor had no way of helping themselves. This prohibition was due to the fact that if the poor planted *tlacolol,* the rich or *caciques* would not have the peones during the rainy season to seed their lands. . . ." [13]

. . . In the years immediately following the Revolution, that is between 1920 and 1927, relatively few individuals became *tlacoloeros.* The population of the village was still small (the Revolution having reduced the population to about half its previous figure) and there was a relative abundance of rentable land. . . .

In 1927 the municipio lost control of the *tlacolol* lands, which passed to the jurisdiction of the forestry department. . . . With the rapid increase of population in the thirties, the shortage of land became acute and the need for the *tlacolol* land urgent. Many individuals began to open *tlacolol* plots and were fined.

In 1938 a group of Tepoztecans . . . stated that they would open *tlacolol* even if it meant violence and arrest. Following this demonstration the *tlacoloeros* were allowed to work without government interference, and the number of *tlacoloeros* increased.[14] . . . one of the crucial problems in Tepoztlán . . . [now is] the rapid increase of population with no accompanying increase in resources or improvement in production techniques. On the contrary, the increase in the number of *tlacoloeros* represents a return to a more primitive type of production in an effort to escape the devastating effects of a money economy during a period of inflation. . . . Although it is helping to resolve the immediate problem, it by no means offers a satisfactory solution. In fact, it increases the problems to be faced.[15]

The writer knows of no better demonstration than that above of the manner in which two tools and their associated techniques form the core of social subdivision within a society. While it would certainly be unjustifiable to attribute the land-use system and its attendant problems in Tepoztlán solely to the cooccurrence of plow culture and *tlacolol,* it is equally unjustifiable to say that they are unrelated. Lewis' material indicates specifically that the introduction of plow agriculture and its coexistence with

---

[11] *Ibid.,* p. 130.
[12] *Ibid.,* p. 131.
[13] *Ibid.,* p. 93.
[14] *Ibid.,* pp. 148-149.
[15] *Ibid.,* p. 157.

hoe agriculture is directly related to phenomena of population density, family cooperation, market economy, group solidarity, and conflicts indicative of social disorganization. What is more, this heterogeneity of technique seems to be related to shifts in the other variables away from the folk and, hence, toward the urban type. Tepoztlán is rural, in that it is an agricultural community, but it has a rural culture which shows definite urban influences and characteristics.

> (3) Some of the criteria used in the definition of the folk society are treated by Redfield as linked or interdependent variables, but might better be treated as independent variables. . . .

The argument supporting this statement cites Tax's work and Lewis' own material showing that commercialism is accompanied by little evidence of family disorganization in Tepoztlán. This point is obviously a more generalized statement of that immediately preceding it. The only comment required is to note that the continuum, as defined, does not require that the type traits change at the same rate or that they are all interdependent in the same way in all circumstances. This is implicit in Redfield's statement, ". . . the societies of the world do not range themselves in the same order with regard to the degree to which they realize all of the characteristics of the ideal folk society." [16] It is explicit in his comparison of the Yucatan and Guatemala evidence.[17]

> (4) The typology involved in the folk–urban classification of societies tends to obscure . . . the wide range in the ways of life and in the value systems among so-called primitive peoples . . . the criteria used . . . are concerned with the purely formal aspects of society. . . . Focusing only on the formal aspects of urban society reduces all urban societies to a common denominator and treats them as if they all had the same culture. . . . It should be clear that the concept "urban" is too much of a catchall to be useful for cultural analysis. Moreover, it is suggested here that the question posed by Redfield, namely, what happens to an isolated, homogeneous society when it comes into contact with an urbanized society, cannot possibly be answered in a scientific way because the question is too general and the terms used do not give us the necessary data. What we need to know is what kind of an urban society, under what conditions of contact, and a host of other specific historical data.

We should amend two of these statements slightly to bring them in line with the facts before discussing them. Obviously the reduction of "all urban societies to a common denominator" treats them as though they had *something in common,* but not "as if they all had the same culture." Secondly, we see again a confusion between the conceptualization of the continuum

---

[16] *Op. cit.,* "The Folk Society," p. 306.
[17] *Op. cit., The Folk Culture of Yucatan,* pp. 364-369.

and Redfield's research concern with a particular kind of loss of isolation, namely urban contact.

Granted that it is desirable to study the total configuration of a society and the specific historical factors which gave rise to that pattern, limiting our interests to such inquiry produces a methodological and descriptive science, such as linguistics. If we want to develop a social science with general principles applicable to all societies, despite their cultural differences, we are forced to abstract categories of phenomena which are applicable to all cultures.

Differences in ethos are important in understanding culture, as Lewis says in his discussion, citing the individualism and competitiveness of the Plains Indians. But because the urbanite and the Indian hunter share these features, does this mean we should cease to consider individualism and competition as specifically related to other aspects of urban life? It may also argue that we need to know how and in what circumstances individualism is systematically related to other systems than the urban.

As for the polar types being "catchalls," too generally defined for scientific investigation, Lewis seems to be restating Redfield's remarks:

> The problems suggested in that earlier paper defining the types are too comprehensive in scope and too vague in definition to be suitable guides for research. Nine or ten characters, each simply denoted by a phrase or two, are thrown together and called a "type." It is not clear how we are to determine how any particular society partakes more or less of any of these characters. It is not made clear how we are to determine which of these characters is naturally associated with any other. It is necessary to ask many more special questions, and to relate them to particular fact, to define more precise lines of inquiry.[18]

The continuum is an oversimplification, but at least it is a simplification of a mass of data on cultural variation and change. As a rudimentary conceptual device, the continuum requires elaboration—elaboration which will produce a different conceptual scheme. Science does advance by asking the general questions. The crude answers to the general questions are the basis of increasingly more specific inquiry. The real query is, do we have a better initial answer than the folk–urban continuum to the general question of how to account for the similarities and differences observable among societies.

> (5) The folk–urban classification has serious limitations in guiding field research, because of the highly selective implications of the categories themselves and the rather narrow focus of problem. The emphasis upon essentially formal aspects of culture leads to neglect of psychological data and, as a rule, does not give insight into the character of the people. . . .

---

18 *Ibid.,* p. 344.

The new element of critique here is that the continuum is not specifically concerned with psychological variables. This is perfectly true. The continuum does, however, invite the use of any body of theory which can explain the nature of the interrelationships among the variables.

(6) Finally, underlying the folk–urban dichotomy as used by Redfield, is a system of value judgments which contains the old Rousseauan notion of primitive people as noble savages, and the corollary that with civilization has come the fall of man. . . . It is assumed that all folk societies are integrated while urban societies are the great disorganizing force. . . .

To the extent that this is a criticism of Redfield rather than the continuum, we are not here concerned with the argument. This is, in part, the case, for there are no explicit value judgments placed on the polar types in their definition. The organization–disorganization variable, however, does lead to questions of value orientation. The concepts of "function" and what Merton calls "dysfunction," along with the idea of "degree of integration," are all closely allied in this problem. Social scientists do sometimes treat organization, function, and integration as though they were better than disorganization, dysfunction, and lack of integration. Much of our theory about culture change relies upon the belief that people experience conflict as punishing and that they restructure their behavior so as to eliminate the conflict. The fact that culture change often introduces new conflicts gives us pause to consider, but we still use this motivation of conflict-reduction as an essential element in explaining culture change. The basis for such motivation in the noncultural reactions of organisms is quite clear. The value connotation of "organization" and "integration" seems to be a quality of data, not of the investigator, and as such is not bias.

Quite a different consideration concerning disorganization as a feature of urban society is that this characteristic may not be dependent upon the other variables of the polar type, but may be a function of the rate of social change. Such an explanation is consistent with change theory, and might explain why ancient urban civilizations seem to have been less disorganized.

The foregoing discussion has introduced many of the sorts of inadequacies which some social scientists have seen in the folk–urban concept. Rather than to continue here piecemeal treatment, further questions will be introduced into any attempted systematic formulation of all of the arguments, with a view to making some judgment as to what the status of the continuum might profitably be in our theoretical thinking.

Criticisms of the folk–urban concept might be classed under three general headings: (1) the problem of lack of fit between the empirical evidence on particular societies and the nature of these societies which one might expect from the ideal type construct; (2) the problem of definition of the characteristics of the ideal types; (3) the limited theoretical insight provided by the continuum.

(1) *The problem of fit.* Redfield deals with the ideal type as a mental construct which will be productive of testable hypotheses concerning society. This construct itself is commonly referred to as a hypothesis. It is the testing of this hypothesis which we here refer to as "the problem of fit." The fundamental hypothesis inherent in the formulation of the ideal type and the related continuum is that "There is some natural or interdependent relation among some or all of these characters (of the ideal type) in that change with regard to certain of them tends to bring about or carry with it change with respect to others of them." [19] Implied also is a general tendency for the characters to change in the same direction.

A. L. Kroeber raises two questions which essentially involve problems of fit.[20] One, which he does not develop, concerns the nature of the characteristics of the neglected, urban polar type. He asks if we can project the urban characteristics "forward into the future to a vanishing point." In other words, how can we conceive of a completely nonisolated, secular, heterogeneous, individualistic society? Kroeber's question is also applicable to the folk pole, although somewhat less so. While we might conceive of a completely isolated, sacred, personal, and kin-oriented society, what is a completely small or homogeneous society? These questions do not destroy the rationale of the continuum. They point up the fact that the empirically possible polarities must be located short of the logical extremes. Answers to the problem of what the minimal and maximal societal requisites are in this regard involve important knowledge about the basic nature of society.

Kroeber's other concern is the fact that if culture change is considered as movement along the continuum, it is an irregular progression, sometimes reversing its trend and moving at varying rates. These facts about culture change would only vitiate the continuum if it contended that change is always at the same rate or in the same direction. This it does not do. . . .

The diffuseness of the hypothesis implied by the continuum is such that many specific cases of lack of fit do not in themselves invalidate the concept. If, considering all known societies, there is shown to be no general tendency for the elements of the type to co-occur, then obviously the ideal type is not valid. So far as the writer knows, no one has claimed that the general tendency does not exist.

•

(2) *Definition of characteristics.* Attempts to find the degree of fit between actual societies and the ideal type presupposes a precise definition of the characteristics of the type. The definition must be operationalized so

---

[19] *Op. cit., The Folk Culture of Yucatan,* p. 343.

[20] A. L. Kroeber, *Anthropology* (New York: Harcourt, Brace and Co., 1948), pp. 280-286.

that all observers of societies can categorize the cultural characteristics in the same way. Inasmuch as the traits of the ideal type are variables, there must be some way not only to identify them but also to quantify them, or at least to rank the variations of each trait in some consistent fashion.

Widely different societies conceivably might be ranked by judicious rule-of-thumb methods. There is definite evidence, however, that even this procedure is unsatisfactory. The difference between Redfield and Lewis in their conclusions concerning Tepoztlán is in large part attributable to the use of different standards by the two workers.

•

The study of Timbuctoo may also be open to different interpretation from that which the writer has made. The attention given to cases of conflict may be seen by others as observer bias. Actually instances of conflict were specifically sought, as they were regarded as indicative of disorganization. There is nothing novel about this approach, but it suggests that some scale of conflict indices should be applied to the whole range of the organization–disorganization variable, instead of using it solely at one pole. Past practice has often been to categorize organization by a "see how well it all fits together" description. This led, for example, to the anomaly of Lewis' discovering that there were over a hundred cases of crime in Tepoztlán during the time that Redfield was observing the integrated nature of folk culture there. In his later work Redfield came to recognize four different categories of organization.[21] Disorganization, in the sense of lack of internal consistency, stands as the polar opposite to only one of these. All four need some uniformly applicable and scalable treatment.

Others of the characteristics of the ideal type lend themselves to more explicit handling than has been accorded them. Population size and density are easily metricized. Indices of amount of isolation could be developed on the basis of amount of movement of persons and goods in and out of the community, as well as the amount of mail and mechanical communication. The degree of functional importance of these contacts to the society is less readily dealt with, but this factor is probably more significant than the gross quantity of contact.

The presence of three distinct culture groups in Timbuctoo, and their organization in a ramifying division of labor and class structure, was used as indicative of marked heterogeneity. An itemization of distinctive roles based on kinship, economy, politics, religion, etc., might fruitfully be derived from such data for single numerical comparison with similar material from other societies. Taking population size into account, one would have an index of heterogeneity of roles. It is not suggested that this is the only important kind of heterogeneity, but its relevance to degree of individualization and impersonalization is clear.

---

[21] Op. cit., The Folk Culture of Yucatan, p. 346.

•

The weight of evidence seems to be that, irrespective of the merits of the folk–urban continuum for theory building, the characteristics of the ideal type must be operationalized before relevant theory can be reliably tested cross-culturally.

(3) *The limited theoretical insight.* G. P. Murdock has criticized the folk–urban concept because it does not make use of historical, functional, or psychological theory and method.[22] Melville Herskovits antedates Lewis in dissatisfaction with the type categories because they emphasize form rather than process.[23] These criticisms point up accurately the basic nature of the continuum. It does deal with the form rather than with the content of culture traits. As a predictive device it is a weak hypothesis. This doubtless accounts for the fact that Redfield does not refer to it as a hypothesis at all.

It will place the continuum in its proper perspective if we ask what utility remains for it, if it provides little exact fit or predictive value and if no theory concerning function or process is involved. To answer simply, we can only rephrase Redfield's original exposition. The ideal type is a conceptual recognition of a general tendency for certain formal characteristics of cultures to vary together. The continuum stands as an insistence that social science has something to explain here. Any body of theoretical knowledge in the social sciences can be related to the continuum if it can contribute to our understanding of the processes through which the characteristic traits are interrelated.

We note the Spencerian principle that as population density increases, so does differentiation, *i.e.*, heterogeneity. This principle must be refined by the addition of Durkheim's idea of "social density," or frequency of contact and interchange within a population. This essential intervening variable lends itself not only to ecological treatment, but also to sociopsychological considerations of communication. In other words, there are bodies of theory which, when applied to the heterogeneity of population, and size and density characteristics, can go a long way toward explaining the processes through which they tend to vary together.

Probably the most valuable feature of the continuum is the fact that it provides a framework within which various theoretical fields may be integrated to provide greater understanding of the nature and course of culture change. It is clear that such theoretical progress will involve the clarification, refinement, and addition of important variables in such change. Whether or not these developments take place with the continuum spe-

---

[22] G. P. Murdock, Review of *The Folk Culture of Yucatan, American Anthropologist*, XIV (1943), 133-136.

[23] Melville Herskovits, *Man and His Works* (New York: Alfred A. Knopf, 1948), pp. 604-607.

cifically in mind, they will, of necessity, have to take into account the cultural facts upon which the continuum rests. It is hardly prophetic to predict that the linear continuum will evolve into a more complex and more insightful construct. The ideal types are useful as a basis for such development.

CHAPTER 19

MERVYN L. CADWALLADER

The Cybernetic Analysis
of Change

Cybernetic theory has been extensively applied in electronics, telecommunications, automation, and neurology. Some first attempts at the application of cybernetics in experimental psychology are reported in *Information Theory in Psychology*.[1] Communication theory has been slower in gaining attention among the social scientists interested in large social systems. The pioneers include economist Kenneth E. Boulding and the electrical engineer Arnold Tustin, who have suggested a variety of empirical applications to the problems of economic analysis.[2] Karl W. Deutsch has undertaken a cybernetic analysis of the emergence of nationalism in political communities.[3] The work of these men demonstrates that cybernetics can be employed as a theoretical system in social analysis. The present essay sketches how some of the concepts and principles of cybernetics might be used in the analysis of change in formal social organizations.

The ultrastable system—The fundamental theme of cybernetics is always regulation and control in open systems. It is concerned with homeostasis in organisms and the steady states of social organizations. Its orientation is the source of considerable misunderstanding because many of the sociologists who are interested in the subject of social change object to the use of

From Mervyn L. Cadwallader, "The Cybernetic Analysis of Change in Complex Social Organizations," *American Journal of Sociology*, LXV (1959), No. 2, pp. 154-157. Copyright 1959 by The University of Chicago Press, and reprinted by permission of the author and The University of Chicago Press.

[1] Henry Quastler, ed., *Information Theory in Psychology* (Glencoe, Ill.: The Free Press, 1955).

[2] Kenneth E. Boulding, *The Organizational Revolution* (New York: Harper & Bros., 1953); Arnold Tustin, *The Mechanism of Economic Systems* (Cambridge, Mass.: Harvard University Press, 1953).

[3] Karl W. Deutsch, *Nationalism and Social Communication* (New York: John Wiley & Sons, 1953).

all concepts of equilibrium, homeostasis, or stability, arguing that to include such ideas as a central part of social theory is to preclude the possibility of dealing with change.[4] They seem to believe that stability and change are not only contradictory ideas, but that the processes themselves are totally incompatible. The difficulty here is not merely semantic: some kinds of stability do negate certain kinds of change. What has been overlooked is that at least one category of stability depends upon and is the consequence of change. Just this kind of stability is of prime interest to cybernetics.

An open system, whether social or biological, in a changing environment either changes or perishes. In such a case the only avenue to survival is change. The capacity to persist through a change of structure and behavior has been called "ultrastability."[5] If a complex social organization is to survive critical changes in its environment, it can do so only by changing its structure and behavior. That Great Britain has survived through medieval, mercantile, and capitalist periods means that as a national state it has ultrastability. Any industrial corporation, such as International Business Machines or General Electric, that has survived the last fifty years of social change in the United States has done so through a process of self-transformation and not through the continuation of original organizational and operational patterns. Therefore, the concept of ultrastability will aid in distinguishing between systems that achieve stability under specific constant conditions and those that can learn or evolve new structures and behavior so as to remain stable under changing conditions. The latter is the focus here.

Another way of expressing the above is to say that some classes of open systems adapt to a fluctuating environment through processes of learning and innovation. There is nothing new in such a statement if the reference is to biological organisms. The novelty here lies in the proposal that complex formal social organizations, such as industrial corporations, armies, churches, and so on, be regarded as learning and innovating systems. Or, to put it another way, largescale formal organizations are treated as open problem-solving systems, studied with a variety of theoretical problem-solving models, i.e., as learning and innovating systems.

By common convention we are used to thinking in terms of individual human beings as inventing or innovating, but not of social groups. But it is valid to talk about innovations produced by a social organization taken as a whole, and this is not to deny the fact of individual innovation. Any such

---

[4] Such objections can be found in the following: Wayne Hield, "The Study of Change in Social Science," *British Journal of Sociology*, V (1954), 1-11; David Lockwood, "Some Remarks on 'The Social System,'" *British Journal of Sociology*, VII (1956), 134-146; and Barrington Moore, "Sociological Theory and Contemporary Politics," *American Journal of Sociology*, LXI (1955), 107-115.

[5] For a full discussion of this concept see W. Ross Ashby, *An Introduction to Cybernetics* (New York: John Wiley & Sons, 1956), pp. 82-85; H. S. Tsien, *Engineering Cybernetics* (New York: McGraw-Hill, 1954), pp. 253-267.

system capable of purposeful problem-solving behavior and of learning from the past and innovating for the future is an ultrastable system.

Cybernetics and the analysis of ultrastable organizations—From the point of view of cybernetics, any largescale formal social organization is a communication network. It is assumed that these can display learning and innovative behavior if they possess certain necessary facilities (structure) and certain necessary rules of operation (content).

First, consider the structure of the system—as it might be represented in the language of cybernetics. Any social organization that is to change through learning and innovation, that is, to be ultrastable, must contain certain very specific feedback mechanisms, a certain variety of information, and certain kinds of input, channel, storage, and decision-making facilities. This can be stated in the form of an axiomatic proposition: that complexity of purposeful behavior is a function of the complexity of the communication components or parts of the system. More specifically, every open system behaving purposefully does so by virtue of a flow of factual and operational information through receptors, channels, selectors, feedback loops, and effectors. Every open system whose purposeful behavior is predictive—and this is essential to ultrastability—must also have mechanisms for the selective storage and recall of information; it must have memory. Does the social organization under scrutiny behave purposefully, does it solve problems, and does it forecast future events? If the answers are in the affirmative, then one must find in it certain kinds of communications, information, and control mechanisms.

In addition to the requisite structural components mentioned above, the communication net must contain or acquire information that makes learning and innovating behavior possible. This is a "program." That is to say, it must acquire or discover rules of behavior, instructions regarding internal mechanisms and processes—all of which will result in performance to be identified as learning, problem-solving, and innovating.

Innovation by any system is subject to the limitations and possibilities established by the quantity and variety of information present in it at a particular time and by the information available to it from the environment. Something cannot be created from nothing, much less something new. Therefore the range of possible new combinations that may be formed by an innovating system depends upon the possible range of output, the range of available information stored in the memory, and the operating rules (program) governing the analysis and synthesis of the flow of information within the system. In order to innovate, the system must be able to analyze information, that is, it must separate it into constituent parts. In a social system this is a consequence of certain explicit operating rules about what can and should be done, by whom, when, and why.

The ulitilization by a system of a particular part of its fund of information as an output for the solution of an environmental problem is not usually determined by pure chance, unless the system, in dealing with a totally un-familiar situation, is trying completely random outputs.[6] In the long run there must emerge an organization of the trial process in any open system capable of storing information about past behavior. Purposeful and predic-tive behavior depends upon memory, whether the system is organismic or social. Continuing behavior is modified by the results of specific acts. This is one kind of negative feedback and one which introduces a bias into the program of the system which changes the probabilities of various kinds of future acts in terms of present and past successes and failures.

If the problem-solving output of the system is organized solely in terms of past successes and failures, a point would be reached in its development at which it would not try anything new: all obstacles would be attacked with the techniques which had already proved successful. Innovation depends, therefore, on preventing such a freezing of the behavior of the system in old patterns. This is accomplished in a variety of ways. "Mistakes" in the identification, analysis, and synthesis of information may be the source of novel behavior. The loss of information (forgetting) about the past counter-mands the freezing process, to some extent, in all open systems complex enough to learn. In addition, the program of the system may contain specific instructions preventing the synthesis of all information into old familiar pat-terns and explicitly supporting certain kinds and amounts of novel action. Whenever novel behavior is successful, a negative feedback of information reinforces the creation and use of novelty. Not only will the system innovate, but it will remember that the act of innovating enabled it to circumvent ob-stacles and reach its goals. It will have discovered that a technique which worked in the past can be improved upon. Finally, in doing so, the system will have achieved the state of ultrastability which, for an open system, is the optimum road to survival.

Elements of a model, empirical indicators, and sample hypotheses[7]— One of the main tasks which a theoretical model performs for the scien-tist is the selection of relevant variables and significant hypotheses from the infinite number of possibilities. A cybernetic model would focus the investi-gator's attention on such things as the following: (1) the quantity and variety of information stored in the system; (2) the structure of the com-munication network; (3) the pattern of the subsystems within the whole; (4) the number, location, and function of negative feedback loops in the system and the amount of time-lag in them; (5) the nature of the system's

---

[6] The randomized strategy of certain games as described in game theory is one ex-ample. However, it is assumed that goal-seeking behavior is guided by random trial-and-error process during the early history of such systems.

[7] The reader who is unfamiliar with the terminology of cybernetics will find a general discussion of the discipline in Colin Cherry, *On Human Communication* (New York: John Wiley & Sons, 1957); Norbert Wiener, *The Human Use of Human Beings* (Boston: Houghton Mifflin Co., 1950).

memory facility; (6) the operating rules, or program determining the sys-tem's structure and behavior.

The operating rules of the system and its subsystems are always numerous. Relevant for the present problem are (1) rules or instructions determining range of input; (2) rules responsible for the routing of the information through the network; (3) rules about the identification, analysis, and classification of information; (4) priority rules for input, analysis, storage, and output; (5) rules governing the feed-back mechanisms; (6) instructions for storage in the system's memory; (7) rules regarding the synthesis of information for the output of the system—especially those concerned with the matter of usual or novel output.

It is now possible to suggest a few cybernetic propositions determining the presence, absence, and nature of innovative processes in complex communications systems. For example, it can be said that: (1) the rate of innovation is a function of the rules organizing the problem-solving trials (output) of the system; (2) the capacity for innovation cannot exceed the capacity for variety or available variety of information; (3) the rate of innovation is a function of the quantity and variety of information; (4) a facility, mechanism, or rule for forgetting or disrupting organizing patterns of a high probability must be present; (5) the rate of change for the system will increase with an increase in the rate of change of the environment (input). That is, the changes in the variety of the inputs must force changes in the variety of the outputs or the system will fail to achieve "ultrastability." [8]

While no exact mathematical relationship between the elements of such a system has been specified, it is assumed that this is possible in principle but that its realization must wait for the results of actual experimentation and field tests. The use of mathematical devices for the measurement of information and the representation of networks will be a necessary and crucial first step in research programs designed to test hypotheses derived from the theory above. Research might be carried out along the following lines: (1) the volume of mail, telegrams, telephone calls, and memos could be sampled at input terminals, output terminals, and at crucial points in the network; (2) the volume of printed and written materials stored in the libraries and files of the system could be measured; (3) tracer messages would enable the observer to map channel connections, one-way couplings, two-way couplings, and to locate relatively independent subsystems; (4) the time taken by regular or tracer messages to move through a feedback loop would give information on time-lag; (5) the many techniques already in use by the social scientist for measuring values and attitudes will be useful tools for the detection and measurement of implicit operating rules. The techniques of content analysis could be put to use for the abstraction of critical

[8] For a sophisticated development of this idea see W. Ross Ashby, "The Effect of Experience on a Determinate System," *Behavioral Science,* I (1956), 35-42.

operating rules contained in the official documents of the formal organization, in order to isolate and index those parts of the program of the system which constrain and determine the range, routing, identification, analysis, storage, priority, feedback, and synthesis of information. Above all else, the rules supporting the synthesis and use of unusual as against usual patterns of action would be of special concern in a description and analysis of the ultrastable system in the process of change, or of a system with a certain potential for purposeful change.

CHAPTER 20

DAVID C. McCLELLAND

Business Drive and National Achievement

What accounts for the rise in civilization? Not external resources (*i.e.,* markets, minerals, trade routes, or factories), but the entrepreneurial spirit which exploits those resources—a spirit found most often among businessmen.

Who is ultimately responsible for the pace of economic growth in poor countries today? Not the economic planners or the politicians, but the executives whose drive (or lack of it) will determine whether the goals of the planners are fulfilled.

Why is Russia developing so rapidly that—if it continues its present rate of growth—it will catch up economically with the most advanced country in the world, the United States, in 25 or 30 years? Not, as the USSR claims, because of the superiority of its Communist system, but because—by hook or by crook—it has managed to develop a stronger spirit of entrepreneurship among executives than we have today in the US.

How can foreign aid be most efficiently used to help poor countries develop rapidly? Not by simply handing money over to their politicians or budget makers, but by using it in ways that will select, encourage, and develop those of their business executives who have a vigorous entrepreneurial spirit or a strong drive for achievement. In other words: *invest in a man, not just in a plan.*

What may be astonishing about some of these remarks is that they come from a college professor and not from the National Association of Manufacturers. They are not the defensive drum rattlings of an embattled capitalist, but are my conclusions, based on nearly 15 years of research, as a strictly academic psychologist, into the human motive that appears to be largely

From David C. McClelland, "Business Drive and National Achievement," *Harvard Business Review,* XL (1962), No. 4. Reprinted by permission of the author and the publisher.

responsible for economic growth—research which has recently been summarized in my book, entitled *The Achieving Society*.[1]

Since I am an egghead from way back, nothing surprises me more than finding myself rescuing the businessman from the academic trash heap, dusting him off, and trying to give him the intellectual respectability that he has had a hard time maintaining for the last 50 years or so. For the fact is that the businessman has taken a beating, not just from the Marxists, who pictured him as a greedy capitalist, and the social critics, who held him responsible for the Great Depression of the 1930's, but even from himself, deep in his heart.

•

But now the research I have done has come to the businessman's rescue by showing that everyone has been wrong, that it is *not* profit per se that makes the businessman tick but a strong desire for achievement, for doing a good job. Profit is simply one measure among several of how well the job has been done, but it is not necessarily the goal itself.

The Achievement Goal

But what exactly does the psychologist mean by the "desire for achievement"? How does he measure it in individuals or in nations? How does he know that it is so important for economic growth? Is it more important for businessmen to have this desire than it is for politicians, bishops, or generals? These are the kinds of questions which are answered at great length and with as much scientific precision as possible in my book. Here we must be content with the general outline of the argument, and develop it particularly as it applies to businessmen.

To begin with, psychologists try to find out what a man spends his time thinking and daydreaming about when he is not under pressure to think about anything in particular. What do his thoughts turn to when he is by himself or not engaged in a special job? Does he think about his family and friends, about relaxing and watching television, about getting his superior off his back? Or does he spend his time thinking and planning how he can "sell" a particular customer, cut production costs, or invent a better steam trap or toothpaste tube?

If a man spends his time thinking about doing things better, the psychologist says he has a concern for achievement. In other words, he cares about achievement or he would not spend so much time thinking about it. If he spends his time thinking about family and friends, he has a concern for affiliation; if he speculates about who is boss, he has a concern for power, and so on. What differs in my approach from the one used by many psycholo-

---

[1] David C. McClelland, *The Achieving Society* (Princeton, N.J.: D. Van Nostrand Co., 1961).

gists is that my colleagues and I have not found it too helpful simply to *ask* a person about his motives, interests, and attitudes. Often he himself does not know very clearly what his basic concerns are—even more often he may be ashamed and cover some of them up. So what we do is to try and get a sample of his normal waking thoughts by asking him just to tell a few stories about some pictures.

Stories within Stories

Let us take a look at some typical stories written by US business executives. These men were asked to look briefly at a picture—in this case, a man at a worktable with a small family photograph at one side—and to spend about five minutes writing out a story suggested by the picture. Here is a very characteristic story:

> The engineer is at work on Saturday when it is quiet and he has taken time to do a little daydreaming. He is the father of the two children in the picture —the husband of the woman shown. He has a happy home life and is dreaming about some pleasant outing they have had. He is also looking forward to a repeat of the incident which is now giving him pleasure to think about. He plans on the following day, Sunday, to use the afternoon to take his family for a short trip.

Obviously, no achievement-related thoughts have come to the author's mind as he thinks about the scene in the picture. Instead, it suggests spending time pleasantly with his family. His thoughts run along *affiliative* lines. He thinks readily about interpersonal relationships and having fun with other people. This, as a matter of fact, is the most characteristic reaction to this particular picture. But now consider another story:

> A successful industrial designer is at his "work bench" toying with a new idea. He is "talking it out" with his family in the picture. Someone in the family dropped a comment about a shortcoming in a household gadget, and the designer has just "seen" a commercial use of the idea. He has picked up ideas from his family—he is "telling" his family what a good idea it is, and "confidentially" he is going to take them on a big vacation because "their" idea was so good. The idea will be successful, and family pride and mutual admiration will be strengthened.

The author of this story maintains a strong interest in the family and in affiliative relationships, but has added an achievement theme. The family actually has helped him innovate—get a new idea that will be successful and obviously help him get ahead. Stories which contain references to good new ideas, such as a new product, an invention, or a unique accomplishment of any sort, are scored as reflecting a concern for achievement in the person who writes them. In sum, this man's mind tends to run most easily along the lines of accomplishing something or other. Finally, consider a third story:

> The man is an engineer at a drafting board. The picture is of his family. He has a problem and is concentrating on it. It is merely an everyday occurrence—a problem which requires thought. How can he get that bridge to take the stress of possible high winds? He wants to arrive at a good solution of the problem by himself. He will discuss the problem with a few other engineers and make a decision which will be a correct one—he has the earmarks of competence.

The man who wrote this story—an assistant to a vice president, as a matter of fact—notices the family photograph, but that is all. His thoughts tend to focus on the problem that the engineer has to solve. In the scant five minutes allowed, he even thinks of a precise problem—how to build a bridge that will take the stress of possible high winds. He notes that the engineer wants to find a good solution by himself, that he goes and gets help from other experts and finally makes a correct decision. These all represent different aspects of a complete achievement sequence—defining the problem, wanting to solve it, thinking of means of solving it, thinking of difficulties that get in the way of solving it (either in one's self or in the environment), thinking of people who might help in solving it, and anticipating what would happen if one succeeded or failed.

Each of these different ideas about achievement gets a score of + 1 in our scoring system so that the man in the last incident gets a score of + 4 on the scale of concern or need for achievement (conventionally abbreviated to n achievement). Similarly, the first man gets a score of − 1 for his story since it is completely unrelated to achievement, and the second man a score of + 2 because there are two ideas in it which are scorable as related to achievement.

Each man usually writes six such stories and gets a score for the whole test. The coding of the stories for "achievement imagery" is so objective that two expert scorers working independently rarely disagree. In fact, it has recently been programed for a high-speed computer that does the scoring rapidly, with complete objectivity and fairly high accuracy. What the score for an individual represents is the frequency with which he tends to think spontaneously in achievement terms when that is not clearly expected of him (since the instructions for the test urge him to relax and to think freely and rapidly).

Thinking Makes It So

What are people good for who think like this all the time? It doesn't take much imagination to guess that they might make particularly good business executives. People who spend a lot of their time thinking about getting ahead, inventing new gadgets, defining problems that need to be solved, considering alternative means of solving them, and calling in experts for help should also be people who in real life *do* a lot of these things or at the very best are readier to do them when the occasion arises.

I recognize, of course, that this is an assumption that requires proof. But, as matters turned out, our research produced strong factual support. . . . In three countries representing different levels and types of economic development managers or executives scored considerably higher on the average in achievement thinking than did professionals or specialists of comparable education and background. Take two democratic countries:

> In the United States the comparison was between matched pairs of unit managers and specialists of the same position level, age, educational background, and length of service in the General Electric Company. The managers spent more of their time in the test writing about achievement than the specialists did.
>
> The same was true of middle-level executives from various companies in Italy when contrasted with students of law, medicine, and theology who were roughly of the same intelligence level and social background.

In other words, it takes a concern for achievement to be a manager in a foreign country like Italy, for instance, just as it does in the United States. It is worth noting in passing, however, that the level of achievement thinking among Italian managers is significantly lower than it is among American managers—which, as will be shown later, quite probably has something to do with the lower level and rate of economic development in Italy.

What about a Communist country? The figures for Poland are interesting, because (1) the level of concern for achievement is about what it is in the United States and (2) even in businesses owned and operated by the state, as in Poland, managers tend to have a higher concern for achievement than do other professionals.

Another even more striking result, . . . is the fact that there is *no real difference* between the average *n* achievement score of managers working for the US government (9.3) and those in US private business generally (8.90). Apparently, a manager working for the Bureau of Ships in the Department of the Navy spends as much time thinking about achievement as his counterpart in Ford or Sears, Roebuck; government service does not weaken his entrepreneurial spirit. Whether he is able to be as effective as he might be in private business is another matter, not touched on here.

Careful quantitative studies of the prevalence of achievement concern among various types of executives also yield results in line with what one would expect. Thus, sales managers score higher than other types of managers do.

In general, more successful managers tend to score higher than do less successful managers (except in government service where promotion depends more on seniority). The picture is clear in small companies, where the president tends to score higher than his associates. In large companies, the picture is a little more complicated. Men in the lowest salary brackets (earning less than $20,000 a year) definitely have the lowest average n achievement scores, while those in the next bracket up ($20,000 to $25,000 a year) have the highest average n achievement level. Apparently an achievement concern helps one get out of the ranks of the lowest paid into a higher income bracket. But from there on, the trend fades. Men in the highest income brackets have a somewhat lower average concern for achievement, and apparently turn their thoughts to less achievement-oriented concerns. Possibly these men are doing well enough to relax a little.

•

Achieving Nations

If the theory underlying the experiments with determining n achievement in individuals is correct, then what is true for groups of individuals might well prove true for nations. Does a high achievement concern herald a nation's rise? Let's take a look at the facts.

Naturally, tests of individual businessmen in particular countries would not prove very much about the influence of achievement concern on the nation's success. However, we figured that, by coding popular literature of past and present, we could get a rough estimate of the strength of the concern for achievement in a given country at a given time period. So we took samples from various time periods of a wide variety of the most popular imaginative literature we could find—poems, songs, plays—and scored them for n achievement just as we had scored the simple stories written by individuals.

When we plotted the number of achievement ideas per hundred lines sampled in a given time period against economic indexes for the same time period, we got two curves that showed a very interesting relationship to each other. Normally, we found, a high level of concern for achievement is followed some 50 years or so later by a rapid rate of economic growth and prosperity. Such was certainly the case in ancient Greece and in Spain in the late Middle Ages. Furthermore, in both cases a decline in achievement concern was followed very soon after by a decline in economic welfare. The relationship between the two curves is shown most dramatically in Figure 20-1, which plots the data for the 300-year time span from Tudor times to the Industrial Revolution in England:

There were two waves of economic growth in this time period, one smaller one around 1600 and a much larger one around 1800 at the beginning of the Industrial Revolution. Each wave was preceded by a wave of concern for achievement reflected in popular literature, a smaller one prior to the growth spurt around 1600 and a larger one prior to the Industrial Revolution.

What clearer evidence could one ask for? What people are concerned about determines what they do, and what they do determines the outcome of history!

Present Confirms Past

In modern nations, too, the picture is very much the same. Children's stories used in public school textbooks proved to be the most standardized form of popular literature that we could get from a large number of different countries. As a matter of fact, the simple imaginative stories that every country uses to teach its children to read are very similar in format to the stories produced by individuals when we test them as described earlier, particularly if one concentrates as we did on second-, third-, and fourth-grade readers, where normally political influences are quite unimportant. The stories could be coded quite easily by the standard n achievement scoring system.

Growth rates had to be estimated from the only figures available that could be trusted on such a wide variety of countries—namely, the figures showing electric power consumption—but there is ample evidence to show that electricity consumed is probably the best single available index of gross national income in modern times.

The n scores, when compared with the subsequent rates of economic growth for various countries, confirm the findings of the historical studies to a surprising extent. The higher the n achievement level in the children's readers around 1925, the more rapid the subsequent rate of economic growth. (For 22 countries, the correlation was actually a substantial .53.) Furthermore, the higher the n achievement level in a country's children's readers around 1950, the more rapid its rate of growth between 1952-1958. In fact, of 20 countries above average in n achievement in 1950, 13 (or 65 per cent) showed a rapid rate of economic growth in 1952-1958. Whereas, of 19 low in n achievement, only 5 (or 26 per cent) achieved a rapid rate of growth.

Prediction Possibilities

How meaningful are these findings, especially when one realizes the crudity of the data? In a certain sense, the cruder one admits the data to be, the more remarkable the findings appear. After all, the data suggest that one could have got a pretty good line on the economic future of various countries by studying its stories for children in 1925—regardless of a major depression, a World War, and a host of other political and economic factors.

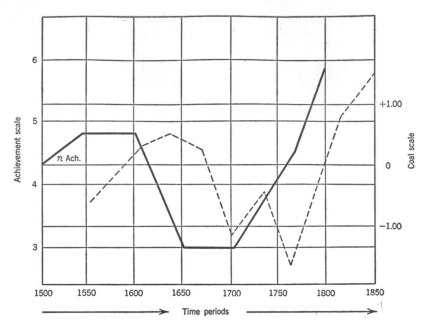

Achievement thinking (*n*. Ach.) = Mean number of achievement images per 100 lines.
Rate of industrial growth = Rate of gain in coal imports at London, as deviations from average trend (standard deviation units).

FIGURE 20-1. How achievement thinking expressed in English literature predicts the rate of industrial growth fifty years later.

Is it possible that we have stumbled on a way of predicting the future course of history? And from such an almost laughable source—stories for children—rather than the serious pronouncements of statesmen, generals, and economists? How is it possible?

The best interpretation of such findings would appear to run something as follows. The stories tell us what is on the minds of significant elites in the country, what these influential persons tend to think about most naturally, when they are "off guard," so to speak, and not under any particular pressure to think one thing or another. In this sense, the stories are exactly analogous to the ones written for us by individuals. If you ask a man whether he is interested in achievement, the chances are that he will tell you that of course he is. Similarly, if you were to ask a country's leaders whether they wanted their nation to forge ahead, they would find it unpatriotic to say no. But, regardless of what such leaders say in public, the stories in the children's readers of many nations will show whether their peoples' thoughts turn naturally to achievement or to matters other than achievement.

Here is an illustration. Take a simple story theme like one in which some children are building a boat. Such themes are frequently borrowed by one culture from another and appear in several different readers, but the way they are embroidered may be quite different and quite revealing. For example:

> In Country A, an *achievement*-oriented country, the emphasis is on making the boat, on constructing something that will work and not sink or tip over in a strong wind.
> In Country B, the emphasis may be on *affiliation,* on the fun that the children have in playing together to sail their boat. Here little may be said about the details of constructing a seaworthy craft and much about the personal interaction of the children.
> In Country C, the story may center on *power,* and describe how the children were organized to produce the boat. One boy might set himself up as a leader, coordinating the work of the other children and telling them what to do.

Apparently, what comes most readily to the minds of these authors—whether concepts of achievement, affiliation, or power—reflects sufficiently well what is on the minds of key people in the country. And not only will these concepts seem natural and pleasing to the readers of these stories but will determine what they spend their time doing in the years to come. Thus, if the stories stress achievement, it means that an entrepreneurial spirit is abroad in the land. It indicates that many key people are thinking in achievement terms even when they do not need to.

In a nation, a strong achievement orientation affects particularly the business or economic sector of the population. And if the entrepreneurial types are strongly motivated to do well, they apparently succeed in getting the economy moving at a faster rate. So the children's stories are a symptom of the quality or "drive" of the entrepreneurial sector of an economy.

Rising and Falling Nations

With this in mind it is interesting to look at scores for particular countries —if only to make a better guess as to where to invest one's money! A generation ago, the North European countries, particularly Sweden and England, were very high in *n* achievement, but both have fallen in the 1950's to well below average. Is it just a coincidence that one hears reports of stagnation or "maturity" in both economies? Are England's present difficulties the fault of outside circumstances, or do these difficulties stem from the fact that its citizens have lost their achievement drive? For some reason, the Central European countries—France, Germany, and Russia—were all low in achievement concern in 1925, but by the 1950's all had increased sharply.

The case of Russia is particularly critical for us. How does the United States stand in achievement motivation as compared to the USSR? According to a historical study, achievement concern in the United States increased regularly from 1800 to around 1890 but has decreased more or less regularly since, although there is a possibility that the decline has leveled off in the past 30 years. We are still above average and, in fact, were at approximately the same level as Russia in 1950, although we were probably on the way down while they were certainly on the way up.

From the point of view of this analysis, the argument as to whether a socialist or a free enterprise system is the better way of stimulating an economy has been based on a false premise all along. Americans claimed that the success of their economy resulted, naturally, from the free enterprise system. Then, when the Soviet Union scored successes in outer space and in other fields, the Russians immediately claimed these great economic and technological achievements stemmed from the superiority of their system.

Both contentions may well be wrong. Economic success and technological development depend on achievement motivation, and the rapid rate of Russian economic growth is due to an increase in her achievement concern just as ours was a generation or so earlier. There are other issues involved in comparing the two social systems, of course, but so far as this particular issue is concerned it has been misunderstood by both sides.

Need for Acceptance

There is one final question that must be answered before we move on. Is it possible that achievement motivation will be aroused in *any* nation which comes in contact with modern technology and vividly sees the opportunity for a better life? Can't achievement motivation be "borrowed" or assimilated from one nation to another? Are there not good illustrations of countries in which need for achievement has risen as they see more and more clearly the possibilities of growing and developing into modern, economically advanced nations? Are we just describing the "revolution of rising expectations" in fancy psychological jargon?

Opportunity is part of the story, of course. It does arouse people to act, but it arouses precisely those who have some need for achievement *already*. The soil must be ready for the seeds, if they are to grow. After all, many countries have been in touch with Western technology for generations—for example, the Islamic nations around the Mediterranean; yet they have been very slow to respond to the possibilities of a better life clearly presented to them all this time.

Consider, for example, a nation like Nigeria, which provides a good illustration of how opportunity and motivation must interact. Nigeria is essentially a federation of three regions, each of which is dominated by a different cultural group. Only one of these groups—the Yoruba—is known to be very high in need for achievement. In fact, long before the Yoruba had much contact with the West, this tribe was noted for its skill and interest in trade and native financial transactions. An indication of the validity of the achievement theory is shown by the fact that the Yoruba tribe, when exposed to new opportunities, produced a much stronger and more successful economic response than did the other tribes—as would be predicted. The regional bank operated by the Yoruba is in a much sounder position, for example, than the other two regional banks in Nigeria.

Opportunity challenges those who are achievement-oriented. Like two other groups high in *n* achievement, American Jews and American Catholics between the ages of 35 and 45, . . . the Yoruba reacted vigorously to develop economic opportunities as they became available. Exposure to economic and technological opportunities did not produce as vigorous a response from groups lower in *n* achievement in Nigeria any more than a similar exposure has done through the years to similar low *n* achievement groups in the United States.

What Can We Do?

Is it inevitable that the achievement concern shown by US citizens should continue to decline? Must we fade out in time as all other civilizations have in the past? Not if we understand what is happening and take steps to change it. Not if we move decisively and quickly to influence the sources of achievement concern in individuals and in our nation.

What are those sources? Clearly, not race or climate—those traditional external explanations of the superior energies of some nations. For Russia's *n* achievement level has increased decisively since 1925, while Sweden's and England's have dropped. Certainly there have been no equally decisive changes in the gene pools or the climates of those nations in that time period.

In fact, external factors are usually unimportant, though occasionally they may play a role, as they have in helping to create generally high levels of *n* achievement in immigrant countries like the United States, Canada, and Australia. Such nations tended to attract immigrants higher in *n* achievement, because:

1. They drew their population initially from countries that were higher in achievement concern than those from which the Latin American countries drew.

2. They provided a haven for many persecuted religious minorities whose achievement concern was very strong.

3. They did not provide as many opportunities for getting rich quick as did Mexico and Peru, for example, with their plentiful supplies of gold and silver.

In short, countries like the United States were lucky. The barrier to migration was so formidable that primarily those with high *n* achievement climbed it.

Historians have sometimes claimed that it was the great frontier in the United States that provided the challenge and stimulus to development. Nonsense. Great frontiers have existed and still exist in many South American countries without eliciting a similar response. It was the achievement-oriented

immigrants to America who regarded the frontier as a challenge to be overcome. It was not the frontier that made them achievement-oriented. Opportunities, like new frontiers, always exist, but it takes a certain kind of person
to see them and believe he can exploit them.

While our distance from Europe, our tolerance for religious minorities, our
good fortune in drawing immigrants initially from countries high in n achievement tended to ensure that we got more citizens with high achievement motivation, our later restrictive immigration policies have drastically reduced our
chances of continuing to receive such people. These policies continue to give
preference to immigrants from the North European countries, whose achievement drive has dropped significantly, and to restrict immigration from other
countries where the n achievement has been rising sharply. It would be a
tragic irony of history if in an endeavor to protect ourselves, we managed to
shut off the supply of that entrepreneurial spirit that made our country great!

Sources of Achievement

Where does strong achievement motivation come from? Values, beliefs,
ideology—these are the really important sources of a strong concern for
achievement in a country. Studies of the family have shown, for instance, that
for a boy three factors are important in producing high n achievement—
parents' high standards of achievement, warmth and encouragement, and a
father who is not dominating and authoritarian. Here is a typical study that
reveals this fact:

> A group of boys were blindfolded and asked to stack irregularly shaped
> blocks on top of each other with their left hands, at home in front of their
> parents. Separately, the mothers and fathers were asked how high they thought
> their sons could stack the blocks. Both parents of a boy with high n achieve-
> ment estimated that their boys should do better; they expected more of him
> than did the parents of a boy with low n achievement. They also encouraged
> him more and gave him more affection and reward while he was actually
> doing the task. Finally, the fathers of boys with high n achievement directed
> the behavior of their sons much less when they were actually stacking the
> blocks; that is, they told them less often to move their hands this way or that,
> to try harder, to stop jiggling the table, and so forth than did the fathers of
> boys with low n achievement.

Other studies have shown that fathers must be respected by their sons; but
after the boy is capable of achieving something for himself, his father must
stop directing every step he takes if the boy is to develop a strong concern for
achievement.

In a sense, however, these family studies only push the question further
back. Where did the parents get their standards? Why do some emphasize
achievement and affectionately reward self-reliance? Because, very simply,
they themselves believe in achievement for their family or for their political,

social, or religious group. For one reason or another they are caught up in some great wave of achievement ideology.

One of the paradoxes of history is that often the achievement concern was not itself initially directed toward business or economics. For instance, the two great waves of achievement concern in the history of England shown in Figure 20-1 were each associated with waves of Protestant reform or revival, whose explicit aims were not secular but strictly religious. The Methodists, for example, in the second wave of the English Protestant revival, stressed religious perfection in this life; yet even John Wesley recognized with some puzzlement that devout Methodists tended to get rich, a fact which he considered a handicap in attaining religious perfection.

But now we can understand what happened. The strong concern for Christian perfection in this world tended to produce an achievement orientation in Methodist parents and their sons that turned the boys toward business because, as we have shown above, an achievement concern is most easily satisfied in business. In our day, it is the secular religions of nationalism and communism that have placed the highest emphasis on achievement and tended to create higher levels of n achievement in underdeveloped and Communist countries. Communism lays the same claims to superiority as a means of salvation that Christianity once did. However wrong we may feel it to be, we must recognize that it tends to create a strong atmosphere of achievement that has important consequences for economic growth.

The Achievement Challenge

If we are to compete successfully with Russia in the economic sphere, we must develop an achievement ideology at least as strong as hers. If we are to help poor countries develop rapidly and become self-reliant, we must recognize that the first order of priority lies in fostering the entrepreneurial spirit in those countries, not in simply providing them with material capital or in meeting their physical needs.

Oddly enough, a businessman knows this about his own company. He knows that in the final analysis it is the spirit in the company that counts most—the entrepreneurial drive of the executives, the feeling of all that they are working together to achieve a common goal; it is not "hardware" that counts in the long run—the size and slickness of the plant or the money in the bank. These assets will melt away like snow in a hot sun without the proper achievement orientation in the company. Knowing this, the wise executive acts accordingly. He is concerned to keep the achievement orientation of the company alive by talking about its aims, by setting moderate but realizable goals for himself and his associates, by assigning personal responsibility, by making sure that people know how well they are doing, by selecting executives with high n achievement or by developing it in those who need it.

What is true for a business is also true for a country, but this is not widely recognized. And we must realize that it is important to foster the achieving spirit not only at home but abroad if we are to be effective as a nation. American foreign policy is currently based on two main strategies: (a) the provision of political freedom and (b) material aid. Both are excellent goals, but they are not enough. How long would a company last if its chief goals were freedom from interference by others and freedom from want? It needs positive, specific goals such as a more effective marketing program, or a strict cost reduction program; something dynamic is necessary to keep a company —and a country—alive and growing.

Over and over again we have failed to learn the lesson that political freedom without a strong drive for progress is empty and impossible to maintain for long. China was politically free under Chiang Kai-shek, but it lacked the dynamic of a really self-sacrificing achievement effort until it was taken over by the Communists. Unless we learn our lesson and find ways of stimulating that drive for achievement under freedom in poor countries, the Communists will go on providing it all around the world. We can go on building dikes to maintain freedom and impoverishing ourselves to feed and arm the people behind those dikes, but only if we develop the entrepreneurial spirit in those countries will we have a sound foreign policy. Only then can they look after their own dikes and become economically self-sufficient.

Compare India and China, for example. Despite newspaper reports to the contrary, economic experts assure us that China is developing much more rapidly economically today than is India. Why? Is it because the West has given less material help to India than the Communist world has to China? Probably not. Is it because there is less political freedom in India than in China? Certainly not. Yet if the keystones of our foreign aid policy are the ensuring of political freedom and the granting of economic aid, these measures are clearly not doing very well as far as developing India is concerned. Russia has apparently exported something more important to China—namely, an achievement dynamic that has galvanized the whole country. There is absolutely no evidence that this dynamic needs to be associated with regimentation and lack of personal freedom as it is in China, for the United States had this dynamic once, still has quite a lot of it, and could export it more effectively—if we really tried.

•

If there is one thing that all this research has taught me, it is that men can shape their own destiny, that external difficulties and pressures are not nearly so important in shaping history as some people have argued. It is how people respond to those challenges that matters, and how they respond depends on how strong their concern for achievement is. So the question of what happens to our civilization or to our business community depends quite literally on how much time tens of thousands or even millions of us spend thinking about achievement, about setting moderate achievable goals, taking calculated risks, assuming personal responsibility, and finding out how well we have done our job. The answer is up to us.

PART III

SPHERES OF CHANGE

The Modern Society

CHAPTER 21

Introduction

With all due respect for the differences among societies, it can be said that they all do seem to change from a traditional to a modern type. Once all societies were "traditional"; probably one day they will all be "modern." It cannot be denied that, for the past three centuries or so, a number of nations have been the forerunners of modernization, the first to reach a new type of social structure which many other countries now seem bent on acquiring. This part of the volume is devoted to the examination of the emergence of modern society, not on the general societal level—this was discussed earlier, for instance in the work of Toennies—but in one social sphere after another.

In the most general terms, the transition from traditional to modern society involves: (1) a demographic revolution, in which both the death rate and the birth rate sharply decline; (2) a decrease in the size, scope, and pervasiveness of the family; (3) an opening of the stratification system to much higher rates of mobility; (4) a transition from a tribal or feudal structure to a bureaucracy of the democratic or totalitarian type; (5) a decline in the influence of religion; (6) the separation of education from family and community life, the lengthening and enrichment of the educational process, the development of schools and universities and, more recently, the enormous spread of education, from a monopoly of the few to a property of the many; (7) the growth of a "mass culture" nourished by mass education and the development of mass media of communication; (8) the emergence of a "market economy," and, even more important, of industrialization. (Economic institutions, not discussed in this section, are extensively reviewed in the next.)

But even as these revolutionary changes go on, as traditional societies become modern, important changes are taking place within modern society itself. These may be in line with the major modernization trends, or they may be smaller cross- and counter-currents in the major streams of history.

For instance, Kingsley Davis' discussion of the demographic aspects of modernization points to the radical decline in the death rate which, in

Western societies, was followed by a drastic decline in the birth rate. The "population explosion," which occurs when the decline in the birth rate lags way behind the decline in the death rate, has been a crucial problem for countries now in the process of modernization (discussed in the next part of the volume). Western countries, however, did not suffer from this problem, because they began with a more favorable population–resources ratio, so that resources increases always outweighed population increases; moreover, in later periods, the birth rate declined. Some of them—France, for instance—were even concerned with the opposite problem, the birth rate declining more rapidly than the death rate. This trend, had it continued, would have led to the slow extinction of Western society. Actually, however, after World War II, a cross-current set in, when an upsurge of the birth rate led to a population increase in Western countries. Of course premodernization birth rates were not regained; the major demographic trend of modernization was somewhat offset but not reversed.

In comparison with primitive or traditional society, the importance of the family in modern society has largely declined. With modernization, the nuclear family has been disconnected from the extended one, and kinship ties have been greatly weakened. The family is no longer the unit of production nor the major agency of education. The significance of familial values, too, has been greatly reduced. Still, as can be seen from Burgess' discussion, this has not led toward the extinction of the family. The economic and educational functions of the family have declined, but its importance as a source of companionship and emotional security in a mobile and competitive society has, if anything, increased.

In traditional societies, most people die in the social positions in which they are born. People tend to accept their positions as God-given and do not attempt to change them. Some channels of vertical mobility exist in most traditional societies—for instance, the Church in medieval society—but, as a rule, society is stratified into castes or estates, with fairly rigid social, cultural, economic, and often legal barriers. Modernization involves the opening up of the stratification system. In modern societies, many people die in higher, some in lower, statuses than they were born into; a large proportion of any social group moves upward or downward; and the social groups themselves change their place in the social structure. In the United States, for instance, ethnic groups have moved up the ladder as assimilation progressed, and newer groups have entered at the bottom. Barber's discussion centers around changes within two premodern systems of stratification approximating the "closed" type and around changes within two modern systems of stratification approximating the "open" type. It also deals with the revolutionary changes experienced in the transition from the first to the second type. As we see from these discussions, modernization involves a major trend toward the opening up of the class structure.

The picture is less clearcut so far as the changes within modern society are concerned. Some observers claim that, in the United States for instance, mobility has been diminishing—among other reasons, because largescale immigration has ceased and the economy has not been expanding at the previous rate. Barber, however, points out that what may seem a reversal of the trend is merely a consolidation of its achievements; several social processes are presently going on which serve to "strengthen the American open-class stratification system." But though the channels of mobility are still opening up, this of course is not to suggest that the opening of these channels can continue at anything like its initial pace. According to this view, the major trend that set in with modernization was not reversed or even stopped, but did slow down to some extent.

The degree of mobility directly affects the dynamics of politics. As Mosca points out, in each society there is a ruling minority and a majority that is being ruled. However, the structure of this ruling class as well as the criteria of recruitment into it change with the changes in its predominant societal function. One change that occurred in premodern times was the shift from military skills, first to land-ownership and then to wealth, as criteria of access to the ruling class. While wealth may still facilitate recruitment to the ruling class (or political elite) even in modern times, one of the main characteristics of modernization in the political sphere is that access to the political elite has become open to wider and wider strata of the population. In addition, the potential political power of nonpoliticians has increased enormously. This is true in modern democratic as well as nondemocratic countries, where it becomes evident from the constant flow of communication oriented toward the population at large to sustain its commitment to the regime.

Another major aspect of modernization in the political sphere has been the emergence of the modern state, whose boundaries mostly correspond to those of national identification. Scattered and loosely related smaller units have become integrated into largescale, tightly-knit political entities. The trend of modernization has been one of an ever-increasing concentration of power in the hands of a state that carries out and regulates more and more functions. This is closely connected with a drastic change in the mode of organization of the political structure: the transition from feudalism to bureaucracy. Political bureaucracy, Mosca suggests, first came into being with absolutism, but since then it has been enormously developed and elaborated, and has evolved into the democratic and totalitarian bureaucratic states.

There seems to be no reversal of these trends with the further developments within modern society. However, they do appear to have mostly exhausted themselves. Thus, the scope of political participation has been widened so far that there is little room for further expansion other than on the racial front. Similarly, the process of bureaucratization can no longer proceed at the same rate. As far as the process of state planning and regulation is concerned, there seems to be a movement in opposite directions in the two major sub-types of modern societies: while totalitarian societies, especially those whose industrialization is advanced, seem to somewhat reduce the very pronounced dominance of the state, democratic societies, especially those of the welfare type, seem slowly to increase the comparatively limited role of government; though even at its most extreme, the power of the government in democratic societies is much smaller than in totalitarian ones.

With the advent of modern society, religion retreated so far so fast that it was expected to dissappear. The influence religion had exerted in various social spheres rapidly declined; the proportion of religious people in society diminished; the intensity of religious feelings decreased. The main value system of modern society, the major focus of identification, became secular, of the national-historical type. But, as Herberg points out, over the last decades, especially in the United States, these trends of modernization were largely stopped and to a degree reversed. The number of Americans affiliated with religious bodies has been growing; militant anti-religiousness has practically disappeared; the scope of religion's influence in society has been broadened. This is usually referred to as a "religious revival," although, as Herberg suggested, present-day religion has become largely man-centered, a way of "belonging" socially, and a way of attaining peace of mind. It has little in common with the religion of yesteryear. One can hardly expect society to return to the religious state of premodern times, but on the other hand, within modern society, the trend toward more and more secularization has been arrested and to some degree reversed. It has become increasingly clear that religion is not about to disappear.

One of the unique features of modern society is its vast system of formal education. In this sphere, modernization has meant the vesting of education in specialized institutions, schools of all types. As can be seen from Drucker's discussion, in recent years this kind of education has vastly expanded. Today, more students study more subjects for more years in more schools than ever before. There has been an enormous increase in high school and college attendance in the United States; the educational revolution in Russia has been even more explosive.

The fact that education is no longer exclusive to an elite but has been opened to the masses, as well as the general trend in American society to emphasize adjustment to the group over achievement in work (see Riesman's discussion, Part V), resulted in a certain relaxation of academic standards in many schools and colleges. This trend has been reversed to some extent in the last few years, especially after Russia's achievements in space threw into dramatic relief the importance of high standards of education for a nation's stature. While education can never again become the refined leisure activity of a cultured minority, techniques are being developed to combine mass education with high standards. A combination of screening through high tuition fees in combination with fellowships, honor programs, tutoring, specialized schools, and other devices make it easier for education to aim both for quantity and for quality.

In the sphere of culture, some of the problems and patterns of modern education are repeated on the adult level. Like education, culture in today's sense was once confined to a minority. With the development of mass education and of mass media of communication, there came into being what has been widely called "mass culture," passive submission to undemanding entertainment. While mass culture certainly is an advance in comparison to previous periods, when the majority of the population had little if any access to any culture whatever, it is often held to block the way for the masses to attain higher levels of culture and, indeed, to endanger the very existence of a higher culture.

In addition to the major revolution out of which mass culture was born, important changes have occurred within mass culture, or parts of it, since its emergence. Lowenthal, examining biographies in popular magazines, traces a shift in emphasis from "heroes of production" to "idols of consumption," drawn predominantly from the world of entertainment. We see from this how the content of mass culture itself reflects the growing pervasiveness of mass culture. This change in the focus of hero-worship, from production to consumption, and the growing pervasiveness of "entertainment," though discerned more than twenty years ago, have immediate relevance today: they prefigure the general character change from "innerdirectedness" to "otherdirectedness" that Riesman discusses below. But it seems that in this area, too, some cross-currents have to be recognized. While the media of mass communication are utilized largely for the dissemination of mass culture, these same media also spread genuine culture. Radio has made it possible for much larger audiences to hear classical music. Many newspapers give accurate and thorough information on political developments and also help readers to get acquainted with the latest works of literature. Television, too, is in the process of developing an increasing number of educational programs. Since education is constantly expanding, it is possible that a larger and larger number of people will be able (and hopefully also willing) to take advantage of these opportunities. Thus, while improved communications have brought pseudoculture to the masses, these same technological developments have made it possible for more people than ever before to gain the real thing.

The general pattern of the changes, then, seems to suggest that the processes of modernization, at least in some Western countries and especially in the United States, have been more or less "completed," that in a sense the dramatic changes of modernization have exhausted themselves. Many trends have been slowed down or halted; and in some areas, in which modernization has been "overdone," some limited "correcting" cross-currents have set in. Obviously no society can maintain itself if its birth rate falls below its death rate, hence the importance of the increase in the birth rate in Western countries. The decline in the educational, economic, and other functions of the family has been compensated for by an ascent of its "companionship" function. Though many people desire absolute equality, it is questionable whether this can ever be attained. At any rate, the trend toward the opening up of channels of mobility, if not reversed or halted, has slowed down. The revival of religion may suggest that there are certain basic questions—especially concerning the creation of the universe and the meaning of death—that no secular ideology can answer satisfactorily. In education and culture there has been no reversal of the trend of encompassing larger and larger numbers; rather a balancing trend has set in, consisting of the attempt to combine quantity and quality. In politics, the trend of bureaucratization has slowed down. The movement toward higher concentration of functions in the hands of the state continues in democratic countries, but has, to a limited extent, been reversed in totalitarian ones.

In general, old (traditional) structures have been replaced by new (modern) ones, after which some further changes on a smaller scale have modified this trend. In other words, since the old equilibrium was disrupted and a new one came into being, further changes have tended to restore balance where disproportionate changes made for excessive strains. These changes may be viewed as re-equilibrating processes but not as processes pushing for return to the old traditional equilibrium.

While some people may evaluate the slowing down and the occasional reversals of the larger trends as consolidating the gains of modernization, others may view them as "reactionary." In any case, we do not wish to imply that a perfect balance has been reached, making for permanent stability. But for the near future, modern societies seem comparatively stable, and—barring a major nuclear disaster—unlikely to change rapidly on a large scale.

CHAPTER 22

KINGSLEY DAVIS

The Demographic Transition

The Revolutionary Decline in Mortality

The most significant and farreaching modern population trend is the worldwide decline in the death rate. This was not only the *first* major change to be observed in the evolution of the modern demographic cycle, but also the one that has triggered most of the changes, for it was upon mortality that the technological and economic revolution of modern times had its first and main demographic impact.

As early as the eighteenth century in northwestern Europe, the death rate was noticeably undergoing a gradual though fluctuating retreat. The drop became faster and steadier in the nineteenth century, but did not reach its most precipitous fall until early in the present century. (*See* Table 22-1.) A notion of how drastic the reduction was is seen in the fact that in five west European countries, the number of people surviving *to age 60* out of each 1,000 born was greater in the 1940's than the number surviving *to age fifteen* in the 1840's (763 as against 674). Or, to put it another way, in the 1840's, in these five countries on the average, half the population was dead by age 44½, whereas in the 1940's half had not died until age 73½.[1] Among eleven Western countries for which long series of life-tables are available, seven had their most rapid short-run gains in life-expectancy after 1915, three had their most rapid gains between 1900 and 1915, and one fell into the first period with respect to males and into the second period with respect to females. None of the eleven countries had its most rapid extension of life-expectancy prior to 1900.

From Kingsley Davis, "Social Demography," *The Voice of America Forum Lectures,* Behavioral Science Series 17, pp. 3-12. Reprinted by permission of the author and the publisher. This paper was originally prepared for use in the Voice of America's program titled "Forum—The Arts and Sciences in Mid-Century America."

[1] Derived from George J. Stolnitz, "A Century of International Mortality Trends: I," *Population Studies,* IX (1955), 29. The countries are Belgium, England and Wales, France, Netherlands, and Sweden.

The gains in life-expectancy in the Western industrial nations, though unprecedented at the time, are now being eclipsed by faster improvement in the underdeveloped countries. Most of these enjoyed a gradual lowering of mortality prior to World War I, but the fall was not generally remarkable until after that conflict. Since then the drop in the death rate has accelerated in a spectacular way, until it has become faster than anything ever experienced by the industrial nations. For seventeen underdeveloped countries for which fairly reliable death rates are obtainable, for example, the decline in the average crude death rate in 1940-1959, as against 1920-1939, was 37 per cent.[2] This is nearly three times the drop found in the four Scandinavian countries between the same periods (*See* Table 22-1), and it is greater than any preceding drop in those four countries as between two successive twenty-year periods.

Causes of the Decline in Mortality

The more gradual drop in death rates in the industrializing Western nations arose from a basically different set of causes from those currently operating in backward lands. In northwestern Europe and among the northwest-European peoples overseas, the mortality gains were comparatively slow because they depended on self-generated economic and scientific advance. Until late in the nineteenth century the main factor was economic—improvement in commerce, agriculture, and manufacturing—which provided a higher level of living, better housing, education, sanitation, etc. The quickening of the pace of death control around 1900 was due to the fact that, along with continued economic improvement, discoveries in scientific medicine and public health were at last beginning to yield fruit in the massive saving of lives. However, the scientific discoveries had to be slowly invented and applied.

In today's underdeveloped countries, on the other hand, the spectacular declines of mortality are being made by importing the latest medical discoveries from the most industrialized countries, usually with the help of medical personnel and funds from the latter nations. Modern techniques, applied on a mass basis under government sponsorship, have achieved almost miraculous results in the control of infectious diseases and other ailments among backward peoples. These results do not depend on economic development within the areas in question, because funds and personnel can be brought in from outside. They do not depend on scientific discoveries

---

[2] The countries used in the analysis were Barbados, Ceylon, Costa Rica, Cyprus, El Salvador, Fiji Islands, Jamaica, Malaya, Mauritius, Mexico, Panama, Philippines, Puerto Rico, Surinam, Taiwan, Thailand, and Trinidad-Tobago. These countries are still, for the most part, very underdeveloped economically.

within the areas in question, because the research is done in the laboratories of America, Australia, and Europe. This is why the extremely fast drop in the death rate in the world's backward areas is occurring at a more primitive stage of economic development than it did in the Western industrial nations. As noted above, the most rapid death-rate declines in the latter countries came after 1900, a time when these countries were already industrialized and when their birth rates had already started down. In the backward lands today, death rates are being brought down at a faster clip among peoples who in some cases are scarcely removed from savagery and in other cases are overwhelmingly agrarian.

The speed of the drop in the death rate of nonindustrial countries can be seen by comparison with Japan, the latest country to industrialize. One would expect that, owing to the recency of Japan's industrialization, rapid economic improvement *plus* twentieth-century medical advance would enable her to reduce her mortality faster than the older industrial nations did at a similar stage of development. And this is true. Her average death rate in 1940-1959 (despite her war losses) was 37 per cent lower than her average rate in 1920-1939. This, it will be recalled, is exactly the percentage reduction made by our seventeen underdeveloped countries between the two twenty-year periods! The fact that countries like El Salvador, Fiji, and Mauritius can make gains in lengthening life as fast as a rapidly industrializing country shows that such gains are now independent of local economic development.

Demographic Consequences of Death Control

The first, most obvious result of the dramatic lowering of mortality was rapid population growth. Again, however, the story in the underdeveloped countries of today differs from what it was earlier in the currently advanced nations. Since the death rate fell first among the industrializing West European peoples, these peoples experienced a remarkable colonization of new regions and continents. The same social and economic advances that were giving them control over deaths were giving them dominance over more backward races. But another consequence of their falling mortality was a drop in their birth rates. The latter began to turn down noticeably in the 1870's, long before the death rate had reached its present low level and before it had exhibited its fastest drop. The reason was that since the gains in saving lives were made primarily in infancy and early childhood, parents were having to contend with larger numbers of living children than they had ever had to contend with before, precisely at a time when, with industrialization and urbanization, large broods were more of a handicap. Accordingly, people reduced their procreation, partly by postponing marriage and partly by practicing abortion or contraception within marriage. Eventually, from about 1900 to 1932 (depending on the particular country) the birth rate in the industrial nations fell even faster than the death rate, thus decreasing the speed of population growth.

In the 1930's, then, it looked as though the industrial nations had passed through a cycle of rapid population growth and were heading for a normal condition of virtual demographic stability. It was naïvely believed that this might be the transition through which the whole world would move in an orderly fashion.

But two things happened to change this outlook: first, the birth rate went up again in the industrial nations themselves; second, the death rate went down faster in the underdeveloped nations than it had done previously among the advanced European peoples and at a more primitive stage of economic and social development. As a consequence of the way death control was being brought to backward regions, their birth rates were not dropping; and this, with the extremely rapid fall in mortality, gave them the fastest rates of population growth ever experienced by whole nations. The total result, since 1940, has been an increase in the world's population so unprecedented and unpredicted that it has been appropriately called a "population explosion." With more than 2.9 billion today, humanity is multiplying at better than 2 per cent per year. This rate, if continued, will double the population every 35 years.

Most of the world's increase is occurring in precisely the areas least able to accommodate increased numbers, the poorer and more underdeveloped regions. Between 1920 and 1960, for example, the increase in the world's underdeveloped regions amounts to 70.5 per cent, as compared to 41.1 per cent in the industrialized regions.

Social and Economic Consequences

Rapid population growth is impeding economic development in the underdeveloped regions by causing the gains in national income to be used to maintain swelling numbers of people at the old level of living, rather than to improve the level of living itself. Furthermore, when mortality is reduced rapidly without any reduction in the high birth rate the resulting population is abnormally young. Costa Rica, whose death rate dropped 50 per cent during the last thirty years, has 105 children aged 0-14 for each hundred adults aged 20-59; whereas Belgium has only 41. Such young populations mean a heavy child-dependency ratio, added to the burden of total population increase. An underdeveloped country tends to compensate by starting children to work at an early age, a practice that lowers the productivity of labor because education is cut short. The entry of large numbers of youth into the labor market each year tends to bring largescale unemployment and political instability. Costa Rica, for example, has one-fourth as many youths in the five-year age span fifteen to nineteen as she has adults in the forty-year age span 20-59; whereas Belgium has a little more than one-tenth as many.

It seems that the agrarian nations must make a choice between rapid population growth and rapid economic progress. If they decide to cut their population growth, it will presumably be by way of reducing the birth rate. . . . There is every indication from field studies that peasant women do not like having a large number of children, especially when most of them remain alive. All such studies show that on the average women prefer only two, three, or four children, not five to fifteen. Peasant men, however, since the burden of children does not fall directly on them, are less resistant to having large numbers of children except when hard-pressed economically. Actually, as long as the costs of children impinge directly on the parents, the economic incentive to limit offspring is mounting, because the aspirations of the people in peasant lands are running ahead of the actual economic growth. Insofar as the costs fall on the joint family (as in certain traditional social systems) or on the government (as in the welfare state), the potential parent can reproduce without economic penalty. No state has yet seen fit, however, to relieve parents of all the economic costs of reproduction, much less the noneconomic costs in terms of energy and inconvenience.

As the aspirations of the agrarian peoples rise while their economic growth falters, the burden of unusually large families will tend to force parents to reduce their reproduction. If they are encouraged in this by educational measures, by the availability of birth control devices, measures, and by a system that holds parents responsible for their children, the lag of the birth rate behind the declining death rate will be less than otherwise, and the alternative of increasing the death rate will more likely be avoided.

But even if the birth rate around the world is reduced, the question still remains, "Will it be reduced enough to match the low mortality?" Such a depressed birth rate would entail a heavy sacrifice. The sacrifice is commonly thought to consist in the abandonment of traditional values extolling large families; yet it must be emphasized that under conditions of high mortality—the normal situation during nearly all of human history—families were *not* large despite the high birth rate. There were, to be sure, large *households* in many societies, but this was due to living arrangements of kinsmen, not to the high birth rate. There was also a wider *range* in the number of living children than there is today, since couples varied sharply in their biological fecundity and in their capacity to keep their infants alive. The price of adjusting fertility to low mortality is therefore not small numbers of living children, for this has been the normal situation of mankind. Rather, what would be sacrificed is the *chance* of having a sizable family and the *proportion of life* spent with children. If the incidence of death falls so low that most couples need have only two children to replace the population, and if the average lifetime is extended to 83 years, each parent will spend only about a fourth of his adulthood with a child of his own under age fifteen in the household, and only about a tenth of it with a child under five. In view of the love for children, which cannot be unquestionably attributed to culture, one can question whether people will make such a sacrifice.

Perhaps an even greater cost of really low fertility is its effect on the age structure. Although lessening the child-dependency burden, it would enormously expand the old-age-dependency problem. Already, in countries where the birth rate has long been rather low, the population has become topheavy with oldsters. France, for example, now has 33 persons aged 60 or over for each 100 aged 20-59. In the future, as life-expectancy is continually lengthened, a rate of reproduction low enough just to replace the population will yield a higher ratio of elderly. For instance, the life-expectancy of white females in the north central region of the United States is now 73 years. If the whole population reached this figure and maintained it indefinitely, and if the birth rate constantly matched the death rate, the United States would have 45 persons aged 60, and 48 under fifteen, for each hundred aged 20 through 59. If we imagine future mortality improving by an orderly continuance of the fall in age-specific rates observed between 1900 and 1950, until the life-expectancy at birth reaches 83 years, a birth rate that just sustained the population would produce an age structure with 60 persons aged 60-plus, and 38 children under fifteen, for each hundred aged 20-59. This would be nearly double the old-age-dependency ratio in France, which thinks it has too old a population now.

Partly because the price is so high, no nation has yet reduced its reproductive effort sufficiently to match regularly a low modern death rate. Although such a reduction is not inconceivable (especially under radically new institutional arrangements), it should not be complacently assumed to be inevitable or probable or to entail no cost.

National Population Policies

. . . Numerous governments have tried to influence demographic behavior, but the particular nations concerned and the nature of their efforts have shifted markedly. During the 1930's the industrial nations became worried about their low birth rates, and some of them—notably Sweden, Germany, Italy, and France—adopted policies designed to stimulate reproduction. Although the more radical measures for this purpose have now been abandoned, family-allowance legislation and other measures favorable to reproduction are now common, being found in nations as diverse as Russia, Canada, Belgium, and Britain.

This governmental effort to raise the birth rate was based on fallacious reasoning. The birth rates of the 1930's were low, to be sure, but it was a mistake to assume that they would stay that way unless measures were taken. The subsequent baby-boom in industrial countries, especially after World War II, was not the result of the depression-born pronatalist policies, for it occurred in countries that had no such policies. It was mainly a result of prosperity and full employment permitting couples to get married and to have children. Although in most European countries the baby-boom has subsided in recent years, it has remained at such a high level in the new-world industrial countries (Canada, U.S.A., Australia, New Zealand) that, with a continued influx of immigrants, they are still experiencing very fast rates of population growth, their combined population being expected to increase by 22 per cent from 1960 to 1975. In both the old-world and the new-world industrial countries, rising levels of living are added to population growth to create ever more congestion. Escape from the nuisances created by crowding—noise, smog, traffic—cannot be found, because there is not enough space. In the United Kingdom, for example, there are 62 motor vehicles per square mile of land; in the United States there are 22 and in France 25. For this reason, even in the most prosperous countries, voices are beginning to be heard which urge the official encouragement of birth control.

So far, however, the only industrial country that has really carried out an anti-natalist policy is Japan. There the government's permissiveness with respect to abortion and its sponsorship of birth control clinics and family-planning education have helped reduce the crude birth rate 26 per cent below its lowest wartime bottom (1945) and 50 per cent below its postwar peak (1947). This is probably the sharpest birth-rate decline ever experienced by a large nation.

Some of the underdeveloped countries, worried by rapid population growth in the face of poverty and chronic overcrowding, have adopted policies designed to diminish births. The most successful of these has been Puerto Rico, where the birth rate, though still high, has steadily declined since the postwar peak in 1947. Red China vigorously pursued such a policy for awhile and still takes certain measures that lessen reproduction, such as the de-emphasis on the family and the use of women in the labor force. India is strengthening her nationwide anti-natalist policy, and countries such as Mauritius, Bermuda, El Salvador, Haiti, and the Federation of the West Indies are considering a similar policy.

The limitation of population growth, however, is not easy. The reduction of mortality in underdeveloped countries has been so fast and so unconnected with fundamental economic and social change in those countries, that parents cannot be expected yet to limit their offspring by their own efforts. In trying to hasten such an adjustment, no government can succeed by appealing to patriotism or to enlightened awareness of the population problem. It has to influence behavior by altering the conditions. In general, the alterations consist in increasing the effectiveness and availability of contraceptives and/or abortion and sterilization, increasing the participa-

tion of women in the labor force (making them not only personally ambitious but also economically independent), allowing the costs of children to
fall on the parents themselves rather than upon the joint family or the
state, and raising the parents' aspirations for their children's future. These
are conservative measures. If they do not succeed, some governments may
eventually consider radical means.

There is, of course, the possibility that the world's present climatic population increase will be stopped by a rise in mortality rather than a drop in
fertility. The death rate can rise faster and higher than the birth rate,
wiping out whole populations in a matter of days or weeks. . . .

Table **22-1**

Average Crude Death Rate in Four Scandinavian Countries, 1740 to
1958[a]

Period	Average Annual Deaths per 1000 Inhabitants[b]	Per Cent Drop from Prior Period[c]
1740-1759	29.1	——
1760-1779	28.1	3.6
1780-1799	26.2	7.2
1800-1819	25.8	1.6
1820-1839	23.0	12.1
1840-1859	21.4	7.4
1860-1879	20.9	2.3
1880-1899	18.0	15.6
1900-1919	15.4	17.2
1920-1939	11.7	31.3
1940-1959	10.2	13.3

[a] The countries are Denmark, Finland, Norway, Sweden.

[b] Average rates for the eighteenth century calculated from H. Gille, "Demographic History of the
Northern European Countries in the Eighteenth Century," *Population Studies*, III (1949), 65.

[c] Crude death rates do not afford an accurate basis for comparing the force of mortality from one
time to another, because they are influenced by the age structure independently of mortality. The
effect of changes in the age structure is particularly important when birth rates are declining rapidly.
However, since the alterations in the crude rate from one twenty-year period to the next are not
markedly distorted in this way, the percentage changes give a fair index of the rate of change with
time.

CHAPTER 23

ERNEST W. BURGESS

The Family in
a Changing Society

Never before in human history has any society been composed of so many divergent types of families. Families differ by section of the country, by communities within the city, by ethnic and religious groups, by economic and social classes, and by vocations. They are different according to the family life-cycle and by number and role of family members. They vary by the locus of authority within the family and by widely different styles of life. There are families of the Hopi Indian (primitive maternal), of the old Amish of Pennsylvania (patriarchal), of the Ozark mountaineers (kinship control), of the Italian immigrant (semipatriarchal), the rooming-house (emancipated), the lower middle class (patricentric), the apartment house (egalitarian), and the suburban (matricentric).

Unity in Diversity

With due recognition of all the diversity among American families, it is still possible and desirable to posit a concept of *the* American family. In a sense this is an ideal construction, in that it attempts to concentrate attention upon what is distinctive about families in the United States in comparison with those of other countries. These differential characteristics are largely in terms of process rather than of structure, and represent relative rather than absolute differences from families in other cultures. Chief among these distinctive trends are the following:

1. *Modifiability and adaptability* in response to conditions of rapid social change;

From Ernest W. Burgess, *The American Journal of Sociology*, LIII (1948), No. 6, pp. 417-422. Copyright 1958 by University of Chicago Press, and reprinted by permission of the author and the University of Chicago Press.

2. *Urbanization,* not merely in the sense that the proportion of families living in cities is increasing, but that rural as well as urban families are adopting the urban way of life;

3. *Secularization,* with the declining control of religion and with the increasing role of material comforts, labor-saving devices and other mechanical contrivances, like the automobile, the radio, and television;

4. *Instability,* as evidenced by the continuing increase in divorce, reaching in 1945 the proportion of one for every three marriages;

5. *Specialization,* on the functions of the giving and receiving of affection, bearing and rearing of children, and personality development, which followed the loss of extrinsic functions, such as economic production, education, religious training, and protection;

6. The *trend to companionship,* with emphasis upon consensus, common interests, democratic relations, and the personal happiness of family members.

•

The Family and Society

With all the variations among American families, it is apparent that they are all in greater or lesser degree in a process of change toward an emerging type of family that is perhaps most aptly described as the "companionship" form. This term emphasizes the point that the essential bonds in the family are now found more and more in the interpersonal relationship of its members, as compared with those of law, custom, public opinion, and duty in the older institutional forms of the family.

Not that companionship, affection, and happiness are absent from the institutional family. They exist there in greater or lesser degree, but they are not its primary aims. The central objectives of the institutional family are children, status, and the fulfillment of a social and economic function in society.

The distinctive characteristics of the American family, as of the family in any society, are a resultant of (1) survivals from earlier forms of the family, developing under prior or different economic and social conditions; (2) the existing social and economic situation; and (3) the prevailing and evolving ideology of the society.

Survivals

The American family has had a rich and varied historical heritage, with strands going back to all European countries and to the religious ideologies of the Catholic, Jewish, and Protestant faiths. What is distinctive in the American family, however, has resulted from its role, first, in the early rural situation of the pioneer period and, second, in the modern urban environment.

The growth of democracy in the family proceeded in interaction with the development of democracy in society. Pioneer conditions promoted the emancipation both of women and of youth from subordination to the family and to the community. Arrangements for marriage passed from the supervision of parents into the control of young people.

The rural family of the United States before World War I, however, had progressed toward, but had not achieved, democratic relations among its members. Control was centered in the father and husband as the head of the farm economy, with strict discipline and with familistic objectives still tending to be dominant over its members. Children were appraised in terms of their value for farm activities, and land tenure and farm operations were closely interrelated with family organization and objectives.

The Evolving Urban Environment

The modern city, growing up around the factory and serving as a trade center for a wide area, provided the necessary conditions for the development of the distinctive characteristics of the American family. It still further promoted the equality of family members and their democratic interrelationships, initiated and fostered to a certain degree by the rural pioneer environment. In the urban community the family lost the extrinsic functions which it had possessed from time immemorial and which continued, although in steadily diminishing degrees, in the rural family. The urban family ceased to be, to any appreciable extent, a unity of economic production. This change made possible a relaxation of authority and regimentation by the family head. Then, too, the actual or potential employment of wife and children outside the home signified their economic independence and created a new basis for family relations. In the city the members of the family tended to engage in recreational activities separately, in their appropriate sex and age groups. Each generation witnessed a decline of parental control over children.

This increased freedom and individualization of family members and their release from the strict supervision of the rural neighborhood was naturally reflected in the instability of the family. The divorce rate has averaged a 3 per cent increase each year after the Civil War.

Urbanization involves much more than the concentration and growth of population. It includes commercialization of activities, particularly recreational; specialization of vocations and interests; the development of new devices of communication—telephone, telegraph, motion picture, radio, the daily newspaper, and magazines of mass circulation. All these still further promote the urbanization and secularization of families residing not only in cities but even in remote rural settlements.

The Ideology of American Society

Democracy, freedom and opportunity for self-expression are central concepts in the American ideology. The frontier situation favored their expression in the social, economic and political life of the people. As they found articulation in the American creed, they reinforced existing tendencies toward democracy and companionship within the family.

Urban life in its economic aspects provided less opportunity than did the rural environment for the exemplification of the American ideology. For example, the development of big business and enormous industries decreased the opportunities for the husband and father to run his own business. But the city greatly increased the economic freedom and independence of the wife and children by providing employment outside the home. The social conditions of the modern city led to the emancipation of family members from the institutional controls of the rural family. The urban family tended to become an affectional and cultural group, united by the interpersonal relations of its members.

The Family in Process

The paradox between the unity and the diversity of the American family can be understood in large part by the conception of the family in process. This means, first of all, that it is in transition from earlier and existing divergent forms to an emergent generic type and, second, that it is in experimentation and is developing a variety of patterns corresponding to the subcultures in American society.

The Family in Transition

Much of what is termed the "instability" of the American family arises from the shift to the democratic companionship type from the old-time rural family of this country and the transplanted old-world family forms of immigrant groups.

Many of the current problems within the family are to be explained by the resulting conflicting conceptions in expectations and roles of husbands and wives and of parents and children. The husband may expect his wife to be a devoted household slave like his mother, while she aspires to a career or to social or civic activities outside the home. Immigrant parents attempt to enforce old-world standards of behavior upon their children, who are determined to be American in appearance, behavior, and ideas.

The Family in Experimentation

The changes taking place in the family have constituted a vast experiment in democracy. Hundreds of thousands of husbands and wives, parents and children, have participated in it. Couples have refused to follow the pattern of the marriages of their parents and are engaged in working out new designs of family living more-or-less of their own devising. This behavior has been fully in accord with the ideals and practices of democracy and has exemplified the American ideology of individual initiative and opportunity for self-expression.

This experiment in family formation, while apparently proceeding by individual couples, has been essentially collectivistic rather than pluralistic behavior. Each couple has naturally cherished the illusion that it was acting on its own. To be sure, individual initiative and risk-taking were involved.[1] Many individual ventures have ended in disaster. But actually it has been a collective experiment in the sense that the couples were acting under the stimulus of current criticisms of family life and were attempting to realize in their marriage the new conceptions of family living disseminated by the current literature, presented by the marriages of friends, or developed in discussion by groups of young people.

Adaptability versus Stability

In the past, stability has been the great value exemplified by the family and expected of it by society. This was true because the family was the basic institution in a static society. American society, however, is not static but dynamic. The virtue of its institutions do not inhere in their rigid stability, but in their adaptability to a rapid tempo of social change.

The findings of two recent studies underscore the significance of adaptability for the American family. Angell began his study of the family in the depression with the hypothesis that its degree of integration would determine its success or failure in adjustment to this crisis.[2] He found, however, that he needed to introduce the concept of adaptability to explain why certain families, highly integrated and stable before the depression, failed and why some moderately integrated families succeeded, in adjusting to the crisis. A restudy of these cases indicated that adaptability was more significant than integration in enabling families to adjust to the depression.

---

[1] *See* Floyd Dell, *Love in Greenwich Village* (New York: Doubleday, Doran & Co., 1926).

[2] Robert C. Angell, *The Family Encounters the Depression* (New York: Charles Scribner's Sons, 1936).

Another study[3] arrived at a similar conclusion. In predicting success and failure in marriage, data were secured from couples during the engagement period. Certain couples with low prediction scores were later found to be well adjusted in their marriage. The explanation seemed to lie in the adaptability of one or both members of the couple, which enabled them to meet and solve successfully difficult problems as they developed in the marriage.

Adaptability as a personal characteristic has three components. One is psychogenic, and represents the degree of flexibility in the emotional reaction of a person to a shift from an accustomed to a different situation. The second component is the tendency of the person, as culturally or educationally determined, to act in an appropriate way when entering a new situation. The third component of adaptability is the possession of knowledge and skills which make for successful adjustments to a new condition.

Successful marriage in modern society, with its divergent personalities, diversity of cultural backgrounds, and changing conditions, depends more and more upon the adaptability of husbands and wives and parents and children. The crucial matter, then, becomes the question of the adaptability of the family as a group, which may be something different from the adaptability of its members.

The growing adaptability of the companionship family makes for its stability in the long run. But it is a stability of a different kind from that of family organization in the past, which was in large part due to the external social pressures of public opinion, the mores, and law. The stability of the companionship family arises from the strength of the interpersonal relations of its members, as manifested in affection, rapport, common interests and objectives.

Flexibility of personality is not sufficient to ensure adaptability of the family to a changing society. Its members should also be culturally and educationally oriented to the necessity for making adjustments. For example, the prospects of successful marriage would be greatly improved if husbands on entering wedded life were as predisposed in attitudes as are wives to be adjustable in the marital relation. Finally, adaptability in marriage and family living demands knowledge and skills on the part of family members. These are no longer transmitted adequately by tradition in the family. They can be acquired, of course, the hard way, by experience. They can best be obtained through education and counseling based upon the findings of social science research.

---

[3] *See* E. W. Burgess and Paul Wallin, "Engagement and Marriage," chapter on "Adaptability" (unpublished manuscript).

The Family and Social Science

The instability of the American family as evidenced by its rising divorce rate is, in general, incidental to the trial-and-error method by which divorced persons ultimately find happiness in a successful remarriage.[4] But trial and error is a wasteful procedure. It involves tragic losses both to husbands and wives and to their children. So far as possible, it should be replaced by a more rational and less risk-taking planning.

The solution, however, does not lie fundamentally in legislation. Laws, within limits, may be helpful as in the ensuring of economic and social security, the improvement of housing and nutrition, in the exemptions from income taxes for wives and children, and in family allowances for children.

State and federal governments have taken steps to undergird the economic basis of the family and are likely to be called upon for further aid. But assistance to young people entering marriage and to the family in attaining its cultural objectives is coming from other institutions and agencies.

The school and the church have for some time shown a growing interest in assuming responsibility for education for marriage and family life. This is most marked in colleges and universities, a large majority of which, upon demand of the student body, now offer one or more courses in the family, family relations, marriage and the family, and preparation for marriage. High schools are experimenting with different types of courses in human relations and in family relations or with the introduction of family-life education material in existing courses. Churches, through Sunday school classes, young peoples' societies, young married couples' clubs, and Sunday evening forums, have promoted programs in family-life education. Community programs have been organized under the auspices of the Y.M.C.A., the Y.W.C.A., settlements, social centers, associations for family living, parent–child study associations, and other agencies.

Marriage and family counseling are developing under both older and newer auspices. The public still turns to the minister, the physician, and the lawyer for assistance upon spiritual, physical, and legal aspects of marriage. Theological, medical, and law schools are beginning to realize their responsibilities for training their students for this activity. The family social caseworkers, particularly those with psychiatric training, are at present the persons best trained professionally for marriage and family counseling. The identification in the public mind of family-service societies with relief-giving has largely limited this service to dependent families, although in some cities special provision has been made to extend marriage and family counseling on a fee basis to middle-class clientele.

---

[4] Harvey J. Locke, "Predicting Marital Adjustment by Comparing a Divorced and a Happily Married Group," *American Sociological Review*, XII (1947), 187-191.

Beginning with the Institute of Family Relations in Los Angeles, established in 1930, and the Marriage Council of Philadelphia two years later, marriage-counseling centers under the independent auspices are now functioning in an increasing number of our largest cities, in some smaller communities, and in a growing number of colleges and universities.

The growing disposition of young people is, as we have seen, to make their own plans for marriage and family living. They are, at the same time, interested in the resources available in education, in counseling, and in the findings of research in the psychological and social sciences. Leaders in the family-life educational and counseling movement are also looking to research to provide the knowledge which they may use in giving more efficient service.

. . . This paper attempts to state the role of research in relation to the solution of the problems of the family in our modern society. Its role is to provide the knowledge which an increasing number of young people are desirous of using in planning marriage and parenthood.

The outstanding evidence of this attitude and expectation is the reliance upon science of upper- and middle-class parents in the rearing of children. Their diet is determined upon the advice of a pediatrician, and their rearing is guided by the latest book on child psychology. This is a wide and significant departure from the older policy of bringing up the child according to methods carried down by tradition in the family.

A second illustration is the growing interest of young people in the factors making for the wise selection of a mate and for success or failure in marriage, as derived from psychological and sociological studies.

A third significant fact is the widespread public interest in A. C. Kinsey's book, *Sexual Behavior in the Human Male*, containing the first report of sex behavior of 5,300 male Americans, based upon a very complete schedule and a carefully organized interview.

These are but three of the indications of the receptivity of intelligent young people to the findings of the psychological and social sciences and of their willingness to utilize them in planning for marriage and parenthood. In short, these activities are being taken out of the realm of the mores and are being transferred to the domain of science.

The findings of research do not, in and of themselves, provide the data for a design for marriage and family life. It is, however, the function of social science research to collect and to analyze the fund of experience of young people in their various experiments in achieving happiness in marriage and family life. Therefore, these findings of research should be made available to them through books, magazines, and newspapers; through motion pictures and radio; and through marriage counseling and programs of family-life education. . . .

CHAPTER 24

BERNARD BARBER

Change and Stratification
Systems

Change and the Stratification Systems in Feudal and Early Modern France and England

The long history of France and England from feudal times in the eleventh century to early modern times in the eighteenth century cannot, of course, be described in any simple terms. There were changes over this long period in every aspect of these societies and in the European world which was their setting. Yet there is a sense in which it is possible to say that both France and England remained relatively constant during this time. Though all the different social changes that occurred did change their stratification systems in some measure, nevertheless these systems maintained the same basic structural type and processes through some six or seven hundred years. Our first case or cases, then, are intended as examples of changes in stratification systems that are changes *within type,* not changes *of type.* Such changes within type are often important, of course, but sociologically they are different from changes of type.

Essentially, during the feudal and early modern periods, France and England had stratification systems that were nearer to the caste than to the open-class type. That is to say, on the whole the predominant institutional norms disapproved of social mobility, and in fact there was relatively little mobility. But . . . there was an important admixture of open-class norms that gave the stratification systems of these societies a somewhat more mixed character. In addition, there was always a steady, though relatively small, stream of actual social mobility in France and England during the feudal and early modern periods. . . .

Though there was always a small amount of mobility during this period, most of it gradual, the relative importance of the different processes of mobility changed somewhat. In the feudal period, of course, the achievement of knighthood was an important process of mobility. In the early feudal period, up to about the year 1100, knighthood could often be achieved through deeds of prowess on the field of battle. This was a time when French and English society was relatively disorganized, subject to continual petty and private warfare among the knightly class, and when people lived in fear of unlawful violence. Knightly skill was highly valued, but the training and equipment necessary to obtain and practice this skill were so expensive that they were usually available only to members of the upper classes. As Coulborn has put it, the would-be knight "needed special training from the age of twelve, a horse specially bred for fighting, and expensive armor." [1] Where a wealthy knight was willing to pay for the equipment of a good warrior whom he desired as his vassal and military support, however, this avenue of mobility remained open. With the rise of the centralized feudal states in the twelfth and thirteenth centuries, individual knights had fewer occasions for engaging in their own petty private wars. After the middle of the twelfth century in France, says Painter, "a noble who wished to follow the traditional occupation of his class was obliged to do so under the authority of a feudal prince or feudal monarch." [2] The knight was no longer, so to speak, a small entrepreneur, but a kind of employee or retainer of the great princes. During the twelfth century also, says Bloch in his account of French feudal society, "the right to be dubbed a knight was transformed into an hereditary privilege." [3] But some mobility into the knightly class through skill and valor on the actual field of battle still occurred, though there was less of it than in the more violent, more disorganized earlier period of feudal society.

But if the emergence of the centralized feudal state made individual mobility through military prowess less common, it enlarged the scope of other processes of social mobility. A man could now more often rise through service in the administrative and legal bureaucracies of the great princes and monarchs. Or men who had accumulated wealth in urban commerce could buy land and a patent of nobility. Kings and great princes were always in need of more money to strengthen their positions. From the time of the thirteenth century and the reign of St. Louis onwards, there is evidence of the granting of letters of ennoblement by the royal court. The king still sometimes used his right of making knights to reward some act or career

---

[1] Rushton Coulborn, ed., *Feudalism in History* (Princeton University Press, 1956), p. 9.

[2] Sidney Painter, *French Chivalry: Chivalric Ideas and Practices in Mediaeval France,* (Baltimore: Johns Hopkins Press, 1940), p. 17.

[3] Marc Bloch, *La Société Féodale* (2 vols.; Paris: Editions Albin Michel, 1939, 1940), Vol. II, p. 59.

of military bravery or administrative service. But often also he used this right merely to obtain funds. By about 1300 there were French royal commissioners traveling about selling nobility to wealthy merchants, as well as freedom to some of the royal serfs. To be sure, this selling of nobility, though it fluctuated in amount, was always kept under control, in both the feudal and early modern periods. This door into the nobility was never open more than a relatively small way. Bloch is correct when he says, "In truth, the period that extends from 1250 to about 1400 was, on the continent, one in which there was a most rigid hierarchization of the social strata." [4] With only slight qualification, the same could have been said not only of England in the same period, but of both France and England for the next four hundred years as well. . . .

Although there was some change of balance among the processes of mobility during this long period, there was no basic change either in the structure of influence or in the predominant ideological conception of the nature of society and of the stratification system. The structure of influence rested fundamentally on landholding and associated rights, and the land remained in the hands of the nobles or was bought up by those who wished to become nobles. There was some change in the relative predominance of the king and court as against the rest of the nobles during this long period, of course. The rise of the centralized state in the feudal period marked an increase in the influence of the king. But by the seventeenth and eighteenth centuries—a little earlier in England, a little later in France—the king's influence in society relative to that of the rest of the nobles had declined somewhat. Always, however, predominant influence remained with the landholding noble class as a whole, whatever the changes in the relative share of influence possessed by the king as premier noble.

This enduring structure of influence was supported by an equally enduring ideological conception, the organic conception of society in which a predominant value was placed upon the roles of the noble warriors, noble rulers, and noble clergymen. . . . No counter-ideology gained any strength among the nonnoble, middle-class people in France or England. The middle-class elements—the merchants, the lesser gentry, and the well-to-do yeomanry—wished, as individuals, to change their own class position in society; they wished to rise into the nobility. But they did not give their allegiance to any ideology that recommended a change in the caste type of stratification system itself.

One sphere in which there was considerable change during the feudal and early modern periods in France and England was the domestic "style of life" of the noble class. This change did not, however, have any fundamental effect on the stratification system. In the early feudal period, in the eleventh century, for example, the standard of living even for the knightly class was low. A petty

[4] *Ibid.*, p. 66.

noble had to be content with coarse woolen clothes, an abundance of simple food, and a two-room wooden house surrounded by a moat and palisade. A great lord might have enough serf labor at his command to build a high artificial mound on which to erect his large and fine residence. He might also have servile artisans to produce clothes and armor of reasonably good quality. But even the greatest lords in the eleventh century did not have fine stone castles, silken garments, or spices for their food. By the end of the eleventh century, however, the French noble class became enriched from several sources. The conquest of Spain, the Holy Land, England, and Sicily brought not only wealth in the form of gold but also new skills, new foods, and new fabrics.

After the Conquest, this new domestic "style of life" spread to England. Also, in the twelfth century, there began to be more and larger towns and commercial fairs in France and England. From both the towns and the fairs the nobles received money rents from the merchants and also new goods of all kinds to make their standard of living better. The greatest of the lords were now extremely wealthy and could command great resources of labor and whatever goods were on the market. Such men built themselves fine stone castles, wore costly silks imported from the East and rare furs brought from the north of Europe, drank good wines for the first time, and added rarities like sugar and spices to their tables. . . .

And from the sixteenth century onwards, with the opening up of the Western world and the continuing slow economic advance in Europe, the noble standard of living improved still further. But none of the change in this area of society, although over the period of six hundred years or more it was considerable and important in other respects, such as the economic, resulted in basic change in the caste type of stratification system in France and England.

Perhaps if the caste system had not had admixtures of open-class elements, there might sooner have occurred a basic change in its character, either through revolution or incrementally. Perhaps if there had not been opportunities for social mobility, opportunities for men to rise in the church, in the service of the state, or by purchasing land and titles with the money accumulated in commerce, there might sooner have occurred a basic change in the stratification system. But these opportunities were continuously available in France and England, and they served to dissolve social strains and personal resentments that might otherwise have supported ideologies and movements opposed to the existing society and its stratification system. It is, of course, often said that "the rising bourgeoisie" did constitute a group suffering from such social strains and personal resentments and that they did, consequently, form an inherently revolutionary element in French and English society. But . . . there is good evidence that although some individual members of the bourgeoisie did rise in every century of the feudal and early modern periods, the bourgeois group as a whole was not at all self-consciously or otherwise revolutionary. A bourgeois, as we have seen, was in basic agreement with the caste norms and ideologies. Fundamentally, what he wanted was either to pass on his class position to his children or to move himself or his children into the noble class. He did not believe in equality for all, at least not here on earth, though he might, if he was a firmly believing Christian, look forward to it in Heaven. If the successful bourgeois had any deviant sentiments about the virtues of earthly universalism, they were soon driven out by his rise into a noble social class where such sentiments no longer suited his own social interests.

How, then, did the change from a basically caste type of stratification system to a basically open-class one occur in modern France and England? We cannot, of course, give a very satisfactory answer. In France, it was the Revolution and the social changes in every aspect of society which the Revolution involved that ushered in the change to an open-class stratification system. But there is no consensus among historians on what the causes of the Revolution were. Almost every conceivable social factor has been defined by some historian as the essential cause. Until there is a good deal more historical research and the kind of theory of change in societies as a whole considered at the beginning of this chapter, a satisfactory account of the origins and development of the French Revolution will be lacking. Nor can we do much better in explaining the fundamental changes in the stratification system that occurred in England. Although the historical evidence has not yet been collected to prove the point firmly, it does seem that the admixture of open-class elements *may have been* a little larger in England than in France and that these elements *may have been* sufficient to obviate a revolutionary solution to the necessity for social change. Moreover, the example of the social costs of the Revolution in France probably had an important influence in keeping the changes in England on the whole on peaceful paths. There was some violence in England too in the late eighteenth and early nineteenth centuries, but by and large England moved into an open-class stratification system peaceably.

How precisely can we assign an historical date to the change from the caste to the open-class type of stratification system in France and England? Not very precisely, because we do not have the evidence with regard to changes in the balance of institutional norms and in the actual amounts of mobility which would be the best indicators of the fundamental social transformation. In France we know that the basic legal changes took place during the Revolution. How soon these were effective in producing changes in stratificational norms and in amounts of mobility we do not know. A great deal of change in these respects took place during the Revolution itself, and this change was enlarged and consolidated in the early-middle nineteenth century. In England, where changes in all respects were more gradual, less violent, more unplanned, it is perhaps even harder to set a definite date for the transformation of the stratification system. Probably there, as in France, the change did not occur until sometime during the early-middle nineteenth century. In both societies, of course, there persisted an admixture of caste elements after the establishment of a basically open-class type. In all complex societies there is some mixture of institutional elements and social processes. The sociologist must always keep this fact in mind, since the mixture is often the source of fundamental social change.

•

Change and the Stratification System in Russia

Social change occurs not only at varying rates of speed, but as the result of varying amounts of social planning. In this, our third case, we have an example of a society where the change from a basically caste type of stratification system to an open-class one has been brought about by revolution and by overall state social planning.

•

In legal terms, prerevolutionary Russia was, like eighteenth-century France, an "estate" society. The law defined special rights and duties for each of the three estates: the clergy, hereditary nobility, and a third estate consisting of peasants and town-dwelling merchants and workers. In terms of social stratification, prerevolutionary Russia was, again like eighteenth-century France, basically of the caste type, but with a much larger admixture of open-class elements. Indeed, since Russia had begun to industrialize, and this with increasing speed in the twentieth century, the admixture of open-class elements was large enough that some scholars have argued that Russia was already more nearly an open-class than a caste society. Certainly there was a small but increasing number of industrialists, merchants, and skilled workers; moreover, many upper-class intellectuals were ardently devoted to universalistic values and ideologies. Hence the appeal of various democratic, constitutional, socialist, and Marxist social philosophies. Many of the mobile bourgeois, however, did not approve in principle of social mobility for all but, like their eighteenth-century proto-types in France, wanted only to move into the hereditary noble class them-selves. Just how much actual social mobility and institutionalized approval existed in prerevolutionary Russia, we do not know. We can only venture the estimate that these open-class elements were probably somewhat sub-ordinate to the basically caste type of stratification system. This is not to imply, of course, that over the longer run there would not have occurred inevitably a slow and gradual increase in the open-class elements, eventuat-ing in a basically open-class society.

But social change in Russia was not to take place gradually or peace-ably. A violent revolution initiated, and social planning has carried to completion, basic changes in every part of Russian society: in the organiza-tion of production, in the property system, in the political and legal systems, in education, in science, in the family, in religion, and, not least of all, in values and ideologies. Just how the revolution was begun or the social transformation completed is not, like many great historical events, entirely clear even to those who have studied the history and sociology of Russian society most intensively. However, the fundamental importance of Marxist-Leninist theory and of Communist Party organization in initiating and consolidating the revolution is unmistakable. In the beginning, in fact, Marxist-Leninist theory gave the revolution a utopian cast. It proclaimed that such fundamental social structures as the stratification system, the state bureaucracy, and the family would ultimately be unnecessary. Eventually, however, though basic changes in these and other structures were made, the Russians have had to recede from their utopian views or at least announce the postponement of the realization into the indefinite future.

Even in a revolution, basic social changes do not occur overnight, nor sometimes even in a single generation. The deaths and destruction, the expropriation of property, and the social disfranchisement of the formerly privileged classes did, in the period of revolutionary violence and immediately thereafter, cause a great increase in both upward and downward social mobility in Russia. But as Lenin recognized in his "Testament," there is a limit to the extent to which "new" men can immediately take the place of the "old" social groups. It takes time especially to train technical specialists; it also takes time to allow "new" men to gain the necessary experience even in positions that require no special technical training. Lenin and the other revolutionary leaders were compelled, therefore, to allow many of the former middle- and upper-class industrial, civil-service, and free-professional experts to remain in their old positions. Looking to the future, however, the Communists began to train their own experts. During the 1920's, special privileges in education were given to industrial workers and their children. This facilitated the social mobility of these "proletarian" groups. Undoubtedly, though, some of the children of those members of the old upper classes who had been retained in high positions were able to profit from their family advantages and maintain unchanged the social class position in which they were born. That is the consequence, or "price," of preserving some stable continuity in a society even though it has undergone a fundamental social revolution.

Probably the period of maximum social mobility and of the most rapid increase in open-class norms and ideologies occurred in Russia in the late twenties, the thirties, and the forties, the period in which there was the greatest proportionate expansion of Russia's industrial, governmental, military, scientific, and educational systems. The absolute number of middle- and higher-ranking positions in Soviet society was vastly increased in this period, and probably the proportion of these positions relative to the lower ones was also somewhat increased. These increases created a vast expansion of the opportunities for social mobility of both large and small degree. Along with the expansion resulting from industrialization, the recurrent "purges" of prerevolutionary groups from the higher-ranking positions also enlarged the opportunities for social mobility during the thirties and forties.

By now, Soviet society has settled down with an open-class stratification system very much like that of the other industrialized countries of Europe and in the United States. . . . The educational system is now as much one of the key elements in the process of mobility in Russia, as it is in other open-class industrial societies that require and provide opportunities for individual achievement. . . . Actual access to what is formally a universally available education system is influenced by social class position in Russia as it is in other open-class societies. The settling down of Russian society probably has lessened, relative to the thirties and forties and earlier, the amount of social mobility that now occurs. Nevertheless, there is still a considerable amount of social mobility. . . . Probably a fairly large minority of the population remains in the class into which it was born; another large minority moves up or down in relatively small degree; and a small minority moves up or down in the class structure in large degree. Until we have better comparative evidence for Russia and other industrial countries which will reveal subtle differences in the amount and processes of mobility, the safest estimate of the Russian stratification system is that it consists of norms, structure, and processes basically similar to those of other open-class industrial societies in Europe and the United States. That is the estimate supported by all the good evidence now in hand.

•

Change and the Stratification System in Great Britain

It has often been said that during and since the end of World War II Great Britain has gone through a "social revolution." Great social changes have indeed occurred during the last fifteen years in many different parts of the society, and these have been important to nearly every member of the society. But are these changes "revolutionary"? In some sense, perhaps they are. But not in the sense of involving fundamental changes *of type* in any of the major social institutions. The changes have been planned and carried through by means of long-established democratic political techniques. They have been agreed to, on the whole, by the adherents of both of the major political parties. In short, they have been built on long-standing social consensus. In this . . . case, then, we shall consider recent changes in the stratification system of Great Britain as examples of changes within a stable and institutionalized open-class system.

As we have suggested earlier in this chapter, Great Britain may have had a predominantly open-class type of stratification since at least the early-middle part of the nineteenth century. All during that century, and continuing up to the present, a series of incremental changes have tended to make the stratification system approximate ever more nearly the open-class type. Social change has often not come as fast or as easily as many Britons wished; there have always been many people to criticize the persistence of caste elements in British society. But the general direction of change in the stratification system has been constant. And in this perspective especially, the post-World War II changes in Britain represent another large increment of a long trend of change within the open-class type of stratification system. During the last one hundred and fifty years, for example, the availability of education, both as to amount and quality, has been spreading in Britain. The recent increases in scholarships, the improvement of schools for the poorer groups, and the "opening up" of the "public schools" and of Oxford and Cambridge, then, are social changes that build upon earlier and similar changes in the educational system. Further, the diminution of family advantages for the maintenance of high social class position through the levying of progressive income and inheritance taxes is also not new to Britain, though these instruments of an open-class society have been applied with increased force in the postwar period. Finally, if the political influence of the lower classes reached a peak in Britain after the war through the Labour Party and the Labour Government, this too was a development founded on a long history of slowly increasing political influence among the lower classes.

A long series of peaceable, slow, and interrelated social changes have made the stratification system of Great Britain approach ever more nearly, though not absolutely achieve, the open-class type. There seems to have occurred a general "flattening" of the class structure, that is, there has been a trend toward relatively fewer people in the upper and lower classes. The proportion of people in that broad range of the class structure ideologically defined as "the middle classes" has been increasing. Differences of evaluation and of the associated social privileges still exist, but they are less obvious than formerly because more subtly graded and more subtly expressed. The rise in the standard of living of the lower and lower-middle classes—their better food, better education, better health, better housing, and better clothes—has not only increased their chances for social mobility, but has eliminated some of the most striking of the former symbols of their social class inferiority.

•

. . . There seem to be on all sides stronger sentiments of approval of social mobility; equality of opportunity for individual achievement in all socially valued roles is now a more common ideal in all social classes. Great Britain, then, is not now a classless society; nor has she undergone a major social revolution such as that of 1789 in France or of 1917 in Russia. She has, rather, taken somewhat longer steps than at other times in the past down a path of change toward a more nearly open-class type of stratification system—a path she has been following for a long time.

Change and the Stratification System in the United States

Our . . . final case is the United States. . . . The United States is an example of a society in which the changes of the stratification system are changes *within type*. . . . Just how much change there has been in the American open-class stratification system, we cannot precisely say. Nor can we be absolutely sure about the general direction of the change that has occurred within that type. The social changes taking place recently may, as some Americans have thought, be in the direction of a somewhat less open-class society. But it seems more likely that these changes have generally strengthened the conditions necessary for an open-class stratification system and made that system a little bit more realizable in practice. For example, there is no evidence that Americans now approve any less of social mobility than they ever have in the past. Indeed, there seems to be a persistence of open-class sentiments and aspirations, even in the face of widespread social depression or individual "failure" . . . and an equally persistent amount of social mobility. Even the Negroes, with regard to whom the caste elements in American society have always been strongest, have recently won a set of social improvements, among which not the least is the weakening of the prejudices against them among their white fellow Americans.

Certainly we can point to a number of social processes and social changes that have probably served to strengthen the American open-class stratification system. Education and educational opportunity, though still not equal for all, are changing in the direction of greater availability and equality. Political and other forms of social influence are becoming somewhat less unequally distributed among the social classes. The development of labor union organizations and their participation in national and local politics has been one of the basic sources of the reduction of political and social inequality among the classes. As in England, the American tax system serves to diminish the differential advantages provided by accumulated family wealth; this system has recently become an even more effective instrument of this open-class function. Science and technology have continually been creating in American society new opportunities for entrepreneurial ability and new jobs requiring valued social and technical knowledge and skill. And these in turn provide continuing opportunities for social mobility. In general, conservative or reactionary inequalitarian ideologies and movements have either been lacking or strikingly unsuccessful in their appeals for support. Other social changes have at least not weakened, and sometimes they have actively strengthened, the set of conditions required for enlarging the realization of an open-class type of stratification system in the United States.

To many people, the account given above of social change and the

American stratification system will seem excessively optimistic. But perhaps it will seem so only because Americans have tended to have utopian expectations with regard to their stratification system and have been impatient of any hindrance to completely free social mobility. . . . Such mobility does not occur. Therefore Americans can be optimistic without being utopian. Optimism, of course, does not mean that they should be complacent. Because the stratification system is a system in process, continuous social action of many different kinds is required either to maintain it in the state Americans desire or to improve it. They must therefore pay constant attention to the social arrangements and policies that foster the kind of stratification system and change they want. Increasingly, as social science develops, social change can be planned and foreseen. The choice for Americans now is not between an open-class and a caste type of stratification system; it is among degrees of approximation to the openclass system and to the American ideals. Perhaps this is also true now for societies all around the world.

CHAPTER 25

GAETANO MOSCA

The Varying Structure of
the Ruling Class

The Concept of the Ruling Class

In all societies—from societies that are very meagerly developed and have barely attained the dawnings of civilization, down to the most advanced and powerful societies—two classes of people appear, a class that rules and a class that is ruled. The first class, always the less numerous, performs all the political functions, monopolizes power, and enjoys the advantages that power brings. The second, the more numerous class, is directed and controlled by the first, in a manner that is now more-or-less legal, now more-or-less arbitrary and violent; it supplies the first class, in appearance at least, with material means of subsistence and with the instrumentalities that are essential to the vitality of the political organism.

In practical life we all recognize the existence of this ruling class. We all know that, in our own country, whichever it may be, the management of public affairs is in the hands of a minority of influential persons, to which, willingly or unwillingly, the majority defers. We know that the same thing goes on in neighboring countries, and in fact we should be hard put to it to conceive of a real world otherwise organized—a world in which all men would be directly subject to a single person without relationships of superiority or subordination, or in which all men would share equally in the direction of political affairs. If we reason otherwise in theory, that is due partly to inveterate habits that we follow in our thinking and partly to the exaggerated importance that we attach to two political facts that loom far larger in appearance than they are in reality.

The first of these facts—and one has only to open one's eyes to see it—

From Gaetano Mosca, *The Ruling Class* (New York: McGraw-Hill, 1939), pp. 50-58, 65-68, 80-83, 371-376. Copyright 1936 by the McGraw-Hill Book Company Inc., and reprinted by permission of the publisher.

is that in every political organism there is one individual who is chief among the leaders of the ruling class as a whole and stands, as we say, at the helm of the state. That person is not always the person who holds supreme power according to law. At times, alongside of the hereditary king or emperor, there is a prime minister or a major-domo who wields an actual power that is greater than the sovereign's. At other times, in place of the elected president, the influential politician who has procured the president's election will govern. Under special circumstances, there may be, instead of a single person, two or three who discharge the functions of supreme control.

The second fact, too, is readily discernible. Whatever the type of political organization, pressures arising from the discontent of the masses who are governed, from the passions by which they are swayed, exert a certain amount of influence on the policies of the ruling, political class.

But the man who is at the head of the state would certainly not be able to govern without the support of a numerous class to enforce respect for his orders and to have them carried out; and granting that he can make one individual, or indeed many individuals, in the ruling class feel the weight of his power, he certainly cannot be at odds with the class as a whole or do away with it. Even if that were possible, he would at once be forced to create another class, without the support of which action on his part would be completely paralyzed. On the other hand, granting that the discontent of the masses might succeed in deposing a ruling class, inevitably, as we shall later show, there would have to be another organized minority within the masses themselves to discharge the functions of a ruling class. Otherwise all organization and the whole social structure would be destroyed.

From the point of view of scientific research the real superiority of the concept of the ruling, or political, class lies in the fact that the varying structure of ruling classes has a preponderant importance in determining the political type, and also the level of civilization, of the different peoples.

. . . We think it may be desirable . . . to reply at this point to an objection which might very readily be made to our point of view. If it is easy to understand that a single individual cannot command a group without finding within the group a minority to support him, it is rather difficult to grant, as a constant and natural fact, that minorities rule majorities, rather than majorities minorities. But that is one of the points—so numerous in all the other sciences—where the first impression one has of things is contrary to what they are in reality. In reality the dominion of an organized minority, obeying a single impulse, over the unorganized majority, is inevitable. The power of any minority is irresistible as against each single individual in the majority, who stands alone before the totality of the organized minority. At the same time, the minority is organized for the very reason that it is a minority. A hundred men acting uniformly in concert, with a common understanding, will triumph over a thousand men who are not in accord and can therefore be dealt with one by one. Meanwhile, it will be easier for the former to act in concert and have a mutual understanding, simply because they are a hundred and not a thousand. It follows that the larger the political community, the smaller will the proportion of the governing minority to the governed majority be and the more difficult will it be for the majority to organize for reaction against the minority.

However, in addition to the great advantage accruing to them from the fact of being organized, ruling minorities are usually so constituted that the individuals who make them up are distinguished from the mass of the governed by qualities that give them a certain material, intellectual or even moral superiority; or else they are the heirs of individuals who possessed such qualities. In other words, members of a ruling minority regularly have some attribute, real or apparent, which is highly esteemed and very influential in the society in which they live.

From the Warriors to the Wealthy

In primitive societies that are still in the early stages of organization, military valor is the quality that most readily opens access to the ruling or political class. In societies of advanced civilization, war is the exceptional condition. It may be regarded as virtually normal in societies that are in the initial stages of their development; and the individuals who show the greatest ability in war easily gain supremacy over their fellows, the bravest becoming chiefs. The fact is constant, but the forms it may assume in one set of circumstances or another vary considerably.

As a rule, the dominance of a warrior class over a peaceful multitude is attributed to a superposition of races, to the conquest of a relatively unwarlike group by an aggressive one. Sometimes that is actually the case: we have examples in India after the Aryan invasions, in the Roman Empire after the Germanic invasions and in Mexico after the Aztec conquest. But more often, under certain social conditions, we note the rise of a warlike ruling class in places where there is absolutely no trace of a foreign conquest. As long as a horde lives exclusively by the chase, all individuals can easily become warriors. There will of course be leaders who will rule over the tribe, but we will not find a warrior class rising to exploit, and at the same time to protect, another class that is devoted to peaceful pursuits. As the tribe emerges from the hunting stage and enters the agricultural and pastoral stage, then, along with an enormous increase in population and a greater stability in the means of exerting social influence, a more-or-less cleancut division into two classes will take place, one class being devoted exclusively to agriculture, the other class to war. In this event, it is inevitable that the warrior class should little by little acquire such ascendancy over the other as to be able to oppress it with impunity.

Poland offers a characteristic example of the gradual metamorphosis of a

warrior class into an absolutely dominant class. Originally the Poles had
the same organization by rural villages as prevailed among all the Slavic
peoples. There was no distinction between fighters and farmers—in other
words, between nobles and peasants. But after the Poles came to settle on
the broad plains that are watered by the Vistula and the Niemen, agriculture began to develop among them. However, the necessity of fighting with
warlike neighbors continued, so that the tribal chiefs, or voivodes, gathered
about themselves a certain number of picked men whose special occupation was the bearing of arms. These warriors were distributed among the
various rural communities. They were exempt from agricultural duties, yet
they received their share of the produce of the soil along with the other
members of the community. In early days their position was not considered
very desirable, and country dwellers sometimes waived exemption from
agricultural labor in order to avoid going to war. But gradually as this order
of things grew stabilized, as one class became habituated to the practice of
arms and military organization while the other hardened to the use of the
plow and the spade, the warriors became nobles and masters, and the peasants, once companions and brothers, became villeins and serfs. Little by
little, the warrior lords increased their demands, to the point where the
share they took as members of the community came to include the community's whole produce, minus what was absolutely necessary for subsistence on the part of the cultivators; and when the latter tried to escape such
abuses, they were constrained by force to stay bound to the soil, their
situation taking on all the characteristics of serfdom pure and simple.

In the course of this evolution, around the year 1333, King Casimir the
Great tried vainly to curb the overbearing insolence of the warriors. When
peasants came to complain of the nobles, he contented himself with asking
whether they had no sticks and stones. Some generations later, in 1537, the
nobility forced all tradesmen in the cities to sell such real estate as they
owned, and landed property became a prerogative of nobles only. At the
same time the nobility exerted pressure upon the king to open negotiations
with Rome, to the end that thenceforward only nobles should be admitted to
holy orders in Poland. That barred townsmen and peasants almost completely from honorific positions, and stripped them of any social importance
whatever.

•

Everywhere—in Russia and Poland, in India and medieval Europe—
the ruling warrior classes acquire almost exclusive ownership of the land.
Land, as we have seen, is the chief source of production and wealth in
countries that are not very far advanced in civilization. But as civilization
progresses, revenue from land increases proportionately. With the growth
of population there is, at least in certain periods, an increase in rent, in the
Ricardian sense of the term, largely because great centers of consumption
arise, such at all times have been the great capitals and other large cities,

ancient and modern. Eventually, if other circumstances permit, a very important social transformation occurs. Wealth rather than military valor comes to be the characteristic feature of the dominant class: the people who rule are the rich rather than the brave.

The condition that in the main is required for this transformation is that social organization shall have concentrated and become perfected to such an extent that the protection offered by public authority is considerably more effective than the protection offered by private force. In other words, private property must be so well protected by the practical and real efficacy of the laws as to render the power of the proprietor himself superfluous. This comes about through a series of gradual alterations in the social structure whereby a type of political organization, which we shall call the "feudal state," is transformed into an essentially different type, which we shall term the "bureaucratic state." We are to discuss these types at some length hereafter, but we may say at once that the evolution here referred to is as a rule greatly facilitated by progress in pacific manners and customs and by certain moral habits which societies contract as civilization advances.

Once this transformation has taken place, wealth produces political power, just as political power has been producing wealth. In a society already somewhat mature—where, therefore, individual power is curbed by the collective power—if the powerful are as a rule the rich, to be rich is to become powerful. And in truth, when fighting with the mailed fist is prohibited whereas fighting with pounds and pence is sanctioned, the better posts are inevitably won by those who are better supplied with pounds and pence.

There are, to be sure, states of a very high level of civilization which in theory are organized on the basis of moral principles of such a character that they seem to preclude this overbearing assertiveness on the part of wealth. But this is a case—and there are many such—where theoretical principles can have no more than a limited application in real life. In the United States all powers flow directly or indirectly from popular elections, and suffrage is equal for all men and women in all the states of the union. What is more, democracy prevails not only in institutions, but to a certain extent also in morals. The rich ordinarily feel a certain aversion to entering public life, and the poor a certain aversion to choosing the rich for elective office. But that does not prevent a rich man from being more influential than a poor man, since he can use pressure upon the politicians who control public administration. It does not prevent elections from being carried on to the music of clinking dollars. It does not prevent whole legislatures and considerable numbers of national congressmen from feeling the influence of powerful corporations and great financiers.

•

In all countries of the world, those other agencies for exerting social influence—personal publicity, good education, specialized training, high rank in church, public administration, and army—are always readier of access to the rich than to the poor. The rich invariably have a considerably shorter road to travel than the poor, to say nothing of the fact that the stretch of road that the rich are spared is often the roughest and most difficult.

•

The Ruling Class in Periods of Renovation and Crystallization

. . . As soon as there is a shift in the balance of political forces—when, that is, a need is felt that capacities different from the old should assert themselves in the management of the state, when the old capacities therefore lose some of their importance or changes in their distribution occur— then the manner in which the ruling class is constituted changes also. If a new source of wealth develops in a society, if the practical importance of knowledge grows, if an old religion declines or a new one is born, if a new current of ideas spreads, then, simultaneously, farreaching dislocations occur in the ruling class. One might say, indeed, that the whole history of civilized mankind comes down to a conflict between the tendency of dominant elements to monopolize political power and transmit possession of it by inheritance, and the tendency toward a dislocation of old forces and an insurgence of new forces; and this conflict produces an unending ferment of endosmosis and exosmosis between the upper classes and certain portions of the lower. Ruling classes decline inevitably when they cease to find scope for the capacities through which they rose to power, when they can no longer render the social services which they once rendered, or when their talents and the services they render lose in importance in the social environment in which they live. So the Roman aristocracy declined when it was no longer the exclusive source of higher officers for the army, of administrators for the commonwealth, of governors for the provinces. So the Venetian aristocracy declined when its nobles ceased to command the galleys and no longer passed the greater part of their lives in sailing the seas and in trading and fighting.

In inorganic nature we have the example of our air, in which a tendency to immobility produced by the force of inertia is continuously in conflict with a tendency to shift about as the result of inequalities in the distribution of heat. The two tendencies, prevailing by turn in various regions on our planet, produce now calm, now wind and storm. In much the same way in human societies, there prevails now the tendency that produces closed, stationary, crystallized ruling classes, now the tendency that results in a more or less rapid renovation of ruling classes.

The oriental societies which we consider stationary have in reality not always been so, for otherwise, as we have already pointed out, they could not have made the advances in civilization of which they have left irrefutable evidence. It is much more accurate to say that we came to know them at a time when their political forces and their political classes were in a period of crystallization. The same thing occurs in what we commonly call "aging" societies, where religious beliefs, scientific knowledge, methods of producing and distributing wealth have for centuries undergone no radical alteration and have not been disturbed in their everyday course by infiltrations of foreign elements, material or intellectual. In such societies political forces are always the same, and the class that holds possession of them holds a power that is undisputed. Power is therefore perpetuated in certain families, and the inclination to immobility becomes general through all the various strata in that society.

So in India we see the caste system become thoroughly entrenched after the suppression of Buddhism. The Greeks found hereditary castes in ancient Egypt, but we know that in the periods of greatness and renaissance in Egyptian civilization political office and social status were not hereditary. We possess an Egyptian document that summarizes the life of a high army officer who lived during the period of the expulsion of the Hyksos. He had begun his career as a simple soldier. Other documents show cases in which the same individual served successively in the army, civil administration, and priesthood.

The best known and perhaps the most important example of a society tending toward crystallization is the period in Roman history that used to be called the Low Empire. There, after several centuries of almost complete social immobility, a division between two classes grew sharper and sharper, the one made up of great landowners and high officials, the other made up of slaves, farmers and urban plebeians. What is even more striking, public office and social position became hereditary by custom before they became hereditary by law, and the trend was rapidly generalized during the period mentioned.

On the other hand it may happen in the history of a nation that commerce with foreign peoples, forced emigrations, discoveries, wars, create new poverty and new wealth, disseminate knowledge of things that were previously unknown, or cause infiltrations of new moral, intellectual and religious currents. Or again—as a result of such infiltrations, or through a slow process of inner growth, or from both causes—it may happen that a new learning arises, or that certain elements of an old, long forgotten learning return to favor, so that new ideas and new beliefs come to the fore and upset the intellectual habits on which the obedience of the masses has been founded. The ruling class may also be vanquished and destroyed in whole or in part by foreign invasions, or, when the circumstances just mentioned arise, it may be driven from power by the advent of new social elements who are strong in fresh political forces. Then, naturally, there comes a period of renovation, or, if one prefer, of revolution, during which individual energies have free play and certain individuals, more passionate, more energetic, more intrepid or merely shrewder than others, force their way from the bottom of the social ladder to the topmost rungs.

Once such a movement has set in, it cannot be stopped immediately. The example of individuals who have started from nowhere and reached prominent positions fires new ambitions, new greeds, new energies; and this molecular rejuvenation of the ruling class continues vigorously until a long period of social stability slows it down again. We need hardly mention examples of nations in such periods of renovation. In our age that would be superfluous. Rapid restocking of ruling classes is a frequent and very striking phenomenon in countries that have been recently colonized. When social life begins in such environments, there is no ready-made ruling class, and while such a class is in process of formation, admittance to it is gained very easily. Monopolization of land and other agencies of production is, if not quite impossible, at any rate more difficult than elsewhere. That is why, at least during a certain period, the Greek colonies offered a wide outlet for all Greek energy and enterprise. That is why, in the United States, where the colonizing of new lands continued through the whole nineteenth century and new industries were continually springing up, examples of men who started with nothing and have attained fame and wealth are still frequent—all of which helps to foster in the people of that country the illusion that democracy is a fact.

Suppose now that a society gradually passes from its feverish state to calm. Since the human being's psychological tendencies are always the same, those who belong to the ruling class will begin to acquire a group spirit. They will become more and more exclusive and learn better and better the art of monopolizing to their advantage the qualities and capacities that are essential to acquiring power and holding it. Then, at last, the force that is essentially conservative appears—the force of habit. Many people become resigned to a lowly station, while the members of certain privileged families or classes grow convinced that they have almost an absolute right to high station and command.

•

From Feudalism to Bureaucracy

Before we proceed any further, it might be wise to linger briefly on the two types into which, in our opinion, all political organisms may be classified, the feudal and the bureaucratic.

This classification, it should be noted, is not based upon essential, unchanging criteria. It is not our view that there is any psychological law peculiar to either one of the two types and therefore alien to the other. It seems to us, rather, that the two types are just different manifestations, different phases, of a single constant tendency whereby human societies become less simple, or, if one will, more complicated in political organization, as they grow in size and are perfected in civilization. Level of civilization is, on the whole, more important in this regard than size, since, in actual fact a liter-

ally huge state may once have been feudally organized. At bottom, therefore, a bureaucratic state is just a feudal state that has advanced and developed in organization and so grown more complex; and a feudal state may
derive from a once bureaucratized society that has decayed in civilization
and reverted to a simpler, more primitive form of political organization,
perhaps falling to pieces in the process.

By "feudal state" we mean that type of political organization in which all
the executive functions of society—the economic, the judicial, the administrative, the military—are exercised simultaneously by the same individuals,
while at the same time the state is made up of small social aggregates, each
of which possesses all the organs that are required for self-sufficiency. The
Europe of the Middle Ages offers the most familiar example of this type of
organization—that is why we have chosen to designate it by the term "feudal"; but as one reads the histories of other peoples or scans the accounts of
travelers of our own day, one readily perceives that the type is widespread.

•

In the bureaucratic state, not all the executive functions need to be concentrated in the bureaucracy and exercised by it. One might even declare
that so far in history that has never been the case. The main characteristic
of this type of social organization lies, we believe, in the fact that, wherever
it exists, the central power conscripts a considerable portion of the social
wealth by taxation, and uses it first to maintain a military establishment and
then to support a more-or-less extensive number of public services. The
greater the number of officials who perform public duties and receive their
salaries from the central government or from its local agencies, the more
bureaucratic a society becomes.

•

Feudalism introduced . . . the political supremacy of an exclusively
warrior class. . . . Another characteristic of the feudal system was the centralization of all administrative functions and all social influence in the
local military leader, who at the same time was master of the land—virtually the one instrument for the production of wealth which still existed.

Feudalism, finally, created a new type of sovereignty that was intermediate between the central, coordinating organ of the state and the individual.
Once their position had become hereditary, the more important local leaders bound lesser leaders to themselves by subgrants of land, and these lesser
chiefs were tied by oaths of feudal homage and fidelity to the man who
made the grant. They had, therefore, no direct relations with the head of
the feudal confederation as a whole, the king. In fact, they felt obliged to
fight the king if the leader to whom they were directly bound was at war
with him. This, certainly, was the main cause of the long resistance which
the feudal system offered to the continuous efforts of the central power to
destroy it.

. . . Down to the fourteenth century, the memory of the old unity of all civilized and Christian peoples, guided in religious matters by the Roman pontiff, who little by little gained recognition as supreme hierarch of the universal church, and in temporal matters by the successor of the ancient Roman emperor, lingered alive and vigorous in the intellectual classes, the clergy and the doctors of the law. Unless such memories had been very much alive, we should be at a loss to explain the attempt to restore the Empire that took place under Charlemagne and Pope Leo III in the year 800, or another somewhat more successful attempt that was made by Otto I of Saxony in 962.

A name and an idea may exercise a great moral influence, but they are not enough to restore a centralized, coordinated political system once that system has fallen to pieces. In order to effect such a restoration, they have to have a material organization at their disposal, and in order to have such an organization the agencies required for establishing it must be available. Such agencies Charlemagne's successors and the Germanic emperors lacked. They had neither a sound financial organization nor a regular bureaucracy nor, finally, a standing army that was capable of enforcing obedience to imperial edicts.

In Charlemagne's day, the old Germanic band still furnished a fairly well-disciplined militia for the Frankish armies, and the local lords were not yet omnipotent. For the same reason the emperors of the House of Saxony, and the first two emperors of the House of Franconia, could count on the cooperation of the German military class, which was not yet solidly grouped about a few leaders. Imperial and regal power attained its maximum efficiency in Germany under Henry III of Franconia. That emperor managed for some time to keep a few of the principal duchies unfilled, or to have them occupied by relatives of the reigning house. He held the duchy of Franconia and, for a time, the duchy of Swabia under his personal dominion and further retained the exclusive right to name the holders of the great ecclesiastical fiefs, bishoprics and abbacies, which were not hereditary and which covered almost half of the territory of Germany. Henry III died an untimely death. Henry IV at that moment was a minor, and he was personally weak. His struggles with the papacy permitted the higher German nobility to regain the ground it had lost.

But the moment the feudal system had taken a strong hold in Germany, the military base of the empire became shaky. Then the struggle between the Empire and the Church gave the local sovereignties the support of a great moral force in their clash with imperial authority. The effort to reestablish the worldwide political unity of Christian peoples, which Charlemagne had made and which Otto I of Saxony had repeated, may be considered a complete and final failure with the death of Frederick II of Hohenstaufen.

But the state of semibarbarism which characterized the darkest period of the Middle Ages in central and western Europe was not to be eternal. Civilization was to rise again. The process of reabsorbing local powers into the central organ of the state had, therefore, to start anew under a different form; and, in fact, what the representative of the ancient Roman Empire had been unable to do became the task of the various national monarchies.

Meantime, from about the year 1000 on, another sort of local sovereignty had begun to rise alongside of the fief: the medieval town, the commune. The commune was a federation of guilds, neighborhood organizations and trade corporations—all the various associations of people who were neither nobles nor subject vassals—which were organized in the more troublous periods of feudal anarchy, in order that those who belonged to them might enjoy a certain measure of personal security through mutual defense. The communes became powerful first in northern Italy, then in Germany and Flanders and in those countries they were among the greatest obstacles to the growth of the power of the . . . emperors. They achieved more modest positions in France, England, the Iberian kingdoms and southern Italy. In those countries they supported the crown against feudalism.

In general, the national monarchies claimed historical connections with the old barbarian monarchies which the invading Germans had set up on the ruins of the ancient Roman Empire. But after the period of political dissolution that occurred under Charlemagne's first successors, they began to take shape again following geographic and linguistic lines rather than historic traditions. The France of St. Louis, for instance, did not correspond to the old territory of the Franks. In one direction it embraced ancient Septimania, which the Visigoths had formerly controlled. In the other it withdrew from Flanders, Franconia and the Rhineland, which were all Germanic territories and were eventually attracted into the orbit of the Holy Roman Empire.

Furthermore, though his title might derive officially from the titles with which the old barbarian kings had adorned their persons, the national king was at first only the head, and sometimes the nominal head, of a federation of great barons—first among them, but first among peers. Hugh Capet and Philip Augustus were looked upon in just that way in France. King John of England appears in that guise in the text of the Magna Charta, and so do the kings of Aragon in the oath which they were obliged to take before the Cortes. As is well known, the barons of Aragon, in council assembled, invited the new king to swear that he would keep all the old agreements. Before enumerating them, they repeated a declaration: "We, who one by one are your equals and all united are more than your equals, name you our king on the following conditions." And when the conditions had been read, they concluded: "And otherwise not."

More than six centuries of struggle and slow but constant ferment were needed for the feudal king to develop into the absolute king, the feudal hierarchy into a regular bureaucracy, and the army made up of the nobles in arms and their vassals into a regular standing army. During those six hundred years, there were periods when feudalism was able to take advantage of critical moments that country and crown chanced to be passing through and regain some of its lost ground. But in the end victory rested with centralized monarchy. The kings little by little succeeded in gathering into their hands assemblages of material agencies that were greater than the feudal nobility could match. They also made shrewd use of the support of the communes and of powerful and constant moral forces, such as the widespread belief that reigning dynasties had been divinely appointed to rule, or a theory of the doctors of law that the king, like the ancient Roman Emperor, was the sovereign will that created law and the sovereign power that enforced it.

The process by which feudal monarchy evolved into an absolute bureaucratic monarchy might be called typical or normal, since it was followed in France and in a number of other countries in Europe. Nevertheless, there were other processes which led, or might have led, to the same results. The commune of Milan, for instance, in the valley of the Po, developed first into a signoria, or tyranny, and then into a duchy. In the first half of the fifteenth century it subjected many other communes and acquired a fairly extensive territory. It might easily have become a modern national kingdom. Elsewhere great feudatories enlarged their domains and transformed them into kingdoms. That was the case with the margraves of Brandenburg, who became kings of Prussia and then emperors of Germany, and with the dukes of Savoy, who became kings of Sardinia and finally of Italy.

Economic causes seem to have exercised very little influence on the transformation of the feudal state into the bureaucratic state, and that evolution certainly is one of the events that have most profoundly modified the history of the world. Systems of economic production did not undergo any very radical changes between the fourteenth century and the seventeenth, especially if we compare them with the changes that took place after bureaucratic absolutism was founded. On the other hand, between the end of the fifteenth century and the second half of the seventeenth—in other words, during the period when the feudal system was losing ground every day and was being permanently tamed—a farreaching revolution was taking place in military art and organization, owing to improvements in firearms and their wider and wider use. The baronial castle could easily and rapidly be battered down as soon as cannon became common weapons. The heavy cavalry had been made up of nobles, the only ones who could find time for long training and money for the expensive knightly equipment. But cavalry ceased to be the arm that decided battles, once the arquebus had been perfected and the infantry had generally adopted it.

•

The absolute bureaucratic state may be regarded as permanently established and fully developed in France at the beginning of the personal reign of Louis XIV—in 1661, that is. At the same time, or soon after, the strengthening of central authority and the absorption of local sovereignties became more or less completely generalized throughout Europe. The few states, such as Poland or Venice, that would not, or could not, move with the times and transform their constitutions, lost power and cohesion, and disappeared before the end of the eighteenth century.

Thus the origins of absolute monarchy are relatively recent. Inside it, and under its wing, new ruling forces, new intellectual, moral and economic conditions, rapidly grew up, so that in less than a century and a half its transformation into the modern representative state became inevitable. The rapidity of that evolution strikes us as one of the most interesting phenomena in history.

CHAPTER 26

WILL HERBERG

Religious Revival in the United States

The Contemporary Upswing in Religion

No one who attempts to see the contemporary religious situation in the United States in perspective can fail to be struck by the extraordinary pervasiveness of religious identification among present-day Americans. Almost everybody in the United States today locates himself in one or another of the three great religious communities. . . .

In the quarter of a century between 1926 and 1959, the population of continental United States increased 28.6 per cent; membership of religious bodies increased 59.8 per cent: in other words, church membership grew more than twice as fast as population. Protestants increased 63.7 per cent, Catholics 53.9 per cent, Jews 22.5 per cent. Among Protestants, however, the increase varied considerably as between denominations: Baptist increase was well over 100 per cent, some "holiness" sects grew even more rapidly, while the figure for the Episcopal Church was only 36.7 per cent, for the Methodist Church 32.2 per cent, for the Northern Presbyterians 22.4 per cent, and for the Congregationalists 21.1 per cent.[1] In general, it may be said that "practically all major types of American religion have staged what is popularly called a 'comeback.' "[2]

In 1950 total church membership was reckoned at 85,319,000, or about 57 per cent of the total population. In 1958 it was 109,557,741, or about 63

From Will Herberg, *Protestant—Catholic—Jew* (New York: Doubleday and Company, Inc., 1955). Copyright © 1955 by Will Herberg, and reprinted by permission of the author and Doubleday and Company, Inc., pp. 46-53, 256-272.

[1] "Trends of Church Membership in the Larger Religious Bodies," *Information Service,* issued by the National Council of the Churches of Christ in the United States of America, March 8, 1952.

[2] Herbert W. Schneider, *Religion in 20th Century America* (Cambridge: Harvard University Press, 1952), p. 16.

per cent, marking an all-time high in the nation's history.[3] Indeed, all available information tends to show that the proportion of the American people religiously affiliated as church members has been consistently growing from the early days of the republic. In his address to the Evanston Assembly of the World Council of Churches, President Eisenhower pointed out that "Contrary to what many people think, the percentage of our population belonging to churches steadily increases. In a hundred years, that percentage has multiplied more than three times." [4]

President Eisenhower was here probably understating the case. Comparisons are difficult, and figures even approximately accurate are not available for earlier times, but it seems to be generally agreed that church membership in the United States at the opening of the nineteenth century was not much more than 10 or 15 per cent of the population; [5] through the century it grew at a varying rate, reflecting many factors, but above all the success of the evangelical movement in bringing religion to the frontier and the vast influx of Roman Catholic immigrants with a high proportion of church membership. At the opening of the present century, church membership stood at something like 36 per cent of the population; in 1926, when the Census of Religious Bodies established a new basis of calculation, it was about 46 per cent; in 1958, 63 per cent.[6] The trend is obvious, despite the lack of precision of the particular figures.

It is not easy to understand just what these figures reveal beyond a steady increase through a century and a half. Church membership does not mean the same today as it meant in the eighteenth or early nineteenth century, when something of the older sense of personal conversion and commitment still remained. Further, such factors as recent population trends and the increased mobility conferred by the automobile cannot be ignored in any serious effort to estimate the reasons for the growing proportion of Americans in the churches. There is also the significant fact that considerably more Americans regard themselves as church members than the statistics of church affiliation would indicate. Asked, "Do you happen at the present time to be an active member of a church or of a religious group?", 73 per cent of Americans over eighteen answered in the affirmative: of those identifying themselves as Catholics, 87 per cent said "yes"; of those identifying themselves as Protestants, 75 per cent; and of those identifying

---

[3] *Yearbook of American Churches,* Benson Y. Landis, ed., issued annually by the National Council of the Churches of Christ in the United States of America, New York, edition for 1960, pp. 258, 279.

[4] *The New York Times,* August 20, 1954.

[5] Cf. Winfred E. Garrison, "Characteristics of American Organized Religion," *The Annals of the American Academy of Political and Social Science,* Vol. 256, March 1948, p. 20.

[6] *Yearbook of American Churches, op. cit.,* edition for 1955, pp. 288-289; edition for 1960, pp. 278-279.

themselves as Jews, 50 per cent.[7] The overall total of 73 per cent is considerably higher than the percentage indicated in church membership statistics: 57 per cent in 1950 and 63 per cent in 1958. It would seem that many more people in the United States regard themselves as members, even "active" members, of a church than are listed on the actual membership rolls of the churches. The fact of the matter seems to be that: "In America, there is no sharp division between those within the religious fold and those outside, as there tends to be in Europe. It is extremely difficult, in fact, to determine just how many members the churches have, since no clear boundary marks off members from those who participate without formal membership." [8]

About 70 to 75 per cent of the American people, it may be safely estimated, regard themselves as members of churches; [9] another 20 or 25 per cent locate themselves in one or another religious community without a consciousness of actual church membership; they constitute a "fringe of sympathetic bystanders," [10] so to speak. Only about 5 per cent of the American people consider themselves outside the religious fold altogether.

•

That public opinion is markedly more favorable to religion today than it has been for a long time is recognized by all observers. "A hostile attitude toward religion as such," Schneider notes, "gets less of a hearing today than a century ago, or even half a century ago." [11] . . . It is probably true that "in no other modern industrial state does organized religion play a greater role" than it does in the United States.[12]

With institutional growth and enhanced public status has come a notable increase in the self-assurance of the spokesmen of religion, who no longer feel themselves defending a losing cause against a hostile world. . . . Spokesmen of religion are now beginning to speak with the confidence of those who feel that things are going their way and that they are assured of a respectful hearing. Indeed, there have lately arisen voices among the "irreligious" minority who profess to see their "freedom *from* religion" threatened by the increasingly proreligious climate of our culture and the new aggressiveness of the churches.[13] It is a far cry indeed from the 1920's, when religion and the churches were in retreat, faith was taken as a sign of intellectual backwardness or imbecility, and the initiative had passed to the "emanci-

---

[7] "Who Belongs to What Church?" *The Catholic Digest,* January 1953.

[8] Robin M. Williams, Jr., *American Society: a Sociological Interpretation* (New York: Alfred A. Knopf, 1951), p. 325.

[9] *See* Jerald C. Brauer, *Protestantism in America* (Philadelphia: Westminster Press, 1953), p. 286.

[10] *American Society, op. cit.,* p. 325.

[11] *Religion in 20th Century America, op. cit.,* p. 32.

[12] *American Society, op. cit.,* p. 304.

[13] *See e.g., Religion in 20th Century America, op. cit.,* p. 33.

pated" debunkers of the superstitions of the "Babbitts" and the "Bible Belt." That age has disappeared almost without a trace, and the generation that has arisen since finds it well-nigh impossible to imagine what those days were like, so remote from our consciousness have they become.

Particularly significant as reflecting a reversal of trend is the new intellectual prestige of religion on all levels of cultural life. On one level, this means the extraordinarily high proportion of socalled "religious books" on the best-seller lists; on another, the remarkable vogue in intellectual circles of the more sophisticated religious and theological writing of our time. Kierkegaard (rediscovered in this generation), Tillich, Maritain, Reinhold Niebuhr, Buber, Berdyaev, Simone Weil—these writers have standing and prestige with the intellectual elite of today in a way that no religious writers have had for many decades. Religious ideas, concepts, and teachings have become familiar in the pages of the "vanguard" journals of literature, politics and art.

•

The Triple Melting Pot

The outstanding feature of the religious situation in America today is the pervasiveness of religious self-identification along the tripartite scheme of Protestant, Catholic, Jew. From the "land of immigrants," America has . . . become the "triple melting pot," restructured in three great communities with religious labels, defining three great "communions" or "faiths." This transformation has been greatly furthered by what may be called the dialectic of "third generation interest": the third generation, coming into its own with the cessation of mass immigration, tries to recover its "heritage," so as to give itself some sort of "name" or context of self-identification and social location, in the larger society. "What the son wishes to forget"—so runs "Hansen's Law"—"the grandson wishes to remember." But what he can "remember" is obviously not his grandfather's foreign language, or even his grandfather's foreign culture; it is rather his grandfather's *religion.* America does not demand of him the abandonment of the ancestral religion as it does of the ancestral language and culture. This religion he now "remembers" in a form suitably "Americanized," and yet in a curious way also "retraditionalized." Within this comprehensive framework of basic sociological change operate those inner factors making for a "return to religion" which so many observers have noted in recent years—the collapse of all secular securities in the historical crisis of our time, the quest for a recovery of meaning in life, the new search for inwardness and personal authenticity amid the collectivistic heteronomies of the present-day world.

Self-identification in religious terms, almost universal in the America of today, obviously makes for religious belonging in a more directly institutional way. It engenders a sense of adherence to a church or denomination and impels one to institutional affiliation. These tendencies are reinforced by the pressures of other-directed adjustment to peer-group behavior, which today increasingly requires religious identification and association with some church. Thus a pattern of religious conformism develops, most pronounced, perhaps, among the younger, "modern-minded" inhabitants of suburbia, but rapidly spreading to all sections of the American people.

The picture that emerges is one in which religion is accepted as a normal part of the American way of life. Not to be—that is, not to identify oneself and be identified as—either a Protestant, a Catholic, or a Jew is somehow not to be an American. It may imply being foreign, as is the case when one professes oneself a Buddhist, a Muslim, or anything but a Protestant, Catholic, or Jew, even when one's Americanness is otherwise beyond question. Or it may imply being obscurely "un-American," as is the case with those who declare themselves atheists, agnostics, or even "humanists." . . . Americanness today entails religious identification as Protestant, Catholic, or Jew in a way and to a degree quite unprecedented in our history. To be a Protestant, a Catholic, or a Jew is today the alternative way of being an American.

•

The Religion of "Belonging"

The ultimate ambiguity of the present religious situation in this country is obvious on the face of it. Every manifestation of contemporary American religion reveals diverse sides, of varying significance from the standpoint of Jewish-Christian faith. No realistic estimate of the present religious situation is possible unless this fundamental ambiguity is recognized.

The new status of religion as a basic form of American "belonging," along with other factors tending in the same direction, has led to the virtual disappearance of anti-religious prejudice, once by no means uncommon in our national life. The old-time "village atheist" is a thing of the past, a folk curiosity like the town crier; Clarence Darrow, the last of the "village atheists" on a national scale, has left no successors. The present generation can hardly understand the vast excitement stirred up in their day by the "atheists" and "iconoclasts," who vied for public attention less than half a century ago, or imagine the brash militancy of the "rationalist" movements and publications now almost all extinct. Religion has become part of the ethos of American life to such a degree that overt anti-religion is all but inconceivable.

The same factors that have led to the virtual disappearance of overt anti-religion have also made for a new openness to religion and what religion might have to say about the urgent problems of life and thought. In many ways the contemporary mind is more ready to listen to the word of faith than Americans have been for decades.

Yet it is only too evident that the religiousness characteristic of America today is very often a religiousness without religion, a religiousness with almost any kind of content or none, a way of sociability or "belonging" rather than a way of reorienting life to God. It is thus frequently a religiousness without serious commitment, without real inner conviction, without genuine existential decision. What should reach down to the core of existence, shattering and renewing, merely skims the surface of life, and yet succeeds in generating the sincere feeling of being religious. Religion thus becomes a kind of protection the self throws up against the radical demand of faith.

Where the other-directed adjustment of peer-group conformity operates, the discrepancy becomes even more obvious. The other-directed man or woman is eminently religious in the sense of being religiously identified and affiliated, since being religious and joining a church or synagogue is, under contemporary American conditions, a fundamental way of "adjusting" or "belonging." But what can the other-directed man or woman make of the prophets and the prophetic faith of the Bible, in which the religion of the church he joins is at least officially grounded? The very notion of being "singled out," of standing "over against" the world, is deeply repugnant to one for whom wellbeing means conformity and adjustment. Religion is valued as conferring a sense of sociability and "belonging," a sense of being really and truly *of* the world and society, a sense of reassurance; how can the other-directed man then help but feel acutely uncomfortable with a kind of religion—for that is what biblical faith is—which is a declaration of permanent resistance to the heteronomous claims of society, community, culture and cult? The other-directed man generally protects himself against this profoundly disturbing aspect of biblical faith by refusing to understand it; indeed, insofar as he is other-directed, he really cannot understand it. The religion he avows is still formally the Christian or Jewish faith rooted in the prophetic tradition; it is, however, so transformed as it passes through the prism of the other-directed mind that it emerges as something quite different, in many ways, its opposite.

•

"The 'unknown God' of Americans seems to be faith itself." [14] What Americans believe in when they are religious is . . . religion itself. Of course, religious Americans speak of God and Christ, but what they seem to regard as really redemptive is primarily religion, the "positive" attitude of *believing*. It is this faith in faith, this religion that makes religion its own object, that is the outstanding characteristic of contemporary American religiosity.

---

[14] Reinhold Niebuhr, "Religiosity and the Christian Faith," *Christianity and Crisis,* XIV (1955), No. 24.

•

Religion Becomes Man-Centered

Prosperity, success, and advancement in business are the obvious ends for which religion, or rather the religious attitude of "believing," is held to be useful. There is ordinarily no criticism of the ends themselves in terms of the ultimate loyalties of a God-centered faith, nor is there much concern about what the religion or the faith is all about, since it is not the content of the belief but the attitude of believing that is felt to be operative.

Almost as much as worldly success, religion is expected to produce a kind of spiritual euphoria, the comfortable feeling that one is all right with God. Roy Eckardt calls this the cult of "divine-human chumminess" in which God is envisioned as the "Man Upstairs," a "Friendly Neighbor," who is always ready to give you the pat on the back you need when you happen to feel blue. "Fellowship with the Lord is, so to say, an extra emotional jag that keeps [us] happy. The 'gospel' makes [us] 'feel real good.' " [15] Again, all sense of the ambiguity and precariousness of human life, all sense of awe before the divine majesty, all sense of judgment before the divine holiness, is shut out; God is, in Jane Russell's inimitable phrase, a "livin' Doll." What relation has this kind of god to the biblical God who confronts sinful man as an enemy before he comes out to meet repentant man as a savior? Is this he of whom we are told, "It is a fearful thing to fall into the hands of the living God" (*Heb.* 10.31)? The measure of how far contemporary American religiosity falls short of the authentic tradition of Jewish-Christian faith is to be found in the chasm that separates Jane Russell's "livin' Doll" from the living god of scripture.

The cultural enrichment that is looked for in religion varies greatly with the community, the denomination, and the outlook and status of the church members. Liturgy is valued as aesthetically and emotionally "rewarding," sermons are praised as "interesting" and "enjoyable," discussions of the world relations of the church are welcomed as "educational," even theology is approved of as "thought-provoking." On another level, the "old-time religion" is cherished by certain segments of the population because it so obviously enriches their cultural life.

But in the last analysis, it is "peace of mind" that most Americans expect of religion. "Peace of mind" is today easily the most popular gospel that goes under the name of religion; in one way or another it invades and permeates all other forms of contemporary religiosity. It works in well with the drift toward other-direction characteristic of large sections of American so-

---

[15] Roy Eckardt, "The New Look in American Piety," *The Christian Century*, November 17, 1954.

ciety, since both see in adjustment the supreme good in life. What is desired and what is promised is the conquest of insecurity and anxiety, the overcoming of inner conflict, the shedding of guilt and fear, the translation of the self to the painless paradise of "normality" and "adjustment"! Religion, in short, is a spiritual anodyne designed to allay the pains and vexations of existence.

•

The burden of the criticism of American religion from the point of view of Jewish-Christian faith is that contemporary religion is so naïvely, so innocently *man-centered*. Not god, but man—man in his individual and corporate being—is the beginning and end of the spiritual system of much of present-day American religiosity. In this kind of religion there is no sense of transcendence, no sense of the nothingness of man and his works before a holy god; in this kind of religion the values of life, and life itself, are not submitted to Almighty God to judge, to shatter, and to reconstruct; on the contrary, life, and the values of life, are given an ultimate sanction by being identified with the divine. In this kind of religion it is not man who serves god, but god who is mobilized and made to serve man and his purposes—whether these purposes be economic prosperity, free enterprise, social reform, democracy, happiness, security, or "peace of mind." . . . The American is a religious man, and in many cases personally humble and conscientious. But religion as he understands it is not something that makes for humility or the uneasy conscience: it is something that reassures him about the essential rightness of everything American, his nation, his culture, and himself; something that validates his goals and his ideals instead of calling them into question; something that enhances his self-regard instead of challenging it; something that feeds his self-sufficiency instead of shattering it; something that offers him salvation on easy terms instead of demanding repentance and a "broken heart." Because it does all these things, his religion, however sincere and well-meant, is ultimately vitiated by a strong and pervasive idolatrous element.

•

Yet we must not see the picture as all of one piece. Within the general framework of a secularized religion embracing the great mass of American people, there are signs of deeper and more authentic stirrings of faith. Duncan Norton-Taylor, in his comments on the new religiousness of businessmen, may not be altogether wrong in noting that "particularly among the younger men, there *is* a groping for a spiritual base." [16] Norman Thomas, though recognizing that the "return to religion," which is "one of the significant phenomena of our confused and troubled times," is a "phenomenon of many and contradictory aspects," nevertheless finds it, in part at least,

---

[16] Duncan Norton-Taylor, "Businessmen on Their Knees," *Fortune,* October, 1953.

"definitely characterized by an awareness of, or search after God." [17] Certainly among the younger people, particularly among the more sensitive young men and women on the campuses of this country, and in the suburban communities that are in so many ways really continuous with the campus, there are unmistakable indications of an interest in and concern with religion that goes far beyond the demands of mere social "belonging." [18] These stirrings are there; they are not always easily identified as religion on the one hand, or easily distinguishable from the more conventional types of religiousness on the other; but they constitute a force whose range and power should not be too readily dismissed. Only the future can tell what these deeper stirrings of faith amount to and what consequences they hold for the American religion of tomorrow. . . .

---

[17] Norman Thomas, "Religion and Civilization," *The Atlantic Monthly*, August, 1947.

[18] Will Herberg, "The Religious Stirring on the Campus," *Commentary*, XIII (1952), No. 2.

CHAPTER 27

PETER F. DRUCKER

The Educational Revolution

An abundant and increasing supply of highly educated people has become the absolute prerequisite of social and economic development in our
world. It is rapidly becoming a condition of national survival. What matters is not that there are so many more individuals around who have been
exposed to long years of formal schooling—though this is quite recent. The
essential new fact is that a developed society and economy are less than
fully effective if anyone is educated to less than the limit of his potential.
The uneducated is fast becoming an economic liability and unproductive.
Society must be an "educated society" today to progress, to grow, even to
survive.

A sudden, sharp change has occurred in the meaning and impact of
knowledge for society. Because we now can organize men of high skill and
knowledge for joint work through the exercise of responsible judgment, the
highly educated man has become the central resource of today's society, the
supply of such men the true measure of its economic, its military, and even
its political potential.

This is a complete reversal of man's history within the last fifty years or
so. Until the twentieth century, no society could afford more than a handful of educated people; for throughout the ages, to be educated meant to
be unproductive.

•

It has always been axiomatic that the man of even a little education
would forsake the hoe and the potter's wheel and would stop working with
his hands. After all, our word "school"—and its equivalent in all European
languages—derives from a Greek word meaning "leisure."

To support more educated people than the barest minimum required
gross exploitation of the "producers," if not strict rules to keep them at work

and away from education. The short burst of education in the Athens of Pericles rested on a great expansion of slavery, the intellectual and artistic splendor of the Italian Renaissance on a sharp debasement of the economic and social position of peasant and artisan.

Idealists tried to break this "iron law" by combining manual work and education; the tradition goes back to the Rule of St. Benedict with its mixture of farmwork and study. It found its best expression in the mid-nineteenth century, in Emerson's New England farmer who supposedly read Homer in the original Greek while guiding a plow. But this, of course, never worked. The Benedictines—imperiling their salvation, to the lasting benefit of mankind—very soon left farming to villeins and serfs and concentrated on study. Long before Emerson's death, those New England farmers who cared for the plow had left both Homer and New England for the rich soils of the Midwest, while those few who had cared for Homer had left farming altogether to become lawyers, preachers, teachers or politicians. The "iron law" was indeed inescapable as long as manual labor was the really productive labor.

Thomas Jefferson believed in higher education and in equality as much as any American. He considered the founding of the University of Virginia and the authorship of the Declaration of Independence, rather than the Presidency, his greatest achievements. Yet in his educational master plan he proposed to limit access to higher education to a handful of geniuses. It was obvious that only a few could be spared from manual labor.

Today the dearth of educated people in the formerly colonial areas appears such a handicap as by itself to be adequate condemnation of colonialism and proof of the "wickedness" of the imperialists. But education did not come first in the scale of social needs even fifty years ago; flood control and land boundaries, equitable taxation and improved agriculture, railroads and incorruptible magistrates, all ranked much higher. If the colonial powers were then criticized on the score of education, it was for forcing it on too many, for destroying thereby the native culture, and for creating an unemployable, overeducated proletariat. The educated person was then still a luxury rather than a necessity and education a preparation for dignified leisure rather than for productive work.

In my own childhood forty years ago, schools still assumed that education was for "nonwork." They preached that the educated man should not despise the honest worker, as schools had preached since the days of Seneca in the first century.

The Scale of the Explosion

Thirty years ago, only one out of every eight Americans at work had been to high school. Today four out of every five of the young people of high school age in the United States attend high school. Twenty years hence, when today's middleaged will have retired, practically every working American will be a high school graduate. We have already passed the halfway mark.

Even greater has been the jump in college and university attendance. Thirty years ago, it was still an almost negligible 4 per cent or less of the appropriate age group. Today the figure is around 35 per cent for the nation; this takes in groups such as the southern Negro or the southern "poor white," for whom going to college is still all but unknown. In the metropolitan areas of the country—even in such predominantly working-class cities as Detroit—the figure is nearly 50 per cent. It will, barring catastrophe, be that high for the nation as a whole in another fifteen years. By then two out of every three young Americans in the metropolitan areas will, regardless almost of income, race, or sex, be exposed to higher education.

In the American work force of thirty years ago, there were at most three college graduates for every hundred men and women at work. There are eighteen today; the figure will be thirty-five, twenty years hence—even if, contrary to all expectations, going to college becomes no more general than it is already among the two-thirds of our people who live in metropolitan areas.

On top of all this, adult education is booming. Fifty years ago, only those adults went back to school who had been unable to get a formal education as children. Adult education was for the educationally underprivileged— the immigrant from southern Europe who wanted to learn English, or the man who had gone to work at age fourteen and wanted to improve himself. In England adult education was the "Workers Educational Alliance" or the "Home University Library," both offering standard school subjects to workers and clerks. The German *Volkshochschule* served the same purpose.

Adult education during the last fifteen years has been growing faster in this country than college enrollment. And now, increasingly, it means advanced education for the already highly educated. It is almost routine for the experienced and successful physician to go back to school for advanced training every two or three years. Refresher courses are increasingly demanded of our teachers. Some fifty universities—in addition to a dozen large companies and professional management associations—offer advanced management courses to successful men in the middle and upper ranks of business, who usually already have college if not advanced degrees. Yet before World War II only two such programs existed, both new and both struggling to get students.

The educational revolution has been even more explosive in Soviet Russia. Thirty years ago, basic literacy was confined to a small minority and had probably fallen even below the low standards of czarist Russia. The educational push hardly began until the mid-thirties. Today, because of Russia's larger population, the proportion of young people in secondary or higher education is still quite a bit lower than in this country, but the absolute numbers are fast approaching ours.

In the total population of the Soviet Union, educated people must still be a small group. Few if any of the top people in the Soviet Union have had more than elementary formal schooling; certainly of those over forty in the Soviet Union, even high school graduates are still only a tiny fraction. But in Russia, too, it has become evident that education is the capital resource of a modern, industrial society. We know now that the Russian achievement does not rest on the Communist tenets of "socialist ownership of productive resources," the "dictatorship of the proletariat," "collectivization of agriculture," or "national planning." Every one of them has been as much an impediment as a help, a source of weakness fully as much as a source of strength. The achievement rests squarely upon the tremendous concentration of resources, time, and effort on producing an educated society.

The two outstanding success stories among small nations, Switzerland and Mexico, have nothing in common save extraordinary educational development. Switzerland is the one European country where secondary education, in the last thirty years, has become almost universal. Mexico is the only country in the world that, since the mid-thirties, has spent no money on defense but has instead made education the first charge on its national income. And is it entirely coincidence that the major countries in the Free World that have found the going the roughest since World War II, Great Britain and France, are also the countries in which the educational revolution has advanced the least, in which the supply of educated people, though of high quality, is today still not much larger proportionately than it was in 1930 or even in 1913? In England the supply may well be smaller, considering the steady emigration of so many of the highly educated young people.

We are undergoing the educational revolution because the work of knowledge is no longer unproductive in terms of goods and services. In the new organization, it becomes the specifically productive work. The man who works exclusively or primarily with his hands is the one who is increasingly unproductive. Productive work in today's society and economy is work that applies vision, knowledge, and concepts—work that is based on the mind rather than on the hand.

There will therefore be no permanent oversupply of educated people. On the contrary, the more there are, the greater should be the demand for them. Educated people are the "capital" of a developed society. The immediate impact of, say, using physicians instead of barbers is to uncover needs, opportunities, and areas of ignorance, leading to the need both for more physicians and for more medical and biological research. The same process can be seen in every other field—and with particular force in the economic field of production and distribution. Every engineer, every chemist, every accountant, every market analyst immediately creates the opportunity and the need for more men who can apply knowledge and concepts, both in his own field and all around it.

This may sound obvious. But it is so new that it is not yet recognized. Our accountants, for instance, still base their terms and measurements on the eighteenth-century tenet that manual labor creates all value. They still call it "productive labor"; the work of men of knowledge is "nonproductive labor" or "overhead," a term reeking of moral disapproval. When economists talk of "capital" they rarely include "knowledge." Yet this is the only real capital today. The development of educated people is the most important capital formation, their number, quality, and utilization the most meaningful index of the wealth-producing capacity of a country.

The Impact on Society

What is today called "automation," that is, the rapid substitution of work by knowledge and concept for work by human hands, is a first impact of the educated society. It is a moot question whether the essence of automation lies in specific machinery and technical ideas, or whether it lies rather in basic concepts about the nature of work.

But there can be little doubt that the driving force in automation is the fact that people who have been exposed to formal schooling for twelve or sixteen years have expectations in respect to work and jobs which manual work, no matter how well paid, does not fulfill. They increasingly demand jobs in which they can apply knowledge, concepts, and system. They increasingly refuse to accept jobs in which they cannot apply what they have learned, namely, to work with their minds. They may be satisfied with a job of little skill—and there are a good many semiskilled knowledge jobs— but they expect work that draws on mental rather than manual faculties.

In the United States, where most of the young people in the metropolitan areas go at least to high school, the assembly line is already obsolete. The labor necessary to run it is becoming scarce. Young people with a high school education do not want to work as human machine tools. Moreover, to use people with that degree of education for the semiskilled and unskilled manual jobs of the assembly line would be a gross waste of valuable, expensive, and scarce resources.

Tomorrow everybody—or practically everybody—will have had the education of the upper class of yesterday and will expect equivalent opportunities. Yet only a small minority can get ahead, no matter what work they choose. This is why we face the problem of making every kind of job meaningful and capable of satisfying an educated man. This is why the new organization must create an effective relationship of function, rank, rewards, and responsibility, not only for its professionals, but for all those employed in knowledge jobs.

•

The educational revolution has had an equal impact on the world economy. Educational capacity, as much as natural resources or industrial plants, is becoming a crucial factor in international trade, economic development, and economic competition. Educational development, above all, has become a central problem of the poor countries.

Many of these underdeveloped countries spend today a larger proportion of their national income on education than does the United States. Yet where we complain that one-fifth of our young people still do not finish high school, many of these countries can barely keep one-fifth of their young people in elementary school. They cannot finance the cost of a literate society, let alone that of an educated society.

This educational inequality is a serious international and interracial problem. Its inevitable result is to make inequality greater, to make the rich richer and the poor poorer. Even greater is the danger that it will push poor, underdeveloped countries into the totalitarian camp; for a totalitarian tyranny, so it appears to them, can raise enough money for the rapid development of education even in the poorest. (This is a delusion. Practically all the poor underdeveloped countries are much poorer than Russia was in 1917 and much further behind in education. They are unlikely therefore to repeat her performance in education even by faithfully copying every Russian tenet and action. But this may be found out only when it is too late.)

Here, it would seem, is a highly promising area for international aid and cooperation. There is need and opportunity for financial aid to help the underdeveloped countries pay for the rapid expansion of education. There is need for systematic cooperative effort in training and developing people, especially future teachers. There is need and opportunity to help think through the purposes, the structure and the methods of education needed in those countries. Above all, there is need for the developed countries, and especially for the United States, to accept a national policy of assisting underdeveloped countries in building education.

•

"The Battle of Waterloo," it is said, "was won on the playing fields of Eton." Perhaps, but no one asserts that it was won in Eton's classrooms. "The Prussian schoolmaster," another saying goes, "defeated France in the War of 1870 that created imperial Germany." But long ago this was exposed as empty boast; the credit belongs to the German railway and the German armaments designers.

With the launching of Russia's Sputnik, however, the old pleasantry became a grim fact. The higher education of a country controls its military, its technological and its economic potential. In an age of superpowers and absolute weapons, higher education may indeed be the only area in which a country can still be ahead, can still gain decisive advantage.

The greatest impact of the educational revolution is therefore on international power and politics. It has made the supply of highly educated people a decisive factor in the competition between powers—for leadership and perhaps even for survival. . . .

CHAPTER 28

LEO LOWENTHAL

Biographies in Popular Magazines: From Production Leaders to Consumption Idols

Rise of Biography as a Popular Literary Type

The following study is concerned with the content analysis of biographies, a literary topic which has inundated the book market for the last decades and has for some time been a regular feature of popular magazines. Surprisingly enough, not very much attention has been paid to this phenomenon, none whatever to biographies appearing in magazines, and little to those published in book form.

It started before the first World War, but the main onrush came shortly afterward. The popular biography was one of the most conspicuous newcomers in the realm of print since the introduction of the short story. The circulation of books by Emil Ludwig, André Maurois, Lytton Strachey, Stefan Zweig, etc. reached a figure in the millions, and with each new publication the number of languages into which they were translated grew. Even if it were only a passing literary fad, one would still have to explain why this fashion has had such longevity and is more and more becoming a regular feature in the most diversified media of publications.

Who's Who, once known as a title of a specialized dictionary for editors and advertisers, has nowadays become the outspoken or implied question in innumerable popular contexts. The interest in individuals has become a

From Leo Lowenthal, "Biographies in Popular Magazines," in Paul F. Lazarsfeld and Frank N. Stanton, eds., *Radio Research 1942-1943* (New York: Essential Books, 1944), pp. 507-519. Reprinted by permission of the author and the editors.

kind of mass gossip. The majority of weeklies and monthlies, and many dailies too, publish at least one life story or a fragment of one in each issue; theater programs present abridged biographies of all the actors; the more sophisticated periodicals, such as *The New Republic* or *Harper's,* offer short accounts of the main intellectual achievements of their contributors; and a glance into the popular corners of the book trade, including drug store counters, will invariably fall on biographies. All this forces the conclusion that there must be a social need seeking gratification by this type of literature.

One way to find out would be to study the readers' reactions, to explore by means of various interviewing techniques what they are looking for, what they think about the biographical jungle. But it seems to be rather premature to collect and to evaluate such solicited response until more is known about the content structure itself.

As an experiment in content analysis, a year's publication of *The Saturday Evening Post (SEP)* and of *Collier's* for the period from April, 1940 to March, 1941 was covered.[1] It is regrettable that a complete investigation could not be made for the most recent material, but samples taken at random from magazines under investigation showed that no basic change in the selection or content structure has occurred since this country's entry into the war.

Biographers' Idols

Before entering into a discussion of our material we shall briefly look into the fate of the biographical feature during the past decades.

Production—Yesterday

Biographical sections have not always been a standing feature in these periodicals. If we turn back the pages we find distinct differences in the number of articles as well as in the selection of people treated.

Table 28-1 gives a survey of the professional distribution of the "heroes" in biographies between 1901 and 1941.

Table 28-1 indicates clearly a tremendous increase in biographies as time goes on. The average figure of biographies in 1941 is almost four times as high as at the beginning of the century. The biography has nowadays become a regular weekly feature. Just to illustrate how relatively small the

---

[1] It should not be inferred that the results as presented here are without much change applicable to all other magazines which present general and diversified topics. From a few selections taken from less widely circulated and more expensive magazines, ranging from *The New Yorker* to the dollar-a-copy *Fortune,* it seems very likely that the biographies presented there differ in their average content structure and therefore in their social and psychological implications from these lower-priced popular periodicals. The difference in contents corresponds to a difference in readership.

number of biographies was forty years ago: in 52 issues of the *SEP* of 1901-1902 we find altogether 21 biographies, as compared with not less than 57 in 1940-1941. The smallness of the earlier figure in comparison to

Table **28-1**

Distribution of Biographies According to Professions in *Saturday Evening Post* and *Collier's* for Selected Years between 1901 and 1941

	1901-1914 (5 sample yrs.)		1922-1930 (6 sample yrs.)		1930-1934 (4 years)		1940-1941 (1 year)	
	No.	%	No.	%	No.	%	No.	%
Political life	81	46	112	28	95	31	31	25
Business and professional	49	28	72	18	42	14	25	20
Entertainment	47	26	211	54	169	55	69	55
TOTAL NUMBER	177	100	395	100	306	100	125	100
Yearly average of biographies	36		66		77		125	

the present day is emphasized by the fact that nonfictional contributions at that time far outnumbered the fictional material. A fair average of distribution in the past would be about three fictional and eight nonfictional contributions; today we never find more than twice as many nonfictional as fictional contributions and in the majority of cases even fewer.

We put the subjects of the biographies in three groups: the spheres of political life, of business and professions, and of entertainment (the latter in the broadest sense of the word). Looking at our table we find for the time before World War I very high interest in political figures and an almost equal distribution of business and professional men, on the one hand, and of entertainers on the other. This picture changes completely after the war. The figures from political life have been cut by 40 per cent, the business and professional men have lost 30 per cent of their personnel, while the entertainers have gained 50 per cent. This numerical relation seems to be rather constant from 1922 up to the present day. If we reformulate our professional distribution by leaving out the figures from political life, we see even more clearly the considerable decrease of people from the serious and important professions and a corresponding increase of entertainers. The social impact of this change comes to the fore strikingly if we analyze the composition of the entertainers. This can be seen from Table 28-2.

While at the beginning of the century three-quarters of the entertainers were serious artists and writers, we find that this class of people is reduced by half twenty years later and tends to disappear almost completely at present.

Table 28-2

Proportion of Biographies of Entertainers from the Realm of Serious Arts[a] in *SEP* and *Collier's* for Selected Years between 1901 and 1941 (in Per Cent of Total Biographies of Entertainers in Each Period)

Period	Proportion Entertainers from Serious Arts	Total No. Entertainers
1901-1914 (5 sample yrs.)	77	47
1922-1930 (6 sample yrs.)	38	211
1930-1934 (4 yrs.)	29	169
1940-1941 (1 yr.)	9	69

a This group includes literature, fine arts, music, dance, theater.

As an instance of the selection of biographies typical of the first decade of the century, it is notable that out of the 21 biographies of the *SEP* 1901-1902, eleven came from the political sphere, seven from the business and professions, and three from entertainment and sport. The people in the political group are numerically prominent until before Election Day in the various years: candidates for high office, *i.e.,* the President or senators; the Secretary of the Treasury; an eminent state governor. In the business world, we are introduced to J. P. Morgan, the banker; his partner, George W. Perkins; James J. Hill, the railroad president. In the professions, we find one of the pioneers in aviation; the inventor of the torpedo; a famous Negro educator; an immigrant scientist. Among the entertainers there is an opera singer, Emma Calvé; a poet, Eugene Field; a popular fiction writer, F. Marion Crawford.

If we look at such a selection of people, we find that it represents a fair cross-section of socially important occupations. Still, in 1922 the picture is more similar to the professional distribution quoted above than to the one which is characteristic of the present-day magazines. If we take, for example, *Collier's* of 1922, we find in a total of twenty biographies only two entertainers, but eight business and professional men and ten politicians. Leaving out the latter ones, we find among others: Clarence C. Little, the progressive President of the University of Maine; Leonard P. Ayres, the very outspoken Vice-President of the Cleveland Trust Company; Director-General of the United States Railroad Administration, James C. Davis; President of the New York Central Railroad, A. H. Smith; and the City Planner, John Nolen. From the entertainment field, we have a short résumé of the stage comedian, Joe Cook (incidentally, by Franklin P. Adams) and an autobiographical sketch by Charlie Chaplin.

We might say that a large proportion of the heroes in both samples are idols of production, that they stem from the productive life, from industry, business, and natural sciences. There is not a single hero from the world of sports, and the few artists and entertainers either do not belong to the sphere of cheap or mass entertainment or represent a serious attitude toward their art, as in the case of Chaplin. The first quarter of the century cherishes biography in terms of an openminded liberal society which really wants to know something about its own leading figures on the decisive social, commercial and cultural fronts. Even in the late Twenties, when jazz composers and the sports people are admitted to the inner circle of biographical heroes, their biographies are written almost exclusively to supplement the reader's knowledge of the technical requirements and accomplishments of their respective fields.[2] These people, then, are treated as an embellishment of the national scene, not yet as something that in itself represents a special phenomenon which demands almost undivided attention.

We should like to quote from two stories which seem to be characteristic of this past epoch. In a sketch of Theodore Roosevelt, the following comment is made in connection with the assassination of McKinley: "We, who give such chances of success to all that it is possible for a young man to go as a laborer into the steel business and before he has reached his mature prime become, through his own industry and talent, the president of a vast steel association—we, who make this possible as no country has ever made it possible, have been stabbed in the back by anarchy." [3]

This unbroken confidence in the opportunities open to every individual serves as the leitmotiv of the biographies. To a very great extent they are to be looked upon as examples of success which can be imitated. These life stories are really intended to be educational models. They are written—at least ideologically—for someone who the next day may try to emulate the man whom he has just envied.

A biography seems to be the means by which an average person is able to reconcile his interest in the important trends of history and in the personal lives of other people. In the past, and especially before the first World War, the popular biography lived in an optimistic atmosphere where understanding of historical processes and interest in successful people seemed to integrate pleasantly into one harmonious endeavor: "We know now that the men of trade and commerce and finance are the real builders of freedom, science, and art—and we watch them and study them accordingly. . . . Of course, Mr. Perkins is a 'self-made man.' Who that has ever made

---

[2] *See,* for instance, the *SEP,* September 19, 1925, where the auto-racer, Barney Oldfield, tells a reporter details of his racing experiences and of the mechanics of racing and automobiles; September 26, 1925, in which the vaudeville actress, Elsie Janis, comments on her imitation acts and also gives details of her techniques. The same holds true for the biography of the band leader, Sousa, in the *SEP,* October 31, 1925, and of the radio announcer, Graham McNamee, May 1, 1926; after a few remarks about his own life and career, McNamee goes on to discuss the technical aspects of radio and his experiences in radio with famous people.

[3] *Saturday Evening Post,* October 12, 1901.

a career was not?" [4] This may be taken as a classical formulation for a period of "rugged individualism" in which there is neither the time nor the desire to stimulate a closer interest in the organizers and organization of leisure time, but which is characterized by eagerness and confidence that the social ladder may be scaled on a mass basis.

Consumption—Today

When we turn to our present-day sample, we face an assortment of people which is both qualitatively and quantitatively removed from the standards of the past.

Only two decades ago, people from the realm of entertainment played a very negligible role in the biographical material. They form now, numerically, the first group. While we have not found a single figure from the world of sports in our earlier samples given above, we find them now close to the top of favorite selections. The proportion of people from political life and from business and professions, both representing the "serious side," has declined from 74 to 45 per cent of the total.

Let us examine the group of people representing nonpolitical aspects of life. Sixty-nine are from entertainment and sports; 25 from that which we called before the "serious side." Almost half of the 25 belong to some kind of communications professions: there are ten newspapermen and radio commentators. Of the remaining fifteen business and professional people, there are a pair of munitions traders, Athanasiades and Juan March; Dr. Brinkley, a quack doctor; Mr. Angas, judged by many as a dubious financial expert; Pittsburgh Phil, a horse race gambler in the "grand style"; Mrs. D'Arcy Grant, a woman sailor, and Jo Carstairs, the owner of an island resort; the Varian brothers, inventors of gadgets, and Mr. Taylor, an inventor of foolproof sports devices; Howard Johnson, a roadside restaurant genius; Jinx Falkenburg, at that time a professional model; and finally, Dr. Peabody, a retired rector of a swanky society prep school.

The "serious" people are not so serious after all. In fact there are only nine who might be looked upon as rather important or characteristic figures of the industrial, commercial, or professional activities, and six of these are newspapermen or radio commentators.

We called the heroes of the past "idols of production"; we feel entitled to call the present-day magazine heroes "idols of consumption." Indeed, almost every one of them is directly or indirectly related to the sphere of leisure time; either he does not belong to vocations which serve society's basic needs (e.g., the heroes of the worlds of entertainment and sports), or he amounts, more or less, to a caricature of a socially productive agent. If we add to the group of the 69 people from the entertainment and sports world

---

[4] *Saturday Evening Post,* June 28, 1902.

the ten newspaper and radio men, the professional model, the inventor of sports devices, the quack doctor, the horse race gambler, the inventors of gadgets, the owner of the island resort, and the restaurant chain owner, we see 87 of all 94 nonpolitical heroes directly active in the consumers' world.

Of the eight figures who cannot exactly be classified as connected with consumption, not more than three—namely, the automobile producer, Sloan; the engineer and industrialist, Stout; and the airline tsar, Smith— are important or characteristic functionaries in the world of production. The two armament magnates, the female freight boat skipper, the prep school head, and the doubtful market prophet remind us of the standardized protagonists in mystery novels and related fictional merchandise—people with a more-or-less normal and typical personal and vocational background who would bore us to death if we did not discover that behind the "average" front lurks a "human interest" situation.

By substituting such a classification according to spheres of activity for the cruder one according to professions, we are now prepared to present the vocational stratifications of our heroes in a new form. It is shown in Table 28-3 for the *SEP* and *Collier's* of 1940-1941.

Table **28-3**

The Heroes and Their Spheres

	Number of Stories	Per Cent
Sphere of production	3	2
Sphere of consumption	91	73
Entertainers and sports figures	69	55
Newspaper and radio figures	10	8
Agents of consumers' goods	5	4
Topics of light fiction	7	6
Sphere of politics	31	25
TOTAL	125	100

. . . The idols of the masses are not, as they were in the past, the leading names in the battle of production, but the headliners of the movies, the ballparks, and the nightclubs. While we found that around 1900 and even around 1920 the vocational distribution of magazine heroes was a rather accurate reflection of the nation's living trends, we observe that today the hero-selection corresponds to needs quite different from those of genuine information. They seem to lead to a dream world of the masses who no longer are capable or willing to conceive of biographies primarily as a means of orientation and education. They receive information not about the agents and methods of social production, but about the agents and methods of social and individual consumption. During the leisure in which they read, they read almost exclusively about people who are directly, or indirectly, providing for the reader's leisure time. The vocational setup of the dramatis personae is organized as if the social production process were either completely exterminated or tacitly understood and needed no further interpretation. Instead, the leisure-time period seems to be the new social riddle on which extensive reading and studying has to be done.

The human incorporation of all the social agencies taking care of society as a unity of consumers represents a literary type which is turned out as a standardized article, marketed by a tremendous business, and consumed by another mass institution—the nation's magazine reading public. Thus biography lives as a mass element among the other elements of mass literature. . . .

PART IV

MODERNIZATION

CHAPTER 29

Introduction

Many contemporary societies are still predominantly traditional, in the sense that their demographic, economic, educational, religious, and political structure is much like that which existed centuries ago before modernization set in. Still, even these societies, in addition to having their own internal dynamics, are affected by contacts with other modern societies. Most of them, therefore, have already started on the way toward modernization, though they differ considerably in the point and time of departure, the stage they have reached, the pace, orderliness, and the path their development follows, as well as in the end result for which they strive.

Selections in this part examine modernization mainly from the viewpoint of contemporary traditional or transitional societies. Though some of the generalizations suggested below would apply to all modernization processes, including those of the first traditional societies to modernize, they mostly concern modernization in the contemporary world.

Smelser draws on a differentiation model of the kind presented above by Parsons, to provide an analytical framework for the study of modernization. He analyzes the process by which the major social functions gain structural independence. Previously, the same social units served a large variety of functions. With modernization, special social units evolve for the separate performance of each set of functions. Once the family was the unit in which, among other things, work, religious devotion, and education were carried out. Now work is delegated to the factory and the office, religious services to the church, and formal education to the school. Each of these units has its own authority structure, its own sets of norms prescribing the appropriate forms of behavior, and its own systems of rewards and sanctions to induce conformity and discourage deviation.

Thus differentiation is not just a type of technical specialization, but is profoundly connected with the whole social process of modernization. The crucial link between differentiation and modernization lies in the fact that for every social function there is a distinct set of structural conditions under which it is optimally served. While production can be carried out in the family, it is maximized when delegated to a unit of its own, where actors are detached, calculative, and limited in their orientation to the specific tasks at hand. Education requires an asymmetric relationship in which the students are more involved with the teacher than the teacher with the students. That is to say, to allow for communication of values and voluntary discipline, the students must identify with the teacher; the teacher, on the other hand, must combine an emotional commitment to his work and to students in general with a somewhat detached orientation to each individual student, so as to ensure the objectivity of his judgment. Such an asymmetrical relationship is easier to maintain in the school than in the family. Similar points could be made about other structural differentiations. The total effect of differentiation is that the various societal functions—especially the economy, science, and administration, which "suffered" most from the fusion into the particularistic, diffuse, affective family—are now being served by units "designed" to fit their needs and hence are served more effectively.

The transition is not always smooth; modernization cannot come about without the disruption of the old patterns. Frequently it is accompanied by *anomie,* expressed for instance in outbursts of violence or mass hysteria. It becomes necessary for the new system to find ways of relating the newly differentiated units so as to provide new mechanisms to integrate society. The frequent rise of religious sects and the ascent of radical political movements are indicative of the need for reintegration. Nationalism as an ideology serves this need.

Each of the subsequent selections deals with one major facet of modernization and confronts the twofold problem of developing specialized sectors and relating them in a new fashion. These articles cast light on some of the central problems of modernization, but obviously do not exhaust their analysis. The student interested in developing nations will find a rich literature on almost every subject discussed here.

Rostow's key contribution to the analysis of economic development is the concept of "takeoff." The term, by now used in political science and sociology as well, is borrowed from the field of aeronautics: an airplane must gain a certain amount of speed before it has enough momentum to take off and continue to higher altitudes and greater speeds on its own. Similarly in the process of economic development: up to a certain level, growing investments in—and increased outputs of—an economy are absorbed by the population growth and by increased consumption. Only after the increase of production rises above that of consumption can a flow of investment allow the economy to grow continuously, on its own, without the aid of capital investment from the outside and without additional changes in the consumption, saving, and investment habits of the population. Rostow suggests that this transition, or takeoff point, occurs within a fairly limited period—a generation or less—and that it is likely to result from the development of particular economic sectors.

If Smelser's work is part of the modern theoretical work employing the differentiation model, Rostow is a neo-evolutionist reviving an earlier tradition. He expects societies to follow a sequence of similar stages and to move in the same general direction—toward the attainment of high productive ability. To what use societies put this ability is a different question altogether. Some use much of their newly gained capacities to buy a large military machinery, increase national status, and for purposes of territorial expansion; others are more inclined to use their new resources to increase the citizen's standard of living, while still others reinvest much of their yield to make future national income even higher.

The most crucial aspect of modernization is industrialization. Industrialization may be perceived as part of the general process of differentiation, in that its advent implies the growing structural independence of the production and exchange function. Industrialization is also the base for economic takeoff in that increased production and exchange make it possible for output to exceed consumption. While industrialization is primarily a technological and economic process, it is closely related to the dynamics of other social spheres. The two selections dealing with industrialization—those of Moore and Bendix—emphasize the noneconomic aspects of industrialization, primarily its effect on value systems and motivational complexes. Industrialization tends to lead to a separation of labor and management. If industrialization is to proceed, each group must develop the value orientations enabling it to play its part. Moore deals with the changes in the values, habits, and outlooks of workers that are required to sustain their motivation to participate, while Bendix discusses the changing ideologies of management by means of which it justifies its own role in the process.

As Moore points out, there is at least an initial period in which the members of a traditional society have fixed economic needs that are more-or-less satisfied by the traditional economy. The prospects of a higher standard of living leave these people largely indifferent. An incentive such as increased wages is largely ineffective so long as the additional purchasing power so established has no social meaning. It seems, though, that following education and the development of new commitments and tastes, the economic demands of these workers can be expected to increase. It is more difficult to induce them to attain the kind of self-discipline without which it is impossible to build up a modern economy. Long training, regular performances, punctuality, precision, and so on are all patterns of behavior new to the members of these societies and impose a high strain on their motivation. It remains to be seen whether a sufficient number of workers in all or even most transitional societies will develop such patterns or whether they will in practice prefer a lower standard of living as an unavoidable consequence of a less demanding work life.

Though dealing with industrialization in Europe, Bendix's analysis casts light on a process which at present is especially relevant to newly developing areas. Bendix studies the changes in management's conception of its relations with workers, the justifications devised for the new modes of subordination. These ideologies as well as the relationships they deal with, are, as Bendix emphasizes, affected by many elements of the social structure: the degree of interclass tensions and conflicts; the availability of mechanisms of peaceful adjustments on the political level; cultural traditions of the managerial groups, and many other factors. The different development of the same authority relationship in various societies, and the many factors affecting this development, discussed by Bendix, illustrate the fact that societies change as systems and that hence the study of industrialization requires the study of modernization in general.

As all the sectors of society are changing and adjusting to each other under the influence of industrialization, the basic political framework is altered as well. In part, the changes in the political sphere are a response to industrialization; in part they follow their own dynamics and the changes in value systems; in turn they exert an influence on the pace and pattern of industrialization. Eisenstadt's analysis, though primarily concerned with the processes of political development itself, also points to their impact on economic development. Like Moore's article, it implies that the emergence of rationalized economies and industrial systems is by no means historically "necessary" and may be retarded or distorted if the appropriate attitudes and institutions are not established.

Eisenstadt points to the fact, often ignored by students of the economic aspect of industrialization, that many of the developing countries are new nations—that is, colonies that recently gained or are about to gain political independence after some form of tutelage under, and rebellion against, a colonial power. The revolts and drives for independence are expressions of nationalistic ideologies and of growing resentment against the colonial powers. One major source of this resentment lies in the fact that the colonial powers expect "natives" to perform various economic and administrative roles within modern frameworks of action, but deny them the rewards that would otherwise accompany these performances, such as full participation in the political system. As a reaction to this political frustration, coupled with the emergence of nationalist values and ideologies, charismatic movements are created that aim to eliminate colonial interference and gain political independence. Understandably, in the preindependence period these movements focus on political emancipation more than on economic development. When political independence is finally attained, often neither the rank and file nor the leaders of the movements have the necessary skills and orientations that could provide effective political guidance for the development of a modern economy and state. The future modernization of these nations depends to a large degree on the extent to which they can overcome the political biases created by the struggle for independence and develop managerial and administrative elites capable of guiding the construction of modern economies—as against continuing to view political action, sometimes even military expansionism, as the main outlet for their newly gained powers.

Marriott concludes the discussion of modernization with a descriptive examination of the concrete changes that have taken place in an Indian village. Drawing on firsthand knowledge, he traces the changes in various institutional spheres of village life, utilizing conceptual schemes of the kind developed in earlier presentations. The changing village provides an illuminating illustration of the strains involved in the disruption of old patterns and of the attempts to cope with them.

CHAPTER 30

NEIL J. SMELSER

Toward a Theory of Modernization

A thorough analysis of the social changes accompanying economic development would require an ambitious theoretical scheme and a vast quantity of comparative data. Because I lack both ingredients—and the space to use them if I possessed them—I shall restrict this exploratory statement in two ways: (1) Methodologically, I shall deal only with ideal-type constructs in the Weberian sense; I shall omit discussion of any individual cases of development, as well as discussion of the comparative applicability of particular historical generalizations. (2) Substantively, I shall consider only modifications of the social structure; I shall omit discussion of factor-allocation, savings and investment, inflation, balance of payments, foreign aid, size of population, and rate of population change, even though these variables naturally affect and are affected by structural changes. These restrictions call for brief comment.

Max Weber defined an ideal-type construct as a "one-sided accentuation . . . by the synthesis of a great many diffuse, discrete, more or less present and occasionally absent *concrete individual* phenomena, which are arranged . . . into a unified *analytical* construct. In its conceptual purity, this mental construct cannot be found anywhere in reality." [1] The analyst utilizes such ideal constructs to unravel and explain a variety of actual historical situations. Weber mentioned explicitly two kinds of ideal-type constructs—first, "historically unique configurations" such as "rational bourgeois capitalism," "medieval Christianity," etc. and second, statements concerning

From Neil J. Smelser, "Mechanisms of Change and Adjustment of Changes," in Wilbert E. Moore and Bert F. Hoselitz, eds., *The Impact of Industry* (Paris: International Social Science Council, in press). Reprinted by permission of the author and the publisher.

[1] Max Weber, *The Methodology of the Social Sciences* (Glencoe, Ill.: The Free Press, 1949), pp. 90, 93.

historical evolution, such as the Marxist laws of capitalist development.[2] While the second type presupposes some version of the first, I shall concentrate on the dynamic constructs.

Economic development generally refers to the "growth of output per head of population."[3] For purposes of analyzing the relationships between economic growth and the social structure, it is possible to isolate the effects of several interrelated technical, economic, and ecological processes frequently accompanying development: (1) In the realm of technology, the change *from* simple and traditionalized techniques *toward* the application of scientific knowledge. (2) In agriculture, the evolution *from* subsistence farming *toward* commercial production of agricultural goods. This means specialization in cash crops, purchase of nonagricultural products in the market, and frequently agricultural wage-labor. (3) In industry, the transition *from* the use of human and animal power *toward* industrialization proper or "men aggregated at power-driven machines working for monetary return with the products of the manufacturing process, entering into a market based on a network of exchange relations."[4] (4) In ecological arrangements, the movement *from* the farm and village *toward* urban centers. These several processes often occur simultaneously; this is not, however, necessarily the case. Certain technological improvements—*e.g.,* the use of improved seeds—can be introduced without automatically and instantaneously producing organizational changes; agriculture may be commercialized without accompanying industrialization, as in many colonial countries; industrialization may occur in villages; and cities may proliferate in the absence of significant industrialization. Furthermore, the specific social consequences of technological advance, commercialized agriculture, the factory, and the city, respectively, are not in any sense reducible to each other.

Despite such differences, all four processes tend to affect the social structure in similar ways. All give rise to the following ideal-type structural changes which ramify throughout society: (1) Structural differentiation, or the establishment of more specialized and more autonomous social units. I shall illustrate this process in several different spheres—economy, family, religion, and stratification. (2) Integration, which changes its character as the old social order is made obsolete by the process of differentiation. The state, the law, political groupings, and other associations are particularly salient in this integration. (3) Social disturbances—mass hysteria, outbursts of violence, religious and political movements, etc.—which reflect the uneven march of differentiation and integration.

---

[2] *Ibid.,* pp. 93, 101-103.

[3] W. A. Lewis, *The Theory of Economic Growth* (London: George Allen & Unwin, 1955), p. 1.

[4] N. Nash, "Some Notes on Village Industrialization in South and East Asia," *Economic Development and Cultural Change,* III (1954), No. 3, p. 271.

Obviously, the implications of technological advance, agricultural re-organization, industrialization, and urbanization differ from society to society, as do the resulting structural realignments. Some of the sources of variation in these ideal patterns of pressure and change follow:

(1) Variations in premodern conditions. Is the society's value-system congenial or antipathetic to industrial values? How well integrated is the society? How "backward" is it? What is its level of wealth? How is the wealth distributed? Is the country "young and empty" or "old and crowded?" Is the country politically dependent, recently independent, or altogether autonomous? Such pre-existing conditions shape the impact of the forces of economic development.

(2) Variations in the impetus to change. Do pressures to modernize come from the internal implications of a value-system, from a desire for national security and prestige, from a desire for material prosperity, or from a combination of these? Is political coercion used to form a labor force? Or are the pressures economic, as in the case of population pressure on the land or loss of handicraft markets to cheap imported products? Or do economic and political pressures combine, as in the case of a tax on peasants payable only in money? Or are the pressures social, as in the case of the desire to escape burdensome aspects of the old order? Such differences influence the adjustment to modernization greatly.

(3) Variations in the path toward modernization. Does the sequence begin with light consumer industries? Or is there an attempt to introduce heavy, capital-intensive industries first? What is the role of government in shaping the pattern of investment? What is the rate of accumulation of technological knowledge and skills? What is the general tempo of industrialization? All these affect the nature of structural change and the degree of discomfort created by this change.

(4) Variations in the advanced stages of modernization. What is the emergent distribution of industries in developed economies? What are the emergent relations between state and economy, religion and economy, state and religion, etc.? While all advanced industrialized societies have their "industrialization" in common, unique national differences remain. For instance, social class differs in its social significance in the United States and the United Kingdom, even though both are highly developed countries.

(5) Variations in the content and timing of dramatic events during modernization. What is the significance of wars, revolutions, rapid migrations, natural catastrophes, etc. for the course of economic and social development?

Because of these sources of variation, it is virtually impossible to discover hard and fast empirical generalizations concerning the evolution of social structures during economic and social development. My purpose, therefore, in this paper, is not to search for such generalizations, but rather to outline certain ideal-type directions of structural change which modernization involves. On the basis of these ideal types we may classify, describe and ana-lyze varying national experiences. Factors such as those just described de-termine in part the distinctive national response to these universal aspects of modernization, but this in no way detracts from their "universality." While I shall base my remarks on the vast literature of economic development, I can in no sense attempt an exhaustive comparative study.

Structural Differentiation in Periods of Development

The concept of structural differentiation can be used to analyze what is frequently referred to as the "marked break in established patterns of social and economic life" in periods of development.[5] Simply defined, differentia-tion refers to the evolution from a multi-functional role structure to several more specialized structures. The following are typical examples: (1) In the transition from domestic to factory industry, the division of labor increases, and the economic activities previously lodged in the family move to the firm. (2) With the rise of a formal educational system, the training functions previously performed by the family and church are established in a more specialized unit—the school. (3) The modern political party has a more complex structure than tribal factions and is less likely to be fettered with kinship loyalties, competition for religious leadership, etc. Formally defined, then, structural differentiation is a process whereby *"one* social role or or-ganization . . . differentiates into *two or more* roles or organizations which function more effectively in the new historical circumstances. The new social units are structurally distinct from each other, but taken together are func-tionally equivalent to the original unit." [6]

Differentiation concerns only changes in role-structure. We should not, therefore, confuse differentiation with two closely related concepts: (1) The cause or motivation for entering the differentiated role. Wage-labor, for instance, may result from a desire for economic improvement, from po-litical coercion, or indeed from a desire to fulfill traditional obligations (*e.g.,* to use wages to supply a dowry). These "reasons" should be kept conceptu-ally distinct from differentiation itself. (2) The integration of differentiated roles. As differentiated wage-labor begins to appear, for instance, there also appear legal norms, labor exchanges, trade unions, and so on, which regu-late—with varying degrees of success—the relations between labor and management. Such readjustments, even though they sometimes produce a new social unit, should be considered separately from role-specialization in other functions.

---

[5] S. Kuznets, "International Differences in Income Levels," in S. Kuznets, W. E. Moore, and J. J. Spengler, eds., *Economic Growth: Brazil, India, Japan* (Durham, N.C.: Duke University Press, 1955), p. 23.

[6] N. J. Smelser, *Social Change in the Industrial Revolution* (Chicago: University of Chicago Press, 1959), p. 2.

Let us now inquire into the process of differentiation in several different social realms.

Differentiation of Economic Activities

Typically, in underdeveloped countries, production is located in kinship units. Subsistence farming predominates; other industry is supplementary but still attached to kin and village. In some cases occupational position is determined largely by an extended group such as the caste.

Similarly, exchange and consumption are deeply embedded in family and village. In subsistence agriculture there is a limited amount of independent exchange outside the family; this means that production and consumption occur in the same social context. Exchange systems proper are still lodged in kinship and community (e.g., reciprocal exchange), in stratification systems (e.g., redistribution according to caste membership), and in political systems (e.g., taxes, tributes, payments in kind, forced labor). Under such conditions market systems are underdeveloped, and the independent power of money to command the movement of goods and services is minimal.

As the economy develops, several kinds of economic activity are removed from this family-community complex. In agriculture, the introduction of money crops marks a differentiation between the social contexts of production and consumption. Agricultural wage-labor sometimes undermines the family production unit. In industry it is possible to identify several levels of differentiation. Household industry, the simplest form, parallels subsistence agriculture in that it supplies "the worker's own needs, unconnected with trade." "Handicraft production" splits production and consumption, though frequently consumption takes place in the local community. "Cottage industry," on the other hand, frequently involves a differentiation between consumption and community, since production is "for the market, for an unknown consumer, sold to a wholesaler who accumulates a stock." [7] Finally, manufacturing and factory systems segregate the worker from his capital and frequently from his family.

Similar differentiations appear simultaneously in the exchange system. Goods and services, previously exchanged on a noneconomic basis, are pulled more and more into the market. Money now commands the movement of more and more goods and services and thus begins to supplant—and sometimes undermine—the religious, political, familial, or caste sanctions which previously had governed economic activity. Such is the setting for the institutionalization of relatively autonomous economic systems which show

---

[7] These "levels," which represent points on the continuum from structural fusion to structural differentiation, are taken from J. H. Boeke, *The Structure of the Netherlands Indian Economy* (New York: International Secretariat, Institute of Pacific Relations, 1942), p. 90.

a greater emphasis on values such as universalism, functional specificity, and rationality.

Empirically we may classify underdeveloped economies according to how far they have moved along this line of differentiation. Migratory labor, for instance, may be a kind of compromise between full membership in a wage-labor force and attachment to an old community life; cottage industry introduces extended markets but retains the family-production fusion; the hiring of families in factories maintains a version of family production; the expenditure of wages on traditional items such as dowries also shows this half-entry into the more differentiated industrial-urban structure. The reasons for these partial cases of differentiation may lie in resistances on the part of the populace to give up traditional modes, in the economics of demand for handmade products, in systems of racial discrimination against native labor, or elsewhere. In any case, the concept of structural differentiation provides a yardstick to indicate the distance which the economic structure has evolved toward modernization.

Differentiation of Family Activities

One implication of the removal of economic activities from the kinship nexus is that the family loses some of its previous functions and thereby itself becomes a more specialized agency. The family ceases to be an economic unit of production; one or more members now leave the household to seek employment in the labor market. The family's activities become more concentrated on emotional gratification and socialization. While many halfway houses such as family hiring and migratory systems persist, the tendency is toward the segregation of family functions and economic functions.

Several related processes accompany this differentiation of the family from its other involvements: (1) Apprenticeship within the family declines. (2) Pressures develop against the intervention of family favoritism in the recruitment of labor and management. These pressures often lie in the demands of economic rationality. The intervention often persists, however, especially at the managerial levels, and in some cases (*e.g.,* Japan) family ties continue as a major basis for labor recruitment. (3) The direct control of elders and collateral kinsmen over the nuclear family weakens. This marks, in structural terms, the differentiation of the nuclear family from the extended family. (4) One aspect of this loss of control is the growth of personal choice, love, and related criteria as the basis for courtship and marriage. Structurally this is the differentiation of courtship from extended kinship. (5) One result of this complex of processes is the changing status of women, who become generally less subordinated economically, politically, and socially to their husbands than under earlier conditions.

In such ways structural differentiation undermines the old modes of integration in society. The controls of extended family and village begin to dissolve in the enlarged and complicated social setting which differentiation creates. New integrative problems are posed by this growing obsolescence. We shall inquire presently into some of the lines of integration.

Differentiation of Value Systems

The concept of differentiation can also elucidate the delicate problem of the role of values in economic development. It is clear that values affect development significantly, though in many different ways. Max Weber's analysis of Protestantism is an illustration of the force of religious values in encouraging development. In addition, secular nationalism plays an important role in the industrial "takeoff."

> . . . with the world organized as it is, nationalism is a *sine qua non* of industrialization, because it provides people with an overriding, easily acquired, secular motivation for making painful changes. National strength or prestige becomes the supreme goal, industrialization the chief means. The costs, inconveniences, sacrifices, and loss of traditional values can be justified in terms of this transcending, collective ambition. The new collective entity, the nation-state, that sponsors and grows from this aspiration is equal to the exigencies of industrial complexity; it draws directly the allegiance of every citizen, organizing the population as one community; it controls the passage of persons, goods, and news across the borders; it regulates economic and social life in detail. To the degree that the obstacles to industrialization are strong, nationalism must be intense to overcome them.[8]

In fact, nationalism seems in many cases to be the very instrument designed to smash those traditional religious systems—such as the classical Chinese or Indian—which Weber himself found to be less permissive than Protestantism for economic modernization. Yet nationalism too, like many traditionalistic religious systems, may hinder economic advancement by "reaffirmation of traditionally honored ways of acting and thinking," [9] by fostering anti-colonial attitudes after they are no longer relevant, and, more indirectly, by encouraging passive expectations of "readymade prosperity." [10] It seems possible to distinguish between these contrasting forces of "stimulus" and "drag" that value-systems have on economic development by using the logic of differentiation. . . .

In the early phases of modernization, many traditional attachments must

---

[8] K. Davis, "Social and Demographic Aspects of Economic Development in India," in *Economic Growth: Brazil, India, Japan, op. cit.,* p. 294.

[9] B. F. Hoselitz, "Non-Economic Barriers to Economic Development," *Economic Development and Cultural Change,* I (1952), No. 1, p. 9.

[10] J. van der Kroef, "Economic Development in Indonesia: Some Social and Cultural Impediments," *Economic Development and Cultural Change,* IV (1955), No. 2, pp. 116-133.

be modified in order to set up more differentiated institutional structures. Because these established commitments and methods of integration are deeply rooted in the organization of traditional society, a very generalized and powerful commitment is required, in the nature of the case, to "pry" individuals from these attachments. The values of ascetic and this-worldly religious beliefs, xenophobic national aspirations, and political ideologies such as socialism provide such a lever. Sometimes these various types of values combine into a single system of legitimacy. In any case, all three have an "ultimacy" of commitment in the name of which a wide range of sacrifices can be demanded and procured.

The very success of these value-systems, however, breeds the conditions for their own weakening. In a perceptive statement, Weber noted that by the beginning of the twentieth century, when the capitalistic system was already highly developed, it no longer needed the impetus of ascetic Protestantism. Capitalism had, by virtue of its conquest of much of Western society, solidly established an institutional base and a secular value-system of its own—"economic rationality." These secular economic values no longer needed the "ultimate" justification required in the newer, unsteadier days of economic revolution.

Such lines of differentiation, we might add, constitute the secularization of religious values. In this process, other institutional spheres—economic, political, scientific, etc.—come to be established more nearly on their own. The values governing these spheres are no longer sanctioned directly by religious beliefs, but by an autonomous rationality. Insofar as such rationalities replace religious sanctions in these spheres, secularization occurs.

Similarly, nationalistic and related value-systems undergo a process of secularization as differentiation proceeds. As a society moves toward more and more complex social organization, the encompassing demands of nationalistic commitment give way to more autonomous systems of rationality. The Soviet Union, for instance, as its social structure grows more differentiated, seems to be introducing more "independent" market mechanisms, "freer" social scientific investigation in some spheres, and so on. These measures are not, moreover, directly sanctioned by an appeal to nationalistic or communistic values. Finally, it seems a reasonable historical generalization that in the early stages of development nationalism is heady, muscular, and aggressive; as the society evolves to an advanced state, however, nationalism tends to settle into a more remote and complacent condition, rising to fury only in times of national crisis.

Thus the paradoxical element in the role of religious or nationalistic belief-systems; insofar as they encourage the breakup of old patterns, they may stimulate economic modernization; insofar as they resist their own subsequent secularization, however, the very same value-systems may become a drag on economic advance and structural change.

Differentiation of Systems of Stratification

In analyzing systems of stratification, we concentrate on two kinds of issues:

(1) To what extent are ascribed qualities subject to ranking? Some ascription exists in all societies, since the infant in the nuclear family always and everywhere begins with the status of his parents. The degree to which this ascribed ranking extends beyond the family to race, ethnic membership, etc. varies from society to society. In our own ideology we minimize the ascriptive elements of class and ethnic membership, but in practice these matter greatly, especially for Negroes.

(2) To what extent do ascribed qualities determine membership in occupational, political, religious, and other positions in society? In theory, again, the American egalitarian ideology places a premium on the maximum separation of such positions from ascribed categories, but in fact family membership, minority group membership, etc. impinge on the ultimate "placing" of persons. In many nonindustrialized societies this link between ascription and position is much closer. Such criteria as these reveal the degree of "openness," or social mobility, in a system.

Under conditions of economic modernization, structural differentiation increases along both these dimensions:

(1) Other evaluative standards intrude on ascribed memberships. For instance, McKim Marriott has noted that in the village of Paril in India:

> . . . Personal wealth, influence, and morality have surpassed the traditional caste-and-order alignment of kind groups as the effective bases of ranking. Since such new bases of ranking can no longer be clearly tied to any inclusive system of large solidary groupings, judgments must be made according to the characteristics of individual or family units. This individualization of judgments leads to greater dissensus (sic).[11]

Of course, castes, ethnic groups, and traditional religious groupings do not necessarily decline in importance *in every respect* during periods of modernization. As political interest groups or reference groups for diffuse loyalty, they may even increase in salience. As the sole bases of ranking, however, ascriptive standards become more differentiated from economic, political, and other standards.

(2) Individual mobility through the occupational hierarchies increases. This signifies the differentiation of the adult's functional position from his point of origin. In addition, individual mobility is frequently substituted

---

[11] McKim Marriott, "Social Change in an Indian Village," Chapter 35, this book; J. S. Coleman, *Nigeria: Background to Nationalism* (Berkeley and Los Angeles: University of California Press, 1958), pp. 70-73.

for collective mobility. Individuals, not whole castes or tribes, compete for higher standing in society. This phenomenon of increasing individual mobility seems to be one of the universal consequences of industrialization. After assembling extensive empirical evidence on patterns of mobility in industrialized nations, Lipset and Bendix concluded that "the overall pattern of [individual] social mobility appears to be much the same in the industrial societies of various Western countries." [12] Patterns of class symbolization and class ideology may, however, continue to differ among industrialized countries.

The Integration of Differentiated Activities

One of Emile Durkheim's remarkable insights concerned the role of integrative mechanisms under conditions of growing social heterogeneity. Launching his attack against the utilitarian view that the division of labor would flourish best without regulation, Durkheim demonstrated that one of the concomitants of a growing division of labor is an *increase* in mechanisms to coordinate and solidify the interaction among individuals with increasingly diversified interests.[13] Durkheim found this integration mainly in the legal structure, but one can locate similar kinds of integrative forces elsewhere in society.

Differentiation alone, therefore, is not sufficient for modernization. Development proceeds as a contrapuntal interplay between differentiation (which is divisive of established society) and integration (which unites differentiated structures on a new basis). Paradoxically, however, the process of integration itself produces more *differentiated* structures—*e.g.,* trade unions, associations, political parties, and a mushrooming state apparatus. Let us illustrate this complex process of integration in several institutional spheres.

Economy and Family

Under a simple kind of economic organization—subsistence agriculture or household industry—there is little differentiation between economic roles and family roles. All reside in the kinship structure. The *integration* of these diverse but unspecialized activities also rests in the local family and community structures and in the religious traditions which fortify both of these.

---

[12] S. M. Lipset and R. Bendix, *Social Mobility in Industrial Society* (Berkeley and Los Angeles: University of California Press, 1959), pp. 13 ff.

[13] Émile Durkheim, *The Division of Labor in Society* (Glencoe, Ill.: The Free Press, 1949), chs. 3-8. A recent formulation of the relationship between differentiation and integration may be found in R. F. Bales, *Interaction Process Analysis* (Cambridge, Mass.: Addison-Wesley Press, 1950).

Under conditions of differentiation, the social setting for production is separated from that for consumption, and productive roles of family members are isolated geographically, temporally, and structurally from their distinctively familial roles. Such differentiation immediately creates integrative problems. How is information concerning employment opportunities to be conveyed to workpeople? How are the interests of families to be integrated with the interests of firms? How are families to be protected from market fluctuation? Whereas such integrative exigencies were faced by kinsmen, neighbors, and local largesse in premodern settings, modernization gives birth to dozens of institutions and organizations geared to these new integrative problems—labor recruitment agencies and exchanges; labor unions; government regulation of labor allocation; welfare and relief arrangements; cooperative societies; savings institutions. All these involve agencies which specialize in integration.

Community

If industrialization occurs only in villages or if villages are "built around" paternalistic industrial enterprises, many ties of community and kinship can be maintained under industrial conditions. Urbanization, however, frequently creates more anonymity. As a result, one finds frequently in expanding cities a growth of voluntary associations—churches and chapels, unions, schools, halls, athletic clubs, bars, shops, mutual aid groups, etc. In some cases this growth of integrative groupings may be retarded because of the back-and-forth movement of migratory workers, who "come to the city for their differentiation" and "return to the village for their integration." In cities themselves the original criterion for associating may be common tribe, caste, or village; this criterion may persist or give way gradually to more "functional" groupings based on economic or political interests.

Political Structure

In a typical premodern setting, political integration is closely fused with kinship position, tribal membership, control of the land or control of the unknown. Political forms include chieftainships, kingships, councils of elders, powerful landlords, powerful magicians and oracles, etc.

As social systems grow more complex, political systems are modified accordingly. Fortes and Evans-Pritchard have specified three types of native African political systems, which can be listed according to their degree of differentiation from kinship lineages: (1) small societies in which the largest political unit embraces only those united by kinship; thus political authority is coterminous with kinship relations; (2) societies in which the political framework is the integrative core for a number of kinship lineages; (3) societies with an "administrative organization" of a more formal nature.

Such systems move toward greater differentiation as population grows and economic and cultural heterogeneity increases.[14] In colonial and recently-freed African societies, political systems have evolved much further, with the appearance of parties, congresses, pressure groups, and even "parliamentary" systems.[15] In describing the Indian village, Marriott speaks of the "wider integration of local groups with outside groups." [16] Sometimes this wider political integration, like community integration, is based on an extension and modification of an old integrative principle. Harrison has argued that modern developments in India have changed the significance of caste from the "traditional village extension of the joint family" to "regional alliances of kindred local units." This modification has led to the formation of "new caste lobbies" which constitute some of the strongest and most explosive political forces in modern India.[17] We shall mention some of the possible political consequences of this persistence of old integrative forms later.

These examples illustrate how differentiation in society impinges on the integrative sphere. The resulting integrative structures coordinate and solidify—with varying success—the social structure which the forces of differentiation threaten to fragment. In many cases the integrative associations and parties display tremendous instability—labor unions turn into political or nationalistic parties; religious sects become political clubs; football clubs become religious sects, and so on.[18] The resultant fluidity points up the extremely pressing needs for reintegration under conditions of rapid, irregular, and disruptive processes of differentiation. The initial response is a kind of trial-and-error floundering for many kinds of integration at once.

We have sketched some structural consequences of modernization and integration. These changes are not, it should be remembered, a simple function of "industrialization." Some of the most farreaching structural changes have occurred in countries which have scarcely experienced the beginnings of industrialization. For instance, colonialism—or related forms of economic dominance—creates not only an extensive differentiation of cash products and wage labor but also a vulnerability to world price fluctuations in commodities. Hence many of the structural changes described above—and the resulting social disturbances to be described presently—

---

[14] M. Fortes and E. E. Evans-Pritchard, eds., *African Political Systems* (London: Oxford University Press, 1940), pp. 1-25.

[15] D. Apter, *The Gold Coast in Transition* (Princeton: Princeton University Press, 1956); T. Hodgkin, *Nationalism in Colonial Africa* (New York: New York University Press, 1957), pp. 115-139; G. A. Almond and J. S. Coleman, *The Politics of Developing Areas* (Princeton: Princeton University Press, 1960).

[16] "Social Change in an Indian Village," *loc. cit.*

[17] S. E. Harrison, *India: The Most Dangerous Decades* (Princeton: Princeton University Press, 1960), pp. 100 ff.

[18] *Nationalism in Colonial Africa, op. cit.*, pp. 85 ff.

characterize both societies which are industrializing and some that are still "preindustrial."

Discontinuities in Differentiation and Integration: Social Disturbances

The structural changes associated with modernization are disruptive to the social order for the following reasons:

(1) Differentiation demands the creation of new activities, norms, rewards and sanctions—money, political position, prestige based on occupation, and so on. These often conflict with old modes of social action, which are frequently dominated by traditional religious, tribal, and kinship systems. These traditional standards are among the most intransigent of obstacles to modernization, and when they are threatened, serious dissatisfaction and opposition arise.

(2) Structural change is, above all, *uneven* in periods of modernization. In colonial societies, for instance, the European powers frequently revolutionized the economic, political, and educational frameworks, but simultaneously encouraged or imposed a conservatism in traditional religious, class, and family systems.

> . . . the basic problem in these [colonial] societies was the expectation that the native population would accept certain broad, modern institutional settings . . . and would perform within them various roles—especially economic and administrative roles—while at the same time, they were denied some of the basic rewards inherent in these settings . . . they were expected to act on the basis of a motivational system derived from a different social structure which the colonial powers and indigenous rulers tried to maintain.[19]

Under noncolonial conditions of modernization similar discontinuities appear. Within the economy itself, rapid industrialization, no matter how coordinated, bites unevenly into the established social and economic structure. And throughout the society, the differentiation occasioned by agricultural, industrial and urban changes always proceeds in a seesaw relationship with integration; the two forces continuously breed lags and bottlenecks. The faster the tempo of modernization, the more severe are the discontinuities. This unevenness creates *anomie* in the classical sense, for it generates disharmony between life experiences and the normative framework by which these experiences are regulated.

(3) Dissatisfactions arising from conflict with traditional ways and those arising from *anomie* sometimes aggravate one another when they come into contact. *Anomie* may be relieved in part by new integrative devices such as unions, associations, clubs, and government regulations. Such innovations

---

[19] S. N. Eisenstadt, "Sociological Aspects of Political Development in Underdeveloped Countries," *Economic Development and Cultural Change*, V (1957), No. 4, p. 298.

are often opposed, however, by traditional vested interests because the new forms of integration compete with the older undifferentiated systems of solidarity. The new result is a three-way tug-of-war among the forces of tradition, the forces of differentiation, and the new forces of integration. Such conditions create virtually unlimited potentialities for group conflict.

Three classic responses to these discontinuities are anxiety, hostility, and fantasy. These responses, if and when they become collective, crystallize into a variety of social movements—peaceful agitation, political violence, millenarianism, nationalism, revolution, underground subversion, etc. There is plausible—though not entirely convincing—evidence that those drawn most readily into such movements are those suffering most severely the pains of displacements created by structural change. For example,

> [Nationalism appeared] as a permanent force in Southeast Asia at the moment when the peasants were forced to give up subsistence farming for the cultivation of cash crops or when (as in highly colonized Java) subsistence farming ceased to yield a subsistence. The introduction of a money economy and the withering away of the village as the unit of life accompanied this development and finally established the period of economic dependence.[20]

Other theoretical and empirical evidence suggests that social movements appeal most to those who have been dislodged from old social ties by differentiation but who have not been integrated into the new social order.

Many belief-systems associated with these movements envision the grand and almost instantaneous integration of society. In many cases the beliefs are highly emotional and unconcerned with realistic policies. In nationalistic colonial movements, for instance, "the political symbols were intended to develop new, ultimate, common values and basic loyalties, rather than relate to current policy issues within the colonial society." [21] Furthermore, such belief-systems reflect the ambivalence resulting from the conflict between traditionalism and modernization. Nationalists alternate between xenophobia and xenophilia; they predict that they will "outmodernize" the West in the future and simultaneously "restore" the true values of the ancient civilization; they argue for egalitarian and hierarchical principles of social organization at the same time.[22] Nationalistic and related ideologies unite these contradictory tendencies in a society under one large symbol; then, if these ideologies are successful, they are often used as a means to modernize and thus erase those kinds of social discontinuity which gave rise to the original nationalistic outburst.

---

[20] E. H. Jacoby, *Agrarian Unrest in Southeast Asia* (New York: Columbia University Press, 1949), p. 246.

[21] "Sociological Aspects of Political Development," *op. cit.*, p. 294.

[22] M. Matossian, "Ideologies of Delayed Industrialization," *Economic Development and Cultural Change*, VI (1957), No. 3, pp. 217-228.

Naturally not all the cases of early modernization produce violent nationalistic or other social movements. When such movements do arise, furthermore, they take many different forms. I shall merely list what seem to be the five most decisive factors in the genesis and molding of social disturbances:

(1) The scope and intensity of the social dislocation created by structural changes. "The greater the tempo of these changes . . . the greater the problems of acute malintegration the society has to face." [23]

(2) The structural complexity of the society at the time when modernization begins. In the least developed societies, where "the language of politics is at the same time the language of religion," protest movements more or less immediately take on a religious cast. In Africa, for instance, utopian religious movements seem to have relatively greater appeal in the less developed regions, whereas the more secular types of political protest such as trade union movements and party agitations have tended to cluster in the more developed areas. The secularization of protest increases, of course, as modernization and differentiation proceed.

(3) The access of disturbed groups to channels of influencing social policy. If dislocated groups have access to those responsible for introducing reforms, agitation tends to be relatively peaceful and orderly. If this access is blocked, either because of the isolation of the groups or the intransigence of the ruling authorities, demands for reform tend to take more violent, utopian, and bizarre forms. Hence the tendency for fantasy and unorganized violence to cluster among the disinherited, the colonized, and the socially isolated migrants.

(4) The overlap of interests and lines of cleavage. In many colonial societies, the social order broke more-or-less imperfectly into three groupings: first, the Western representatives who held control of economic enterprises and political administration, and who frequently were allied with large local landowners; second, a large native population who—when drawn into the colonial economy—entered as tenant farmers, wage laborers, etc.; and third, a group of foreigners—Chinese, Indians, Syrians, Goans, Lebanese, etc.—who fitted "in between" the first two as traders, moneylenders, merchants, creditors, etc. This view is oversimplified, of course, but many colonial societies approximated this arrangement. The important structural feature of such a system is that economic, political, and racial-ethnic memberships *coincide* with each other. Hence *any* kind of conflict is likely to assume racial overtones and arouse the more diffuse loyalties and prejudices of the warring parties. Many colonial outbursts did in fact follow racial lines. Insofar as such "earthquake faults" persist after inde-

---

[23] "Sociological Aspects of Political Development," *op. cit.,* p. 294; J. S. Coleman, "Nationalism in Tropical Africa," in L. W. Shannon, *Underdeveloped Areas* (New York: Harper & Row, 1957), pp. 42 ff.; *Nationalism in Colonial Africa, op. cit.,* p. 56.

pendence, these societies are likely to be plagued by similar outbursts. If, on the other hand, the various lines of cleavage crisscross, it is more nearly possible to insulate and manage specific economic and political grievances peacefully.

(5) The kind and extent of foreign infiltration and intervention on behalf of protest groups.

Structural Bases for the Role of Government

Many have argued on economic grounds for the presence of a strong, centralized government in rapidly modernizing societies. Governmental planning and activity are required, for instance, to direct saving and investment, to regulate incentives, to encourage entrepreneurship, to control trade and prices, and so on. To such arguments I should like to add several considerations arising out of the analysis of structural change in periods of rapid development:

(1) Undifferentiated institutional structures frequently constitute the primary social barriers to modernization. Individuals refuse to work for wages because of traditional kinship, village, tribal, and other ties. Invariably a certain amount of political pressure is required to pry individuals loose from these ties. The need for such pressure increases, of course, with the rate of modernization desired.

(2) The process of differentiation itself creates those conditions which demand a larger, more formal type of political administration. A further argument for the importance of government in periods of rapid and uneven modernization lies, then, in the need to accommodate the growing cultural, economic, and social heterogeneity, and to control the political repercussions from the constantly shifting distribution of power which accompanies extensive social reorganization.

(3) The apparent propensity for periods of early modernization to erupt into explosive outbursts creates delicate political problems for the leaders of developing nations. We might conclude this essay on the major social forces of modernization by suggesting what kinds of government are likely to be most effective in such troubled areas. First, political leaders will increase their effectiveness by open and vigorous commitment to utopian and xenophobic nationalism. This commitment serves as a powerful instrument for attaining three of their most important ends: (a) the enhancement of their own claim to legitimacy by endowing themselves with the mission for creating the nation-state; (b) the procurement of otherwise impossible sacrifices from a populace which may be committed to modernization in the abstract but which resists the concrete breaks with traditional ways; (c) the use of their claim to legitimacy to hold down protests and to prevent generalized symbols such as communism from spreading to all sorts of particular grievances. These same political leaders should not, however,

take their enthusiasm for this claim to legitimacy too literally. They should not rely on the strength of their nationalistic commitment to ignore or smother grievances altogether. They should play politics in the usual sense with aggrieved groups in order to give these groups an access to responsible political agencies and thereby reduce those conditions which give rise to counterclaims to legitimacy. One key to political stability would seem to be, therefore, the practice of flexible politics behind the façade of an inflexible commitment to a national mission.

•

In this essay I have attempted to sketch, in ideal-type terms, the ways in which economic and social development are related to the social structure. I have organized the discussion around three major categories—differentiation, which characterizes a social structure moving toward greater complexity; integration, which in certain respects balances the divisive character of differentiation; and social disturbances, which result from the discontinuities between differentiation and integration.

To this analysis must be added four qualifications: (1) I have not attempted to account for the determinants of economic development itself. In fact, the discussion of differentiation, integration, and social disturbance takes as given a certain attempt to develop economically. These three forces condition the *course* of development, however, once it has started. (2) For purposes of exposition I have presented the three major categories in a certain order—differentiation, integration, social disturbances. We should not assume from this, however, that any one of them assumes causal precedence in the analysis of social change. Rather they form an interactive system. Disturbances, for instance, may arise from discontinuities created by structural differentiation, but these very disturbances may shape the course of future processes of differentiation. Likewise, integrative developments may be set in motion by differentiation, but in their turn they may initiate new lines of differentiation. (3) Even though the forces of differentiation, integration, and disturbance are closely linked empirically, we should not "close" the "system" composed of the relationship among the three forces. Differentiation may arise from sources other than economic development; the requirement of integration may arise from conditions other than differentiation; and the sources of social disturbance are not exhausted by the discontinuities between differentiation and integration. (4) The "all-at-once" character of the transition from less differentiated to more differentiated societies should not be exaggerated. Empirically the process evolves gradually and influences the social structure selectively. The emphasis on various halfway arrangements and compromises throughout the essay illustrates this gradualness and irregularity.

CHAPTER 31

W. W. ROSTOW

The Takeoff into
Self-Sustained Growth

The purpose of this article is to explore the following hypothesis: that the process of economic growth can usefully be regarded as centering on a relatively brief time interval of two or three decades, when the economy and the society of which it is a part transform themselves in such ways that economic growth is, subsequently, more-or-less automatic. This decisive transformation is here called the takeoff.

The takeoff is defined as the interval during which the rate of investment increases in such a way that real output *per capita* rises, and this initial increase carries with it radical changes in production techniques and the disposition of income flows, which perpetuate the new scale of investment and perpetuate thereby the rising trend in *per capita* output. Initial changes in method require that some group in the society have the will and the authority to install and diffuse new production techniques; and a perpetuation of the growth process requires that such a leading group expand in authority and that the society as a whole respond to the impulses set up by the initial changes, including the potentialities for external economies. Initial changes in the scale and direction of finance flows are likely to imply a command over income flows by new groups or institutions; and a perpetuation of growth requires that a high proportion of the increment to real income during the takeoff period be returned to productive investment. The takeoff requires, therefore, a society prepared to respond actively to new possibilities for productive enterprise; and it is likely to require political, social, and institutional changes which will both perpetuate an initial increase in the scale of investment and result in the regular acceptance and absorption of innovations.

From W. W. Rostow, "The Takeoff into Self-Sustained Growth," *The Economic Journal*, LXVI (1956), No. 261, pp. 25-48. Reprinted by permission of the author and the Royal Economic Society, London.

In short, this article is an effort to clarify the economics of industrial revolution where an industrial revolution is conceived of narrowly with respect to time and broadly with respect to changes in production functions.

Three Stages in the Growth Process

The historian examining the story of a particular national economy is inevitably impressed by the long-period continuity of events. Like other forms of history, economic history is a seamless web. The cotton-textile developments in Britain of the 1780's and 1790's have a history stretching back for a half century at least; the United States of the 1840's and 1850's had been preparing itself for industrialization since the 1790's, at the latest; Russia's remarkable development during the two pre-1914 decades goes back to 1861 for its foundations, if not to the Napoleonic Wars or to Peter the Great; the remarkable economic spurt of Meiji Japan is incomprehensible outside the context of economic developments in the latter half of the Tokugawa era; and so on. . . . From the perspective of the economic historian, the isolation of a takeoff period is, then, a distinctly arbitrary process. It is to be judged, like such other arbitrary exercises as the isolation of business cycles and secular trends, on whether it illuminates more of the economic process than it conceals; and it should be used, if accepted, as a way of giving a rough framework of order to the inordinately complicated biological problem of growth, rather than as an exact model of reality.

There is difficulty in this set of conceptions for the statistical analyst of economic development as well as for the historian. At first sight, the data mobilized, for example, by Clark, Kuznets, Buchanan and Ellis exhibit a continuum of degrees of development both within countries over time and as among countries at a given period of time, with no *prima facie* case for a clearly marked watershed in the growth process.[1] In part, this statistical result arises from the fact that historical data on national product and its components are only rarely available for an economy until after it has passed into a stage of more-or-less regular growth; that is, after the takeoff. In part, it arises from the fact that, by and large, these authors are more concerned with different levels of *per capita* output (or welfare)—and the structural characteristics that accompany them—than with the growth

---

[1] Colin Clark, *The Conditions of Economic Progress* (2nd ed.; London, 1951); Simon Kuznets, "International Differences in Capital Formation and Financing," mimeographed, Conference on Capital Formation and Economic Growth, November 1953 (New York: National Bureau of Economic Research, 1953); Norman Buchanan and Howard Ellis, *Approaches to Economic Development* (New York: Twentieth Century Fund, 1955). *See also* the United Nations data presented as a frontispiece to H. F. Williamson and John A. Buttrick, *Economic Development* (New York: Prentice-Hall, 1954).

process itself. The data they mobilize do not come to grips with the inner determinants of growth. The question raised here is not how or why levels of output *per capita* have differed, but rather how it has come about that particular economies have moved from stagnation, to slow, piecemeal advance, to a situation where growth was the normal economic condition. Our criterion here is not the absolute level of output *per capita,* but its rate of change.

In this argument, the sequence of economic development is taken to consist of three periods: a long period (up to a century or, conceivably, more) when the preconditions for takeoff are established; the takeoff itself, defined within two or three decades; and a long period when growth becomes normal and relatively automatic. These three divisions would not, of course, exclude the possibility of growth giving way to secular stagnation or decline in the long term. It would exclude from the concept of a growing economy, however, one which experiences a brief spurt of expansion which is not subsequently sustained; for example, the United States industrial boom of the War of 1812, or the ill-fated spurts of certain Latin American economies in the early stages of their modern history.

Takeoffs have occurred in two quite different types of societies; therefore, the process of establishing preconditions for takeoff has varied. In the first and most general case, the achievement of preconditions for takeoff required major change in political and social structure and, even, in effective cultural values. . . . In the second case, takeoff was delayed not by political, social, and cultural obstacles, but by the high (and even expanding) levels of welfare that could be achieved by exploiting land and natural resources. In this second case, takeoff was initiated by a more narrowly economic process, as, for example, in the northern United States, Australia and perhaps Sweden. . . . As one would expect in the essentially biological field of economic growth, history offers mixed as well as pure cases.

In the first case the process of establishing preconditions for takeoff might be generalized in impressionistic terms as follows:

We start with a reasonably stable and traditional society, containing an economy mainly agricultural, using more-or-less unchanging production methods, saving, and investing productively little more than is required to meet depreciation. Usually from outside the society, but sometimes out of its own dynamics, comes the idea that economic progress is possible; and this idea spreads within the established elite, or (more usually) in some disadvantaged group whose lack of status does not prevent the exercise of some economic initiative. More often than not, the economic motives for seeking economic progress converge with some noneconomic motive, such as the desire for increased social power and prestige, national pride, political ambition, and so on. Education, for some at least, broadens and changes to suit the needs of modern economic activity. New enterprising men come forward willing to mobilize savings and to take risks in pursuit of profit, notably in commerce. The commercial markets for agricultural products, domestic handicrafts, and consumption-goods imports widen. Institutions for mobilizing capital appear, or expand from primitive levels in the scale, surety, and time horizon for loans. Basic capital is expanded, notably in transport and communications, often to bring to market raw materials in which other nations have an economic interest, often financed by foreign capital. And here and there modern manufacturing enterprise appears, usually in substitution for imports.

Since public health measures are enormously productive in their early stages of application, and, as innovations go, meet relatively low resistance in most cultures, the death rate may fall and the population begin to rise, putting pressure on the food supply and the institutional structure of agriculture, creating thereby an economic depressant or stimulus (or both in turn), depending on the society's response.

The rate of productive investment may rise up to 5 per cent of national income; but this is unlikely to do much more than keep ahead of the population increase. And, in general, all this activity proceeds on a limited basis, within an economy and a society still mainly characterized by traditional low-productivity techniques and by old values and institutions which developed in conjunction with them. The rural proportion of the population is likely to stand at 75 per cent or over.

In the second case, of naturally wealthy nations, with a highly favorable balance between population and natural resources and with a population deriving by emigration from reasonably acquisitive cultures, the story of establishing the preconditions differs mainly in that there is no major problem of overcoming traditional values inappropriate to economic growth and the inert or resistant institutions which incorporate them; there is less difficulty in developing an elite effective in the investment process; and there is no population problem.[2] Technically, much the same slow-moving process of change occurs at high (and, perhaps, even expanding) levels of *per capita* output and with an extensive growth of population and output still based on rich land and other natural resources. Takeoff fails to occur mainly because the comparative advantage of exploiting productive land and other natural resources delays the time when self-reinforcing industrial growth can profitably get under way.

The beginning of takeoff can usually be traced to a particular sharp stimulus. The stimulus may take the form of a political revolution which affects directly the balance of social power and effective values, the character of economic institutions, the distribution of income, the pattern of investment outlays and the proportion of potential innovations actually applied; that is, it operates through the propensities. It may come about through a tech-

---

[2] Even in these cases, there have often been significant political and social restraints which had to be reduced or eliminated before takeoff could occur; for example, in Canada, the Argentine and the American South.

nological (including transport) innovation, which sets in motion a chain of secondary expansion in modern sectors and has powerful potential external economy effects which the society exploits. It may take the form of a newly favorable international environment, such as the opening of British and French markets to Swedish timber in the 1860's or a sharp relative rise in export prices and/or large new capital imports, as in the case of the United States from the late 1840's, Canada and Russia from the mid-1890's; but it may also come as a challenge posed by an unfavorable shift in the international environment, such as a sharp fall in terms of trade (or a wartime blockage of foreign trade) requiring the rapid development of manufactured import substitutes, as in the case of the Argentine and Australia in the 1930's and during the Second World War. . . .

What is essential here is not the form of stimulus but the fact that the prior development of the society and its economy result in a positive sustained, and self-reinforcing, response to it: the result is not a once-over change in production functions or in the volume of investment, but a higher proportion of potential innovations accepted in a more-or-less regular flow and a higher rate of investment.

In short, the forces which have yielded marginal bursts of activity now expand and become quantitatively significant as rapid-moving trends. New industries expand at high rates, yielding profits which are substantially reinvested in new capacity; and their expansion induces a more general expansion of the modern sectors of the economy where a high rate of ploughback prevails. The institutions for mobilizing savings (including the fiscal and sometimes the capital-levy activities of government) increase in scope and efficiency. New techniques spread in agriculture as well as in industry, as increasing numbers of persons are prepared to accept them and the deep changes they bring to ways of life. A new class of businessmen (usually private, sometimes public servants) emerges and acquires control over the key decisions determining the use of savings. New possibilities for export develop and are exploited; new import requirements emerge. The economy exploits hitherto unused backlogs in technique and natural resources. Although there are a few notable exceptions, all this momentum historically attracted substantial foreign capital.

The use of aggregative national-income terms evidently reveals little of the process which is occurring. It is nevertheless useful to regard as a necessary but not sufficient condition for the takeoff the fact that the proportion of net investment to national income (or net national product) rises from (say) 5 per cent to over 10 per cent, definitely outstripping the likely population pressure (since under the assumed takeoff circumstances the capital –output ratio is low), and yielding a distinct rise in real output *per capita*. Whether real consumption *per capita* rises depends on the pattern of income distribution and population pressure, as well as on the magnitude, character, and productivity of investment itself.

As indicated in Table 31-1, I believe it possible to identify at least tentatively such takeoff periods for a number of countries which have passed into the stage of growth.

The third stage is, of course, the long, fluctuating story of sustained economic progress. Overall capital per head increases as the economy matures. The structure of the economy changes increasingly. The initial key industries, which sparked the takeoff, decelerate as diminishing returns operate on the original set of industrial tricks and the original band of pioneering entrepreneurs give way to less single-minded industrial leaders in those sectors; but the average rate of growth is maintained by a succession of new, rapidly growing sectors, with a new set of pioneering leaders. The proportion of the population in rural pursuits declines. The economy finds its (changing) place in the international economy. The society makes such terms as it will with the requirements for maximizing modern and efficient production, balancing off, as it will, the new values against those retarding values which persist with deeper roots or adapting the latter in such ways as to support rather than retard the growth process. This sociological calculus interweaves with basic resource endowments to determine the pace of deceleration.

Table **31-1**

Some Tentative, Approximate Takeoff Dates

Country	Takeoff	Country	Takeoff
Great Britain	1783-1802	Russia	1890-1914
France	1830-1860	Canada	1896-1914
Belgium	1833-1860	Argentine[c]	1935-
United States[a]	1843-1860	Turkey[d]	1937-
Germany	1850-1873	India[e]	1952-
Sweden	1868-1890	China[e]	1952-
Japan[b]	1878-1900		

[a] The American takeoff is here viewed as the upshot of two different periods of expansion: the first, that of the 1840's, marked by railway and manufacturing development, mainly confined to the East— this occurred while the West and South digested the extensive agricultural expansion of the previous decade; the second the great railway push into the Middle West during the 1850's marked by a heavy inflow of foreign capital. By the opening of the Civil War the American economy of North and West, with real momentum in its heavy-industry sector, is judged to have taken off.

[b] Lacking adequate data, there is some question about the timing of the Japanese takeoff. Some part of the post-1868 period was certainly, by the present set of definitions, devoted to firming up the preconditions for takeoff. By 1914 the Japanese economy had certainly taken off. The question is whether the period from about 1878 to the Sino-Japanese War in the mid-1890's is to be regarded as the completion of the preconditions or as takeoff. On present evidence, I incline to the latter view.

[c] In one sense the Argentine economy began its takeoff during the First World War. But by and large, down to the pit of the post-1929 depression, the growth of its modern sector, stimulated during the war, tended to slacken; and, like a good part of the Western World, the Argentine sought during the 1920's to return to a pre-1914 normalcy. It was not until the mid-1930's that a sustained takeoff was inaugurated, which by and large can now be judged to have been successful despite the structural vicissitudes of that economy.

[d] Against the background of industrialization measures inaugurated in the mid-1930's, the Turkish economy has exhibited remarkable momentum in the past five years, founded in the increase in agricultural income and productivity. It still remains to be seen whether these two surges, conducted under quite different national policies, will constitute a transition to self-sustaining growth, and whether Turkey can overcome its current structural problems.

[e] As noted in the text it is still too soon (for quite different reasons) to judge either the Indian or Chinese Communist takeoff efforts successful.

It is with the problems and vicissitudes of such growing economies of the third stage (and especially with cyclical fluctuations and the threat of chronic unemployment) that the bulk of modern theoretical economics is concerned, including much recent work on the formal properties of growth models. The student of history and of contemporary underdeveloped areas is more likely to be concerned with the economics of the first two stages; that is, the economics of the preconditions and the takeoff. If we are to have a serious theory of economic growth or (more likely) some useful theories about economic growth, they must obviously seek to embrace these two early stages—and notably the economics of the takeoff. The balance of this article is designed to mobilize, tentatively and in a preliminary way, what an economic historian can contribute to the economics of takeoff.

The Takeoff Defined and Isolated

There are several problems of choice involved in defining the takeoff with precision. We might begin with one arbitrary definition and consider briefly the two major alternatives.

For the present purposes the takeoff is defined as requiring all three of the following related conditions:

(*a*) a rise in the rate of productive investment from (say) 5 per cent or less to over 10 per cent of national income (or net national product);

(*b*) the development of one or more substantial manufacturing[3] sectors, with a high rate of growth;

(*c*) the existence or quick emergence of a political, social and institutional framework which exploits the impulses to expansion in the modern sector and the potential external economy effects of the takeoff and gives to growth an on-going character.

The third condition implies a considerable capability to mobilize capital from domestic sources. Some takeoffs have occurred with virtually no capital imports, *e.g.,* Britain and Japan. Some takeoffs have had a high component of foreign capital, *e.g.,* the United States, Russia and Canada. But some countries have imported large quantities of foreign capital for long periods, which undoubtedly contributed to creating the preconditions for takeoff, without actually initiating takeoff, *e.g.,* the Argentine before 1914, Venezuela down to recent years, the Congo currently. In short, whatever the role of capital imports, the preconditions for takeoff include an initial ability to mobilize domestic savings productively, as well as a structure which subsequently permits a high marginal rate of savings.

This definition is designed to isolate the early stage when industrialization

---

[3] In this context "manufacturing" is taken to include the processing of agricultural products or raw materials by modern methods, *e.g.,* timber in Sweden, meat in Australia, dairy products in Denmark. The dual requirement of a "manufacturing" sector is that its processes set in motion a chain of further modern sector requirements and that its expansion provide the potentiality of external economy effects.

takes hold rather than the later stage when industrialization becomes a more massive and statistically more impressive phenomenon. In Britain, for example, there is no doubt that it was between 1815 and 1850 that industrialization fully took hold. If the criterion chosen for takeoff was the period of most rapid overall industrial growth, or the period when largescale industry matured, all our takeoff dates would have to be set forward: Britain, for example, to 1819-1848, the United States to 1868-1893, Sweden to 1890-1920, Japan to 1900-1920, Russia to 1928-1940. The earlier dating is chosen here because it is believed, on present (often inadequate) evidence, that the decisive transformations (including a decisive shift in the investment rate) occur in the first industrial phases; and later industrial maturity can be directly traced back to foundations laid in these first phases.

This definition is also designed to rule out from the takeoff the quite substantial economic progress which can occur in an economy before a truly self-reinforcing growth process gets under way. British economic expansion between (say) 1750 and 1783, Russian economic expansion between (say) 1861 and 1890, Canadian economic expansion between 1867 and the mid-1890's—such periods, for which there is an equivalent in the economic history of almost every growing economy—were marked by extremely important, even decisive, developments. The transport network expanded, and with it both internal and external commerce; new institutions for mobilizing savings were developed; a class of commercial and even industrial entrepreneurs began to emerge; industrial enterprise on a limited scale (or in limited sectors) grew. And yet, however essential these pre-takeoff periods were for later development, their scale and momentum were insufficient to transform the economy radically or, in some cases, to outstrip population growth and to yield an increase in *per capita* output.

With a sense of the considerable violence done to economic history, I am here seeking to isolate a period when the scale of productive economic activity reaches a critical level and produces changes which lead to a massive and progressive structural transformation in economies and the societies of which they are a part, better viewed as changes in kind than merely in degree.

•

The Inner Structure of the Takeoff

Following the definition of takeoff . . . we must consider not merely how a rise in the investment rate is brought about, from both supply and demand perspectives, but how rapidly growing manufacturing sectors emerged and imparted their primary and secondary growth impulses to the economy.

Perhaps the most important thing to be said about the behavior of these variables in historical cases of takeoff is that they have assumed many different forms. There is no single pattern. The rate and productivity of investment can rise, and the consequences of this rise can be diffused into a self-reinforcing general growth process by many different technical and economic routes, under the aegis of many different political, social and cultural settings, driven along by a wide variety of human motivations.

The purpose of the following paragraphs is to suggest briefly, and by way of illustration only, certain elements of both uniformity and variety in the variables whose movement has determined the inner structure of the takeoff.

The Supply of Loanable Funds

By and large, the loanable funds required to finance the takeoff have come from two types of sources: from shifts in the control over income flows, including income-distribution changes and capital imports and from the ploughback of profits in rapidly expanding particular sectors.

The notion of economic development occurring as the result of income shifts from those who will spend less productively to those who will spend more productively is one of the oldest and most fundamental notions in economics.

Historically, income shifts conducive to economic development have assumed many forms. In Meiji Japan and also in Tsarist Russia, the substitution of government bonds for the great landholders' claim on the flow of rent payments led to a highly Smithian redistribution of income into the hands of those with higher propensities to seek material advance and to accept innovations. In both cases, the real value of the government bonds exchanged for land depreciated; and, in general, the feudal landlords emerged with a less attractive arrangement than had first appeared to be offered. Aside from the confiscation effect, two positive impulses arose from land reform: the state itself used the flow of payments from peasants, now diverted from landlords' hands, for activity which encouraged economic development; and a certain number of the more enterprising former landlords directly invested in commerce and industry. In contemporary India and China, we can observe quite different degrees of income transfer by this route. India is relying to only a very limited extent on the elimination of large incomes unproductively spent by large landlords, although this element figures in a small way in its program. Communist China has systematically transferred all nongovernmental pools of capital into the hands of the State, in a series of undisguised or barely disguised capital levies; and it is drawing heavily for capital resources on the mass of middle and poor peasants who remain.

In addition to confiscatory and taxation devices, which can operate effectively when the State is spending more productively than the taxed individuals, inflation has been important to several takeoffs. In Britain of the late

1790's, the United States of the 1850's, Japan of the 1870's there is no doubt that capital formation was aided by price inflation, which shifted resources away from consumption to profits.

The shift of income flows into more productive hands has, of course, been aided historically not only by government fiscal measures but also by banks and capital markets. Virtually without exception, the takeoff periods have been marked by the extension of banking institutions which expanded the supply of working capital; and in most cases also by an expansion in the range of longrange financing done by a central, formally organized, capital market.

Although these familiar capital-supply functions of the State and private institutions have been important to the takeoff, it is likely to prove the case, on close examination, that a necessary condition for takeoff was the existence of one or more rapidly growing sectors whose entrepreneurs (private or public) ploughed back into new capacity a very high proportion of profits. Put another way, the demand side of the investment process, rather than the supply of loanable funds, may be the decisive element in the takeoff—as opposed to the period of creating the preconditions, or of sustaining growth once it is under way. The distinction is, historically, sometimes difficult to make, notably when the state simultaneously acts both to mobilize supplies of finance and to undertake major entrepreneurial acts. There are, nevertheless, periods in economic history when quite substantial improvements in the machinery of capital supply do not, in themselves, initiate a takeoff, but fall within the period when the preconditions are created: *e.g.,* British banking developments in the century before 1783, Russian banking developments before 1890, etc.

One extremely important version of the ploughback process has taken place through foreign trade. Developing economies have created from their natural resources major export industries; and the rapid expansion in exports has been used to finance the import of capital equipment and to service the foreign debt during the takeoff. United States, Russian, and Canadian grain fulfilled this function, Swedish timber and pulp, Japanese silk, etc. Currently, Chinese exports to the Communist Bloc, wrung at great administrative and human cost from the agricultural sector, play this decisive role. It should be noted that the development of such export sectors has not in itself guaranteed accelerated capital formation. Enlarged foreign-exchange proceeds have been used in many familiar cases to finance hoards (as in the famous case of Indian bullion imports) or unproductive consumption outlays.

It should be noted that one possible mechanism for inducing a high rate of ploughback into productive investment is a rapid expansion in the effective demand for domestically manufactured consumers' goods, which would direct into the hands of vigorous entrepreneurs an increasing proportion of income flows under circumstances which would lead them to expand their own capacity and to increase their requirements for industrial raw materials, semi-manufactured products and manufactured components.

A final element in the supply of loanable funds is, of course, capital imports. Foreign capital has played a major role in the takeoff stage of many economies: *e.g.,* the United States, Russia, Sweden, Canada. The cases of Britain and Japan indicate, however, that it cannot be regarded as an essential condition. Foreign capital was notably useful when the construction of railways or other large overhead capital items with a long period of gestation, played an important role in the takeoff. After all, whatever its strategic role, the proportion of investment required for growth which goes into industry is relatively small compared to that required for utilities, transport and the housing of enlarged urban populations. And foreign capital can be mightily useful in helping carry the burden of these overhead items either directly or indirectly.

What can we say, in general, then, about the supply of finance during the takeoff period? First, as a precondition, it appears necessary that the community's surplus above the mass-consumption level does not flow into the hands of those who will sterilize it by hoarding, luxury consumption or low-productivity investment outlays. Second, as a precondition, it appears necessary that institutions be developed which provide cheap and adequate working capital. Third, as a necessary condition, it appears that one or more sectors of the economy must grow rapidly, inducing a more general industrialization process, and that the entrepreneurs in such sectors plough back a substantial proportion of their profits in further productive investment, one possible and recurrent version of the ploughback process being the investment of proceeds from a rapidly growing export sector.

The devices, confiscatory and fiscal, for ensuring the first and second preconditions have been historically various. And, as indicated below, the types of leading manufacturing sectors which have served to initiate the takeoff have varied greatly. Finally, foreign capital flows have, in significant cases, proved extremely important to the takeoff, notably when lumpy overhead capital construction of long gestation period was required; but takeoffs have also occurred based almost wholly on domestic sources of finance.

The Sources of Entrepreneurship

It is evident that the takeoff requires the existence and the successful activity of some group in the society which accepts borrowers' risk, when such risk is so defined as to include the propensity to accept innovations. As noted above, the problem of entrepreneurship in the takeoff has not been profound in a limited group of wealthy agricultural nations whose populations derived by emigration mainly from northwestern Europe. There the problem of takeoff was primarily economic; and when economic incentives for industrialization emerged, commercial and banking groups moved over easily into industrial entrepreneurship. In many other countries, however, the development of adequate entrepreneurship was a more searching social process.

Under some human motivation or other, a group must come to perceive it to be both possible and good to undertake acts of capital investment; and, for their efforts to be tolerably successful, they must act with approximate rationality in selecting the directions toward which their enterprise is directed. They must produce not only growth, but tolerably balanced growth. We cannot quite say that it is necessary for them to act as if they were trying to maximize profit; for the criteria for private profit maximization do not necessarily converge with the criteria for an optimum rate and pattern of growth in various sectors. But in a growing economy, over periods longer than the business cycle, economic history is reasonably tolerant of deviations from rationality, in the sense that excess capacity is finally put to productive use. Leaving aside the question of ultimate human motivation, and assuming that the major overhead items are generated, if necessary, by some form of state initiative (including subsidy), we can say as a first approximation that some group must successfully emerge which behaves as if it were moved by the profit motive, in a dynamic economy with changing production functions; although, risk being the slippery variable, it is under such assumptions that Keynes' dictum should be borne in mind: "If human nature felt no temptation to take a chance, no satisfaction (profit apart) in constructing a factory, a railway, a mine or a farm, there might not be much investment merely as a result of cold calculation." [4]

In this connection, it is increasingly conventional for economists to pay their respects to the Protestant ethic.[5] The historian should not be ungrateful for this light on the gray horizon of formal growth models. But the known cases of economic growth which theory must seek to explain take us beyond the orbit of Protestantism. In a world where Samurai, Parsees, Jews, North Italians, Turks, Russian and Chinese civil servants (as well as Huguenots, Scotsmen and British Northcountrymen) have played the role of a leading elite in economic growth, John Calvin should not be made to bear quite this weight. More fundamentally, allusion to a positive scale of religious or other values conducive to profit-maximizing activities is an insufficient sociological basis for this important phenomenon. What appears to be required for the emergence of such elites is not merely an appropriate value system, but two further conditions: first, the new elite must feel itself denied the conventional routes to prestige and power by the tradi-

---

[4] John M. Keynes, *The General Theory of Employment, Interest and Money* (New York: Harcourt, Brace and Company, 1936), p. 150.

[5] *See, for example,* N. Kaldor, "Economic Growth and Cyclical Fluctuations," *Economic Journal,* March 1954, p. 67.

tional less acquisitive society of which it is a part; second, the traditional society must be sufficiently flexible (or weak) to permit its members to seek material advance (or political power) as a route upward alternative to conformity.

Although an elite entrepreneurial class appears to be required for takeoff, with significant power over aggregate income flows and industrial investment decisions, most takeoffs have been preceded or accompanied by radical change in agricultural techniques and market organization. By and large, the agricultural entrepreneur has been the individual landowning farmer. A requirement for takeoff is, therefore, a class of farmers willing and able to respond to the possibilities opened up for them by new techniques, landholding arrangements, transport facilities, and forms of market and credit organization. A small, purposeful elite can go a long way in initiating economic growth; but, especially in agriculture (and to some extent in the industrial working force), a wider-based revolution in outlook must come about.[6]

Whatever further empirical research may reveal about the motives which have led men to undertake the constructive enterpreneurial acts of the takeoff period, this much appears sure: these motives have varied greatly from one society to another; and they have rarely, if ever, been motives of an unmixed material character.

Leading Sectors in the Takeoff

. . . The overall rate of growth of an economy must be regarded in the first instance as the consequence of differing growth rates in particular sectors of the economy, such sectoral growth rates being in part derived from certain overall demand parameters (*e.g.,* population, consumers' income, tastes, etc.), in part from the primary and secondary effects of changing supply factors, when these are effectively exploited.

On this view the sectors of an economy may be grouped in three categories:

---

[6] Like the population question, agriculture is mainly excluded from this analysis, which considers the takeoff rather than the whole development process. Nevertheless, it should be noted that, as a matter of history, agricultural revolutions have generally preceded or accompanied the takeoff. In theory we can envisage a takeoff which did not require a radical improvement in agricultural productivity: if, for example, the growth and productivity of the industrial sector permitted a withering away of traditional agriculture and a substitution for it of imports. In fact, agricultural revolutions have been required to permit rapidly growing (and urbanizing) populations to be fed without exhausting foreign exchange resources in food imports or creating excessive hunger in the rural sector; and as noted at several points in this argument, agricultural revolutions have in fact played an essential and positive role, not merely by both releasing workers to the cities, and feeding them, but also by earning foreign exchange for general capital-formation purposes.

(*a*) *Primary growth sectors,* where possibilities for innovation or for the exploitation of newly profitable or hitherto unexplored resources yield a high growth rate and set in motion expansionary forces elsewhere in the economy;

(*b*) *Supplementary growth sectors,* where rapid advance occurs in direct response to—or as a requirement of—advance in the primary growth sectors, *e.g.,* coal, iron and engineering in relation to railroads. These sectors may have to be tracked many stages back into the economy, as the Leontief input–output models would suggest;

(*c*) *Derived growth sectors,* where advance occurs in some fairly steady relation to the growth of total real income, population, industrial production or some other overall, modestly increasing parameter. Food output in relation to population, housing in relation to family formation are classic derived relations of this order.

Very roughly speaking, primary and supplementary growth sectors derive their high momentum essentially from the introduction and diffusion of changes in the cost-supply environment (in turn, of course, partially influenced by demand changes); while the derived-growth sectors are linked essentially to changes in demand (while subject also to continuing changes in production functions of a less dramatic character).

At any period of time, it appears to be true even in a mature and growing economy that forward momentum is maintained as the result of rapid expansion in a limited number of primary sectors, whose expansion has significant external economy and other secondary effects. From this perspective, the behavior of sectors during the takeoff is merely a special version of the growth process in general; or, put another way, growth proceeds by repeating endlessly, in different patterns, with different leading sectors, the experience of the takeoff. Like the takeoff, longterm growth requires that the society not only generate vast quantities of capital for depreciation and maintenance, for housing and for a balanced complement of utilities and other overheads, but also a sequence of highly productive primary sectors, growing rapidly, based on new production functions. Only thus has the aggregate marginal capital–output ratio been kept low.

•

What can we say, then, in general about these leading sectors? Historically, they have ranged from cotton textiles, through heavy-industry complexes based on railroads and military end products, to timber, pulp, dairy products and finally a wide variety of consumers' goods. There is, clearly, no one sectoral sequence for takeoff, no single sector which constitutes the magic key. There is no need for a growing society to recapitulate the structural sequence and pattern of Britain, the United States or Russia. Four basic factors must be present:

(1) There must be enlarged effective demand for the product or products of sectors which yield a foundation for a rapid rate of growth in output. Histori-

cally, this has been brought about initially by the transfer of income from consumption or hoarding to productive investment; by capital imports; by a sharp increase in the productivity of current investment inputs, yielding an increase in consumers' real income expended on domestic manufactures; or by a combination of these routes.

(2) There must be an introduction into these sectors of new production functions as well as an expansion of capacity.

(3) The society must be capable of generating capital initially required to detonate the takeoff in these key sectors; and especially, there must be a high rate of ploughback by the (private or state) entrepreneurs controlling capacity and technique in these sectors and in the supplementary growth sectors they stimulated to expand.

(4) Finally, the leading sector or sectors must be such that their expansion and technical transformation induce a chain of Leontief input–output requirements for increased capacity and the potentiality for new production functions in other sectors, to which the society, in fact, progressively responds.

Conclusion

This hypothesis is, then, a return to a rather old-fashioned way of looking at economic development. The takeoff is defined as an industrial revolution, tied directly to radical changes in methods of production, having their decisive consequence over a relatively short period of time.

This view would not deny the role of longer, slower changes in the whole process of economic growth. On the contrary, takeoff requires a massive set of preconditions going to the heart of a society's economic organization and its effective scale of values. Moreover, for the takeoff to be successful, it must lead on progressively to sustained growth; and this implies further deep and often slow-moving changes in the economy and the society as a whole.

What this argument does assert is that the rapid growth of one or more new manufacturing sectors is a powerful and essential engine of economic transformation. Its power derives from the multiplicity of its forms of impact, when a society is prepared to respond positively to this impact. Growth in such sectors, with new production functions of high productivity, in itself tends to raise output per head; it places incomes in the hands of men who will not merely save a high proportion of an expanding income but who will plough it into highly productive investment; it sets up a chain of effective demand for other manufactured products; it sets up a requirement for enlarged urban areas, whose capital costs may be high, but whose population and market organization help to make industrialization an ongoing process; and, finally, it opens up a range of external economy effects which, in the end, help to produce new leading sectors when the initial impulse of the takeoff's leading sectors begins to wane.

We can observe in history and in the contemporary world important changes in production functions in nonmanufacturing sectors which have powerful effects on whole societies. If natural resources are rich enough, or new agricultural tricks are productive enough, such changes can even outstrip population growth and yield a rise in real output per head. Moreover, they may be a necessary prior condition for takeoff or a necessary concomitant of takeoff. Nothing in this analysis should be read as deprecating the importance of productivity changes in agriculture to the whole process of economic growth. But in the end takeoff requires that a society find a way to apply effectively to its own peculiar resources what D. H. Robertson once called the tricks of manufacture; and continued growth requires that it so organize itself as to continue to apply them in an unending flow, of changing composition. Only thus, as we have all been correctly taught, can that old demon, diminishing returns, be held at bay.

CHAPTER 32

WILBERT E. MOORE

Motivational Aspects
of Development

In the literature on economic development a certain notable division between optimists and pessimists is apparent. This division is highly predictive of disciplinary origin. Economists—representatives of the "dismal science"—are customarily optimistic about economic growth and its social consequences. Anthropologists and sociologists are customarily pessimistic about the possibilities of economic growth and particularly about its consequences. Although possibly these fields attract different personality types —the manic and the depressed—it seems more likely that conventional theory and habits of thought explain the difference.

Some Contrasting Theory

Theory of Motives and Consequences

Traditional economic theory has not been strongly concerned with attitudes and motives. Human attitudes and motives are simply assumed to be appropriate to rational choice of means effective for maximizing satisfactions, as economically defined and measured. Human wants are thought to be essentially unlimited, and human nature pretty much the same wherever encountered. A monetary market system coordinates the factors of production and allocates rewards, and financial incentives are assumed to be effective in allocating labor. The movement of labor between sectors of the economy is regarded as a function of its differential marginal productivity, which is principally determined by relative states of capitalization, technique, and, possibly, enterprise.

From Wilbert E. Moore, "Labor Attitudes toward Industrialization in Underdeveloped Countries," *The American Economic Review*, XLV (1955), No. 2, pp. 156-165. Reprinted by permission of the author and the American Economic Association.

Given these assumptions, such hints of pessimism that economists have about economic growth in underdeveloped areas could be expected to center on questions of capital, market organization, and entrepreneurial activity, but not on the willingness of potential workers to work. And since the economist has a normal prejudice toward the view that improvements in levels of production and consumption are consistent with universal human aspirations, he is certainly inclined to optimism about the consequences of economic growth.

Anthropological and sociological theory stands in sharp contrast to this set of views. Attitudes and motives are of more central concern as variables, related to differential positions within any social system. The person is viewed as having been socialized in ways appropriate to differential social roles, to hold values appropriate to group activity and its survival, and to behave in ways that are "irrational" and "nonrational" as judged on economic grounds. Wants are thus viewed as limited and relative to social position. The social system is viewed as strongly resistant to change, in part because of secondary and tertiary consequences of changes in a complex functional network. If these considerations are important within societies, they are even more marked between them. To contrast with the economist's "similarity of human nature" assumption, the anthropologist or sociologist offers "cultural relativity." He is likely to emphasize differences in values and aspirations in space and time, and to be extremely reluctant to assume that Western experience can be used as a guide to behavior in Dahomey, Nepal, or even Peru.

Given these assumptions, such hints of optimism that anthropologists or sociologists have about economic growth in undeveloped areas could be expected to center on the adaptability of economic incentives and organization to traditional attitudes and patterns, and especially on the willingness of potential workers to work. And since the anthropologist-sociologist has a normal prejudice toward the view that bread or all purchasable goods and services are not enough to satisfy human values, he is certainly inclined to pessimism about the consequences of economic change.

These contrasts are, of course, moderately unfair to both professional groups. Many economists, and especially those who have studied labor mobility, the operation of labor markets, and worker behavior, have expressed strong misgivings about the assumptions of traditional theory. Many anthropologists and sociologists, and especially those who have studied the actual impact of modern economic forms in undeveloped areas, have noted the stresses and tensions in traditional systems and the considerable success of the new employment alternatives in recruiting labor.

Theory of Organized Cooperation

The literature on economic development has included very little material on another aspect of theory, on which our two professional groups tend to disagree. There are differing views on the nature of business and industrial organization as related to the attitudes or motives of participants.

Traditional economic theory has little to say on this subject, since labor is viewed as allocated by market mechanisms and the relation between employer and employee the same in principle as any other economic contract. The productive efficiency of the division of labor has received consistent attention, but the problems associated with the authoritative coordination of labor implicit in factory organization remain relatively unexplored. Only in Marxist economic theory and, more recently, in attempts to construct alternative theories of the labor movement and management–union relations, have variables such as power and group loyalties been considered.

Traditional anthropological and sociological theory also has little to say on business or industrial organization, partly because of a concentration on the structure of society generally, partly because economic organization was thought to be the proper province of economists. Only in Weberian sociological theory and, more recently, in attempts to treat "the factory as a social system" have variables such as the authority of office, communication systems, and "informal organization" been considered.

Despite the recent and still somewhat peripheral attention given industrial organization in the disciplines we have been comparing, some differences between the disciplines can be detected. There is a notable tendency for the economist to emphasize—and exaggerate—individual, competitive aspirations, and an equally notable tendency for the anthropologist or sociologist to emphasize—and exaggerate—group cooperative aspirations. If the economist's model of behavior tends to be the prize fight, the sociologist's model tends to be the quilting bee.

Some Empirical Evidence

Faced with such contrasting views of economic behavior and its motivational sources, the analyst may be forgiven some confusion and permitted to seek refuge in the data. Unfortunately, evidence has not been collected or analyzed in ways that permit a clear resolution of theoretical disputes. It is possible, however, to get some leverage on the issues by reference to the reported experience in the recruitment and utilization of labor in undeveloped areas.[1]

Apathy and Opposition

A considerable body of evidence runs contrary to the notions that human wants are unlimited, that financial incentives will transfer labor from non-

---

[1] This section represents a selective summary of a rather extensive discussion, with citations to the literature, in Wilbert E. Moore, *Industrialization and Labor* (Ithaca: Cornell University Press, 1951).

industrial to industrial pursuits, and thus that the potential worker may be viewed as welcoming release from traditional restraints. Some of this evidence can be interpreted in terms of "rational conduct," but not in terms of economic maximization. The potential worker in undeveloped areas is typically required to give up traditional forms of organization and reciprocal obligations that have combined to afford him security, both material and affective. The kinship system in any nonindustrial society is likely to provide a major barrier to individual mobility, because it is a social security system, because it is the focus of positive values and advantages, and because extended kin obligations are likely to reduce the effective appeal of individual rewards. With an extended kinship system, if the individual faces adversity, his kinsmen are obliged to come to his aid. If he prospers, he is obliged to share his good fortune with great-uncles and second cousins once removed. Industrialization breaks up such units by geographical separation and, more importantly, by social separation.

The other side of the coin (an inappropriate metaphor in its connotations) is the lack of appreciation of the new status system. This may take the form of a relatively low and highly particular appeal of wages, often commented on with reference to "native" laborers, but also commented on by preclassical writers in economic theory with reference to workers in the early stages of the Industrial Revolution. The principle bears extension, however. New occupations simply do not fit traditional standards of prestige, or are valued negatively because they involve manual labor and merit placement irrespective of age, kinship position, caste, or other forms of "ascribed" status. To the extent that the potential worker operates as an independent producer, the change to wage labor involves some loss of "freedom," even if it offers higher rewards. To the extent that the potential worker operates as the equivalent of a craftsman, the change to factory employment is likely to involve a loss of socially recognized skills, of "workmanship," in the division of labor and its subordination to machine processes.

It would be hard to deny that a considerable part of this apathy and opposition is "reasonable," but equally hard to deny that its explanation lies partly in social standards and values that are badly served by wage incentives and by industrial forms of labor allocation.

The Force of Circumstances

If wages have a limited appeal to nonindustrial populations and new employments are negatively valued, it is not surprising that workers are more commonly "pushed" than "pulled" into modern forms of economic activity. Much of the "push" is in fact the largely unintentional consequence of external intervention. The successful attempt to reduce mortality has the effect of deteriorating man–land ratios, thus increasing agricultural underemployment and causing the landless and impoverished rural dweller to seek and accept other means of livelihood. The introduction of cheap manufactured goods may well displace the handicraft worker and make available an additional pool of workers, either directly or through increased dependency on agriculture. Even the trader may be displaced by largescale distribution, or simply by more efficient organization of established markets.

The coercion of hunger does not exhaust the available pressures. Direct political coercion also has an extensive record, ranging from forced labor to the indirect coercion of taxation—a system which has been widely used as a device in colonial Africa.

Not all of the sources of pressure on the potential worker are so clearly external in origin. Any society exhibits some degree of tension and strain, some evidence of dissatisfaction. The presence of new alternatives may allow the deviant who seeks to evade the sanctions of the traditional order to escape from unwanted and oppressive controls.

Again it would be hard to deny that the attitudes implicit in these types of behavior are reasonable and again equally hard to deny that they do not correspond to notions of high sensitivity to slight differences in incentives and opportunity.

The Efficacy of Positive Inducements

Not all of the empirical evidence involves such negative attitudes toward industrial labor. Wages do have an appeal, particularly if they can be used for goods and services that form part of traditional patterns of consumption and traditional modes of relationship. The transitional forms are many, and often oddly at variance with Western conceptions of market operation. The African from the native reserve who works long enough in the mines to pay his hut tax is presumably not highly integrated into a market system. He becomes slightly more integrated when he uses wages to buy cattle for use as a bride price, but this still has a distinctly exotic flavor. His behavior fits our standard conceptions better when he proves interested in all sorts of commercialized goods and services, but of course by then he is likely to have little in common with the values of the preindustrial community.

In some places other inducements to work seem to have operated, although not necessarily in the absence of financial incentives or contrary to their economically expected effect. Patriotic motives and other collective goals have formed the basis of appeals to workers in most industrial societies, with what effect it is difficult to say precisely. Certainly it is likely that a sense of voluntary participation in a worthwhile common enterprise offers some source of satisfaction to workers, although the standard forms of productive organization are not well adapted to making the use of such appeals very convincing. Here, it may be noted, is a possible positive role for union-type organization. Certainly the communists have attempted to involve workers in undeveloped areas in the organized building of the new, as well as the destroying of the old forms of social allegiance and power.

Toward a Tenable Theory

The discussion to this point implies the rejection of two extreme theoretical positions, both of which constitute alternatives available in the literature. The one extreme may be attributed to economics, although by no means all economists would subscribe. To traditional economists, labor attitudes are simply unproblematical, as they are adequately subsumed under the assumptions of maximizing want satisfactions. The other extreme may be attributed to anthropology, in the same unrepresentative sense. To the anthropologist, labor attitudes are so problematical, because they are so conditioned by variable cultures, that no other general statement about them is possible.

The attempt to formulate here the elements of a low-order theory rests upon the assumption that it is possible to give a general characterization to the undeveloped areas, to specify some of the crucial characteristics of modern economic organization, and to indicate some of the labor attitudes which are significant for transition from one to the other.

The Nature of Undeveloped Areas

Although it is true that cultures differ, and in many ways, it is possible at a higher level of generalization to detect common and essential functions in the organization of society. Every society has provisions and rules for reproduction, socialization of the young, production and allocation of goods and services, adjustment to the nonhuman environment, maintenance of order. It is also possible to detect some common bases in cognitive orientations and values. All societies encourage some material aspirations (although not necessarily expanding and competitive), some rational, technical orientation to the use of the environment (although not necessarily innovative), and some positive value on health and length of life.

There are internal sources of tension and strain in all societies. The model of the perfectly integrated society is a useful analytical fiction for many purposes, but ought not to be confused with primitive or agrarian societies. The sources of strain include, at least, uncertainties in socialization from generation to generation, chance innovations, and competing role demands given scarcities of time, treasure, and energy (or affective loyalty).

All undeveloped areas have already been disrupted in some form and degree by the "external" influence of Western patterns. The consequences of this interference may or may not be favorable to continuous economic development, but this will depend in some measure on the strategy adopted in view of the situation, as well as on the probable effects of influences so far.

One negative generalization is also negative in its implications for labor attitudes toward industrialization. Mobility on the basis of individual performance is generally not markedly present in undeveloped areas, and does not generally form a part of the positive value system. Whether for the individual or for the system as a whole, continuity and not change is likely to be the major value.

The Nature of Modern Economic Organization

It is now commonly recognized that modern economic enterprise depends upon a complex institutional structure. For purposes of simplification, this may be partially summarized as a monetary-market mechanism for allocation of the factors of production and for achieving distribution of goods and services. For the nonhuman factors of production, this involves at least transferable property rights and rational cost accounting. For the human factors of production, this involves a wage system for putting into the hands of the specialized worker a medium for commanding the necessary and appropriate goods and services for himself and his dependents.

Although part of the division of labor will be coordinated by impersonal market mechanisms, the fixed capital and economies of scale in the productive unit characteristic of industrial organization imply also administrative coordination and the development of scales of authority.

If labor is to be rationally allocated and optimally utilized, it appears essential to select on the basis of technical competence, to coordinate on the basis of relationships specific to the interdependent tasks, and to tie rewards to types of activities. These rewards need not be exclusively financial and indeed rarely will be. All of the rewards imply a system of social ranking closely related to position in the productive system.

The Nature of the Transition

Whether one looks at undeveloped areas or the most highly industrialized ones, a fundamental theoretical point is evident. That point is the great complexity of human motivation. Men will work for as many reasons as there are values to be served by such activity and will refuse to work where that serves his values. The fact that industrial systems emphasize values that are commanded in a market and incentives that provide monetary claims on a market should not blind us to the diversity of ends or the diversity of means for their satisfaction.

The effectiveness of wage incentives is relative to the availability of goods and services in the market that form part of the effective wants of workers.

This is essentially a common-sense static principle. But it is quite limiting, and failure to recognize it accounts for some of the exasperation of observers of "irrational" natives. The worker in an undeveloped area is typically not accustomed to expect, or even to aspire to, any considerable raising of ceilings on his consumption and social position. And there are many wants typically not satisfiable by market mechanisms. So we have both limited demand and limited supply.

To translate this principle into dynamic terms, the available evidence indicates that we should expect an increase in demand through knowledge, education, and the development of new values, and in supply through the addition of goods newly available because of industrialization and the movement of services into the market.

This view of market-oriented attitudes can be broadened, with considerable benefit to its theoretical importance.

The effectiveness of the appeal of new employment alternatives is relative to the availability of need-satisfying rewards. This principle will still apply if material or even financial wellbeing is held constant. The potential rewards include prestige and esteem within an acceptable system of social valuation. This also is a common-sense static principle and is also limiting. The traditional system of social valuation will not typically include the new activities, and the latter compete or conflict with the former. Both change and choice tend to be devalued. If some relationship between wages and markets has been established, higher wage levels can be used as a principal lever on conservative traditions, and this has been their historic role. The private employer is unlikely to act "correctly" in this matter, and this may be a major area for governmental policy in economic development.

Over time, we should expect an increase in aspiration and the addition of values associated with status mobility, merit evaluation, and a realistic sense of choice and initiative. We should also expect new systems of social organization and stratification to which these aspirations and values are appropriate.

Economic growth, insofar as it is affected by labor attitudes, is likely to be radically retarded or contained by any one of several vicious circles. There is considerable evidence of a reciprocal relationship between low wages and low productivity, whether the connection works through mere physical energy or through more subtle frustration and apathy. The failure to detect and utilize convertible craft skills, the assumption that initially unskilled local labor is incapable of training, and the adoption of the "color bar" as an extreme and open manifestation of these practices, constitute waste in the short run and possible failure of continued development in the long run.

It appears evident that neither the available skills nor the appropriate attitudes can be assumed to be adequate among the potential workers in undeveloped areas. Growth seems to have been most rapid and most probably continuous in the future where considerable resources have been devoted to formal education and where education and in-service training have been most closely geared to the skill demands of an industrial economy. Now, clearly, education in many colonial areas has encouraged anything but the development of mechanical and technical skills, and the opportunities for use of any such skills have not been made available to natives. That the new native leaders tend to be political agitators rather than economic administrators is scarcely surprising in view of colonial political and economic policies.

The development of positive labor attitudes toward industrialization would probably be enhanced by the fostering of a sense of social participation, as well as by the expansion of individual opportunity and the provision of amenities and security at least equivalent to those available in traditional organization. A sense of social participation has been consistently neglected even in advanced industrial societies. We do not know how flexible industrial organization may be made. But if economic development entails a revolutionary change in the organization of society, as it does, there is at least some theoretical reason for supposing that workers as well as managers or government officials might welcome positive participation in partial compensation for their uprooting.

In view of the complex richness of human motivation, the idea that economic and noneconomic incentives are necessarily competitive for a limited supply is untenable. Both may be increased simultaneously and continuously within very high limits. . . .

CHAPTER 33

REINHARD BENDIX

Industrialization, Ideologies, and Social Structure

Changes in Ideology

At the inception of industrialization in England, an ideology of tradition-alism prevailed; John Stuart Mill called it the "theory of dependence." According to this view the laboring poor are children, who must be gov-erned, who should not be allowed to think for themselves, who must per-form their assigned tasks obediently and with alacrity, who must show def-erence to their superiors, and who—if they only conduct themselves virtuously—will be protected by their betters against the vicissitudes of life. This interpretation of authority is self-confirming and self-serving. But it sets up the presumption that the dependence of the poor and the responsi-bility of the rich are the valid moral rules of the social order. In the course of industrial development, these ideas were gradually modified. As the re-sponsibility of the rich was increasingly rejected by the advocates of *laissez-faire,* the dependence of the poor was turned from an inevitable into a self-imposed fate. As it was "demonstrated" that the rich cannot care for the poor without decreasing the national wealth, it was also asserted that by abstinence and exertion the poor can better their lot. The same virtues which in the eighteenth century were extolled so that the lowly will not aspire above their station were praised by the middle of the nineteenth century because they enable a man to raise himself by his own efforts.

In England, and even more in America, this praise of effort led toward the end of the nineteenth century to an apotheosis of the struggle for exist-ence. The militant language of an ethics of the jungle was applied to the relations between employers and workers. Riches and poverty merely re-

From Reinhard Bendix, "Industrialization, Ideologies, and Social Structure," *American Sociological Review,* XXIV (1959), No. 5, pp. 616-623. Reprinted by permission of the author and the American Sociological Association.

flect differences of ability and effort. The employer's success is evidence of his fitness for survival, and as such justifies his absolute authority over the enterprise. This assertion of authority has a clearcut meaning only as long as most managerial functions are in the hands of one man. The idea becomes ambiguous as the use of expertise in the management of enterprises increases and the managerial function becomes subdivided and specialized. Yet the idea of the employer's absolute authority over his enterprise coincided with the "scientific management" movement which sought to give him expert advice on what to do with that authority. It may be suggested, therefore, that the doctrines of Social Darwinism gradually lost their appeal, in part because changes in industrial organization gave rise to a changing imagery of men in industry. From the Gilded Age to the 1920's, workers and managers were self-evident failures or successes in a struggle for survival, in which they were the recalcitrant objects or the exasperated originators of managerial commands. Today they have become individuals-in-groups whose skills must be improved and allocated systematically, and whose productivity must be maximized by appropriate attention to their psychological makeup. Thus, over the past two hundred years, managerial ideologies in Anglo-American civilization have changed from the "theory of dependence" to *laissez-faire,* to Social Darwinism, and finally to the "human relations" approach.

In the Russian development we also find the assertion of paternal authority and of childlike dependence, and in much the same terms as in England. But in Russia this ideology of traditionalism was a very different thing from what it was in England, because of the Tsar's assertion of supreme authority over all the people. This authority remained intact regardless of how many privileges the Tsar granted to the landlords and regardless of how rarely he interfered in fact with the use and abuse of these privileges. Ideologically, the Tsar maintained his pre-eminence through repeated assertions concerning his paternal care and responsibility for all of "his" people. Through repeated petitions and sporadic revolts, the people used this Tsarist claim in order to obtain redress for their grievances against landlords and employers. Finally, because of the early centralization of authority under the Muscovite rulers, the whole distribution of wealth and rank among the aristocracy turned upon the competition for favors at the Court and hence reinforced the Tsar's supremacy.

During the second half of the nineteenth century this pattern of Tsarist autocracy had farreaching consequences. The dislocations incident to the emancipation of the serfs (1861) and the development of industry brought in their train assertions of absolute authority by the employers, efforts of the workers to organize themselves, and sporadic attempts of the government to regulate the relationship between them. Although ostensibly acting on an equitable basis, the government in fact supported the employers against the workers. Much of this is again broadly familiar from the English experience; but Russia's historical legacies prevented the shift in ideology which has been described for England. As long as Tsarist autocracy remained intact, neither the rejection of responsibility by the Tsar and the ruling strata nor the demand for the self-dependence of the workers developed. Instead, the Tsar and his officials continued to espouse the ideology of traditionalism. Quite consistently, Tsarist officials sought to superintend both employers and workers in order to mitigate or suppress the struggles between them. That is, the officials aided *and* curbed the employers' exercise of authority, as well as the workers' efforts to formulate grievances and organize protest movements.

Tsarist autocracy was overthrown in the Russian revolutions of 1905 and 1917. Although vast differences were brought about by the revolutions, the managerial ideology of Tsarism lived on in a modified form. In theory, Tsarist officials had regarded employers and workers as equally subject to the will of the Tsar; loyal submission to that will was the mark of good citizenship. In theory, Lenin believed that all workers were equal participants in the management of industry and government; their loyal submission to the Communist party represented their best interest and expressed their sovereign will. The logic of Lenin's as of the Tsarist position is that under a sovereign authority the same person or organization can and should perform both subordinate and superordinate functions. For example, Soviet labor unions approach the ideal of workers' control of industry when they are called upon to participate in the management of industry. But they also function in a managerial capacity when they inculcate labor discipline among their members under the authoritative direction of the Communist Party.

Ideologically, this position is defended on the ground that the party represents the historical interests of the proletariat against the shortrun interests of individuals and factions. In this orientation one can still see survivals of Tsarist autocracy, since all wisdom and responsibility reside in a small group or indeed in one man who, like the Tsar, knows better than private persons what is the good of all, and cannot but wish the wellbeing of the people. But there is also an important difference. The leaders of the Russian revolution were faced with the task of developing self-discipline and initiative among workers if a suitable industrial workforce was to become available. They proceeded to inculcate these qualities by the direct or indirect subordination of everyone to the discipline of the Communist Party. This policy continued the Tsarist tradition by making all matters the object of organizational manipulation rather than of personal striving; but it also represented a break with the past in that it was no longer restricted to personal submission.

Historical Significance of Ideological Change

What are the historical implications of this analysis of managerial ideologies? Ruling groups everywhere, including the rulers of developing industrial societies, justify their good fortune as well as the ill fortune of those subject to their authority. Their self-serving arguments may not appear as a promising field of research; in fact, the whole development of industrialization has been accompanied by an intellectual rejection of such ideologies as unworthy of consideration. Yet the fact is that all industrialization involves the organization of enterprises in which a few command and many obey; and the ideas developed by the few and the many may, I believe, be considered a symptom of changing class relations, and hence as a clue to an understanding of industrial societies.

Historically, ideologies of management became significant in the transition from a preindustrial to an industrial society. The authority exercised by employers was recognized as distinct from the authority of government. This was a novel experience even in Western Europe where there was precedent for such autonomy in other institutions, because the industrial entrepreneurs were "new men" rather than a ruling class buttressed by tradition. This was also the period during which the discipline of sociology originated. Under the impact of the French revolution, society came to be conceived in terms of forces that are independent from, as well as antagonistic to, the formal institutions of the body politic. Some early elaborations of this key idea enable us to see the historical significance of ideologies of management.

The authority of employers rests on the contractual acquisition of property, which the eighteenth-century philosophers made the conceptual basis of the social order. In Rousseau's view, that order can be and ought to be based on a general will which presupposes that the individual acts for the whole community. In such a society, as George Herbert Mead has pointed out, ". . . the citizen can give laws only to the extent that his volitions are an expression of the rights which he recognizes in others . . . [and] which the others recognize in him. . . ." [1] This approach provides a model for a society based on consent, so that the power of rule-making is exercised by all and for all. This foundation of society upon a "general will" was directly related to the institution of property. As Mead has stated,

> If one wills to possess that which is his own so that he has absolute control over it as property, he does so on the assumption that everyone else will possess his own property and exercise absolute control over it. That is, the in-

---

[1] George Herbert Mead, *Movements of Thought in the Nineteenth Century* (Chicago: University of Chicago Press, 1936), p. 21.

dividual wills his control over his property only insofar as he wills the same sort of control for everyone else over property.[2]

Thus, the idea of a reciprocal recognition of rights specifically presupposed the equality of citizens as property-owners.

This implication gave pause to some eighteenth- and nineteenth-century philosophers. They noted that the reciprocity of rights among property owners based on freedom of contract does not apply to the relations between employers and workers. As early as 1807 the German philosopher Hegel formulated the problematic nature of this relationship in a manner which anticipates the modern psychology of the self, just as Rousseau's "general will" anticipates the sociological analysis of interaction. Hegel maintains that men come to a recognition of themselves through a process whereby each accepts the self-recognition of the other and is in turn accepted by him. That is, each man's sense of identity depends upon his acceptance of the identity of others and upon their acceptance of himself. In Hegel's view, this reciprocity is lacking in the relation between master and servant. The master does not act toward himself as he acts toward the servant; and the servant does not do toward others what his servitude makes him do against himself. In this way the mutuality of recognition is destroyed, and the relations between master and servant become one-sided and unequal.[3]

In Western Europe, this inequality of the employment-relationship coincided with the ideological and institutional decline of traditional subordination. Yet while the old justifications of subordination crumbled, and new aspirations were awakened among the masses of the people, their experience of inequality continued. According to De Tocqueville, this problem had a differential impact upon masters and servants. In the secret persuasion of his mind the master continues to think of himself as superior; but he no longer recognizes any paternal responsibilities toward the servant. Still, he wants his servants to be content with their servile condition. In effect, the master wishes to enjoy the age-old privileges without acknowledging their concomitant obligations; and the servant rebels against his subordination, which is no longer a divine obligation and is not yet perceived as a contractual obligation.

> Then it is that [in] the dwelling of every citizen . . . a secret and internal warfare is going on between powers ever rivals and suspicious of each other: the master is ill-natured and weak, the servant ill-natured and intractable; the

---

[2] *Ibid.,* p. 17.

[3] Georg Friedrich Wilhelm Hegel, *Phänomenologie des Geistes* (Leipzig: Felix Meiner, 1928), pp. 143, 147. My paraphrasing attempts to convey Hegel's meaning without use of his language. The relevant passages are readily accessible in C. J. Friedrich, ed., *The Philosophy of Hegel* (New York: Modern Library, 1953), pp. 399-410.

one constantly attempts to evade by unfair restrictions his obligation to protect and to remunerate, the other his obligation to obey. The reins of domestic government dangle between them, to be snatched at by one or the other. The lines that divide authority from oppression, liberty from license, and right from might are to their eyes so jumbled together and confused that no one knows exactly what he is or what he may be or what he ought to be. Such a condition is not democracy, but revolution.[4]

In the nineteenth century men like Hegel, De Tocqueville, and Lorenz von Stein pointed out that the spread of egalitarian ideas was causing a transition in the relations between masters and servants. This transition may be called a crisis of aspirations. . . . As a consequence, most European countries witnessed the rise of a "fourth estate" which struggled against existing legal liabilities and for basic civil rights, above all the right to suffrage. In a parliamentary debate on Chartism, Disraeli remarked that this struggle was invested with a degree of sentiment usually absent from merely economic or political contests. To the extent that such complex movements can be characterized by a common denominator this sentiment referred, I think, to the workers' quest for a public recognition of their equal status as citizens. Where this and other civil rights became accepted, such recognition compensated for the continued social and economic subordination of the workers and thus assuaged the crisis of aspirations. Moreover, the political utilization of these civil rights could lead to a recognition of basic social rights which today is embodied in the institutions of social welfare characteristic of many Western democracies. The initial crisis of aspirations continued, on the other hand, where civil rights were rejected or where their acceptance was postponed for too long, leading either to an eventual revolutionary upheaval as in Tsarist Russia, or to a more-or-less damaging exacerbation of class-relations as in Italy and France.

My hypothesis is that the break with the traditional subordination of the people gave rise to a generic problem of many industrial societies. The question of nineteenth-century Europe concerned the terms on which a society undergoing industrialization will incorporate its newly recruited industrial work force within the economic and political community of the nation. Ideologies of management are significant because they contribute to each country's answer to this question. In England the workers were invited to become their own masters, if they did not wish to obey; in Russia they were told that their subordination was less onerous than it seemed, because their own superiors were also servants of the almighty Tsar.

---

[4] Alexis de Tocqueville, *Democracy in America* (New York: Vintage Books, 1945), Vol. II, p. 195. Some phrases in the preceding paragraph are also taken from this chapter of De Tocqueville's work.

•

Ideologies, Industrial Bureaucracy, and Totalitarianism

Since the eighteenth century Anglo-American and Russian civilizations have witnessed a growing managerial concern with the attitudes as well as the productivity of workers. It is possible to relate this change of ideology to a large number of the developments which comprise the transition from an early to a mature industrial society. The changing structure of industrial organizations was only one of these developments. Yet the bureaucratization of economic enterprises is of special importance for any attempt to "interpret the difference of fact and ideology between a totalitarian and nontotalitarian form of subordination in economic enterprises." [5] Bureaucratization is also especially suitable for a comparative study of authority relations in industry, since it involves processes that are directly comparable in two such different civilizations as England and Russia. This choice of focus deliberately eschews a comprehensive theory of society in favor of selecting a problem which, if suitable for comparative analysis, will also lead to an analysis of social structures. For, if comparable groups in different societies confront and over time resolve a common problem, then a comparative analysis of their divergent resolutions will reveal the divergence of social structures in a process of change.[6]

Problems of a systematic management of labor come to the fore where the increasing complexity of economic enterprises makes their operation more and more dependent upon an *ethic of work performance*. This ethic involves a degree of steady intensity of work, reasonable accuracy, and a compliance with general rules and specific orders that falls somewhere between blind obedience and unpredictable caprice. Where personal supervision is replaced by impersonal rules, the efficiency of an organization will vary with the degree to which these attributes of work-performance are realized, and this realization is part of the ongoing bureaucratization of economic enterprises. That is to say, management subjects the conditions of employment to an impersonal systematization, while the employees seek to modify the implementation of the rules as their personal interests and their commitment (or lack of commitment) to the goals of the organization dictate. As everyone knows, there is no more effective means of organizational sabotage than a letter-perfect compliance with all the rules and a consistent refusal of the employees to use their own judgment. . . . In the

---

[5] Reinhard Bendix, *Work and Authority in Industry* (New York: John Wiley & Sons, 1956), p. xx.

[6] Here I am indebted to the work of Max Weber, although more to what he did in his own studies than to what he wrote about them in his methodology. *See* my *Max Weber, An Intellectual Portrait* (New York: Doubleday, 1960), Ch. 8.

literature on organizations, the exercise of discretion by subordinates is known by a number of terms: Veblen called it the "withdrawal of efficiency"; Max Weber referred to it as the bureaucratic tendency toward secrecy; Herbert Simon might call it the "zone of nonacceptance." I have suggested the phrase "strategies of independence" so as to get away from the negative connotations of the other terms, since the exercise of discretion may serve to achieve, as well as to subvert, the goals of an organization.

Now, the great difference between totalitarian and nontotalitarian forms of subordination consists in the managerial handling of this generic attribute of all authority relations. The historical legacies of some Western countries have encouraged management to presuppose the existence of a common universe of discourse between superiors and subordinates, and this presupposition is related to the successful resolution of the crisis of aspirations. From the evangelism and the tough-minded *laissez-faire* approach of eighteenth-century England to the latest refinement of the "human relations" approach, managerial appeals have been addressed to the good faith of subordinates in order to enlist their cooperation. Whether such good faith existed is less important than that such appeals were made, though it is probable that in England and the United States large masses of workers in one way or another accepted managerial authority as legitimate even if they were indifferent to, or rejected, the managerial appeals themselves. In Russia, on the other hand, historical legacies did *not* encourage management (under the tsars) to presuppose the existence of a common universe of discourse between superiors and subordinates. From the time of Peter the Great to the period of rapid industrial growth in the last decades preceding World War I, managerial appeals were addressed to the workers' duty of obedience toward all those in positions of authority. Whether or not the workers actually developed a sense of duty, the appeals presupposed that they had not. Accordingly, officials and managers did not rely on the good faith among their subordinates, but attempted instead to eliminate the subordinates' strategies of independence.

This managerial refusal to accept the tacit evasion of rules and norms or the uncontrolled exercise of judgment is related to a specific type of bureaucratization which constitutes the fundamental principle of totalitarian government. In such a regime the will of the highest party authorities is absolute in the interest of their substantive objectives. The party may disregard not only all formal procedures by which laws are validated, but also its own previous rulings; and where norms may be changed at a moment's notice, the rule of law is destroyed. Totalitarianism also does away with the principle of a single line of authority. Instead of relying on an enactment of laws and on the supervision of their execution from the top, totalitarian regimes use the hierarchy of the party in order to expedite and control at each step the execution of orders through the regular administrative channels. This may be seen as the major device by which such regimes seek to prevent officials from escaping inspection, while compelling them to use their expertise in an intensified effort to implement the orders of the regime. A totalitarian government is based, therefore, on two interlocking hierarchies of authority. The work of every factory, of every governmental office, of every unit of the army or the secret police, as well as every cultural or social organization, is programmed, coordinated, and supervised by some agency of government. But it is also propagandized, expedited, criticized, spied upon, and incorporated in special campaigns by an agency of the totalitarian party, which is separately responsible to the higher party authorities.

The rationale of this principle of a double government can be stated within the framework of Max Weber's analysis of bureaucracy. An ideally functioning bureaucracy in his sense is the most efficient method of solving largescale organizational tasks. But this is true only *if* these tasks involve a more-or-less stable orientation toward norms which seek to maintain the rule of law and to achieve an equitable administration of affairs. These conditions are absent where tasks are assigned by an omnipotent *and* revolutionary authority. Under the simulated combat conditions of a totalitarian regime, the norms that govern conduct do not stay put for any length of time, although each norm in turn will be the basis of an unremitting drive for prodigies of achievement. In response, subordinates will tend to use their devices of concealment for the sake of systematic, if tacit, strategies of independence. They will do so not only for reasons of convenience, but because the demands made upon them by the regime are "irrational" from the viewpoint of expert knowledge and systematic procedure. The party, on the other hand, seeks to prevent the types of concealment that make such collective strategies possible by putting every worker and official under maximum pressure to utilize their expertise to the fullest extent. This is the rationale of a double hierarchy of government, which places a party functionary at the side of every work unit in order to prevent concealment and to apply pressure. The two hierarchies would be required, even if all key positions in government and industry were filled by party functionaries. For a functionary turned worker or official would still be responsible for "overfulfilling" the plan, while the new party functionary would still be charged with keeping that official under pressure and surveillance.

In this way totalitarianism replaces the old system of stratification by a new one based on criteria of activism and party orthodoxy. The ethic of work performance on which this regime relies is not the product of century-long growth as in the West, but of material incentives and of a political supervision that seeks to prevent evasion from below as well as from above. For example, the collective "bargaining" agreements of Soviet industry are in fact declarations of loyalty in which individuals and groups pledge themselves publicly to an overfulfillment of the plan, while the subsequent organization of public confessionals, the manipulation of status differences between activists and others, the principle of collective leadership, and further devices seek to maximize performance and prevent the "withdrawal of efficiency." The individual subordinate is surrounded almost literally. Aside from ordinary incentives, he is controlled by his superior and by the party agitator who stands at the side of his superior; but he is also controlled "from below" in the sense that the social pressures of his peer group are manipulated by party agitators and their agents. This institutionalization of suspicion and the consequent elimination of privacy are justified on the ground that the party "represents" the masses, spearheads the drive for Russian industrialization, and leads the cause of world communism. . . .

CHAPTER 34

S. N. EISENSTADT

Political Development

In this paper I shall try to outline, in a systematic way, some of the main sociological factors influencing the political developments in underdeveloped countries, and the social characteristics and internal dynamics of their political systems.

Uneven Change in Colonial Societies

A characteristic of the whole process of transition and change in underdeveloped societies is that it has been, and continues to be, unbalanced. Certain main elements of this lack of balance have long been recognized and more-or-less correctly attributed to the basic nature of colonialism. Although many of the underdeveloped societies did not have officially colonial status, most of the changes have occurred under the impact of the clash with the West. As a result of this, these societies have been put in an inferior, dependent, and unbalanced position in relation to European powers. This situation, moreover, has been evaluated within a framework of European institutions and values. But in order to understand some of the dynamic problems to which this process has given rise, certain additional aspects of this uneven and unbalanced change should be analyzed.

The first major aspect is the lack of balance in processes of change and transition that can be found between the "central" level and the local level. Most changes introduced either directly or indirectly by the colonial powers (or by the "traditional" authorities of the independent societies which co-operated with the European powers) have been focused on the central institutions of the society. The most obvious changes were in the broad frameworks of political and economic institutions. In the political field, the

From S. N. Eisenstadt, "Sociological Aspects of Political Development in Underdeveloped Countries," *Economic Development and Cultural Change,* V (1957), No. 4, pp. 289-307. Copyright 1957 by the University of Chicago Press, and reprinted by permission of the author and the publisher.

introduction of unitary systems of administration, the unification or regularization of taxation, the establishment of modern court procedures, and at later stages, the introduction of limited types of representation, have greatly changed overall political structures and orientations. In the relatively independent states, innovation in military techniques was prevalent. The changes have introduced certain universalistic criteria, that is, orientations toward general rules and modern procedures. Even where various forms of indirect rule were practiced (as in many British South-East Asian, and particularly African territories), some change necessarily took place in political organization, though this change was much slower than in cases of direct rule.

Similarly, many changes have been effected in the economy, notably the change to a market economy. Similar attempts to change the central foci of the institutional framework were made on a more limited scale in the educational field by endeavoring to provide new types of modern education for selected local elites.

The common factor in these changes was their direction toward promotion of systematic change in the society as a whole. There was a more-or-less conscious awareness that such change was necessary (and presumably good) and that new general institutional structures and principles should be established. At the same time, however, the colonial powers (or indigenous traditional rulers) saw it as part of their task to effect these changes only within the limits set by the existing institutions and their own interests.

This is manifest in their orientation toward change at the local level, *i.e.,* the level of the village, community, or tribal unit. Here colonial or indigenous rulers attempted to contain most changes within the limits of traditional groups and/or to limit, as much as possible, the extent of any change. But many changes did develop within the local communities, as the literature on detribalization, social and economic disorganization in villages, and disorganization of the family indicates. The important thing for our analysis is that the rulers tried, insofar as possible, to contain these changes within traditional systems, and most of their administrative efforts on the local level were aimed at the strengthening of the existing organizations and relations, at maintaining peace and order, and at reorganizing the systems of taxation. Thus, while the administration attempted to introduce innovations —particularly new taxes and improved methods of revenue administration —it tried to accomplish this within a relatively unchanging social setting, with the implicit goal of limiting changes to technical matters. Here existed a basic contradiction: on the one hand, attempts were made to establish broad, modern, administrative, political, and economic settings, while on the other hand, these changes were to be limited and based on relatively unchanged subgroups and on traditional attitudes and loyalties. This contradictory attitude could be found in most spheres of social action.

In the economic field, the major efforts were made to facilitate the functioning of a market-oriented economy, albeit of a very specific kind. This economy had to operate, as it were, without full development of new economic motivations, which would have disturbed the existing social order. In the field of education, where innovations were much less broad, there existed the tendency to impart rudiments of technical education without changing the system of values and aspirations. In economic and educational fields of action at least partial solutions could be found. Some indigenous groups found a place in newly established economic, educational, and professional organizations. Literacy grew to some extent, and the expectation of monetary rewards became customary and permissible for most groups.

Internal contradictions were most pronounced in the political field. Since the colonial powers or the indigenous rulers were interested in political loyalty, they aimed at maintaining a relatively passive type of obedience and identification and were always ready, whenever possible, to utilize existing traditional loyalties or to transfer them to the new setting without much change in their basic social and cultural orientations.

While the colonial powers and most indigenous rulers were interested in loyalty and were concerned with the transformation of certain institutional aspects—especially technical aspects—of the social structure, they wanted at the same time to base these innovations not on new types of solidarity and general political orientations and participation of the main strata of the population. Rather they tried to base the new political-administrative structure on orientations limited to technical, administrative changes for the bulk of the population, and on more general and active identification for a very limited and select group at the center.

The full dynamic implications of this unbalanced development can only be understood if some additional aspects of the unevenness of change are analyzed. These are aspects derived from the colonial or semicolonial political situation. Most of them were present also in the noncolonial "independent" societies (China, Ottoman Empire, Arab states) but appeared in a different light, to be analyzed in more detail later.

The two chief results derived from the colonial nexus were (1) segregation between Europeans and natives, and (2) discrimination against the natives in most of the newly developed institutions. The extent of segregation and the intensity of discrimination varied in different institutional spheres and was often coupled with attempts to maintain the traditional native culture and even to idealize and romanticize it. The attempts at "segregation" and at minimal developments of a common framework were most prominent in the fields of politics and social solidarity; they were somewhat less so in the fields of administration and the economy. But the paradox of the situation was that the more overt attempts at segregation in the traditional as well as more modern spheres were gradually being given up, due to situational exigencies and as more and more natives were drawn into the modern spheres, the more acute became the discrimination against them in terms of the basic premises of these institutions.

Thus the basic problem in these societies was the expectation that the native population would accept certain broad, modern institutional settings organized according to principles of universalism, specificity and common secular solidarity, and would perform within them various roles—especially economic and administrative roles—while at the same time, they were denied some of the basic rewards inherent in these settings. They were denied above all full participation in a common political system and full integration in a common system of solidarity. In other words, they were expected to act on the basis of a motivational system derived from a different social structure which the colonial powers and indigenous rulers tried to maintain. Quite obviously these societies faced acute problems of integration which could not be solved, except momentarily, within the framework of colonial or semicolonial societies.

These processes of uneven change did not and could not stop at a given time and freeze, as it were, a society's development at a certain stage. Many such attempts were made—as is evidenced by the attempts at indirect rule, on the one hand, and by widespread efforts of indigenous rulers to limit changes to purely technical matters, on the other. But such devices could not succeed for long. The economic needs of the colonial powers and/or of the indigenous ruling groups, their growing dependency on international markets, and on the international political system and the changes within it, precluded any freezing of development at a given stage. Thus, all these processes tended to affect "native" social systems to an increasing degree and to draw ever wider strata of these societies into the orbit of modern institutional settings. Different countries are even today at different stages of development in this process. But the greater the tempo of these changes, the greater the unevenness and lack of balance and the greater the problems of acute malintegration the society has to face.

As has been shown earlier, these problems of malintegration arose at various levels and in different social spheres—in the economic and ecological spheres, in education, in family life, and others. But they were necessarily most acute in the political and solidarity spheres; there the colonial or Western impact had undermined most of the old integrative principles and organizations both at the local and at the national level. While partial solutions could sometimes be found for economic and technical problems, their very partiality only tended to emphasize the alien political framework and the malintegration in the solidarity sphere.

The Influence of Uneven Change on Political Movements in Colonial Societies

It is not within the province of this paper to analyze the various attempts by colonial powers to find solutions to these problems within the framework of colonial society. Our main concern will be to analyze the repercussion of these developments on the nationalistic political and social movements which have been of prime importance for the future of these countries.

These movements have their origin in the dynamic situation of change, whose imprint can be discerned in their structure and development. Naturally, most of the nationalistic and social-nationalistic movements were especially sensitive to the manifestations of lack of balance and evenness of change. Yet, at the same time, they usually could not overcome easily the problems that this imbalance had created.

This sensitivity can be discerned in two basic characteristics of these movements: first, in their strong emphasis on new secular, modern symbols of solidarity and on their strong orientation toward solidarity-political activity (aiming ultimately at political independence); and second, in their attempts, especially in the later stages of development, to break through the "freezing" at the local level and to reach the broad masses of the population. But, at the same time—and this is most important for our analysis—the common bond which they tried to create with the masses was almost entirely couched in modern solidarity-political terms and did not emphasize the solution of immediate economic and administrative problems. The political symbols used were intended to develop new, ultimate, common values and basic loyalties, rather than relate to current policy issues within the colonial society. This emphasis was caused by their exclusion from effective power and by their fear of compromising the basic issue through participation in current affairs when opportunity arose.

A somewhat similar attitude can be observed in respect to economic, administrative and instrumental problems. Most nationalist movements did develop an economic ideology either stressing romantically the maintenance of the old village community or the necessity of state planning. All decried the injustices of the economic policies and discrimination of the colonial powers. But the nationalist leaders did not deal concretely with current economic problems or problems of daily administration. It is significant that members of the social groups among colonial peoples who participated relatively successfully in economic or administrative areas and who developed new types of social organization (as, for example, native business communities or membership in the colonial services) usually did not participate actively in the nationalistic movements and often were looked upon as traitors, or, at least, as "compromisers," by the members and leaders of these movements. The nationalistic leaders appealed to those groups of the population which were in an acute state of transition from the traditional to the modern setting, and which therefore suffered most from social disorganization, rather than to the groups which could adapt tolerably to the new institutional spheres.

Thus, most nationalistic movements, though obviously opposed to the colonial regime, inherited from it some important social characteristics. On the one hand, the leaders attempted to formulate new symbols of solidarity which would transcend the limitations of the colonial situation and which were couched in modern nationalistic and universalistic terms. But at the same time, they did not make any special efforts to transform other spheres of institutional life and to solve the problems created there by the processes of uneven change. Although the nationalist leaders did not try to prevent the development of new types of social organization, they did not explicitly deal with problems provoked by these changes. They seemed to be content to base the new movement, within the instrumental fields, either on traditional types of attitudes and organization, or on transitory types of attitudes and motivations which were not fully stabilized. Their major assumption, common to many revolutionary movements, was that all of these problems would be more-or-less automatically solved once political independence were achieved.

•

The social peculiarities of nationalist movements produced various characteristics which have often been described in the literature. The emphasis on solidarity symbols, without attention on other aspects of social organization, has necessarily given rise to a relative lack of stability in the sphere of political organization itself. This is evidenced by the divisions between different political movements and between the leaders of political movements and the more traditional powers in the society, such as tribal chiefs, princes, and colonial elites. Whenever competing nationalist movements developed within any one society, they became usually totally opposed to one another in terms of ultimate values and symbols of identification, and not merely in terms of differences over policies. This was not only true in the relations between modern and traditional forces, but also—and perhaps even more so—between the different modern groups, such as nationalistic, socialistic, communistic groups. Although on certain occasions all groups entered into uneasy alliances and coalitions; this did not change greatly their basic attitudes and their mutual ideological antagonisms.

A further characteristic of political structure in colonial countries is the relative weakness of various economic and professional organizations, *e.g.,* trade unions, cooperatives, chambers of commerce, and the talk of their mutual integration as well as their uneasy relationship with the political movements. These weaknesses usually are of two kinds. Either the economic organizations, whatever their strength, held themselves apart from one another and from the political movements, did not participate in them, and thus did not exert their influence on them; or they became entirely subordinate to the political leaders (especially in the case of the Belfast movements) who did not take account of the specific problems and needs of economic organizations.

Another characteristic of colonial politics was the way in which various interest groups, *e.g.*, local merchants, exerted influence on the administration or on political organizations in lower levels of government. The most common techniques of exerting influence included various types of lobbying, *i.e.*, personal pressure, and sometimes attempts at bribery. Whatever the exact nature and diversity of these activities, they were not closely related to the major political movements and did not envisage to any great extent the mobilization of public opinion. Whenever one of these issues became important for political groups and public opinion, it became transformed into an overall problem of political independence and subsumed under the general solidarity symbols.

The combination of all these factors perhaps explains the importance of the urban "mob" in the politics of many colonial countries—and the parallel weakness of organized public opinion.

The different characteristics of the political process which we enumerated varied greatly from one country to another in their concrete details and in their relative importance and intensity. . . . But at this stage, a general analysis with illustrations will have to suffice. The illustrations point out some inherent weaknesses, or perhaps more accurately, the lack of balance in political developments and organizations in colonial countries. All these problems did not seem acute as long as the main issue was the attainment of political independence and as long as the movements were acting within the framework of colonial rule which was responsible for the daily running of the country. It was only when independence was attained, or when a definite transfer of power was planned and realized, that all these problems became of crucial importance for the stability of the new political system. In those countries which still retain their colonial status, the former characteristics are still predominant in different degrees. Only in those countries which have attained independence, or are in the process of attaining it, or in those areas in which a traditional ruling group has been supplanted by some more modern nationalistic elite (as in China, or some of the Middle Eastern countries) are all these problems coming to the surface.

The Transformation of Political Movements after Attainment of Independence

The full sociological significance of the attainment of independence becomes apparent and can be more exhaustively analyzed within the framework described above. Let us first analyze some basic structural changes which were brought about by the attainment of independence.

1. The attainment of political independence and the establishment of a new state always entails the establishment of new spheres of power, of new power positions which exercise a strong influence on the economic structure of the society and greatly widen the various instrumental rewards and gratifications which can be allocated through political and administrative channels.

2. The attainment of political independence necessarily also gives rise to the promotion of new collective symbols of identification, mostly borne by the new political elites which also claim special acceptance by the population because of the successful attainment of this aim. It may be said that because of the extension of the field of instrumental rewards and of new spheres of power, we find here also an intensification of claims by these elites to solidarity acceptance and prestige.

Let us briefly enlarge on these two points.

The enlargement of the spheres of power, and the concomitant increase in rewards through new political and administrative agencies, is self-evident. It is significant that most "new" states have attained their independence in an historical period which has witnessed a growing concentration of economic power and direction by government. Moreover, most of the new states were relative latecomers to the international economy and found that many of the best positions had already been monopolized by the older, long-established states. They were also relatively poor in original capital and entrepreneurial skill. For all these reasons the importance of the state and consequently its growing power in the economic sphere is evident in all former colonial societies.

The growing power of the government manifests itself in the expansion of its administrative services and in the continuous growth of the bureaucratic apparatus. This expansion is not purely quantitative. It gives rise to a relatively new social group, the political elite and bureaucracy, which, whatever the extent of its internal cohesion and homogeneity, tends to claim special positions of power and prestige and attempts to supervise many activities of other professional, economic, and cultural groups in the society.

These claims to social *importance* are usually raised both by the active political top circles and the top and middle strata of the bureaucracy. They derive their strength not only from their holding of important power positions, but also—especially among the political elite—from their close attachment to the collective solidarity values of the community, from the would-be personification of the attainment of political independence, and from the glory of the "revolutionary" days when they formed the nucleus of revolutionary political and social movements. Moreover, the elites quite often justify their claim to power and instrumental rewards in terms of their solidarity activities and values. After the attainment of independence—unlike the preindependence days, when their claim to prestige and influence were solely based on collective-solidarity grounds—the claims of the elite became strongly interwoven with claims based on acquisition of power and oriented to rewards in the instrumental field. The most outstanding feature of this process is the potential claim of the political and bureaucratic elite to the monopolization of the highest positions of prestige and power in the instrumental, the solidarity, and the cultural fields alike.

Generally speaking, then, the attainment of political independence has meant the extension of modern political and social institutions from the purely solidarity to the technical, adaptive, and instrumental fields, as well as the first stages in the routinization of the charisma of the older political movements. The new political system had to incorporate within its framework the existing administrative organs and/or create new ones and had to orient itself toward various economic and instrumental problems. In other words, the sphere in which modern, universalistic principles of administration and politics prevailed became greatly extended and coordinated in one common framework with that of solidarity symbols and institutions. In a way, this constituted a total reversal of the colonial situation. But this reversal did not necessarily mean that all the problems of uneven development and change have been successfully solved. Rather, these problems became transformed, in keeping with the new framework, and constitute the main new problems of formerly dependent countries.

New Patterns of Political Participation and Motivation

With the attainment of independence the new elites faced several tasks in the area of political organization. They could not confine political participation to its former level, but had to extend its scope to the politically more passive or inarticulate groups from which new types of allegiance, political involvement, and loyalties were being demanded. The new regimes could not maintain themselves entirely on passive allegiance that had been predominant in the colonial times, since they themselves had undermined this kind of allegiance. Through their emphasis on governmental activities in many spheres of the society, they penetrated more and more into various social layers. Because of this, the new governments could not rely on traditional motivations and attitudes in the instrumental and administrative fields to the same extent the old colonial regimes had. They had, in one way or another, to foster the development of new motivations and social and political participation. Schemes for community development, for new industrial and agrarian organizations, as well as agrarian reforms, whenever they were undertaken—all implied the necessity for new orientations and incentives and the development of many new motivational patterns.

The new elites had to develop the allegiance of the masses to the new symbols of solidarity and the all-embracing political system as a whole. At the same time, they had also to develop in the masses some identification with and loyalty to the new administrative and bureaucratic institutions, and—even more important—to the new rules of the political game. They had simultaneously to develop a basic loyalty to the new system and to foster new types of political participation and competition within that system. They had to assume that these new patterns of competition would not disrupt the system as a whole. In other words, they had to work for the simultaneous establishment of two new kinds of legitimization: a new solidarity one and a new legal-rational one. Between the two there could easily develop many tensions and incompatibilities.

These tensions were due to a growing contradiction between the aspirations of various social, professional and economic groups and the policies and aspirations of the ruling elites. The attainment of independence extended the sphere and increased the value of economic, administrative, and professional activities. Moreover, most of these activities were no longer performed within the framework of an alien political system, and a place had to be found for them within the new national framework.

The increase of the scope of these activities has naturally increased the potential power and the social and political aspirations of the various groups performing them. These groups constituted also the potential participants in the political game within the new states. But the aspirations of these groups have come up against the inherent tendency of the political elite and bureaucracy with respect to the monopolization of power and prestige. This tendency, which is closely related to the social transformations attendant on the attainment of independence, has manifested itself in: (1) attempts to create a strong unified hierarchy of status in terms of political power; (2) efforts to subject most processes of social mobility to control by the different political elites; and (3) efforts to subject a large number of economic, professional, and cultural activities to political control.

As a result, there tends to develop a continuous tension and ambivalence in the relations between the political elite, other elite groups, and potential new centers of power. The bureaucracy is inclined to belittle the importance and efficiency of purely economic activities and the claims of economic groups toward social autonomy. It tends to superimpose extra-economic criteria on economic activities and on their bearers, not only by stipulating broad, general "social goals," but also by the daily regulation and direction of activity. In other words, the bureaucracy claims great, if not absolute, power over these activities and claims greater prestige than their bearers. In this way many aspects of economic activity and entrepreneurship are stifled and discouraged. Moreover, the political elite attempts, in some cases, to undermine the autonomous development of the middle and working classes and link their positions entirely to political directives. A similar and sometimes even more intensive pattern can be found in the relations of the political elite and bureaucracy toward professions and cultural elites. If direct regimentation is not often attempted (this feature is usually limited to post-revolutionary totalitarian societies), a general tendency toward the direct linking of these activities with collective goals as represented by the elite and bureaucracy can still be found. Thus the emphasis put on cultural professions (teaching, creation of new traditional symbols) is greater than that placed on medicine, engineering and other technical professions which seem to be more "neutral" in relation to collective goals.

Closely related are the attempts of the political elite and bureaucracy to direct and control all social developments of the country, especially those relating to the standard of living and the availability of new occupations and mobility within them. In this way they tend to maintain their hold on potential centers of power and to control their evolution. But these attempts are often self-contradictory because the close control exercised by the bureaucracy undermines efforts for economic development. More aspirants are created for new posts than there are posts available, and thus the bureaucracy itself is put in an insecure position.

The ambivalent position of the political elite, and especially of the bureaucracy, is clearly shown by the following facts (which are found in varying degrees in most of the countries studied): (1) the bureaucracy itself experiences difficulties in recruiting adequately trained personnel; and (2) because of financial stringency officials are underpaid, with the result that corruption develops. Hence the efficient functioning of the bureaucracy becomes problematic. On the one hand, the bureaucracy increases its attempts to attain social prestige and political power; on the other hand, it alienates large parts of the population and undermines some of the social and economic aims of its activities.

All these tendencies impede the development of social and institutional differentiations which would facilitate the emergence of diversified centers of power and prestige in the society. Attempts to establish a monolithic hierarchy of power and prestige have often impeded the development of relatively autonomous groups and organizations in society and weakened the development of independent public opinion. The wellknown weakness of different nonspecific voluntary associations in many poor countries is a case in point.

All this may be summed up by saying that the main problem in the development of the political institutions in the new countries is the necessity of developing social support for the maintenance of different and even contradictory aspects of modern, institutional frameworks.

The difficulty of a simultaneous development of different types of political institutions, and of the social attitudes necessary for their maintenance and functioning, is obviously rooted in the specific heritage of uneven change analyzed earlier in this paper. The unevenness of change resulted in an uneven development of different types of motivation and orientation to different aspects of a modern institutional setting. In some institutional spheres the development has, as we have seen, overemphasized new types of motivations, especially in the solidarity field. This overemphasis was reinforced by a relatively unorganized and unstable development of motivations and by a high extent of social disorganization in other spheres. Stabilization of these fields of action may have weakened the intensive solidarity orientation. With the attainment of independence and a growing emphasis on wider administrative activities and power relations, all new developments tended to be subordinated to the activities of the political elite, which attempted also to assure its control over these new developments. Autonomous developments of outlying centers of power and the stabilization of new political groups or interests were viewed by the elite as interfering with the stabilization of the new basic institutional framework and with universal allegiance to the new common symbols. Faced with this problem, the residing elites of the new countries tended to undertake one of two possible courses of action. In some cases the elites attempted to "solve" this problem by slowing down the tempo of modern development and by maintaining, wherever possible, traditional authorities and loyalties. Perhaps the most outstanding examples of this may be found in some Middle Eastern countries, in Pakistan, and formerly in the Philippines. In other cases, the new ruling elites attempted to speed up the destruction of traditional forces and loyalties and to replace them as rapidly as possible with a new nationalism. At the same time they attempt to control this new ideology and to place it in the service of their own aims and power-positions. In these countries the ruling elites also tended to impede the development of autonomous and independent centers of social and political power. Examples of this are Indonesia, Ghana, and India. But in neither of the two cases can the ruling elites avoid the dilemma, and neither solution seems to contribute significantly to the maintenance of governmental stability.[1]

The Structure of Political Institutions

In the formal structure of government some parallel tendencies can also be discerned, in varying degrees, in different new countries. The first is the obvious preponderance of the executive over all other branches of government. This development clearly flows from the need of the new governments to take over and to operate the governmental machinery smoothly. It is connected with the strong emphasis on governmental economic activity

---

[1] The analysis presented here on the different levels of motivation has some affinities with Boeke's analysis of dual societies. But it seems to me that Boeke does not realize sufficiently that the "duality" of motivation and of economic attitudes is not that between traditional and modern setting, but is a part of the whole process of change.

and the necessity to promote overall identification with and loyalty to the new state. The legislature is usually passive and subservient to the executive or so unruly as to minimize the effects of its own influence and power. This does not mean that the different legislative bodies in all new countries are totally ineffective, although in some (especially the Middle East) they may be nonexistent. It does indicate, rather, that their effective power of control over the executive and their function as mediators between the executive and the population at large is rather weak. This is closely connected with the often observed fact that in most new countries there has not existed, until recently, an effective opposition. The opposition party is too weak to constitute a real alternative (as in India), or there exists a multiplicity of parties between whom shifting coalitions are tried out (as in Indonesia), or any opposition that may arise is suppressed because it is seen as totally disloyal (as formerly in Pakistan). Closely connected with this also is the tendency for dictatorial regimes or movements with dictatorial tendencies to develop.

The judicial branch is characterized by a similar weakness. In some cases, there is no tradition of judicial independence. In others, the inability to promulgate a constitution and to organize the basic juridical norms of the state have been important factors in the absence of full legitimization of the judicial branch of government. India and Burma seem to be outstanding here, and the comparison with Pakistan and Indonesia is very instructive.[2]

But the most important manifestation of the predominance of the executive can perhaps be seen, paradoxically enough, in the uneasy relations between the executive and the administrative bureaucracies. Whatever the initial separation between the branches of government, they seem to come closer to one another and to share more values. Yet there exist many difficulties in establishing a proper division of labor between them. The two extremes of an administration engaging in political contests (or being used by the parties in power to this end), and an executive and legislative interfering in the working of the administration, are situations to be found frequently, and quite often together.

Perhaps the most extreme example of this may be found in those countries where parts of the administration, especially the military, engage in independent political action. While this is a pattern common in the Middle East, some of its embryonic manifestations may also be seen in Indonesia and Pakistan. These problems indicate the relative weakness of the concept of legal-rational legitimation and of the adherence to the universalistic

---

[2] See J. H. Boeke, *Economics and Economic Policy of Dual Societies* (New York: The Institute of Pacific Relations, 1953); and "Three Forms of Disintegration in Dual Societies," *Indonesie*, VIII (1953-1954), 278-295. *See also* B. Higgins, "The 'Dualistic Theory' of Underdeveloped Areas," *Economic Development and Cultural Change*, IV (1956), No. 2, 94-116.

norms in these societies. Here, two points are of special importance. The first is the uneasy relationship between the bureaucracy and the executive, which may easily impede the smooth functioning of administrative procedures and the maintenance of a wide sphere of universal rules beyond the province of current political disputes and differing interests. In other words, the capacity of the bureaucracy to mediate according to universalistic criteria between different interests and groups may be sometimes strongly curtailed.

Secondly, the weakness of universalistic rules and of legal-rational legitimization affects most acutely adherence to parliamentary procedures and "rules of the game," as well as the possibility of maintaining discussion and organizing an independent public opinion. Here the two traits of "total" opposition and divisiveness, as well as of various types of direct pressures for different allocations, have been transplanted into the new political framework and have been continued in the new setting—sometimes with more intensity. They can be discerned most clearly in political parties and movements in the new countries.

•

These and other aspects of the formal organization of governmental institutions clearly indicate the relative weakness of representative institutions and of the democratic process. In some countries, as in many Middle Eastern ones, such institutions are almost entirely absent or ineffective. In others they are stronger, but the problem of their successful development is still unsolved. But it is not so much the lack of procedural experience and other formal qualifications that is so important, but rather that it is difficult for these institutions to perform one of their basic functions in a democracy: that of mediating and integrating different interests in terms of common issues and in accordance with general rules of the political game. . . .

•

The problems described in this paper seem to be, to some extent, common to most underdeveloped countries. This is largely due to the basic impact of Western colonialism. But obviously there exist also many differences between these countries, conditioned by different rates and types of the impact, by different social and cultural traditions of different underdeveloped countries, and by many other factors. These differences are beyond the scope of this paper, and it is hoped that they will be dealt with in a subsequent publication.

CHAPTER 35

McKIM MARRIOTT

Social Change in an
Indian Village

The focal village of Kishan Garhi was selected to represent the social structure of a Hindu agricultural community in full complexity. Kishan Garhi is both large and complex. It has about 160 houses and 850 residents, to be compared with the U.P. average of 527 persons per village. Among its twenty-four castes, the largest are, in order: Brahman Chamars, Jats, Kumhars, and Muslim Faqirs—all large and common castes of the district and province. Essential servant, commercial and artisan castes are well represented; they serve the specialized needs of many nearby villages, in addition to Kishan Garhi's. From his office here, a government accountant (*patwari*) does the land-recording work of six other villages. Landlord rights (*zemindari*) are held mainly by Jats who reside both in the village and outside, although a total of four lineages in three castes hold shares. Six households in the village derive some income from *zemindari,* some in Kishan Garhi, some elsewhere.

•

Kishan Garhi in the Past: A Reconstruction of Its Society
30 Years Ago

The year 1920, approximately 30 years ago, is chosen as a convenient base mark for reconstructing social structure and other social behavior in Kishan Garhi. Thirty years is convenient because it falls within easy memory of elder persons, and within the time range of many official documents

This paper consists of revised excerpts from a report to the Social Science Research Council on field work carried out under its sponsorship in 1951-1952 in Uttar Pradesh, India. From *Economic Development and Cultural Change,* I (1952), No. 2, pp. 145-155. Copyright 1952 by the University of Chicago Press, and reprinted by permission of the author and the publisher.

and descriptions of this and other villages not far away. Thirty years also encompasses a number of known and appreciable alterations of Kishan Garhi's social structure.

Solidary groupings in Kishan Garhi 30 years ago may be listed under the four large headings of (1) kinship, (2) rank, (3) economic, and (4) associational structures. Certain other social behavior will be summarized in connection with each classification of solidary groupings.

(1) *Kinship groupings* included about 100 families containing on the average a little more than five persons each. These 100 families, or 525 persons, were divided among about 37 local lineage groups (*kunba, khandan*) of 30 clans (*gotra*).

All of the reticulate units of male descent, being exogamous with respect to the village, had necessary ties with clans and lineages in other villages. Marriage ties ran on the average to a distance of about twelve miles. Since all descent groups were further divided into 24 endogamous castes, their marital ties, though coinciding occasionally in the same distant villages, were wholly divided in actual relationship into 24 distinct marriage groups. Kishan Garhi's own resident caste groups varied in size from one family to about 30 families, the average caste comprising about four families. Each resident cluster of families of a single caste belonged, however, to a vast regional assembly of families linked by name, marriage, and traditions.

Families closely related within one lineage grouping cultivated jointly any lands which their members held as tenants. Such were small units averaging only two families in size. Families of different groupings in the same lines carried on frequent but less intense cooperation, lending and selling to one another. Loyalty, some sharing of resources, and common action were expected in case of need by any lineage member. The clan had active meaning outside Kishan Garhi only for the Jat *zemindars,* as an aristocratic dynasty.

Castes, and also some of the largest clans, had their internal councils, informal in membership, to decide internal quarrels. Their decisions were not always effective. For the same purpose, several of the lower caste groups sent representatives to regional caste councils which might be either formal or informal in constitution. Outside the village the strongest ties of most families were with caste-fellows, their relatives by marriage. Between such relatives there were frequent and lengthy visits as well as large gifts or purchases. Castes and lineages were repositories of distinctive cultural traits, the traits being sometimes connected with their traditional occupations or ritual duties.

(2) *Rank groupings* 30 years ago corresponded with the largest kinship units, which were the 24 castes. Castes were placed with nearly perfect agreement (by informants) in five or six major groups of castes which may be called "blocs," and these blocs were ranked with perfect consensus in relation to one another. Within one bloc, there was less perfect agreement on the ranking of particular castes, however. Power and wealth were strongly

correlated with the ranking of castes and blocs, since most land rights lay with the four or five highest castes. Whatever differences there may have been in individual judgments, these could have little effect on public behavior. Gestures of precedence and deference, rules for the handling of food and water, smoking and sitting arrangements, terms of address—all of these followed the ranked arrangement of blocs very closely.

(3) *Economic groupings* could be classified in three types: (a) work groups, (b) dependencies, and (c) classes. (a) Work groups were small, since cultivation of Kishan Garhi's crops required the labor of only two men and a boy for even the most elaborate operation. One or two families, related as lineage brothers or as master and servant, could supply all the labor needed for an average holding. (b) Economic dependencies constituted much larger groupings, each cutting across kinship and rank groupings and focusing upon a few persons of wealth and power. Such groups of dependents were not on the whole cooperative groups, but rather consisted of clusters of concentric pair-relations. They had to do with land, credit, and service. For access to an adequate holding of land, the cultivator was dependent on an unwritten short-term lease granted by one of three families of a single lineage of *zemindars*. *Zemindars* granted lands to only about 40 tenants, keeping more than one-fifth of the total lands for their own cultivation through laborers. The 30 families of laborers having one bullock or none worked year after year for the same *zemindar,* to whom they were often deeply indebted. For credit in money or grain, borrowers—including most persons in the village—turned to *zemindars,* to wealthier tenants, or to professional lenders both in the village and outside. Since interest rates were high, such relationships once begun were not easily broken off; the mortgaging of one crop could barely finance the cultivation of the next. Specialized servants and artisans, forming another third of Kishan Garhi's population, were likewise bound closely to their employers, frequently indebted to the more powerful of these. . . . *Zemindars* and a few others had permanent groups of dependent followers in all ranks and kin groups. *Zemindars,* as collectors of land taxes for the government, were always given the office of police agent (*mukhya*). This combination of powers delegated by government and by their followers allowed the *zemindars* to arbitrate and dispute and to punish summarily any petty crime, real or suspected. Village disputes could generally reach formal trial only when the case was taken to the court by or with the help of one of the *zemindars* or bigger tenants. (c) Economic class groupings were most effective among the *zemindars,* to a much lesser extent among the wealthier tenants, and not at all among the rest of the society.

(4) *Associational or convivial groupings* were small and impermanent. On three or four days of the year the whole village gathered, but most of these were occasions for an audience to watch rather than for mutual interaction. The one exception was *Holi,* when there was a general ceremonial breaking of group barriers. On *Holi* and for a month before, the only formal con-

vivial group, a singing society, joined members of several castes in an activity of common interest. Other associations were informal and irregular. Children's play and probably most women's visiting followed neighborhood patterns. Certain sports provided occasions for participation by boys of all castes for a few days of the year. Marriages brought larger random assortments of friends and neighbors together for a few daily rituals. But rules of rank as between the six blocs and 24 castes prohibited many kinds of public reciprocity among friends. Arrangements by which all persons could dine from one house—at separate times and places—were found only at the feasts of the highest-ranking persons, occasions of great expense and rarity.

Alterations in Social Structure Effected in 30 Years

Past alterations—(1) *Economic developments* in Kishan Garhi and outside over the past 30 years have been responsible for numerous changes in solidary groupings.

A near doubling of population stimulated more extensive and intensive use of Kishan Garhi's land for agriculture. Pasture and forest wastes, constituting one-tenth of the village lands, once had been held for common use by the *zemindar*. Now they have been parceled out as fields. This has lessened the value of the landlord's bounty and enhanced the value of competition for private access to scarce lands.

Increased pressure on local lands has brought about an increase in the number of groups in the village whose members have dispersed to the outside urban world. One or two persons of almost every line have joined with outsiders to earn a living instead of staying to work with kinsmen and neighbors.

The world depression brought a period of lowered crop prices and an increase of debt. Two families of *zemindars* were themselves bankrupt. Nearly half of Kishan Garhi's *zemindari* rights changed hands, one part going to a local money lender, another to an outside owner.

Despite a generally regressive movement of Kishan Garhi's internal economy, with much more competition for nearly static resources, there began ten years ago an enormous increase in the prices paid on outside markets for the crops grown by people in Kishan Garhi. The huge increase of money in the hands of tenants has unbound many of the dependencies on lenders that existed in the past. Laborers, their wages rising, were released from the debts that kept them in the exclusive charge of one master. The rise in crop prices has also left more food with more cultivators; more can now give the expensive feasts and ceremonies which once symbolized the status of the few wealthiest persons in the village. Feasts demonstrate the power of the feeder to his neighbors and relatives and strengthen cooperative friendly relations across rank lines.

(2) *Tenancy laws,* notably the Agra Tenancy Act of 1926 and the U.P. Tenancy Act of 1939, have steadily broadened the distribution of wealth and power in Kishan Garhi.

Tenants and subtenants (generally sharecroppers) long in occupancy of the same lands, were given permanent, even hereditary rights, where previously they could have been ejected at the pleasure of the *zemindar* or superior tenant. The writing of deeds and receipts has encouraged formal subdivision and registration of lands previously held loosely in common by lineal groups of families. Not only has the number and formality of work groups increased but their size has, if anything, decreased in response to the fall in holding size from eleven to nine acres on the average. Moreover, nine new lineages have settled in Kishan Garhi to take up permanent land rights gained through relatives by marriage. This increases the differentiation of kin groups by nearly 25 per cent.

Zemindars' private lands have been slowly diminished and all rents limited by law. Closely controlled groups of landlords' followers have ceased to exist as an inclusive type of solidary grouping in Kishan Garhi. There now remains but a single tenant-at-will of one *zemindar.* Because of the threat of their securing permanent tenancy, subtenants and tenants-at-will are shifted with greatly increased frequency.

(3) *Legislation and administrative measures* for social welfare have had light effects. Usury has been limited and the professional lender has nearly disappeared. More provision of cheap education and special political patronage for the lowest castes has placed in favorable relations with higher outside organizations people who otherwise stand at the bottom of village society.

(4) *Political changes* in the larger society, especially the paraphernalia of limited democracy—elections, appointment of an advisory *panchayat* and of a local rationing board—these have encouraged persons of local power to align themselves with the powers of other villages in the area and with the dominant party in fairly permanent informal organizations for mutual aid.

Current alterations. The time of my field research in Kishan Garhi spans the early stages of three new government measures which are effecting a slightly broader and different organization of wealth and power. All three are conceived by their authors as leading toward a more egalitarian and democratic social structure.

(1) *The U.P. Panchayat Raj Act,* designed to restore village political life to its "original" state of "Athenian democracy" was promulgated about three years ago. *Panchayats* were elected and had been operating for more than a year before the beginning of this field research.

The village assembly (*gram sabha*) and village council (*gaon panchayat*) set up under this law are larger and more localized interest groups than have ever existed before in Kishan Garhi. The assembly includes Kishan Garhi with two small villages—a constituency of 1300 persons. The council is a committee of fifteen to twenty persons, given responsibility for village welfare. The council has also been given several minor powers and duties formerly belonging to the police, to the police agent, to the earlier appointed *panchayat,* and to other higher authorities. The council has the power to give formal legal trial to minor disputes and to collect a tax. Persons elected to the village council in the first election include members of most of the large castes in Kishan Garhi, along with a strong majority of large tenants and higher caste persons.

The rural court (*adalti panchayat*), with 25 elected members, represents and has jurisdiction over twenty villages. It can give legal trial to disputes of larger consequence than can a village council, and can levy larger fines. Elections to the rural court were held before the plans for *zemindari* abolition act had become widely known. Almost every member of Kishan Garhi's rural court is a *zemindar,* and the weekly meetings of the court at a *zemindar's* house constitute a new formal convivial occasion, strengthening the supralocal class solidarity of the *zemindars.* It is to be noted, however, that the *zemindars* now must exercise their arbitrating powers in a group —a group that comprises opposing cliques based in neighboring villages. The exclusive local power of each in his own village is a thing of the past. . . .

(2) *The U.P. Zemindari Abolition Act,* a device for eliminating landlords as middlemen in the tax system and for reducing their social influence, is being put into effect slowly.

Zemindars are to be replaced by governmental tax collectors after July, 1952. The new role of government is still unclear. *Zemindars* will be paid dwindling compensation over many years out of money collected now from tenants by government. Tenants will begin to profit by lowered rent only after twenty years, since they are now required to purchase their plots from the government for a price equal to ten times their former legal rent; for the next few years they will be poorer.

Land-purchasing "drives" have been held, one drive shortly before my coming to Kishan Garhi and another since. In these drives, government officers and party allies urge, entice and threaten tenants into paying. Two-thirds of the tenants in Kishan Garhi have already paid about one-half of the amount demanded from them.

Tenants and *zemindars,* sharply differentiated in the past, will have nearly equal powers over their lands and nearly equal permanency. New subtenants will not be able to gain occupancy rights as they could in the past, for the new tenants' lands will be like the private lands of the old *zemindar.*

The formal registration of lands that accompanies payment of ten times rent is stimulating further advance subdivision of many lineage holdings in

Kishan Garhi. It seems probable that these formal land divisions will hasten divisions of joint families.

(3) *Election* of representatives to the national Parliament and to the state Assembly will be held in Kishan Garhi on January 28, 1952. For the first time, all adults will have the power to vote. Campaigners of five parties —Congress, Socialist, Peasant-Worker Party (KMP), Rule of God Organization (Ram Rajiya Parishad), and Independent—visit Kishan Garhi frequently seeking support. All candidates are Jats, two being of the clan of Kishan Garhi's own *zemindars*.

Thus far, as in the past, those seeking support have first applied to persons in the village who have known power, wealth and influence. But voting powers now lie with all adults, that is, with nearly three times as large a number as in preceding elections. Party leaders in the village are now trying to extend greatly their groups of followers. It remains to be seen whether alterations of social structure may develop from this activity.

Summary of Alterations. The alterations of solidary structures which have occurred over 30 years in Kishan Garhi may be subsumed under four headings: (a) broader distribution of power—lowering the power of landlords and lenders, loosening the ties binding large groups of dependents to them, emergence of autonomous tenants; (b) wider integration of local groups with outside groups—organizing political contacts at the top of village society, making a few high connections for lesser persons, placing some members of many groups in urban situations; (c) increase in the complexity of the strongest solidary groupings—subdividing of old lineages, adding on of new lineages, dissolving of large and permanent economic dependencies, all leading to more irregularity and fluidity in the pattern of those relationships which are most binding; (d) addition of new formal associations—village assembly and village council. The sum of these induced alterations is not small.

Kishan Garhi in the Present: Some Further Changes

Over and beyond these four major types of alteration which have been specifically induced in Kishan Garhi's social structure through 30 years there have been noted further changes in other social behavior connected with kinship, rank, and political groupings. The following paragraphs on recent changes are impressions of the trend of the evidence to date, plus a few facts. Analysis of full results is by no means complete.

Rank groupings, once well agreed upon, have now become a subject of much disagreement and conflict. Competition for higher rank is now great. At least eight of Kishan Garhi's caste groups are now actively making claims to higher caste standing. The status claims of all are stimulated by areal organizations of the respective castes with which local people have come in contact.

Individuals, especially of the tenant class, are devoting great energies to back-biting and to a general informal jockeying for positions of leadership and influence.

Lineages and castes which once had distinctive customs are tending to drop them in favor of a more generalized culture. Many are beginning to feel defensive about their unique customs. This is true especially of the ritual customs of the lower castes, and also true of some of the customs of the highest lines which have to do with their traditional or ritual occupations. Such distinctive kin-group cultures, when they pass away, are being replaced by a general highest-bloc complex on the one hand and by a very-low-bloc complex on the other hand. The loss by a caste of its shared unique rituals is the loss of a bond of caste unity.

At the same time that a generalized culture is spreading, individuals are no less bent on elaborating their personal rituals and on competing for ritual virtue.

Caste and clan councils, which formerly attempted to handle minor disputes within the larger kin group, have now nearly ceased to be distinguishable as solidary groupings. The old formal councils have, except in one of the two lowest castes, passed away entirely. The remaining informal councils meet rarely, if at all, and are even more rarely able to achieve composition. Yet disputes are by no means less. Indeed, there are major and disabling divisions within each of the larger castes. Such divisions are generally organized around opposing persons of wealth and their striving for dominance in the group. Villagers say that lesser persons cannot be disciplined because they can find refuge in the group's internal divisions. Outcasting cannot occur, and the old remedy of flight is unnecessary.

Legal conflict, often involving large numbers of persons in opposed factions, has enormously increased in Kishan Garhi. Quarrels of the vaguest and most trivial sort, which would formerly have been settled by group decision of the caste council or by arbitration of the *zemindar,* are now readily given legal form in the rural court. Once legally formalized, quarrels are protracted long beyond the heated feelings that gave rise to them. A case lasts on the average nearly seven weeks in the rural court. Since a new case begins once a month, there are always two or three in progress. An adult male spends an average of more than a day each month in litigation, and for each day he may travel from eight to 25 miles.

Cases are deviously framed. One vague issue easily shifts and diffuses into other issues as new persons join in the same legal battle. To engage in litigation and to practice dishonesty are felt to be synonymous.

Litigation is outstandingly the pastime of Kishan Garhi's tenants who have recently gained in wealth and power, although loud public quarrels are not unpopular among lesser persons. *Zemindars,* formerly themselves the all-powerful arbitrators, now maneuver and manipulate tenants' cases through the rural court. They play their game of influence and wits with litigant pawns, preferring to keep themselves aloof. For the tenants, newly secured property rights and ready cash are the materials of litigation. But in villagers' talk, all material contents of cases are polarized around the struggle to gain or keep respect in a world that is felt to be losing the quality of respect.

An individual rarely engages in conflict alone. The litigating groups, which were once generally the following of single *zemindars,* are now more often impermanent congeries of small cliques which may well include a *zemindar.* Each participant clique may have its distinct reasons for joining the conflict. The factions thus formed cannot well become stabilized as secondary associations, for they share only a temporary common activity, and that one charged with divisive rivalry. Besides this inherent reason, formation of any large regular clique would be strongly disapproved by the clan or caste, for the involvement of one member may require the involvement of others. When there is conflict inside a caste or clan, as is now common, however, formation of a non–kin-based faction becomes essential to both participants in the conflict. They must seek allies outside their kin group, despite the negative evaluation of their secondary grouping that will certainly be made by the village as a whole. It thus appears that factions are both despised and made necessary because of the same structural fact—that the community is differentiated into a highly complex pattern of large solidary kinship groups and small economic dependencies.

The new *village associations,* the assembly and council, are in these circumstances unable to operate effectively, whether to promote village welfare or to compose disputes. There is no dominant *zemindar* member in the council, although, since the council amalgamates three villages, it infringes upon the territory of two resident *zemindars.* Only cliques of the *zemindars* are in the council, not their overbearing power. Little agreement has yet developed as to leadership by and among the contesting tenants.

The complex pattern of primary solidarities restrains all of the kinds of secondary convivial and interest groupings that might promote community solidarity. Individual friendship, individual membership in any permanent association, individual delegation of allegiance to a leader outside of the kin group—all of these are discouraged. Of themselves, kin groups as wholes move into larger associations only slowly.

Summary. From contrasting Kishan Garhi society of 30 years ago with that of the present, it is apparent that: . . . (a) Dissensus and competition in ranking is increased by broader distribution of power, by a fluid and complex pattern of solidary relationships and by a widening of group relations outside the villages. (b) Loss of distinctive kin-group culture is hastened by competition for rank. (c) Legal conflict and the formation of factions increases with alteration of local power groups, with complexity of social structure, with failure of caste councils, and with integration of local political structures into a wider grouping of powers. (d) Caste councils pass away when they are disrupted by reorganization of power and by competition for rank within themselves. (e) The new village associations' effectiveness is hampered by the complexity of social structure, by the shift of power and by competition for higher rank.

PART V

Levels of
Change

CHAPTER 36

Introduction

Society may be viewed as a set of Chinese nesting boxes; smaller social units exist and function within larger ones, and these within still larger ones. While all these "boxes" ultimately have the same building stones, each has some characteristics of its own, or "emergent properties," as they are called. Some rely chiefly on formal, others mainly on informal communication; some may use force, others are forbidden to use it; and so on.

The following selections call attention to the comparative study of change on various social levels, a dimension of the study of change that has hardly been explored. They illustrate the importance of taking into account emergent properties.

Inkeles' study discusses changes in what is the basic unit of all social collectivities—the role. The problem, which is being examined by means of an empirical study, is whether, and to what degree, the role of parents as agents of socialization changes as society changes. Since all societies do change, at least to some extent, it follows that if parents continue to educate their children in the ways in which they themselves were educated, a gap is created between the children's personality and the demands of society, a gap whose scope is affected by the speed of societal change, as well as by the degree to which corrective socialization is carried out by socialization agents other than the parents—schools, for example. Inkeles' study clearly establishes that the parents' conception of their educational role and their ways of carrying it out do adjust to "the changing times." The degree to which this change is adequate has yet to be established.

The studies and work of Kurt Lewin and Elton Mayo have initiated a school often referred to as "group dynamics" or "human relations." Its influence is especially large in social psychology and education, as well as in the applied social sciences; it has been somewhat critically received by several leading sociologists.[1]

---

[1] The student interested in additional reading on this school might turn to Dorwin Cartwright and Alvin Zander, eds., *Group Dynamics: Research and Theory* (2nd ed.;

From the selection here presented, it might seem at first as if Lewin were dealing with modification in the behavior of individuals, more specifically with changes in their food habits. But it soon becomes clear that actually Lewin is interested in the dynamics of the social climate of small, face-to-face groups. As a result of several experimental studies, only one of which could be presented here, Lewin concluded that people are more reluctant to modify their behavior—and if they do, are less likely to persist in their new behavior—if they are approached as individuals, that they are more apt to change if they are approached as members of a group, so that their individual modification of behavior goes hand in hand with changes in the climate of the group and that these personal modifications are more likely to persist if they can be anchored in group support. As Lewin sees it, the individual, in need of his group's approval, tends to adjust his behavior to the group's standards. Hence it is easier for him to change when the group standards change as well.

The Lewin study and that of Inkeles, though they deal with different problems from different viewpoints, both serve to call attention to a major controversy within social science, of much importance to the study of social change: the relative flexibility, as against stability, of the personality. The orthodox Freudians are on the one extreme, often more extreme than the master himself. They view the basic personality as relatively stabilized in early childhood, hence determined largely by the parent–child relationship. As the person moves from group to group through his social life, he expresses his personality, but it hardly changes. At the other extreme are some students of Lewin, more extreme than the master himself, who view the personality as a kind of radar that constantly picks up clues from the immediate social environment and adjusts behavior to it. Hence the ability to change is almost unlimited.

Most social scientists take some kind of middle view, recognizing both the role of personality and that of social groups in determining behavior and viewing the two as factors affecting each other. But there are important differences among them, according to the relative weight they tend to attribute to the two factors. Since the evidence is far from clearcut, each student will have to decide for himself which interpretation is more satisfactory to him. The conclusions reached are, of course, of much consequence for one's view of such problems as the efficacy and limits of adult education, rehabilitation of criminals, and therapy of mental patients.

Moving to larger and more encompassing social units, Haire deals with

---

Chicago: Row, Peterson and Co., 1960); and to Warren B. Bennis, Kenneth D. Beme, Robert Chin, eds., *The Planning of Social Change* (New York: Holt, Rinehart & Winston, 1961). For a critical discussion of this school and arguments in its favor see various articles collected in Part II of Amitai Etzioni, ed., *Complex Organizations: A Sociological Reader* (New York: Holt, Rinehart & Winston, 1961).

collectivities which specialize in the service of specific goals, often referred to as complex organizations, while Park deals with the ethnic group, one kind of collectivity that has no such goals. Both Haire and Park work with neo-evolutionary models, but while Haire is ultimately concerned, as are most students of organizations, with the question of effectiveness, Park is interested in that of integration and elimination of social conflict. Haire deals with the growth of one unit, Park with the merger of two or more.

The special characteristics of complex organizations are that they tend to be large, bureaucratic, run from one center with an effort to enforce a disciplined service to a given set of goals. Many organizations, at least of the general type Haire discusses, include a large number of persons that only partially or indirectly accept the organizational goals. This creates problems of communication and morale, which become more pronounced the larger the organization grows. Here, Haire resorts to a biological model. When the organism evolves and becomes more complex and differentiated, it develops a specialized nervous system for the purpose of intrasystem communication and coordination. Similarly, when the organization grows, becomes more complex, and develops a specialization of functions, it too must face up to the increased problem of integration and must counter the growing communication blocks. This is why the organization, as it grows, must provide for an increased ratio of clerical personnel largely concerned with communication and for the disproportionate growth of staff in general, one of whose functions it is to provide information for coordination, control, and integration.

Park studies the relationships between ethnic or racial groups as they change under the impact of their mutual interaction. Reviewing a large variety of cultural contacts and group interaction, Park finds a specific pattern repeating itself, a set of stages often referred to as a "natural history." The stages, formulated slightly differently in various of Park's articles, are four: contact, competition, accommodation, and assimilation. Of much interest is Park's notion of the source of the forces that move intergroup relations along the course from contact to assimilation: they lie in these relations themselves. Each phase triggers certain processes that carry the relationship a step further. Contact between two groups leads to competition, which brings them to know each other more intimately, which results in accommodation, which creates the conditions for deeper interaction, which removes the barrier to assimilation. The central point is that, after the initial step, the process is one of increasingly harmonious relations, of declining differences. The harmonious relationship begins with the formation of economic, instrumental ties, proceeding to much deeper social, emotional, normative bonds.

Park had little doubt that all social groups follow these steps, in this order, and that eventually not just ethnic but racial groups too will assimilate (though in his earlier writings this position is somewhat more qualified).

The key word is "eventually," which accompanies many of Park's statements and makes it practically impossible to validate or invalidate his assertions. Whether all intergroup relations really go through the same set of stages, in the same order, is a question that must be answered empirically. While the evidence is far from clear, a case at least equally strong could be made for the proposition that they follow different patterns which lead to different "end-states."

Riesman moves the discussion of change to a higher level, that of the study of societies. The study of units of this size and complexity confronts the contemporary sociologist with serious dilemmas. On the one hand, there is the danger of statements that are extremely difficult to document, on the other, of shying away from the study of societies altogether. Riesman approaches the subject in the manner of the classical sociologist, studying society and its course, leaving much of the detailed documentation to his colleagues and students.

Before the full meaning of Riesman's insight can be understood, it is important to realize that his discussion of the changes in the character structure of modern man is actually concerned with the changes in the character of society; like many an anthropologist, he learns about societal change by studying changes in the characters of its typical members.

Riesman's conclusion was probably the most oft-cited statement of sociology in the 1950's. He found that the behavior based on self-direction, on internalized sets of values, often referred to as the Protestant Ethic, is being replaced by behavior largely directed from the outside by the social environment. One might say that Riesman found that character can be explained neither by an orthodox Freudian nor by a strict Lewinian view, but that a shift has occurred from behavior approximating the one type to behavior approximating the other.

The normative issues Riesman's findings raise are evident, nor does Riesman avoid them. He does not think that the moral value of the inner-directed person and his way of life is "higher" than that of the other-directed. Both types have their appealing and appalling sides; the inner-directed person is likely to be self-reliant but rigid and intolerant; the other-directed person is flexible but spineless. Riesman closes by depicting a third personality type that emerges as a synthesis of the character struggle of the two, that of the autonomous man. The autonomous man is not compulsive either in following his milieu or in ignoring it. He relates to people through affection and to objects through creativity; he is both sociable and creative. At present the autonomous type is in the minority, but it may become a "saving remnant," laying the groundwork for a new society, Riesman's utopia.

It is important to note that these concepts were developed by Riesman in the early fifties. International developments and their repercussions on the national society have resulted in several major changes that could not have been foreseen on the basis of an analysis of American society itself. Using Riesman's terms, there seems to be a heightened other-directedness in some areas and a considerable revival of inner-directedness in others. The pressure of the global struggle with Communism brought first the McCarthy period, in which intellectual and political inner-directedness was highly penalized. In the last years there has been some untightening, though much of the pressure of earlier periods has become institutionalized. In an effort to counter the impact of an international movement supporting radical social changes in other societies, and on the global level, America has largely curtailed the number, importance, and power of groups and individuals supporting such changes in its own society.

At the same time, the arms race and the competition in space (and in underdeveloped countries) have created new pressures for larger scientific, educational, technological, and economic efforts, which have caused the return of a certain amount of the striving, achievement-oriented spirit. The importance of education has been growing; constantly indirect federal aid to education has been increased; and demands put on students have generally been heightened. To some degree the emphasis in the school has returned from social adjustment to higher grades, from group integration to increased individual knowledge.

As mentioned above, these unanticipated changes in American society must be accounted for, at least in part, by relating them to changes on the next higher level of analysis—the international level. Basically, the global system differs from that of societies in that it has no implementation in a state. National societies are social groups that share not only values and social bonds, but also an integration supported by police forces, courts, and prisons. While the tendency of sociologists is to underplay the role of this feature of society, this is the major demarcation line that distinguishes it from other social collectives, *e.g.,* ethnic groups, private organizations, and international systems. The importance of such a framework of coercion lies in the fact that its potential or actual use is likely to limit the conflicts resulting from social change, thus both limiting the scope and pace of change and at the same time safeguarding, to a large extent, the continued peaceful adjustment of society to new needs and pressures. The international system is not only practically without an order-enforcing framework (despite the few instances of use of force by the United Nations to impose order, as in the Middle East and the Congo), but it also has far fewer common values, universal sentiments, and shared interests than the national system.

Parsons studies the sociological basis of changes in the global system, assessing the degree to which it is moving in the direction of a more firmly established collectivity. In general, Parsons sees more movement toward a global community than do most political scientists and many sociologists.[2] He identifies some universal processes shared by all modern nations, surely by the two superpowers: industrialization and modernization. He then points to some issues on which the two blocs differ, but on which they are in the process of converging or of approaching each other. As a result of industrialization, the two blocs share the high evaluation of products and services; they disagree, however, on the manner in which these ought to be controlled and allocated. But this disparity too is constantly decreasing. The United States has already moved toward a more egalitarian allocation of resources, while the USSR may well be moving closer to a political structure resembling Western democracy. Two trends seem to point in the latter direction: the decline in Russia of the political control of various social spheres including that of the arts, sciences, and religion and the increased division of labor and specialization, which might well be pushing the system in the direction of increased pluralism, which in turn could generate increased interest in objective sets of "rules of the game" in which the different interest-groups could peacefully work out their differences.

Thus Parsons sees the two blocs not as two utterly antagonistic, conflicting forces, but as two systems that, despite some differences, already share some values and structural features and are destined to move even closer to each other. The conditions under which such convergence would proceed, and, if it did proceed, the conditions under which the two blocs could form one community, remain to be explored.

---

[2] Parsons' view is supported by a parallel examination of "World Government and Supernationalism" in Chapter 8 of Amitai Etzioni, *The Hard Way to Peace: A New Strategy* (New York: Collier Books, 1962).

CHAPTER 37

ALEX INKELES

Social Change and Social Character: The Role of Parental Mediation

In his general essay on national character, Geoffrey Gorer[1] provides a clear and succinct formulation of one of the major premises underlying most of the related literature. Gorer indicates that we can deal with the simple but imposing fact that "societies continue, though their personnel changes" only because we can assume that "the present generation of adults will be replaced in due course by the present generation of children who, as adults, will have habits very similar to their parents." Implicit in this general pattern, of course, is the further assumption "that the childhood learning of the contemporary adults was at least very similar to the learning which contemporary children are undergoing."

Gorer recognizes, and indeed explicitly states, that this model is probably not applicable to "societies which are in the process of drastic change." As Margaret Mead[2] points out, however, so few individuals may now hope to grow up under conditions of sociocultural stability that we may regard this situation as almost unusual and its products as in a sense "deviants." Gorer's model, therefore, requires elaboration, extension, and adjustment to enable it to deal adequately with national character as it develops and emerges under conditions of social change. The question is essentially this: Insofar as rapid social change interrupts the simple recapitula-

---

From Alex Inkeles, "Social Change and Social Character: The Role of Parental Mediation," *The Journal of Social Issues,* XI (1955), No. 2, pp. 12-22. Reprinted by permission of the author and the American Psychological Association.

[1] Geoffrey Gorer, "The Concept of National Character," in J. L. Crammer, ed., *Science News* (Harmondsworth Middlesex: Penguin Books, 1950), pp. 105-122.

[2] Margaret Mead, "The Implications of Culture Change for Personality Development," *American Journal of Orthopsychiatry,* XVII (1947), 633-646.

tion of childtraining practices and produces new modal personality patterns, by what means are such changes mediated or effected?

The literature on national character contains several important and interesting efforts to answer this question. Mead,[3] for example, has explored the significance for personality development of growing up in a culture that is no longer homogeneous and posits the development under those circumstances of what she calls a "tentative" personality syndrome. David Riesman,[4] developing in full detail a point also made by Mead,[5] has discussed the significance for social character of growing up under the strong influence of peer-group pressures and standards. Erikson[6] has stated the implications for personality development that arise from the absence of adequate and valued role models with which to identify and from the associated lack of roles through which the individual can find socially sanctioned and culturally meaningful outlets for the discharge of his emotions.

Despite the diversity of these studies they seem to have one element in common in their approach to the role of the parent as "childrearer" under conditions of social change. Implicitly, if not explicitly, the parent is conceived as having available a relatively fixed repertory of childtraining procedures provided by his culture and learned by him in the period of his own childhood. Two main alternatives as to his utilization of those techniques are then generally considered. On the one hand, the parent is seen as acting as the passive agent of his culture, raising his children according to the procedures he had learned earlier in his own childhood, even though these techniques may have lost their appropriateness. It is assumed in that case that, as his children grow up, the gulf between parent and child will rapidly grow great, and relations will become strained as the child meets and learns the conflicting behavior patterns and underlying values of his "own" new culture. On the other hand, the parent may know enough not to try to apply the training procedures under which he was raised, and in that case he either surrenders to other cultural surrogates such as peer group, teachers, mass media, etc. or borrows, and of course generally ineptly applies, some prefabricated set of rules. In the lower classes the borrowing might be from the local baby clinic, and in the upper classes from books and lectures on childrearing. In short, the parents will manifest what Mead[7] terms "disturbed and inconsistent images of their children's future."

Without doubt these descriptions are faithful to the facts in many situations. Nevertheless, they seem to have made inadequate allowance for the positive adjustive capacity of human beings and for the process of con-

---

[3] *Loc. cit.*

[4] David Riesman, *The Lonely Crowd* (New Haven: Yale University Press, 1950).

[5] Margaret Mead, "Social Change and Cultural Surrogates," *Journal of Educational Psychology,* XIV (1940), 92-110.

[6] Erik Erikson, *Childhood and Society* (New York: Norton, 1950).

[7] "The Implications of Culture Change for Personality Development," *loc. cit.*

tinuous interaction that goes on between them and their sociocultural environment. Very often the global impact of Western contacts on a non-literate people may be almost totally disorienting, but parents need not be either unimaginative and passive agents of their culture, raising their children by rote, nor so disorganized and disoriented as is suggested by Mead's discussion. Although parents are adults, they may nevertheless still *learn,* and learn what they feel to be major "lessons," from their experiences under conditions of social change. This learning, furthermore, may influence the parents to seek purposefully to bring their children up in a way different from that in which they were raised and in a manner intended better to suit the children for life in the changed social situation. This has been clearly recognized by Aberle and Naegele,[8] who in a passage not easily duplicated elsewhere in the literature affirm that:

> All in all child rearing is future oriented to an important extent. The picture of the desired end product is importantly influenced by the parents' experiences in the adult world, as well as by their childhood experiences. When adult experience changes under the impact of major social change, there is reason to believe that there will ultimately, although not necessarily immediately, be shifts in the socialization pattern as well.

. . . One very probable reaction to the experience of social change is to adjust the training of children to better prepare them for life in the future as the parent now anticipates that life in the light of his own experience. There is reason to assume, therefore, that the influence of largescale social change occurring at any one time may be reflected in the character of the *next* generation, because of mediation by parents living under and experiencing the change.

To test these assumptions, one would ideally want a research design permitting the exploration of two distinct although intimately related questions. The first involves the hypothesis that parents who have experienced extreme social change seek to raise their children differently from the way in which they were brought up, purposefully adapting their childrearing practices to train children better suited to meet life in the changed world as the parent now sees it. To test this hypothesis we would need detailed information about the childrearing practices utilized by two consecutive generations of parents in the same culture, the first of which lived and raised its children in a period of relative stability, whereas the second lived and brought up its children under conditions of fairly extreme social change. A different requirement is posed by the question of how effective the parents in the second generation are in developing new traits or combinations of traits in

---

8 D. F. Aberle and K. D. Naegele, "Middle-Class Father's Occupational Role and Attitude toward Children," *American Journal of Orthopsychiatry,* XXII (1952), 366-378.

their children. The extension of the ideal research design in this direction would require that we secure data on the modal personality patterns prevalent in the third generation. We would anticipate that as a result of their different socialization experience, those in the third generation would manifest modal personality patterns different in important respects from those of their parents in the second generation.

Clearly such a design is extremely difficult to execute. Fortunately, however, we can approximate the ideal, although admittedly very imperfectly, through the utilization of some of the materials collected by the Harvard Project on the Soviet Social System. In that research program, detailed life history interviews were conducted with about 330 former Soviet citizens, yielding a well-balanced sample in regard to such factors as age, sex, and occupation. The interview extensively explored the life of the respondent in both his family of orientation and procreation. Particular attention was paid to the values in regard to character development and occupational goals that dominated in childrearing as practiced by the respondent's parents and by the respondent himself in the role of parent. Through an exploration of these data we may hope to see some of the effects of social change in the Soviet Union as the parents who "lived" the change adjusted their childrearing practices in response to their own adult experiences, and thus acted as intermediaries in transmitting the effects of their current change to a future generation.

We may begin by testing the first assumption, namely that a generation experiencing extreme social change in adulthood will adapt the methods whereby it raises its children and that as a result its children will be reared differently than it had been and yet more in keeping with the changed social realities. For our first generation, which we shall call the "Tsarist" generation, we need a group that raised its children during a period of relative social stability. The most recent period of that sort in Russia unfortunately falls as far back as the time immediately preceding the First World War, roughly from 1890 to 1915. Since we are interested in childrearing practices, and particularly of people who raised their children to adulthood (taken here as age fifteen) in those years, then eligible respondents would have been at least 33 by 1915 and at least 68 by the time of our interview in 1950. Indeed, most of those who could qualify as parents in our first generation were probably dead by 1950, and in any event only three of those living appear in our sample. We can learn about the childrearing practices utilized by that generation, therefore, only by relying on what their children report to have been true of the parents. The children of the Tsarist generation do, of course, appear in our sample. In this group we include all respondents over 45 in 1950, and we call it the "Revolutionary" generation because its members, born in 1905 or before, were young adults at the time of the Revolution and lived as mature individuals through the subsequent Civil War and the later periods of momentous social change represented by the forced collectivization and industrialization programs. It was this second generation that was raising its children to adulthood during the main period of Soviet development.

It will be recognized, therefore, that, although dealing with the child-rearing practices of two different generations of parents, we draw our information from but a single set of respondents, namely those in our sample over 45 years of age in 1950. In telling us how their parents brought them up they provide us with data about the childrearing practices of the Tsarist generation, whereas in describing the training of their own children, they provide our materials on the childrearing practices of the Revolutionary generation. Although limits of space do not permit presentation of the evidence, we have data that indicate that this procedure of ascertaining the childrearing values of an earlier generation by accepting the description given by those who had been the children of the group being studied, is methodologically less suspect than might appear to be the case. The description by the youngest generation in our sample of the manner in which it was reared agrees so closely with the report of how the training was done as related by the middle generation, which actually reared the children, as to yield correlations of .89 and .95 on the two available comparisons.

Relative to the childrearing materials we have a detailed summary code of the dominant values governing childrearing, both as to character and occupational goals, characteristic for each generation acting as parents. In no case, however, is the rating of the parent based on his observed behavior, but only on the values deduced by us to have been operative on the basis of the interview. Furthermore, as already noted, the respondents from the prerevolutionary Tsarist generation could not speak for themselves, and we had to rely on the retrospective report of their children.

In the following analysis, a larger number of code categories has been grouped into a set of six major dimensions that were prominent value orientations in the childrearing efforts of those in our sample. The value of "tradition" was coded mainly for emphasis on religious upbringing, but it included as well references to maintenance of strong family ties and traditions; "adjustment" reflects emphasis on "getting along," staying out of trouble, keeping an eye on your security and safety, etc.; "achievement" was coded when parents stressed attainment, industriousness, mobility, material rewards, and similar goals; "personalistic" was checked when the parent was concerned with such personal qualities as honesty, sincerity, justice, and mercy; "intellectuality," where the emphasis was on learning and knowledge as ends in themselves; and "political," when the focus was on attitudes, values, and beliefs dealing with government and particularly with *the* government of the land.

When we consider the profound differences, during their years of child-rearing, in the life experience of the Revolutionary generation as contrasted with that of its parents in the Tsarist generation, what differences may we

expect in their values with regard to childrearing? The revolutionary upheaval of 1917 and the subsequent programs of forced social change struck
a great blow at the traditional structure of Russian society and profoundly
altered it. Massive programs of expansion were undertaken in industrialization, in urbanization, in formal organization and administration. The pattern of rural life, in which the bulk of the population was involved, was
drastically revised through the forced collectivization of agriculture. Centralized political control and political terror were ruthlessly imposed. Opportunities for mobility increased greatly. Under these circumstances we
might well expect the traditional values to suffer the greatest loss of
emphasis, with a consequent shift to stress on either simple successful adjustment or the more secularized morality represented by the personalistic
values and the pursuit of knowledge as an end in itself. In addition, our
knowledge of the growing opportunities for advancement, associated with
the generally expanded development of the formal occupational structure,
leads us to anticipate that greatly increased weight would be given to
achievement. Finally the central role played by the state in Soviet affairs,
the existence of the political terror, and the additional fact that our respondents were disaffected from the political system, lead us to anticipate
heightened concern with political considerations in childrearing.

Table **37-1**

Childrearing Values of Parents in Russian Prerevolutionary and Post-
revolutionary Times

Areas	Distribution[a] of Emphasis in	
	Tsarist Period	Postrevolutionary Period [b]
Tradition	75%	44%
Achievement	60	52
"Personalistic"	32	44
Adjustment	16	21
Intellectuality	12	22
Politics	12	20
NUMBER OF RESPONDENTS	77	78

[a] These per cents total more than 100, since respondents were scored for as many themes as cited, but
percentaging is on the basis of total respondents.
[b] The percentages in this column have been adjusted to equalize for the effect created by the larger
number of responses given by our informants in describing their own activity as parents, as against the
manner in which they had been raised by the Tsarist generation.

In Table 37-1 we have indicated the distribution of emphasis among
the dimensions in our set of dominant value orientations. The relative
stability of the gross rank order is testimony to the fact that both genera-

tions of parents represented a common cultural tradition which they carried forward through time. Nevertheless, it is clear that there have been very substantial shifts in the relative weight of several value orientations, and they go largely in the expected direction. Perhaps the most striking finding is the sharp decrease in emphasis on the traditional values, accounted for overwhelmingly by the decreased emphasis on religious training and belief. Under the impact of industrialization and urbanization, perhaps abetted by the anti-religious and "proscientific" propaganda conducted by the regime, parents in the Revolutionary generation clearly shifted toward an emphasis on more secular values. This shift is reflected in the increased emphasis on learning (intellectuality) and positive personal qualities *as ends in themselves* rather than as *means* to the attainment of the good life lived, as it were, "in the sight of God." Thus secular morality replaced traditional and religiously based morality.

Perhaps most directly and explicitly related to the intervening experience of the parents under conditions of social change is the increased attention paid to political considerations in the education of one's children. The greater emphasis on political problems arises from the fact that the Soviet regime has progressively "politicized" more and more areas of human activity that in most Western societies fall outside the political realm. A person at all alert to his situation and surroundings could therefore hardly fail to realize that if he wished to prepare his child adequately for life under Soviet conditions he must train him to an awareness concerning the political realities of the system, even though such training had not been important in his own childhood. This interpretation is borne out by the statements made by our interviewers.

Finally, it is necessary to comment on the major instance in which the data fail to confirm expectation, namely in regard to emphasis on achievement values. This failure is, of course, only relative, since achievement was the most emphasized value in the rearing of children by those in the Revolutionary generation. Nevertheless, in absolute weight it declined in importance even though it had been expected to increase. It might be that since our respondents were refugees from the system, and since many of them looked upon too active pursuit of a career as suggesting involvement with the regime, they did not admit fully the importance they actually attributed to inculcating achievement strivings in their children. On the other hand, it may be that the expectation was unrealistic quite apart from specific Soviet conditions. There is some evidence that values such as security, adjustment, and personal attractiveness are becoming ever more important foci in childrearing in the United States[9] and that stress on achievement *as an end in itself,* although still prevalent, has become some-

---

[9] *The Lonely Crowd, loc. cit.*

what old-fashioned. This pattern may be associated with the combination of mass industry, education and communication, and the consumer culture of which the Soviet Union is but one example.

All told, however, the data certainly seem strongly to support the assumption that the experience of extreme social change that the Revolutionary generation underwent did have a marked effect on that generation's approach to the rearing of its children. As compared with the way their parents raised them, they can hardly be assumed to have merely "recapitulated" the earlier pattern of childrearing. On the contrary, having experienced marked social change, they adjusted their childrearing practices, the better to prepare their children for the life they expected those children to lead.

To test the effectiveness of the changed general childrearing orientations of the Revolutionary generation, we would need data on the personality patterns prevalent among their children in the third generation, which we unfortunately do not have. Nevertheless, we can make a very approximate approach to our second question concerning the effectiveness of the changed childrearing emphases if we shift our attention to the realm of occupational choices. In that area we have data not only on the values stressed by parents, but we also have information on the values which the individual held in regard to himself. In treating value orientations relative to the occupational world we are, of course, dealing not with personality patterns in a psychodynamic sense, but rather with something more closely akin to "social character" as it has been defined by Riesman[10] and Inkeles.[11]

The influence of their experience with social change on the childtraining practices adopted by the Revolutionary generation is perhaps even more strikingly evident in the area of occupational choices. In addition to asking about the specific occupations for which parents wished to prepare their children, we asked the reasons for the selection. The reasons cited provide us with a guide to the values that were dominant in the home atmosphere created by the parent for the child. Considering the nature of the social change experienced by the Revolutionary generation and described above, we might again well expect that as part of the general weakening of the traditional way of life there would have been a decline in the importance of family tradition, as against self-expression or free choice, as values emphasized in orienting the child toward the occupational world. In addition it is reasonable to assume that economic and material rewards would have come to be much more stressed among the goals set before the child, as would the necessity of finding work that permitted an appropriate ac-

10 *Loc. cit.*

11 Alex Inkeles, "Some Sociological Observations on Culture and Personality Studies," in C. M. Kluckhohn, H. A. Murray, and D. M. Schneider, eds., *Personality in Nature, Society, and Culture* (2nd ed.; New York: Alfred A. Knopf, 1953), pp. 577-592.

commodation to the highly politicized occupational structure in Soviet society.

Table **37-2**

Changing Values Concerning the Occupational Realm

Value Areas	Distribution of Emphasis among Values Stressed		
	in Childrearing by		in Hypothetical Choice by
	"Tsarist" Generation	*"Revolutionary" Generation*	*"Soviet" Generation*
Rewards	41%	25%	14%
Tradition	35	14	11
Self-expression	21	38	62
Politics	3	23	13
NUMBER OF RESPONSES (equal to 100%)	58	63	931

As a comparison of the first and second columns of Table 37-2 indicates, three of these four expectations are rather strongly supported by the responses of our interviewees. We see, to begin, a sharp decline in the importance of family tradition as a criterion in shaping the child's occupational orientation, along with a marked increase in the role played by self-expression or free job choice. In addition, we may note the much greater emphasis on guiding the child toward a job that is politically desirable, which for our respondents generally meant one safe from danger of political arrest and not too directly involved in the regime's political objectives. Finally, it should be observed that here again the data fail to support our expectation that the material and psychic rewards on the job—roughly equivalent to earlier discussed achievement value—would be more emphasized by the Revolutionary generation than by the Tsarist generation. Indeed, the relative weight of such rewards as values to be emphasized in orienting children toward the occupational world declined markedly from the one generation to the next.

Now, to return to our original research design, do we have any evidence that the different childrearing patterns utilized by the middle generation as a response to their experience of social change actually were effective? Or did the parents in that second generation, despite their apparent intention, act in fact as passive agents of the culture and, *nolens volens,* raise their children in their own image and much as the first generation would have done the job? For a proper answer to this question we should have access to the children of the Revolutionary generation and to data on their job choices coded by the same categories used to describe the childtraining values of their parents. Unfortunately, we can only approximate each requirement. Respondents on both our written questionnaire and oral interview remained anonymous, and we therefore have no way of identifying the actual children of the Revolutionary generation. But we can secure a reasonable equivalent of that third group, which we call the "Soviet" generation, by taking all respondents under 35 in 1950. Most of them were raised and reached adulthood in the same period in which the Revolutionary generation was acting in the parental role and could well have been their children. As for the values that governed their job choices, we are obliged to draw on our written questionnaire, which presented the respondents with a choice of precoded categories not strictly comparable with those used in assessing childtraining values. For example, the check list included the omnibus category "I feel suited to it," which we have equated here with "self-expression," but which obviously could have meant many more things to the respondents.

Quite apart from such methodological difficulties, it would be naïve to expect a near-perfect correlation between the values that the parents in the Revolutionary generation stressed while they reared the Soviet generation and the ones which that generation emphasized in its own job choices. Such training always produces only an approximation of the parents' desire. More important, those in the Soviet generation have had their values shaped by many influences other than those exerted by their parents. Nevertheless, our expectation is that on the whole the pattern of value orientations of the Soviet generation will be quite close to those that were stressed in childtraining by their parents in the Revolutionary generation as contrasted with those inculcated in an earlier era by the Tsarist generation. The relative degree of fit between the two sets of orientations may be taken as a rough measure of how successful the Revolutionary generation was in training the Soviet generation to orient in new directions.

The appropriate comparison may be obtained by examining the third column of Table 37-2—which contains the distribution of emphasis in the operative values guiding the job choices of the younger generation—in relation to the first and second columns. The overall comparison strongly suggests that those in the Revolutionary generation were highly successful in their purposive effort to shape the values their children would carry into adulthood. This is most evident in the marked emphasis that the Soviet generation places on self-expression rather than family tradition as a criterion for its job choices, much in keeping with the lesser emphasis that its parents had put on tradition in orienting their children's thoughts about the world of jobs and work. Even if we make allowance for the strong pull of the actual code category, "I feel suited for it," this interpretation would clearly not be materially affected.

It will be noticed, further, that in raising children those in the Tsarist generation gave extremely slight attention to political considerations, whereas those in the Revolutionary generation stressed it very heavily, indeed more heavily than tradition. In their own job choices, those in the Soviet generation again show the apparent influence of their parents' concern for this dimension, although in their own value scheme it does not loom quite so large as it did in their parents' efforts at socialization. Finally, we may note that material and psychic rewards such as income and prestige had roughly similar relative weight, as compared to politics and tradition, in the childrearing practices of the Revolutionary generation and in the actual job choices of the Soviet generation.

It seems reasonable to conclude again, therefore, that the Revolutionary generation did not merely act passively as the agent of the old culture, recapitulating in its own parental activities the socialization practices that had earlier been used by *its* parents. On the contrary, it may be said that the middle generation, responding to its experience of social change under the Soviet regime, in large measure turned away from the pattern of childrearing under which it had been raised earlier and in its approach to the new Soviet generation stressed goals and values of a different sort. It appears, furthermore, that this training of the youth in new value orientations was relatively successful. . . .

CHAPTER 38

KURT LEWIN

Group Dynamics and Social Change

Promoting Change: Lecture versus Group Decision

A preliminary experiment in changing food habits[1] was conducted with six Red Cross groups of volunteers organized for home nursing. Groups ranged in size from thirteen to seventeen members. The objective was to increase the use of beef hearts, sweetbreads, and kidneys. If one considers the psychological forces which kept housewives from using these intestinals, one is tempted to think of rather deepseated aversions requiring something like psychoanalytical treatment. Doubtless a change in this respect is a much more difficult task than, for instance, the introduction of a new vegetable such as escarole. There were, however, only 45 minutes available.

In three of the groups attractive lectures were given which linked the problem of nutrition with the war effort, emphasized the vitamin and mineral value of the three meats, giving detailed explanations with the aid of charts. Both the health and economic aspects were stressed. The preparation of these meats was discussed in detail, as well as techniques for avoiding those characteristics to which aversions were oriented (odor, texture, appearance, etc.). Mimeographed recipes were distributed. The lecturer was able to arouse the interest of the groups by giving hints of her own methods for preparing these "delicious dishes" and her success with her own family.

For the other three groups Mr. Alex Bavelas developed the following

From Kurt Lewin, "Group Decision and Social Change," in Eleanor E. Maccoby, Theodore M. Newcomb, and Eugene L. Hartley, eds., *Readings in Social Psychology* (New York: Holt, Rinehart, and Winston, Inc., 1958). Reprinted by permission of the publisher.

[1] The studies on nutrition discussed in this article were conducted at the Child Welfare Research Station of the State University of Iowa for the Food Habits Committee of the National Research Council (Executive Secretary, Margaret Mead).

procedure of group decision. Again the problem of nutrition was linked with that of the war effort and general health. After a few minutes, a discussion was started to see whether housewives could be induced to participate in a program of change without attempting any high-pressure salesmanship. The group discussion about "housewives like themselves" led to an elaboration of the obstacles which a change in general and particularly change toward sweetbreads, beef hearts, and kidneys would encounter, such as the dislike of the husband, the smell during cooking, etc. The nutrition expert offered the same remedies and recipes for preparation which were presented in the lectures to the other groups. But in these groups preparation techniques were offered after the groups had become sufficiently involved to be interested in knowing whether certain obstacles could be removed.

In the earlier part of the meeting a census was taken on how many women had served any of these foods in the past. At the end of the meeting, the women were asked by a showing of hands who was willing to try one of these meats within the next week.

A follow-up showed that only 3 per cent of the women who heard the lectures served one of the meats never served before, whereas after group decision 32 per cent served one of them.

If one is to understand the basis of this striking difference, several factors may have to be considered.

Degree of Involvement

Lecturing is a procedure in which the audience is chiefly passive. The discussion, if conducted correctly, is likely to lead to a much higher degree of involvement. The procedure of group decision in this experiment follows a step-by-step method designed (*a*) to secure high involvement and (*b*) not to impede freedom of decision. The problem of food changes was discussed in regard to "housewives like yourselves" rather than in regard to themselves. This minimized resistance to considering the problems and possibilities in an objective, unprejudiced manner, in much the same way as such resistance has been minimized in interviews which use projective techniques, or in a sociodrama which uses an assumed situation of role-playing rather than a real situation.

Motivation and Decision

The prevalent theory in psychology assumes action to be the direct result of motivation. I am inclined to think that we will have to modify this theory. We will have to study the particular conditions under which a motivating constellation leads or does not lead to a decision or to an equivalent process through which a state of "considerations" (indecisiveness) is changed into a state where the individual has "made up his mind" and is ready for action, although he may not act at that moment.

The act of decision is one of those transitions. A change from a situation of undecided conflict to decision does not mean merely that the forces toward one alternative become stronger than those toward the other alternative. If this were the case, the resultant force should frequently be extremely small. A decision rather means that the potency of one alternative has become zero or is so decidedly diminished that the other alternative and the corresponding forces dominate the situation. This alternative itself might be a compromise. After the decision people may feel sorry and change their decision. We cannot speak of a real decision, however, before one alternative has become dominant so far as action is concerned. If the opposing forces in a conflict merely change so that the forces in one direction become slightly greater than in the other direction, a state of blockage or extremely inhibited action results rather than that clear onesided action which follows a real decision.

Lecturing may lead to a high degree of interest. It may affect the motivation of the listener. But it seldom brings about a definite decision on the part of the listener to take a certain action at a specific time. A lecture is not often conducive to decision.

Evidence from everyday experience and from some preliminary experiments by Bavelas in a factory indicate that even group discussions, although usually leading to a higher degree of involvement, as a rule do not lead to a decision. It is very important to emphasize this point. Although group discussion is in many respects different from lectures, it shows no fundamental difference on this point.

Of course, there is a great difference in asking for a decision after a lecture or after a discussion. Since discussion involves active participation of the audience and a chance to express motivations corresponding to different alternatives, the audience might be more ready "to make up its mind," that is, to make a decision after a group discussion than after a lecture. A group discussion gives the leader a better indication of where the audience stands and what particular obstacles have to be overcome.

In the experiment on hand, we are dealing with a group decision after discussion. The decision itself takes but a minute or two. (It was done through raising of hands as an answer to the question: Who would like to serve kidney, sweetbreads, beef hearts next week?) The act of decision, however, should be viewed as a very important process of giving dominance to one of the alternatives, serving or not serving. It has an effect of freezing this motivational constellation for action. We will return to this point later.

Individual versus Group

The experiment does not try to bring about a change of food habits by an approach to the individual as such. Nor does it use the "mass approach" characteristic of radio and newspaper propaganda. Closer scrutiny shows that both the mass approach and the individual approach place the individual in a quasiprivate, psychologically isolated situation with himself and his own ideas. Although he may, physically, be part of a group listening to a lecture, for example, he finds himself, psychologically speaking, in an "individual situation."

The present experiment approaches the individual as a member of a face-to-face group. We know, for instance, from experiments in level of aspiration[2] that goal setting is strongly dependent on group standards. Experience in leadership training and in many areas of re-education, such as re-education regarding alcoholism or delinquency,[3] indicates that it is easier to change the ideology and social practice of a small group handled together than of single individuals. One of the reasons why "group-carried changes" are more readily brought about seems to be the unwillingness of the individual to depart too far from group standards; he is likely to change only if the group changes. We will return to this problem.

One may try to link the greater effectiveness of group decision procedures to the fact that the lecture reaches the individual in a more individualistic fashion than group discussion. If a change of sentiment of the group becomes apparent during the discussion, the individual will be more ready to come along.

It should be stressed that in our case the decision which follows the group discussion does not have the character of a decision in regard to a group goal; it is rather a decision about individual goals in a group setting.

Expectation

The difference between the results of the lectures and the group decision may be due to the fact that only after group decision did the discussion leader mention that an inquiry would be made later as to whether a new food was introduced into the family diet.

Leader Personality

The difference in effectiveness may be due to differences in leader personality. The nutritionist and the housewife who did the lecturing were persons of recognized ability, experience, and success. Still, Mr. Bavelas, who led the discussion and subsequent decision, is an experienced group worker and doubtless of unusual ability in this field.

To determine which of these or other factors are important, a number of

---

[2] K. Lewin, "Behavior and Development as a Function of the Total Situation," in L. Carmichael, ed., *Manual of Child Psychology* (New York: John Wiley, 1946), pp. 791-844.

[3] K. Lewin and P. Grabbe, eds., "Problems of Re-education," *Journal of Social Issues*, I (1945), No. 3.

systematic variations have to be carried out. To determine, for instance, the role of the decision as such, one can compare the effect of group discussion with and without decision. To study the role of group involvement and the possibility of sensing the changing group sentiment, one could introduce decisions after both, lecture and discussion, and compare their effects.

•

Quasistationary Social Equilibriums and the Problem of Permanent Change

The Objective of Change

The objective of social change might concern the nutritional standard of consumption, the economic standard of living, the type of group relation, the output of a factory, the productivity of an educational team. It is important that a social standard to be changed does not have the nature of a "thing," but of a "process." A certain standard of consumption, for instance, means that a certain action—such as making certain decisions, buying, preparing and canning certain food in a family—occurs with a certain frequency within a given period. Similarly, a certain type of group relations means that within a given period certain friendly and hostile actions and reactions of a certain degree of severity occur between the members of two groups. Changing group relations or changing consumption means changing the level at which these multitudinous events proceed. In other words, the "level" of consumption, of friendliness, or of productivity is to be characterized as the aspect of an ongoing social process.

Any planned social change will have to consider a multitude of factors characteristic for the particular case. The change may require a more-or-less unique combination of educational and organizational measures; it may depend upon quite different treatments or ideology, expectation, and organization. Still, certain general formal principles always have to be considered.

The Conditions of a Stable Quasistationary Equilibrium

The study of the conditions for change begins appropriately with an analysis of the conditions for "no change," that is, for the state of equilibrium.

From what has been just discussed, it is clear that by a state of "no social change" we do not refer to a stationary, but to a quasistationary equilibrium; that is, to a state comparable to that of a river which flows with a given velocity in a given direction during a certain time interval. A social change is comparable to a change in the velocity or direction of that river.

A number of statements can be made in regard to the conditions of quasistationary equilibrium.

(1) The strength of forces which tend to lower that standard of social life should be equal and opposite to the strength of forces which tend to

raise its level. The resultant of forces on the line of equilibrium should therefore be zero.

(2) Since we have to assume that the strength of social forces always shows variations, a quasistationary equilibrium presupposes that the forces against raising the standard increase with the amount of raising and that the forces against lowering increase (or remain constant) with the amount of lowering. . . .

(3) It is possible to change the strength of the opposing forces without changing the level of social conduct. In this case the tension (degree of conflict) increases.

Two Basic Methods of Changing Levels of Conduct

For any type of social management, it is of great practical importance that levels of quasistationary equilibriums can be changed in either of two ways: by adding forces in the desired direction, or by diminishing opposing forces. If a change from the level L_1 to L_2 is brought about by increasing the forces toward L_2, the secondary effects should be different from the case where the same change of level is brought about by diminishing the opposing forces.

In both cases the equilibrium might change to the same new level. The secondary effect should, however, be quite different. In the first case, the process on the new level would be accompanied by a state of relatively high tension; in the second case, by a state of relatively low tension. Since increase of tension above a certain degree is likely to be paralleled by higher aggressiveness, higher emotionality, and lower constructiveness, it is clear that as a rule the second method will be preferable to the high pressure method.

The group decision procedure which is used here attempts to avoid high pressure methods and is sensitive to resistance to change. In an experiment by Bavelas on changing production in factory work, for instance, no attempt was made to set the new production goal by majority vote, because a majority vote forces some group members to produce more than they consider appropriate. These individuals are likely to have some inner resistance. Instead, a procedure was followed by which a goal was chosen on which everyone could agree fully.

It is possible that the success of group decision and particularly the permanency of the effect is, in part, due to the attempt to bring about a favorable decision by removing counterforces within the individuals, rather than by applying outside pressure.

•

Social Habits and Group Standards

Viewing a social stationary process as the result of a quasistationary equilibrium, one may expect that any added force will change the level of the process. The idea of "social habit" seems to imply that, in spite of the application of a force, the level of the social process will not change because of some type of "inner resistance" to change. To overcome this inner resistance, an additional force seems to be required, a force sufficient to "break the habit," to "unfreeze" the custom.

Many social habits are anchored in the relation between the individuals and certain group standards. An individual may differ in his personal level of conduct from the level which represents group standards by a certain amount. If the individual should try to diverge "too much" from group standards, he would find himself in increasing difficulties. He would be ridiculed, treated severely, and finally ousted from the group. Most individuals, therefore, stay pretty close to the standard of the groups they belong to or wish to belong to. In other words, the group level itself acquires value. It becomes a positive valence corresponding to a central force field with the force keeping the individual in line with the standards of the group.

Individual Procedures and Group Procedures of Changing Social Conduct

If the resistance to change depends partly on the value which the group standard has for the individual, the resistance to change should diminish if one diminishes the strength of the value of the group standard or changes the level perceived by the individual as having social value.

This second point is one of the reasons for the effectiveness of "group-carried" changes resulting from procedures which approach the individuals as part of face-to-face groups. Perhaps one might expect single individuals to be more pliable than groups of like-minded individuals. However, experience in leadership training, in changing of food habits, work production, criminality, alcoholism, prejudices, all indicate that it is usually easier to change individuals formed into a group than to change any one of them separately.[4] As long as group standards are unchanged, the individual will resist changes more strongly the further he is to depart from group standards. If the group standard itself is changed, the resistance which is due to the relation between individual and group standard is eliminated.

Changing as a Three-Step Procedure: Unfreezing, Moving, and Freezing of a Level

A change toward a higher level of group performance is frequently short-lived: after a "shot in the arm," group life soon returns to the previous level. This indicates that it does not suffice to define the objective of a planned change in group performance as the reaching of a different level. Perma-

---

[4] "Problems of Re-education," *op. cit.*

nency of the new level, or permanency for a desired period, should be included in the objective. A successful change includes therefore three aspects: unfreezing (if necessary) the present level L_1, moving to the new level L_2, and freezing group life on the new level. Since any level is determined by a force field, permanency implies that the new force field is made relatively secure against change.

The "unfreezing" of the present level may involve quite different problems in different cases. Allport [5] has described the "catharsis" which seems to be necessary before prejudices can be removed. To break open the shell of complacency and self-righteousness, it is sometimes necessary to bring about deliberately an emotional stir-up.

Although in some cases the procedure is relatively easily executed, in others it requires skill and presupposes certain general conditions. Managers rushing into a factory to raise production by group decisions are likely to encounter failure. In social management as in medicine, there are no patent medicines and each case demands careful diagnosis. . . .

---

[5] G. W. Allport, "Catharsis and the Reduction of Prejudice" in "Problems of Reeducation," *op. cit.,* pp. 3-10.

CHAPTER 39

MASON HAIRE

Biological Models and Empirical Histories of the Growth of Organizations

The Biological Model

The biological model for social organizations—and here, particularly for industrial organizations—means taking as a model the living organism and the processes and principles that regulate and describe its growth and development. It means looking for lawful processes in organizational growth grounded in factors inside the firm and for the forces shaping it as it grows. It means restating, in specific terms, the interdependence of size, shape, and function in organizations. . . .

An outstanding characteristic of a social organization is simply that it is a special kind of aggregation of individuals. Many of the problems of organization seem to arise from two facets of this fact—first, that it is made up of individuals and, second, that it is an aggregation of them. From the first comes the problem of conflict between individual and organization and the organizational necessity of resisting the centrifugal force associated with individuals—each with his own goal and each tending to fly off from the path of the whole. From the second comes the pressure, as the size of the aggregation increases, to provide communication among the parts, integration of the parts into the whole, and the possibility of specialization of function.

It is in these last areas particularly—those growing out of the size of the aggregation—that the biological model seems most appropriate. Here, too, we have the problem of integrating the parts into a single functioning unit, of maintaining communication among them, and of developing and coor-

From Mason Haire, ed., *Modern Organization Theory* (New York: John Wiley & Sons, Inc., 1959). Reprinted by permission of the author and the publisher.

dinating specialized functions. If we look at the living organism for a moment, while we think of the problems of an organization, the relevance of the model may become clear.

The first step—the interdependence of size, shape, and function—can be seen particularly well in D'Arcy Thompson's example.[1] Taking the story of Jack the Giant Killer, Thompson points out that Jack had nothing to fear from the Giant. If he were, as he is pictured, ten times as large as a man and proportioned like one, Jack was perfectly safe. The Giant's mass would be 10^3, or a thousand times a man's, because he was ten times as big in every dimension. However, the cross-section of his leg bones would have increased only in two dimensions, and they would be 10^2, or a hundred times as big as a man's. A human bone simply will not support ten times its normal load, and the Giant, in walking, would break his legs and be helpless. He was trapped by a simple principle called the square-cube law which points out that, in normal spatial geometry, as volume increases by a cubic function, the surface enclosing it increases only by a square.

. . . We see here the force of gravity acting to put a limit on increase in size without a corresponding change in shape. The organism exists under the pressures of the environment, and a simple relationship drawn from the geometry of its shape expresses the factor through which the environmental pressure is exerted. A man cannot grow as big as a giant and still have the shape of a man. A deer cannot grow as big as an elephant and still look like a deer; it has to look (something) like an elephant to support the elephant's mass. The size cannot vary completely independently of the shape.

A similar application of the principle shows the interdependence of functions with size and shape. Small, unicellular organisms can take in oxygen directly through the skin, and one side is sufficiently near the other so that oxygen permeates the entire organism. As an organism gets bigger, however, the same square-cube law, operating with atmospheric pressure, demands a change in structure and shape. In a larger mass, oxygen no longer permeates throughout, and it is necessary to provide specialized veins and arteries to carry the blood through the whole system. At the same time, the skin surface has become inadequate—growing only by a square— to assimilate adequate oxygen. New folds of spongy tissue, maximizing surface in relation to mass, develop (as lungs), providing a specialized function and shape to accommodate a change in size.

In dealing with the growth of industrial organizations, it has been customary to see the specialized function of the chief executive as the limiting factor leading to diminishing returns with increase in size. Since the supply of this specialty is inelastic within a firm but infinitely elastic within an industry, a limit is seen to profitable expansion. It seems likely, however,

---

[1] Sir D'Arcy Thompson, *On Growth and Form* (2nd ed.; Cambridge, England: Cambridge University Press, 1952).

and empirical evidence seems to suggest, that the limitation also comes from other implications of the size-shape-function relationship. As the organization grows, its internal shape must change. Additional functions of coordination, control, and communication must be provided and supported by the same kind of force that previously supported an organization without these things. If the relationship were linear, there would be no problem. If each increment in size produced one increment (or one plus) in productive capacity and needed one increment of additional supportive function, there would be no limit. However, in the organism, the proportion of skeleton needed to support the mass grows faster than the mass itself and puts a limit on size as a function of the environmental forces playing on it. Similarly, it is suggested that, as the size of a firm increases, the skeletal structure (needed to support it against the forces tending to destroy it) grows faster than the size itself and hence comes to consume a disproportionate amount of the productive capacity of the organization. If this is so, it becomes important to identify the skeletal support of the firm, the forces it resists, and the rates at which the support must grow. Some empirical findings will be presented along these lines.

In the organismic examples used above, it was the force of gravity, and the closely related atmospheric pressure, which impressed modifications on a living form as its size changed. In organisms of other scales of size, other forces seem primarily determinative. In small insects, for example, where the ratio of wet weight to dry weight is high, it seems to be surface tension which determines modifications in form.[2] In still smaller microscopic organisms, it may be the shocks and jars associated with Brownian movement. What kind of force field can be the relevant one for social organisms? It is hard to hypothesize. However, knowing something of the forces operating on living organisms, we could study the modifications with growth and see the operation, for example, of gravity. In industrial organizations, we can study the history of growth and infer the operation of the forces from the direction of changes in shape and function as size changes. With adequate empirical histories, it should be possible to infer some of the characteristics of the force, even before it is possible to identify it.

•

Some kinds of clues seem to exist to help in this job. For one thing, in physical organisms, the form itself shows where the force tending to destroy the organism is strongest. A shelf bracket is thickest and strongest where the tendency for the loaded shelf to break from the wall is greatest. The bowstring arch of a bridge is shaped as it is, not for aesthetic reasons, but to provide maximum support where the weight associated with the size of the bridge tends to destroy it. In general, as physical objects get bigger but retain the same proportions, they get weaker, and a larger and larger propor-

---

[2] G. R. de Beer, *Growth* (London: Edward Arnold, 1924).

tion must go toward supporting their own mass. Consequently, with in-crease in size their forms are modified to resist the force associated with size. The appropriate modification is a clue to the force. The appropriate support for a physical structure is a perfect diagram of the forces tending to destroy it. Similarly, in the industrial organization, special attention to the modification of form as size increases may give us at least a clue to the strength of the force tending to destroy it, and to its point of application.

•

Empirical Histories of Firms

In order to see some of the phenomena of growth in industrial organizations, let us look at the histories of some actual firms. Four companies will be reported on here. These reports are the first results of a research project designed to study growth, and the sample is not necessarily representative of all of industry along any dimension. Several factors dictated the choice of companies. One of them was the simple availability of the firm and the cooperation of the management. To make accurate studies, it was necessary to take payroll records, telephone books, organizational charts, and similar data back to the beginning of the company; finally, sometimes we had to interview the oldest living inhabitants about the origins. These procedures were expensive both for the companies and for the research workers, but accurate data on size and assignment were seldom readily available. Another selective factor, associated with the first, was size. To encompass data of this kind in the early stages of investigation, it was necessary to use relatively small groups. The four firms reported here recently totaled about 2,000; 200; 275; and 300 employees; larger organizations will come later. Still another criterion was youth; in the first studies it seemed useful to try to get companies in which it was still possible to trace histories from the start. Finally, an attempt was made to choose firms where the growth was rapid and where technological advantage in the company materially reduced the pressure of competition on the firm's growth.

•

Internal Changes Associated with Growth

Physical models of organizations lead us to notice the relative proportions of parts as the size of the whole changes and to measure the proportion progressively assigned to such functions as communications and integration. A look at the internal changes in the organizations studied will give us some suggestions about these problems and will provide also some data on growth of functions which have been conspicuously lacking in discussion of organizations.

The relative proportions assigned to line and staff are shown in figures

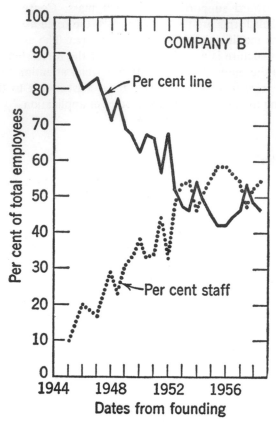

FIGURE 39-1. Per cent of line and staff personnel.

39-1 to 39-4. It was necessary to provide some definitions of line and staff
to make these measures comparable from one firm to another. In industrial
practice there seems to be no uniformity in the use of the terms. Here the
distinction is made as follows: the "line" includes those who directly make
and sell a product; the "staff" includes those who provide specialized support, advice, and help. In borderline cases, the proximity to the product
and direct control over it were taken as determinative. For example, product
planning, when intimately connected with the actual production organization, is here considered as line; product research is not. Similarly, a quality-
control function may operate as part of the line, if it is immediately in the
operation and stops production, modifies practice directly, and rejects output. In some instances, it serves a staff function when, for example, it is a
more removed reportorial service comparable to the financial control afforded by bookkeeping practices.

   Two patterns seem to appear. Two of the firms stabilize at about 50 per
cent devoted to staff, and two at about 25 per cent. All four companies seem

to show a relatively stable proportion in recent years. In all of them the initial proportion, of course, was virtually 100 per cent line. The average size of these companies in the first year of their operation was about eight people, a figure which neither requires nor leaves much room for functional specialization. Beyond this point, however, all four show a rapid shift toward a higher proportion of staff, and the first six to ten years in each firm showed a steep increase in the per cent of staff until the figures stabilized.

There seems to be less relation between absolute size and the steady state of the line-staff proportion than with age. The sizes varied considerably, but the age of six to ten years at the time of steadying gave a narrower range. The fact that three of the four companies are young, with their staff growth in the recent postwar years, suggests that it is perhaps more a function of the times than of growth in general. The fourth company, however, shows much the same pattern, though its main staff growth reached just into the depression thirties, suggesting that the particular times are not determinative.

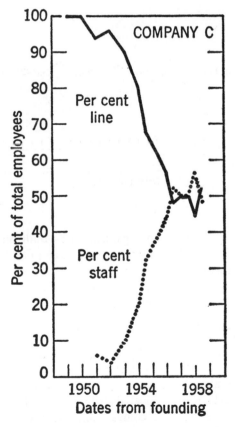

FIGURE 39-2. Per cent of line and staff personnel.

The rapid rise of the proportion of the whole allocated to staff function with early growth takes us back to the argument about the shelf bracket. The brace is strongest where the force tending to destroy it is greatest. If this is true in industrial organizations, the force tending to destroy is greatest at the point where it is shored up by increased staff. What can that force be? The two main functions of the staff are to provide information for control and coordination, and to provide expert assistance beyond the skill or training of line executives. The pressures which threaten to crack the organization as size increases must be in these areas.

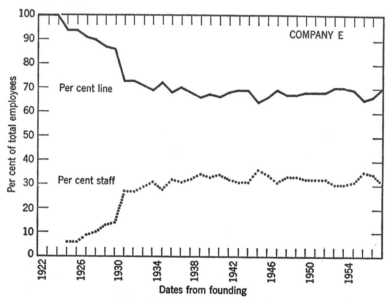

FIGURE 39-3. Per cent of line and staff personnel.

It seems fruitful to think of an organization as built on a module determined by the amount and kind of work one man can do. The best definition of a superior in the hierarchy is that he is responsible for more work than one man can do. As the job grows to be more than he can do, he is given subordinates to help him get it done. In this manner a new level is created in the organization. When the job of supervising these subordinates grows too big, he is given subsubordinates. In general, the vertical extent of the organization grows out of this simple module of the amount of line work one man can do or supervise. To be sure, this same pressure sometimes expands the organization horizontally—divisions are created for line specialties or, more often, to accommodate geographical distributions of the basic activities— but the real branch organization comes from another pressure. Levels are formed, in general, when a man has more than he can do of essentially the same kind of responsibility he has had. However, where a special expertise is required, usually somewhat different from the basic function, the horizontal extent is increased by the addition of branches. It is still the same module—what one man can do—but in a slightly different realm of competence. The specialized functions are of two rough types: control and coordination, as in the case of personnel function, financial control, quality control, and the like; and technical specialties such as research and development, advertising, legal counsel, and, perhaps, industrial relations.

These two pressures flowing from the amount of work one man can do seem to be at the base of the direction of growth of companies. Roughly, when it is more work of the same kind, we have vertical extension; when it is special competences, horizontal. Can these be said to be the pressures tending to destroy the organization? I think so. Whyte[3] gives a delightfully

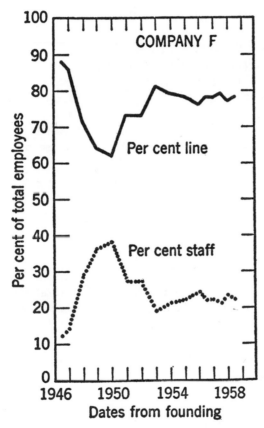

FIGURE 39-4. Per cent of line and staff personnel.

3 W. F. Whyte, *Human Relations in the Restaurant Industry* (New York: McGraw-Hill, 1948).

succinct history of the growth and decline of a restaurant—the industry in which more organizations fail early than in any other. Here the one-man diner flourishes. The owner has been cook, counterman, and cashier, as well as greeter and purchasing agent. He expands and now must keep the cook cooking well, the waitresses efficient and happy, and the cashier honest. He has functions of public relations to supervise (but not to perform) as well as those of labor relations, purchasing, and the like. Very often, in the Shakespearian mold, the very qualities that lent him his worth in his individual operation lead him to fail, as he cannot effectively assume his new responsibilities. They are of two kinds: as supervisor, he must get the subordinates to help him get the work done and keep information flowing back and forth for control and coordination; as manager, he must have the specialized skills of the staff branches, often before he can afford to represent them in individuals.

In the cases reported here, it is the support for these supervisory and managerial tasks which grow most rapidly in the first six to ten years. Apparently the basic line function grows without much threat to the life of the social organism. The structure is strengthened most to provide support for control and coordination on the one hand, to extend assistance for policy-making and planning on the other. It seems reasonable to argue that the relative growth of staff to line provides a parallel to the shelf bracket or the bridge arch—the organization grows fastest where the force tending to destroy it is strongest; the shape of the support is a diagram of the forces acting against the structure.

Before we leave the staff-line relationship, one or two other points are worth noticing. It has been argued that, as the line grows by a linear function, the staff will grow geometrically.[4] This old wives' tale—which, like many pronouncements having to do with organization theory, is completely unsupported by empirical evidence—seems to be widely accepted. Only one study of the facts in the case has come to light. Baker and Davis[5] have shown that, in surveying about 200 companies, the line and staff both grow linearly. Unfortunately, Baker and Davis' data are also misleading on this point. They questioned companies at a point in time, to get a cross-sectional rather than a longitudinal result. Then, when they plot size of staff against size of total, they get a spurious growth curve. It is not a curve of growth representing the dynamics within an organization, but a set of static measurements arranged by size.

The four companies studied here, while differing considerably in their patterns of growth, all show both the points mentioned above. In the early

---

[4] R. C. Davis, *The Fundamentals of Top Management* (New York: Harper & Row, 1951).

[5] A. W. Baker and R. C. Davis, *Ratios of Staff to Line Employees and Stages of Differentiation of Staff Function* (Columbus, Ohio: Ohio State University, 1954), Monograph No. 72.

years, while the line grows linearly, the staff grows by some exponential function (though no single one seems to describe the curve well). Later, in another period of growth, they grow at quite similar rates. In terms of rough averages, during the period when the line first doubled, the staff grew about six times as large. When the line next doubled, the staff grew about five times; the next doubling of the line was accompanied by a tripling of the staff, and from then on they (approximately) each doubled. Early, the staff grows geometrically as the line grows linearly, but this relation tapers off to parallel growth.

Two other points might be noticed with regard to the staff before we leave it. One is the remarkable resistance of the staff to negative growth. The companies studied did not all grow uniformly larger. At times they cut the total personnel. In the total histories observed, there were nineteen such cases of layoffs, totaling 311 people from all firms. What proportion of these were line and what were staff? During the time in which 311 were laid off, there were actually 325 line workers furloughed; fourteen new staff people were hired during the very layoff period. Many reasons might be advanced for this. Staff people are specialists and harder to come by than line; it is simple economy to save them. Cutting down line and saving staff builds for the future. When business picks up again the line workers can be rehired to take places in the organization the staff has held intact. A more cynical interpretation might be that the staff plans and designs the layoffs, though line management makes the policy. No one ever plans to let himself go. Indeed, the process of laying off apparently required more staff to do it. Whatever the reason, it is clear that the staff is the place to take a job. It seems to have built-in tenure.

A second point which might be mentioned is the considerable regularity shown in the point of introduction of one staff function—personnel. The four companies had separate personnel people when their sizes were 177, 152, 138, and 248. Except for the last one, the figures are remarkably close together.

The Growth of Supervision and the Span of Control

Earlier we referred to the idea that the limiting condition leading to diminishing returns is based on the fact that the pyramidal shape of an organization always has a single individual at the apex and that this chief executive's function is inexpandable within the firm. This view of the function of the executive seems to be based on two notions: one, that there is a unit of decision-making potential of finite size, which can be stretched to cover only a certain amount of operation; and two, that there is a "span of control" which limits, more-or-less absolutely, the rate at which the pyramid can spread out beneath the top executive. The first notion—of an indivisible, inexpandable unit of decision-making—seems to leave out the possibility of decentralization, and the extreme of virtually autonomous organization within a single skin in the style, for example, of General Motors. While there may be an eventual upper limit on size associated with the operation of a factor of this kind, it does not seem to be limiting in the range of sizes which characterizes most of the industry. The second assumption, about the span of control, is even more tenuous. For one thing, even granting the reality of this span, it is not very sharply limiting. A figure of eight subordinates controlled by each superior occurs quite frequently in writings about span of control. In practice, a company with six levels of command below the vice-presidents is not out of the question. This would give us six levels of superiors with each man supervising eight subordinates. Such an organization would have a total payroll of 8^6, or about a quarter of a million; if we increase the span of control to ten, the same-shaped organization would give us a million employees. Surely this factor does not limit the size of industrial firms in the ranges with which we are familiar. Again, in practice, this kind of span of control does not seem to fit observed facts; Sears Roebuck is the classic example in which the number of subordinates reporting directly to policy-making levels has been increased well beyond the number usually discussed. Sears often has 50 subordinates reporting to a single man. To man a full organization of six levels, with 50 men reporting to each superior, would take 100 times the population of the United States.

The idea of the span of control in itself is an interesting one. It is often discussed as if there were some absolute answer to the question—"How many subordinates can a superior manage?"—as if the span were a kind of inflexible constant in social organizations, rather than a factor which itself is variable as a result of a number of such things as the training of the subordinates; the objectives of the group; the situation in which they find themselves; the communication facilities available to them; and the like. . . .

In dealing with principles of management, one often sees references to Graicunas' formulation of the limitations of authority.[6] Graicunas stresses the number of relationships with and between subordinates as their number increases. Using almost all possible relationships, he comes to a formula of

$$r = N \left(\frac{2^N}{2} + N - 1 \right)$$

where r is the number of relationships and N is the number of subordinates. With three subordinates, for example, we get a total of eighteen relationships, with four, 44. These surprising totals, however, are achieved only by taking a most elaborate view of human interactions. We must consider A's relationship with B in C's presence separately from his relationship with B alone and separately from his relationship with C in B's presence and in-

---

[6] L. Gulick and L. F. Urwick, *Papers on the Science of Administration* (New York: New York Institute of Public Administration, 1937).

clude B's relationship with C as well as C's with B. While all these relationships are logically contained in the system, it is not clear how they limit the span of control. Koontz and O'Donnell,[7] for example, say:

> An executive with four subordinates may well hesitate before adding a fifth member to the group when by doing so he increases the total possible relationships *for which he is responsible* [italics mine] by 127 per cent (from 44 to 100) in return for a 20 per cent increase in subordinate working capacity.

Surely this is just plain silly. Students must have been misled by the mathematical nicety Graicunas introduced in a previously foggy field. Making the superior responsible in any direct sense for all the relationships between and among his subordinates seems to extend unduly the functions of the executive. It would seem to me that these figures point again to the complexity of communication required to maintain contact within a growing organization, rather than to a limit on the realm of authority of the manager. . . .

When we look at the average number of line production workers supervised by first-line foremen, the simple ratio of one to eight does not stand up. In 1958, the four companies had an average of thirteen production workers reporting to each line foreman. The companies varied among themselves. Over their total life, the average number of men reporting to a supervisor were 19, 18, 7, and 13 for the four companies—a ratio of about 1 to 14 for

Table **39-1**

Average Number of Employees per Supervisor

Size of Company	Average Number Supervised
20-50	11.5
50-100	14
100-200	12
Over 200	21

Table **39-2**

Top and Middle Management as a Percentage of Total

Size of Firm	Per cent in Top and Middle Management
20-50	13.6
50-100	10.5
100-200	5.9
Over 200	4.1

---

[7] H. Koontz and C. O'Donnell, *Principles of Management* (New York: McGraw-Hill, 1955), p. 91.

all four companies for their total life span. The ratio of supervisors to supervised does not go up as the company grows. On the contrary, as the line increased, each supervisor was responsible for more men. To return to the argument from the shelf bracket, more supervision is not one of the supports against the destructive forces associated with size.

The ratio of top and middle management shows an even greater decline with increasing size. Table 39-2 shows the general relationship. When the firms are small the ratio is somewhat misleading, since there is an almost irreducible minimum of management no matter how small the total. Using a table similar to that given for first-line supervisors, the decreasing ratio is clear. Management grows in size as the total grows, but more slowly than the total, and it is an increasingly smaller part of the whole. The strength that management provides does not need to be increased more than proportionately as the company grows. Contrary to the argument that diminishing returns come from a pinch at the top, in the range of sizes studied here, the top seems perfectly adequate.

The Rise of the Clerical Function

Parkinson has made us all self-conscious about the clerical function in modern organization. To look at this, a special tabulation was kept in these four firms of all the people who were primarily paper handlers of one sort or another. The total number of clerical workers does increase as the company increases. In general, as the companies went from 40 to 80 employees, the clerical staff doubled, and the doubling of total size and clerks roughly continued. The table shows some variation, but not the alarming growth one

Table **39-3**

Clerical Workers as a Percentage of Total

Size of Company	Per cent of Clerks
20-50	12
50-100	15
100-200	12
Over 200	14

might expect. . . . As a company ages, the tendency to acquire a larger percentage of clerks appears. Part of this may be the staying power of the staff mentioned earlier. Or, in part, it may be a kind of agglutinative accretion, as when a line promotion requires a new secretary because there is no room for salary increase. In any case, the number and proportion of clerks tends to grow and grow.

The clerks have been treated separately from the staff for the present study because of the timeliness of the interest. They belong to the staff, however, and, as such, it is worthwhile considering their function for a moment. They are part of the general function of control, coordination, and communication which increases rapidly as the size increases. These functions are the responsibility of the line, but they are largely implemented by the staff. We saw that the staff increased by a factor of six when the line first doubled; the steady growth of the clerical function gives another clue to what is happening. The clerk's job is largely concerned with information —recording, duplicating, disseminating, keeping, and finding information —to support the integrative function.

In the biological organism, there is the same pressure for information in the interest of integration. Part of it is answered by the growth of the nervous system into a more complex network. Part of it is met by a simple increase in the speed of the transmission of the signal. For example, in a sea-urchin egg, without a proper nervous system, a signal barely moves along the membrane at a centimeter an hour; in the sponge it is already up to a centimeter a minute. A differentiated communication system—a nervous system—greatly improves the situation. In a jellyfish a signal goes 10 cm/sec, in a worm about ten times as fast. The arthropods step up the rate by another factor of ten; and finally the anthropoids—including man—again show a tenfold increase to something like 100 m/sec. Two things might be noticed; one, that in larger and more complex organisms there is a marked increase in transmissive capacity and hence in adaptive response; and, two, in very complex organisms two specialized branches develop— one for internal adjustments (the autonomic nervous system) and one for handling external information.[8]

In social organisms we cannot do much to speed the actual transmission of the nerve impulse, but we can and do develop, like the biological model, separate specialized functions for internal and external adjustments. Instead of increasing the actual transmission speed, there is one thing which we can do. It is a truism in communication engineering that it is always possible to trade band-width for time. If a message takes a channel of x frequencies to travel in y time, one can usually use $2x$ frequencies, and, by simultaneous transmission, achieve $\frac{1}{2}y$ time. This is essentially what happens in the combined staff-clerical function. Unable to speed up transmission, we duplicate messages and transmit simultaneously, achieving a measure of the desired speed.

. . . With the great deal of attention currently paid to the rise of the staff, it will perhaps make us happier with it if we realize its true role. The tendency to refer to staff as "nonproductive workers," "overhead personnel," or "burden personnel" expresses a frustration that is quite common, but it represents a bookkeeping fiction more than it does a factual reflection of the true organizational role of the function. . . .

---

[8] R. Redfield, *Levels of Integration in Biological and Social Sciences* (Lancaster, Pa.: Jacques Cattell Press, 1942), *Biological Symposia*, VIII, pp. 67-78.

CHAPTER 40

ROBERT E. PARK

The Race-Relations Cycle

The impression that emerges from the review of international and race relations is that the forces which have brought about the existing interpenetration of peoples are so vast and irresistible that the resulting changes assume the character of a cosmic process. New means of communication enforce new contacts and result in new forms of competition and of conflict. But out of this confusion and ferment, new and more intimate forms of association arise.

The changes which are taking place on the Pacific Coast—"the last asylum," in the language of Professor Ross, "of the native-born"—are part of the changes that are going on in every other part of the world. Everywhere there is competition and conflict; but everywhere the intimacies which participation in a common life enforces have created new accommodation, and relations which were merely formal or utilitarian have become personal and human.

In the relations of races there is a cycle of events which tends everywhere to repeat itself. Exploration invariably opens new regions for commercial exploitation; the missionary, as has frequently been said, becomes the advance agent of the trader. The exchange of commodities involves in the long run the competition of goods and of persons. The result is a new distribution of population and a new and wider division of labor.

The new economic organization, however, inevitably becomes the basis for a new political order. The relations of races and people are never for very long merely economic and utilitarian, and no efforts to conceive them in this way have ever been permanently successful. We have imported labor as if it were mere commodity, and sometimes we have been disappointed to find, as we invariably do, that the laborers were human like ourselves. In this way it comes about that race relations which were economic later be-

From Robert E. Park, *Race and Culture* (Glencoe, Ill.: The Free Press, 1950), pp. 149-151. Reprinted by permission of the publisher.

come political and cultural. The struggle for existence terminates in a struggle for status, for recognition, for position and prestige, within an existing political and moral order. Where such a political and moral order does not exist, war, which is the most elementary expression of political forces, creates one. For the ultimate effect of war has been, on the whole, to establish and extend law and order in regions where it did not previously exist.

The race relations cycle, which takes the form, to state it abstractly, of contacts, competition, accommodation, and eventual assimilation, is apparently progressive and irreversible. Customs regulations, immigration restrictions, and racial barriers may slacken the tempo of the movement, may perhaps halt it altogether for a time, but cannot change its direction; cannot at any rate, reverse it.

In our estimates of race relations we have not reckoned with the effects of personal intercourse and the friendships that inevitably grow up out of them. These friendships, particularly in a democratic society like our own, cut across and eventually undermine all the barriers of racial segregation and caste by which races seek to maintain their integrity.

It was the intimate and personal relations which grew up between the Negro slave and his white master that undermined and weakened the system of slavery from within, long before it was attacked from without. Evidence of this was the steady increase, in spite of public opinion and legislation to the contrary, of the number of free Negroes and emancipated slaves in the South. Men who believed the black man foreordained to be the servant of the white were unwilling to leave the servants they knew to the mercy of the system when they were no longer able to protect them.

In spite of the bitter antagonism that once existed toward the Chinese, the attitude of the Pacific Coast is now generally amiable, even indulgent, and this in spite of the nuisance of their *tong* wars and other racial eccentricities. The Chinese population is slowly declining in the United States, but San Francisco, at any rate, will miss its Chinese quarter when it goes.

There has never been the antagonism toward the Japanese in this country that there once was toward the Chinese. Even such antagonism as existed has always been qualified by a genuine admiration for the Japanese people as a whole. Now that the exclusion law seems finally to have put an end to Japanese immigration, there is already a disposition to relax the laws which made the permanent settlement of Orientals on the Pacific Coast untenable.

It does not follow that because the tendencies to the assimilation and eventual amalgamation of races exist, they should not be resisted and, if possible, altogether inhibited. On the other hand, it is vain to underestimate the character and force of the tendencies that are drawing the races and peoples about the Pacific into the ever-narrowing circle of a common life. Rising tides of color and Oriental exclusion laws are merely incidental evidences of these diminishing distances.

In the Hawaiian Islands, where all the races of the Pacific meet and mingle on more liberal terms than they do elsewhere, the native races are disappearing, and new peoples are coming into existence. Races and cultures die—it has always been so—but civilization lives on.

CHAPTER 41

DAVID RIESMAN

From "Inner-Directed" to "Other-Directed"

My purpose here is to trace a shift I believe to have occurred in very recent times in the character structure of modern man: a shift from the predominance of a type I have called "inner-directed," whose source of guidance in life is an internalized authority, to a type I have called "other-directed," dependent on external authorities. We shall further explore the relationship between these two types of character and the changing feelings in people as to their power to resist social pressures. For obviously, given the objectively identical social pressure, the individual's feeling and experience will depend upon his character, in which his previous life-experiences, especially those of mastery and submission, have been crystallized.

While our helplessness in the world is historically the condition of every advance in our mastery of it, the feeling of helplessness may today be so overpowering that regression, and not advance, ensues. But only when we have understood those forces that make for helplessness can we assay the probable outcome, and see what might be required for a new leap to security and freedom. . . . One requirement is a type of character structure that can tolerate freedom, even thrive on it; I call persons of such type "autonomous," since they are capable of conscious self-direction. The very conditions that produce other-direction on the part of the majority today, who are heteronomous—that is, who are guided by voices other than their own—may also produce a "saving remnant" who are increasingly autonomous and who find strength in the face of their minority position in the modern world of power.

From David Riesman, "The Saving Remnant," in J. W. Chase, ed., *The Years of the Modern* (New York: David McKay, 1949), pp. 115-147. Reprinted by permission of the author and the publisher.

The Inner-Directed Type

Throughout most of history, people have lived in the bosom of nature, and at her mercy. They have sought a kind of defensive power and command of nature through magic and animism, by which they attempted to personalize and to propitiate the environment. The Pueblo Indians of the American Southwest, for instance, still cope with fear of drought by preoccupation with word-perfect rituals of rain-making—and by very practical communal organization of the available water supply. These tribes quiet their anxiety over the weather by substituting for it anxiety over the ritual, which remains in their control. In such a society, as in the feudal past, people live on a relatively unawakened level, with limited life-expectations and limited potentialities for choice. An overall balance is struck between helplessness and power; institutions mediate this balance, and character structure builds upon it.

This balance altered radically in the West during the age that opens with the Renaissance and closes, to set an equally arbitrary date, with the virtual cutting off of immigration from Europe following World War I. During this period, men were forced to face a world of changed dimensions, changed social relations, and changed meanings. As a result, some felt increasingly helpless and alone; the Calvinist doctrines appealed to them because those doctrines stressed man's helplessness to secure grace, the "chosen" being predestined by a terrifying and inscrutable God. The practical Calvinist, however, did not merely wait for the day of judgment; he tried to force God's hand by a ritual. This ritual, unlike the Pueblo Indian's rain-making, was symbolized by hard work in the worldly processes of production—even though the ultimate aim was otherworldly. The result for many was success in mundane pursuits, which was regarded as a sign of election. Thus both hard work and its practical fruits assuaged the feeling of helplessness in the new conditions of life and led to the attainment of a new balance between power and weakness.

This period was the age of the early physical and industrial frontiers—the frontiers of expanding industry and trade, as well as expanding geographical frontiers. This age also enlarged the frontiers of intellectual and emotional discovery, excavating man's past and acquainting him with other cultures. To pioneer on a frontier—whether an external one, at the edge of a white settlement, or an internal one, at the edge of the known in science, art, or industry—requires a somewhat new type of character that is, to a degree, capable of self-piloting, a type that can act when the guidance of custom breaks down or when a choice must be made among several different sets of customs.

I call this type inner-directed, since the source of direction is internalized. By inner-direction, however, I do not mean genuine autonomy, but rather obedience to an internal psychic "gyroscope" which, installed in childhood, continues to pilot the person as he struggles to master the exigent demands of the frontier. This gyroscope is set going by the parents, or rather by their idealized image (the Freudian superego); or by heroes or great men of antiquity or revered elders taken as models. Driven by these internal voices, the inner-directed person is often ambitious—for fame, for goodness, for accomplishment in the world; and this is as true of the bold men of the Renaissance as of the hard, ascetic Puritans. By their own efforts at self-discipline and self-development, these men often helped to "produce" their own characters; the conquering of this internal frontier was accompanied and rewarded by mastery over others and over nature.

In all I have said, I speak primarily of the middle classes, for it was among them that inner-directed types arose; the lower classes moved more slowly out of feudalism. In time, as the doctrine of predestination became attenuated or forgotten, these middle classes developed an ideology of liberalism and individualism that proclaimed for all men the values of freedom and self-reliance compatible with characterological inner-direction. The inner-directed person came to *feel* free and to *feel* self-made: in his psychological innocence, he was not aware how many of "his" choices had been made for him already by his parents and his conditioning generally. He might have read the famous phrase of Heraclitus—"Character is fate"—to mean that he, as an individual, possessed his own fate, working in him through his own self-mastery; while we today would read the same sentence to mean that our own character is not truly ours, but is produced by our social environment, our "fate" of living in a particular place and time—a new, more sophisticated doctrine of predestination. Moreover, the inner-directed person, living in a time of expanding frontiers, could in fact achieve a small degree of the freedom that he felt. Many inner-directed persons achieved a measure of psychic autonomy and independence as theocratic controls declined in the eighteenth and nineteenth centuries.

•

Inner-direction was never very widespread, but rather represented the ideal model toward which people strove. We have evidence that many people of that era tried desperately to conduct themselves in the approved inner-directed way, but were unable to conform. Thus, in Vermont of the eighteenth and nineteenth centuries, many more people started diaries and account books—perfect symbols of inner-direction—than kept them up. Such people must have felt helpless in their efforts at self-mastery, particularly since they took as models those pre-eminent men, from George Washington to Andrew Carnegie, who then stood unshaken by disciples of Marx and Freud. Thus, in a very special sense, the feelings of potency were monopolized by those whose inner-direction was relatively stable and successful in the public mind, while a reservoir of hidden impotence existed. Yet for many of the unsuccessful, failure never seemed quite final, and so long as the future beckoned, or the belief in grace persisted, helplessness could be staved off.

The Other-Directed Type

Individual helplessness and collective power play leapfrog with each other throughout history. Today, the helplessness foreseen by a few thinkers, and sensed even in the earlier age of frontiers by many who failed, has become the common attribute of the mass of men. We turn now to discuss some of the factors responsible for this development: in economic and political life, in methods of childrearing, and in their consequences for character structure.

When immigration from Europe was cut off in 1924, a great symbol of hope in the Western world was destroyed. The "no help wanted" sign had been posted on the American frontier in 1890, but it was now hung out along our borders for all to see. Today, in the advanced industrial countries, there is only one frontier left—that of consumption—and this calls for very different types of talent and character.

The inner-directed type fitted the conditions of essentially open capitalism, which rewarded ability to envisage new possibilities for production, and zeal to realize those possibilities. To a degree, this is still the case. Nevertheless, we think that, on the whole, contemporary society, especially in America, no longer requires and rewards the old enterprise and the old zeal. This does not mean that the economic system itself is slowing down; total production may continue to rise; but it can be achieved by institutionalizing technological and organizational advance, in research departments, management counsel, and corporate planning staffs. The invention and adoption of new improvements can be routinized, built into the system, so to speak, rather than into the men who run the system. Therefore, the energies of management turn to industrial and public relations, to oiling the frictions not of machines but of men.

Likewise, with the growth of monopolistic competition, the way to get ahead is not so much to make a better mousetrap but rather to "package" an old mousetrap in a new way, and then to sell it by "selling" oneself first. People feel they must be able to adapt themselves to other people, both to manipulate them and to be manipulated by them. This requires the ability to manipulate oneself, to become "a good package," to use a phrase current among personnel men. These pressures are, of course, not confined to business, but operate also in the professions, in government, and in academic life.

As work becomes less meaningful and intense, however, leisure grows, and men who are discarded as workers are cultivated in the one role that still matters, that of consumer. This is not an easy role, and people become almost as preoccupied with getting the "best buys" as they once were with finding their proper "calling" in the production economy. They turn, then, to the mass media of communication for advice in how to consume; at the same time, these media help make them anxious lest they fail in the role of consumer. We speak here not merely of "keeping up with the Joneses"—this is part of an older pattern—but rather of the much more unsettling fear of missing those leisure-time experiences, including sex, love, art, friendship, food, travel, which people have been induced to feel they should have.

These changes in the nature of work and leisure have made themselves felt most strongly among the middle classes of the American big cities in the last 25 years or so. It is here that we find developing the character type that I call other-directed, a type whose source of direction is externalized. The clear goals and generalized judgments of the inner-directed types are not implanted in the other-directed person in childhood. Rather, he is taught, vaguely, to do the "best possible" in any given situation. As soon as he can play with other children, he is made sensitive to the judgments of this play group, looking to it for approval and direction as to what is best. Parents and other adults come to value the child in terms of his ability to live up to the group's expectations and to wrest popularity from it.

The adult never loses this dependence, but continues to live psychologically oriented to his contemporaries—to what might be called his "peer group." Of course, it matters very much who these others are: whether they are his immediate circle of the moment, or a higher circle he aspires to, or the anonymous circles of whose doings he learns from the mass media of communication. But the great psychological difference from inner-direction is that this modern type needs open approval and guidance from contemporaries. This new need for approval goes well beyond the human and opportunistic reasons that lead people in any age to care very much what others think of them. People in general want and need to be liked, but it is only the other-directed character type that makes others its chief source of direction and its chief area of sensitivity and concern.

These differences in the source looked to for direction lead to different modes of conformity in the two types. The inner-directed person will ordinarily have had an early choice made for him among the several available destinies of the middle-class child. What holds him on course is that he has internalized from his elders certain general aims and drives—the drive to work hard, or to save money, or to strive for rectitude or for fame. His conformity results from the fact that similar drives have been instilled into others of his social class. As against this, the other-directed person grows up in a much more amorphous social system, where alternative destinations cannot be clearly chosen at an early age. The "best possible" in a particular situation must always be learned from the others in that situation. His conformity to the others is thus not one of generalized drives, but of details—the minutiae of taste or speech or emotion which are momentarily "best." Hence he internalizes neither detailed habits nor generalized drives, but instead an awareness of and preoccupation with the *process* of securing direction from others.

We can find exemplars of the other-directed character in leisured urban circles of the past, where the preoccupations were those of consumption, not production, and where status depended on the opinion of influential others. What is new is the spread of such an outlook over large sectors of a middle class that was once inner-directed. Elements of this outlook, moreover, have now filtered down in America to many members of the lower-middle class.

It is my tentative conclusion that the feeling of helplessness of modern man results from both the vastly enhanced power of the social group and the incorporation of its authority into his very character. And the point at issue is not that the other-directed character is more opportunistic than the inner-directed—if anything, the contrary is true. Rather, the point is that the individual is psychologically dependent on others for clues to the meaning of life. He thus fails to resist authority or fears to exercise freedom of choice even where he might safely do so.

An illustration may clarify my meaning. I have sometimes asked university students why they come to class so regularly day after day, why they do not—as they are technically free to do—take two or three weeks off to do anything they like on their own. The students have answered that they must come to class or otherwise they will flunk, though the fact is that many students get ahead when they finally do break through the routines. It has become apparent that the students cling to such "rational" explanations because, in their feeling of helplessness, freedom is too much of a threat. They fail to see those loopholes of which they could take advantage for their own personal development; they feel safer if they are obeying an authoritative ritual in sympathetic company. Their attendance at class has much the same meaning as the Pueblo Indian's rain-making dance, only the student has less confidence that his "prayer" will be heard. For he has left "home" for good, and all of modern thought teaches him too much for comfort and too little for help. . . .

Some Factors in the Transition

Let us examine several further factors that have robbed the middle-class individual of his defenses against the pressure of the group. We shall deal in somewhat more detail with changes in the nature of private property of work and of leisure, all of which at one time functioned as defenses.

In the feudal era, the individual was attached to property, largely land, by feudal and family ties. The breakdown of feudalism meant helplessness for many peasants, who were thrown off the land; but for the middle class the result was a gradual gain in consciousness of strength. A new type of relationship between persons and property developed: the person was no longer attached to property, but attached property to himself by his own energetic actions. Property, including land, became freely alienable; at the same time, it was felt to be an individual, not a family, possession. And property was satisfying, substantial—an extended part of the self. Inside the shell of his possessions, the inner-directed person could resist psychological invasion.

Today, however, property is not much of a defense. Taxes and other state activities, inflation and the panicky desire for liquid assets, have made it factually friable. Moreover, the fears of property-holders outrun the actual dangers. Thus, even powerful groups in America feel more frightened of Communism than its actual power warrants. Property no longer represents the old security for those who hold it, and the fear that it may vanish any day makes it as much a source of anxiety as of strength. The rich no longer dare flaunt wealth, but tread softly, guided by considerations of "public relations." Wealthy students often act as if ashamed of their wealth; I have sometimes been tempted to point out that the rich are a minority and have rights, too.

The change in the meaning of work is even plainer. For the inner-directed person, work seemed self-justifying: the only problem was to find the work to which one felt called. As we have seen, the age of expanding frontiers provided the individual with an inexhaustible list of tasks. Work, like property, moreover, was considered a mode of relating oneself to physical objects, and only indirectly to people. Indeed, the work-hungry inner-directed types of this period sometimes found that they were cut off from family and friends, and often from humanity in general, by their assiduity and diligence. And work, like property, was a defense against psychological invasion, a "do not disturb" sign guarding the industrious man of the middle class.

Today the meaning of work is a very different one, psychologically, though in many professions and industries the older modes still persist. To an increasing degree, the self is no longer defined by its productive accomplishments but by its role in a "Friendship" system. As the "isolate" or "rate-buster" is punished and excluded from the work force in the shop, so the lone wolf is weeded out of management; up-to-date personnel men use deep-probing psychological tests to eliminate applicants, whatever their other gifts, who lack the other-directed personality needed for the job.

To be sure, out of anxiety, a lingering asceticism, and a need for an impressive agenda, the professional and business men and women of the big cities continue to work hard, or more accurately, to spend long hours in the company of their fellow "antagonistic cooperators"; "work" is seen as a network of personal relationships that must be constantly watched and oiled. Increasingly, both work and leisure call on the same sort of skills—sociability, sensitivity to others' feelings and wants, and the exercise of taste-preferences freed from direct considerations of economic advantage. Work in this case has a certain unreality for people, since it has almost floated free from any connection with technical crafts. The latter have been built into machines or can easily be taught; but people must still go to the office and find ways of keeping, or at least looking, busy. Thus in many circles work and leisure are no longer clearly distinguished, as we can see by observing a luncheon or a game of golf among competitors.

The feeling of powerlessness of the other-directed character is, then, the result in part of the lack of genuine commitment to work. His life is not engaged in a direct struggle for mastery over himself and nature; he has no long-term goals since the goals must constantly be changed. At the same time, he is in competition with others for the very values they tell him are worth pursuing; in a circular process, one of these values is the approval of the competing group itself. Hence he is apt to repress overt competitiveness, both out of anxiety to be liked and out of fear of retaliation. In this situation, he is likely to lose interest in the work itself. With loss of interest, he may even find himself little more than a dilettante, not quite sure that he is really able to accomplish anything.

•

When we turn from the sphere of work to the sphere of leisure, we see again that roles in which the individual could once find refuge from and defense against the group have become stylized roles, played according to the mandates and under the very eyes of the group. The individual in the age of inner-direction had little leisure; often he was so work-driven that he could not even use the leisure given him. On occasion, however, he could escape from the pressures and strains of the workaday world into a private hobby or into the resources of culture, either "highbrow" or popular. In either case, the stream of entertainment and communication was intermittent; to come into contact with it required effort. Leisure, therefore, by its very scarcity, provided a change of pace and role. Moreover, beyond these actual leisure roles stood a group of fantasy roles—roles of social ascent, of rebellion against work and inhibition, dreams of world-shaking achievement; the individual was protected against invasion at least of his right to these dreams.

Today, leisure is seldom enjoyed in solitude, nor is it often used for unequivocal escape. Hobbies of the older craft type seem to have declined, and a baseball game is perhaps the only performance where the mass audience can still judge competence. The torrent of words and images from radio, the movies, and the comics begins to pour on the child even before he can toddle; he starts very early to learn his lifelong role of consumer. The quantity of messages impinging on the child becomes increasingly "realistic"; instead of "Just-So Stories" and fairy tales, children are given "here and now" stories of real life, and escape into imaginative fantasy is therefore held at a minimum.

Likewise, movies, fiction, and radio for adults increasingly deal with "here and now" problems: how to handle one's relations with children, with the opposite sex, with office colleagues away from the office. Story writers for the better woman's magazines are instructed to deal with the intimate problems faced by the readers, and soap opera is one long game of Going to Jerusalem; when one problem sits down, another is left standing. Indeed, we might claim, there is no "escape" from leisure. Wherever we turn, in work or in popular culture, we are faced by our peers and the problems they present, including the pressure they put on us to "have fun." A kind of ascetic selflessness rules much of the greatly expanded leisure of the other-directed person—selflessness disguised by the craving for comfort, fun, and effortlessness, but ascetic nonetheless in its tense use of leisure for preparing oneself to meet the expectations of others.

Thus, the newly reached horizons of leisure and consumption made possible by our economic abundance have not been as exhilarating for the individual as the realized horizons of work and production proved to be for many in the age of expanding frontiers. . . .

I do not mean to imply that our society "produces" other-directed people because such people are in demand in an increasingly monopolistic, managerial economy. The relations between character and society are not that simple. Moreover, neither character nor society changes all at once. But it would take us too far afield to trace the many formative agencies in the shift, still far from complete, from inner-direction to other-direction in the middle classes.

Furthermore, I must guard against the implication that I think inner-direction is a way of life preferable to other-direction. Each type has its virtues and its vices: the inner-directed person tends to be rigid and intolerant of others; the other-directed person, in turn, is likely to be flexible and sensitive to others. Neither type is altogether comfortable in the world. But in different ways each finds the discomforts it needs psychologically in order, paradoxically, to feel comfortable. The inner-directed person finds the struggle to master himself and the environment quite appropriate; he feels comfortable climbing uphill. The other-directed person finds equally appropriate the malaise that he shares with many others. Engrossed in the activities that the culture provides, he can remain relatively unconscious of his anxiety and tonelessness. Moreover, the character type must always be judged in context. Many persons who are inner-directed and who, in an earlier age, would have gone through life in relative peace, today find themselves indignant at a big-city world in which they have not felt at home. Other-directed persons also may not feel at home, but home never had the same meaning for them. It would appear to the envious inner-directed observer that the other-directed manage their lives better in a mass society. Conversely, the other-directed may envy the seeming firmness of the inner-directed, and look longingly back on the security of nineteenth-century society, while failing to see that firmness was often merely stubbornness and security merely ignorance. . . .

The Saving Remnant

Nevertheless, even under modern conditions, and out of the very matrix of other-directed modes of conformity, some people strive toward an autonomous character. An autonomus person has no compulsive need to follow the other-direction of his culture and milieu—and no compulsive need to flout it, either. We know almost nothing about the factors that make for such positive results; it is easier to understand the sick than to understand why some stay well. It hardly helps to repeat our point that man's helplessness is the condition for his every advance, because this generalization tells us too little about individual cases. However, it seems that the helplessness of modern man in a world of power has been one element in the genesis of some of the extraordinary human achievements of our age. Some of these achievements are the physical and literary productions of men's hands and minds, but other achievements lie in the internal "productions" of men—their characters; it is of these that I speak here.

There were autonomous people of course, in the era of inner-direction, but they were made of sterner stuff; the barriers they encountered were the classic ones: family, religion, poverty. On the other hand, the person who seeks autonomy today in the upper socio-economic levels of the Western democracies is not faced with the barriers that normally restricted him in the past. The coercions against his independence are frequently invisible. An autonomous person of the middle class must work constantly to detach himself from shadowy entanglements with his culture—so difficult to break with because its demands appear so "reasonable," so trivial.

For our study of autonomy, we have drawn freely on Erich Fromm's concept of the "productive orientation" in *Man for Himself*. Fromm shows the orientation of a type of character that can relate itself to people through love, and to objects and the world generally through the creative gift. The struggle for a productive orientation becomes exigent at the very moment in history when solution of the problem of production itself, in the technical sense, is in sight.

All human beings, even the most productive, the most autonomous, are fated, in a sense, to die the death of Ivan Ilyitch, in Tolstoy's "The Death of Ivan Ilyitch," who becomes aware only on his deathbed of his underlived life and his unused potentialities for autonomy. All of us realize only a fraction of our potentialities. Always a matter of degree, always blended with residues of inner-direction or other-direction, autonomy is a process, not an achievement. Indeed, we may distinguish the autonomous by the fact that his character is never a finished product, but always a lifelong growth.

I speak of autonomy as an aspect of character structure, and not in terms of independence of overt behavior. The autonomous person may or may not conform in his behavior to the power-requirements of society; he can choose whether to conform or not. (The Bohemians and rebels are not usually autonomous; on the contrary, they are zealously tuned in to the signals of a defiant group that finds the meaning of life in a compulsive nonconformity to the majority group.) Yet the separation of "freedom in behavior" from "autonomy in character" cannot be complete. Autonomy requires self-awareness about the fact of choice, about possible ways of living. The autonomous person of today exists precisely because we have reached an awareness of the problem of choice that was not required among the Pueblos, or, for the most part, in the Middle Ages, or even in the period after the Reformation, when the concepts of God's will and of duty confined choice for many within fairly narrow bounds.

The very fluidity of modern democratic social systems, that, for the mass of people, results in anxiety and "escape from freedom," forces those who would become autonomous to find their own way. They must "choose themselves," in Sartre's phrase, out of their very alienation from traditional ties and inner-directed defenses which inhibited true choice in the past. However, I think Sartre mistaken in his Kantian notion that men can choose themselves under totalitarian conditions. Likewise, if the choices that matter are made for us by the social system, even if it is in appearance a democratic system, then our sense of freedom also will atrophy; most people need the opportunity for some freedom of behavior if they are to develop and confirm their autonomy of character. Nevertheless, the rare autonomous character we have been describing, the man of high, almost precarious, quality, must arise from that aloneness, that helplessness of modern man, that would overwhelm a lesser person. It is in this quality and in the mode of life he is groping to achieve, that he has made a contribution to the problem of living in a power-world.

•

If these conjectures are accurate, then it follows that, by a process of unconscious polarization which is going on in society, a few people are becoming more self-consciously autonomous than before, while many others are losing their social and characterological defenses against the group. The latter, though politically strong, are psychically weak, and the autonomous minority, by its very existence, threatens the whole shaky mode of adaptation of the majority.

Nevertheless, joy in life has its own dynamic. . . . Character structure is not completely fixed for the individual, so long as life lasts, or for the group. Men have some control over the fate by which their characters are made. By showing how life can be lived with vitality and happiness even in time of trouble, the autonomous people can become a social force, indeed a "saving remnant." By converting present helplessness into a condition of advance, they lay the basis of a new society, though they may not live to see it.

CHAPTER 42

TALCOTT PARSONS

Communism and the West: The Sociology of the Conflict

Without underestimating the seriousness of the elements of conflict between the two systems of social organization which seem to dominate the contemporary scene, I should like to use this opportunity to suggest a few respects in which the dichotomy is more relative than it tends to be painted in the ideological interchanges from both sides and to present reasons why there may be a better prospect of an eventual resolution than appears on the surface.

In spite of the very hard things which have been said on both sides which seem to imply absolute irreconcilability; both are outcomes of the same basic cultural roots; both are involved in promoting the social changes which have come to be called "modernization"; and, I venture to say, both in the last analysis are concerned with promotion of a general pattern of "human freedom and welfare" which transcends their differences. It will sometime become clear that on both sides there is more concern with the substance of this welfare than with whether it has been arrived at by our path or by theirs. Clearly this implies that the two paths in fact converge more than is generally realized.

Let us attempt to formulate what seem to be the principal issues between the systems, issues which are only imperfectly expressed in their respective ideological pronouncements. Then let us try to explore a little bit the paths by which the main forces of social change are making for convergence which, under favorable conditions (which are possible but by no means necessary), may lead to an eventual integration in a wider system which includes both.

This paper is published here for the first time.

It is an essential premise of this analysis that movements and conflicts of this magnitude are involved with the great developmental trends and stages of social change. There would be little doubt that in this case it is in the broadest sense the industrial revolution and its consequences which are the focus of the problem. The process has of course been going on for some two centuries, and even now is far from complete, even in the most advanced countries of its development. However complex the variegated threads which run through the history of industrialization, there seem to be some main trends. The focal one is perhaps the increase of productivity through the division of labor and technological advancement, including of course effective organization of the factors of production. This promises an altogether new level of facilities available in society for *whatever* purposes may be valued. These purposes, however, may on a general level be classified as economic "welfare," whatever the reference to group or subgroup, and political—in an analytical sense broader than governmental—power. In the former context, a major reference is to the egalitarian spread of welfare to the masses of a population—the "end of the line" in this sense being consumption standards.

Beyond this, of course, the facilities available for a variety of functions other than individual consumption become increasingly important in any society which is strongly impressed by developmental possibilities. The continuing furtherance of economic productivity itself must figure prominently in this picture. Then comes the concern for the foundations of power, both at the level of collective units within a given politically organized system, pre-eminently the territorial "state," and the political power of such units *vis-à-vis* each other. Of course the symbol and a pre-eminently central intrinsic fact is the impact of this general increase in economic effectiveness on the technology of war and hence the absolute imperativeness of commanding an industrial economy for any territorial unit which claims to "count" in the higher power struggle of the international world.

The basic desirability of industrialization can hardly be said to be in question; it seems to be assumed as one of the central givens of the modern world—somewhat surprisingly, in view of the recent vogue of the doctrine of an indefinite relativity of values. Thus, from the communist point of view, the essential immorality of capitalism does not consist in its having abandoned the virtues of preindustrial economic systems; nor, from the other side is it the "crime" of Soviet Russia to have promoted industrialization. Quite the contrary on both sides, as is evidenced by the continuing stress in Soviet pronouncements on their imminent "catching up" with the United States and a less obvious, sometimes indeed grudging, Western admiration for Soviet achievements.

The primary issues, then, are two, which are related to each other in a complex way. These are the distribution of the benefits of the process on the one hand, the mechanisms by which it is to be controlled on the other. Each of these issues needs, however, to be carefully interpreted and interrelated. The basic reference point is the "politically organized society," *i.e.,* the territorial unit which has been more-or-less of a "national state." The original socialist definition was internal to this unit and hence spoke of the "working class" as the claimant to an enhanced share of distributive benefits. In fact, however, the most important tendency of the socialist movement has not been directed to raising the relative standards of living of the working classes within predominantly socialist countries, but rather to bring new and previously underdeveloped countries under the socialist movement and accelerating their economic development. This naturally has been accompanied by a strongly antagonistic attitude toward the traditional elites of these countries. Hence, they could be said to be working class societies in one sense, namely that the new dominant groups—party people, managerial groups, and "intellectuals"—were predominantly recruited from the old lower or middle classes. On the other hand, the tendency has not been to any very pronounced internal egalitarianism—rather, to a subordination of consumption interests generally to those of rapid industrialization and political power position.

This problem presents the first major case of complication of the pattern of conflict. This results from the fact that, in the societies where the industrialization process had taken hold previous to and independent of the socialist movement, there has been a process of diffusion of the benefits to the population as a whole, including the working classes, and hence not only a generalized rise in living standards, but a substantial diminution in the inequalities of the preindustrial persists. There seem to have been three main aspects of this "equalization," which is a phase of a more general process of upgrading of standards. The one which has been most discussed is, of course, that of "consumption," with no further questions asked. The second is "welfare," in the sense of direct action, either by the state or by lower-class organized groups, such as trade unions, to alleviate their difficulties. The third, which is most likely to be overlooked in these discussions, is the increasing participation of lower groups in the general growth, not only through opportunities for upward mobility, but through the generalization of levels of education and access to cultural goods of various sorts.

Very generally, the trend in the "capitalistic" societies—*i.e.,* those which have combined industrialization (thus Spain is dubiously capitalistic in this sense) with continuity of control and status on the part of non-"working-class" elements—has been, contrary to the Marxian predictions, clearly one of both absolute and relative upgrading of the lower elements; lower first by the standards of standard of living and relative political power, but beyond that of levels of education, cultural interest, and the like.

This, of course, poses a critical problem for the action-collectivity which starts with espousal of a cause. If the problem is simply how to alleviate the condition of the "toiling masses," it may be that they do better within the

normal framework of a socalled "capitalistic" system than they have so far
and presumptively ever would under regimes which are ostensibly dedicated
to the interests of the "working classes."

From the "capitalistic" point of view, it is hence not unreasonable to suggest that there is a conspicuous tendency of Communist regimes to shift
away from the attempt to gain control by revolutionary overturn of the political machinery of the pioneering industrial societies, notably Britain, Germany, and the US, and instead to become the international role model for
the process of *new* industrialization. This can then be interpreted as a "con-
fession" that the original position was an untenable one, that there is indeed no inherent tendency to "exploitation" in the capitalistic system, but
that what the communists say they want would emerge anyway and "why
all the fuss"? Indeed, the case can be pressed one stage further by pointing
out that there is also a strong tendency to extension of the "metropolitan"
pattern of benefits to the internal lower elements, to that of upgrading of the
external dependencies under metropolitan control.

It will probably never be possible to decide the question of whether the
desired developments would or would not have occurred "anyway," or
under what circumstances and on what time schedule. However that may
be, the accumulating sense of urgency of such a goal as not only industrialization, but its spread with maximal distributive emphasis, has in fact led to
a polarization, on the one hand and more weakly *within* political societies,
on the other hand and more drastically *between* them. The internal "class
struggle" was for a time a major factor in Western continental Europe, less
intense in Great Britain, and least in the United States, where social conflicts
are well known but have never been clearly polarized about industrial production in the strict Marxian sense.

Externally, however, the polarization has become much more marked as
between socalled "imperialist" and "colonial" countries, and surely this
rather than the internal one is the polarity which dominates the current
scene, with of course the expected "feedback" of a counterimperialism,
namely that of the control of "satellites" by the previously anti-imperialist
powers.

The process I have emphasized, of gradual extension of the benefits of
industrialization to the previously disadvantaged classes and nations, has on
the whole occurred by relatively undramatic processes, so that it could appear to be a matter of gradual erosion of the earlier positions. On the other
side, there has been the sense of immediate urgency on which I have remarked and a certain pre-eminent position in the range of ideological justification. Broadly, the socialists have, with respect to the industrial complex,
been the "young men in a hurry," who have professsed not to believe that
their slower elders really "meant it" that the general pattern of industrialization—with respect not only to total productivity, but to distribution and
the other aspects of the process—would be implemented.

The combination of being in a hurry and of basic distrust of the older "parental" auspices of the process provides the setting for what we have called the problems of political control. Being in a hurry places the immediate goals of industrialization and its concomitants in the paramount position, and distrusting the parental auspices has been interpreted to mean that the movement for implementing these goals in a hurry must be declared to be absolutely independent of any connection with the older system.

The communist system is not, however, basically divergent from the more general normative pattern of Western civilization; indeed, *vis-à-vis* the world outside the latter, it functions as one primary symbol and agency of westernization. In relation to its parent system, however, it comes into an acute conflict at one major point, namely that of the system of political control over both the process of economic development itself and the allocation of claims to the utilization of the products of the developmental process. The older "capitalistic" system is permissive and pluralistic in these respects, whereas the insurgent "socialistic" system is not only suspicious of all competing claims, but tends to repress them entirely in the interest of a monolithic centralized control—claiming that all limitations on this are, if internally oriented, "exploitation" of the working class by "monopoly" interests, if external, "imperialistic" exploitation of the weak and underdeveloped. What are some of the structural antecedents of this conflict?

The key fact is of course that the initial processes of what we are calling industrialization occurred under the auspices of "private enterprise," *i.e.,* not of political authority which could be presumed to represent the "public interest." From the point of view of the institutional matrix within which it developed, this could readily be interpreted as usurping the prerogatives of the public interest in favor of private "self"-interest. It was an innovative process of fateful scope and importance which took place within a range of public permissiveness, rather than directly in the name of a public interest.

The key concept here came to be that of *property*. It has been common to think of this as in some sense a simple "economic" category. But the main problem at issue is precisely what is meant by economic? In terms of institutional development, I think the best characterization of property is as that aspect of *political* authority—or power—which has not been kept in or absorbed in, as the case may be, the authority of government. It is the private sphere of power, which in turn serves to *control* what in a more specifically analytical sense should be called the economic aspect of societal function. To this extent Marxian theory is right; capitalism is essentially a "political" phenomenon, in that it is founded on authority to control the process of production, and this control in turn operates through the institution of property. The basic capitalist–socialist difference is, seen in these terms, a political difference, as between a diffused and a centralized distribution of power. The common presumption of course is the desirability of industrial level economic development, and a "just" distribution of benefits and opportunities.

Capitalist production was first defined as political by Marx when it became clear, in the nineteenth century, that the typical unit of production was no longer either the individual or his immediate household—as in peasant agriculture—but included an employed class. This feature has of course not only remained, but been vastly increased and ramified, with the development of largescale organization of what Max Weber called the "bureaucratic" aspect of modern capitalism. What has become attenuated is not the employment of labor by organizations, but the monolithic unity of the employed class as "workers" and the character of the managerial control over them. Here "property" in the older simple sense has ceased to be the primary focus of control; and whereas, in the case of private enterprise, property has continued to play its part, it is no longer the simple private aspect of political power that it once was.

The basic issue now is no longer as such the prerogatives of "ownership" but the modes and degrees of autonomy which are to be exercised by the management and fiduciary controls of organizations, centering in the sphere of economic production to be sure, but ramifying into the fields of education, research, welfare functions, and various others what in the Western world we call the "private, nonprofit sector." Socialism therefore presents an issue of "political liberty," in the sense of the relation of functionally important operating units of the social system to the central decision-making authority. For understandable historic reasons, there is in the West a deepseated moral valuation of rights of autonomy in these spheres, though perhaps it is correct to say also a certain pragmatism in attitudes toward the proper line of division between governmental and private agency in promoting legitimate functions. It is by no means a matter of whether it must be one or the other. A good example would be the sharing of responsibility for higher education in the United States between public state and privately endowed universities.

The problem, being political, is not however confined to the relations of operative units, notably of economic production, to central authority. It also concerns the political machinery of control over governmental authority as such, namely the question of "dictatorship" *versus* "democracy" in the Western sense. Property, in the sense in which it came to be the focal "enemy" of socialism, was a basis of *diffuse superiority* within the society, which may be compared to that of the religious orders within the Catholic church, or to hereditary aristocracy in postmedieval Europe. Socialism is aimed basically at abolishing the two-class system which is involved in the concept of a duality between the propertied (the "proprietors") and the propertyless worker. We have suggested that the internal process of the free enterprise system itself has, in the industrially advanced countries, been eliminating or at the least very greatly attenuating this duality.

The socialist path has, however, been to deprive private property of its power of control altogether by transferring it to government. The effect of course is not to abolish power, but to fuse the two main sectors of the power-system, the public and the private, into one. Socialist ideology has tended to claim that they always were essentially one, in that under "capitalism," government can have no genuine independence but is only in Marx's famous phrase, the "executive committee of the bourgeoisie"—a claim which is surely at best an oversimplification. This fusion, however, necessarily means a great increase in the power of government and hence again raises the question of "who is to control the controllers"?

All three of the great "reform" movements of postmedieval Western history, starting with the "Reformation" itself, have produced radical groups who have undertaken to impose their interpretation of the correct position on others, by gaining control of major political units and drastically reorganizing them. In the case of the Reformation it was the Calvinist branch which in this sense was the most radical, in the era of the democratic Revolutions it was the Jacobins, and in the socialist period it is of course the Communists.

In all three of these cases a drastically difficult position was assumed, in that in effect a *self*-appointed elite has claimed the right to control the system as a whole, whether it be in the name of a "Divine mandate" through predestinarian election, in the name of Rousseau's "general will" of the people, or in the name of the "historic mission" of the proletariat. In this process, of course, not only are the prerogatives of private property carried away but, with them, for the time being, legally protected civil liberties against both government and political democracy.

In the same sense in which strict Calvinism and Jacobinism were short-lived, it seems as certain as such things can be that Communism also will prove to be short-lived. The basis of this judgment is the hypothesis, first of all, that iron dictatorship of a self-appointed elite cannot be legitimized in the long run. Even more than other comparable movements the Communist is bound to be deeply undermined by its own success; its drastic controls can in the nature of the case apply only to the transition to the desired state, not to the state itself, as is quite explicit in the ideology. On the other hand, the orthodox Communist view of the outcome, the "withering away" not only of the state, but even more important, presumably also of the party, simply cannot happen. This is the strictly utopian element in the movement (which has never been better analyzed than by Ernst Troeltsch in the discussion of Marx in his *Historimus*). So long as there is human society there will always be government, with coercive powers and law which imposes *binding* obligations. The question is not the existence of these institutions, but their character and the modes in which they are controlled.

Just as Calvinism in time gave way to a more "liberal" Protestantism which acknowledged that all men of faith could have access to Divine

Grace and Jacobinism gave way (considerably more quickly) to the conception of political democracy which has given real power to an electorate based on universal adult suffrage, so it seems a safe prediction that Communism will, from its own internal dynamics, evolve in the direction of the restoration—or where it has not yet existed, the institution—of political democracy. The basic dilemma of the Communists is that it is not possible in the long run either to legitimize dictatorship of the Party or to abolish all governmental and legal controls of behavior, as the "withering-away" doctrine would have it. Political democracy is the *only* possible outcome—except for general destruction or breakdown.

In the light of these considerations, one of the most conspicuous features of the Communist story becomes particularly significant, namely that it has not gained ascendancy in a *single* political society where the process of industrialization has become advanced under "capitalist" auspices. Indeed, as Seymour Martin Lipset in particular has made clear,[1] there is a close relation between such advancement and the decline of political radicalism of the left, a situation which of course stands in direct contradiction to the Marxian predictions. It is of course our view that this can only very partially be explained by the strengthening of vested interests opposed to change, usually referred to as "monopoly capitalism"; the most important explanation is that through industrial development under democratic auspices, the most important legitimately-to-be-expected aspirations of the "working class" have in fact been realized.

Besides the centrally important matter of political democracy, there is reason to believe that in other respects the trend of change in communist societies is likely to be in a direction which converges with that of the Western world. Two of these trends may be mentioned. One is the pressure for increasing autonomy of the proponents of elements of culture other than political ideology itself, notably in science and the arts, but also including traditional religion, which, though pushed into a very subordinate place, is by no means dead—for example, in the Soviet Union. The most immediately powerful of these is science, because of its strategic importance to the industrialization process itself and to military technology. There seems to be inherent in the professions of science and the fields of its application, a tendency to become autonomous relative to *any* centralized system of control. In the decisively important sphere of technical competence, no one can compete with the scientist except his own peers in the field. Basically, a major component of responsibility for science and its uses must focus in the scientists themselves and cannot be carried out by persons lacking in this competence. Since, however, a modern society develops not one but many sciences and since totalitarian political control is necessarily centralized, the increasing importance of science cannot but have a centrifugal

---

[1] *See* Seymour M. Lipset, *Political Man* (New York: Doubleday, 1959).

effect on the social system, the development of centers of power independent of the central authority. Not least important here is extension of scientific patterns into the sphere of social phenomena themselves where science comes into direct competition with ideology.

Similar considerations apply more generally to the effects of the increasing division of labor, which operate in the direction of pluralism. We already hear of problems of complicated balances of power among groups in Soviet society, *e.g.,* the Party, the "bureaucrats" of the central government, the industrial managers, the military establishment, the intellectuals, scientists, artists, and the like. It can, I think, be definitely said that the further this differentiation of the social structure proceeds, the more difficult it becomes to press it into the mold of a rigid line of authority from the top down.

There is one further aspect of the Communist movement, which in a broad way is shared with socialism generally, which deserves comment. This is the fact that, though by no means alone, it has been one of the main forces working for the transcending of the older conceptions of nationalism. It is with justice referred to as the *international* Communist movement, which from the point of view of the antagonists makes it all the more formidable, but seen in a broader perspective may well be a major agency in the integration of society on wider bases. It is not unimportant that the two principal antagonists of the present world conflict are something more than nation-states in the nineteenth-century European sense, both are more-or-less "continental" polities, and both, in different ways, have worked out modes of assimilation of ethnically and otherwise diverse elements, the US through the absorbtion of mass immigration of very diverse origins, the USSR through assimilating the populations of many different federated republics. It is not surprising that our own time has seen another major attempt at international "community" in the British Commonwealth and just now is seeing the emergence of the European Common Market, with its tendencies toward political as well as economic integration. Without these lower level integrations beyond the earlier national level, it is doubtful that even the relative and qualified success of the United Nations to date could have been possible.

The basic conclusion seems to me clear, simple, and of the utmost importance. It is simply that the present major polarization of the world is not the collision between two deeply alien cultural and societal trends, but a conflict between two very closely related ones. They have diverged relatively recently—after all, Karl Marx was a German Jew who spent most of his mature life in England and whose ideas were built on the pre-eminently British classical enonomics and the German philosophical idealism of Hegel. Similarly, there is already clearly discernible a major process of convergence by which on the one hand the "social gains" of the Western democracies have already gone far to bring the older working class fully into the general social community, and, on the other hand the Communist world, notably in Soviet Russia, has already begun to move away from the rigid patterns which were the source of the most serious conflict of institutional structure with the Western world.

This is not to underestimate the seriousness of the difficulties and dangers of our world. Conflicts of interest, of nations, and of supranational groups of course remain. But the most dangerous feature of the developing Cold War situation has not been this, but the tendency to polarization which may be interpreted to be leading toward a head-on collision between two "moral crusades," each party feeling that absolute right was on its side and absolute evil on that of its opponents. The convergent trend of the development of social structures and their attendant cultures makes the further deepening of *this* order of antagonism unlikely, though the dangers involved in retreating from positions already taken—on both sides—should not be underestimated.

PART VI

PROCESSES OF CHANGE

Initiation, Diffusion, Termination

CHAPTER 43

Introduction

Every process has a beginning, a middle, and an end—which is hardly a revelation, but does provide a helpful way of organizing some insights concerning modes of change. The following discussions deal with the conditions under which social changes are initiated, spread from the initial sector or sectors to others (rarely do all parts of a society change simultaneously), and finally, in one way or another, terminated. With few exceptions, the statements made in this section, though they are illustrated by application to one specific kind of social change, are applicable to a variety of social processes on several levels and in different institutional spheres. In this sense they are general. On the other hand, they are limited in scope, since, unlike classical or contemporary theories, they do not provide broad analytical frameworks but just one or two elements of such constructions.

Underlying the analysis of most processes described in this section is the assumption that the various parts of any social system are interdependent, so that changes in one sector will be followed by strains which necessitate adjustive changes in other sectors if the social system is to maintain its viability. This seems to be the basic common denominator of the various viewpoints represented.

The beginning of social change is to a large degree a response to the presence of some degree of social disorganization, caused either internally or externally. This is just another way of saying that strains in a social system call for new adjustments. A well-integrated social system, in which needs are effectively fulfilled and men are largely satisfied, is rather rare. This is especially true of modern society, which tends to contain a comparatively high amount of social disorganization, because of its size and complexity and the rapid pace of change generated in part as a response to earlier disorganization. Hence, the central question for the student of modern society is not, "Is there social disorganization?" for which the answer is invariably, "Yes, there is," but rather, "What is its scope, what institutional areas are affected, how strategic are the affected areas, and is disorganization accelerating or subsiding?" Faris' analysis suggests that presentday processes of disorganization, while still accelerating, can be expected to slow down. For even though many forms of disorganization are a byproduct of modern life itself, their unusual upsurge is related not to modern society but to modernization. The crest of these disruptions coincides with the transition from a preindustrial, folk society to an industrial urban one; the crest subsides with the stabilization of a modern society in which at least some change is routine. This is not to say that the present forms of disorganization will disappear. Furthermore, it is quite likely that new forms of disorganization will emerge as the result of further technological advances and international tensions.

Warfare raises the possibility that disorganization or disintegration will proceed to such an extent that a society will cease to exist due to physical destruction or absorption by another society. Although warfare is not the only process by which one society can be absorbed by another, this phenomenon is uncommon, and as a rule disorganization tends to assume less extreme forms. When disorganization occurs, there is a likelihood that some responses will be generated in an attempt to check or to counter it. The kind of responses generated depend on the type, strength, and scope of disorganization. Frequently the regular mechanisms of social control are sufficient to check it. Disorganization, for instance, might generate dissatisfaction on the part of individuals, resulting in what March and Simon call "search behavior."[1] But the discontent of individuals rarely becomes a threat to the system, unless it finds expression in the "search behavior" of a group or of groups, and the decisiveness of the latter process depends on the number, size, strategic power, and communication positions of these groups.

When disorganization grows to the degree that it can no longer be contained within the prevailing system, attempts at reorganization are likely to be made, sometimes involving farreaching changes of the social structure. In these cases, "search behavior" of groups may result in social movements advocating and implementing basic changes. If the advocated changes are blocked rather than accepted by the regime, a revolutionary potential is created, and the social movements are likely to become revolutionary movements. Note, though, that Brinton, studying the uniformities of revolutions, sees revolutionary movements as originating not in the despair of totally crushed groups, but in the discontent of groups on their way up whose further ascent has been wholly or partially blocked. Usually, many intellectuals and some members of the upper classes desert the existing regime and join the revolutionary forces. When forces, so fortified, are confronted with a government that is inflexible and inefficient, a revolution is likely to occur.

Revolution is by no means the only method for effecting basic social change, although its dramatic character inevitably attracts much attention.

---

[1] James G. March and Herbert A. Simon, *Organizations* (New York: John Wiley & Sons, 1958), Ch. 7.

Other farreaching changes are introduced gradually, when the government and/or the ruling classes, apprehensive of the increasing pressures and responsive to the needs of various social groups, meet them halfway. Bismarck first outlawed the Social Democrats, but then, in effect, introduced a large portion of their platform into his legislation. Disraeli, the Conservative prime minister of Great Britain, in his competition with the liberal Whigs over the lower-class vote, initiated much social legislation. The famous Industrial Revolution was no revolution at all, but rather a gradual process of change that lasted two generations (approximately 1760-1830). In this period, Britain was transformed from a traditional and agricultural to a modern and industrial society, without any major outbreaks of violence or overthrow of government and despite considerable disorganization. In short, reform is a major mode of response to acute social needs and to social disorganization. Only when the ruling classes or the government do not adequately adjust the social structure to mounting needs and demands does alienation and social disorganization accumulate to such a degree that a revolutionary potential is accumulated. When the pace of social adjustment required is rapid—let us say, due to quick succession of changes in the social environment—few governments are likely to respond by adequate reforms.

Viewing the initiation of processes of social change—either revolutions or reforms—largely as a response to social disorganization, caused either internally or externally, implies that change is the outcome of an interplay among a variety of factors. Some factors are mere background conditions, while others are more closely related to the initiation of change. In addition, there often is a definite event that actually precipitates a major social change. Discussing the role of such a precipitant, MacIver points out that it should not be viewed in isolation, as the sole generator of social change, but rather in conjunction with the entire system as it is being changed. Frequently, the precipitant appears to be the decisive factor in bringing about a drastic change, while in fact the system was "ripe," and the specific event only "triggered" rather than "caused" the transformation. However, the precipitant is not without importance, since it exerts an influence on the timing and concrete manifestation of the particular change and thus plays a not negligible role in altering the course of events.

Turning from the conditions and factors of change to change itself, we recognize that each process which involves a new pattern of behavior, new attitudes, new techniques, etc. might be referred to as an innovation. This is the case whatever the nature of the change, whether introduced violently or peacefully, abruptly or gradually, by a sudden occurrence or after long preparation. The term "innovation" suggests that deliberation has taken place, but actually, as Kallen points out, this is not necessarily the case.[2]

---

[2] The terms "invention" and "discovery" as used by Linton cover roughly the same ground as the term "innovation" as discussed by Kallen.

While some innovators consciously plan their innovations, others may not seek to innovate at all and may not be aware of doing so. Innovation may be spontaneous or unconscious, unplanned, and even undesired; so long as a new pattern of human thought or action has emerged, an innovation has occurred.

Innovation and acceptance of innovation do not occur at random, but depend on the urgency of social needs, the degree of disorganization, as well as the flexibility of society and the degree to which change has been institutionalized. As a rule, the more dynamic a society, the more tolerant it is toward innovation. Whereas traditional societies actively suppress innovation, modern societies actively encourage it. But, as Kallen points out, even in modern society innovation encounters resistance, due to emotional investment in old patterns and distrust of new ones. Linton demonstrates that even in the same society not all innovations stand an equal chance of being accepted. In order to be accepted an innovation must be in line with a society's needs and interests, and it must be compatible with the society's existing framework. Modern society, for instance, is unlikely to pay attention to innovations in the field of magic, but is likely to encourage innovations in the field of science and technology. In fact, innovation in these areas is highly institutionalized. Universities, industries, and the military establish special research divisions and devote large amounts of resources to the search for new information and its application. Part of the education system, especially scientific training, is geared to the encouragement of innovations. Once an innovation is favorably judged, special divisions (*e.g.,* development units in corporations) are devoted to its implementation and to promoting its acceptance in society (marketing and advertising). In some cases, not only the new product but even the need for it is produced.

Acceptance of innovations is really nothing more than the receiving end of the diffusion of an innovation. The term diffusion has been used mostly to indicate the spread of items from one culture to another. But the term diffusion applies here also, and is used to refer to the spread of an item within a culture—from the innovator to a group, from one group to another. Crosscultural diffusion is discussed in Part II by Kroeber in his analysis of the diffusionist approach. We included here an empirical study about intracultural diffusion. The article by Coleman, Menzel, and Katz traces the diffusion of a medical innovation—more specifically, a new drug —among physicians. Analysis of the data collected suggests, as the authors point out, that the physician's readiness to use a new drug, *i.e.,* his tendency to accept an innovation, is a function not only of his individual traits, but also of his relations with other physicians. The more integrated he is in the community of physicians, the sooner will he accept the new drug.

Like the concept of diffusion, the principle of accumulation deals with the spread of an innovation as the process of social change moves from the sector in which it was initiated to other sectors. Myrdal's central claim is that by the very fact that a process starts rolling, it gains additional momentum, that change in one sector triggers changes in others. The importance of this insight in the particular area Myrdal studied, that of race relations, lies in that there is a vicious circle in which discrimination makes for lower education, which makes for less employment opportunities, which makes for a lower standard of living, all of which, in turn increase (and "justify") discrimination, and so on. Myrdal's point is that if one could break into this circle at any one place, bring about an improvement in any one of the sectors, this in turn would bring about cumulative improvements. This raises some questions: Will any initial "push" do to start the process rolling, or must it have a certain magnitude? And, if the latter, how does one establish what it is? Are all factors equally potent in setting the cumulative process in motion or are some more potent than others? And finally, how far can the momentum thus gained carry a process such as desegregation?

Ogburn addresses himself to the same general problems of change in one sector expanding to other sectors. Ogburn's basic assumption, like that of the other authors in this section is, that the various parts of a sociocultural system or subsystem are interrelated, hence changes in one sector necessitate adaptive changes in others. But unlike the previous authors, he is concerned with the gap in time between the initial changes and the adaptive responses. This cultural (or social) lag makes for maladjustments in the society in which it occurs—the longer the lag, the greater the strain—so that eventually, if the lags occur in significant spheres, the society faces the possibility of complete or partial disintegration.

An altogether different question is whether there is one single sector or set of sectors that always leads and others that always lag, or whether different sectors lead in different processes of social change. Ogburn puts more stress on cases where material factors change first and cultural factors adapt, but he points out that it is also possible for nonmaterial factors to start the process of change.

Since the time period in which the change in one sector has already occurred but adaptive changes in other sectors have not yet taken place is, as Ogburn points out, a period of maladjustment, the question is raised of whether many such strains could not be significantly reduced by adequate planning. On the other hand, it might be feared that planning, while reducing strain in one sphere, would increase strain in other spheres by entailing excessive restrictions on the individual.

The question of what is the optimal degree of social planning is a highly controversial issue because it involves questions concerning the social conditions of freedom, socialism *versus* free enterprise, etc. Mannheim's concern is the construction of a viable democratic system that will combine planning with freedom. In his contribution, Mannheim stresses that democracy must be secured by planning. While at a previous stage, freedom was a synonym for *laissez-faire,* at the present stage freedom can no longer be left to the interplay of random forces; provision must be made for it. Society must be planned, and freedom must be incorporated in the plan itself. Thus, planning and freedom would not exclude each other; rather, "planning for freedom is the only logical form of freedom which remains."

The idea of combining freedom and planning is now well established in practice, though many people still find the theory unacceptable. Even in the societies most committed to free enterprise, a combination of progressive income tax, governmental spending on welfare, regulatory commissions, antitrust laws, and labor acts set clear and deliberate limits to the play of economic and social forces. Even in the societies most committed to central planning, the idea of total planning has been relinquished, and large pockets of free enterprise are tolerated, especially in agriculture, small business, and services. Other freedoms, as that of scientific research and artistic expression, pose constant dilemmas in these latter societies. The problem each society struggles with is no longer whether to combine freedom with planning, but where to draw the line.

The question of how a process starts and how it spreads has been raised much more frequently than the question of how it terminates. As the study of termination develops, one would expect a certain symmetry to emerge; parallel to the question of what launched a process would be the question of what stopped it. The question: "Was the process initiated in all spheres simultaneously, and if not, in what spheres did it start and which spheres 'lagged' behind?" could be matched by the question: "Did the process cease in all spheres at the same time, and if not, in which sphere did it cease first?" This is not to say that the pattern of termination must be symmetrical with the pattern of initiation. Often, initiation may come first in one sphere, while termination may emerge from an altogether different sphere, or the factors making for termination may be unrelated to the factors making for initiation. Sometimes, as can be seen from Coser's study, a process may cease because it has exhausted itself or because the point of termination is institutionalized as part of the process itself. Furthermore, some processes may go on "indefinitely," ceasing only with the distintegration of one or more of the units by which they are carried. In other cases a process which could otherwise go on, provides opportunities at which it can be deliberately stopped.

The termination of conflict, studied by Coser, can take any one of these forms: a duel, for instance, has an institutionalized termination point; a quarrel, on the other hand, may go on until both sides have reached a point of exhaustion; war may continue until one or both of the contending parties cease to exist. In this sphere, in which the continuation of the process may make for the destruction of one or more of the units which perpetuate it, institutionalized or deliberate termination is of course of special interest.

Termination, it must be noted, need not be final. After a certain interval, the process may be resumed. There is also the possibility that the termination point of one process serves as the initiation point of another process and that the factors making for the termination of the old process are also the factors which bring about the initiation of the new process. Kaplan's article links the study of termination with the study of initiation. When certain rules of equilibrium are transgressed, the present system ceases to exist, and a new system comes into being. This transformation does not occur at random, but follows certain patterns. One can delineate a universe of possible structures of a given system. Kaplan presents six such possible structures, as sufficient for the effective study of international relations. Once such a universe of possible structures has been established, one can safely state that, when a system which has one of these structures is strained to the breaking point, one of the five others will emerge. (The breakdown of the system into its elementary units must be one possibility in any such universe of structures.) The next question is then: "Which of the other structures is likely to emerge, and to what degree can this be predicted on the basis of our knowledge of the present structure, of the strains making for its disintegration, and of the interstructural rules of transformation?"

Though Kaplan studies rules of transformation on the level of international systems, there is no reason why his method cannot be applied to other social systems. Thus one could predict that if a modern democracy were to disintegrate, either anarchy would prevail or a totalitarian regime would emerge, which would be controlled either from the inside or, to varying degrees, from the outside (though there is always at least a logical possibility of the resurrection of the initial structure). One could then analyze the conditions under which each of the possible structures would emerge; *e.g.,* when is the fall of a democracy more likely to lead to anarchy, when to dictatorship.

The study of the rules of transformation adds an entirely new dimension to the exploration of social change. Many earlier studies analyzed change *in* a structure or *of* a structure, but had little to say about what new structure would emerge if an existing one were to disintegrate. While a notion of rules of transformation might be too stringent for sociological theory at this stage, it seems that movement in this direction constitutes one of the most promising lines of thought and research for the whole area of social change.

Drawing on insights like those represented earlier in this part, Etzioni suggests a model for the functional analysis of one type of process from its initiation to its termination. The conditions under which political unification proceeds are explored, the development of supranational communities serving as a prime example. The development of a new unit is viewed as a multilevel process that proceeds on the performance, communication, and power level, though not necessarily at an even pace. The epigenesis of supranational communities is studied in terms of its initiation and takeoff points, its expansion through secondary priming, and the various states at which the process might come to rest or be terminated. Like many other ideas reported in this final part of the volume, the present contribution, though directed toward the specific problem of supranational unification, applies also to other processes of social change.

Initiation

CHAPTER 44

ROBERT E. L. FARIS

Contemporary and Prospective Social Disorganization

As a sociological concept, disorganization refers to the failure of institutional mechanisms, to the disintegration of the bonds and controls which make social teamwork carry out its functions. Total disorganization means the disappearance of the group or organization as an entity. Partial disorganization—far more common in actual occurrence—refers to some defectiveness in the social organization which results in incomplete fulfilling of its functions.

The transition from primitive to civilized society has brought with it the reduction and even the elimination of many of the natural perils which early man constantly faced. Modern man has approached the long-sought states of freedom from hunger, from wild animals, from diseases and other natural dangers. But in place of these ancient menaces, there has arisen the far greater threat of extreme social disorganization, which has at least the possibility of destroying the human race. The contemporary danger to man is man himself, but not as an individual. The great menace lies in the possibility that in his corporate relation to others he may bring things to an end through either destruction or neglect.

Contemporary Forms of Social Disorganization

There is justification for the rich and fruitful sociological interest that has been shown in the standard forms of urban pathology, for these ex-

From Robert E. L. Faris, "Contemporary and Prospective Social Disorganization," *Sociology and Social Research,* XXXII (1948), No. 3. Reprinted by permission of the author and the University of Southern California Press.

pressions of social disorganization are sources of heavy costs, much misery, and even menace to the general fabric of society. Furthermore, each decade brings an increase, sometimes almost spectacular, in the incidence of these conditions. Crime, for instance, involves an annual cost to the United States which runs into billions of dollars. No figures are available to define a trend for all types of crime; but if Federal Bureau of Investigation figures on such conventional crimes (as reported to police) as burglary, robbery, auto theft, and the like are representative, the population of our nation is now more lawless than ever, for the figures for 1946 broke all previous records, in some cases by a large amount.[1]

The trend for mental disorders continues upward, reflecting various defects in the social mechanism which ordinarily produces and supports normality of mind and behavior. Although figures for hospitalization cannot be considered as accurate reflections of incidence of psychoses, the increases have been such as to make it highly unlikely that growing recognition and hospitalization facilities alone could account for them. Some years ago a shocking calculation was made that, in New York State at least, one person in twenty may be expected to spend some time in a mental hospital during his life. . . .

The situation is somewhat similar for the other conventional urban types of disorganization. The rise in the divorce rate is well known. . . . Suicide has had a long upward trend, usually temporarily interrupted by warfare, but accelerated by depressions. Vice behavior is difficult to measure, but rates for alcoholism, drug addiction, gambling, and minor vices are probably also on an irregular upward trend.

•

In still another aspect of modern life, that of government, the disorganization has been notable, though not so invariably progressing. During the past quarter of a century most urban governments in the United States have been corrupt at least in certain aspects, and in a few cases the disintegration approached the point of inability to function. Scandals in county, state, and even federal governments have been common enough to reveal an inadequacy in the total political process. The degree of such corruption has not yet been great enough to constitute a general danger to the survival of the United States, although the example of the fall of France stands to warn of the consequences of political fragility in a hostile world.

---

[1] In a news release of August, 1946, FBI figures showed a six-month increase in major crimes (in 1,997 cities with a total population of 66 million) from 460,303 to 520,307.

•

The Main Causes of Modern Disorganization

Present evidence does not force the student to an acceptance of the despondent outlook of the cosmic historians who foresee the downfall of modern man. It is true that most of the trends mentioned above have appeared to move in a single direction, but an examination of the underlying processes which produce them suggests that at least part of the disruption is related to conditions which are probably only temporary.

Many of the conventional urban forms of social pathology are clearly related to the fact of rapid population increase and city growth—an aspect of human history which cannot last indefinitely. Related to these processes is the unprecedented swiftness of the settling of the North American continent, involving at the peak an immigration of over a million persons a year.

These population changes are aspects of a great transition that has a beginning and an end. It is the change from preindustrial folk society to urban civilization. The population increase appears to occur as a result of the differential rates at which the civilization process affects birth and death rates. All primitive peoples live in a wasteful equilibrium of high birth and high death rates. Civilized populations have much lower rates of both kinds. But the fall of the death rate invariably occurs first, and in the interval before birth rates make their decline there occurs a spectacular population growth. This cycle has ended in certain European countries and is soon to end in the United States, when the present excess of women in the child bearing ages passes into the nonfertile years. Java, India, Russia, Argentina, and other regions are in the phase of rapid growth, and other nonindustrial regions have yet to begin the process.

Urban expansion may continue for a time beyond the period of total population growth, as rural populations, displaced by farm mechanization, flow to the cities. But rural birth rates are also falling—even faster than urban rates in the United States—and the rural manpower surplus will in time run out, possibly within a few decades. There is the possibility of continued growth by immigration from other countries, but this is slight unless there should occur a remarkable shift in political temper regarding immigration policy.

The previously mentioned forms of urban disorganization—professional organized crime, vice, suicide, mental disorders, family disorganization and the rest—all have their highest incidence in the slum areas of large cities. The causal connections differ in each case, but it seems clear that extreme disruption of the normal agencies of society, particularly the family and neighborhood primary groups, constitutes an important aspect of the causation of the pathological behavior. It is further evident that this disruption is

no inevitable consequence of poverty, but rather of the instability of residence, the novelty of city life to persons of rural and even foreign origin,
and the heterogeneity of cultural types—all of which result from the fact
of rapid growth. Cessation of growth promises to permit the development of
a kind of stability, in even the low-income urban population, which may be
found in old European cities but which is not a familiar phenomenon in
America.

This stability will not be merely a return to the settled form of social life
of earlier times, but will undoubtedly be a new equilibrium, evolved slowly
and adapted to an ever-changing modern urban civilization.

This does not of course mean instantaneous utopia. There will continue
to be crime, unhappy families, eccentric personalities; but the crimes will
probably be on the more manageable scale found, for example, in English
cities, whose relatively favorable crime conditions have often been errone-
ously attributed to superiority of police methods. And the other forms of
pathological behavior should also give far less threat of general catastrophe.

Processes of Reorganization

The historical origin of social disorganization may have been at the time
of, or shortly after, the development of trade relations between peoples of
different cultures. If so, disorganization has been developing continuously
for thousands of years. This is surely enough time to destroy civilization if
this process could do it; yet mankind lives on, for during all this period
there have been occurring, just as continually, certain anabolic social processes which have reorganized social relations almost, if not quite, as rapidly
as they have been broken down.

Sumner has described the slow, unwitting, trial-and-error process by
which new folkways, mores, and institutions arise and find their place in a
social organization. His discussion was written mainly in terms of early man
or preliterate peoples, but it should be recognized that folkways were not
merely generated once in the beginning of things, but are being continuously produced by the same means today as they were twenty thousand
years ago.

There is also a type of reorganization process which is not slow, continuous, and unwitting, but rather sudden, episodic and dramatic. In this
classification are found revivals, reform crusades, social movements, and
revolutions. These begin at a definite time and place, have leadership, consciousness of destiny, and deliberate invention of methods. There is of
course a trial-and-error process involved here too, for many movements rise,
all hoping to succeed, but few of them leave any lasting impression upon
the society. There are, however, so many of these efforts in critical periods
of history that it can be asserted that almost every conceivable solution gets
some actual trial. In the depression of the 1930's there were back-to-the-

farm movements of various kinds, currency reform movements, technocracy and similar developments, revolutionary and fascist movements, mystical and religious movements, and others by the hundreds. Some of these were resurrections, or imitations, of movements from earlier crises or from foreign lands; others—Townsend, Ham and Eggs, and the like—were novel inventions. Some died quickly; others found a steady and apparently permanent level of membership and, like the Townsend organization, remain today to exert a constant pressure on legislatures. Still others formed spores which lay dormant in southern California, preparing to resume growth when times become appropriate. It is only a few, such as the great revolutions of France and Russia, that succeed to the extent of making a sudden, drastic, and enduring alteration of a society.

But the assessment of the effects of social movements is best made in the aggregate and over a considerable period of time. . . . The New Deal may be regarded as the culmination of more than a century of social and political movements, including Granger, Populist, Silver, labor union, Wilson's New Freedom, and many others perhaps even unrecognized by officials of the New Deal administration. The eventual result of the many kinds of organized agitation could not easily have been foreseen a half century ago, nor is it easy today to know what eventual results will flow from the host of contemporary organizations for human betterment. Cause and effect are complex, and it can only be said that to counter the forces that disorganize a society in transition there occurs a broad general process that works toward reorganization and new equilibrium.

There is no intention here to suggest that final perfection is only five decades away. Even if our present forms of disorganization dwindle to insignificance we still have as a source of tragic concern a possibility of a War of the Hemispheres, which might well present examples of new degrees of social disorganization. Even without this catastrophe, there loom population crises in various parts of the world. And, finally, since there is no indication that technological advance will cease, it can be taken for granted that entirely novel forms of social disorganization will continue to arise and test our adaptiveness and ingenuity.

CHAPTER 45

CRANE BRINTON

The Anatomy of Revolution: Tentative Uniformities

We have studied four revolutions which on the surface seem to have certain resemblances, and deliberately avoided certain other types of revolution. Our four took place in the postmedieval Western world, were "popular" revolutions carried out in the name of "freedom" for a majority against a privileged minority, and were successful, that is, they resulted in the revolutionists becoming the legal government. Anything like a complete sociology of revolutions would have to take account of other kinds of revolution. . . .

When all necessary concessions are made to those who insist that events in history are unique, it remains true that the four revolutions we have studied do display some striking uniformities. Our conceptual scheme of the fever can be worked out so as to bring these uniformities clearly to mind. We shall find it worthwhile, in attempting to summarize the work of these revolutions, to recapitulate briefly the main points of comparison on which our uniformities are based.

We must be very tentative about the prodromal symptoms of revolution. Even retrospectively, diagnosis of the four societies we studied was very difficult, and there is little ground for belief that anyone today has enough knowledge and skill to apply formal methods of diagnosis to a contemporary society and say, in this case revolution will or will not occur shortly. But some uniformities do emerge from a study of the old regimes in England, America, France, and Russia.

First, these were all societies on the whole on the upgrade economically before the revolution came, and the revolutionary movements seem to originate in the discontents of not unprosperous people who feel restraint, cramp, annoyance, rather than downright crushing oppression. Certainly these revolutions are not started by down-and-outers, by starving, miserable people. These revolutionists are not worms turning, not children of despair. These revolutions are born of hope, and their philosophies are formally optimistic.

Second, we find in our prerevolutionary society definite and indeed very bitter class antagonisms, though these antagonisms seem rather more complicated than the cruder Marxists will allow. It is not a case of feudal nobility against bourgeoisie in 1640, 1776, and 1789 or of bourgeoisie against proletariat in 1917. The strongest feelings seem generated in the bosoms of men—and women—who have made money, or at least who have enough to live on, and who contemplate bitterly the imperfections of a socially privileged aristocracy. Revolutions seem more likely when social classes are fairly close together than when they are far apart. "Untouchables" very rarely revolt against a God-given aristocracy, and Haiti gives one of the few examples of successful slave revolutions. But rich merchants whose daughters can marry aristocrats are likely to feel that God is at least as interested in merchants as in aristocrats. It is difficult to say why the bitterness of feeling between classes *almost* equal socially seems so much stronger in some societies than others—why, for instance, a Marie Antoinette should be so much more hated in eighteenth-century France than a rich, idle, much publicized heiress in contemporary America; but at any rate the existence of such bitterness can be observed in our prerevolutionary societies, which is, clinically speaking, enough for the moment.

Third, there is the desertion of the intellectuals. This is in some respects the most reliable of the symptoms we are likely to meet. Here again we need not try to explain all the hows and whys, need not try to tie up the desertion of the intellectuals with a grand and complete sociology of revolutions. We need simply state that it can be observed in all four of our societies.

Fourth, the governmental machinery is clearly inefficient, partly through neglect—through a failure to make changes in old institutions; partly because new conditions—in the societies we have studied, conditions attendant on economic expansion and the growth of new monied classes, new ways of transportation, new business methods—these new conditions laid an intolerable strain on governmental machinery adapted to simpler, more primitive, conditions.

Fifth, the old ruling class—or rather, many individuals of the old ruling class—come to distrust themselves, or lose faith in the traditions and habits of their class, grow intellectual, humanitarian, or go over to the attacking groups. Perhaps a larger number of them than usual lead lives we shall have to call immoral, dissolute, though one cannot by any means be as sure about this as a symptom as about the loss of habits and traditions of command effective among a ruling class. At any rate, the ruling class becomes politically inept.

The dramatic events that start things moving, that bring on the fever of revolution, are in three of our four revolutions intimately connected with the financial administration of the state. In the fourth, Russia, the breakdown of administration under the burdens of an unsuccessful war is only in part financial. But in all our societies the inefficiency and inadequacy of the governmental structure of the society come out clearly in the very first stages of the revolution. There is a time—the first few weeks or months—when it looks as if a determined use of force on the part of the government might prevent the mounting excitement from culminating in an overthrow of the government. These governments attempted such a use of force in all four instances, and in all four their attempt was a failure. This failure indeed proved a turning point during the first stages and set up the revolutionists in power.

Yet one is impressed in all four instances more with the ineptitude of the governments' use of force than with the skill of their opponents' use of force. We are here speaking of the situation wholly from a military and police point of view. It may be that the majority of the people are discontented, loathe the existing government, wish it overthrown. Nobody knows. They don't take plebiscites *before* revolutions. In the actual clash—even Bastille Day, Concord, or the February Days in Petrograd—only a minority of the people is actively engaged. But the government hold over its own troops is poor, its troops fight half-heartedly or desert, its commanders are stupid, its enemies acquire a nucleus of the deserting troops or of a previous militia, and the old gives place to the new. Yet, such is the conservative and routine-loving nature of the bulk of human beings, so strong are habits of obedience in most of them, that it is almost safe to say that no government is likely to be overthrown until it loses the ability to make adequate use of its military and police powers. That loss of ability may show itself in the actual desertion of soldiers and police to the revolutionists, or in the stupidity with which the government manages its soldiers and police, or in both ways.

The events we have grouped under the name of first stages do not of course unroll themselves in exactly the same order in time, or with exactly the same content, in all four of our revolutions. But we have listed the major elements, and they fall into a pattern of uniformities: financial breakdown, organization of the discontented to remedy this breakdown (or threatened breakdown), revolutionary demands on the part of these organized discontented, demands which if granted would mean the virtual abdication of those governing, attempted use of force by the government, its failure, and the attainment of power by the revolutionists. These revolutionists have hitherto been acting as an organized and nearly unanimous group, but with the attainment of power it is clear that they are not united.

The group which dominates these first stages we call the moderates. They are not always in a numerical majority in this stage—indeed, it is pretty clear that if you limit the moderates to the Kadets, they were not in a majority in Russia in February, 1917. But they seem the natural heirs of the old government, and they have their chance. In three of our revolutions, they are sooner or later driven from office to death or exile. Certainly there is to be seen in England, France, and Russia a process in which a series of crises—some involving violence, street fighting, and the like—deposes one set of men and puts in power another and more radical set. In these revolutions power passes by violent or at least extralegal methods from Right to Left, until at the crisis period the extreme radicals, the complete revolutionists, are in power. There are, as a matter of fact, usually a few even wilder and more lunatic fringes of the triumphant extremists—but these are not numerous or strong and are usually suppressed or otherwise made harmless by the dominant radicals. It is therefore approximately true to say that power passes on from Right to Left until it reaches the extreme Left.

The rule of the extremists we have called the crisis period. This period was not reached in the American Revolution, though in the treatment of Loyalists, in the pressure to support the army, in some of the phases of social life, you can discern in America many of the phenomena of the Terror as it is seen in our three other societies. We cannot here attempt to go into the complicated question as to why the American Revolution stopped short of a true crisis period, why the moderates were never ousted in this country. We must repeat that we are simply trying to establish certain uniformities of description and are not attempting a complete sociology of revolutions.

The extremists are helped to power, no doubt, by the existence of a powerful pressure toward centralized strong government, something which in general the moderates are not capable of providing, while the extremists—with their discipline, their contempt for half measures, their willingness to make firm decisions, their freedom from libertarian qualms—are quite able and willing to centralize. Especially in France and Russia, where powerful foreign enemies threatened the very existence of the nation, the machinery of government during the crisis period was in part constructed to serve as a government of national defense. Yet though modern wars, as we know in this country, demand a centralization of authority, war alone does not seem to account for all that happened in the crisis period in those countries.

What does happen may be a bit oversimply summarized as follows: emergency centralization of power in an administration, usually a council or commission, and more-or-less dominated by a "strong man"—Cromwell, Robespierre, Lenin; government without any effective protection for the normal civil rights of the individual—or if this sounds unrealistic, especially for Russia, let us say the normal private life of the individual; setting up of extraordinary courts and a special revolutionary police to carry out the decrees of the government and to suppress all dissenting individuals or groups; all this machinery ultimately built up from a relatively small group—Independents, Jacobins, Bolsheviks—which has a monopoly on all governmental action. Finally, governmental action becomes a much greater part of all human action than in these societies in their normal condition; this apparatus of government is set to work indifferently on the mountains and molehills of human life—it is used to pry into and poke about corners normally reserved for priest or physician, or friend, and it is used to regulate, control, plan, the production and distribution of economic wealth on a national scale.

•

In all of our societies the crisis period was followed by a convalescence, by a return to most of the simpler and more fundamental courses taken by interactions in the old network. . . . The equilibrium has been restored and the revolution is over. But this does not mean that nothing has been changed. Some new and useful tracks or courses in the network of interactions that makes society have been established, some old and inconvenient ones—you may call them unjust if you like—have been eliminated. . . .

CHAPTER 46

R. M. MacIVER

The Role of the Precipitant

Wherever, in the more practical or in the more theoretical type of investigation, we distinguish some factor that is introduced from the outside, or else emerges from within, so that it evokes a series of repercussions or reactions significantly changing the total situation, we may call such a factor a "precipitant." The search for precipitants in this sense is one of the favorite forms of the limited causal quest.

Often we envisage a situation as dependent on the balance of two opposing forces, or on the equilibrium of a number of forces. The balance or equilibrium is unstable, temporary, precarious. One of the simplest of cases would be where public opinion is nearly equally divided in favor of and against a particular policy. Some event, some accident, some act of leadership, may decisively turn the scales. In a larger sense, we may think of one set of forces making for the perpetuation of an established order and another making for change or revolution. The forces of change are held in leash by the resisting forces. Again, some event, a war, an invention, the rise of a new prophet, a local outbreak of the suppressed forces, may be conceived as destroying the pre-existing equilibrium. Some writers actually go so far as to interpret all change along similar lines. Thus the German legal philosopher Binding maintains that "the causation of a change is identical with a change in the balance between the restraining and the promoting conditions" and adds that "man is the cause of an effect insofar as he causes any superiority of the promoting over the deterring conditions." [1] But what right have we to assume that equally matched opposites meet in every situation until some precipitant overthrows their balanced neutrality? Why should change advance by a series of jumps and halts as disturbances successively interrupting states of equilibrium? The conception arbitrarily denies the reality of geniune causal *process*. It is more

From R. M. MacIver, *Social Causation* (New York: Ginn and Company, 1942), pp. 163-164, 169-172, 177-178. Reprinted by permission of the author and the publisher.
[1] Karl Binding, *Normen und ihre Übertretung* (Leipzig, 1914), Vol. II, pp. 472-510.

pertinent to inquire under what conditions and with what limitations the principle of precipitant and preceding equilibrium is justified.

•

As a device for interpreting social and economic changes, the concept of equilibrium and disturbance is less serviceable than the concept of equilibrium and precipitant. The former never introduces us to any vital source of change, it always minimizes change in favor of the *status quo*. But since, as we have seen, it is precisely the difference, the contrast, between social phenomena or social situations that we must seize upon if we are to make any effective advance in our causal inquiries, we cannot expect much enlightenment in that regard from a viewpoint that looks on change itself as the incidental and temporary interruption of a persistent order. It is quite otherwise when the change-provoking factors are thought of as precipitants. For now we need postulate no self-maintaining order, we are committed to no doctrine of permanence, to no distinction between primary and secondary causes. All that is implied is a condition of things that endures, for no matter how short a time, until some intrusive or explosive factor converts it into another condition of things. It may be that we are dealing with a relatively closed system, or a system that slowly changes, or with a mere moment of seeming inertia. Then something decisive occurs. A class order that has been dominant for centuries is overturned. A mode of production that has been long established is, in a relatively brief period, transformed into another. A political party that commanded a majority allegiance is suddenly overthrown. A leader, a general, a popular hero, falls from his eminence to oblivion or disrepute. In all such situations we usually conceive that some one factor has intervened, has emerged within or thrust itself into the total situation, in such a way as to bring about a state of disequilibrium, a change of direction, or a realignment of forces.

Innumerable changes occur that seem to conform to this pattern. But an immediate caution is necessary, for a danger besets this mode, as indeed all other modes, of isolating a factor as distinctively causal. It is the danger of attaching an undue weight or role to the designated factor. We omit for the present any consideration of the evidence required to assure us that a particular event, or some narrow conjuncture of events within a total changing situation, effectively disturbs or disrupts a pre-existing equilibrium. We will assume that the designated factor does function as precipitant. A single thrust may set a landslide moving. A spark may set a whole forest afire, with all its entailments. The mistake of a general may lose a war and thus have farreaching repercussions on a whole civilization. One invention may revolutionize an industry. "A grain of sand in a man's flesh, and empires rise and fall." These things are in the record. But there are empires that do not fall because an emperor dies, and there are wars that are not lost because a general makes a mistake, and the thrust sends the landslide moving only because the conditions are all prepared for it. The situation may be ripe for change, and for change only in the particular direction congenial to the complex of forces controlling it. The landslide would have happened sooner or later apart from the particular thrust, or from any thrust at all. The appeal or the manifesto that seemed to change the fortunes of political parties may merely accentuate or bring to light the till then inarticulate but deeper-working trends of public opinion. The storm may shake from the trees only the ripe fruit or the dead leaves.

•

On the other hand there are events, intrusive forces, interventions, discoveries, even accidents, that in the light of our best knowledge still appear decisive, changing the direction of the whole stream of human affairs. If, to take a much quoted example, the Persians had defeated the Greeks at Marathon, the history of civilization would doubtless have been a quite different story. And there are frequent instances in which a single event has a train of consequences so dependent upon it that we cannot assume they would have been brought about apart from this event. The act of an assassin at Sarajevo precipitated a world war. Who can say with assurance that this kind of war would have occurred, sooner or later, had there not been this event? And even if the absence of the particular precipitant should only have delayed such a war, who can affirm that it would not have followed an entirely different course, had it broken out at some different time?

It is apparent, then, that the role of the precipitant may vary enormously in significance and that in each instance we can assess its causal importance only if we understand the whole dynamic system into which it enters. The causal efficacy we impute to any factor must always be contingent not only on the other factors, but also on the dynamic interdependence of them all within the total situation. It is only as a temporary heuristic expedient that we can select any item as "cause" and speak of the rest as "conditions." . . .

While a particular complex of social attitudes may enter very significantly into the causal process, it is difficult to ever assign to a factor of this sort the salience and immediate causal decisiveness suggested by our term "precipitant." These qualities are more appropriately looked for in the *event,* the dated conjecture of forces that perceptibly disturbs or disrupts a pre-existing order or coherence. A war, a revolution, a bold stroke of policy, a drastic new law, a quarrel between leaders, the assassination of a ruler, are obvious examples of precipitant in this sense. Any of these may, under certain conditions, decisively disrupt the going system, and yet, any of them may reasonably be regarded, at the hour of its occurrence, as not inevitably the outcome or expression of the conditions or forces inherent in the particular system it disrupts. There is an element of conjuncture, if not a sheer chance, in the mode and time of the occurrence. The most indubitable type is that in which the decisive factor comes wholly or essentially from outside the affected system. A war, for example, might precipitate important changes in the economic employment of women, in the credit structure of a country, or even in an artistic style. The settlement of missionaries or of traders among a primitive people may initiate profound changes in the life of that people. Again, wherever a system is relatively closed, that is, when it rigorously clings to pre-established lines and resists all innovations or new adaptations, it is likely that significant change will await the impact of some definite precipitant and be more drastic or shattering when it occurs. A caste system, for example, is usually broken open only by some powerful intrusive factor, such as revolt, invasion, a new gospel appealing to the masses, or the introduction of an externally developed industrial technique.

CHAPTER 47

HORACE M. KALLEN

Innovation

The changes or novelties of rites, techniques, customs, manners, and mores which constitute innovation are usually thought of as purposive. The actualities of the social process, however, do not validate this connotation. The attribution of intent is always retrospective. But the causes of innovation are too complex to be covered by merely personal intent. Insofar as human existence is a process and not sheer repetition, the rise, the forms, the life cycles, and the influence of innovations are the vital theme of history and the social sciences. Innovation includes in its range the transformations in food, clothing, shelter, defense against enemies and disease, tools and technologies of production and consumption, forms of play and sport, rituals and liturgies of religion, precedents of law, inventions in science and thought, styles and attitudes in literature and the arts. Every social institution is a field of innovation, no matter how conservative its intent and how standardized its techniques and procedures. The limit to innovation comes only at the point where the identity of an establishment itself is menaced.

Within this limit innovations may be numerous and rapid; the very individuality of the institution may consist in them. This is the case among the various divisions of science. The essential of each of these is the process of deliberate innovation which goes by the name of scientific method. Scientific method is simply another name for the gathering, testing, and applying of innovations. How these innovations are reached is indifferent. Every innovation involves a certain contingency, a dimension of chance and luck; every innovation also begins as focal to some particular individual or very small group. Once a "scientific" mind has become aware of it, it is developed formally and tested experimentally, given its chance to succeed or fail. The work of breeders of animals, legumes, fruits; the invention and elaboration of machines; the transformations of the art of medicine in the last fifty years, insofar as these have anything deliberate in them, all rest on the presumption and use of scientific method. This is postulated wherever innovation is both deliberate and follows the gradients of social change. Where innovation is incongruous with those, it must either struggle for its survival, establishing itself by means of a process of give and take with its environment, or be imposed by *force majeure,* as when after a revolution or a war the victor imposes upon the defeated a new way of doing or thinking.

Innovation may be slow or rapid, manifold or simple, but it is ineluctable. In a sense, the mere lapse of time is innovating. Aging takes place in institutions and societies no less than in woods and wines. This autogenous transformation through invariant repetition seems, however, never to occur in isolation. It is crossed and modified by other processes which add novelties a priori. Such are inventions, wars, crises and catastrophes, migrations, exhaustion of materials, exhaustion of interest (*i.e.* boredom). Boredom is a psychic force of innovation which deserves more attention than it has received. The revulsion which it generates and the subsequent searching and seeking are no small part of the dynamics of fashion, gaming, sport, crusades, exploration, scientific investigations, and the like. All these involve contacts with changing environments, natural and human, osmosis or more violent impacts of cultures, and consequent innovations.

The optimal conditions for innovation are a certain flexibility and readiness in the organic pattern of a society itself. These develop as a rule more easily in new societies, where a fresh start is being made; they develop also during a crisis such as a war, a profound business depression, a natural catastrophe or a revolution. At such times, playing upon a ground of fear and uncertainty, is a feeling of the significance of the social adventure. Novelties are invited, projected, and perhaps installed and domesticated; experiments are made, and change may become a standard of public policy. Such was the case in Athens from the Persian wars through the Peloponnesian War, and in the United States while the frontier lasted; it is now the case in Soviet Russia. Where custom coheres too firmly and authority is unshaken, the situation is reversed. In primitive societies the new way must be assimilated to the ways of the fathers before it can be accepted. Theocracies require that it shall confirm before it can be confirmed by the divine authority which they wield. Military or bureaucratic establishments reject it if it does not conform to the customary patterns and rituals of conduct. So does the institution of the law. In all these cases, the variant is seen as a disorderly interruption of set routine and therefore a priori a heresy, a sedition and a danger. If its import is acknowledged and it is adopted, it is usually denatured of all qualities inharmonious with the established procedure. Apparently only a crisis, the feeling of danger at hand, can transform this habitual inertia into a readiness to try new tools and ways.

•

Innovators are not necessarily rebels, and the temper of innovation is not by any means the temper of revolt. Novelties, spontaneous deviations of the same energy, continually pour from the main stream of custom and convention. Thus the industrial revolution in England, the growth and diffusion of the factory system in the United States, in Germany, and in Japan, took place mainly in the context of the old mores and on the initiative and by the effort of persons who were on the whole champions of those mores. Now the mores are being transformed and displaced by what they allowed. Again, the impact of photography and the theory of color vision on the painter's art constituted a fecundation of method and a diversion of ideals. The impressionists began by affirming the novelty, and were forced into a defensive denying of the tradition. Socalled modern movements are innovations only because of reaction against the innovation which photography itself represented. The intent of the postimpressionist schools was conservative; their achievements were innovations.

Nevertheless, innovators are forced into a combative position. For their novelties enter a social organization most of whose establishments are going concerns and enter as competitors and deprecators of one or another. If they succeed in establishing themselves, they become embodied in the organic flow of the mores. They cause that flow to deviate to a slightly different gradient definable by what they represent. This is what the city life of the Renaissance did to Christian society in Europe, what the fusion of the scientific with the technological attitude did to the eighteenth century mind, and what the industrial system is doing to contemporary civilization. Of course there are programs of innovation whose dynamic is a reaction against the established order. Such programs sometimes function as precipitates of deep-lying emotions which are not disturbing enough to change the social order, but do nourish a formulated opposition to it. The opposition becomes organized into cults and movements whose rituals and programs then identify it as a sort of antibody in the social organism. So Methodism grew to maturity in the Episcopal milieu of England. The single tax movement in the United States is such a development, and such also are cults of diet (like vegetarianism), of dress (like nudism), of health and of other goods of life. They arise as variants and survive as orderly antagonists within the nexus of the social process.

Since all innovations animate readjustments in the distribution and organization of social forces they automatically evoke the antagonism of those who are disturbed. If the antagonism is pervasive and deep, the innovation perforce lapses. If, however, it satisfies a want or nullifies an annoyance, however illusorily, it gathers a following. . . .

Innovations are mostly resisted out of motives of self-interest and fear.

The new is quite usually synonymous with the unreasonable, the dangerous, the impossible. As William James pointed out long ago, rationality is a sentiment in which the feeling of familiarity is fused with that of congruity with our fundamental hopes and desires. Sometimes mere familiarity may become identical with this congruity. Thus people resist changing their dietary habits in spite of the fact that this change is required by health, the social setting, or religion; there are freethinking Jews who get indigestion at the very thought of pork and "liberated" Hindus who are upset by the idea of meat. Between love of food and love of God or country the difference is in degree, not in kind. All involve clinging to the habitual, familiar and secure. . . . Where innovations have finally established themselves and compel recognition, they are assimilated to the old order—or the old order is assimilated to them—by means of some formula. Thus in the United States, "trusts" were feared at their origin and laws were passed to constrain them. But they developed into the dominant controls of the economic process; the established order has had to count with them and acquiesce in them. The Supreme Court of the United States celebrated this necessity by the well known decision concerning "the rule of reason" (Standard Oil Co. *versus* United States, 221 U.S. 1 [1911]), which has resulted in the virtual nullification of the original intent to control the trusts rigorously. . . .

CHAPTER 48

RALPH LINTON

Discovery, Invention, and Their Cultural Setting

Discovery and Invention

Discovery and invention are the obvious starting points for any study of cultural growth and change, since it is only by these processes that new elements can be added to the total content of man's culture. Although developed cultural traits can be transmitted from one culture to another and most cultures owe the bulk of their content to this process, every culture element can ultimately be traced to a discovery or invention or to a more or less complex combination of various discoveries and inventions, which arose at a particular time and place.

We may define a discovery as any addition to knowledge, an invention as a new application of knowledge. To give a concrete example, on an individual rather than a social basis, when a small child pulls a cat's tail and gets scratched, this particular sequence of cause and effect is a discovery as far as the child is concerned. The observed fact that cats will scratch when their tails are pulled is an addition to his store of knowledge. If the child pulls the cat's tail when someone else is holding it, so that that person will get scratched, this is in the nature of an invention. The knowledge is employed in a new way to achieve a particular end. If the child is then spanked, he will have another discovery to his credit.

Since it is the application of knowledge, *i.e.,* invention, which is functionally important to culture, we will refer to all new active elements which are developed within the frame of a particular culture and society as inventions.

From Ralph Linton, *The Study of Man* (New York: Appleton-Century-Crofts, 1936), pp. 304, 306, 316-323, 341-343. Copyright 1936 by D. Appleton-Century Co., and reprinted by permission of the publishers.

Inventions—Classified

. . . There have been numerous attempts to classify inventions, none of them altogether successful and all depending for their utility upon the particular problem in which they are to be employed. There is the simple division of inventions into religious, social, and technological. This is useful for descriptive purposes, yet there are practical difficulties in drawing lines between even such elementary divisions. Almost every religious invention has numerous purely social aspects. The revelation, if such happens to be the starting point of the new cult, nearly always includes regulations for human relationships as well as for the relationship between believers and the supernatural. It may even include fairly complicated rules as to how the faithful should dress, what food they should eat, and how they should kill their meat. Moreover, such a classification is of little value for the study of the dynamics of culture. The classification most useful in this appears to be the simple one of *basic inventions* and *improving inventions*.

A basic invention may be defined as one which involves the application of a new principle or a new combination of principles. It is basic in the sense that it opens up new potentialities for progress and is destined, in the normal course of events, to become the foundation of a whole series of other inventions. The bow would be a good example of such an invention. It involved the use of a new principle and became the starting point for a whole series of improving inventions, such as those which culminated in the laminated bow, crossbow, and so on. A more modern example of such a basic invention would be the vacuum tube, whose potentialities for use are only beginning to be understood. An improving invention, as the name implies, is a modification of some pre-existing device, usually made with the intention of increasing its efficiency or rendering it available for some new use. Thus the modern hand telephone instrument is an improving invention superimposed upon the basic telephone invention. Although certain inventions are clearly basic and others as clearly improving, the assignment of many others rests upon the observer's judgment of when any modification is important enough to be said to involve a new principle. Perhaps the best test is a pragmatic one, classing any invention as basic when it becomes the starting point for a divergent line of inventions and improving when it does not.

•

Although a certain romantic interest attaches to basic inventions . . . , the bulk of cultural progress has probably been due to the less spectacular process of gradual improvement in pre-existing devices and the development of new applications for them. In fact, basic inventions seem to be valuable mainly as the starting point for series of improving inventions. Very few of them are efficient or satisfactory in the condition in which they first appear. Thus the first automobiles were little better than toys or scientific curiosities. They did not begin to play their present important role in our culture until they had been refined and perfected by literally hundreds of improving inventions.

A sufficient number of improving inventions can even transform an appliance into something quite different from the original and with totally different applications. Thus the wheel appears to have been, in its inception, a development of the roller and something employed exclusively in transportation. As the potentialities of the device were recognized, it was turned to other uses, as for drawing water for irrigation and for the manufacture of pottery. Still later came a realization of its potentialities for transforming direct into rotary motion and for transmitting power, until this transportation appliance became an integral part of thousands of devices which were in no way related to transportation. Again, the bow, beginning as a weapon, or more probably as a toy, not only underwent a series of modifications which perfected it for its original use but, through a divergent line of inventive evolution, became ancestral to the harp and ultimately to all stringed musical instruments. In both of these cases, the development of the new appliances rested upon a long series of improving inventions, no one of which seemed to be of tremendous importance in itself, but which, in the aggregate, produced something fundamentally different from the original appliance. For this reason it is extremely hazardous to class any appliance as the result of a . . . basic invention unless its actual history is known. The new principle which gives it its basic quality may have crept in little by little, entering by such gradual degrees that its point of first appearance can hardly be detected.

The Cultural Setting

Hitherto we have discussed . . . inventions from the point of view of their own qualities, but the picture would be quite misleading if we stopped there. There is a constant and intimate association between the inventor and his products and the cultural setting in which inventions are produced and must function. We have defined an invention as a new application of knowledge, a definition which at once implies that the knowledge must precede the invention. Although the knowledge incorporated into a new invention may derive in part from a fresh discovery, most of it always derives from the culture of the inventor's society. Every inventor, even the one who produces a basic invention, builds upon this accumulation of previously acquired knowledge, and every new thing must grow directly out of other things which have gone before. Thus no inventor reared in a culture which was ignorant of the wheel principle could conceivably produce even such simple appliances as the potter's wheel or lathe. The wheel would have to be invented first. The content of the culture within which the inventor operates thus imposes constant limitations upon the exercise of his inventive abilities. This applies not merely to mechanical inventions but to invention in all other fields as well. The mathematical genius can only carry on from the point which mathematical knowledge within his culture has already reached. Thus if Einstein had been born into a primitive tribe which was unable to count beyond three, lifelong application to mathematics probably would not have carried him beyond the development of a decimal system based on fingers and toes. Again, reformers who attempt to devise new systems for society or new religions can only build with the elements with which their culture has made them familiar. It is ridiculous to try to understand the form and content of such sects as Christianity and Mohammedanism until we know the cultural background from which they sprang.

•

Acceptance

New traits are accepted primarily on the basis of two qualities, utility and compatibility: in other words, on the basis of what they appear to be good for and how easily they can be fitted into the existing culture configuration. Both these qualities are, of course, relative to the receiving culture and are influenced by such a long series of factors that an outsider can hardly ascertain all of them. . . . Cultural change is mainly a matter of the replacement of old elements by new ones, and every culture normally includes adequate techniques for meeting all the conscious needs of the society's members. When a new trait presents itself, its acceptance depends not so much on whether it is better than the existing one as on whether it is enough better to make its acceptance worth the trouble. This in turn must depend upon the judgment of the group, their degree of conservatism, and how much change in existing habits the new appliance will entail. Even in . . . mechanical appliances, superiority cannot be judged simply in terms of increased output. There are pleasant and unpleasant forms of work, and even such a simple change as that from the use of adzes to axes for tree-felling entails a change in muscular habits which is unpleasant for the time being. . . .

Very much the same situation holds with regard to the problem of compatibility. The acceptance of any new culture element entails certain changes in the total culture configuration. Although the full extent of these changes can never be forecast, certain of them are usually obvious. If the new trait is of such a sort that its acceptance will conflict directly with important traits already present in the culture, it is almost certain to be rejected. One cannot conceive of techniques of mass production being accepted by a culture which had a pattern of uniqueness. There actually are societies which believe that no two objects should ever be the same and never make any two things exactly alike.

•

In the matter of compatibility, as in that of utility, there is a broad zone of uncertainty. There are new elements which may be recognized as slightly superior to existing ones and other elements which may be seen to be somewhat incompatible, but not enough so as to make their acceptance impossible. Very often the advantages and disadvantages are so evenly balanced that the acceptance of the new trait may seem desirable to certain members of the society and undesirable to others. The ultimate acceptance or rejection of elements which fall within this zone is controlled by still another series of variable factors about which we know very little. One of the most important of these is certainly the particular interests which dominate the life of the receiving group. A new trait which is in line with these interests will be given more serious consideration and has a better chance of adoption than one which is not. A slight gain along the line of these interests is felt to be more important than a larger one in some other line in which the group takes little interest. Thus the Hindus have always been highly receptive to new cults and new philosophic ideas as long as these did not come into too direct conflict with their existing patterns, but have shown an almost complete indifference to improved techniques of manufacture. The material world was felt to be of so little importance that minor advances in its control were not considered worth the trouble of changing established habits.

•

In our own civilization, invention itself has become a focus of interest as long as it confines itself to mechanical lines. Social and religious invention is still frowned upon, but this attitude may change as the necessity for advance in these fields becomes increasingly apparent. However, there has never been a time in history when individuals were afforded a better opportunity to add to the material aspects of a culture. In most societies the way of both the inventor and his inventions are hard, and surprisingly few inventions survive to be actually incorporated into culture. For every invention which has been successful in the cultural and social sense, there have probably been at least a thousand which have fallen by the wayside. Many of these have been successful in the practical sense, being actually more efficient than the appliances which were used before and continued to be used after. However, society rejected them, and if they have not been completely forgotten they survive simply as antiquarian curiosities. We know that the Alexandrian Greeks had a steam-engine which was effective enough for one to be installed on the Pharos and used to haul up fuel for the beacon. Leonardo da Vinci's notebooks provide a perfect mine of inventions, many of which show a surprising similarity to modern ones. Perfectly feasible repeating rifles and machine-guns were developed during the first hundred years that hand firearms were in use. All of these inventions failed to "take."

It seems that any invention which fails of acceptance by society within the first generation after it appears may be set down as a total loss. Even when, as in Europe, there are methods for recording it and preserving it as a latent element within the culture, it is rarely if ever revivified. The examples cited above had nothing to do with the modern inventions which they foreshadowed. The inventor works from his own knowledge and his own sense of needs and rarely pores over archives. The same things are invented again and again and rejected again and again until changes in the culture continuum have prepared a place for them. The process is slow and, from the point of view of the inventor, most discouraging. In the progressive enrichment of its culture, no society has ever employed even a tithe of its members' inventive ability. There are few cultures which can show more than a mere handful of traits which have been invented by members of the societies which bear them. All cultures have grown chiefly by borrowing. . . .

Diffusion

CHAPTER 49

JAMES COLEMAN, HERBERT MENZEL, and
ELIHU KATZ

Social Processes in Physicians' Adoption of a New Drug

Over the past twenty years, the practice of medicine has undergone profound changes, not the least of which has been the accelerated rate of change itself. Again and again, new diagnostic techniques, new laboratory tests, new drugs, new forms of anesthesia, new surgical procedures, and new principles of patient management make their appearance. Most of these innovations are minor steps which alter the medical scene only by gradual accretion, if at all; many, indeed, are short-lived or quickly superseded; a few have been milestones in medical developments. Whatever the ultimate significance of a new practice may be, its immediate fate, once it has been launched from the laboratory or research clinic, rests in the hands of the practicing physician in the field.

The pathways by which a successful innovation in medical practice spreads through the profession have seldom been systematically investigated. The present study is a contribution toward that end. It concerns the fate of a single innovation in four cities, a new variant in a well-established family of drugs. Such a case study can hardly claim to represent the course of all types of medical innovation under all circumstances, but it does illuminate some important paths and processes through which medical innovations can make their way into the practice of physicians. One may add that drugs are peculiarly suitable as tracers of these paths, because they are

From James Coleman, Herbert Menzel, and Elihu Katz, "Social Processes in Physicians' Adoption of a New Drug," *The Journal of Chronic Diseases,* IX (1959), No. 1, pp. 1-19. Reprinted by permission of the authors and Pergamon Publishers.

physical objects with standardized names, their release dates are easily ascertainable, and pharmacists maintain exact prescription records.

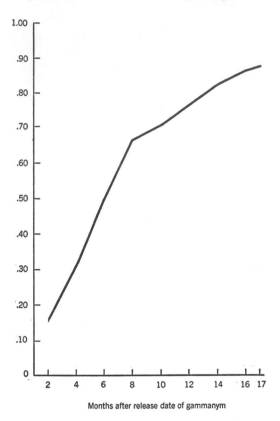

FIGURE 49-1. Cumulative proportion of doctors introducing gammanym over a sixteen-month period (N = 125).

The data of this study stem from two sources. In four Midwestern communities, interviews were conducted with 125 general practitioners, internists, and pediatricians, who generously contributed an average of 1½ hours of their time. They constituted 85 per cent of all practitioners of their specialties in these cities. In addition, data on the prescriptions written by these 125 physicians were obtained from almost all the pharmacies in these communities.[1] The prescription data covered a period of sixteen months

_____

[1] Ninety-one additional interviews were held with practitioners of other specialties, but their prescription record was not examined. The communities had altogether 356 physicians in active private practice. The sample was designed to include all the general practitioners, internists, and pediatricians and a selected group of other specialists. The population of the four cities ranged from about 25,000 to just over 100,000.

beginning with the release date of a new drug which will here be called "gammanym." At this time, two older drugs of the same general type were in widespread use. They had appeared some years earlier and are here designated as "alphanym" and "betanym." The three medications belong to a well-established family of drugs which has widespread applicability in the hands of general practitioners and many specialists. By the end of the survey period, sixteen months after its release, gammanym had become at least a part of the standard medication of most practicing physicians; 87 per cent of the general practitioners, internists, and pediatricians in the sample under study had introduced it into their practice. But this change had been neither immediate nor all-encompassing. The overall rate of introduction of gammanym by these doctors is seen in Figure 49-1. This cumulative curve indicates for each stated date the percentage of doctors who had already prescribed the drug up to that time. As can be seen, more and more doctors introduced the drug during this sixteen-month period until almost 90 per cent had used it; then the curve finally leveled off.

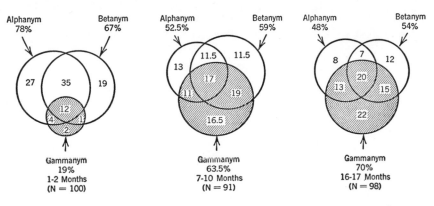

Months after release of gammanym

FIGURE 49-2. Overlapping use of alphanym, betanym, and gammanym during three time intervals.

To be sure, the rapid rise in the use of gammanym did not mean that its predecessors, alphanym and betanym, were dropped from use. The degree of overlapping use of two or three of the drugs by the same doctor is pictorially represented in Figure 49-2, for three time intervals, representing the beginning, middle, and end of the period studied. Thus, for example, as late as sixteen and seventeen months after the release of gammanym, only 22 per cent of the doctors were prescribing gammanym exclusively, while 15 per cent were prescribing both betanym and gammanym, 13 per cent were prescribing both alphanym and gammanym, and 20 per cent were writing prescriptions for all three drugs during these same two months (more accurately, during the six sampling days representing these two months). The introduction of gammanym meant for most doctors an addition to whatever drugs of this type they were already using, rather than a substitution. Only slowly, if at all, did some of the doctors stop using the older drugs.

Drug Adoption and Individual Characteristics of Physicians

This, then, describes the overall course of the acceptance of gammanym in these four communities, from the time it first arrived on the drugstore shelves to the time when it appeared on prescription slips of most of the doctors in town. But what exactly happened during this period? Through what paths and processes did the new drug find its way into the prescribing habits of the local physician? As one essential step in answering these questions, it is necessary to examine and compare the doctors who introduced the new drug quickly with those who prescribed it only after most of their colleagues had done so. By ascertaining the backgrounds, types of practice, and other characteristics of these doctors, we can begin to sketch a picture of the "innovator" among the local practicing physicians.

Let us first look at specialty differences. Pediatricians introduced gammanym into their practices more quickly than internists, and internists introduced it more quickly than general practitioners. The average pediatrician first prescribed the drug 6.6 months after its release, the average internist 8.2 months, and the average general practitioner 9.0 months after release. This result is somewhat surprising in view of the general impression that internists are the pace setters. But the contradiction is only apparent and results from the different prescription volume of the different specialties. The pediatricians' average number of prescriptions for alphanym, betanym, and gammanym combined was 13.6 per three-day sampling period; for internists it was 2.7; and for general practitioners 3.6. When doctors with roughly the same volume of prescriptions are compared, the contradiction disappears. Internists then introduce the new drug more rapidly than pediatricians or general practitioners.

Less surprising is the finding that doctors who expose themselves frequently to the primary sources of information were much more likely to be innovators than those who do not. . . . The rate of gammanym introduction was more rapid among those who receive many journals, among those who attend many out-of-town specialty meetings, and among those who conscientiously attend conferences in their own hospitals than among those who do not. It is difficult to assess to what extent this is due to an actual effect of these means of communication on the doctor's prescription habits. Quite possibly it means merely that doctors who are sensitive to new developments read more and go to more meetings. What we do know is that the relationship of drug introduction to journal reading and meeting attendance is independent of the doctor's specialty. . . . In fact, reading and attendance . . . have a considerably stronger relationship to early use of gammanym than does the doctor's specialty. It appears that the innovator is less characterized by his specialty than by voluntary activities like attendance at meetings and reading journals which bring him into closer contact with events in the profession.

But this is not equally true for *all* information-getting activities. There are some potential sources of influence or information, exposure to which shows no relationship to early use of gammanym. . . . Doctors who read many pharmaceutical house organs, those who attend many nonspecialty meetings (American Medical Association, state and regional medical societies, etc.), and those who attend county medical society meetings regularly were little or no quicker to introduce the drug than their colleagues who attend those media less regularly. These media apparently attract a fairly representative audience of doctors among whom sensitivity to new developments is not more prevalent than among physicians in general.

Drug Adoption and Physicians' Contacts with Colleagues

The media discussed so far have been the relatively obvious channels through which innovations may be diffused to local doctors. But doctors were also found to be affected in their drug adoptions in some less obvious ways. One path which might not have been anticipated is the office arrangement of the doctor. By simply dividing doctors into those who share offices with one or several colleagues and those who have an office alone, we find a considerable difference. The doctors who share offices introduced the drug an average of 2.3 months sooner than their colleagues who practice alone.

It is useful to ask just what social and psychologic processes may produce this effect. Two hypotheses seem quite reasonable. First, being in close professional contact with colleagues keeps a doctor well informed, so that he is saved the difficulty of finding out for himself about each new development. He has surrogates to carry part of the burden of finding out about new developments, for, as soon as any of his office partners seriously considers trying a new therapy or even just finding out about a new development, he will discuss it with him.

A second interpretation of the results, however, seems equally reasonable. Introducing a new technique into his practice is always somewhat dangerous for the physician. He has no firsthand knowledge of possible ill effects, yet he must shoulder the blame if ill effects should occur. Because of this, the doctor needs all the reassurance he can get from his fellows to lessen the uncertainty which he faces. The doctor who shares an office with others can, in a sense, depend upon their support and use it for reassurance, while the doctor who practices alone must make the bold step without this added support. It is difficult to determine which of these two interpretations is most valid without knowing whether the primary barrier to drug innovation among doctors who are alone is lack of information or lack of assurance.

But for whatever reason office-sharing leads to earlier use of new drugs, it is apparent that a doctor's social location in the community of his local colleagues affects his drug use by giving him access to information, by providing him with assurance, or in some other way. This leads to a more general question. What about the dozens of other relations that a doctor may have with his colleagues, beside that of office partnership? What, for example, might be the importance of his contact with colleagues in the hospital during leisure hours? Would it affect his use of new practices and products? In order to answer questions like these, one must know the relations among the doctors of the community, that is, one must know the social structure of the medical community which these relations make up. To uncover the most important facets of this structure, three questions were asked of each doctor in the interview: (1) "When you need information or *advice* about questions of therapy, where do you usually turn?" (2) "Who are the three or four physicians with whom you most often find yourself *discussing* cases or therapy in the course of an ordinary week—last week, for instance?" (3) "Would you tell me who are your three *friends* whom you see most often socially?" In answer to each of these questions, three names of other doctors were requested. The replies to the three questions yielded three cross-sections of the structure of the medical communities, much like a biologist's sections of a plant fiber along several axes. Figure 49-3 presents, as an illustration, one of these cross-sections for one of the four cities covered in the survey. This particular diagram pictures that city's

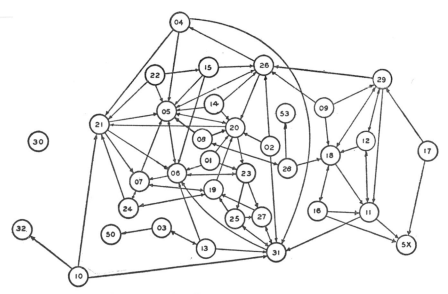

FIGURE 49-3. Discussion network in City D.

structure of discussion partnerships, that is, a sectioning according to the replies to the second question above. In this sociogram, as such a diagram is called, each circle represents a physician, who is identified by a code number. An arrow pointing from Circle 04 to Circle 05 means that Dr. 04 named Dr. 05 as one of his most frequent partners in the discussion of cases. The double-headed arrow connecting Circle 05 and Circle 06 means that Dr. 05 and Dr. 06 each named the other as a frequent partner in the discussion of cases. The fact that seven different arrows point to Circle 31 (near bottom) means that seven different colleagues named Dr. 31 as a frequent discussion partner; in other words, Dr. 31 is quite popular as a discussion partner.

Our general question now becomes: How does this social structure of the community of physicians in a city facilitate or inhibit the diffusion of a new drug? This is an immensely complex question to answer—as complex as the social structures themselves. But it is possible to break the structure and the question into simpler components and to investigate them one by one. Perhaps the simplest question that can be asked in this connection is what is the difference in the rate of drug adoptions between doctors who have contact with many and with few colleagues? This question is a direct parallel to the earlier question about the difference in the rate of drug adoption between doctors who have office partners and those who have none. One can ask more specifically: What is the difference in the rate of drug adoptions between doctors who are named as advisors (or as discussion partners, or as friends) by many of their colleagues and those who are not named by any? One may call the first group socially integrated and the second group socially isolated.

We have pointed out that doctors with office partners introduced gammanym more quickly than those who practice alone. This leads to the hypothesis that the well-integrated doctors would be quicker to introduce this new drug than their more isolated colleagues. This is indeed what is found to be true, and it is true for each of the three cross-sections of the social structure which are under examination here. . . . The effect is quite strong in the predicted direction. Doctors highly integrated into each of the structures[2] were much quicker to introduce the new drug than the more isolated doctors. The average doctor among those most frequently named as advisors introduced the new drug 3.1 months before the average of those who are never named as advisors. The corresponding mean difference between those integrated and isolated as discussion partners is 4.1 months and between those integrated and isolated as friends is 4.3 months. The importance of these factors can be gauged from the fact that no other factor examined in the entire study yielded a mean difference of more than four

---

[2] *I.e.,* those named four times or more as advisors or three times or more as discussion partners or friends.

months, with the single exception of total volume of prescriptions for this general type of medicine. These results suggest that the networks of informal relations among doctors were highly effective as chains of information and influence in the diffusion of this innovation.

Yet, one might reasonably object, is it not likely that these differences in integration and isolation merely reflect different individual characteristics among these doctors and that it is really these personality differences, and not the contacts with other doctors, which account for the striking results found? This is especially plausible in the case of the advisorship network. After all, the doctors who are often designated as advisors may very well be chosen by their colleagues precisely because they are aware of new medications. In that case, their early introductions of new drugs would be a cause rather than a consequence of their high integration. Yet, contrary to this interpretation, the effect of the advisorship network is smaller, not larger, than that of the networks of discussion partners and friends. It is the friendship network which yields the largest difference (4.3 months) between the average adoption times of the integrated and isolated doctors. Since an "integrated" doctor here means one named by many colleagues as a "friend . . . seen most often socially," it is very unlikely that his integration is a result of some professional habit which is accompanied by early introduction of new drugs. It is much more likely that early introduction of the new drug was conditioned by the doctors' informal contacts with one another, through the network of friendships, and through the more strictly professional relationships as well.

Two Processes of Diffusion

But even stronger evidence for this claim can be found in another place. If the socially integrated doctors tended to introduce the drug early merely because of some personality characteristic, the use of the new drug should have spread among these integrated doctors in very much the same way as among the isolates, except earlier. If, on the other hand, it is true that the socially integrated doctors owe their early introduction of gammanym to the networks of contacts which surround them, then the use of the new drug should not only spread *earlier* among them than among the isolates, but the very *nature of the process* of diffusion should then be different. At the extremes, there would be these two processes of diffusion: (1) Among the isolated doctors, it would be an individual process. The effective stimuli—such as detail men, medical journals, advertising from drug houses, and so on—remain fairly constant throughout the diffusion period. The number of doctors introducing the new drug each month would remain a constant percentage of those who have not already adopted the drug. A typical graph for this process would look like the lower curve of Figure 49-4. (2) Among the integrated doctors, it would be an interpersonal or "snowball" process. If, for example, one pioneer introduces the new drug and converts a col-

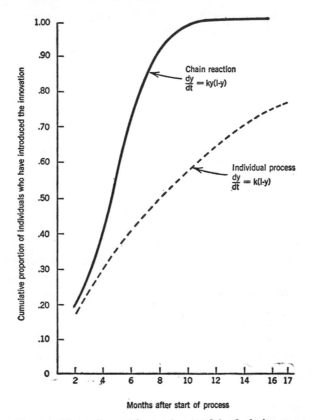

FIGURE 49-4. Comparison of a model of chain-reaction innovation with a model of individual innovation.

league to it during the first month, then these two doctors will convert two others during the second month; during the third month, there would be four doctors making new converts; and so on. The number of doctors introducing the new drug each month would not remain a constant percentage of those yet to be converted, but would gain headway in proportion to those who have already been converted. A typical graph for this process would look like the upper curve in Figure 49-4.

The difference in the shape of the two theoretical curves shown in Figure 49-4 corresponds closely to the differences between the empirical curves obtained for the doctors termed "socially integrated" and "socially isolated" according to the criteria mentioned earlier.[3] In each instance, the curves start

---

[3] The empirical curves referred to here may be inspected in the original article from which this text is excerpted. More concise numerical documentation will be found in our "The Diffusion of an Innovation among Physicians," *Sociometry*, XX (1957), 253-270. A detailed examination of the correspondences and contrasts will be found in our forthcoming *Medical Innovation—A Case Study* (New York: Bobbs-Merrill Company).

out with roughly the same proportion of users in the first two months and then diverge sharply. The curves for the integrated doctors continue steeply upward to their ceiling, indicating at least in part a person-to-person process. The curves for the isolated doctors become gradually less steep, as would be expected in the case of an individual diffusion process. (None of the empirical curves, to be sure, fit the extremes shown in Figure 49-4 exactly.)

No such contrast appears when doctors are categorized according to specialty, number of journals received, specialty meetings attended, or similar individual characteristics. In each instance, one group of doctors adopted the drug faster than the other, as has already been pointed out; but the difference in adoption rates between the two groups appears from the very beginning and does not change systematically as time progresses. In graphic representation, the corresponding upper and lower curves diverge from the beginning and have essentially the same shape. This is as expected, if the doctors represented by these upper and lower curves differ in individual receptivity to or awareness of innovations, but not in their location in effective networks of interpersonal relations.

While these results constitute only a case study of the diffusion of one new product among the doctors of four cities, they have important implications. They suggest that a doctor's tendency to innovate is not only a function of something about him as an individual, but also—and more strongly —a function of his social location among other doctors. The social and professional contacts a doctor has with his colleagues evidently serve important functions in the diffusion of a new practice which are not duplicated by journals, meetings, detail men, or drug house advertisements.

But this result leaves much unsaid. What is it about the social networks that affects the innovating behavior of men within them? Is it merely transmission of information, or do these networks provide the doctor in an unclear situation with the security of numbers? And what are the various stages of the diffusion process as the new drug changes from one used by a small minority into one used by almost the whole community? These are the questions to be considered now.

The Question of Simultaneous Adoptions by Doctors Who Associate with One Another

How can some of these more complex questions about the stages of diffusion be examined? One way, though certainly not the only way, is to examine pairs of doctors who maintain some specified form of contact with one another. Each doctor, it will be recalled, had been asked three questions about his relations to his colleagues. (To whom did he turn for *advice?* With whom did he most often *discuss cases?* What *friends* did he see most often socially?) A doctor and any colleague whom he named in reply to any of these questions constitute a pair of related doctors.

If the networks of doctor-to-doctor contacts are effective, then pairs of related doctors should be more alike in their behavior than pairs assorted at random. More specifically, if a chain-reaction process of drug introduction is at work, then, it seems, adjacent links in the chain—that is, pairs of related doctors—should introduce the drug at about the same time, ideally, during the very same months. If, on the other hand, the use of gammanym was not transmitted through these networks, then the interval between the gammanym adoption dates of doctors and their advisors, doctors and their discussion partners, and doctors and their friends would be no shorter than those of any two doctors picked at random.

Actually, the average intervals between the dates of gammanym adoption of each doctor and those whom he had named as his advisors, discussion partners, or friends were almost identical to the average intervals for pairs picked at random. This meant the rejection of our original hypothesis that pairs of doctors in contact would introduce the drug more nearly simultaneously than pairs of doctors assorted at random. There was, on the other hand, the earlier evidence that the doctor's integration was important to his introduction of gammanym. This dictated a more intensive look at the behavior of pairs of doctors. Accordingly, we raised the question of whether the networks, though ineffective for the *whole* period studied, may have been effective for the *early* period, immediately after the drug was marketed. This, indeed, proved to be the case.

The Stages of Social Diffusion

In order to describe this tendency more precisely, an *index of simultaneity* has been devised, constructed separately for each month. As applied here, it measures how closely the drug introduction of doctors during a given month followed the introductions by any associates who had adopted the drug during the same month or earlier. This index would have a value of +1 if each doctor had introduced the drug during the same month as his discussion partner (or friend or advisor); it would be zero if the introduction dates of the two doctors in a pair were as far apart as expected by chance.[4] In Figure 49-5, the values of this index are plotted. Separate curves are plotted for pairs of friends, pairs of discussion partners, and advisor-advisee pairs. Comparing the three structures, it appears that the discussion network and the advisor network are much alike in their effects. Both are most effective during the earliest period. Both are somewhat more effective than the friendship network during these early periods. The friendship network, on the other hand, appears to have its maximum

---

[4] For further details on the index of simultaneity and the model of randomness used therein, *see* our "The Diffusion of an Innovation among Physicians," *Sociometry,* XX (1957), 253-270.

effectiveness later, about five months after gammanym appeared on the market. Finally, after about six months, none of the networks any longer show an effect.

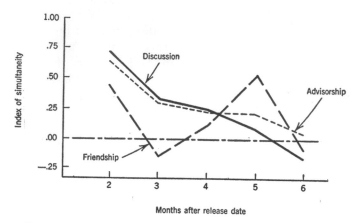

FIGURE 49-5. Index of pair-simultaneity for three networks at different times.

These findings, which show different effectiveness of the social networks at different times after the drug's release, have several implications which will be examined shortly. But first, the very structure of the networks has its own implication. Whatever effect these networks have should operate first in the more dense parts of the structure, where a number of lines of social relationship converge and should only then spread out to the more open parts of the structure, that is, to the relatively isolated doctors. It has already been shown that the more isolated doctors, on the average, introduced gammanym considerably later than the socially more integrated doctors. We propose, however, that, when more isolated doctors did introduce the drug early, it was not with the help of the social networks. While the networks were operative as channels of influence early for the integrated doctors, they were operative only later for the more isolated ones. This is what seems to have occurred. Figure 49-6 plots the index of simultaneity separately for more and less integrated doctors. (The graphs show weighted averages for all three networks; separately the numbers of cases would be so small as to produce erratic trends.)

The peak of effectiveness of doctor-to-doctor contacts for the well-integrated doctors appeared in the earliest month for which it can be plotted (the second month), after which effectiveness sharply declined. For the relatively isolated doctors, by contrast, the networks were not so effective at first as were those for the integrated doctors, but they maintained their effectiveness longer. Thus it appears that the networks of relations were effective not only for the more integrated doctors, but also for those relatively isolated doctors who introduced the drug during the first five months of the drug's availability.

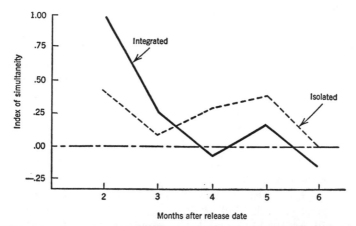

FIGURE 49-6. Index of pair-simultaneity at different times for doctors differing in integration.

To summarize the results so far, it appears that social influence in the process of drug adoption occurred in several stages. First, it operated only among the doctors who are most integrated into the community of their colleagues through ties of a professional nature (as advisors or as discussion partners). Then it spread through the friendship network to doctors who are closely tied to the medical community through their friendship relations. By this time, social influence had also become operative in the more diffuse parts of the social structure, that is, among the relatively isolated doctors. Finally, there came a phase during which an occasional doctor still introduced gammanym, but in complete independence of the time at which his associates introduced it; the networks now showed *no* effect. For the integrated doctors, this phase began four or five months after the drug's release. For the isolated doctors, it began about six months after the drug's release. By this time, the social structure seems to have exhausted its effect. Doctors who introduced gammanym into their practices after this time apparently responded exclusively to influences outside the social networks, such as the professional journals, detail men, drug house advertisements, and so on. They did not, it appears, depend upon their personal relations with other doctors for information and influence. The channels of influence between doctors had operated most powerfully during the first few months after the release of the new drug. Such influence as any doctor had upon his immediate associates by his introduction of the drug occurred very soon after the drug became available. Why is this?

The Role of Contacts with Colleagues in Clearcut and Ambiguous Situations

One answer is that it is only in the early months after a drug's appearance that a doctor needs the support and judgment of his colleagues. It is chiefly when the drug is new that the doctor who is to adopt it needs his colleagues to confirm his judgment and to share the feeling of responsibility in case the decision to adopt the drug should be wrong. At this time, familiarity with the new drug is minimal and the doctor is in an uncertain situation. Several sociopsychological experiments have shown that it is precisely in situations which are objectively unclear, situations in which the individual's own senses and other objective resources cannot tell him what is right and what is wrong, that he needs and uses social validation of his judgments most fully. The first months following the release of a new drug appear to present just this kind of situation. To be sure, the particular drug innovation with which this research has dealt was not a dramatic one. Presumably the effects shown here would be much stronger in the case of a more radical innovation. It is nevertheless suggested that the reason for the greater effectiveness of contacts with gammanym users during the earliest months after the release of the drug was due to the greater uncertainty about the drug that prevailed at that time. It is proposed that a doctor will be influenced more by what his colleagues say and do in uncertain situations than in clearcut situations.

This hypothesis also implies that the necessity for support and validation of judgments by colleagues would be much greater in decisions about some medical conditions than about others. It would be great where the physiology of the illness is not well understood and the treatment is subject to much trial and error. It would be small in conditions which are well understood and in which the action of the medication is well known. It is possible, in fact, to test this implication with certain data of this study. This time the data do not refer to the time of introduction of a new drug, but rather to the habitual use or nonuse of certain classes of modern drugs for two specified conditions. These were respiratory infections and mild-to-moderate cases of essential hypertension. Respiratory infections allow few alternatives of treatment, and their success or failure becomes quickly apparent. They present a clearcut situation. Hypertension, on the other hand, allows many kinds of treatment, and their success can be gauged only slowly and with difficulty. Hypertension presents an uncertain situation.

The implication of the general hypothesis is therefore that pairs of related doctors should be more alike (compared to chance expectations) in their treatment of hypertension than in their treatment of respiratory infections. In order to test this hypothesis, the doctors were classified first according to whether or not they named a broad-spectrum antibiotic as "the antibiotic or sulfonamide [they] most commonly used in infectious conditions of the respiratory tract." They were also classified according to whether or not they included Rauwolfia serpentina drugs in their "usual treatment for essential hypertension in mild or moderate cases." Finally, the Rauwolfia users were divided according to whether they preferred reserpine or other Rauwolfia preparations. With respect to the first classification, a doctor and his friend were considered alike if both or neither named a broad-spectrum drug; with respect to the second, doctors were considered alike if both or neither included Rauwolfia drugs; and, with respect to the third, they were considered alike if both or neither preferred reserpine to other Rauwolfia drugs.

Table 49-1 gives the results in terms of an index of homogeneity. This index would be +1 if all pairs were alike; it would be zero if pairs of related doctors were no more often alike than expected by chance; and it is

Table **49-1**

Homogeneity of Pairs of Related Doctors in Treatment of Respiratory Infections and Hypertension[a]

	Advisor-Advisee Pairs	*Discussion Pairs*	*Friendship Pairs*
Respiratory infections (broad-spectrum versus other antibiotics)	−0.056	−0.016	0.029
Hypertension (Rauwolfia included or not)	0.054	0.095	0.109
Hypertension (reserpine versus non-reserpine)	0.280	0.410	0.233
N (number of pairs)	(253)	(258)	(211)
	(165)	(151)	(121)
	(111)	(97)	(71)

[a] These data refer to all 216 interviewed physicians, not only to the 125 whose prescription record was examined. Cf. footnote 1.

negative if pairs of related doctors are less often alike than expected by chance.[5] The results confirm the hypothesis: in all three networks, pairs are homogeneous beyond chance expectations in hypertension treatment but hardly at all in the treatment of respiratory infections. This finding, like that of the simultaneity of gammanym adoptions by pairs of doctors in the early months, presumably arises from the need for social support and social validation in situations where authoritative objective validation is scant.

[5] For details, *see loc. cit.*

Summary

Two hundred and sixteen physicians in four cities were interviewed, and the prescription records of 125 general practitioners, internists, and pediatricians among them were searched, in order to study how the use of a new drug termed "gammanym" spread through these communities of physicians. The main findings are:

(1) Gammanym was introduced earlier by doctors with a large volume of prescriptions for this general type of drug, by those who exposed themselves frequently to certain media of information, and by those who shared their offices with one or several partners.

(2) Doctors who maintained a variety of contacts with a large number of colleagues, the socially integrated doctors, typically introduced the new drug into their practices months before their relatively isolated colleagues. The degree of a doctor's integration was measured by the number of his colleagues who named him, in response to certain interview questions, as an advisor, frequent discussion partner, or frequently visited friend.

(3) Among the integrated doctors, the use of the new drug spread at an accelerating rate, indicating an interpersonal process of diffusion, while among the isolated doctors use of the new drug spread at a constant rate, indicating largely individual responses to constant stimuli outside the community of doctors.

(4) The hypothesis that a doctor and his friend, a doctor and his advisor, and a doctor and his discussion partner would tend to introduce the new drug at about the same time was not borne out for the period as a whole.

(5) During the early months following the drug's release, however, doctors who introduced the drug tended to follow closely upon any associates who had adopted it earlier.

(6) This phenomenon was strongest during the very earliest months in the case of pairs of discussion partners and advisor-advisee pairs. In the case of pairs of friends, it reached its peak about two months later. In all three cases, the phenomenon occurred among the relatively isolated doctors as well as among the integrated doctors, but it reached its peak much later in the case of the isolated doctors.

(7) The apparent greater effectiveness of contacts with colleagues during the early months was attributed to the greater uncertainty about the new drug that prevailed at that time. This interpretation is supported by comparisons of uncertain and clearcut situations of another sort; pairs of related doctors were found to be more alike in the drugs they use for essential hypertension than in the drugs they use for respiratory infections. . . .

CHAPTER 50

GUNNAR MYRDAL, with the assistance of RICHARD STERNER and ARNOLD ROSE

The Principle of Cumulation

In social science we have been drawing heavily on the notions and theories of the much farther developed natural sciences, particularly physics. The notion of equilibrium, for instance, has been in all our reasoning for centuries. Actually it is present in most research of the present day, even when it is not formally introduced. In most social research, we have restricted our utilization of the equilibrium notion to that simple and static variant of it, the *stable equilibrium*. It is this equilibrium notion which is implicit in the sociological constructions of "maladjustment" and "adjustment" and all their several synonyms or near-synonyms, where equilibrium is thought of as having a virtual reality in determining the direction of change. We propose the utilization of *other equilibrium notions* besides this simplest one. For dynamic analysis of the process of change in social relations, it is highly desirable that we disengage our minds from the stable equilibrium scheme of thinking. The other types of equilibrium notions are often better descriptions of social reality than the stable one.

If we succeed in placing a pencil upright on its end, it is also in equilibrium, but an unstable one, a "labile status" of balancing forces, as we easily find if we touch it. No "adjustment," "adaptation," or "accommodation" toward the original position will follow the application of a push, but only an accelerated movement away from the original state of balance. A third type of equilibrium is present when a pencil is rolling on a plane surface—it may come to rest anywhere. A fourth type is what we might call "created equilibrium," that is, arranging a disordered pile of pencils into a box by intelligent social engineering.

The most important need is to give place in our hypothetical explanatory scheme to a rational recognition of the cumulation of forces. In one branch of social science, economics, these various types of equilibrium notions have lately been used with great advantage. The principle of cumulation has given us, for the first time, something which approaches a real theory of economic dynamics. We have referred to the theory of the "vicious circle" as a main explanatory scheme for the inquiry into the Negro problem. The following brief notes are intended to give an abstract clarification of the theory and a perspective on some of its future potentialities as a method of social research.

In considering the Negro problem in its most abstract aspect, let us construct a much simplified mental model of dynamic social causation. We assume in this model society of our imagination a white majority and a Negro minority. We assume, further, that the interrelation between the two groups is in part determined by a specific degree of "race prejudice" on the side of the whites, directed against the Negroes. We assume the "plane of living" of the Negroes to be considerably lower than that of the whites. We take, as given, a mutual relationship between our two variables, and we assume this relationship to be of such a type that, on the one hand, the Negroes' plane of living is kept down by discrimination from the side of the whites while, on the other hand, the whites' reason for discrimination is partly dependent upon the Negroes' plane of living. The Negroes' poverty, ignorance, superstition, slum dwellings, health deficiencies, dirty appearance, disorderly conduct, bad odor, and criminality stimulate and feed the antipathy of the whites for them. We assume, for the sake of simplicity, that society, in our abstract model, is in "balance" initially. By this we mean that conditions are static, that our two variables are exactly checking each other; there is—under these static conditions—just enough prejudice on the part of the whites to keep down the Negro plane of living to that level which maintains the specific degree of prejudice, or the other way around.

If now, in this hypothetically balanced state, for some reason or other, the Negro plane of living should be lowered, this will—other things being equal—in its turn increase white prejudice. Such an increase in white prejudice has the effect of pressing down still further the Negro plane of living, which again will increase prejudice, and so on, by way of mutual interaction between the two variables, *ad infinitum*. A cumulative process is thus set in motion which can have final effects quite out of proportion to the magnitude of the original push. The push might even be withdrawn after a time, and still a permanent change will remain or even the process of change will continue without a new balance in sight. If, instead, the initial change had been such a thing as a gift from a philanthropist to raise the Negro plane of living, a cumulative movement would have started in the other direction, having exactly the same causal mechanism. The vicious circle works both ways.

The Negroes' "plane of living" is, however, a composite entity. Let us, while retaining our major assumptions, approach a more realistic conception by splitting up this quantity into components, assuming that the cumulative principle works also in their causative interrelations. Besides "relative absence of race prejudice on the side of whites," we introduce a number of variables: levels of "Negro employment," "wages," "housing," "nutrition," "clothing," "health," "education," "stability in family relations," "manners," "cleanliness," "orderliness," "trustworthiness," "law observance," "loyalty to society at large," "absence of criminality," and so on. All these variables, according to our hypothesis, cumulate. In other words, we assume that a movement in any of the Negro variables in the direction toward the corresponding white levels will tend to decrease white prejudice. At the same time, white prejudice is assumed to be, directly or indirectly, one of the causative factors effective in keeping the levels low for the several Negro variables. It is also our hypothesis that, on the whole, a rise in any single one of the Negro variables will tend to raise all the other Negro variables and thus, indirectly as well as directly, result in a cumulatively enforced effect upon white prejudice. A rise in employment will tend to increase earnings, raise standards of living, and improve health, education, manners, and law observance, and *vice versa;* a better education is assumed to raise the chances of a higher salaried job, and *vice versa;* and so all the way through our whole system of variables. Each of the secondary changes has its effect on white prejudice.

If, in actual social life, the dynamics of the causal relations between the various factors in the Negro problem should correspond to our hypotheses, then—assuming again, for the sake of simplicity, an initially static state of balanced forces—*any change in any one of these factors, independent of the way in which it is brought about, will, by the aggregate weight of the cumulative effects running back and forth between them all, start the whole system moving* in one direction or the other as the case may be, with a speed depending upon the original push and the functions of causal interrelation within the system.

Our point is not simply that many forces are "working in the same direction." Originally we assumed that there was a balance between these forces and that the system was static, until we introduced one push coming in at one point or the other. When the system starts rolling, it is true that *the changes in the forces*—though not all the forces themselves—work in one direction; but this is because the variables are assumed to be interlocked in such a causal mechanism that a change of any one causes the others to change *in the same direction,* with a secondary effect upon the first variable, and so on.

We may further notice that the "balance" assumed as initial status was not a stable equilibrium at all—of the type which is tacitly assumed in the notions of "maladjustment," "adjustment," "accommodation," "social lag"— and, further, that in our scheme of hypotheses there is not necessarily assumed to exist any new "balance," or "equilibrium," or "harmony" toward which the factors of the system "adjust" or "accommodate." In the utilization of this theoretical model on problems of actual social reality, the initial state of labile balance, which we assumed for simplicity in our demonstration, will, of course, never be found. What we shall have to study are *processes of systems actually rolling* in the one direction or the other, systems which are constantly subjected to all sorts of pushes from outside through all the variables, and which are moving because of the cumulative effect of all these pushes and the interaction between the variables.

CHAPTER 51

WILLIAM F. OGBURN

The Hypothesis of Cultural Lag

The thesis is that the various parts of modern culture are not changing at the same rate, some parts are changing much more rapidly than others and that since there is a correlation and interdependence of parts, a rapid change in one part of our culture requires readjustments through other changes in the various correlated parts of culture. For instance, industry and education are correlated, hence a change in industry makes adjustments necessary through changes in the educational system. Industry and education are two variables, and if the change in industry occurs first and the adjustment through education follows, industry may be referred to as the independent variable and education as the dependent variable. Where one part of culture changes first, through some discovery or invention and occasions changes in some part of culture dependent upon it, there frequently is a delay in the changes occasioned in the dependent part of culture. The extent of this lag will vary according to the nature of the cultural material, but may exist for a considerable number of years, during which time there may be said to be a maladjustment. It is desirable to reduce the period of maladjustment, to make the cultural adjustments as quickly as possible.

A first simple statement of the hypothesis we wish to investigate now follows. A large part of our environment consists of the material conditions of life, and a large part of our social heritage is our material culture. These material things consist of houses, factories, machines, raw materials, manufactured products, foodstuffs, and other material objects. In using these material things we employ certain methods. Some of these methods are as simple as the technique of handling a tool. But a good many of the ways of using the material objects of culture involve rather larger usages and adjustments, such as customs, beliefs, philosophies, laws, governments. One important function of government, for instance, is the adjustment of the population to the material conditions of life, although there are other governmental functions. Sumner has called many of these processes of adjustments "mores." The cultural adjustments to material conditions, however, include a larger body of processes than the mores; certainly they include the folkways and social institutions. These ways of adjustment may be called, for purposes of this particular analysis, "the adaptive culture." The adaptive culture is therefore that portion of the nonmaterial culture which is adjusted or adapted to the material conditions. Some parts of the nonmaterial culture are thoroughly adaptive culture such as certain rules involved in handling technical appliances, and some parts are only indirectly or partially so, as for instance, religion. The family makes some adjustments to fit changed material conditions, while some of its functions remain constant. The family, therefore, under the terminology used here is a part of the nonmaterial culture that is only partly adaptive. When the material conditions change, changes are occasioned in the adaptive culture. But these changes in the adaptive culture do not synchronize exactly with the change in the material culture. There is a lag which may last for varying lengths of time, sometimes indeed, for many years.

An illustration will serve to make the hypothesis more clearly understood. One class of material objects to which we adjust ourselves is the forests. The material conditions of forestry have changed a good deal in the United States during the past century. At one time the forests were quite plentiful for the needs of the small population. There was plenty of wood easily accessible for fuel, building, and manufacture. The forests were sufficiently extensive to prevent in many large areas the washing of the soil, and the streams were clear. In fact, at one time the forests seemed to be too plentiful, from the point of view of the needs of the people. Food and agricultural products were at one time the first need of the people, and the clearing of land of trees and stumps was a common undertaking of the community in the days of the early settlers. In some places, the quickest procedure was to kill and burn the trees and plant between the stumps. When the material conditions were like these, the method of adjustment to the forests was characterized by a policy which has been called exploitation. Exploitation in regard to the forests was indeed a part of the mores of the time and describes a part of the adaptive culture in relation to forests.

As time went on, however, the population grew, manufacturing became highly developed, and the need for forests increased. But the forests were being destroyed. This was particularly true in the Appalachian, Great Lakes and Gulf regions. The policy of exploitation continued. Then, rather suddenly, it began to be realized in certain centers of thought that if the policy of cutting timber continued at the same rate and in the same manner, the forests would in a short time be gone and very soon indeed they would be inadequate to supply the needs of the population. It was realized that the custom in regard to using the forests must be changed and a policy of conservation was advocated. The new policy of conservation means not only a restriction in the amount of cutting down of trees, but it means a more scientific method of cutting and also reforestation. Forests may be cut in such a way, by selecting trees according to their size, age and location, as to yield a large quantity of timber and yet not diminish the forest area. Also by the proper distribution of cutting plots in a particular area, the cutting can be so timed that by the time the last plot is cut the young trees on the plot first cut will be grown. . . . There of course are many other methods of conservation of forests. The science of forestry is, indeed, fairly highly developed in principle, though not in practice in the United States. A new adaptive culture, one of conservation, is therefore suited to the changed material conditions.

That the conservation of forests in the United States should have been begun earlier is quite generally admitted. We may say, therefore, that the old policy of exploitation has hung over longer than it should before the institution of the new policy. In other words, the material conditions in regard to our forests have changed but the old customs of the use of forests which once fitted the material conditions very well have hung over into a period of changed conditions. These old customs are not only not satisfactorily adapted, but are really socially harmful. These customs of course have a utility, since they meet certain human needs; but methods of greater utility are needed. There seems to be a lag in the mores in regard to forestry after the material conditions have changed. Or translated into the general terms of the previous analysis, the material conditions have changed first; and there has been a lag in the adaptive culture, that is, that culture which is adapted to forests. The material conditions changed before the adaptive culture was changed to fit the new material conditions.

●

The foregoing discussion of forestry illustrates the hypothesis which it is proposed to discuss. It is desirable to state more clearly and fully the points involved in the analysis. The first point concerns the degree of adjustment or correlation between the material conditions and the adaptive nonmaterial culture. The degree of this adjustment may be only more-or-less perfect or satisfactory; but we do adjust ourselves to the material conditions through some form of culture; that is, we live, we get along, through this adjustment. . . .

Another point to observe is that the changes in the material culture precede changes in the adaptive culture. This statement is not in the form of a universal dictum. Conceivably, forms of adaptation might be worked out prior to a change in the material situation, and the adaptation might be applied practically at the same time as the change in the material conditions. But such a situation presumes a very high degree of planning, prediction and control. The collection of data, it is thought, will show that at the present time there are a very large number of cases where the material conditions change and the changes in the adaptive culture follow later. . . . It is not implied that changes may not occur in nonmaterial culture while the material culture remains the same. Art or education, for instance, may undergo many changes with a constant material culture.

Still another point in the analysis is that the old, unchanged, adaptive culture is not adjusted to the new, changed, material conditions. It may be true that the old adaptive culture is never wholly unadjusted to the new conditions. There may be some degree of adjustment. But the thesis is that the unchanged adaptive culture was more harmoniously related to the old than to the new material conditions and that a new adaptive culture will be better suited to the new material conditions than was the old adaptive culture. Adjustment is therefore a relative term, and perhaps only in a few cases would there be a situation which might be called perfect adjustment or perfect lack of adjustment. . . .

CHAPTER 52

KARL MANNHEIM

Planning for Freedom

Planning raises the fundamental philosophical question: "Is not an ideally planned society a prison, a strait-jacket, even compared with the almost intolerable life led by many classes in an unplanned society? In the latter many people may be threatened with insecurity, but the individual is still (potentially at least) a free agent and can cope with his difficulties himself. Does not the continual development of social technique lead to the complete enslavement of the individual?" The question is only too justified, and if a human solution of our present problems is to be possible at all, an answer must be found.

It is all the more necessary to consider the possibility of freedom in an age of highly developed social technique, as a conception of freedom modeled on the preceding age is an obstacle to any real understanding of our problems and hinders the transition to a new type of action. Both the man in the street and the practical politician have vague conceptions of freedom, so that a historical and sociological explanation of the term is no barren speculation, but the prelude to action.

To the abstract approach of a naïve mind which conceives of freedom in general terms without reference to the concrete historical situation, freedom corresponds to the strength of human initiative, the desire to influence social conditions which are as yet uncontrolled or uncontrollable. This definition is vague, so that the question how far and in which form initiative is possible in a given society, can receive many different answers according to the nature of the social structure. It is equally indeterminate with regard to another question: How far can a definite type of social environment be changed, and where are the best points to intervene? The answer to these inquiries will again depend on the nature of the historical situation.

From Karl Mannheim, *Man and Society in an Age of Reconstruction* (New York: Harcourt, Brace and Company, 1951), pp. 369-370, 372-381. Copyright 1951 by Harcourt, Brace and Company, and reprinted by permission of the publisher.

•

The conception of freedom only becomes significant when we consider
the problem . . . from the standpoint of three stages in the development
of social technique. . . .

At the stage of chance discovery, of trial and error, freedom expresses
itself in direct action on and reaction to the stimuli of the surroundings.
Lack of freedom is felt if one is prevented from taking the necessary steps
to satisfy one's wishes as they arise. At this stage, not unlike an animal
which feels hampered when it is prevented from using its body as it wishes,
man feels his freedom at stake when he is not allowed to handle things or
people as he hoped to do. The immediacy with which freedom expresses
itself at this stage is not essentially changed when man has learned to use
the simple tools. The difference is only that by identification with these tools
he will feel frustrated when he is denied their use or possession, just as
though they were an extension of his body. Although the use of the simple
tools does not surpass the stage of chance discovery, it marks an advance,
for the process of adjustment is becoming more active. The equilibrium
between man, his desires and his environment is now brought about by
altering part of the surroundings instead of snatching at any pleasure which
offers itself. Any obstacle to the occasional alteration of these surroundings
is regarded as a threat to freedom.

In the process of this active adjustment to the surroundings we pass to
the second stage—that of invention. Owing to an accumulated knowledge
of tools and their combined uses, we can set more and more intermediate
ends and means between ourselves and some ultimate goal which might
still be very vague. At the stage of invention, we learn to make ourselves
more and more independent of natural conditions as they happen to occur,
so that this increased command over intermediate aims becomes the most
vital expression of our freedom. . . .

Technique, while freeing us from the tyranny of nature, gives rise to
. . . new forms of dependence. All progress in technique is bound up with
additional social organization. If I use better weapons in a hunting expedi-
tion or irrigate the soil to make it more fertile, the necessary preliminaries,
such as the production of the weapons or the construction of canals, can
only be completed by means of a collective division of labor. Thus no
sooner has technique made me independent of nature than it subjects me
in the same measure to the inevitable social coercion which cooperation
entails.

•

At the second stage (that of invention), a far more complicated "second
nature" replaces the first. This "second nature" is technique—and the organized relationships which the mastery of technique demands. The more
technique frees us from the arbitrary force of circumstance, the more we

are entangled in the network of social relationships we have ourselves created. From the human point of view this "second nature" is no less chaotic and menacing than the first, as long as these relationships cannot be grasped in their totality and therefore controlled. It is immaterial whether man be destroyed by hunger and earthquake, or by social maladjustments leading to war and revolution; the effect is just the same, although the original calamity was due in the first case to natural, and in the second to social, causes. The course of events as a whole is unpredictable, just as natural events were unpredictable before they had been studied. We are free to produce and manipulate individual tools or to devise certain organizations and then work them out in detail, but we are powerless at this stage, both theoretically and practically, to master the cumulative effects of mass psychology, or of the trade cycle, or of maladjusted institutions.

•

Although this unregulated mass of institutions is as impenetrable and as uncontrollable as nature itself (if on a different plane), men accept this determinism with the same resignation as they accepted the impossibility of controlling natural forces at an earlier stage. If men who had been molded by the educational tendencies prevailing at the stage of invention had been told that by coordinating social institutions they could bring order out of chaos, they would have felt that this was not merely a foolhardy suggestion but an attack upon the freedom of mankind. Although the blind play of social forces is destroying humanity, they regard this destruction as part and parcel of their freedom, simply because it is anonymous and directed by the invisible hand of history. . . .

The new conception of freedom creates the desire to control the effects of the social surroundings as far as possible. This is no mere daydream, it is based on the fact that enormous advances in social technique allow us to influence the conduct of social affairs from the key positions, according to a definite plan. Once we have realized this, our outlook on life will change, and we shall feel that while this chaotic tangle of institutions continues we are no longer free. . . .

At the stage we have just reached, it seems to be greater slavery to be able to do as we like in an unjust or badly organized society, than to accept the claims of planning in a healthy society which we ourselves have chosen. The realization that fair and democratic planning does not involve the surrender of our freedom is the mainspring of those arguments which show that an unplanned capitalist society is not the basis of the highest form of liberty.

It has rightly been pointed out that the "liberties" of liberal capitalist society are often only available to the rich, and that the "have-nots" are forced to submit to the pressure of circumstances. The real representative of this society would be the free workman, who had the right to sell his labor in a "free" market, or if he preferred, to give up the struggle and starve. What is the use of freedom in teaching and learning to a poor man who has neither the time nor the means to acquire the necessary education? . . .

Those who cling to the forms of freedom which were current at the stage of invention retort: "What use is the best social order if it is simply imposed on the individual and he cannot escape from it? . . . I would rather work out my own solution, however inadequate, to a difficult state of affairs, than be forced into the mold of a situation, however skillfully designed."

This antagonism clearly shows that the question is only insoluble because the concept of freedom of the second stage has been applied to the third. It is just as impossible to want a rational and planned society without foregoing the luxury of arbitrary interference as it was for the individual at the stage of invention to preserve his desire for an absolute spontaneity of adjustment.

The guarantees of freedom are entirely different at the three stages. At the first stage, freedom is really equivalent to freedom to escape. The possibilities of fleeing from a tyrant, of taking one's head out of the noose, of escaping direct pressure, these are the most obvious marks of freedom. At the second stage, where an increasing number of isolated institutions fill up the framework of society and where each is allowed, broadly speaking, to go its own way, the most vital guarantee of freedom consists in playing off these institutions against each other. This is reflected in the political theory of checks and balances. At this stage, the balance of power seems to be guaranteed by the mutual supervision and control of individual institutions. . . .

At the third stage, that of planning, freedom cannot consist in the mutual control of individual institutions, for this can never lead to planned cooperation. At the highest stage, freedom can only exist when it is secured by planning. It cannot consist in restricting the powers of the planner, but in a conception of planning which guarantees the existence of essential forms of freedom through the plan itself. For every restriction imposed by limited authorities would destroy the unity of the plan, so that society would regress to the former stage of competition and mutual control. As we have said, at the stage of planning freedom can only be guaranteed if the planning authority incorporates it in the plan itself. Whether the sovereign authority be an individual or a group or a popular assembly, it must be compelled by democratic control to allow full scope for freedom in its plan. Once all the instruments of influencing human behavior have been coordinated, planning for freedom is the only logical form of freedom which remains.

•

Naturally the advent of planned freedom does not mean that all earlier forms of freedom must be abolished. . . . On the contrary, the planned retention of ancient liberties is a guarantee against exaggerated dogmatism in planning. We have learned to realize that even when society has passed to a new stage in many spheres of its existence, some of the old forms of adjustment could still continue. Wherever it is possible and the plan is not endangered, every effort must be made to maintain the primary form of freedom—freedom for individual adjustment. This was legitimately retained at the stage of invention, and in spite of an increasing mechanization, it helped to preserve vitality and strengthen initiative. Thus one of the guarantees of freedom in a planned society will be the maintenance of the individual capacity for adjustment. In the same way, the freedom achieved at the second stage of invention must be retained in a planned society wherever possible. Constitutional provision must be made for the creation of new institutions through the initiative of small groups, in order to supply the needs of local circles rather than those of the centralized bureaucracy. It is one of the greatest advantages of the Anglo-Saxon tradition that most public institutions, such as hospitals, schools, and universities, are not maintained by the state but are forced as a rule to be self-supporting in order to prove the necessity for their existence. This principle of corporate initiative, these conceptions of the responsibilities and risks which must be borne by small groups, are characteristic of the stage of invention and are genuinely sound. They may mitigate exaggerated tendencies toward centralization, for this technique is a safeguard against bureaucracy and helps to keep the planning authorities in touch with actual conditions. Of course, once society has reached the stage of planning, separatism and local autonomy cannot be allowed to have the last word as at the stage of invention. . . .

All depends on whether we can find ways of transferring democratic, parliamentary control to a planned society. If this control is destroyed in the effort to establish a planned society, planning will be a disaster, not a cure. On the other hand, planning under communal control, incorporating safeguards of the new freedom, is the only solution possible at the present stage of social technique. The chances of achieving this new society, to be sure, are limited. It is not absolutely predetermined. But this is just where our new freedom begins. . . . Human freedom is not extinguished when we reach the stage of mass society; on the contrary, this is where its genuine vigor is needed. The man of today has far more freedom in the determination of his destiny than the unsociological ethics of the past would have us believe. Why search the past with a romantic longing for a freedom that is lost, when that freedom is now ready to come into its own if we only have the courage to see what must be seen, to say what must be said, to do what must be done? Rightly understood, recent tendencies toward a mass society, and our ever-increasing awareness of the determinism of sociological factors do not release us from responsibility for the future; responsibility increases with every advance in the course of history and has never been greater than it is today.

Termination

CHAPTER 53

LEWIS A. COSER

The Termination of Conflict

Certain social processes are finite, *i.e.,* they are defined by their transitory character and the manner of their termination is institutionally prescribed. Other social processes, however, have no precise termination point. They follow a law of social inertia, insofar as they continue to operate if no explicit provision for stopping their course is made by the participants. While in a game, for example, the rules for the process include rules for its ending, in social conflict explicit provisions for its termination must be made by the contenders. If no mutual agreements are made at some time during the struggle, it "ceaseth only in death" or in total destruction of at least one of the antagonists. Hence, the termination of conflict presents problems that do not arise in finite processes.

Various types of conflicts can be classified according to the degree of their normative regulation. Fully institutionalized conflicts, such as duels, may be said to constitute one extreme of a continuum; while absolute conflicts, in which the goal is the total destruction of the enemy rather than a mutually agreed-upon settlement, fall at the other extreme. In the second type, agreement is reduced to a minimum; the struggle ceases only upon the extermination of one or both of the contenders.

It stands to reason that conflicts of this kind—at least between contenders with a rough equality of strength—are exceedingly costly and exhausting. If the contenders wish to prevent their struggle from becoming a zero sum game in which the outcome can only be total defeat or total victory, they have a common interest in establishing mechanisms which can lead to an agreed-upon termination of the struggle. The fact is that most conflicts do indeed end long before the defeated has been totally crushed. "Resistance to the last man" is almost always a phrase. As long as one belligerent survives in

From Lewis A. Coser, "The Termination of Conflict," *The Journal of Conflict Resolution,* V (1961), No. 4, pp. 347-353. Reprinted by permission of the author and the publisher.

one's camp further resistance is always possible; yet combat usually ceases long before this point is reached. This is so because both parties agree upon norms for the termination of the conflict.

While absolute conflicts allow practically no agreements as to their termination, certain types of highly institutionalized conflicts have built-in termination points. Trials by ordeal, duels, and other agonistic struggles are centered upon symbolic endings which give them gamelike features and determine the outcome automatically. A score is kept, a goal line established, maximum injury is conventionally fixed. When the score adds up to a certain number, when a certain type of injury has been established, or the goal line has been crossed, the conflict is over, and the loser as well as the winner can easily perceive the outcome of the contention.

In conflicts not fully institutionalized, assessment of relative strength is not an easy matter, so that the loser may not in fact concede that he has lost, nor may he even be aware of it. Therefore, it is to the interest of both contenders that the point at which victory is attained, or the point beyond which no more gains can be anticipated, be marked as clearly as possible, so as to avoid unnecessary exertions on both sides.

•

For all except absolute conflict, termination involves a reciprocal activity and cannot be understood simply as an unilateral imposition of the will of the stronger on the weaker. Therefore, contrary to what common sense might suggest, not only the potential victor but also the potential vanquished makes crucial contributions to the termination. . . . Victory involves the yielding of the vanquished. By the very act of declaring himself beaten, he achieves a last assertion of power. . . .

If both victor and vanquished are to make a contribution to the termination of their conflict, they must arrive at some agreement. . . . In order to end a conflict, the parties must agree upon rules and norms allowing them to assess their respective power position in the struggle. Their common interest leads them to accept rules which enhance their mutual dependence in the very pursuit of their antagonistic goals. Such agreements make their conflict, so to speak, self-liquidating. To the degree that such rules are provided, the conflict is partly institutionalized and acquires some of the features of the agonistic struggle alluded to earlier.

Agreements as to goals and determination of outcome shorten the conflict. Once a goal has been reached by one of the parties and this accepted as a clue to the acceptance of defeat by the other, the conflict is ended. The more restricted the object of contention and the more visible for both parties the clues to victory, the higher the chances that the conflict be limited in time and extension. . . . The history of trade unionism provides interesting examples.

Struggles engaged in by business unionism, given its limited goals, provide for the contending parties an opportunity for settlement, and furnish them at the same time with recognizable signals as to the opportune moment for ending a conflict. Revolutionary syndicalism, on the other hand, has always been plagued by the problem of ending strike action. Since its goal is the overthrow of the capitalist order rather than improvements within it, it cannot accept as the end of the conflict outcomes which would constitute victories from the point of view of business unionism. Revolutionary syndicalism is faced with the dilemma that no outcome of a strike, short of the overthrow of capitalism, can be considered an acceptable form of conflict resolution, so that its strategy is foredoomed to failure. Not sensitized to clues which would allow them to conclude that a victory has been reached, unable to recognize peace overtures or concessions from the adversary, revolutionary syndicalists are not in a position to take advantage of partial gains. Paradoxically, in this case, those who are under ordinary conditions the *weaker* party demand "unconditional surrender" of the stronger, so that they make it inevitable that the struggle can cease only upon total exhaustion.

The above examples illustrate how closely specific outcomes are related to the aims of the contenders. The smaller the sacrifice a party demands from the opponent, the more limited the aims, the higher the chances that the potential loser will be ready to give up battle. The loser must be led to decide that peace is more attractive than the continuation of the conflict; such a decision will be powerfully enhanced if the demands made upon him are not exorbitant. When the war aims of the winning side are limited—as, say, in the Spanish-American war or the Russo-Japanese conflict of 1905—the making of peace is relatively easy. Once the Japanese war aims—the stopping of Russian penetration into the Far East—had been reached, Japan could afford to make the first move for peace by appealing to Theodore Roosevelt to act as a mediator. Once Cuba was liberated and the Spanish fleet defeated, American war aims were attained, and the United States had no interest in continuing the war through an attack upon the Spanish mainland.

It remains, however, that no matter how the activities of the potential winner have facilitated an early termination of the conflict, the final decision to end the war remains with the potential loser. How, then, is the loser moved to decide that he has, in fact, lost? Not only the objective situation, but the perception of the situation, is crucially important, since only the latter will bring forth the requisite admission of defeat. . . . Different contenders might arrive at variant estimates as to the degree of oppressiveness of a situation and of the value of the sacrifice demanded. Since such assessments are difficult to make and do not depend on rational calculations alone, they are greatly facilitated by the availability of symbolic signposts.

Whenever wars have been strictly limited, as in eighteenth-century warfare, some visible event, such as the taking of a particular fortress, the reaching of some natural barrier, and the like, symbolized to both parties that the desired objective had been reached by one of them and that the conflict could now be considered solved through the subsequent acquiescence of the loser. When such mutually acceptable symbolic clues are not available, the resolution of the conflict will be more difficult.

The nature of such symbolic clues may vary considerably,[1] and it is hence important that the potential winner ascertain which clues will be accepted by the potential loser as symbols of defeat. If, in the common consciousness of the citizens, the capital symbolizes the very existence of the nation, then its fall will be perceived as defeat and will lead to the acceptance of the terms of the victor. The fall of Paris in 1871 and 1940 symbolized to the bulk of Frenchmen the end of the war, despite the fact that Gambetta had rallied significant numbers of undefeated troops in the provinces and that De Gaulle appealed for the continuation of the war from London. Only a relatively small number of Frenchmen refused to accept the fall of Paris as a symbol of defeat. In less centralized nations, however, where the capital has no such symbolic significance, its fall is not perceived as a decisive event. . . . The sacking of Washington in 1812 did not signal defeat to Americans, for whom the open spaces of the country, rather than the federal capital, symbolized national independence. In other situations the capture of charismatic war lords, rather than any taking of a locality, will symbolize defeat.

The structure of the opposing camp furnishes clues as to meaningful symbols of defeat and victory. It is hence of the utmost importance for both sides to have as much knowledge as possible about the characteristic features of their respective structure and symbols. When ignorant armies clash by night, their pluralistic ignorance militates against their ability to come to terms short of mutual exhaustion.

The contenders' ability to make use of one another's symbols of defeat and victory does not only depend on their awareness of the structure of the opposing camp, but also on the dynamics within each camp. Internal struggles may be waged over what set of events may be considered a decisive symbol of defeat. A minority may consider that resistance can be continued even though the majority has accepted defeat. . . . Different parties may disagree violently on whether a given event is to be considered decisive or of only incidental significance. Such contentions are likely to be the more deepgoing the less integrated the social structure. . . . To the extent that a society or group is rent into rival camps so that there is no community of ends between the parties, if one party is not willing to accept the definition of the situation which the other propounds, the making of peace becomes an almost impossible enterprise. In such situations a prior settlement of scores within, an unambiguous definition or redefinition of the balance of power between contending groups, may be the precondition for concluding peace without. The Russian provisional government after the March 1917 revolution, being continuously goaded and challenged by the growing Bolshevik Party, was unable either to wage war effectively or to conclude peace; once the Bolsheviks had seized

---

[1] One must further distinguish between purely symbolic events, such as the capture of a flag, and events which, as in the examples that follow, have realistic as well as symbolic significance.

power their definition of the situation prevailed, and peace could be concluded at Brest-Litovsk.

•

Most conflicts end in compromises in which it is often quite hard to specify which side has gained relative advantage. Hence, one must distinguish between the will to make peace and the will to accept defeat. Quite often the former may be present although the latter is not. The parties to the conflict may be willing to cease the battle when they recognize that their aims cannot be attained or that they can be attained only at a price which they are not willing to pay, or, more generally, when they conclude that continuation of the conflict is less attractive than the making of peace. In neither of these cases would they be willing to accept defeat, although they are willing to stop short of victory. In such situations they may be impelled to explore the chances for a compromise. The willingness to negotiate a compromise, that is to stop chasing the mirage of victory, will, of course, depend on correct assessment of the situation and such assessment, just as in the cases discussed earlier, will be facilitated by the availability of indexes of relative standing in the battle. It is one of the key functions of the mediator to make such indexes readily available to both parties. To the extent that the contenders share a common system of symbols allowing them to arrive at a common assessment, to that extent they will be able to negotiate. Symbols of defeat and victory thus turn out to be of relevance in order to stop short of either.

Relative appraisal of power is difficult before the contenders have measured their respective strength in conflict. But accommodation may be reached once such an assessment has been achieved. Such redefinitions in the course of a struggle often bring to the fore elements which remained hidden during its onset. Accommodation is facilitated if criteria are available which allow the contenders to gauge the situation. The chance of attaining peace without victory depends on the possibility of achieving consensus as to relative strength and on the ability to make this new definition "stick" within each camp. When the United States chose the neck of Korea as their symbolic standing place in the Korean war, they succeeded in conveying to the other side, as well as to the American people, their determination to hold it. When enough blood had been let and it became clear to both sides that the other could be beaten only at a cost that neither was willing to incur, negotiations got down to a compromise that took into account the real balance of political and military power and proved acceptable at home. . . .

Although it is true that in many cases an assessment of the relative strength of the opponents is possible only in conflict, it is also true that their travail may be shortened if clear symbolizations of outcome and relative strength are readily available. When recourse to such measures of success or failure has been highly institutionalized, the duration of the conflict can be shortened and its intensity limited. . . .

CHAPTER 54

MORTON A. KAPLAN

Essential Rules and Rules of Transformation

The equilibrium states of going systems, such as political systems, may be described in part in terms of what can be called their essential rules.[1] Essential rules describe the forms of behavior that maintain the equilibrium conditions of the system. In a "balance of power" international system, the essential rules specify that nations pursue additional capabilities: if necessary, fight wars for that purpose; limit the indemnities levied on defeated nations; treat all other nations as acceptable alliance partners; and oppose nations or alliances that seek predominance in the system. Alliances are transitory and limited to immediate objectives in this system. Of course, these rules do not need to be followed in every case for the equilibrium of the system to be maintained, but if they are not followed in general, the system can be expected to change. Thus the rules are regarded as essential.

Different international systems are characterized by different essential rules. Thus the loose bipolar system is not characterized by transitory alliances that are oriented toward immediate and shortterm objectives. Instead, blocs are formed within the system, and the nations that join these blocs subordinate immediate interests to bloc interests. Since members of the opposing bloc are not potential future alliance partners, certain limitations of objectives *vis-à-vis* those nations that would have characterized behavior in the "balance of power" system are not to be expected in the loose bipolar system.

If some dramatic change occurs in a system—*e.g.,* the rules are not followed, the number or types of actors change, relative or absolute capabilities change, etc.—the system undergoes transformation. That is, the old equilibrium becomes unstable and is replaced by a new equilibrium. One of the

This paper is published here for the first time.
[1] Morton A. Kaplan, *System and Process in International Politics* (New York: John Wiley & Sons, 1957), pp. 9-10.

objects of the discipline of international politics is to understand the linkage between the starting state of the system and the change it undergoes if it becomes unstable. Statements that link changes in the behavior of the system to other changes in the system are called the transformation rules of the system, for they specify—if only probabilistically—the changes that are to occur if a particular disturbance affects a particular state of the system.

The transformation rules may be related to the essential rules. The essential rules of a system constitute an equilibrium set. If it becomes impossible to follow one of the rules, at least one other of the rules will necessarily change also. If one relates these changes to the parameters of the system, the transformation rules can in some cases be derived as applications of the theory. For instance, although the evidence for the deduction is not complete, one would deduce from the theory of the "balance of power" system[2] that the changes in Europe after 1870 would incline the system toward rigid rather than flexible alliances and to unlimited rather than limited wars.

The seizure by Prussia of Alsace-Lorraine from France after the war of 1870 set in motion a transformation of the "balance of power" international system. The French public reacted in an outraged way that made it difficult or impossible for the government to reconcile itself to the loss. As a consequence, Germany could not, in the foreseeable future, expect to have France as an alliance partner. Since one of the reasons for limitations of objectives in the "balance of power" system is to optimize the number of potential coalition partners who are able to protect a nation against dismemberment, this constraint ceased to operate with respect to France and Germany. In addition, the potential number of coalitions or alliances was greatly reduced as a result of this and other occurrences. As a result, the system of alliances became rigid. This forced other changes in national objectives and alliance behavior that produced a transformation of the system and that helped produce—although the actual explanation is more complicated than this—the loose bipolar system.

Growing ideological issues and international political movements also made the normal functioning of a "balance of power" system difficult and perhaps impossible. As the national power of the Soviet Union grew after the Second World War, the organizational relationships of the Communist states and the operations of local Communist parties in non-Communist states made the normal alliance arrangements of a "balance of power" system inappropriate and helped to produce a transformation to a loose bipolar system.

The cohesion of the Communist bloc gives that bloc a distinct organizational advantage, if other major nations do not form an antagonistic bloc. This is reinforced by Communist organizations within the democratic nations,

---

[2] For a discussion of the theory of the "balance of power," see Morton A. Kaplan, Arthur Burns, and Richard Quandt, "Theoretical Analysis of the 'Balance of Power,'" *Behavioral Science*, V (1960), No. 3, pp. 240-252.

which may be able to prevent foreign policy measures that are "rational" from an external point of view. If a counterbloc were not formed, one would expect the Communist bloc to secure enormous international victories, which would transform the system in still a different way, that is, in the direction of hegemony.

The formation of the bloc system is not the end of the transformation process that produces bipolarism. The rules governing nonintervention that were followed in the "balance of power" period were also related to the problem of optimizing alliance potential. If alliances become rigid or blocs are formed, the constraints maintaining the rule of nonintervention must weaken. On the other hand, the introduction of nuclear weapons—because of their enormous destructive power—introduces a new factor making for limitation in war, which compensates to some extent for the elimination of the constraint that ceased to operate with the failure of the principle of flexibility of alignment.

If we examine the present loose bipolar system, it is possible to see a number of factors that may produce an eventual transformation of that system. The problems arising from the development and spread of nuclear weapons may necessitate forms of supranational organizational control that change the nature of the international system. If these weapons are not controlled successfully, there may be a nuclear war that produces other kinds of transformation. If the war is a minor one, it may merely serve to emphasize the dangers of the age and may induce the major nations to accept controls that increase the powers of international organizations. However, the war may end in the victory of one side which may then seek to exercise a form of international control that prevents future nuclear wars. Whether such an attempt at hegemony would succeed would depend upon the completeness of victory, the organizational means at the victor's disposal, and the nature of its policies.

The number of possible transformations would be quite large, and efforts at exact prediction would not be worthwhile here in the absence of specification of the relevant variables. The transformations, however, would be the product of efforts at regulation and control carried out by nations and other organized groupings in an effort to maintain certain desired values. The general process that occurs during such transformations could be viewed in terms of Ashby's concept of ultrastability.[3] Ultrastable systems may be said to "search" for stable patterns of behavior. They are capable of recognizing the failure of existing patterns of response and of making changes in themselves that permit them to respond differently. The old patterns are rejected because they fail, and new organizational means and behavioral patterns are adopted. A series of changes may be made until some equilibrial pattern is discovered which is relatively stable, that is, which can be maintained despite disturbances in the environment.

---

[3] W. Ross Ashby, *Design for a Brain* (New York: John Wiley & Sons, 1952), p. 98.

If one examines the present system of international politics, one can see that relations between the United States and the USSR are only partly competitive. Each may desire an eventual international system in which its values predominate. But each is forced to search for patterns of behavior with which the other can live. Indeed, the uncommitted nations participate in this colloquy also. The more radical uncommitted nations are attempting to support a pattern of behavior that permits force to be used only against "colonial" regimes. The US rejects this on the ground that the criterion is insufficiently compelling and that the exception threatens the general rule. The Soviet Union attempts to secure adoption for the rule that intervention is permissible only in behalf of "popular revolutions." The major nations will find it impossible to agree on some of these rules, and such disagreement will serve to focus conflict. Other rules may succeed in satisfying sufficient of the interests and values of most of the parties of the dispute and may come to characterize more-or-less stable aspects of the period. This does not imply that these rules are fair in some abstract or arbitral sense, but that agreement—whether explicit or implicit—is reached on them.

The process by means of which this occurs is an ultrastable process in which a vast and complex social system finds a level of behavior that can be maintained. Any effort to understand these complex systems requires consideration of the ultrastable aspects of the process. This does not imply, however, that ultrastability is an explanatory concept. Equilibrium may be used as an explanatory concept when dealing with mechanical systems because there are independent measures for forces, etc. When we deal with ultrastable systems, we cannot use the concept in an explanatory way, for we lack independent measures. The concept is instead a directive for research. That is, it directs our attention to system properties that are either self-maintaining or that are maintained for external reasons.

There is, of course, no necessary value in any particular equilibrium. And ultrastability focuses our attention on change and transformation. Neither equilibrium nor change possesses any metaphysical value in itself. Attention to equilibrial aspects of systems has some pragmatic value, however. Generally, the factors that maintain equilibrium are more restricted than those which break it down, that is, only a few variables need be included in the theory that explains equilibrium. Thus theoretical development is more likely when attention is turned to problems of equilibrium and less likely when turned to problems of disequilibrium. If one possesses a good equilibrium theory, moreover, he may be able to predict what happens when a factor in the environment upsets the equilibrium, that is, he may discover the transformation rules of the system, since a specific question is being asked, rather than a diffuse set of questions. Reverse inferences are much less likely. Thus, in general, the concept of equilibrium may have a productivity for theory and for research that concepts which focus on disequilibrium and change lack—at least, where the subject matter is exceptionally complex and cannot be subjected to even semicontrolled experiment or good comparative analysis. It is not necessary to state that if the concept is reified and if the possibility of disequilibrium is neglected, there may be exceedingly harmful results of both a theoretical and practical nature.

CHAPTER 55

AMITAI ETZIONI

The Epigenesis of Political Unification

A Model for the Study of Political Unification

Historical and Contemporary Unifications

So long as international relations are governed by highly calculative orientations, or by the exercise of force, there is relatively little that sociology can contribute to their study. However, during recent decades, international relations seem to have changed. Ideology became a major force; nonrational ties among nations were more common; and, recently, institutional bridges became more numerous. Thus, international relations gradually have become more amenable to sociological analysis. Of these trends, probably the most interesting to the sociologist is the formation of new unions whose members are nations (*e.g.,* the European Economic Community [EEC]).

The EEC is by no means an extreme case. There have been many "historical" unions in which units that were previously autonomous merged to such a degree that today they are considered as one unit (Switzerland, the United States, Italy, Germany); and there are quite a few contemporary unifications where the new community is just emerging and is far from complete (the Scandinavian community, the East European one), exists as a treaty and formal organization rather than as a full-fledged sociological entity (the Ghana-Guinea-Mali union, the Latin American Free Trade Area), or is so tenuous that it is more likely to collapse than to reach fuller integration (the Federation of Nyasaland, Rhodesia).

The emerging communities are frequently referred to as supranational communities, a term that is misleading since it implies that the merging units are

From Amitai Etzioni, "The Epigenesis of Political Communities at the International Level," *American Journal of Sociology,* LXVIII (1963), pp. 407-421. Reprinted by permission of the publisher.

nations. Actually, many of the historical unifications occurred before the units were sanctified by nationalism (the Italian cities, the American colonies), and even contemporary unions are not necessarily unions of nations (the federation of Eritrea with Ethiopia, the formation of the Federation of Nigeria, and the merger of the Southern Cameroons with the Cameroon Republic). Moreover, analytically, the emergence of a nation-state from several tribes, villages, or feudal states—let us say in contemporary Ghana, India, or late medieval France—is in many ways similar to supranational unification. Hence, our concern is with unification of political units that previously shared few or no political bonds. The degree to which these units have been foci of identification for their populations, and the degree to which the normative substance of this identification was secular-historical of the kind that marks nationalism, are two variables of our analysis, not part of the definition of the concept. Therefore, we refer to the emerging entities simply as political communities and to the process as one of unification. The term "unions" refers to entities that seem to develop in the direction of a political community, but have not reached such a high level of integration.

Epigenesis versus Preformism

A strategy often used in sociological studies of international relations is to draw on theories developed in the study of interaction among other social units, bearing in mind the special nature of the subject to which they are applied, and checking whether additional variables have to be introduced or whether the theories require revision in view of the new data. Here we draw on a sociological theory of change.

Most studies of social change presuppose the existence of a unit, and ask: How does it change, why, and in what direction? The analytical framework frequently used for this analysis of social dynamics is the *differentiation model*,[1] which assumes that the "primitive" social unit contains, in embryonic form, fused together, all the basic modes of social functions that later become structurally differentiated. While relations originally fused gain their own sub-

---

[1] This model is applied to the study of small groups by Robert F. Bales and Philip E. Slater, "Role Differentiation in Small Decision-Making Groups," in Talcott Parsons, Robert F. Bales, and Edward A. Shils, eds., *Working Papers in the Theory of Action* (Glencoe, Ill.: The Free Press, 1953); to socialization process by Parsons, Bales, *et al.*, *Family, Socialization and Interaction Process* (Glencoe, Ill.: The Free Press, 1953), Ch. IV; to industrialization by Neil Smelser, *Social Change in the Industrial Revolution* (Chicago: University of Chicago Press, 1959); to the study of the family by Morris Zelditch, Jr., "Role Differentiation in the Nuclear Family: A Comparative Study," in *Family, Socialization . . . , op. cit.*, pp. 307-351, and by Smelser, *op. cit.*, chs. VIII-X; to the study of elites by Amitai Etzioni, "The Functional Differentiation of Elites in the *Kibbutz*," *American Journal of Sociology*, LXIX (1959), 476-487; and to the study of underdeveloped countries by Neil Smelser, "Toward a Theory of Modernization," in this volume.

units, no new functions are served or new modes of interaction are molded. There are, for instance, some universalistic relations in the most primitive tribe. According to this viewpoint, every social unit, if it is to exist, must fulfill a given set of functions, those of adaptation, allocation, social and normative integration. On the individual level, the evolution from infancy to maturity can be analyzed in terms of the differentiation of the personality.[2] On the societal level, the evolution of a primitive society, from a traditional into a modern one, is also seen as a differentiation process. All societal functions are fulfilled by the primitive tribe; they merely become structurally differentiated; that is, they gain personnel, social units, and organizational structures of their own. Religious institutions gain churches, educational institutions gain schools, economic institutions gain corporations, and so forth.

Philosophers and biologists have long pointed out that there is an alternative model for the study of change. While Bonnet, Haller, and Malpighi represented the differentiation (or preformism) approach, according to which the first unit or seed possesses in miniature all the patterns of the mature plant, Harvey, Wolff, and Goethe advanced the accumulation (or epigenesis) approach, according to which "adult" units emerge through a process in which parts that carry out new functions are added to existing ones, until the entire unit is assembled. Earlier parts do not include the "representation" of later ones.

The two processes are mutually exclusive in the sense that new units are either institutional "embodiments" of old functions, or serve new ones. They may occur at different times in the same social unit: for example, a unit may first follow a preformistic model of development, then shift to an epigenetic model (or the other way around); or it may simultaneously develop some subunits following one model and some following the other. But unlike the particle and wave theories, which are used to explain the same light phenomena, the change pattern of all sociological units of which we are aware follows at any given period either a differentiation *or* an accumulation model.

Until now, sociology focused almost exclusively on differentiation models. There are, however, several social units whose development cannot be adequately accounted for by a preformistic model. This article presents an outline of an alternative model, drawing for illustration on the formation of various social units, in particular, international unions. The following questions are asked: (1) Where is the power located that controls the accumulation process? (2) What form does the process itself take? (3) What sector is introduced first? (4) How does this affect subsequent development of sectors? (5) What sequences does the entire process follow? (6) What kinds of "products" do different accumulation (or epigenesis) processes produce? It is essential to bear in mind constantly the peculiar system reference of this analysis; it is a system that does not exist, but which the potential members

---

[2] *Family, Socialization* . . . , *op. cit.*, Ch. IV.

are gradually building up. It is like studying the effect of social relations among students in their postgraduate life before they have graduated.

Power and Epigenesis

Locus of Power: Elitism and Internalization

The main distinction between preformism and epigenesis is the function that new subunits serve; that is, old functions versus new ones. Determining the structural location of the power that controls the development of a social unit, especially that of new subunits, is essential both for distinguishing between units whose development follows one model, and for differentiating between those of one model and those of the other. We need to know whether or not any one, two or more elite units specialize in control functions; that is, whether or not control is equally distributed among all or most units. This will be called the *degree of elitism*. To the degree that there are elites, the question arises whether they operate from within or from outside the emerging union. This dimension will be the *degree of internalization* (of control).[3]

(1) *Degree of elitism.*—Organizational analysis shows that there are two major ways of forming a new corporate body: an elite unit may construct the performance units, or several existing organizations that have both elite and performance units may merge. On the international level, a new community is formed in the first way when a nation more powerful than the other potential members "guides" the unification process. Prussia played such a role in the unification of Germany; Ghana, in the formation of the Ghana-Guinea-Mali union; Egypt, in the late UAR. The cases in which one nation played a central role are so numerous that Deutsch *et al.* suggest that unification requires the existence of one "core" unit.[4]

While many organizations and communities are established by one or a few elite units, the control center of others is formed through a merger of many units, each contributing a more-or-less equal part. The power center of the emerging community is a new unit rather than an existing unit subordinating the others. One might refer to the first as elitist, to the second as egalitarian unification. A study of the Northern Baptist Convention in the United States provides a fine illustration of egalitarian unification.[5] The development of the Scandinavian union appears to follow an egalitarian pattern also. While Norway was initially less supportive of the union than Sweden

---

[3] I found this dimension of much value in analyzing the relationship between specialized units and parent organizations (*see* "Authority Structure and Organizational Effectiveness," *Administrative Science Quarterly*, IV [1959], pp. 62-67).

[4] Karl W. Deutsch *et al., Political Community and the North Atlantic Area* (Princeton, N.J.: Princeton University Press, 1957), pp. 28, 38-39.

[5] Paul M. Harrison, *Authority and Power in the Free Church Tradition* (Princeton, N.J.: Princeton University Press, 1959).

and Denmark, the differences in their support to, and in their control of, the emerging union (and the Nordic Council, its formal instrument) comes close to the egalitarian ideal type.[6]

The degree of elitism (or egalitarianism) should be treated as a continuum. In some nation-unions one unit clearly plays a superior role (England in the early Commonwealth); in some, two or more countries are superior (Brazil, Argentina, and to a degree Chile, of the seven members in the Latin America Free Trade Area); in others, participation, contribution, and power are almost evenly distributed among all participants (as in the Scandinavian union).

The degree to which one or more units control the unification process versus the degree to which it is an effort of all participants is closely related to the means of control used. At the elitist end of this continuum, we find mergers in which one country coerces the others to "unify." It seems that on the international level cases of elitist and coerced unification are much more frequent than egalitarian, voluntary unions, especially if we regard the extensive use of economic sanctions, not just military force, as resulting in a nonvoluntary unification.[7] At the egalitarian end, use of normative means, such as appeal to common sentiments, traditions, and symbols, plays a much more central role than coercive means or economic sanctions. Economic factors operate here more in the form of mutual benefits derived from increased intercountry trade than sanctions or rewards given by one country to the others.

This raises an empirical question: How effective are the various means of unification? One is inclined to expect that unification that begins with coercion ends with disintegration. But the Roman empire, despite its coercive techniques, lasted for about five centuries before it finally collapsed. Nor was the German union weak or ineffective because of the methods employed by Bismarck to bring it about. Quite possibly the line that distinguishes effective from ineffective unification efforts lies not between coercion and noncoercion, but between high coercion (of the kind used to keep Hungary in the Communist bloc in 1956 or to hold the Federation of Rhodesia and Nyasaland together in 1961) and lesser coercion.[8] Effectiveness seems also to be highly determined by the degree to which coercion is coupled with other means—for instance, with propaganda.

(2) *Degree of internalization.*—Collectivities whose developments follow an epigenesis model can be effectively ordered by a second dimension, namely,

---

[6] Frantz Wendt, *The Nordic Council and Cooperation in Scandinavia* (Copenhagen: Mumsgaard, 1959), pp. 98-100.

[7] The infrequency of voluntary unions is stressed in Crane Brinton, *From Many to One* (Cambridge, Mass.: Harvard University Press, 1949), pp. 49 ff.

[8] For an outstanding discussion of the Soviet bloc from this viewpoint *see* Zbigniew K. Brzezinski, *The Soviet Bloc* (Cambridge, Mass.: Harvard University Press, 1960), Ch. XII.

the degree to which the elite unit (or units, if they exist) controls the emerging union from the outside or from the inside. This is not a dichotomous variable, for there are various degrees to which an elite unit can be "in" or "out." An elite might be completely "out," encouraging or forcing the merger of two or more units into a union which it does not join, sometimes relinquishing control once unification is initiated. Colonial powers brought together, frequently unwittingly, subordinated units, only to have to withdraw once their union was cemented. For example, resisting the British control was a major force in bringing together the thirteen American colonies, the various tribes in the Gold Coast that became Ghana, and the Jewish colonies in Palestine that formed the Israeli society. On the international level, the United States required some degree of intra-European economic cooperation as a condition for receiving funds under the Marshall Plan; it encouraged the union of the six countries that formed the European Economic Community and is now encouraging the EEC to include Britain, without having joined these unions. Britain was the major force behind the efforts to launch a Federation of the West Indies and the formation of the Federation of Nigeria. In all these cases the center of power was with a nonmember, external unit.

In other cases, the elites that initiate and support unification do not stay entirely out of the emerging community, nor are they a fully integral part of it. The United States, for instance, is an "informal but powerful" member of CENTO. It signed bilateral pacts with Iran, Turkey, and Pakistan, the three members of CENTO, which in 1961 showed signs of becoming more than just a treaty. Similarly France, while not a member of the Conseil de l'Entente (a loose West African custom, communication, and, to a degree, military union of Ivory Coast, Upper Volta, Niger, and Dahomey), is still an active participant in this union through various treaties.

Finally, in still other cases, the elite is a full-fledged member of the union as Britain was in the European Free Trade Area and Prussia in the unification of Germany.

(3) *Power, capability, and responsiveness.*—The units that control the epigenesis of political communities differ not only in their degree of elitism and internalization, but also in their communication capabilities and degree of responsiveness to the needs and demands of participant units. Deutsch pointed out that, when all other conditions are satisfactory, a unification process might fail because the *communication capabilities* of an elite are underdeveloped. This was probably a major reason why empires in medieval Europe were doomed to fail; they were too large and complex to be run from one center, given the existing communication facilities. Sociologists have concerned themselves extensively with communication gaps, but studies frequently focus on the interpersonal and small-group level (even in many of the socalled organizational studies of communication). Sociologists are often concerned with the structure of communication networks (two-step com-

munication systems,[9] as against chain systems[10]), rather than with the articulation of these networks with the power structure.[11] For students of political systems and of complex organization, ideas such as "overloading" of the elite (presenting it with more communication than it is able to digest; requiring more decisions per time unit than it is able to make) is an interesting new perspective that connects communication studies with power analysis much more closely than the widespread human-relations type of communication analysis.

The concept of *responsiveness* further ties communication analysis to the study of power by asking to what degree does the power center act upon communication received and digested in terms of reallocating resources and rewarding the compliance of sectors.

Thus, to analyze epigenesis effectively, we must know not only who has how much power over the process, but also what are the communication capabilities, and what is the degree of responsiveness of the various power centers.

Performance and Control: A Dynamic Perspective

The performance, power, and communication elements of a social unit developing epigenetically do not always develop at the same rate. As the limbs of an infant develop before he has control over them, so new performances might be taken over by the accumulating unit before its power center gains control over them. Frequently, part of the performances of an accumulating unit are controlled by another unit, at least temporarily. The industrial capacity of colonies often developed before they gained political control over industry.

New communities, whose development follows the pattern suggested by epigenesis rather than that of preformism, tend to develop new performance abilities first and to internalize control over these activities later.[12] Just as a child first learns to walk, then gains the right to decide when and where to walk, or as military units in basic training first learn to act as units under the control of the training ("parent") unit's instructors and sanction system before acquiring their own command, so some countries engage in some collective activity under the control of a superior, nonmember power. Later, control is internalized by the evolving supranational system, and a supra-

---

[9] Elihu Katz and Paul Lazarsfeld, *Personal Influence* (Glencoe, Ill.: The Free Press, 1955).

[10] Alex Bavelas, "Communication Patterns in Task-Oriented Groups," *Journal of the Acoustical Society of America*, XXII (1950), 725-730.

[11] For one of the few studies that successfully ties the two *see* R. H. McCleery, *Policy Change in Prison Management* (East Lansing: Michigan State University, 1957).

[12] "Internalize" here means the transfer of power from external elites to internal elites.

national authority is formed, which regulates collective activities previously controlled by the superior external power.

It is the existence of a supranational authority—at first limited, then more encompassing—that distinguishes *unions of nations* from *international organizations*. Unions have at least a limited power center of their own, whose decisions bind the members and are enforceable; they have internalized at least some control. International organizations, on the other hand, are run by intergovernmental bodies, whose "decisions" are merely recommendations to the members and are not enforceable.[13] They have, in this sense, no power of their own.

The special importance of the High Authority, a governing body of the European Coal and Steel Community (ECSC), is that its decisions directly bind the steel and coal industries of the six member nations and it can levy fines on industries that do not conform to its rulings (though national police forces would have to collect the fines, if they were not paid). Moreover, individuals, corporations, and states have the same status before the Court of Justice of the ECSC; they all can sue each other, an individual suing a state, or the High Authority suing a member state.

Until the ECSC was formed in 1952, almost all European cooperation, such as the Organization for European Economic Cooperation (OEEC) and NATO, was intergovernmental. In 1952 the High Authority was formed; this was the first major step toward self-control of the evolving supranational community. (Interestingly, this is also the year NATO developed a supranational authority with the formation of SHAPE, which provided a supranational headquarters for the multination armies.) In the following years, functions and powers of the High Authority gradually increased. In 1957, the more encompassing common market (EEC) was established, which has its equivalent of the High Authority, the Economic Commission, except that its supranational powers cover more "performances"—much of the intercountry economic actions—than does the High Authority, which is limited to matters related to steel and coal.

Attempts to develop supranational control over shared political activities, in which the members of the EEC do engage, have not yet succeeded. Whatever collective political action the Six take is based on intergovernment consultations of these countries, not supranational direction. *Thus, in the development of this union of nations, as in the epigenesis of many other social units, collective performances expand more rapidly than collective control.* (It should be noted that while frequently performance accumulation occurs before power internalization, the reversed sequence might occur, too. Power

---

[13] For an outstanding discussion of the differences between intergovernment and supranational decision-making bodies, *see* Ernst B. Haas, *Uniting of Europe* (Palo Alto: Stanford University Press, 1958), chs. XII, XIII. The following discussion of the High Authority draws on Haas's work

capabilities can be built up before performance. Modern armies, for instance, train groups of officers in headquarters work before they are given command of military units.)

We saw that communities are built up by accumulation of *new* performances (*e.g.,* military ones) and control over them. We now turn to the dynamics of accumulation, recognizing three problems as basic to the analysis of all accumulation processes: Under what conditions does the process start? What factors contribute to its expansion and pace? What is the sequence in which the functional sectors that make a complete community are assembled? The rest of this article is devoted to these problems.

Initiation, Takeoff, and Spillover

Between Initiation and Takeoff

The concept of takeoff, borrowed from aerodynamics, is applied to the first stage of epigenesis to distinguish the initiation point from that where the continuation of the process becomes self-sustained. The image is one of a plane that first starts its engines and begins rolling, still supported by the runway, until it accumulates enough momentum to "take off," to continue in motion "on its own," generating the forces that carry it to higher altitudes and greater speeds. The analogue is that through accumulation, while relying on external support, the necessary condition for autonomous action is produced. Also during "takeoff" the pilot, released from airport tower control, gains control of his plane. (This control takeoff might occur before or after the performance takeoff.)

Economists use this concept in the study of industrialization, especially in reference to foreign aid. An underdeveloped country requires a certain amount of investment before its economy reaches the level at which it produces a national income large enough to provide for current consumption and for increased investment which, in turn, provides for additional growth of the economy. An economy has taken off when additional growth is self-sustained; when no external investment or externally induced changes in saving, spending, or work habits are needed.

The concept of takeoff can also be used in studying political, communication, and other social processes. A group of leaders, some labor unions, or "reform" clubs, join to initiate a new political party. Again, "to initiate" has two meanings, to which the concept of takeoff calls attention. There is the day the leaders decide to launch the new party, a day that, if the launching is successful, will be known as the party's birthday. However, the new party initially draws its funds, staff, and political power from the founding leaders and groups. Gradually, as the party grows, it accumulates followers and contributors directly committed to it, and if it is successful, it eventually reaches the stage at which it can do without the support of its initiators and continue growing "on its own." While this point is far from being sharply defined, obviously it rarely coincides with the actual birth date. Much insight can be gained by comparing different polities with regard to the lapse between their initiation and their takeoff points. For instance, the greater the lapse, the more difficult it is for small or new groups to gain political representation. On the other hand, if the lapse is very small, entering the political competition becomes too easy, and it will be difficult to find a majority to establish a stable government.

In many countries there is a formal barrier that has to be surmounted before political takeoff. Parties that poll less than a certain percentage of the votes are denied parliamentary representation. Frequently, founders' support is given until the election day; then the party either gains representation and becomes a political factor in its own right or it flounders; it either takes off or crashes. One of the special characteristics of the American political system is that the takeoff point for participation in national politics is remote from the initiation point. Many "third-party" movements that polled many hundreds of thousands of votes still could not continue to grow and to become permanent participants on the federal level.

Takeoff is especially important for the study of social units that are initiated by charter, enactment of a law, or signing of a treaty. While sometimes these "paper" units might be expressions of already-existing social units, often the formal structure precedes the development of a social one. While it has been often pointed out that an informal structure is likely to evolve, turning the formal one into a full-fledged social unit, we do not know under what conditions these informal processes take off, as against those conditions under which they never reach such a point. Clearly, not all formal structures become functioning social units. This applies in particular to international relations, where the supranational takeoff, that is, the transition from a formal, intergovernmental structure to self-sustained growth toward a political community, is quite infrequent. Under what conditions, then, does takeoff occur?

While these problems still require much research, there appears to be one central factor bringing unification movements to takeoff: the amount of decision-making called for by intercountry *flows* (*e.g.,* of goods) and by *shared performance* (*e.g.,* holding a common defense line) that, in turn, is determined by the scope of tasks carried out internationally. If the amount is large, intergovernment decision-making will prove cumbersome and inadequate, and pressure will be generated either to reduce the need for international decision-making—by reducing the international tasks—or to build a supranational decision-making *structure,* which is a more effective decision-making body than are intergovernmental ones.

The central variable for the "takeoff" of supranational authority is the amount of international decision-making required. This, in turn, is determined largely by the amounts and kinds of flows that cross the international borders (*e.g.,* tourists, mail) and the amounts and kinds of shared international activities (*e.g.,* maintaining an early-warning system). It should be stressed, however, that each flow or shared activity has its own decision-making logarithm. Some flows can increase a great deal and still require only a little increase in international decision-making; others require much more. Moreover, the relationship seems not to be linear; that is, some increases in a particular flow (or shared activity) can be handled by the old decision-making system, but once a certain threshold is passed, some supranational authority is almost inevitable.

It seems also that expanding the power and scope of a supranational authority is easier than to form the first element of such an authority. Initially a supranational authority is often accepted on the grounds that it will limit itself strictly to technical, bureaucratic, or secondary matters and that the major policy decisions will be left in the hands of a superior, intergovernment body. This was the initial relationship between the High Authority and the Council of Ministers of the ECSC; between the Economic Commission and the Council of Ministers of the EEC; and between NATO's SHAPE and NATO's conferences of ministers.

Once such a bureaucratic structure is established, a process often sets in whereby full-time, professional bureaucrats tend to usurp functions and authority from the parttime, political, "amateur" superior bodies, thereby expanding the scope of the supranational authority. At the same time, the very existence of supranational control in one area tends to promote such control in others. The concept of spillover, or secondary priming, which is used here to study the epigenesis of nation-unions, is applicable to the study of accumulation processes in general.

Secondary Priming of Change

"Spillover" refers to expansion of supranational performances and control from one sphere of international behavior to another. It was introduced by Haas to refer to expansions within the sector in which unification originally started (*e.g.,* from coal and steel industries to transportation) and from sector to sector (*e.g.,* from the economic to the political). Spillover refers only to secondary priming; that is, to processes—in our case, unifications—that have been initiated or have taken off because of epigenesis in *other* social sectors. NATO, for instance, unifies the military organizations of fifteen nations, and the EEC integrates the economies of six of the NATO countries. While these processes probably support each other, only a little spillover has taken place. Basically the military unification did not initiate the economic one or *vice versa*. There was original priming in each area. Both unifications may have had certain common sources (*e.g.,* the conflicts between the United States and Soviet Russia) and may be mutually supportive, but they did not trigger each other. On the other hand, the integration of the economies of the Six generates pressures toward integration of their governments, though so far political unification is mainly a "grand design."

It follows that one can hardly understand supranational spillover without studying the internal structure and dynamics of the participating societies. This must be done from a dynamic perspective, for spillover raises several questions. Under what conditions and at what level of change does unification of one sector lead to the exhausting of its "degrees of freedom" and trigger unification in other sectors? Which sector is likely to be affected first, second, and nth? Which sector will be affected most, second, and nth?

The Sequence of Epigenesis

Clockwise and Counterclockwise Sequences

The concept of takeoff suggests that epigenesis has to gain a certain momentum before it becomes self-sustaining. However, it does not suggest in what sector accumulation takes off, or what the effects of the selection of a particular takeoff sector are on the probability that general unification will ensue. Similarly, the study of spillover traces the relation between sectors once takeoff in one sector has occurred, but it does not specify either in which sector accumulation is likely to start or in what order other supranational sectors are likely to be built up (since it does not account for primary, simultaneous, or successive priming). To put it in terms of the accumulation model, we still have to determine: Which part is assembled first, which ones later?[14]

A hypothesis defining the sequences most functional for the epigenesis of nation unions can be derived from an application of the Parsonian phase model.[15] Parsons suggests that the most functional cyclical fluctuations in the investment of resources, personnel, and time follow one of two patterns: either a clockwise sequence (adaptive, allocative, socially integrative, and normatively integrative), or a counterclockwise sequence.[16] The two patterns can be applied to the study of epigenesis. They suggest that it is most functional for a new community to assemble its subunits and its self-control from the adaptive to the normative, or the other way around; and that all other sequences are less functional.[17]

Before we turn to express this hypothesis in more substantive terms, the difference between the application of the Parsonian phase model to preformism and its application to epigenesis should be pointed out. The phase model, as such, concerns the movement of an existing system, not its pattern of

---

[14] Note that though sector spillover occurs in the member societies, it leads to expansion in the scope of the supranational community.

[15] *Working Papers . . . , op. cit.,* pp. 182 ff.

[16] Here, as well as in an earlier work, I found it fruitful to apply Parsons' concepts with a certain amount of liberty. A long conceptual quibble seems unnecessary. The use of "allocation" instead of "goal attainment," and of "normative integration" instead of "pattern maintenance and tension-management," may serve as a reminder to the reader concerned with such conceptual subtleties that Parsons is not responsible for my way of using his scheme.

[17] This is one of those statements that sounds tautological but is not. Since there are

growth or change in its structure. Unless other processes take place, after a full round of the phase movement the system is the same as it started. Moreover, while each system is once accumulated or differentiated, the phase movement can continue *ad libitum*.[18]

Parsons also suggested a pattern for the analysis of social change, that of differentiation, according to which fused units bifurcate first into expressive and instrumental elements; then, each of these splits. Expressive elements are divided into social and normative ones; instrumental, into adaptive and allocative ones. This, like all preformism models, is a pattern according to which functions that were served by one, fused structure, become structurally differentiated; that is, they gain their own subunits. The accumulation model, on the other hand, knows no bifurcation, but suggests an order in which new structures serving new functions are conjoined. For example, countries that shared only a common market also establish a common defense line; that is, the union acquires a new function, not just a structural wing. The order we expect to be functional for unification movements to follow is either from the adaptive to the normative or the other way around.

In more substantive terms, the major question raised by the hypothesis concerning the sequence of accumulation is this: Is unification initiated in a particular sector more likely to lead to complete unification (to a political community)? If so, which is it: the military, economic, political, or ideological? Is the probability of success higher if accumulation follows a certain sequence? Which sequence (if any)? And is the most effective sequence the same for all types of unifications?

On the basis of the study of ten historical cases, Deutsch and his associates reached the following conclusion:

> It appears to us from our cases that they [conditions of integration] may be assembled in almost any sequence, so long only as all of them come into being and take effect. Toward this end, almost any pathway will suffice.[19]

They added, however, that:

> In this assembly-line process of history, and particularly in the transition between background and process, timing is important. Generally speaking, we

---

four phases in the system, the statement suggests that two modes of movement are more functional than twenty-two possible other ones. The first pattern—adaptive to normative—is referred to as clockwise, because the convention is to present the four phases in a fourfold table in which the adaptive is in the upper left-hand box, the allocative in the upper right-hand box, the social-integrative in the lower right-hand box, and the normative in the lower left-hand box.

[18] Note also that there is no one-to-one relationship between the pattern in which a system is built up (whether accumulated or differentiated) and the pattern in which it is maintained; *e.g.,* the epigenesis of a system might be counterclockwise and the system will "click" clockwise once its epigenesis is completed.

[19] *Political Community* . . . , *op. cit.,* p. 70.

found that substantial rewards for cooperation or progress toward amalgamation had to be timed so as to come before the imposition of burdens resulting from such progress toward amalgamation (union). We found that, as with rewards before burdens, consent has to come before compliance if the amalgamation is to have lasting success.[20]

Deutsch's distinction between sequence and order in time seems unnecessary for our purposes. Especially after examining his important book, *Backgrounds for Community,* in which his historical material is analyzed in great detail and potency, we conclude that Deutsch suggests—if we push the freedom of interpretation to its limit—that the allocative phase tends to come before the adaptive one (rewards before burdens); and that the normative phase (consent) tends to come before the social-integrative phase (compliance). In other words, interpreting liberally, we find Deutsch suggesting that a counterclockwise sequence from normative to adaptive is most common.

Haas compares the findings of his study of a modern unification with the findings of Deutsch *et al.* on historical cases from this viewpoint.[21] He distinguishes between identical expectations (or aims) and converging expectations that make actors cooperate in pursuing their nonidentical aims. The distinction comes close to Durkheim's dichotomy of mechanic and organic solidarity, and is similar to the dichotomy of expressive and instrumental elements. Haas reports that the ECSC has followed a clockwise sequence in which convergent (or instrumental) expectations preceded the identical (or expressive) ones.[22] Interpreting Haas liberally, one could state that in the case of the ECSC adaptive integration (custom union) came first, followed by allocative integration of economic policies (regarding coal and steel and later the formation of a common market). The union is now on the verge of political integration (election of a European parliament; planning group for federal or confederal institutions) and at the beginning of normative integration. Actually, by the time Haas completed his study in 1957, there was hardly any supranational merger of normative institutions, and even attitudes only started to change from convergent to identical.

Any effort to codify Deutsch's and Haas's findings for the benefit of further research on the question of the relative effectiveness of various sequences will have to take into account (1) the nature of the merging units, (2) the nature of the emerging unit (*i.e.,* the kind of union established), and (3) the nature of functional statements.

---

[20] *Ibid.,* p. 71.

[21] Haas, "The Challenge of Regionalism," in Stanley Hoffman, ed., *Contemporary Theory in International Relations* (Englewood Cliffs, N.J.: Prentice-Hall, 1960), pp. 230-231.

[22] *Ibid.,* p. 230.

Merging Units

One might expect that supranational unification of societies that differ in their internal structure will proceed in a different sequence. If, for instance, the merging units are three newly independent states such as Ghana, Guinea, and Mali—states that in themselves are still in the process of building up their "expressive" foundations—the emphasis on normative and social integration on the supranational level might well be higher than when long-established and well-integrated states unify, as the Scandinavian union, where the instrumental elements of the unification are stressed. These observations support the far from earth-shaking hypothesis that sector integration most responsive to the functional needs of the individual societies that are merging will come first in the unification sequence. After takeoff, however, unification is expected to *proceed more and more in accord with the intrinsic needs of the emerging political union, less and less in accord with the internal needs of the merging units.*

The preceding statements should not be read to imply that "political communities develop differently in different historical context"; that, for instance, one can account for the difference between Deutsch's findings and those of Haas by pointing to the fact that Deutsch deals with historical cases, while Haas is concerned with a contemporary one. Such statements are frequently made by historians who believe that each context is unique, hence what needs explanation is not diversity but uniformity—if ever found. For the sociologist the "historical context" is a shorthand phrase referring to the values of a myriad variable; unless these are specified, little is explained by the statement that "the context is different." In our case the question is: Which contextual variables account for the difference in sequences and for how much of the difference? (Often numerous factors have an effect but a small number accounts for most of the variance.)

"Historical cases," for instance, are often preindustrial societies; hence it comes to mind that the level of industrialization might account for part of the difference; industrialized societies might tend to merge in an adaptive-first, normative-last sequence; nonindustrial ones, in a normative-first, adaptive-last sequence. This formulation seems suggestive because, if valid, it points to the direction in which these findings can be generalized. We would expect, for instance, contemporary nonindustrialized societies to unify in the "historical," not in the "contemporary," fashion. The hypothesis also calls attention to the special importance of historical cases in which unification came after industrialization. If these unifications followed a "contemporary" sequence, the hypothesis on the relation of industrialization to the sequence of unification would be strengthened.

Another variable to be teased out of the undifferentiated phrase, "historical context," is the degree of nationalism. There seem to be three major kinds of unions: prenationalist (*e.g.,* the Roman Empire); postnationalist (*e.g.,* the EEC); and unions that are themselves an expression of rising nationalism (*e.g.,* the unification of Italy). All other things being equal, we would expect the initial phases of pre- and post-nationalist unions to stress the adaptive aspect and follow the clockwise pattern; and those unions that express nationalism to be initiated on the normative side, following the counterclockwise sequence.

Kinds of Union

The sequence of unification is determined not only by the *initial* needs of the merging units (*e.g.,* industrialization) and the "period" (*e.g.,* advent of nationalism) but also by the function the union fulfills for the various participant units as it is *completed*. Unions of nations differ greatly on this score. The most familiar type is that of custom unions, which keep up the level of international trade among member countries. The new Central American Union, formed in 1959, and the Latin America Free Trade Area, ratified in 1961, are actually oriented at economic development, international division of labor, sharing of information, and even of capital rather than increased regional trade. Wallerstein points to still a different function of unions: Some serve as instruments of subordination, while others serve to bolster independence.[23] Thus the whites, who are stronger in Southern Rhodesia than in Northern Rhodesia and Nyasaland, use the federation of the three regions to hold the regions in which they are weak.

Functional analysis of social units that develop epigenetically is more complex than such an analysis of existing social units, for here we deal with functional analysis of change where the system itself is changing. Thus, as unification evolves, it comes to fulfill different (either additional or substitute) functions for the participant units and the emerging union. The West European unification might have been initiated in 1947 as a way to gain capital aid from the United States to reconstruct the postwar economies; soon it acquired the additional function of countering Soviet military expansion; then it came to serve economic welfare and, with the "rebellion" of France since de Gaulle has returned to office, it even serves, to a degree, to countervail United States influence in the Western bloc. (It should be mentioned in passing that at a given stage of development the same union may have different functions for different participants. Thus, Germany supported the EEC partially to overcome its "second-class citizen" status in the community of nations; allied control of German steel industry, for instance, was abolished when Germany entered the ECSC. France supported the formation of NATO in part to gain some control over a rebuilt and rearmed Germany.)

---

[23] On these unions *see* Immanuel Wallerstein, *Africa* (New York: Random House, 1962), Ch. VII.

All functional needs—those of individual members, those common to all members, and those of the evolving community—vary with the various stages of the unification process; and they all seem to affect the sequence in which the "parts" are assembled. It remains for future studies to relate differences in sequence to these functional variations, to validate two hypotheses: (1) the higher the degree of unification, the more its pattern of accumulation can be accounted for by common (identical or complementary) needs, rather than by the individual needs of member states, and by needs of the union rather than by common needs of the members, (2) accumulation sequences, whatever their takeoff sector, are most likely to complete the process of unification if they follow the clockwise or counterclockwise sequence than any other.

Functional and "Real" Sequences

An important difference between the statements about sequences made, on the one hand, by Deutsch and Haas, and, on the other, by Parsons, his associates, and in the preceding discussions, is that the former refer to actual occurrences (the ECSC followed this and that pattern) and empirical frequencies (nine out of ten historical cases followed this sequence), while the latter refer to functional sequences. Functional statements suggest that if epigenesis proceeds in a certain sequence, it will be most effectively completed; if it follows another sequence, certain dysfunctions will occur. The nature of the dysfunctions can be derived from the nature of the stages which are skipped (*e.g.,* high social strain is expected if the expressive elements are not introduced), or incorporated in a "wrong" order (*e.g.,* high strain is expected when allocation of resources is attempted before adaptation has been built up). The fact that a particular unification follows a sequence other than the one suggested by the epigenesis model does not invalidate the latter, so long as it is demonstrated that the "deviation" from the model caused dysfunctions. In short, the test of the model lies in its ability to predict which course of action is functional and which one is not, rather than to predict the course of action likely to be followed.[24]

In the construction of epigenesis models for the various kinds of nation unions, the use of two types of functional models must be distinguished: the crude *survival* model, and the more sophisticated and demanding *effectiveness* model. The first specifies the conditions under which a structure exists or ceases to exist; the second also takes into account differences in the degree of success. In the case of nation-unions, then, while many are likely to continue in existence, some will stagnate on a low level of integration while others will continue to grow in scope, function, and authority.

---

[24] Note that the system this statement refers to is not the existing one, but a future state—that of a complete unification—of a community. The use of a future-system reference might prove useful for the general development of the functional analysis of change.

Index of Names